Horror Comics
in Black and White

Horror Comics
in Black and White

A History and Catalog, 1964–2004

RICHARD J. ARNDT

Foreword by STEPHEN R. BISSETTE

McFarland & Company, Inc., Publishers

Jefferson, North Carolina, and London

Library of Congress Cataloguing-in-Publication Data

Arndt, Richard J.
Horror comics in black and white : a history and catalog, 1964–2004 /
Richard J. Arndt ; foreword by Stephen R. Bissette.
p.   cm.
Includes bibliographical references and index.

ISBN 978-0-7864-7025-9
softcover : acid free paper ♾

1. Horror comic books, strips, etc. — United States — History and
criticism.   2. Horror tales, American — History and criticism.   I. Title.
PN6725.A76 2013   741.5′973 — dc23   2012049772

British Library cataloguing data are available

Cover art by Vicente Segrelles from *Nightmare* #13, June 1973

Manufactured in the United States of America

*McFarland & Company, Inc., Publishers
Box 611, Jefferson, North Carolina 28640
www.mcfarlandpub.com*

To my daughters,
Telisha, Mackenzie,
Olivia and Heidi
(hey, gals!)

Acknowledgments

One does not work on such a book in isolation and the direct or indirect help provided by George Warner, who provided many of the art scans for the *Skywald* chapter and has been a rock of encouragement and support, Steve Bissette, who generously provided a foreword, Dan Braun, Peter Normanton, David Kerekes, Piers Casimir, David Horne, Jon B. Cooke and Roy Thomas was helpful and inspiring.

Extensive information was obtained from personal emails and interviews with David Allikas, Terry Bisson, Frank Brunner, Maelo Cintron, Connor Freff Cochran, Gerry Conway, Clark Diamond, Bill DuBay, Steve Englehart, Ed Fedory, Mike Friedrich, Augustine Funnell, Don Glut, Jerry Grandenetti, Al Hewetson, Tony Isabella, Bruce Jones, Michael Kaluta, Barbara Leigh, Michelle Lemieux, Budd Lewis, Don MacGregor, Stefano Marchesini, Tim Moriarty, Denny O'Neil, Bill Pearson, Stephen Perry, Trina Robbins, Chris Ryall, Louis Simonson, Walt Simonson, Dez Skinn, Bob Toomey, Anglique Trouvere, Boris Vallejo, George Warner, and Marv Wolfman. Thanks, folks!

Table of Contents

Pitching Tents in the Darkness: A Foreword by Stephen R. Bissette

"What's black and white and red all over?"

There was a schoolyard joke that opened with that line. I think I first heard it at age seven or eight. Little did I know how completely it would summarize much of my own future reading — and creative — life.

I was a "monster kid," no two ways about it. But it wasn't easy being a "monster kid" in Duxbury, Vermont.

Well, at least I wasn't alone. There were two of us.

Luckily, my best friend Mitch Casey was a little older than me, and he was a "monster kid," too — at least for part of our shared childhood together. Mitch "outgrew" monsters before I did — well, hell. Let's face it: Mitch outgrew 'em, and I never, ever did. I'm still a "monster kid."

I loved monster movies, when I could manage to see them (usually on TV, rarely in theaters). I loved monster comic books, when I could find them (living within biking distance of two stores that sold comic books, that was often, but never frequently enough). I loved monster magazines, when I lucked into them (only one of those two stores within biking distance carried any, and that was rare — it was clear that Vincent, the proprietor of Vincent's Pharmacy, wasn't in the least fond of them).

Within that part of my childhood universe, 1964 was a magical year. I was nine, and it was the year that editor Forrest J Ackerman — FJA, the first real-life "editor" I'd ever heard of, much less knew of, at a time when I couldn't even guess what an "editor" was or did, other than Perry White on the Superman TV show — and publisher James Warren launched a new monster magazine, *Monster World*. While clearly a lesser kin to the bible of monster magazines, *Famous Monsters of Filmland*, *Monster World* had something I truly loved: monster movie comics!

Now, the Dell movie comics were a staple of my comic-reading diet. I'd grown up reading and re-reading them, with certain issues (*Dinosaurus!*) real treasures in my meager, beat-up comics collection (in reality, a stack of comics kept in the bedroom closet I shared with my brother). But these *Monster World* "monster comics" were different: they were in black and white, not color. That, and the subject matter (*Horror of Dracula*, a movie I'd as yet not seen, and *The Mummy's Hand*, a movie I'd see for the first time the very next year), made the short, unsatisfying "monster comics" in *Monster World* seem more — well, grown-up. More adult. They were in black and white, which made them different, really different. Sure, they were too short, and were never enough, but I went back to them often, time and time again. I copied the panels, again and again. Without the obscuring smears of color, these images seemed more vivid, more alive, and more easily recognized as the work of an artist. I could see the lines. I could copy them more clearly. These were different from all the other comic books I'd ever seen or read.

Better yet were the full-page ads for a new kind of comic — a horror comic! — promoted in the same issues of *Monster World*. *Creepy* was coming!

1

I still remember the heart-stopping first glimpse of that Jack Davis cover (or, as we said it then, "that *MAD* guy cover") for *Creepy* #1. It was on the bottom rack of the tallest magazine rack at Vincent's Pharmacy, and it was a tough purchase — it cost more than THREE comic books, a momentous purchase by any nine-year-old standard circa 1964. But I was able to cajole an extra quarter out of my mom and buy it I did.

And life was never the same again.

Like all monster kids, I could go on and on about all that followed, but I won't. Trust me, though: *Creepy* was a game-changer.

Like most monster kids, "my" monster magazines and beloved black-and-white horror comic magazines were creating some trouble for me. By ages ten, eleven, and twelve, *Creepy* was joined in that closet stack by its brother *Eerie* and the grungy, grimy, gory *Weird*.

I was only stupid enough to bring a copy of *Eerie* to school once — only once — and I'll never forget having it taken away from me by a teacher. That I was diligently copying one of the panels only made the enormity of my crime more terrible, and I was punished by the confiscation of that beloved issue of *Eerie* (#5, with that unforgettable Frazetta Tyrannosaurus Rex looming out of the fog).

I'll never forget sweating that one out: I wasn't worried about the teacher telling my parents — hell, my dad had bought me that issue, because of the dinosaur! — but I was worried that she'd refuse to return it, or (horrors!!!) maybe even destroy it. I don't think I slept a wink that first night.

Well, it was returned — two gut-grinding days later — with the stern warning, "I don't approve of these sorts of THINGS, Stevie!" She made it abundantly clear that had it not been for the fact she knew I had it only because of the dinosaur in it, she'd have burned it.

Oh, how that stuck in my craw.

Unlike most monster kids, not only did I never outgrow monsters and comic books, I ended up living the dream: I became a professional cartoonist, and I drew monster comics for a living. I raised two kids on what I earned drawing monster comics, and won multiple industry awards, and now I teach how to draw comics to

a new generation of cartoonists — a few of whom (like Denis St. John, creator of the ironically titled *Monsters and Girls*) are fellow monster kids. Hey, we know each other when we meet each other, I assure you.

Unlike most of my peers who worked in comics, it was my singular dream to change horror comics — I mean, really change them, for the better.

And on that path, black-and-white horror comics were absolutely vital.

My inroad to the professional cartooning life was the Joe Kubert School of Cartoon and Graphic Art, Inc., in Dover, New Jersey. I was a member of the first-ever class, entering the school in the fall of 1976 and graduating in the spring of 1978. That life-changing experience was framed by two black-and-white horror comics.

The first was *Abyss*, a black-and-white underground magazine-format comic book I drew almost all of my final year at Johnson State College in Johnson, Vermont, bankrolled by my pal Tim "Doc" Viereck (200 copies for the then-princely sum of $200). In there was my most ambitious comics work to date: "Not Yeti," scripted by my newfound friend Steve Perry, whose greatest ambition was to write for Marvel Comics. *Abyss* was the portfolio piece that got me into the Kubert School, along with two beaten sketchbooks and the opening wash-art pages of a grim little story entitled "Cell Food" (which I later redrew, with my pal Rick Veitch, for publication in the underground *Dr. Wirtham's Comix & Stories*).

Among the choice outside-work jobs I landed during my senior year (it was a two-year program) at the Kubert School was a three-page horror comic story, "The Villager's Victory," for a new black-and-white "monster magazine" being launched by Scholastic, called *Weird Worlds*. I gave it my all — not only because it was for Joe, who supervised every stage of the work, but because it was for a monster magazine, and a magazine that was going to be given to junior high students in classrooms.

Do you hear that? A monster magazine — distributed in school classrooms.

Oh, how I ached to wave that first issue of *Weird Worlds*, with my werewolf comic story in it, in the face of the teacher who had confiscated that precious copy of *Eerie* #5 at Duxbury Elementary School. It was a taste of vindication, justice, a correcting of the scales, and something baser. Sweet, sweet revenge!

The first pro gig I was given by my mentor, Joe Kubert, was the *Weird Worlds* "contract"—that is, Joe let me take the continuing gig with me. I was proud as punch, and I gave my utmost to each and every story I ever drew for Scholastic. It was easy to do so—I loved the editors, Bob and Jane Stine (yep, THAT Bob Stine, aka R.L. Stine, who later launched the mega-popular *Goosebumps* books), who wrote most of the scripts I drew from; I loved the art director, Bob Feldgus, who was one of the kindest, coolest cats I had the pleasure to work with in those critical first years of freelancing; and it was the best paying gig, offering the highest page rates and the best production and printing of any of my early comic gigs. What's not to love?

And—every job, every story, every lovingly-rendered panel and page—was REVENGE!!! I could go on, but that's the nut of it, really.

The black-and-white horrors were critical to my career from 1978 on. My first pro job for Marvel Comics was for a black-and-white title, *Marvel Preview*, which became *Bizarre Adventures* during my years working for Marvel, much to my great joy: at last, I was working for a newsstand black-and-white–semi-horror comic magazine!

For *Bizarre Adventuress*, I did my best-ever black-and-white horror stories with my pal the late Steve Perry, "A Frog Is a Frog," and our Dracula story, "The Blood Bequest." Yep, I was able to help Steve fulfill his lifelong dream of writing for Marvel Comics—be careful what you wish for, is all I can say.

I would fulfill my own lifelong dream of changing horror comics for the better thanks to the great, grand fortune of working as penciler (and co-plotting stories) with the incredible creative team of Alan Moore, John Totleben, and Rick Veitch on a four-color comic book—DC Comics' *Saga of the Swamp Thing* (beginning in 1983).

But it was another black-and-white horror anthology title, *Taboo*, that cinched the fulfillment of that dream. *Taboo* was co-created with John Totleben, bankrolled by Cerebus creator Dave Sim, and it was my—our, at first, but it became "my" when John chose to step out of editing, a process he found no joy in, prior to the publication of *Taboo* #1 (1988)—best shot at publishing the best-ever adult black-and-white horror comic possible.

I'll leave it to history—and, specifically, to Richard Arndt, in the book you now hold in your hands—to assess whether we managed to do just that.

In and about that, I also contributed to any and all black-and-white horrors that existed: Clifford Neal's *Dr. Wirtham's Comix & Stories*, Larry Shell's *Alien Encounters* and *Fifties Funnies*, Tom Skulan's *Gore Shriek* and *Shriek*, and more.

Me, I've had my shot, thanks to the black-and-white horrors.

My life, in many ways, was shaped by black-and-white horror comics magazines. For three decades (from 1964 to 1994), they irrevocably determined my own path in life—as a reader, as an aspiring writer and artist, as a professional writer and artist, as an editor, as a publisher and co-publisher, as a creator.

What's black and white and read all over?

Read on; I know for a fact that Richard can answer that riddle for you...

Stephen R. Bissette
Mountains of Madness

Stephen R. Bissette, a pioneer graduate of the Joe Kubert School, teaches at the Center for Cartoon Studies and is renowned for Swamp Thing, Taboo, "1963," Tyrant, *co-creating* John Constantine, *and creating the world's second "24-Hour Comic." His latest books include* Teen Angels & New Mutant: Rick Veitch's Brat Pack and the Art, Karma, and Commerce of Killing Sidekicks *(2011); the short story "Copper" in* The New Dead *(2010), and* The Vermont Monster Guide *(2009).*

Preface

This book chronicles the comprehensive history of the black and white horror comic magazines, which flourished on the newsstands from 1964 through 1983, as well as those few full-sized horror magazines that followed through 2004. These magazines provided an important step in the maturation of both the horror genre within comics and the comics field as a whole, as well as providing a market for writers and artists to work outside the narrow confines of the industry's Comics Code.

In this reference work, only magazine titles that featured predominantly original stories in the horror field (or those titles from other genres that had a high degree of horror material in their stories) are included. Those that featured largely reprinted or redrawn versions of color comics are not included. Nor are the hybrid Picto-fiction titles that EC Comics attempted in the mid–1950s or the similar Joe Simon efforts from 1959. In addition, no color horror comics or black and white comic-sized titles are dealt with.

The research included reading all the original magazines in total, studying the few reference books that actually exist on this subject, most of which deal with only one of the many publishers included here, and personal interviews with many of the publishers, editors, writers and artists who worked on these magazines.

Introduction:
A Black and White
Horror Comics Overview

Horror comics had experienced a huge boom of interest and profitability between 1950 and 1954, but their very popularity and the increasing amount of gore that some of the publishers put in their comics also brought down the wrath of supposed child crime authorities, newsstand distributors, state and federal legislators and, ultimately, parents. The advent of the Comics Code, which the comic companies themselves installed in an effort to placate those parents and ward off the many legal actions against comics that cropped up around the country and threatened the publishers' livelihoods, effectively banned genuine horror comics in 1955. Only the greatly toned down "mystery" titles were allowed to keep publishing and most, if not all, of these were pallid, tame fare compared to the "anything goes" nature of the horror craze.

The black and white revival of horror comics began in 1964 with the publication of *Creepy* #1 by Warren Publishing. That first issue was undated but it would have been either the Winter or January 1965 issue and appeared in either October or November 1964. However, publisher James Warren's great experiment was neither the first black and white (or B&W from now on) comic magazine nor the first B&W horror effort in the magazine field.

EC Comics, the leading publisher of horror, crime, war, science fiction and humor comics in the early 1950s, converted its premiere humor comic, *MAD*, to a B&W format in mid–

1955. This was done in an effort to circumvent the Comics Code office as their authority had jurisdiction only over color comic books. B&W magazine-sized comics had never existed before so William Gaines, *MAD*'s publisher, successfully claimed that new magazine version of *MAD* was not a comic book, even though 90 percent of the contents were comics. *MAD* the comic had been a reasonable success that inspired many short-lived imitators. *MAD*, the magazine became a best-selling publishing phenomenon within a year.

Gaines also tried to salvage his crime and horror comics by starting up a magazine line he called Picto-fiction. Although *MAD*'s contents were still mostly comics, the Picto-fiction magazines—*Shock Illustrated*, *Crime Illustrated*, *Terror Illustrated* and *Confessions Illustrated*— were a hybrid between magazines and comics. The stories were prose, with large illustrations by his best comics artists on every page. Unlike *MAD*, however, the Picto-fiction titles were a flop. Perhaps because it was too soon after the horror backlash of 1954–1955, perhaps because the Picto-fiction books were neither fish nor fowl — being neither truly comics nor traditional prose — or perhaps it was because, unlike *MAD*, which only displayed the EC logo on its first two magazine covers, and then in very small type at the bottom of the cover, the Picto-fiction magazines had the EC logo prominently displayed next to the title. Magazine distributors and sellers were very leery of EC by this time and may not have distributed or displayed the magazines strictly because of the publisher's identifying logo. Whatever the reason, none of the four Picto-fiction titles published more than two issues apiece.

In 1959, an effort was made to revive the Picto-fiction idea. Two one-shot titles were published, under different company names, but obviously by the same people. The first was entitled *Weird Mysteries*, from the publishing company Pastime, and cover dated March–April 1959. The second was entitled *Eerie Tales*, published by Hastings, cover dated November 1959. Both titles had the same horror host. No actual publishing credits are given although it is generally accepted that Joe Simon, one-time partner of Jack Kirby and the editor of *Sick* magazine, a B&W humor competitor of *MAD*'s, was the actual editor. The presence of Carl Burgos in so much of the *Weird Mysteries* titles leads one to suspect that gonzo publisher Myron Fass may have had a hand in it as well. Fass was known for publishing magazines under a host of different company names and Burgos was the editor of his *Eerie* Publications line in the 1960s–1970s.

The two titles in question published horror and crime stories. The stories were partly prose but also used word balloons as regular comics did. So they too were not strictly comics or prose but instead a further refinement of Gaines' Picto-fiction effort. The uncredited stories aren't terrible and the artwork is pretty good, with contributions from Al Williamson, Gray Morrow, Angelo Torres, George Tuska (interior work as well as both covers), Joe Orlando and others. Still, neither title was a success.

James Warren then revived full-fledged horror comics in 1964, first tiptoeing in with three adapted (and greatly abbreviated) versions of 1930s–1940s Universal horror movies in his film magazine *Monster World*, with art by Wally Wood, Joe Orlando and Angelo Torres. *Creepy* #1 hit the newsstands almost immediately alongside the appearance of those stories.

Whose idea it was to actually publish a B&W horror comic in magazine form, which could get around Comic Code restrictions, is somewhat of a mystery. James Warren, the publisher; Russ Jones, the first editor; and Larry Ivie, an early writer for *Creepy*, all claim some or all of the credit. Ivie had contacts with many of the early artists, especially EC vet Al Williamson, who contacted many of his friends to contribute, including Frank Frazetta, Angelo Torres and Archie Goodwin. Jones had contacts with Wally Wood and his assistants and had done work for Warren in the past on several of his science fiction film magazines. Warren himself was a comics fan and, as the publisher, had the final say on what actually happened. My guess is that all three had varying levels of influence, along with influence from folks like Joe Orlando and Archie Goodwin. It is known that Warren wanted Orlando, another EC veteran, to be the editor and that Jones got the job when Orlando declined. Nonetheless, Orlando participated in the planning of that first issue and Goodwin, who would become editor when Warren fired Jones, wrote several stories for that first issue and was listed as the story editor by the second issue.

Warren may have been playing it safe with the first issue's cover. Although he had Frank Frazetta doing an interior story, the leadoff cover was a humorous effort by Jack Davis, showing Uncle Creepy, the horror host of the magazine, reading the contents to a collection of monsters, including the Monster of Frankenstein. Frazetta's classic horror covers wouldn't show up until the second issue.

Warren was in a unique place in 1964. Many of the EC veterans were both available and eager to work on *Creepy*, a situation that wouldn't have existed if he'd tried the idea a year or two later. Unlike DC, Marvel, Dell or Gold Key, the leading publishers of the day, Warren had no house style that artists had to conform to. Thus, experimentation by the artists was encouraged or, at least, not discouraged. Without color, the line artwork gained added prominence, enabling fine line artists such as Al Williamson, Reed Crandall or Angelo Torres to really shine. The superior artwork from all of the EC vets pushed other artists to bring their own "A" game to the Warren table.

Warren had one more secret weapon—a huge one—in the presence of writer/editor Archie Goodwin. Goodwin, whose prior comic effort consisted of a single five-page science fiction story written in 1958 and published in 1962 in Harvey Publications' *Alarming Adventures* #1, proved to be Warren's best asset. Goodwin had the technical experience in putting together a magazine from his employment at *Redbook*. He was an artist himself, although his style was more suited to cartoons than straight action or horror comics. He often wrote his scripts in the form of a thumbnail, or rough, comics page, something that other artists apparently liked a great deal. He was also a master at tailoring his stories to appeal to each individual artist's own enthusiasms or strengths. Thus, Al Williamson got character studies and science fiction tales, John Severin received gritty war tales or horror stories set in the old west, Reed Crandall did the bulk of the nineteenth-century story adaptations, Steve Ditko got scripts set in grubby bookstores or sword and sorcery mini-epics and so on. Goodwin also wrote nearly 80 percent of the stories for Warren between 1964 and 1967 and they were generally of such high quality that they are fondly remembered these many years later.

Unlike the earlier efforts already mentioned, *Creepy* was a success right from the start and before long Warren had three full B&W comic magazines running — *Creepy*, its sister magazine *Eerie* and the short-lived war title *Blazing Combat*. The year 1969 saw a third horror title, *Vampirella*, added to the mix.

That same year saw Warren's first true competition on the newsstands with the appearance of *Web of Horror* from Major Publications. Major's claim to fame in the comic magazine field was its *MAD*-inspired humor title *Cracked*, which EC vet John Severin did a huge amount of work for. *Web* didn't last long, only three issues, but it did force Warren to upgrade his own titles (always a good thing) and introduced young artists like Bernie (then Berni) Wrightson, Ralph Reese, Frank Brunner, Bruce Jones, Michael Kaluta and others to the B&W horror field.

The next set of magazines to challenge Warren's dominance of the B&W field came from a new company, Skywald, formed by publisher Israel Waldman (the Wald) and editor Sol Brodsky (the Sky). Skywald had three main titles — *Nightmare* (1970–1975), *Psycho* (1971–1975) and *Scream* (1973–1975). In the beginning, during Brodsky's editorship, both *Nightmare* and *Psycho* basically served as extra copies of the Warren titles. They had many of the same artists and writers and the quality of the stories was on a similar level. However, Brodsky left the company in 1972 and installed his assistant editor, Al Hewetson, in his place. Hewetson had editorial experience with Marvel Comics as Stan Lee's assistant and had written a number of stories for Warren. At Skywald, however, he had the freedom to do horror the way he thought it should be done and he unleashed what he called the "horror-mood," a delirious blend of the works of Edgar Allan Poe, H. P. Lovecraft and Hewetson's own somewhat overwrought imagination. Hewetson loved alliteration, ellipses ... and the word *macabre* ... and he worked them into a story whenever he could.

The result was a style of storytelling that was quite different from a Warren magazine. Many horror stories are grim. Neither Warren or Skywald tales were exceptions to this, but each Warren tale was generally complete, in and of itself. Skywald tales were a feverish concoction of stories that sometimes barely made sense but each story both built on and fed upon each horror tale that appeared before and after them in each issue. A single Skywald story, by itself, never towered as high as a classic Warren tale, but collectively they were as different from Warren's stories as you could get. Warren had superior art, better storytelling and, above all, *depth*. Skywald had decent art, good storytelling and, above all, *mood*.

If Skywald's approach was seat-of-the-pants publishing and Warren's was stay-small-but-be-the-best-at-what-you-do, than Marvel's take on the B&W field was that of a corporate model. Marvel's artists were just as good as Warren's. Its writers were also usually just as strong but those Marvel writers came from a completely different viewpoint. Marvel's writers were trained on superhero or action adventure genres and their B&W titles generally reflected that. With rare exceptions — the Simon Garth adventures from Steve Gerber and Morbius under Don McGregor's hand — most of Marvel's B&W headliners were horror characters appearing in action adventure stories. At both Warren and Skywald, storylines ended, often with the main character's death. Except for Simon Garth, the living zombie, Marvel never intentionally ended a character's run. And even Garth's death was reconsidered.

In addition, Marvel never limited itself to a single genre. Warren was mainly horror. After brief stabs at crime, science fiction and action-adventure, Skywald was all horror, all the time. Marvel's B&W line not only had a full lineup of horror, but two science fiction titles, a half-dozen or more action adventure titles, and a humor magazine. Marvel had financial and publishing resources that Warren and Skywald could only dream of. Still, with rare exceptions, Marvel's horror titles lacked the punch of pure terror that both Warren and Skywald could regularly achieve.

Marvel first tested the waters of B&W publishing in 1968 with a Spider-Man magazine. The results must not have been good because the second and final issue was in color. They came back with a single issue of *Savage Tales* in 1971, which suffered from distribution woes, and then made a full-blown assault on the newsstands in 1973, unleashing a monster film magazine, a humor title, two adventure titles and no fewer than five horror titles in a matter of months. In the long run, Marvel's B&W newsstand efforts outlasted the closing and shutterings of both Skywald and Warren's doors but the longest lived of their horror titles only lasted two years, from 1973–1975.

This was largely a result of their flooding the marketplace with titles. Marvel's domination of the newsstands ensured Skywald's demise in early 1975 and damaged Warren enough that its promising experimentation with high-quality color in 1973–1975 was cut short and the page count of their titles grew noticeably shorter. Skywald carried stories from cover to cover. Two thirds or more of a Warren title of that time featured story content. Early Marvel titles, however, were 50 percent or more filler, with text articles and pre-code reprints taking the place of new stories. Their titles were often a quarter or more cheaper — a big deal back in 1973, when a quarter represented 20 pages of original artwork.

Plus, a reader *knew* the Marvel creators. They'd grown up with the art of John Buscema and Gene Colan. Marvel's writers were often far better known to readers than those employed by both Warren and Skywald. The Marvel artists and writers worked not only at Marvel, but at DC and Charlton (and, usually uncredited, at Gold Key and Dell) as well. Many of Warren's writers worked for Warren Publishing and nobody else. Skywald's writers worked *only* at Skywald while the company existed.

After 1975, Marvel continued with science fiction, fantasy, sword and sorcery, and action-adventure B&W titles, with only rare forays into horror. Warren soldiered on. Its *Spirit* reprint book ran for three years (1974–1976) and was highly acclaimed but couldn't make enough of a profit to keep going. *Heavy Metal*, which reprinted dozens of European stories, came along in 1977 (and is still publishing today) and shocked both Warren and Marvel with its full-process color, European sensibilities — particularly regarding a heavy use of nudity — and beautiful artwork, all of which were combined with remarkably poor, or poorly translated, stories. Most important of all, though, was that it impressed the American companies with its success. Marvel, Warren and even schlock merchant Myron Fass all promptly launched copycat titles. Fass's 1978 effort — *Gasm* — lasted five issues. Warren's effort *1984* (later retitled *1994*), also from 1978, lasted until the company collapsed. Both were still largely B&W titles with only one or two color efforts per issue. Marvel's magazine — *Epic Illustrated* — took longer to appear but, like *Heavy Metal*, was largely color, concentrated on using American artists more than the Europeans, and, under the editorship of one-time Warren editor Archie Goodwin, had far better stories than any of the other publishers' efforts. *Epic Illustrated* (1980–1986) was a classy, well-done magazine.

Under editor Louise Jones (1976–1980), most of Warren's magazines maintained a high level of story and art, despite the somewhat reduced circumstances. Many of the popular American artists from the magazines' beginnings in 1964–1967, such as Russ Heath and Alex Toth, returned. Newer American artists such as Paul

Gulacy and Val Mayerik were providing top-notch art. The many Spanish artists Warren used continued to deliver strong pages and those Filipino artists making their Warren debuts — Alex Nino, Nestor Redondo, Vicatan, and Rudy Nebres, in particular — were the strongest artists from that region.

However, in December 1979 James Warren ordered a freeze on buying new stories. Within a few weeks, Jones left Warren for the greener editorial pastures of Marvel. Bill DuBay, who'd served as either Warren's art director or editor from 1971 to 1976, returned as editor, this time using the name Will Richardson, but under orders to use up a vast stockpile of unproduced scripts, some dating from years earlier. The result was that the quality of the stories at all three of the main Warren titles dropped like a rock. Unable to sell new stories, Warren's best writers at the time either moved on, or back to, the color comic companies (Bruce Jones, Don MacGregor) or retired from comics completely (Bob Toomey). Those few who remained seemed burnt out.

Matters were further exacerbated by publisher James Warren falling ill and being unable to visit the offices for long periods of time or to oversee the publishing operations as he had done in the past. Just as it had been the best possible time for him to have started his comics publishing venture, it was now the worst possible time for him to be absent. Times were changing. The major Spanish artists were no longer appearing regularly in Warren titles. The American artists who Louise Jones had welcomed also largely vanished from Warren pages. The places of both were given over to the lesser Filipino artists, whose styles were often distressingly similar to each other. That sameness of art and the lesser quality of the stories made for often dreary issues, particularly noticeably in *Eerie*.

The newsstands, drug stores and supermarkets, long the traditional selling platforms for the B&W magazines, began to cut back on the shelf space for magazines of all types but especially those of comics. In the mid–1970s a few non-returnable independent comics, such as *Star*Reach*, *Imagine*, *Hot Stuf'* and others had paved the way for small publishing companies to use the advent of comic shops, stores devoted largely to comics alone, as an alternate market. With the absence of Jim Warren, nobody at the company appeared to be able to move Warren's magazines into that new, profitable market, even as the traditional markets continued to shrink.

The format of the magazines themselves began to present a problem as well. The magazine size of Warren's titles didn't fit on spinner racks, while a regular size comic, whether from Marvel, DC or one of the numerous independent comics companies, could. The independent companies became direct competitors of Warren's horror line with their own horror titles, also published outside the purview of the Comics Code Authority and often written or drawn by former Warren writers and artists. Bruce Jones, arguably Warren's best writer from 1976 to 1982, launched his own color horror series, *Twisted Tales*, which boasted not only superior stories but striking artwork from the likes of Mike Ploog, Bernie Wrightson, John Bolton, Tim Conrad, Rick Geary and others, all of them artists who would and should have been appearing in Warren's magazines. Goodwin's *Epic Illustrated* offered better money and a welcoming market for writers and artists who once would have looked to Warren as a place to present new, edgy material. In its last year of publishing, nearly every other issue of a Warren magazine was a reprint issue, showcasing Warren's glory days while providing a steady contrast in quality to the, at best, fair-to-middling original stories appearing in the regular issues.

In late 1982, with issues cover-dated to either February or March 1983, Warren closed up shop. In August 1983 many of the Warren publication rights were auctioned off to Harris Publications. Stanley Harris had been a partner of Myron Fass for many years before they had a falling out and his publishing empire often echoed Fass' own operations. He published an issue of *Creepy* in 1985, continuing Warren's numbering, which consisted mostly of reprints behind a new Richard Corben cover. An issue of *Vampirella* appeared in 1989, also continuing the Warren numbering. It too was mostly reprint material.

With Warren gone and Marvel no longer doing B&W horror, the publishing of magazine-sized B&W comics came largely to an end in the 1990s. In the nearly thirty years since the end of Warren Publishing there have been only a handful of companies who have attempted to take on the task of publishing full-sized B&W horror magazines.

Warrior, a British magazine (1982–1986) heavily distributed in the United States, was published and edited by Dez Skinn, who had previously worked as a Marvel-UK editor. While *Warrior* was not primarily a horror title, both of Alan Moore's ground-breaking series, *Marvelman* and *V for Vendetta*, had heavy horror overtones. In fact, Moore's *Marvelman* may be the most horrific superhero title ever published. In addition they ran straight horror serials such as *Father Shandor*, featuring a medieval priest who battled actual demons, and *Maniac*, a serial that supposedly got its stories from the mind of an insane man wrapped in a strait jacket. They also ran numerous one-off horror tales.

Steve Bissette's *Taboo* (1988–1995) was probably the most important horror title of the 1990s. It is certainly the most disturbing. *Taboo* boasted powerhouse writers such as Alan Moore and Neil Gaiman, both of whom appeared regularly. Warren writers such as Jack Butterworth returned to comics in its pages. New writers such as the excellent Tim Lucas got their start here. The artwork was often superb, with contributions from artists like Michael Zulli, Charles Vess, Moebius, Mike Hoffman, P. Craig Russell, Eddie Campbell, Rolf Stark, Melinda Gebbie, Bissette himself and many more. All of it was done up in handsome trade paperback volumes of well over a hundred pages. An enormous amount of back history was given on the writers and artists as well as considerable information on the history of horror in comics itself via excellent essays and introductions by Bissette.

Taboo died not so much from low sales, although that may have been a factor, but from the combination of the constantly shifting tumult of self-publishing, co-publishers' problems, the distributor intrigues of the early 1990s, the loss of major serials as other publishers, better

equipped and richer, saw the advantages of reprinting (and concluding) the more high-profile stories *Taboo* published and finally, Bissette's own inability to get the magazine out on a regular schedule. In the end, Bissette was simply too exhausted by it all to continue.

It would be a huge and costly task to attempt to reprint the volumes of *Taboo* in archive editions so it is unlikely to ever be done. You will have to search out the original issues to read them. Be warned: Bissette and company regularly trod the razor's edge of acceptability and, according to some, occasionally stepped off it. This is not horror that allows you a measure of reassurance after the story ends. As with the fish that snaps the hook off once it's embedded, the bitter barb of horror contained within these volumes will always remain. Still, this magazine traced, continued and concluded a direct line of horror templates stretching from the pre-code EC Comics of the 1950s, on to the Warren and Skywald titles of the 1960–1970s and continuing in the mini-renaissance of horror in such color titles as *Twisted Tales* or the B&W comic *Gore-Shriek* in the early to mid–1980s. Not content to copy what had gone before, *Taboo* built on the foundations of dead moldering magazines and raised its own horrible edifice. Since its own demise there has been nothing to really take its place.

Both *Monsters Attack* (from Globe Communications, 1989–1990) and Bruce Hamilton's trilogy of titles — *Grave Tales, Maggots* and *Dread of Night* (1991–1992) — aimed themselves at a younger audience than had Warren, Skywald, Marvel, *Taboo* and most of the other short-lived B&W horror titles but both of these companies published some good stories and were getting increasingly better. Unfortunately, the marketplace had simply moved on. Readers, particularly young readers, no longer seemed willing to read comics that weren't in color. Black and white comics, which serve horror tales so much better than color, were simply ignored by the buying public. If you doubt that black and white is better than color for horror, take a look at DC's Showcase volumes of their "mystery" titles from the 1960s and 1970s. In their B&W reproductions, they seem ten times more effective to look at, read, marvel at for the crisp art, and shudder at than the original color versions.

The last effort, to date, at producing a full-fledged horror magazine is IDW's *Doomed* (2005–2006). It wasn't innovative in any way, basing its look, style and editorial outlook squarely on what Jim Warren and company had done in the 1970s, but it was well done. The stories, adapted from four great horror writers, were strong. The artwork was appropriate to the subject matter. The little tidbits and text articles were fun. It just simply didn't make enough of a profit to continue. Since its cancellation, the days of the full-fledged black and white horror magazines seems ended.

To make this book a manageable length I had to come up with some basic rules. First, each publisher's section would have the most complete and up-to-date credits for the magazines included. Each issue would have a commentary on that particular issue, pointing out interesting historical tidbits or reviewing the stories in that issue.

For the most part, only publishers that published new, original stories are covered. That approach does seem to leave what some may see as a gaping hole in the B&W magazine coverage. Both *Eerie* Publications and the similar magazines put out by Stanley Publications are not included in this book because neither were primary publishers of original stories. Stanley Morse's magazines featured reprinted pre-code horror stories. *Eerie* Publications did a few originals but the vast majority of their output consisted of either straight reprints or redrawn versions of pre-code stories. These redrawn stories were gory in the extreme and far more offensive than the original pre-code versions. Whatever value the original story may have had was often buried beneath the juvenile gore and sensationalism.

For example, the pre-code tale "I Killed Mary," which originally appeared in *Weird Mysteries* #8 (January 1954), is a pretty good story dealing with a mentally challenged boy's sexual tempting by a pretty farm girl. In his excitement he kills her in a barn, then goes home and tells his family what happened. As they sit around the dinner table, none of his relatives believe him because he's such a mild-mannered boy and not

quite all there anyway. It's a story that borrows from John Steinbeck's *Of Mice and Men* and clearly foreshadows Bobbi Gentry's song "Ode to Billy Joe." *Eerie*'s retelling of the story became "I Chopped Her Head Off!" and was published in *Tales of Voodoo*, vol. 4 #2 (March 1971), and, like the more gruesome title implies, has the violence factor vastly increased, with the victim's head being lopped off in an extremely jagged fashion, eyeballs popping loose from her face, etc. The original, well-told story is completely buried under the bottom-of-the-drawer, violence-laden approach. *Eerie* Publications' approach to story seemed to be on the gruesome level of a father slowing the car down so the kids can get a really good look at the mangled bodies from the car wreck. Worse, when their stories weren't draped in gore, they were utterly boring. Thankfully for the dedicated collector, there is a book — *The Weird World of Eerie Publications* — that provides a well-written and researched history for those interested.

I have included Warren's war title *Blazing Combat*, because it's my belief that a good war story is inherently a good horror story as well. *Blazing Combat* is one of the five best war comics events ever produced in the field [for the record, the other four are *Two-Fisted Tales* and *Frontline Combat*, edited and written by Harvey Kurtzman for EC Comics from 1950 to 1953, the two serials, *The Lonely War of Capt. Willy Schultz* and *The Iron Corporal*, written by Willi Franz and illustrated by Sam Glanzman circa 1967–1970 for Charlton Comics, Glanzman's solo *U.S.S. Stevens' Tales* (1970–1977) for DC Comics and (1986) for Marvel Comics and, finally, Garth Ennis' two war series, *War Stories* (2003–2006 from DC) and *Battlefields* (2008–2013 — so far — from Dynamite)]. If you've read *Blazing Combat*, you'll know exactly what I'm writing about in terms of the horror content.

So too, I've included several science fiction titles from both Warren and Marvel as well as Skywald's unpublished solo effort in that field. In comics, far more so than in prose, there is a long-standing tradition that science fiction often combines with horror within the SF genre. However, I have not included action-adventure titles, humor titles or sword and sorcery titles where horror is rarely, if ever, addressed. Perhaps a sequel to this book covering those titles will be forthcoming.

For reading ease, each title in each chapter is discussed in the chronological order in which it was originally published. Text articles and stories are identified in the credits, as are writer or artist's pseudonyms and stories or artwork that were incorrectly credited in the original publication. Commentaries follow each issue's credits.

The Warren Magazines

The Warren magazines were the big cheese in the black and white horror magazine boom for the 1960s–1970s, if only because they were there first, they lasted the longest and they published the most. James Warren, the publisher of several different movie magazines, most notably *Famous Monsters of Filmland*, was a long-time lover of comics, particularly the EC comics of the early 1950s. He made a few tentative stabs at comics in 1964, producing a trio of stories adapting movies from the 1930s for his title *Monster World*, a sister magazine of *Famous Monsters of Filmland*. In late 1964 he decided to take the plunge, producing a full-length horror comic anthology. It should be noted that the magazines he published were not comic books but magazines. They had to be.

The Comics Code Authority, established in 1955 to "clean up" comics, had demolished the EC empire of quality horror comics as well as almost all of the lesser publishers of horror comics. It forced those publishers who survived to water down any hint of horror content to near pablum. You couldn't use vampires, zombies, skeletons, ghouls, etc., as characters in a comic book. You couldn't show blood or horrific details. An excessive amount of shadows or darkness was discouraged. You couldn't write a storyline that suggested that the reader was directly involved in the story. No hint of sex or sexual motivation as a backdrop was allowed. Martial discord was not allowed. Nor could you use such words as "horror," "weird," "crime" or "terror" in titles (although only two of those words — "horror" and "terror" — were specifically banned). As the comic industry existed in 1964, a revival of EC-type comics would not have been possible.

Besides, Jim Warren published *magazines*, designed to sit on stands alongside *Life*, *Look*, *Sports Illustrated* or *Playboy*. Well, maybe a few shelves over from those magazines but still in the general vicinity. Nowhere near those tawdry comic book spinner racks.

Plus, the Comics Code Authority had no authority over magazines, since nobody had ever published anything identified as a comic book successfully in magazine form. As mentioned earlier, EC had, in its dying days, published what they called Picto-fiction: prose stories dealing with crime and horror with a heavy amount of art in comic book style from comic book artists. However, this experiment was a failure. They'd also changed their humor comic, *MAD*, into a black and white comic magazine. They promptly stopped calling it a comic, however. It was now a humor magazine.

In 1959 there was a brief two-issue cross-blend of EC Picto-fiction and what Warren would later produce in the 1960s from editor Joe Simon. It, too, was neither fish nor fowl and was unsuccessful.

So Warren decided to publish his comic stories in a format he was comfortable with, for a distribution system he understood and in a style that allowed him a great deal of freedom. Then he aimed those stories at the exact same audience that the regular four-color comics had targeted —12-to-14-year-old boys. It was a smart and, as it turned out, profitable end run around the Comics Code.

The Warren run can be split up into five

distinct eras. The first was the Goodwin era, which ran from 1965 to 1967. Obviously this era was marked by the work of Archie Goodwin, who edited the line and wrote most of the stories for this period. It's hard to overemphasize how important Goodwin's work here is. He not only provided a foundation for Warren Publications to grow upon and succeed, but he also provided a writing template for other comic writers and for many future writers of horror prose.

The early success of *Creepy* and *Eerie*, a major portion of which can be laid at Goodwin's door as much as James Warren's, gave color comic companies like Charlton, DC and Marvel the desire to reenter the horror field, which helped spark the changing of the Comics Code and directly led to the horror boom that comics went through from 1971 to 1975. Warren mainstay and former EC artist Joe Orlando became an editor at DC and, for at least the prime years of 1968–1973, provided a truly good horror line. Charlton revitalized its own horror line, first under Dick Giordano and then Sal Gentile, and provided a home base in the color comics field for Steve Ditko, Pat Boyette, Rocco Mastroserio and other Warren artists. Marvel blatantly copied Warren when it began its own color horror line in 1969. Its horror hosts for both *Tower of Shadows* and *Chamber of Darkness* looked and sounded a great deal like Uncle Creepy and the style of story was modeled much more after the Warren story style than EC's more sardonic brand of horror. Later, Warren artists such as Mike Ploog, Gray Morrow, Gene Colan and Tom Sutton became major forces in creating and refining Marvel characters such as Dracula, Frankenstein's Monster, Werewolf by Night, Man-Thing, Morbius, the Living Vampire, and Ghost Rider.

Recently, while reading *Toybox*, a collection of Al Sarrantonio's stories (a strong writer and probably *the* major editor in the horror field today), I was pleasantly shocked to recognize that his major literary influence appeared to be the Archie Goodwin Warren stories. In fact, there wasn't a story in that collection that would not have fit handsomely in a Warren magazine circa 1965–1967. I suspect that Stephen King read Warren comics during this period. I know he read the Skywald books in the early 1970s.

This is the cover that started it all. Jim Warren was clearly nervous, however, as this Jack Davis painting is more humorous than scary. © New Comic Co./used by permission.

Goodwin also started a fan page in *Creepy*, where young comic artists and writers could display their own *Creepy* efforts. The letters and fan pages of the Warren magazines are crowded with fan letters and art from pre-professional writers, artists and filmmakers.

But even beyond the solid editorial foundation and literary influence that Goodwin built at Warren were his rock-solid stories month after month. This, along with the respect, care and extra effort that every artist seemed to strive for when working on them, coupled with the obvious joy Goodwin took in tailoring stories for each artist's particular skills, created an extremely high-quality magazine. Re-reading this three-year stretch of stories was just a joy.

By the end of 1967, however, Goodwin and almost all of the artists he had worked with left, victims of a money crunch that forced Warren Publishing to drastically cut page rates and launched Warren into its dark age. For the next two and a half years, 50 percent or more of every issue was reprints. Most of the new stories were so-so at best and were greatly hampered by inferior art, with only Tom Sutton (the only Goodwin era artist to regularly contribute during this time) and Harvey artist Ernie Colon providing any steady quality work. Sutton's cover art, in particular, is worth noting.

The end of the dark age was highlighted by the launch of *Vampirella*, a new comic magazine with a sexy vampiress hosting it. From 1969 to 1973, Warren rebuilt its position as the leading black and white horror publisher. In doing so, Warren launched an astonishing number of artists' and writers' careers into mainstream comics, including (although not limited to) Dave Cockrum, Mike Ploog, Doug Moench, Nicola Cuti, Don McGregor, Al Hewetson, Ed Fedory, Bill Black, Rich Corben, Boris Vallejo, Ken Kelly, Paul Neary and many more.

In 1972–73, two events occurred that completely changed the look of a Warren comic magazine. First, was the "invasion" of Spanish artists from the Selecciones Illustrated (from here on in referred to as S.I.) Studio. Many of these artists came from the European romance field and their ability to draw startling beautiful women as well as a much different brand of horror than Amer-

ican readers were used to was certainly a major draw. The second event was a complete graphic redesign of the magazines themselves by new editor Bill DuBay. During his first stint as editor (he held the title three different times) from 1972 to 1976, he was very much a hands-on boss and the quality of the magazines' stories and art greatly improved. Warren introduced color sections with coloring that was better than any of the comic companies except possibly Playboy's *Little Annie Fannie*. They reintroduced Will Eisner's classic *The Spirit* to readers who probably weren't ever born when the original run ended. In addition, DuBay's reign also seemed to feature a uniform approach to the style and mood of the horror in the magazines, an approach that was as strong as, but completely different from, the approach that Goodwin used. It was certainly something that had not been reflected in the scattershot years from 1968 to 1972.

Beginning in 1976, Louise Jones, former wife of artist Jeff Jones and future wife of artist Walt Simonson, headed the editorial staff, maintaining much of the best of the innovations that DuBay introduced while pulling back into the Warren fold some of the classic American artists who had vanished from the pages of the Warren magazines back in 1967.

After Jones left in 1980, the magazines began a slow decline under a series of different editors. Bill DuBay came back twice, once using the nom-de-plume of Will Richardson, but the quality of the magazines took a sharp nosedive both times. The Spanish artists largely left and were replaced by artists from the Philippines. Mind you, these were not bad artists, but, with the notable exceptions of Alex Nino, Alfredo Alcala and Vic Catan, stylistically they tended to be rather dull. By 1983, when the line collapsed, *Creepy* seemed to be just plodding along, while *Eerie* had abandoned horror completely and was a tottering shell of the fine magazine it had used to be. Only *Vampirella* was showing signs of life. Under the editorship of Timothy Moriarty, it seemed to be staging a comeback when the axe fell.

What caused the collapse? There were a number of different reasons, a major one being that publisher James Warren had fallen ill some years earlier and had little to do with the day-to-day operations of the company any longer. The independent comic shop boom had just begun with new comic companies seemingly springing up overnight. The fresh books and, especially, the physical appearance of those books left Warren's magazines looking somewhat obsolete. Many of Warren's best writers and artists were gone, either working for the big two comic companies or for the new independents. The remaining writers, many of whom had delivered fine work over the years, seemed burnt out. The editorial revolving door insured that no strong hand was at the helm. The horror boom of the early 1970s was long over. Distribution was changing, with the old markets of newsstands, drug stores and supermarkets dropping both comic books and magazines from their inventories. The new comic shops which replaced those markets were none too interested in the Warren books, which appeared old fashioned and tired (and didn't fit into spinner racks!). After 18 years the line ended, not with a whimper or bang, but largely with a yawn.

For much of the nearly 30 years since, there seemed to be few who cared. Harris Publications bought up the assets of Warren and relaunched *Vampirella* with some success in the 1990s. Still, Vampi was never that strong of a character to begin with and while the Harris version is actually better storywise than the Warren version, their approach to her adventures doesn't seem to have improved the quality of her character significantly. However, in recent years there's been a rebirth of interest in the original Warren line, beginning with *The Warren Companion*, complied by David A. Roach and Jon B. Cooke, which is an excellent book-length expansion of the fourth issue of the comic history magazine, *Comic Book Artist*. Another decent source is Stephen Sennitt's *Ghastly Terror*, although there are some irritating technical art/text screwups — covers and art pages mentioned don't appear on the appropriate page of text — and, at times, Sennitt's opinions and bias are not supported by his own observations. Nonetheless, there's a great deal of useful information in the book. In 2003, *Spooky*, a fine fanzine dedicated to the history of Warren Publications, debuted in England and

ran for eight issues before being forced out of business by a change in distributor rules. In 2007, New Comics purchased the rights to the *Creepy* and *Eerie* magazines from Jim Warren, who'd had them returned to him via a lawsuit with Harris. In partnership with Dark Horse Comics, they began an archive reprinting of the original magazines, similar in style to the B&W EC archive volumes published by Russ Cochran in the 1980s. As of this writing, eleven volumes of *Creepy* and nine volumes of *Eerie* have appeared. A large *Spooky Yearbook* was published in early 2010 with some interview and article reprints from the earlier run as well as new print appearance of many others (including some of my interviews with Warren veterans). The spring of 2010 brought the news that Dynamite Comics had purchased the rights to the original *Vampirella* magazine and, to date, has published three archive volumes of that title as well. In June 2010 a massive near–700-page checklist/bibliography called *Gathering Horror*, self-published by writer David Horne, appeared. It is the most through reference book on the subject of Warren Publishing that any Warren fan could hope for.

I'd also like to point out a few online credits sources — the blog of Martin O'Hearn at www.martinohearn.com and, of course, the big one — the Grand Comics Database which one can find at www.comics.org, both of which have information on the B&W magazines and their creators.

It's my hope that this checklist is also a worthy addition to those fans and readers interested in the history of Warren Publications. Have fun!

The Goodwin Era

Creepy

1. cover: Jack Davis (January 1965)

(1) Uncle Creepy's Welcome [Russ Jones?/Jack Davis; frontis] 1p; (2) Voodoo! [Bill Pearson/Joe Orlando, story miscredited to Russ Jones and Bill Pearson] 6p; (3) H20 World! [Larry Ivie/Al Williamson and Roy G. Krenkel] 6p; (4) Vampires Fly at Dusk! [Archie Goodwin/Reed Crandall] 6p; (5) Werewolf! [Larry Ivie/Frank

Frazetta] 6p; (6) Bewitched! [Larry Ivie/Gray Morrow] 6p; (7) The Success Story [Archie Goodwin/Al Williamson] 6p; (8) Pursuit of the Vampire! [Archie Goodwin/Angelo Torres] 6p; (9) Creepy ad [illustrated: Frank Frazetta] 1p.

Notes: Publisher: James Warren. Editor: Russ Jones. 35 cents for 48 pages. No cover date but in keeping with the dates on the 3rd issue, this would probably have been dated either January or Winter 1965. Jack Davis provides several head shot drawings of Uncle Creepy for story introductions. Bill Pearson has stated repeatedly in print his displeasure over editor Russ Jones' claiming of a writing credit for the lead-off story. Pearson insists it's all his work. Apparently this first issue was originally intended to be an "all EC artists" effort with the story "Bewitched" intended to be Wally Wood's contribution. Somehow the story was sent to artist Gray Morrow instead, making him the only non–EC artist included. The Frazetta story was his last comic art, except for two "Creepy's Loathsome Lore" pages which may have been done prior to the art for this story, a Tarzan parody page, which appeared in *MAD* in 1966 and an anti-cigarette ad which appeared in *Eerie*, also in 1966. The best story in this issue, Goodwin's "The Success Story," was based on an actual comic strip artist (supposedly Don Sherwood) who apparently conned his ghost penciler, inker and writer, who were unaware of each other, into doing the entire strip while he claimed credit for it. Characters in that story are based on Goodwin, Williamson, Angelo Torres and Al McWilliams. All in all, a very good first issue.

2. cover: Frank Frazetta (April 1965)

(1) Uncle Creepy's Introduction [Archie Goodwin?/Angelo Torres, frontis] 1p; (2) Fun and Games! [Archie Goodwin/Joe Orlando] 6p; (3) Creepy's Loathsome Lore: Vampires! [Archie Goodwin/Bob Lubbers] 1p; (4) Spawn of the Cat People [Archie Goodwin/Reed Crandall] 6p; (5) Wardrobe of Monsters! [Otto Binder/Gray Morrow and Angelo Torres] 8p; (6) Creepy's Loathsome Lore: Werewolves! [Archie Goodwin/Frank Frazetta] 1p; (7) Welcome Stranger [Archie Goodwin/Al Williamson] 7p; (8) I, Robot [Otto Binder/Joe Orlando, from the story by Otto Binder] 7p; (9) Ogre's Castle [Archie Goodwin/Angelo Torres] 6p; (10) Creepy ad [illustrated: Jack Davis] 1p.

Notes: Goodwin was now listed as story editor. Again, no cover date but this would have been the April or Spring 1965 issue. It also turned out to be the first bimonthly issue. The "I, Robot" adaptation by Otto Binder was his third attempt to present this series in comic form. The first was for EC comics in the 1950s (Orlando did the artwork for that attempt too) and a second attempt appeared in 1964 in a fanzine with art by D. Bruce Berry. This version ran irregularly over the next two years. Jack Davis appeared with more illustrations of Uncle Creepy for story introductions. The art from the *Creepy* ad by Davis turned up again as the cover to the *Eerie* #1 ashcan edition. The "Loathsome Lore" pages listed here did not have official titles for the first 25 or so issues. Titles noted are actually coined by me, based on lore content. The first letters page featured letters from Rip Kirby artist John Prentice and Onstage artist Leonard Starr. "Ogre's Castle" is an especially good story although the art for "Spawn of the Cat People" is quite nice as well. "Wardrobe of Monsters" has Gray Morrow doing the first seven pages while Angelo Torres did the eighth and last page. The first Frazetta cover effort featured a man threatened by growling black panthers. Good, but a long ways from what he was soon to show readers. Frazetta's *Creepy* paintings are sometimes listed as his first horror paintings but he was also painting Ballantine's paperback collections of EC stories and the first collection in that series appeared at roughly the same time as *Creepy* #1. All four of those Ballantine paperbacks had knockout horror covers and are worth looking for. Another solid issue.

3. cover: Frank Frazetta (June 1965)

(1) Creepy's Loathsome Lore: Ghouls! [Archie Goodwin/Jack Davis, frontis] 1p; (2) Swamped! [written: Archie Goodwin/Angelo Torres] 8p; (3) Tell-Tale Heart! [Archie Goodwin/Reed Crandall, from the story "The Tell-Tale Heart" by Edgar Allan Poe] 8p; (4) Howling Success! [Archie Goodwin/Angelo Torres] 7p; (5) Haunted! [Archie Goodwin/Gray Morrow] 6p; (6) Incident in the Beyond! [Archie Goodwin/Gray Morrow] 6p; (7) Return Trip! [Arthur Porges/Joe Orlando] 8p; (8) Uncle Creepy ad [Jack Davis, on the inside back cover] 1p.

Notes: Frazetta's cover depicted a ghoul entering a castle. Again, no cover date but this would be the June issue. This is a very good issue with "Swamped!" and the "Tell-Tale Heart" adaptation holding the honors for best stories. The art is at a high level throughout with a special tip of the hat to Crandall's Poe adaptation. Morrow employed very different art approaches for his two stories. Orlando's art appears to be channeling Johnny Craig's EC work at certain points. The "Loathsome Lore" segment featured Jack Davis' only comic art for Warren's horror line. The letters page featured a reprint of a three-panel *Bullwinkle* comic strip featuring Uncle Creepy, illustrated by Al Kilgore.

4. cover: Frank Frazetta (August 1965)

(1) Creepy's Loathsome Lore: Corpses! [Archie Goodwin/Al Williamson, frontis] 1p; **(2)** Monster Rally! [Archie Goodwin/Angelo Torres] 8p; **(3)** Blood and Orchids! [Archie Goodwin/Al McWilliams] 7p; **(4)** The Damned Thing! [Archie Goodwin/Gray Morrow, from the story by Ambrose Bierce] 6p; **(5)** Moon City! [Larry Englehart/Al McWilliams] 6p; **(6)** Curse of the Full Moon! [Archie Goodwin/Reed Crandall] 8p; **(7)** The Trial of Adam Link! [Otto Binder/Joe Orlando, from the story by Otto Binder] 7p; **(8)** *Creepy* ad [Angelo Torres, on the inside back cover] 1p.

Notes: Goodwin is now listed as editor. The magazine increases to 56 pages but most of that is given over to Captain Company ads, which feature merchandise that Jim Warren thought horror fans would like. Over the years this was a very successful side venture for the company. No cover date but this is the August 1965 issue. Frazetta's cover was his best yet — a man is confronted by a werewolf while traveling over the moors. Just beautiful and the first true classic Warren cover. "Monster Rally" revealed the origin of Uncle Creepy. Art honors go to Al McWilliams for two very good jobs — making one wish he had done more for Warren. The best is "Blood and Orchids." Crandall's art job is also quite nice and illustrated the best script for this issue.

5. cover: Frank Frazetta (October 1965)

(1) Creepy's Loathsome Lore: Zombies! [Archie Goodwin/Angelo Torres, frontis] 1p; **(2)** Family Reunion! [Archie Goodwin/Joe Orlando] 8p; **(3)** Blazing Combat ad [John Severin] 1p; **(4)**

Untimely Tomb! [Archie Goodwin/Angelo Torres, title was credited to Anne T. Murphy] 7p; **(5)** Creepy Fan Club ad [Frank Frazetta and Angelo Torres, Torres' art is a reprint, Frazetta's is a B&W reproduction of the Uncle Creepy portrait poster which was one of the fan club's membership offerings] 1p; **(6)** Sand Doom [Archie Goodwin/Al Williamson] 6p; **(7)** The Judge's House! [Archie Goodwin/Reed Crandall, from the story by Bram Stoker] 8p; **(8)** Grave Undertaking [Archie Goodwin/Alex Toth] 6p; **(9)** Revenge of the Beast! [Archie Goodwin/Gray Morrow] 7p.

Notes: Frazetta's vampire cover was okay, but not his best work. The interior, however, was an absolute blast! Williamson's best art job for the early Warren issues, Toth's debut and solid efforts from Orlando, Torres, Crandall and Morrow make this an art fan's delight. Shoot, even the ads had great art! Severin's *Blazing Combat* ad had the same art as *Blazing Combat* #1's frontispiece. All of the stories were by Goodwin and there wasn't a clunker in the lot, with high points probably going to his Stoker adaptation. Anne T. Murphy was Goodwin's wife.

6. cover: Frank Frazetta (December 1965)

(1) Creepy's Loathsome Lore: Mummy's Curse! [Archie Goodwin/Roy G. Krenkel, frontis] 1p; **(2)** The Thing in the Pit! [Larry Ivie/Gray Morrow] 8p; **(3)** Thumbs Down! [Anne T. Murphy/Al Williamson] 6p; **(4)** Adam Link in Business! [Otto Binder/Joe Orlando, from the story by Otto Binder] 7p; **(5)** The Cask of Amontillado! [Archie Goodwin/Reed Crandall, from the story by Edgar Allan Poe] 8p; **(6)** *Eerie* ad [Angleo Torres, Uncle Creepy is featured] 1p; **(7)** The Stalkers [Archie Goodwin/Alex Toth] 6p; **(8)** Abominable Snowman! [Bill Pearson/John Severin] 6p; **(9)** Gargoyle [Archie Goodwin and Roy G. Krenkel/Angelo Torres] 8p.

Notes: Size increases to 64 pages. Frazetta's gargoyle cover is laid out by Roy G. Krenkel. Krenkel did this for several other Frazetta covers. In fact, he did quite a lot of work in the background for Warren but rarely appeared front and center for a solo art job. Much of his cover layouts are printed for the first time in the EC fanzine *Squa Tront* #7 in 1974. It's a shame that many of them never progressed to full paintings as they're all very striking. Anne T. Murphy contributes her only story for Warren and it was quite good, with snazzy Williamson art. The Poe adaptation is the high point for this issue, both storywise and artwise. Goodwin changes (or adds) the ending and it is a pretty good twist on Poe's classic tale. Future comic pro Frank Brunner has a letter published. A rubber Uncle Creepy Halloween mask is used in an ad on the back cover.

7. cover: Frank Frazetta (February 1966)

(1) The Duel of the Monsters! [Archie Goodwin/Angelo Torres] 8p; **(2)** Image of Bluebeard! [Bill Pearson/Bill Draut and Joe Orlando, art credited solely to Orlando] 7p; **(3)** Creepy's Loathsome Lore: Werebeasts! [Archie Goodwin/Frank Frazetta] 1p; **(4)** Rude Awakening! [Archie Goodwin/Alex Toth] 6p; **(5)** Drink Deep! [Otto Binder/John Severin] 7p; **(6)** The Creepy Fan Club: Frank Frazetta profile [Archie Goodwin/Roberto Oqueli, text article with photo] 1p; **(7)** The Body-Snatcher! [Archie Goodwin/Reed Crandall, from the story by Robert Louis Stevenson] 8p; **(8)** Blood of Krylon! [Archie Goodwin/Gray Morrow] 6p; **(9)** Hot Spell! [Archie Goodwin/Reed Crandall] 7p.

Reed Crandall's incredibly detailed artwork was a highlight of the early Warren magazines. This one is from *Creepy* #7. © New Comic Co./used by permission.

Notes: The second classic Frazetta cover featured Dracula and the Werewolf in a battle royale! The layout was again by Roy G. Krenkel. Best art job was Reed Crandall's "Hot Spell," which featured a stunning detailed splash page. Special note should be made here of Angelo Torres' exceptionally high quality of art during the Goodwin years. He had a story (and sometimes two) in every issue of the early *Creepy*s and *Eerie*s and also appeared in *Blazing Combat*. Each story was strongly paced and beautifully drawn. The fellow

who only appeared on the fringes during EC's run had, by the mid–1960s, developed into a damn fine artist in his own right. I don't mean to slight the other folks here. Frazetta, Toth, Severin, Morrow and a second fine job by Crandall make this a dynamite issue for art freaks. Stories aren't bad either. The Creepy Fan Club page debuted. This was Goodwin's attempt (and it worked) to foster a fan base for the magazine, similar to the one that he, and Warren writers like Ron Parker, John Benson, Bill Parente, Bhob

Stewart and others, had done for EC's horror comics in the 1950s in publications like *Ho-Hah!* Many future pros would make their comic debuts on a Warren fan page.

8. cover: Gray Morrow (April 1966)

(1) Creepy's Loathsome Lore: Vampire Traps! [Archie Goodwin/Angelo Torres, frontis] 1p; **(2)** The Coffin of Dracula [Archie Goodwin/Reed Crandall] 10p; **(3)** Death Plane [Larry Ivie/ George Evans] 6p; **(4)** The Mountain [Johnny Craig, story and art credited to Jay Taycee] 6p; **(5)** The Invitation [Larry Englehart, Russ Jones and Maurice Whitman/Manny Stallman] 7p; **(6)** The Creepy Fan Club: Gray Morrow profile [Archie Goodwin/Kirk Henderson, text article with photo] 1p; **(7)** Adam Link's Mate! [Otto Binder/Joe Orlando, from the story by Otto Binder] 8p; **(8)** Vested Interest [Ron Parker/ George Tuska] 6p; **(9)** Fitting Punishment [Archie Goodwin/Gene Colan] 8p.

Notes: With two horror magazines now coming out, Frazetta was too busy to do every cover so Gray Morrow stepped in with a fine cover, highlighting Warren's new serial, "The Coffin of Dracula," which took place directly after the events in Stoker's novel. The art highpoint is Johnny Craig's beautifully shaded pencil art for his own story. Craig used the pen name Jay Taycee so his advertising bosses wouldn't know he was drawing comics again. The stigma that had attached itself to his EC work from the anti-comics Congressional hearings in 1954 may have been a factor also. The story highpoints are the Dracula serial and Craig's work, although none of the stories are bad. Wish I could say the same about the art. Stallman's work is fair, at best, and Tuska's (generally a pretty good artist) effort is pretty limp. EC great George Evans does his only horror work for Warren. It ain't bad but that's about the best you could say about it. Both the Evans' and Stallman's stories were originally done for #1.

9. cover: Frank Frazetta (June 1966)

(1) Creepy's Loathsome Lore: Giant Man-Apes! [Archie Goodwin/Roy G. Krenkel, frontis] 1p; **(2)** Dark Kingdom! [Archie Goodwin/Gray Morrow] 8p; **(3)** The Castle on the Moor! [Johnny Craig, story and art credited to Jay Taycee] 6p; **(4)** Adam Link's Vengeance! [Otto Binder/Joe Orlando, from the story by Otto

Binder] 8p; **(5)** Overworked! [Archie Goodwin/Dan Adkins and Wally Wood] 6p; **(6)** The Creepy Fan Club: Alex Toth profile [Archie Goodwin/Berni Wrightson, text article with photo] 1p; **(7)** The Coffin of Dracula, part 2 [Archie Goodwin/Reed Crandall] 8p; **(8)** Out of Time [Archie Goodwin/Alex Toth] 6p; **(9)** The Spirit of the Thing! [Archie Goodwin/Steve Ditko] 8p; **(10)** Easy Way to a Tuff Surfboard! [Archie Goodwin/Frank Frazetta, an anti-smoking ad, reprinted from *Eerie* #3 (May 1966)] ½ p.

Notes: Frazetta's cover of a swordsman attacked by flying vampires was only fair although the vampires were cool. Morrow's lead character in his story appears to be the same character he later used in his "Edge of Chaos" comic for Pacific Comics in the early 1980s. The Wood/Adkins art was not very impressive but then neither was the story. Berni Wrightson, who spells his name Bernie today, made his comics debut with a pinup showing a man being dragged into a grave by three ghouls. The tombstone in the foreground reads "Berni Wrightson, December 15, 1965." All in all, this is not a very impressive issue with even the great artists appearing to have an off day and Goodwin's stories feeling rushed and uninspired. Best efforts are the conclusion to "Coffin of Dracula" and the Morrow story.

10. cover: Frank Frazetta (August 1966)

(1) Creepy's Loathsome Lore: Witchcraft! [Archie Goodwin/John Severin, frontis] 1p; **(2)** Brain Trust [Archie Goodwin/Angelo Torres] 6p; **(3)** Into the Tomb! [Archie Goodwin/Joe Orlando] 8p; **(4)** The Creepy Fan Club: Reed Crandall profile/Fate's Verdict/Creepy's Loathsome Lore: Old Scratch! [Archie Goodwin, Arnold Bojorquez and Ed Lahmann/Frank Brunner, Ed Lahmann and Brant Withers, text article and story with photo] 2p; **(5)** Monster! [Archie Goodwin/Rocco Mastroserio] 8p; **(6)** Midnight Sail [Johnny Craig, art and story credited to Jay Taycee] 6p; **(7)** Backfire! [Archie Goodwin/Gray Morrow] 6p; **(8)** Thing of Darkness! [Archie Goodwin/Gene Colan] 8p; **(9)** Collector's Edition! [Archie Goodwin/Steve Ditko] 8p.

Notes: What a difference an issue makes! From Frazetta's classic Frankenstein's Monster cover (with a version of the monster specially designed by Frazetta) to the incredible art job by Ditko that closes out this issue, there's just one triumph after another. "Brain Trust" would have been a feather in anyone's cap and easily have been the best story in the issue except that Goodwin outdoes himself with "Collector's Edition." Joe Orlando's art on "Into the Tomb" reminds anyone who didn't like the art or the concept of Adam Link (like me, for instance) that he was as good as anybody in the business. Frank Brunner made his comics debut on the fan page with a nice skeleton bursting from a grave scene. The headstone therein is entitled "Tales from the Tomb." Perhaps it was inspired by the 1962 Dell comic of that name, which featured a ghost also emerging from a grave. Fan Ed Lahmann wrote and illustrated a "Creepy's Loathsome Lore" page for the fan page, and it was pretty good, too! Gray Morrow contributed a tasty art job too but the undeniable classic here was the Goodwin/Ditko story "Collector's Edition!" From the slanted splash page to the slowly closing eyes running along the bottom of each page to the stellar character design (check out the old fat guy with one blind eye and the other obscured behind a coke-bottle lens!), this may well be Ditko's finest hour! It's as impressive in its own way as Krigstein's "Master Race" or Eisner's "Sand Saref." (And yes, I have seen all the Spider-Man and Dr. Strange stories, thank you very much!) This is the kind of art that makes and sustains a reputation, and any praise you can hand him, Ditko richly deserves. Goodwin's story was classic Goodwin and matched Ditko's art every step of the way. Strong, concise and memorable.

11. Frank Frazetta (October 1966)

(1) Creepy's Loathsome Lore: Rochester Rappings! [Ron Parker/John Severin, frontis] 1p; (2) Hop-Frog [Archie Goodwin/Reed Crandall, from the story by Edgar Allan Poe] 8p; (3) Sore Spot [Archie Goodwin/Joe Orlando] 7p; (4) The Doorway! [Archie Goodwin/Dan Adkins] 6p; (5) The Black Death! [Ron Parker/Manny Stallman] 8p; (6) Beast Man! [Archie Goodwin/Steve Ditko] 8p; (7) The Devil to Pay! [Archie Goodwin/Donald Norman] 6p; (8) Skeleton Crew! [Archie Goodwin/Angelo Torres] 7p.

Notes: Nice giant ape cover by Frazetta. The issue's highpoint was the moody and effective "Hop-Frog," which is probably the best Poe adaptation Goodwin and Crandall did. Solid art and stories throughout the issue.

12. cover: Dan Adkins (December 1966)

An example of Frank Frazetti at his best: beautiful girl, fog, and a near Kong-sized gorilla! © New Comic Co./used by permission.

(1) Creepy's Loathsome Lore: Sea Monsters! [Archie Goodwin/Dan Adkins, frontis] 1p; (2) Dark House of Dreams [Archie Goodwin/Angelo Torres] 6p; (3) Turncoat! [Archie Goodwin/Bob Jenney] 6p; (4) Maximum Effort! [Ron Parker/Rocco Mastroserio] 7p; (5) Voodoo Doll! [Archie Goodwin/Jerry Grandenetti] 6p; (6) Blood of the Werewolf! [Archie Goodwin/Steve Ditko] 8p; (7) The Creepy Fan Club: Joe Orlando profile/Tropical Twilight [Archie Goodwin and Ty Bizony/Dick Mosso, Bill DuBay, Donna L. Austin and Jim Pinkoski] 2p [text article/story with photo] 2p; (8) Idol Hands! [Archie Goodwin/Manny Stallman] 6p; (9) Adam Link, Robot Detective [Otto Binder/Joe Orlando, from the story by Otto Binder] 8p.

Notes: A rather ho-hum issue, with Adkins' cover being no match for the covers that Frazetta and Morrow had been delivering. Grandenetti and Ditko's art jobs were good and most of the stories were fair. Bill DuBay made his comics debut on the fan page with a science fiction pinup that was heavily influenced by Wally Wood.

13.   cover: Gray Morrow (February 1967)

(1) Creepy's Loathsome Lore: Becoming a Werewolf! [Archie Goodwin/Gray Morrow, frontis] 1p; (2) The Squaw! [Archie Goodwin/Reed Crandall, from the story by Bram Stoker] 8p; (3) Early Warning! [Archie Goodwin/Jerry Grandenetti] 6p; (4) Scream Test! [John Benson and Bhob Stewart/Angelo Torres] 7p; (5) Madness in the Method! [Carl Wessler/Rocco Mastroserio] 7p; (6) The Creepy Fan Club: Angelo Torres profile/Pipeline [Archie Goodwin and Geoffrey R. Lucier/Danny Chadbourne, Barry Hoffman and Doyle Sharp, text article/text story with photo] 2p; (7) Fear in Stone [Archie Goodwin/Gene Colan] 8p; (8) Adam Link, Gangbuster! [Otto Binder/Joe Orlando, from the story by Otto Binder] 8p; (9) Second Chance! [Archie Goodwin/Steve Ditko] 6p.

Notes: Morrow's cover was just fine although that's got to be the skinniest and ugliest werewolf I've ever seen! "The Squaw" adaptation was the best story here while Crandall and Ditko shared best art honors. Future artist Leslie Cabarga delivered a letter.

14.   cover: Gray Morrow (April 1967)

(1) Creepy's Loathsome Lore: Magicians! [Archie Goodwin/John Severin, frontis] 1p; (2) Where Sorcery Lives! [Archie Goodwin/Steve

Ditko] 8p; (3) Art of Horror [Archie Goodwin/Jerry Grandenetti] 6p; (4) Snakes Alive! [Clark Dimond and John Benson/Hector Castellon] 7p; (5) The Creepy Fan Club: Archie Goodwin profile/Train to the Beyond [Archie Goodwin and Glenn Jones/Randall Larson, Frank Brunner and Joseph J. Dukett, text article/text story with photo] 2p; (6) The Beckoning Beyond! [Archie Goodwin/Dan Adkins] 8p; (7) Piece by Piece [Archie Goodwin/Joe Orlando] 8p; (8) Castle Carrion! [Archie Goodwin/Reed Crandall] 8p; (9) Curse of the Vampire! [Archie Goodwin/Neal Adams] 8p.

Notes: Morrow's sword and sorcery cover was probably his best Warren cover. Good stories and generally good artwork throughout, although Castellon's art doesn't do much for me. The voodoo king in that Dimond-Benson/Castellon tale was supposed to be a black man. Frank Brunner's second appearance on the fan page depicted an ancient and vampiric Batman! Neal Adams made his mainstream comics debut here although he'd been doing the Ben Casey comic strip for at least 3 years and had done some minor gag strips for Archie Comics when he was a teenager. It was a nice job, too! Joe Orlando also had a strong art job.

15.   cover: Frank Frazetta (June 1967)

(1) Thane: City of Doom! [Archie Goodwin/Steve Ditko] 8p; (2) Adam Link, Champion Athlete! [Otto Binder/Joe Orlando, from the story by Otto Binder] 7p; (3) The Adventure of the German Student! [Archie Goodwin/Jerry Grandenetti, from the story by Washington Irving] 8p; (4) The River! [Johnny Craig] 6p; (5) The Creepy Fan Club: Sink and Fade Swiftly [Archie Goodwin and Mike DeLong/Richard Morgan, Roger Hill, John Hall and Ron Lukas, text article/text story] 2p; (6) Creepy's Loathsome Lore: Monsters of Mythology! [Archie Goodwin/Gil Kane] 1p; (7) The Terror beyond Time! [Archie Goodwin/Neal Adams] 16p.

Notes: Frazetta returned with one of his best covers, painted on plywood (actually, it looks like particle board to my eyes) in six hours! The price went up to 40 cents per issue. Thane was a very irregular series about a Conan-like swordsman. The character appeared only four times between 1967 and 1979 and was unique in that he never had the same artist twice, although Archie Goodwin was generally the writer. Thane's physical appearance was also quite different from story to story. The Adams/Goodwin story was the longest tale that Warren had published to date. The best art and story, however, is the Goodwin/Grandenetti adaptation. It is some of Grandenetti's best work. Adam Link appeared for the last time, his series apparently a victim of the upcoming money crunch that dealt a near fatal blow to the Warren comics line. Orlando's new job as a DC editor may have contributed to the series ending prematurely, too.

16. cover: Frank Frazetta (August 1967)

(1) Creepy's Loathsome Lore: Spirits! [Archie Goodwin/Gil Kane, frontis] 1p; (2) A Curse of Claws! [Archie Goodwin/Neal Adams] 6p; (3) Frozen Fear! [Archie Goodwin/Reed Crandall] 6p; (4) Thane: Angel of Doom! [Archie Goodwin/Jeff Jones] 6p; (5) The Frankenstein Tradition! [Archie Goodwin/Rocco Mastroserio] 8p; (6) There Was an Old Lady [Daniel Bubacz and Archie Goodwin/Bill Molno and Sal Trapani, art credited solely to Trapani] 6p; (7) The Creepy Fan Club: Rocco Mastroserio profile/A Stroke of Genius [Archie Goodwin and Tim Stackline/Dan Gosch, Louie Estrada and Philip Marcino, text article/text story with photo] 2p; (8) Haunted Castle! [Archie Goodwin/Donald Norman] 6p; (9) The Sands That Change! [Clark Dimond and Terry Bisson/Steve Ditko] 8p.

Notes: Frazetta's classic cover featured a largely naked blonde with glowing eyes surrounded by a pride of leopards and a single black panther. Jeff Jones made his comics (and possibly professional) debut here. Adams' and Crandall's art jobs were noticeably lackluster. Clark Dimond mentions that Steve Ditko didn't really like "The Sands That Change!" but turned out a professional job nonetheless. The charcoal effect inking on the Ditko story is quite different from his usual style. Mastroserio takes the art honors here. There have been suggestions made on fan sites that most, if not all of Trapani's solo credited stories in the 1960s and 1970s are actually ghost penciled, often by Charleton artists, and that the publishers were largely unaware of this. There's considerable evidence supporting this conclusion in that even the average viewer can see from just looking at the Trapani artwork from this period, that the quality and style of the penciling seems

to veer all over the place. For this issue, Martin O'Hearn's website/blog provided the hidden penciller behind Trapani's inks.

17. cover: Frank Frazetta (October 1967)

(1) Creepy's Loathsome Lore: Werewolves! [Archie Goodwin/Frank Frazetta, frontis, reprinted from *Creepy* #2 (April 1965)] 1p; (2) Zombie! [Archie Goodwin/Rocco Mastroserio] 6p; (3) Thundering Terror! [Clark Dimond and Terry Bisson/John Severin] 6p; (4) Mummy's Hand [Russ Jones/Joe Orlando, story is credited to Orlando alone, from the 1940 Universal movie, reprinted from Monster World #2 (January 1965)] 7p; (5) Heritage of Horror [Archie Goodwin/Donald Norman] 6p; (6) The Creepy Fan Club: Goodwin's Departure/"Miaow" Said the Pussycat [Archie Goodwin, James Warren and Richard Mills/R. David Duvall, Robert Sankner and Craig Thorton, text article/text story] 2p; (7) Image in Wax! [Archie Goodwin/Tom Sutton] 6p; (8) A Night's Lodging! [Rhea Dunne/Maurice Whitman, "Lodging" is misspelled in the title] 7p; (9) The Haunted Sky! [Archie Goodwin/Roger Brand] 6p.

Notes: Frazetta's classic cover depicts an executioner holding a bloody axe. This was his last Warren cover for two years. The money crunch that nearly crippled Warren started to show its effects as Goodwin's departure was announced. (Although he's not listed as the editor of *Eerie* #12, he clearly had a strong hand in it and I've decided that issue was the final Goodwin era title.) Other effects from the money crunch included the massive use of reprints (which began in this issue), the near-devastating loss of Goodwin's stories, and the mass exodus of artists due to page rate cuts. In fact, all of the original artists introduced during Goodwin's run would leave, with the noticeable exceptions of Rocco Mastroserio (who died in 1968) and Tom Sutton. It's interesting to note that Russ Jones, *Creepy's* first editor and the adaptor of the reprinted "Mummy's Hand," routinely had his credits dropped or erased by James Warren after he and Warren had the falling out that led to Jones' departure from Warren Publications. "Thundering Terror!" was originally entitled "Buffaloed" (a title actually used for another Severin story in 1974) and was retitled by Archie Goodwin.

Warren's Dark Age

18. cover: Vic Prezo (January 1968)

(1) Creepy's Loathsome Lore: Giant Man-Apes! [Archie Goodwin/Roy G. Krenkel, frontis, reprinted from *Creepy* #9 (June 1966)] 1p; **(2)** Mountain of the Monster Gods! [Ron White/Roger Brand] 8p; **(3)** The Rescue of the Morning Maid! [Raymond Marais/Pat Boyette and Rocco Mastroserio, art credited solely to Mastroserio] 10p; **(4)** 4) Act, Three! [Johnny Craig] 8p; **(5)** Footsteps of Frankenstein! [Archie Goodwin/Reed Crandall, reprinted from *Eerie* #2 (March 1966)] 8p; **(6)** Out of Her Head! [Clark Dimond and Terry Bisson/Jack Sparling] 8p.

Notes: Editor: James Warren, although Clark Dimond states that both this and *Eerie* were ghost edited during this time by an editor friend of Jim Warren's from Gold Key Comics. This came out a month late but, actually, isn't too bad of an issue. The amount of content pages vs. ad pages was clearly down but the new material here was quite good. Raymond Marais' story was easily the best story so it's too bad he only wrote one other script for Warren. He did do quite a number of stories for DC's mystery books. The Boyette/Mastroserio art team was a good combo as well. Most of the stories were leftovers from the Goodwin era since Warren had initiated a freeze on buying new stories or art until his finances became less shaky. However, the Dimond/Bisson piece was purchased by the nameless Gold Key editor before the freeze took place. The headless woman named Rachel in that story was based on Dimond's fiancée! Terry Bisson would edit the Warren rival *Web of Horror* in 1969–1970 (see "The Best of the Rest!") and later became a major award-winning science fiction writer. Cover artist Vic Prezio had done a number of covers for *Famous Monsters of Filmland* as well as hundreds of covers for Dell and various men's adventure magazines and was the main cover artist during Warren's Dark Age. Future comic book writer Tony Isabella sent in a letter stating he "was less than wildly enthusiastic about Tom Sutton's art while still noting that he was a talented newcomer."

19. cover: Vic Prezo (March 1968)

(1) Creepy's Loathsome Lore: Mummy's Curse! [Archie Goodwin/Roy G. Krenkel, frontis, reprinted from *Creepy* #6 (December 1965)] 1p; **(2)** The Mark of the Beast! [Craig Tennis/Johnny Craig, from the story by Rudyard Kipling, reprinted from Christopher Lee's *Treasury of Terror* (September 1966)] 9p; **(3)** Carmilla [John Benson/Bob Jenney, from the story by Sheridan Le Fanu] 20p; **(4)** Monsterwork! [Archie Goodwin/Rocco Mastroserio, reprinted from *Eerie* #3 (May 1966)] 6p; **(5)** Eye of the Beholder! [Archie Goodwin/Johnny Craig, reprinted from *Eerie* #2 (May 1966)] 6p.

Notes: Prezo's cover for the Kipling story was one of his best. Magazine size was reduced to 48 pages. This was largely a reprint issue. "Carmilla" was the longest stand-alone story that Warren published for many years and was originally intended for the never published second paperback collection of Christopher Lee's *Treasury of Terror*, packaged by Warren's persona non grata former editor, Russ Jones. All the stories that appeared in the first published volume were reformatted for the larger magazine size and ended up appearing in either *Creepy* or *Eerie*.

20. cover: Albert Nuetzell (May 1968) reprinted from Famous Monsters Of Filmland #4 (August 1959)

(1) Thumbs Down! [Anne T. Murphy/Al Williamson, reprinted from *Creepy* #6 (December 1965)] 6p; **(2)** Inheritors of Earth [Hector Castellon] 8p; **(3)** Beauty or the Beast! [Len Brown/Dick Giordano and Sal Trapani, art credited solely to Trapani] 8p; **(4)** The Cask of Amontillado! [Archie Goodwin/Reed Crandall, from the story by Edgar Allan Poe, reprinted from *Creepy* #6 (December 1965)] 8p; **(5)** The Damned Thing! [Archie Goodwin/Gray Morrow, from the story by Ambrose Bierce, reprinted from *Creepy* #4 (August 1965)] 8p; **(6)** A Vested Interest [Ron Parker/George Tuska, reprinted from *Creepy* #8 (April 1966)] 6p.

Notes: The first new stories since the freeze appeared but neither was particularly good. The Castellon story was originally written by Clark Dimond and Terry Bisson but Castellon didn't understand the script and changed the story so drastically that Bisson and Dimond's names were dropped. The Ms. Corey mentioned in the story was based on Terry Bisson's fiancée. As the money crunch continued, it became clear that Warren had two horror magazines to publish but only enough of a budget for one, so each issue between here and early 1970 featured reprinted stories for half or more of its content. The Nuetzell cover appears to be a tree frog, with an arm growing out of one eyeball. Pretty dreadful image (and not in a good way).

21. cover: Gutenberg Monteiro (July 1968)

(1) Creepy's Loathsome Lore: Trees! [Bill Parente/Bob Jenney, frontis] 1p; (2) The Rats in the Walls [Bill Parente?/Bob Jenney, from the story by H. P. Lovecraft] 10p; (3) Room with a View! [Archie Goodwin/Steve Ditko, reprinted from *Eerie* #3 (May 1966)] 6p; (4) The Immortals! [Ron Parker/Sal Trapani] 8p; (5) The Creepy Fan Club: Bill Parente profile/The Choice [Bill Parente and Bill Eddy/Nicola Cuti, Steve Smith, Doyle Sharp and Louie Estrada, text article/text story with photo] 2p; (6) A Reasonable Doubt [Ron Parker/Bill Fraccio and Tony Tallarico, all of the Fraccio/Tallarico art done for Warren was credited to Tony Williamsune] 6p; (7) Swamped! [Archie Goodwin/Angelo Torres, reprinted from *Creepy* #3 (June 1965)] 8p; (8) Timepiece to Terror! [Bill Parente/Gutenberg Mondiero] 7p.

Notes: Editor: Bill Parente. Parente was an EC fan (as were Goodwin, Jones, Ivie, Dimond, Benson, Parker and many others of the early writers) and his appearance as editor was a sign of growing stability for the company after several very shaky months. Like Goodwin, he would write many of the stories during his time as editor but there was only one Archie Goodwin and Parente's stories simply did not display the quality of the Goodwin era. The cover for this issue was probably the worse single cover Warren ever published on their comic magazines. Absolutely awful. "The Rats in the Walls" was not from the Christopher Lee paperback series of adaptations so I'm assuming Bill Parente did the adaptation. New editions of *Creepy*'s "Loathsome Lore" and the Creepy Fan Club appear for the first time since Goodwin's departure. Future writer and artist Nicola Cuti appeared on the Fan Club pages. Fan Louie Estrada's art was quite nice, both here and in future editions, and one wonders why he wasn't offered an art assignment. The Bill Fraccio (pencils) and Tony Tallarico (inks) art team debuts using the name Tony Williamsune (a combo of their first names). This would begin a long run of stories

by them for Warren and although their artwork was often sneered at by fans, on occasion they were quite good. Of course, you had to accept the fact that all of their monsters and aliens tended to look like melted wax candle figures.

22. cover: Tom Sutton (August 1968)

(1) Home Is Where... [Ron Parker/Pat Boyette] 8p; (2) Monster Rally! [Archie Goodwin/Angelo Torres, reprinted from *Creepy* #4 (August 1965)] 8p; (3) No Fair! [Bill Parente/Tom Sutton] 6p; (4) Strange Expedition [Bill Parente/Ernie Colon] 7p; (5) The Creepy Fan Page: Ernie Colon profile/Unseen Tenants [Bill Parente and Gary Carson/Richard Morgan, text article/text story] 1p; (6) The Judge's House! [Archie Goodwin/Reed Crandall, from the story by Bram Stoker, reprinted from *Creepy* #5 (October 1965)] 8p; (7) Perfect Match [Ron Parker/Sal Trapani] 8p.

Notes: Very nice cover by Sutton. Sutton did beautiful painted covers for Charlton between 1972 and 1976 but only a handful for Warren during the Dark Age. Pity, as those covers he did do were all pretty darn good. The only three regular artists who contributed during the Dark Age are present here: Boyette, Sutton and Colon. You'll see a discussion of Tom Sutton in an upcoming *Eerie* commentary. Pat Boyette had only broken into comics a couple of years before over at Charlton. His best work seemed to be with medieval stories, a genre where he really shone. Colon worked on *Caspar, The Friendly Ghost* and *Richie Rich* over at Harvey. Doing Warren's gruesome monsters must have been a welcome change of pace from such kiddie fare!

23. cover: Tom Sutton (October 1968)

(1) Creepy's Loathsome Lore: The Changeling! [Bill Parente/Bill Fraccio and Tony Tallarico, frontis] 1p; (2) Way Out! [James Haggenmiller/Donald Norman] 10p; (3) Gargoyle [Archie Goodwin and Roy G. Krenkel/Angelo Torres, reprinted from *Creepy* #6 (December 1965)] 8p; (4) Jack Knifed! [Bill Parente/Barry Rockwell] 8p; (5) Quick Change! [Bill Parente/Tom Sutton] 7p; (6) Rude Awakening! [Archie Goodwin/Alex Toth, reprinted from *Creepy* #7 (February 1966)] 6p; (7) The Creepy Fan Club: Rendered Helpless [Larry Goldin/Ed Quimby, Frank Brunner and Scott Grenig, text story] 1p; (8) Cat Nipped [Bill Parente/Bill Fraccio and Tony Tallarico] 6p; (9) Uncle Creepy and

Cousin Eerie's Cauldron Contest [Bill Parente/ Ernie Colon, a writer's contest, on the back cover] 1p.

Notes: Tom Sutton's best Warren cover was a beauty. A huge moon hangs over a house on a cliff so undercut that it threatens to dump the entire dwelling into an abyss. Meanwhile, a werewolf howls in the foggy valley below. New artist Barry Rockwell and Sutton share the best art honors for this issue. Frank Brunner's third appearance on the fan page depicted the head of Universal's Frankenstein's Monster. The Cauldron Contest offered new writers a chance to have their story professionally illustrated and published in a Warren magazine.

Tom Sutton was one of Warren's best artists. This is a striking cover example from *Creepy* #23. © New Comic Co./used by permission.

24. cover: Gutenberg Monteiro (December 1968)

(1) Creepy's Loathsome Lore: Becoming a Werewolf! [Archie Goodwin/Gray Morrow, frontis, reprinted from *Creepy* #13 (February 1967)] 1p; (2) Black Magic [Archie Goodwin/ Steve Ditko, reprinted from *Eerie* #5 (September 1966)] 8p; (3) You Do Something to Me [Bill Parente/Tom Sutton] 6p; (4) The Day after Doomsday! [Archie Goodwin/Dan Adkins, reprinted from *Eerie* #8 (March 1967)] 8p; (5) Room for a Guest [Bill Parente/Reed Crandall] 6p; (6) The Creepy Fan Club: Who Are We? [Robbie Edwards/Brian Clifton, text story] 1p; (7) Typecast! [Archie Goodwin/Jerry Grandenetti, reprinted from *Eerie* #8 (March 1967)] 7p; (8) A Silver Dread Among the Gold [George Hagenauer and Bill Parente/Bill Fraccio and Tony Tallarico] 6p; (9) Uncle Creepy and Cousin Eerie's Cauldron Contest [Bill Parente/Ernie Colon, on the back cover] 1p.

Notes: Reed Crandall was the first Goodwin era artist to return, indicating the first signs of the easing of Warren's money problems.

25. cover: Richard Conway (February 1969)

(1) Creepy's Loathsome Lore: Exorcists! [Bill Parente/Ernie Colon, frontis] 1p; (2) Keep Your Spirits Up [Bill Parente/ Reed Crandall] 7p; (3) Witches' Tide [Archie Goodwin/Gene Colon, reprinted from *Eerie* #7 (January 1967)] 8p; (4) Their Journey's End [Bill Parente/Ernie Colon] 7p; (5) It That Lurks! [Archie Goodwin/Dan Adkins, reprinted from *Eerie* #7 (January 1967)] 6p; (6) The Creepy Fan Club: Black Books!/Park Bench [Bill Parente and Joseph Alaskey/D. Cabrera, text article/text story] 1p; (7) Deep Ruby! [Archie Goodwin/Steve Ditko, reprinted from *Eerie* #6 (November 1966)] 6p; (8) An Unlikely Visitor [Bill Parente/Bill Fraccio and Tony Tallarico] 7p.

Notes: Richard Conway, Parente's assistant editor, designed an interesting cover. He photographed a model wearing the *Creepy* rubber mask, dressed in a shabby Santa coat and hat — then set 12 identical poses in the form of Christmas seals. Other than that, this was a fairly average issue for the time, with the Crandall story being the best of the new stuff.

26. cover: Basil Gogos (April 1969), reprinted from *Famous Monsters of Filmland* #20 (November 1962)

(1) Creepy's Loathsome Lore: Sasquatches! [Bill Parente/Bill Fraccio and Tony Tallarico, frontis] 1p; (2) Stranger in Town [Bill Parente/Tom Sutton] 7p; (3) Second Chance! [Archie Goodwin/Steve Ditko, reprinted from *Creepy* #13 (February 1967)] 6p; (4) The Creepy Fan Club: Demons!/The Beginning of the End [Bill Parente, Sam Lambroza and David Jablin/Jose Velez, text article/text story] 1p; (5) Completely Cured [Bill Parente/Bill Fraccio and Tony Tallarico] 7p; (6) Untimely Meeting [Bill Parente/Ernie Colon] 8p; (7) Backfire! [Archie Goodwin/Gray Morrow, reprinted from *Creepy* #10 (August 1966)] 6p; (8) Voodoo Doll! [Archie Goodwin/Jerry Grandenetti, reprinted from *Creepy* #12 (December 1966)] 6p.

Notes: Gogos' reprint cover depicts Lon Chaney in his 1925 role as the vampire from the film *London After Midnight*. The Parente/Colon story "Untimely Meeting" was quite good as was the Parente/Sutton's tale "Stranger in Town."

27. cover: Frank Frazetta (June 1969)

(1) Creepy's Loathsome Lore: Boris Karloff [Forrest J. Ackerman/Bill Fraccio and Tony Tallarico, frontis] 1p; (2) Collector's Edition [Archie Goodwin/Steve Ditko, reprinted from *Creepy* #10 (August 1966)] 8p; (3) Make Up Your Mind [Bill Parente/Bill Fraccio and Tony Tallarico] 6p; (4) The Coffin of Dracula, part 2 [Archie Goodwin/Reed Crandall, reprinted from *Creepy* #9 (June 1966)] 8p; (5) Thane: Barbarian of Fear [Bill Parente/Tom Sutton] 9p; (6) The Creepy Fan Club: Embalming [Bill Parente/Ken Kelly, text article] 1p; (7) Brain Trust! [Archie Goodwin/Angelo Torres, reprinted from *Creepy* #10 (August 1966)] 6p; (8) Surprise Package [Bill Parente/Ernie Colon] 7p.

Notes: Frazetta's first cover in two years was a revised version of his "Mongul" painting, reputedly altered from the original version because his wife found it too threatening. For some reason, the second half of "The Coffin of Dracula" was reprinted without including the first half! Future Warren cover artist (and Frank Frazetta's son-in-law) Ken Kelly made his comics debut on the fan page. The barbarian Thane made his first appearance in two years. He wouldn't appear again for another ten! Uncle Creepy and Cousin Eerie cameo in the story "Surprise Package." The back cover features an ad for a three-foot-tall monster poster that would border and display a photograph, supposedly depicting a monster, that the readers would send in of themselves, with the surrounding art illustrated by Bill Fraccio and Tony Tallarico.

28. cover: Vic Prezo (August 1969)

(1) Creepy's Loathsome Lore: Fakirs! [Bill Parente/Bill Fraccio and Tony Tallarico, frontis] 1p; (2) Madness in the Method! [Carl Wessler/Rocco Mastroserio, reprinted from *Creepy* #13 (February 1967)] 7p; (3) The Creepy Fan Club: Ghoul/Reuben Reid profile [Bill Parente and Reuben Reid/David Fletcher, text articles with photo] 2p; (4) In the Subway [Reuben Reid/Bill Fraccio and Tony Tallarico] 7p; (5) The Worm Is Turning [Kim Ball/Ernie Colon] 8p; (6) Grub! [Nicola Cuti/Tom Sutton] 6p; (7) Valley of the Vampires [Ron Haycock/Bhob Stewart and Steve Stiles, Haycock's story is credited to Arnold Hayes] 6p; (8) The Doorway! [Archie Goodwin/Dan Adkins, reprinted from *Creepy* #11 (October 1966)] 6p; (9) The Adventure of the German Student! [Archie Goodwin/Jerry Grandenetti, from the story by Washington Irving, reprinted from *Creepy* #15 (June 1967)] 8p; (10) Vampirella Is Coming! ad [Bill Parente/Tony Tallarico] 1p.

Notes: Cost of magazine rose to 50 cents. Reuben Reid was the Cauldron Contest winner for *Creepy*. Best story and art was "The Worm Is Turning." Nicola Cuti made his professional debut with "Grub!" The ad at the end shows Uncle Creepy and Cousin Eerie reacting in fear to the coming of an unseen *Vampirella*.

Warren's Rebuilding!

29. cover: Vic Prezo (September 1969)

(1) Creepy's Loathsome Lore: Ghouls! [Archie Goodwin/Jack Davis, frontis, reprinted from

Creepy #3 (June 1965)] 1p; **(2)** The Summer House [Barbara Gelman/Ernie Colon] 8p; **(3)** Thane: Angel of Doom! [Archie Goodwin/Jeff Jones, reprinted from *Creepy* #16 (August 1967)] 6p; **(4)** Spellbound [Ron Haycock/Bhob Stewart, Will Brown and Mike Royer, Haycock's story credited to Arnold Hayes] 7p; **(5)** Bloody Mary [Buddy Saunders/Bill Fraccio and Tony Tallarico] 7p; **(6)** The Devil of the Marsh [Don Glut/Jerry Grandenetti, from the story by Henry Brereton] 6p; **(7)** The Creepy Fan Club: So Speaks the Book [C. A. Howard/Anthony Kowalik, text story] 1p; **(8)** The Frankenstein Tradition! [Archie Goodwin/Rocco Mastroserio, reprinted from *Creepy* #16 (August 1967)] 8p; **(9)** The Last Laugh [Archie Goodwin/Ernie Colon] 4p; **(10)** Vampirella Is Here! [Bill Parente/Bill Fraccio, Tony Tallarico and Frank Frazetta] 1p.

Notes: The beginning of a long period of regrowth and rebuilding began here, even though reprints continued for several more issues. Prezo contributed a good cover for his final Warren effort. Artist Jerry Grandenetti was the second Goodwin era artist to return while Goodwin himself showed up with his only non–*Vampirella* original story for Warren between 1967 and 1974. Pretty darn good little story, too! The other story highlight was "The Summer House," which, like the Goodwin story, was illustrated by Ernie Colon. The *Vampirella* ad features Bill Fraccio and Tony Tallarico's art on Uncle Creepy and Cousin Eerie while *Vampirella* herself is rendered by Frazetta. The Frazetta art is the same drawing that appears as *Vampirella* #1's frontispiece. Mike Royer made his (uncredited) Warren debut by drawing the female heads in the story "Spellbound."

30. cover: Bill Hughes (November 1969)

(1) Creepy's Loathsome Lore: Exorcism! [Tom Sutton, frontis] 1p; **(2)** The Mind of the Monster! [R. Michael Rosen/Ernie Colon] 6p; **(3)** Drop In! [Don Glut/Tom Sutton] 6p; **(4)** The Haunted Sky! [Archie Goodwin/Roger Brand, reprinted from *Creepy* #17 (October 1967)] 6p; **(5)** The River! [Johnny Craig, reprinted from *Creepy* #15 (June 1967)] 6p; **(6)** To Be or Not To Be a Witch [Bill Parente/Carlos Prunes] 7p; **(7)** The Creepy Fan Club: The Man in the Monkey Suit [Sam Bellotto, Jr./Brant Withers and Bill Black, text story, Black's art is credited to Bill Schwartz, his real name?] 2p; **(8)** Piece

by Piece [Archie Goodwin/Joe Orlando, reprinted from *Creepy* #14 (April 1967)] 8p; **(9)** Dr. Jekyll's Jest [R. Michael Rosen/Mike Royer] 6p; **(10)** Easy Way to a Tuff Surfboard! [Archie Goodwin/Frank Frazetta, reprinted from *Eerie* #3 (May 1966), on the inside back cover] ½ p.

Notes: Bill Hughes' cover featured one of the stupidest-looking Frankenstein's monsters I've ever seen! The "Loathsome Lore" section was always at its best when Sutton wrote and illustrated it, and this first example of his work is no exception. The letters page featured an explanation by Jim Warren about the recent price hike. The future Spanish invasion of artists is previewed here by Selecciones Illustrada (S.I.) artist Carlos Prunes' appearance. Future comic artist and publisher Bill Black (aka Bill Schwartz) made his comics debut on the fan page. Mike Royer, best known in comics as the inker for much of Jack Kirby's 1970s and 1980s artwork, delivered a great art job for his official Warren debut (see #29 for his unofficial debut). While his figures were occasionally somewhat stiff, his women were among the most beautiful to ever appear in the Warren magazines.

31. cover: Vaughn Bode and Larry Todd (February 1970)

(1) Creepy's Loathsome Lore: Torture! [Bill Parente/Bill Fraccio and Tony Tallarico, frontis] 1p; **(2)** In the Face of Death [Al Hewetson/Bill Fraccio and Tony Tallarico] 4p; **(3)** Telephoto Troll! [R. Michael Rosen/Roger Brand] 6p; **(4)** A Night's Lodging! [Rhea Dunne/Maurice Whitman, reprinted from *Creepy* #17 (October 1967)] 7p; **(5)** Snowmen! [Tom Sutton] 8p; **(6)** The Creepy Fan Page: The Master [Marc Rendleman, text story] 1p; **(7)** A Wooden Stake for Your Heart! [Don Glut/Bill Black] 6p; **(8)** Death of a Stranger [T. Casey Brennan/Ernie Colon] 6p; **(9)** Laughing Liquid [Kevin Pagan/William Barry] 8p.

Notes: Underground artists Vaughn Bode and Larry Todd did a number of covers for Warren over the next couple of years. This one depicts an odd chicken-like alien, who's apparently just ripped in half a very human-looking robot. The original version of this cover was too bloody, with too many entrails (making one suspect the gentleman torn in half was originally intended to be an actual human), so before publication the original painting was amended by the Warren production department. Reprints began to be eased out, probably in response to the advent of *Web of Horror*, a rival B&W magazine from Major Publications which featured all original stories. Major Publications were also the publishers of the humor magazine *Cracked* at the time. Both *Eerie* Publications and Stanley Publications had copied Warren's lead in publishing B&W magazines in the mid–1960s but Warren, quite rightly, never considered them a threat as those magazines were mostly composed of pretty lousy retouched or redrawn 1950s horror reprints. *Web of Horror* didn't last long (only three issues) but clearly their use of former Warren writers (Otto Binder, Terry Bisson and Clark Dimond) and artists (Bill Fraccio and Tony Tallarico [with a new pen name], Jeff Jones, Donald Norman, Roger Brand and more), along with the brightest young turks from the fanzines (Berni Wrightson, Michael Kaluta, Bruce Jones, Ralph Reese, Frank Brunner, etc.) had a major effect on James Warren. In fact, a letter by one-time Warren editor J. R. Cochran, which appeared in *Canar* #21–22 (May–June 1974), stated clearly that Warren's infamous "war letter" to writers and artists, which basically declared that one could either work for the B&W competition or one could work for Warren but one couldn't work for both, was a direct result of the existence of *Web of Horror*. "Snowmen!" by Tom Sutton was quite good and won the first Warren award for best story. After several appearances on the fan pages, Bill Black made his professional art debut on "A Wooden Stake for Your Heart!" Kevin Pagan also made his professional writing debut.

32. cover: Frank Frazetta (April 1970)

(1) Creepy's Loathsome Lore: Androids! [Tom Sutton, frontis] 1p; **(2)** The Story Behind the Rock God [Bill Parente?/Frank Frazetta and Neal Adams, text article] 1p; **(3)** Rock God [Neal Adams, from the story by Harlan Ellison] 13p; **(4)** Death Is a Lonely Place [Bill Warren/Bill Black] 7p; **(5)** I ... Executioner [Don Glut/Mike Royer] 6p; **(6)** A Wall of Privacy [Nicola Cuti/Ernie Colon, art credited to David Sinclair] 6p; **(7)** The Creepy Fan Page: To Uncle Creepy/Brief Impulse/The Clock/The Horror at Midnight/News Item [Michael Paumgardhen,

Christopher Laube, Paul J. DeBlasio, Steve Casaw, G. S. Boyde and Bill Parente/Kenneth Smith, George Hrycun and Ken Johnson, poems/text stories] 2p; **(8)** V.A.M.P.I.R.E. [Bill Warren/Bill Fraccio and Tony Tallarico] 8p; **(9)** Movie Dissector! [R. Michael Rosen/Bill DuBay] 6p; **(10)** The 3:14 Is Right on Time! [Ken Dixon/Billy Graham] 7p.

Notes: The first all-new issue of *Creepy* since #16 and it was pretty darn good, too! Frazetta's cover, which was supposed to depict Ellison's gigantic Rock God, actually appears to be a human-size monster or troll, looking down at a European village. He doesn't look much like the version drawn by Neal Adams inside the magazine. I've heard various reasons for this — both that Frazetta only had a paragraph of Ellison's prose story to fashion his cover from (which seems likely) or that this was actually an inventory cover from 1967. I'd normally discount the inventory cover version since it's hard to imagine Jim Warren leaving a bought-and-paid-for Frazetta cover sitting on the shelf for two years except for one thing. Warren actually did that with a 1971 Frazetta cover done for a proposed Warren magazine entitled *POW!* That cover, depicting "Queen Kong," went unpublished for seven years! It should also be noted that my giving Neal Adams credit for the adaptation of Ellison's story is taking into account that Ellison wrote his prose story with the full intent that it be adapted (specifically by Adams) for the Warren line. Not the usual state of affairs for adaptations at all. Regardless, it's a very good story. Adams used Jim Warren himself as the model for the villain of the tale. The intro article before the story features Adams-drawn portraits of Ellison, Warren, Frazetta and Adams himself. According to Ellison, his payment for the story was to be Adams' artwork but it vanished from the Warren offices before it could be sent to him. Last I heard, it was still missing in action. Kenneth Smith, an underground and fanzine artist, made his mainstream debut on the fan page. Brant Withers, a fan page artist, suggested on the letters page that an artist contest, similar to the previous year's writer's contest, take place, but it never happened, possibly because *Web of Horror* was sponsoring the same notion in their magazine. Bill DuBay made his professional artist debut. After "Rock God," the best story and art was "The 3:14 Is Right on Time!" by Dixon and Graham.

33. cover: Pat Boyette (June 1970)

(1) Creepy's Loathsome Lore: Mermaids! [Tom Sutton, frontis] 1p; (2) One Too Many [Buddy Saunders/William Barry] 6p; (3) Royal Guest [Pat Boyette] 6p; (4) Blue Mum Day [R. Michael Rosen/Reed Crandall] 6p; (5) Dr. Jekyll Was Right [Bill Warren/Bill Fraccio and Tony Tallarico] 7p; (6) I'm Only in It for the Money [Al Hewetson/Juan Lopez] 7p; (7) The Full Service! [Nicola Cuti/Jack Sparling] 6p; (8) The Creepy Fan Page: Pat Boyette profile/More Poetry/Rockets to Terror/I Love Her/Message from the Dead [Bill Parente, Joseph Westbrook, L. Alain Portnoff, David Martin, Allan Feldman and Mark Aubry, poems/text stories with photo] 2p; (9) Boxed In! [Tom Sutton] 6p.

Notes: Boyette's cover and interior story were quite good, as was the Rosen/Crandall tale. The best story and art, however, came from Tom Sutton's homage to Will Eisner — the excellent "Boxed In!"

34. cover: Ken Barr (August 1970)

(1) Creepy's Loathsome Lore: The Makara! [Dan Adkins, frontis] 1p; (2) X-Tra ... "X" [R. Michael Rosen/Jack Sparling] 7p; (3) Lifeboat! [Bill Parente/Ken Barr] 7p; (4) The *Creepy* Fan Page: The Doomed/The Movie Critic/Lost: A Life/The Search for the Phasimara Plant [Thomas Isenberg, Steven Hart, Anthony Kowalik and John Scorfani/Mondini Gianluigi, Gerald Colucci, Brant Withers, Scot Cassman and Carole MacKinnon, text stories] 2p; (5) The Cool Jazz Ghoul [Al Hewetson/Ken Kelly] 7p; (6) Minanker's Demons [Buddy Saunders/John G. Fantuccio] 6p; (7) Forgotten Prisoner of Castlemare [R. Michael Rosen/Bill Fraccio and Tony Tallarico] 6p; (8) The Swamp in Hell! [Al Hewetson/Don Vaughn] 6p; (9) Ando! [R. Michael Rosen/Syd Shores] 6p; (10) Easy Way to a Tuff Surfboard! [Archie Goodwin/Frank Frazetta, reprinted from *Eerie* #3 (May 1966)] ½ p.

Notes: Editor: James Warren. Ken Barr was a Scottish artist who did quite a lot of work for DC's war comics as well as for Warren over the next several years. He was a very good cover artist but strangely his best cover work never appeared for Warren. Instead, his Warren work often appeared muted in both color and design and was greatly overshadowed by just about everybody else doing covers at the time. Future underground and "Garbage Pail Kids" artist John Pound appeared on the letters page. Future cover artist Ken Kelly made his professional debut by rendering a rare comic story. It's pretty good, too! The "Forgotten Prisoner of Castlemare" was based on the Aurora model kit of the same name, regularly advertised in the back of each Warren issue.

35. cover: Kenneth Smith (September 1970)

(1) An Editorial to the President of the United States and All the Members of Congress [James Warren, frontis] 1p; (2) Tough Customers! [R. Michael Rosen/Tom Sutton] 6p; (3) Legend in Gold [R. Michael Rosen/Roger Brand] 6p; (4) Polly Want a Wizard [Howard Waldrop/Ernie Colon] 6p; (5) Army of the Walking Dead! [R. Michael Rosen/Syd Shores] 7p; (6) The Creepy Fan Page: Ken Barr profile/Rock God/The Littered Trash-Can of Humanity/The Fool's March [Archie Goodwin?, Bradley Burke, Jessica Clerk and Ted Dasen/Winsor McNemo, poem/text article/text stories] 2p; (7) Godslayer [Bill Stillwell] 6p; (8) It's Grim... [Al Hewetson/Syd Shores] 7p; (9) The Druid's Curse [Buddy Saunders/the Bros. Ciochetti] 6p; (10) Gunsmoke Charly! [Alan Weiss] 8p; (11) Justice! [Pat Boyette] 6p.

Notes: Archie Goodwin returned, listed as associate editor but actually he was functioning as the story editor, although he may not have been doing the page layouts. Cost of the magazine went up to 60 cents. This issue was a brief experiment with an all stories/no ads format, usually suggested as a response to the first issue of Skywald's rival B&W magazine, *Nightmare*. But *Nightmare*'s first issue is cover dated December 1970 so it was more likely that this too was a reaction to Major's *Web of Horror* magazine, which had a no-ads format (although the magazine itself had been recently cancelled) rather than the upcoming *Nightmare* or Skywald. Warren's anti-war editorial was the first in only two attempts to use his magazine line as a bully pulpit. The fact that he was confident in being blatantly anti-war in the editorial underscores the massive changes the country had undergone socially and politically in the four years since conservative elements had forced *Blazing Combat* off the stands (see the *Blazing Combat* checklist). Future gonzo SF writer Howard Waldrop made his professional writing debut, while fan artists Bill Stillwell and Alan Weiss also make their mainstream debuts. A good, solid issue.

36. cover: Kenneth Smith (November 1970)

(1) Creepy's Loathsome Lore: The Body Snatchers Who Stole a Giant! [Tom Sutton, frontis] 1p; (2) One Way to Break the Boredom [James Haggenmiller/Jack Sparling] 9p; (3) Weird World [Nicola Cuti/Tom Sutton] 7p; (4) The Creepy Fan Page: *Creepy* Poems/Tunnel of Terror/Doomsday Monsters [Harry Balmforth, Paul E. King and Rodney E. Hammack/Larry Dickison, poem/text stories] 2p; (5) Frankenstein Is a Clown [Bill Warren/Carlos Garzon] 8p; (6) On the Wings of a Bird [T. Casey Brennan/Jerry Grandenetti] 7p; (7) Forbidden Journey! [Greg Theakston/Rich Buckler] 7p; (8) If a Body Meet a Body [R. Michael Rosen/Jack Sparling] 7p; (9) Frozen Beauty [Richard Corben] 6p.

Notes: Price decreased to 50 cents. Underground artist Richard Corben delivered a very good story for his mainstream debut. Best art was by Corben and Jerry Grandenetti. Best story honors go to Corben, Bill Warren and T. Casey Brennan.

37. cover: Ken Barr (January 1971)

(1) Creepy's Loathsome Lore: I Was Buried Alive! [Tom Sutton, frontis] 1p; (2) The Cadaver [Chris Fellner/Bill Stillwell] 8p; (3) King Keller [Nicola Cuti/Syd Shores] 7p; (4) I Hate You! I Hate You! [Bill Warren/Mike Royer] 9p; (5) Tender Machine 10061 [Ernie Colon] 6p; (6) The Creepy Fan Page: To Fill a Bottle of Blood/The Anniversary/Ghouls Power/The Ape Man [Paul E. King, Jr., Brad McEwen, Howard Williams and Jim Erskine/Tony Boatwright, Jim Erskine and Charles Jones, text stories] 2p; (7) Coffin Cure [Doug Moench/Don Brown] 7p; (8) The Castle [Pat Boyette] 8p; (9) The Cut-Throat Cat Blues [T. Casey Brennan/Ernie Colon, last page is on the inside back cover and is in color] 7p.

Notes: The first use of interior color appeared on the last page of "The Cut-Throat Cat Blues." "I Hate You! I Hate You!" is a pretty good story and was an early comics treatment of child abuse in the form of a horror story. Pat Boyette's "The Castle" is also nicely done.

38. cover: Ken Kelly (March 1971)

(1) Creepy's Loathsome Lore: Killer Plants! [Clif Jackson, frontis] 1p; (2) Wooden Cross! [Steve Skeates/Rich Buckler] 6p; (3) The Vengeance of the Hanged! [Chris Fellner/Syd Shores] 8p; (4) Sticks and Stones to Break Their Bones [Stu Schwartzburg/Bill Fraccio and Tony Tallarico] 5p; (5) The Way Home! [T. Casey Brennan/Mike Royer] 8p; (6) Sleepwalker! [Gerry Conway/Mike Royer] 7p; (7) Secret of the Haunted Room [Bill Warren/Ernie Colon] 9p; (8) The Creepy Fan Page: Alpha 3 [Dan Thost/John Cornell, Gary Kaufman, Loper Espi, Jim Pinkoski and Steve Leialoha, text story] 2p; (9) The Cosmic All [Wally Wood] 8p.

Notes: Warren published new artist Gary Kaufman's submission letter on the letters page and previewed his art on the fan page. Future Marvel editor and writer John Warner also sent in a letter. A fine art job by Ernie Colon enhanced "Secret of the Haunted House." Mike Royer and Syd Shores also contributed some nice art. Like Phillipe Druillet, Loper Espi was a professional artist whose submissions, for unknown reasons, were printed on the fan pages next to amateur submissions. Fan artist Jim Pinkoski also appeared on this issue's fan page, as did future comic artist Steve Leialoha, making his comics debut. The big news, though, was the return of Wally Wood with an excellent little SF number.

39. cover: Basil Gogos (May 1971)

(1) Creepy's Loathsome Lore: The Evil Eye! [Richard Grose/Clif Jackson, frontis] 1p; (2) Uncle Creepy: Where Satan Dwells... [Al Hewetson/Ernie Colon? and Sal Trapani, guest-stars Cousin *Eerie*] 8p; (3) C.O.D.—Collects on Death! [Dave Wood/Dave Cockrum] 8p; (4) The Water World! [Buddy Saunders/Pablo Marcos] 6p; (5) Death of the Wizard [Pat Boyette] 6p; (6) Harvest of Horror! [Phil Seuling/Frank Brunner] 7p; (7) The Dragon-Prow! [Steve Skeates/Richard Bassford] 7p; (8) Puzzling Monsters: Who Drew What? [?/Carlos Garzon, Pat Boyette, Tom Sutton, Jack Davis, Jerry Grandenetti, Bill Fraccio—Tony Tallarico, Syd Shores, Ernie Colon, Billy Graham, James Warren and William Barry, a match-the-artist-with-the-monster page] 2p; (9) The Creepy Fan Club: The Lesson/The Gravekeeper/The Year 2,000/The Voice of Death/Little Miss Muffet [Billy Rand, Danuta Kwapisz, Mark Rone, William Buchanan and John Leho/Harry

Glienke, Edgar Maggiani, Daniel Smeddy, Sam Park and Randy Williams, text stories/poems] 2p; (10) Mad Jack's Girl [Gary Kaufman] 8p.

Notes: When the Uncle Creepy story was first announced, Ernie Colon was listed as the artist. The art in the story is so much better than Trapani's usual stuff that it might just be Colon pencils with Trapani inks. Dave Cockrum made his professional debut while Pablo Marcos made his North American one. Richard Bassford, a familiar name from 1960s fanzines, also made his professional debut. Although "Dual Dragon" was supposed to be Kaufman's professional debut, "Mad Jack's Girl" actually appeared first. The "Who Drew What" page featured partly new and partly old monster illustrations with the readers encouraged to guess who drew what.

40. cover: Larry Todd and Vaughn Bode (July 1971)

(1) Creepy's Loathsome Lore: The Loch Ness Monster [Al Hewetson/Clif Jackson, frontis] 1p; (2) The Fade-Away Walk [Don McGregor/Tom Sutton] 12p; (3) The Impersonation! [Steve Skeates/Pablo Marcos] 6p; (4) Swamp Demon [Dave Cockrum] 7p; (5) Disintegrator [Nicola Cuti/Ken Barr] 7p; (6) Lost and Found [Steve Skeates/George Roussos] 5p; (7) The Creepy Fan Page: The Last Tomorrow [?/?, Scott Rogers, Kenneth Tutton, Tony DeSensi and R. Goodwin, text story, however, the author/art for that story didn't sign his name] 2p; (8) Annual Warren Awards at the New York Comicon... [Martin Greim/Ernie Colon, text article, reprinted from Martin Greim's *Comic Crusader* #10

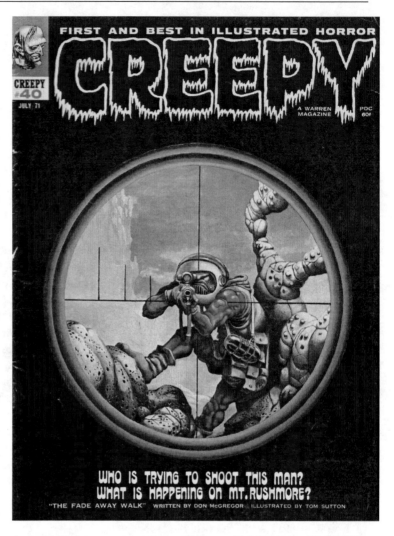

FIRST AND BEST IN ILLUSTRATED HORROR

CREEPY

CREEPY #40

JULY 71

A WARREN MAGAZINE   PDC 60¢

WHO IS TRYING TO SHOOT THIS MAN? WHAT IS HAPPENING ON MT. RUSHMORE?

"THE FADE AWAY WALK"   WRITTEN BY DON McGREGOR   ILLUSTRATED BY TOM SUTTON

A decidedly creepy cover since this Larry Todd/Vaughn Bode effort depicts an alien's gun muzzle that will track you around the room. © New Comic Co./used by permission.

(1970)] 2p; (9) Dual Dragon [Gary Kaufman] 7p.

Notes: Billy Graham became the editor and turned in a pretty solid issue. In an artistic slight-of-hand, the muzzle of the gun on the cover seems to follow you no matter where you are in the room, which is, well — let's fact it, pretty creepy. Don McGregor made his professional debut with a strong story. Nice art and story work also appeared from Dave Cockrum and Gary Kaufman. The first Warren Awards gave "The Ray Bradbury Award" for best story to Tom Sutton for "Snowman" from *Creepy* #31, "The Frank Frazetta Cup" for best illustrated story to Neal Adams for "Rock God" from *Creepy* #32, "The Jack Davis Cup" to Frank Frazetta for best cover from *Eerie* #23, a special award to Harlan Ellison for "Rock God," best all-around artist to Ernie Colon, best all-around writer to Nicola Cuti and an honorable mention for artwork to Billy Graham. There was a bizarre mention in the Award article where James Warren says he wrote his anti-war editorial of the previous year for business reasons! According to the article, it seemed that every time there was a riot or violent anti-war demonstration in an area, sales in surrounding stores plunged, including Warren magazines sales!

41. cover: Kenneth Smith (September 1971)

(1) Creepy's Loathsome Lore: The Hangman of London [Richard Bassford, frontis] 1p; (2) The Thing in Loch Ness [Bruce Jones] 8p; (3) Skipper's Return! [Ernie Colon] 6p; (4) The Final Ingredient! [Bill DuBay] 7p; (5) Prelude to Armageddon [Nicola Cuti and Wally Wood/Wally Wood] 12p; (6) Extra Censory Perception [Steve Skeatess/Gary Kaufman] 5p; (7) The Creepy Fan Club: Gary Kaufman profile/Poem/The Duplicating Machine/Blood River! [Gary Kaufman, Darrell McKenney, Steven Semiatin and ?/ Gary Kaufman, William Fugate, James Boehmer and Martin Greim, text article/text stories/ poem] 2p; (8) A Tangible Hatred [Don McGregor/Richard Corben] 10p.

Notes: Future Marvel editor and writer John Warner sent in a letter. Bruce Jones made his Warren debut. The lead character in Don McGregor's "A Tangible Hatred," police detective Dave Turner, would appear in two more McGregor-scripted stories over the next three years, in both *Creepy* and *Eerie*. Fanzine writer Martin Greim and fanzine artist Bill Fugute did illustrations for the fan page. Pretty impressive issue with good (although not great) art and stories from everyone involved.

42. cover: Manuel Sanjulian (November 1971)

(1) Creepy's Loathsome Lore: Captain Kidd! [T. Casey Brennan/Ken Kelly, frontis] 1p; (2) The Quaking Horror [Gardner Fox/Rafael Auraleon] 6p; (3) A Change of Identity! [Don Glut/Dave Cockrum] 6p; (4) The Amazing Money-Making Wallet [Steve Skeates/Joe Staton] 6p; (5) Spacial Delivery [R. Michael Rosen/Larry Todd] 7p; (6) A Chronicle! [Steve Skeates/Jorge B. Galvez] 4p; (7) Escape from Nowhere World [T. Casey Brennan/Jerry Grandenetti] 8p; (8) The Creepy Fan Page: Jerry Grandenetti profile/The Demon/The Old Lady and the Cats/ The Problem [Jerry Grandenetti, Jim Fadler, Randy Kirk and Robert Nason/Donald MacDonald, text article/text stories] 2p; (9) Ice Wolf [Gary Kaufman] 10p.

Notes: Although it wasn't completely apparent from this issue, the Spanish invasion of artists had begun a couple of months earlier in *Eerie*, which would eventually result in most of the American artists being driven from the Warren pages. The professional artists and writers' debuts, which had highlighted the previous two years, also began to dry up. The sorceress in Sanjulian's first *Creepy* cover was largely naked and while an effort was made to cover up her breasts with a yellow bra overlay, the technique used clearly didn't work. "Escape from Nowhere World" was a sequel to the earlier "On the Wings of a Bird" from #36. Brennan has stated that he wrote the original story but the version published here is not that story. His original script was apparently rewritten by various Warren staffers. Ernie Colon had a letter reprinted from the *New York Times* while future writer/artist Frank Miller also contributed to the letters page. "Ice Wolf" was the best story.

43. cover: Ken Kelly (January 1972)

(1) Creepy's Loathsome Lore: The Golden Sun Disk of the Incas [T. Casey Brennan/Richard Corben, frontis] 1p; (2) Three-Way Split [Dennis P. Junot/Jorge Galvez] 8p; (3) The Mark of Satan's Claw [Fred Ott/Jaime Brocal] 10p; (4) The Men Who Called Him Monster [Don McGregor/Luis Garcia] 14p; (5) 1971 Comicon Awards Go to Frazetta and Goodwin... [?/?, text article with photos] 3p; (6) Quest of the Bigfoot [R. Michael Rosen/Jerry Grandenetti] 6p; (7) Creepy's Fan Club: Richard Corben profile/ The Last Vampire/Now I Know/Friend or Fiend?/The Realm of the Mind/Wanted: A Husband/Unwelcome Visitor [Richard Corben, David Yeske, Rich Cook, Joe Letts, Christopher Caliendo, James Olcott, L. T. Simon and Wayne Carter/Richard Corben, Atherton, Steven Assel, Solano Lopez, Ramiro Bujeiro and Tim Boxell, text article/text stories] 2p; (8) Mirage [Gerry Conway/Felix Mas] 8p.

Notes: The highlight of this issue was Don McGregor's script and Luis Garcia's (in his Warren debut) artwork for "The Men Who Called Him Monster." The story also featured the first inter-racial kiss in comic history, which only came about because the artist misunderstood McGregor's instructions for that panel. In his script, MacGregor wrote "and this is the clincher!"—meaning this is the point of the panel, which the Spanish artist interpreted to mean an actual clinch, so he showed the two main characters in a kiss, even though there was no reason whatsoever for it in the story! The lead character in that story was physically modeled after actor Sidney Poitier. The 1971 Warren Awards went to Frank Frazetta for best cover from *Vampirella* #7, best script to T. Casey Brennan for "On the Wings of a Bird" from *Creepy* #36, best art to Jose Gonzalez for "Death's Dark Angel" from *Vampirella* #12, best all around writer to Archie Goodwin for his work on *Vampirella* and best all-around artist to Wally Wood. Solano Lopez was already a South American professional when his sample work ended up on the fan page. The fan page also underwent a slight retitling while Tim Boxell, who worked on quite a lot of underground and alternative comics as well as an inker for Charlton, made his comics debut there.

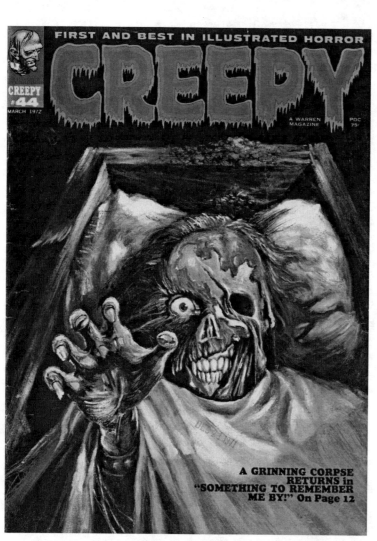

Vincent Segrelles' "corpse reaching from you from the grave" cover is a bit atypical for a Warren work. It actually seems a bit more like a Skywald effort. © New Comic Co./used by permission.

44. cover: Vincente Segrelles (March 1972)

(1) Creepy's Loathsome Lore: The Stars [T. Casey Brennan/Richard Corben, frontis] 1p; (2) With Silver Bells, Cockle Shells and... [F. Paul Wilson/Irv Docktor] 6p; (3) Something to Remember Me By! [Tom Sutton] 9p; (4) A Certain Innocence [Steve Skeates/Nebot] 6p; (5) The Last Days of Hans Bruder [T. Casey Brennan/Frank Bolle] 8p; (6) Like a Phone Booth, Long and Narrow [Jan Strnad/Jose Bea] 8p; (7) The Ultimate High! [Steve Skeates/Martin Salvador] 6p; (8) Creepy's Fan Club: Jan Strnad profile/A Bullet for the Wolf/The Mausoleum/ Nightmare/It's in the Bag! [Jan Strnad, William S. Groginsky, John Ayella, Benjamin Williams and David Michelinie/Gregory R. Suriano, text article/text stories] 1p; (9) Dorian Gray: 2001 [Al Hewetson/William Barry] 8p; (10) Sleep [Kevin Pagan/Mike Ploog] 8p.

Notes: Size and price increased to 72 pages and 75 cents. New Uncle Creepy intro faces, illustrated by Richard Corben, appear. Steve Skeates explained the reasons behind his story "A Chronicle" to a reader on the letters page, leading to a short-lived feature "The Story Behind...," wherein writers explained the origins of their stories. Future comic writer David Michelinie made his comics debut on the fan page. Kevin Pagen and Mike Ploog contributed the best story with the excellent "Sleep." The Strnad/Bea story was quite good, too.

45. cover: Enrich Torres (May 1972)

(1) Creepy's Loathsome Lore: The Chiklil Tablets! [Bill DuBay, frontis] 1p; (2) Creepy Comments/The Story Behind "The Men Who Called Him Monster!" [J. R. Cochran and Don McGregor, text articles on the letters page] 1p; (3) What Rough Beast [Jan Strnad/Frank Brunner] 8p; (4) Targos [Jack Katz/Jack Katz and Nebot] 10p; (5) And Horror Crawls ... from Out of the Sea! [Kevin Pagan/Tom Sutton] 8p; (6) For the Sake of Your Children! [Ed Fedory/ Jaime Brocal] 11p; (7) Dungeons of the Soul [T. Casey Brennan/Felix Mas] 8p; (8) Creepy's Fan Club: Jose Bea profile/Remember Yesterday/The Cold Earth/Hybrid of Hell/The Viewer/Out of the Sea/The Gift/Stare [J. R. Cochran, Tony Boatright, Edgar Dejesus, Randy Williams, Jerome Herskovits, Kevin Schaffer, Barry Aydelotte and Jerry Bradman/Jose Bea, R. Taylor and Surn Iil Oh, text article/text stories] 2p; (9) The Picture of Death [Jose Bea] 11p.

Notes: Editor: J. R. Cochran. A short article entitled "Creepy Comments" appeared on the letters page, as did the official beginning of "The Story Behind..." series. A "Little Orphan Annie" strip from December 1971, featuring a Prof. *Creepy* (who looked nothing like Warren's Uncle Creepy) is reprinted on the letters page. Future artist R. G. Taylor could be the R. Taylor featured on the fan page. A pretty good issue with nice work from Frank Brunner and Tom Sutton, and interesting stories from Jan Strnad, Jack Katz, Ed Fedory and Kevin Pagan. Best story though is Jose Bea's "The Picture of Death."

46. cover: Manuel Sanjulian (July 1972)

(1) Creepy's Loathsome Lore: The Undertaker's Model [Jack Butterworth/Luis Garcia, frontis] 1p; (2) Inside 46/The Story Behind the Story: Like a Phone Booth, Long and Narrow [J. R. Cochran and Jan Strnad, text articles on the letters page] ½ p; (3) Cross of Blood [Doug Moench/Esteban Maroto] 10p; (4) Behold the Cybernite! [Rich Margopoulos/Tom Sutton] 8p; (5) On the Ninth Day of Satan [Kevin Pagan/ Felix Mas] 8p; (6) I, Invisible [Jose Bea] 6p; (7) Spellbound [Lynn Marron/Luis Garcia] 8p; (8) Night Watch [Ed Fedory/Jorge Galvez, from the story "I, The Nightwatchman" by Fedory] 7p; (9) Creepy Book Reviews: The Panic Broadcast/ The Great Radio Heroes/All in Color for a Dime [Doug Moench, text articles] 1p; (10) Creepy's Fan Club: Lynn Marron profile/Instant Replay/After Nightfall/The Spice of Life/ Perpetual Search/The Story Behind the Story: Something to Remember Me By!/*Creepy's* Catchall [Lynn Marron, John C. Salzano, Chris Monzert, Lee Breakiron, George B. Evans, Tom Sutton and J. R. Cochran/Tom Sutton, Terry Harrison and Jack Davis, text articles/text stories with photos] 2p; (11) Friedheim the Magnificent [Greg Potter/Richard Corben] 8p; (12) Creepy's Loathsome Lore: Monsters of the Id! [Clif Jackson, on the inside back cover] 1p.

Notes: Behind a second-rate cover was a decent issue. Best stories were from Doug Moench, Lynn Marron, Ed Fedory and Greg Potter while the best art appeared from Esteban Maroto, Luis Garcia and Richard Corben. Fedory's story had originally appeared as a fan page submission and J. R. Cochran liked it enough to encourage Fedory to rework it into an actual comic script. This was the only time a fan page story contribution directly led to a professional writing career. Rich Margopoulos made his Warren debut.

47. cover: Ron Cobb (September 1972) reprinted from *Famous Monsters* #43 (March 1967) [miscredited to Manuel Sanjulian]

(1) Creepy's Loathsome Lore: Not Sherlock by a Long Shot [Doug Moench/Jose Bea, frontis] 1p; (2) Inside 47/The Story Behind the Story: The Picture of Death [J. R. Cochran and Jose Bea, text article on the letters page] ½ p; (3) The Land of Bone [Buddy Saunders/Esteban Maroto] 8p; (4) Mark of the Phoenix [T. Casey Brennan/Reed Crandall] 8p; (5) The Law and Disorder [Dennis Junot/Luis Garcia] 6p; (6) The Eternity Curse [John Thraxis/Martin Salvador] 6p; (7) Creepy's Fan Club: Reed Crandall profile/The Scarlet Knife/The Shrinking Man/A Moment!/Grin at the Grim Reaper [J. R. Cochran, Jody Gilmore, Terry W. Cloud, Horace Heard and Steve Clement/Reed Crandall, Marc Bilgrey and Pat Boyette, text articles/ text stories] 2p; (8) Point of View [Steve Skeates/ Luis Dominguez] 6p; (9) This Burden — This Responsibility! [Steve Skeates/Jerry Grandenetti] 10p; (10) Futurization Computation! [Bill

DuBay] 3p; (11) Creepy Book Reviews: Dick Tracy/Horror Comics of the 1950s/The Comix [Tom Sutton, Bill DuBay and Greg Potter, text articles] 1p; (12) The Beginning! [Steve Skeates/Tom Sutton] 6p.

Notes: Manuel Sanjulian's cover came in too late for this issue, resulting in it not appearing until *Eerie* #123, nine years later. Cobb's reprinted cover was a last-minute substitute. Reed Crandall returned after almost three years, but his art had sadly deteriorated a great deal since his last appearance. "The Land of Bone" by Saunders and Maroto had the best story and art. The Skeates/Sutton work was also good.

48. cover: montage/back cover: Jack Davis (October 1972), front cover reprints 12 covers from different eras of *Creepy* while the back cover is reprinted from *Creepy* #1 (January 1965)

(1) What Can You Say About an Eight-Year-Old *Creepy*? [J. R. Cochran, text article, frontis] 1p; (2) The Coffin of Dracula [Archie Goodwin/Reed Crandall, reprinted from *Creepy* #8 and #9 (April and June 1966), two pages were edited out from the original second part] 16p; (3) The Castle on the Moor! [Johnny Craig, reprinted from *Creepy* #9 (June 1966)] 6p; (4) Moon City! [Larry Englehart/Al McWilliams, reprinted from *Creepy* #4 (August 1965)] 6p; (5) Swamped! [Archie Goodwin/Angelo Torres, reprinted from *Creepy* #3 (June 1965)] 8p; (6) Thumbs Down [Anne T. Murphy/Al Williamson, reprinted from *Creepy* #6 (December 1965)] 6p; (7) The Cosmic All [Wally Wood, reprinted from *Creepy* #38 (March 1971)] 8p; (8) Drink Deep! [Otto Binder/John Severin, reprinted from *Creepy* #7 (February 1966)] 7p; (9) The Adventure of the German Student! [Archie Goodwin/Jerry Grandenetti, from the story by Washington Irving, reprinted from *Creepy* #15 (June 1967)] 8p.

Notes: The *Creepy* annual now becomes part of the regular numbering.

The DuBay Era, Take 1

49. cover: Manuel Sanjulian (November 1972)

(1) Creepy's Loathsome Lore: No (Horse) Laughing Matter [Doug Moench/Rafael Auraleon, frontis and on the inside back cover] 2p;

(2) Inside 49/The Story Behind the Story: "Behold — The Cybernite!" [Bill DuBay and Rich Margopoulos, text articles on the letters page] ½ p; (3) Buried Pleasure [Doug Moench/Esteban Maroto] 10p; (4) The Severed Hand [Fred Ott/Rafael Auraleon] 12p; (5) The Third Night of Mourning [James Stenstrum/Jaime Brocal] 12p; (6) The Accursed Flower [Jose Bea] 10p; (7) *Creepy*'s Book Reviews: The Pulps/Superman/Batman/Mandrake [Doug Moench, Greg Potter and Tom Sutton, text articles] 1p; (8) Creepy's Fan Club: James Stenstrum profile/Hour for Rest/Mr. Grave's Giant Step/End of the Corridor/Murder Is Not a Fun Game!/Who Can Say? [Jim Stenstrum, George Acevedo, George Hennessey, Calvin L. Cox, Allen Sliwinski, Jack Hennigar/Jim Stenstrum, Victor Kally and Esteban Maroto, text article/text stories with photos] 2p; (9) Wedding Knells [Doug Moench/Jose Gual] 8p.

Notes: Editor: Bill DuBay. The DuBay era started with a great issue! Sanjulian's cover was top notch and the cover story it illustrated, "The Third Night of Mourning," was even more impressive — especially considering that this was author Jim Stenstrum's professional debut (but his second story — #50's "Forgive Us Our Debts" — was his first sale). Just as good as the script, Brocal's artwork was exactly right for the story's French Revolution setting. Jose Bea's bizarre "The Accursed Flower" was almost as good as the Stenstrum/Brocal entry and the remaining tales were more than satisfactory. The Spanish invasion of artists and their artistic takeover of Warren's magazines was now complete, with most of the American artists, with rare exceptions, gone to different pastures.

50. cover: Manuel Sanjulian (January 1973)

(1) Odd Worm! [Al Hewetson/Rafael Auraleon, frontis] 1p; (2) Inside 50/The Story Behind the Story: "Futurization Computation" [Bill DuBay, text articles on the letters page] ½ p; (3) Forgive Us Our Debts [Jim Stenstrum/Esteban Maroto] 18p; (4) Frog God! [Ed Fedory/Adolfo Abellan] 7p; (5) The Critic's Crypt: Buck Rogers/Flash Gordon: Water World/Flash Gordon: Ice Kingdom/Terry and the Pirates [Bill DuBay and Al Milgrom, text articles] 1p; (6) Side-Show [Fred Ott/Jose Bea] 8p; (7) Sum of Its Parts [Doug Moench/Reed Crandall] 10p; (8) Creepy's Fan Club: Esteban Maroto profile/One of Our Policemen Is Missing/Good Morning/The Quarry/Guilty, Guilty, Guilty... [Bill DuBay,

Sandra Chaney, Douglas W. Justice, Don Robers and Nathan Garmon/Bill DuBay, Esteban Maroto, Leslie Fish and Michael Arman, text article/text stories] 2p; **(9)** The Climbers of the Tower [T. Casey Brennan/Felix Mas] 7p.

Notes: After the high quality of the previous issue, this one was a big let-down, especially for a so-called special 50th anniversary issue (it was actually only the 50th issue, not the 50th year of publication). The Sanjulian cover showed Uncle Creepy, Cousin *Eerie*, *Vampirella*, the moronic Warren version of Dracula (currently appearing in *Vampirella*) and Frankenstein's monster along with other various creepy characters sitting around a 50th birthday cake with skull frosting. It was a nice idea that just didn't work. After Stenstrum's powerhouse debut the previous issue, this issue's "Forgive Us Our Debts" came off as long and unfocused, although the Maroto art was nice. With one exception, the remainder of the stories were rather lame, with Brennan's philosophical story in particular showing he had run himself into a creative corner. The exception mentioned was Moench's "Sum of Its Parts," a good story which, sadly, suffered from Crandall's art. It wasn't so much that the art was bad as that it was so far below the quality of the art Crandall had routinely delivered in the 1960s that it made the story look slightly foolish. Fans noticed the drop in quality for the entire issue and heavily criticized this issue, pointing out Crandall's art and Brennan and Stenstrum's stories in particular. The series' title "Creepy's Loathsome Lore" was dropped from the frontis story.

51. cover: Manuel Sanjulian (March 1973)

(1) Possessed from Beyond the Grave [Fred Ott/Rafael Auraleon, frontis and on the inside back cover] 2p; **(2)** Déjà Vu [Doug Moench/Esteban Maroto] 9p; **(3)** Star-Slaughter [Rich Margopoulos/Ramon Torrents] 8p; **(4)** Death Wish! [John D. Warner/Adolfo Abellan] 8p; **(5)** Package Deal [Martin Pasko/Jose Bea] 7p; **(6)** Dracula ad [Esteban Maroto, color] 1p; **(7)** The Viyi [Esteban Maroto, color] 6p; **(8)** Dracula ad [various, color] 1p; **(9)** His Brother's Grave [Kevin Pagan/Rafael Auraleon] 10p; **(10)** The Critic's Crypt: Horror Times Ten/Masters of Horror/Warlocks and Warriors/Wizards and Warlocks [Chuck McNaughton?, text articles] 1p; **(11)** Creepy's Fan Club: John D. Warner profile/Monster/Image in a Puzzle/A Very

Lovely Ghost/Him [John D. Warner, J. C. Bartholomew Del Galzo, Paul G. Ellis, Randall Holmberg and L. R. Slater/Chad Draber, text article/text stories with photo] 2p; **(12)** Bed of Roses [Doug Moench/Felix Mas] 9p.

Notes: Price increased to $1.00 and size increased to 80 pages. A much better issue that the previous one. The first color section appeared, reprinting Maroto's "The Viyi" story from the Dracula color collection. That particular Dracula color album was 120 pages of horror stories that had been previously published in a European magazine entitled *Dracula*. The reprint book was heavily advertised by Warren for several years. This particular color section also appeared in *Vampirella*, the only time the color section stories were repeated. The ads for the Dracula book show only Maroto and Jose Bea artwork. The best story and art in this issue was easily Doug Moench's and Esteban Maroto's "Déjà Vu."

52. cover: Manuel Sanjulian (April 1973)

(1) The Story Behind the Story: "Forgive Us Our Debts"/"Climbers of the Tower"/"The Accursed Flower" [Jim Stenstrum, T. Casey Brennan and Jose Bea, text articles on the letters page] ½ p; **(2)** A Most Private Terror [Budd Lewis/Esteban Maroto, story miscredited to Doug Moench] 12p; **(3)** The Last Hero! [Steve Skeates/Ramon Torrents] 10p; **(4)** Have Your Cake and Eat It Two [Doug Moench/Adolfo Abellan] 10p; **(5)** Them Thar Flyin' Things! [Greg Potter/Jose Bea] 7p; **(6)** The Man with the Brain of Gold [George Henderson/Reed Crandall, from the story by Alphonse Daudet] 6p; **(7)** The Killer [Steve Skeates/Felix Mas] 8p; **(8)** Creepy's Catacombs: Steve Skeates profile/What's News!/Fanzine Reviews: Comic and Crypt/Rockets Blast Comicollector/The Creative Adventure [Steve Skeates, Bill DuBay and Chuck McNaughton?/Steve Skeates, text articles] 1p.

Notes: Back to 75 cents and 72 pages. DuBay continued to revamp the magazines, dropping the fan page — and with it, fan participation and eventually fan support — and replacing them with a feature page (in this case, titled "Creepy's Catacombs") which focused on reviews, profiles and mini-editorials. Unlike the fan pages, which had been unique to each magazine, the feature page displayed the same material in *Creepy*, *Eerie* or *Vampirella*. The magazines also upped their frequency to nine issues per year. Budd Lewis made his professional debut with a great story, easily the best in the issue, only to have it miscredited to Doug Moench! Maroto's art for Lewis' icy winter tale is spot on — as good in its own way as the masterful John Severin's 1966 artwork on "Dark Rider!" Crandall delivers a much better art job than in #50, wrapped around an interesting story adaptation, the first one Warren had done in some time.

53. cover: Manuel Sanjulian (May 1973)

(1) A Scream in the Forest [Greg Potter/Esteban Maroto] 12p; (2) The Stone of Power! [Steve Skeates/Ramon Torrents] 8p; (3) Freedom's Just Another Word [Bill DuBay/Adolfo Abellan] 13p; (4) The Creature of Loch Ness! [Doug Moench/Jose Bea] 10p; (5) The Night the Creatures Attacked [Fred Ott/Rafael Auraleon] 2p; (6) It! [Tom Sutton] 9p; (7) Creepy's Catacombs: Gerry Boudreau profile/What's News!/Fanzine Reviews: Phase/Comic Reader/Heritage [Gerry Boudreau, Bill Dubay and Chuck McNaughton/Reed Crandall, text articles] 1p.

Notes: A great Sanjulian cover of a corpse rising from the swamp (with an odd teddy bear in the foreground) would have been just as much at home over at Skywald's *Horror-Mood* magazines. "A Scream in the Forest" has great artwork by Maroto. Bill DuBay's "Freedom's Just Another Word" was a decent story marred by poor artwork and a somewhat troubling use of racial slurs, especially when one considers some of the stories dealing with African Americans that DuBay wrote in the future. "It!" by Tom Sutton was a fine story that spawned a mediocre series, which would begin in *Eerie* #56.

54. cover: montage of interior panels (July 1973)

(1) A guest editorial by Phil Seuling [Phil Seuling, text article on the letters page] ½ p; (2) Creepy's Catacombs: Jaime Brocal profile/What's News/Fanzine Reviews: File Forty/Remember When/Maxor [Bill DuBay and Chuck McNaughton?/Jaime Brocal, text articles] 1p; (3) The Slipped Mickey Click Flip [Doug Moench/Richard Corben] 10p; (4) This Graveyard Is Not Deserted [Don McGregor/Reed Crandall] 13p; (5) Descent into Hell [Kevin Pagan/Esteban Maroto, color] 8p; (6) Dead Man's Race [Jack Butterworth/Martin

Salvador] 10p; (7) Little Nippers! [R. Michael Rosen/Tom Sutton] 8p.

Notes: Possibly as a cost-cutting measure or perhaps because the increase in frequency had left them short on covers, both *Creepy* and *Vampirella* this month had montage covers composed of interior panels. The response must not have been too good as this was never repeated. "The Slipped Mickey Click Flip!" was a great humorous story. Richard Corben, who, up to this point, had done some great work in the undergrounds and respectable work for Warren, now gave fair warning as to the eye-opening, legendary artwork that would be coming out in the next few years. *Den, Mutant World, Jeremy Brood, A Boy and His Dog, Banner, The House on the Borderlands*, and the Poe and Lovecraft adaptations for Marvel, *Hellboy*, etc., were all clearly forecast by the exceptional work he'd be doing for Warren over the next five years.

55. cover: montage of 12 previous covers (August 1973)

(1) The Creepy-Crawley-Castle Game! [Bill DuBay, game, frontis, one interior page and on the inside back cover] 3p; (2) Brain Trust! [Archie Goodwin/Angelo Torres, reprinted from *Creepy* #10 (August 1966)] 6p; (3) Welcome Stranger [Archie Goodwin/Al Williamson, reprinted from *Creepy* #2 (April 1965)] 7p; (4) Act Three! [Johnny Craig, reprinted from *Creepy* #18, 1968)] 8p; (5) Thundering Terror! [Clark Dimond and Terry Bisson/John Severin, reprinted from *Creepy* #17 (October 1967)] 6p; (6) Incident in the Beyond! [Archie Goodwin/Gray Morrow, reprinted from *Creepy* #3 (June 1965)] 6p; (7) Prelude to Armageddon [Nicola Cuti and Wally Wood/Wally Wood, reprinted from *Creepy* #41 (September 1971)] 12p; (8) The Law and Disorder [Dennis P. Junot/Luis Garcia, reprinted from *Creepy* #47 (September 1972)] 6p.

Notes: The 1973 annual. $1.00 price and 80 pages.

56. cover: Manuel Sanjulian (September 1973)

(1) The *Creepy* Monster Match [Bill DuBay, game, frontis, interior page and on the inside back cover] 2½ p; (2) Creepy's Catacombs: Paul Neary profile/What's New/Fanzine Reviews: The Collector/Graphic Story World/Menomonee Falls Gazette [Bill DuBay and Chuck

McNaughton?/Paul Neary, text articles] 1p; (3) In My Father's House! [Doug Moench/Rafael Auraleon] 10p; (4) Innsmouth Festival [John Jacobson/Adolfo Abellan] 12p; (5) Consumed by Ambition [Jack Butterworth/Martin Salvador] 9p; (6) Lycanklutz [Richard Corben, color] 8p; (7) The Way of All Flesh [Doug Moench/Jose Bea] 10p; (8) The Bell of Kuang Sai [George Henderson/Isidro Mones, from the story by Edward W. Gilbert] 8p.

Notes: Decent issue with the humorous "Lycanklutz" having the best story and art. The Henderson/Mones' adaptation was quite good as well. Isidro Mones' art was credited to Munes for his first dozen or so appearances. Bill DuBay is finally given full editor status (previously his credit had been managing editor).

57. cover: Manuel Sanjulian (November 1973)

(1) Werewolf! The Exciting Game of Detective Skill! [Bill DuBay, game, frontis and on the inside back cover] 2p; (2) Creepy's Catacombs: Bruce Bezaire profile/The Editor's Box/Fanzine Reviews: Barney's Comix/Rocket's Blast/Etcetera [Bill DuBay and Chuck McNaughton?/Rich Buckler, text articles] 1p; (3) The Destructive Image [Don McGregor/Ramon Torrents] 11p; (4) The Hope of the Future [Doug Moench/Jaime Brocal] 8p; (5) The Bloodlock Museum [Jack Butterworth/Martin Salvador] 5p; (6) The Low Spark of High Heeled Noise! [Doug Moench/Richard Corben, color] 8p; (7) The Red Badge of Terror [Doug Moench/Jose Bea] 7p; (8) Sense of Violence [Doug Moench/Isidro Mones] 8p.

Notes: Buckler's artwork on the feature's page was from the story "Snow," which didn't appear until 1975. The sample panel that we see was clearly inked by Buckler as well, although the actual story has inking by Wally Wood. Brocal's art was reproduced from his pencils and it's quite classy looking. Moench and Corben went for another humorous horror story but came up a bit short. None of the stories really jump out at you but all were good, solid tales. Future movie director Brad Bird (*The Iron Giant*, *The Incredibles* and *Ratatouille*) sent in a letter.

58. cover: Manuel Sanjulian (December 1973)

(1) The Old School [Steve Skeates/Vicente Alcazar and Bill DuBay, frontis and on the inside back cover] 2p; (2) Creepy's Catacombs: Manuel Sanjulian profile/Preview: 3 New Warren

Series/Fanzine Reviews: Imagination/Fright and Fantasy/Wonderworld [Bill DuBay and Chuck McNaughton?/Manuel Sanjulian, text articles] 1p; (3) Change ... into Something Comfortable [Doug Moench/Richard Corben] 8p; (4) An Excuse for Violence [Don McGregor/Adolpho Abellan] 10p; (5) Shriek Well Before Dying! [W. Eaton/Jose Bea] 8p; (6) Soul and Shadow [Gardner Fox/Reed Crandall] 10p; (7) The Waking Nightmare! [Don McGregor/Isidro Mones] 12p; (8) Two *Vampirella*'s Stun 5,500 at 1973 Comic Art Convention [Gerry Boudreau, text article with photos] 1p.

Notes: Future comic writer/artist Fred Hembeck and current Warren writer Greg Potter send in letters. Moench and Corben delivered a great Halloween tale! The Fox/Crandall fantasy was quite nice, especially as this turned out to be Crandall's last work in comics. The *Vampirella* text page featured stripper Angelique Trouvere, who did quite of lot of costume work for 1970s-era conventions, as well as 14-year-old (!) Heidi Saha, daughter of fantasy editor Arthur Saha, both in *Vampirella* costumes! Both ladies looked quite nice although Vampi's skimpy costume on a very young girl is rather disturbing. The Saha appearance was the beginning of a rather bizarre publishing venture by Warren Publishing in which James Warren produced both a B&W photo fan magazine and a life-sized wall poster of the teenaged Heidi Saha dressed in often quite revealing costumes. Both Saha's magazine cover and poster shot featured her dressed as Sheena of the Jungle. Saha carries off the costumes quite well but one wonders whether the target audience for such a product might not have been the dirty old men brigade rather than regular comic fans. Regardless, the Saha one-shot fotomag has become one of the hardest to find of the Warren magazines.

59. cover: Manuel Sanjulian (January 1974)

(1) A Few Words and Pictures About Our Brand New Comic Magazine [Bill DuBay/Will Eisner and Bill DuBay, color text article, frontis and on the inside back cover] 2p; (2) Destiny's Witch [John Jacobson/Ramon Torrents] 12p; (3) A Dark and Violent Place [Don McGregor/Adolfo Abellan] 14p; (4) Spare That Tree! [Jack Butterworth/Martin Salvador] 7p; (5) Bless Us, Father... [Bill DuBay/Richard Corben, color] 7p; (6) Curiosity Killed the Cat [Doug Moench/

Paul Neary] 8p; (7) Not a Creature Was Stirring [Don McGregor/Tom Sutton] 13p; (8) Creepy's Catacombs: W. R. Mohalley profile/Warren Magazines Questionnaire [Bill DuBay, text articles with photo] 1p.

Notes: Price increased to $1.00. The killer Santa cover began something of a tradition for Warren, which ran several of these as covers for their Christmas specials over the years. I suspect that the controversial batch of killer Santa Claus movies that provoked protest lines in the early 1980s were directly inspired by these quite gory Warren covers. The new magazine mentioned on the frontispiece was Warren's representation of Will Eisner's *The Spirit*. The same magazine was also advertised on the back cover. W. R. Mohalley was Warren's head of production and his appearance on the features page marked the first time the background staffers were profiled. The best story and art belonged to Bill DuBay and Richard Corben's in-

The first of several annual killer Santa Claus covers, this Manuel Sanjulian effort isn't quite as graphic or gory as they would become. © New Comic Co./used by permission.

spired Christmas tale of a lonely police officer and an crazy Santa Claus killer (well, what did you expect?). It was top notch, even though the reproduction caused the color pages to appear quite muddy. Even that worked to the story's advantage, though, making the grim, dingy city scenes depicted seem even more ugly and sooty. Half of each page (separated cheerfully by mistletoe and candy canes!) told the separate tales of the sad cop and the murderous kook until their Christmas tales combine tragically (?) in the finale. The parallel storyline format clearly inspired many future comic writers, including Alan Moore. The rest of the issue was pretty

good, too, with solid stories from everyone and another excellent Christmas tale from Don McGregor and Tom Sutton. "Not a Creature Was Stirring" is a great story with top-notch art. It was also the third and last story to feature police detective Dave Turner.

60. cover: Manuel Sanjulian (February 1974)

(1) The Exorcist [Bill DuBay, frontis] 1p; (2) Creepy's Catacombs: Ramon Torrents profile/ You're Paying More for Warren Magazines This Month. We Think You Ought to Know Why/ Fanzine Reviews: Dark Fantasy/Quintessence/ CPL [Bill DuBay and Ramon Torrents/Ramon Torrents, text articles with photo] 2p; (3)

Slaughter House [Rich Margopoulos/Adolfo Abellan] 16p; (4) A Most Precious Secret [Rich Margopoulos/Jose Gual] 12p; (5) The Hero Within [Steve Skeates/Richard Corben, color] 8p; (6) Monsieur Fortran's Hoax! [John Jacobson/Martin Salvador] 6p; (7) The Other Side of Hell! [Bill DuBay/Gonzalo Mayo] 8p; (8) Presenting the 1973 Warren Awards [Bill DuBay, text article] 2p.

Notes: The $1.00 price was made permanent. A rather disappointing issue, with only the Skeates/Corben story being particularly memorable. Gonzalo Mayo made his Warren debut. His artwork was quite beautiful, although often overwrought and busy. The 1973 Warren Awards go to Manuel Sanjulian for best covers, Esteban Maroto for best art on "A Scream in the Forest," Bill DuBay for best story with "Freedom's Just Another Word," best writer/artist to Richard Corben for "Lycanklutz," best all around artist to Ramon Torrents, best all around writer to Steve Skeates, and special awards for excellence to Enrich Torres and Richard Corben.

61. cover: Manuel Sanjulian (April 1974)

(1) Child of Hell [Bill DuBay, frontis] 1p; (2) Creepy's Catacombs: Isidro Mones profile/The Return of Archie Goodwin/Fanzine Reviews: Sword and Fantasy/Funnyworld/European Cartoonist [Bill DuBay, Archie Goodwin and Chuck McNaughton?, text articles with photo] 1p; (3) A Stranger in Eternity [T. Casey Brennan/Adolfo Abellan] 9p; (4) Advent of the Scrap-Heap! [Rich Margopoulos/Jose Gual] 10p; (5) The Ghouls! [Carl Wessler/Martin Salvador] 6p; (6) Terror Tomb [Richard Corben, color] 8p; (7) The Blood-Colored Motorbike [Jose Bea] 8p; (8) Twisted Medicine [Steve Skeates/Leo Summers] 7p; (9) Encore Ghastly [Tom Sutton] 6p.

Notes: Archie Goodwin, fresh from his landmark DC editorial turns on Detective Comics and various war titles, returned as editor for a short-lived stint. "A Stranger in Eternity" was a sequel to "A Stranger in Hell" from *Eerie* #38. Richard Corben's latest attempt at a humorous horror story was considerably better than his last. The highlight of the issue was the controversial "Twisted Medicine" from Skeates and Summers (in his Warren debut). Apparently some readers disliked the notion of using a maimed Vietnam vet as a cornerstone to a gory fantasy tale, a re-

action that prompted an excellent defense of the story by Goodwin in a future letter page. Tom Sutton turned in some of his best work on "Encore Ghastly," a sort of grisly valentine to EC artist Graham "Ghastly" Ingels.

62. cover: Ken Kelly (May 1974)

(1) Uncle Creepy's Introduction [Archie Goodwin/Berni Wrightson, frontis] 1p; (2) Creepy's Catacombs: Martin Salvador profile/Alcazar, Corben, Mayo, Mones, Severin, Summers And Wrightson!/Fanzine Reviews: Le Beaver/Exotic Fantasy/The Comic Crusader [Archie Goodwin and Chuck McNaughton?, text articles with photo] 1p; (3) The Black Cat [Berni Wrightson, from the story by Edgar Allan Poe] 12p; (4) Buffaloed [Larry Herndon/John Severin] 8p; (5) Firetrap [Jack Butterworth/Vicente Alcazar] 8p; (6) Judas [Rich Margopoulos/Richard Corben, color] 8p; (7) Survivor or Savior! [Steve Skeates/Gonzalo Mayo] 7p; (8) The Maze [Steve Skeates/Leo Summers] 8p; (9) The Demon Within! [Steve Skeates/Isidro Mones] 7p.

Notes: Behind a gory Ken Kelly cover (depicting the hatcheted head of the gal from "The Black Cat") were clear signs that Archie Goodwin was back in control. Strong stories (with the exception of the rather weak "Judas"), the return of John Severin from the Goodwin era, and the arrival of Berni Wrightson, fresh from his fabled run on DC's *Swamp Thing*, made up an excellent issue. Hard to complain about anything, really. Just a fine, fine issue. There was a sign of trouble ahead, though — Bill DuBay was listed as senior editor, over Goodwin.

63. cover: Ken Kelly (July 1974)

(1) Uncle Creepy's Introduction [Archie Goodwin/Berni Wrightson, frontis] 1p; (2) Creepy's Catacombs: Vicente Alcazar profile/What Do They Have in Common?/1974 New York Comic Art Convention ad [Archie Goodwin/Vicente Alcazar and Berni Wrightson, text articles] 1p; (3) Jenifer [Bruce Jones/Berni Wrightson] 10p; (4) A Touch of Terror [Rich Margopoulos/Adolfo Abellan] 12p; (5) ...A Ghost of a Chance [T. Casey Brennan/Vicente Alcazar] 6p; (6) Demon in the Cockpit [Rich Margopoulos/Richard Corben, color] 8p; (7) Fishbait [Larry Herndon/Leo Summers] 9p; (8) The Clones! [Martin Pasko/Jose Gual] 9p.

Notes: A study in contrasts! "Jenifer" was one of the undeniable classics of this period, with a great Bruce Jones story and top-drawer Wrightson art. Yet it was stuck behind a sub-par Kelly cover, with, at best, fair to downright poor stories surrounding it (please note that the art is generally pretty good in all of these stories). In fact, "The Clones" ranks as one of the worst stories Warren ever published. To be fair, the Alcazar and Corben stories weren't too bad, although the color on "Demon in the Cockpit" seemed to be all of a rather ghastly yellow hue.

64. cover: Larry Todd and Vaughn Bode (August 1974)

(1) Uncle Creepy's Introduction [Archie Goodwin/Berni Wrightson, frontis] 1p; (2) Creepy's Catacombs: Fernando Fernandez profile/The Face That Launched an Issue of *Creepy*!/1974 New York Comic Art Convention ad [Fernando Fernandez and Archie Goodwin/Fernando Fernandez, text articles with photo] 1p; (3) Forgotten Flesh [Doug Moench/Vicente Alcazar] 8p; (4) Mates [Doug Moench/Esteban Maroto, color] 8p; (5) High Time [Steve Skeates/Paul Neary] 7p; (6) Only Losers Win! [Rich Margopoulos/Howard Chaykin] 8p; (7) One Autumn at Arkham [Tom Sutton] 8p; (8) To Sleepy Hollow ... Returned [Jeff Rovin/Leo Summers] 8p; (9) Hard John Apple: An Angel Shy of Hell! [Jim Stenstrum/Richard Corben, color] 8p.

Notes: The first of Warren's themed specials — this one centered around the Todd/Bode cover, which had been done at least two years prior. Each of the stories (with one exception) had a character who ended up looking like the cover painting. The exception was "Forgotten Flesh," which was substituted at the last minute when the Archie Goodwin/Jim Starlin story "Avenger!" missed its deadline. That story wouldn't see print until *Eerie* #128, 8 years later! This was Goodwin's last issue as editor, as he left for Marvel, after alleged tension between him and Bill DuBay over who reported to whom as senior editor. Not Jim Warren's finest hour. The best stories were "An Angel Shy of Hell!" and "One Autumn at Arkham," both in story and art. However, all the stories are good, not a clunker in the bunch. Hard John Apple would return in a series for *Eerie*, beginning in #83 (May 1977). Goodwin wrote a lengthy, intelligent reply on the letters page to Michael Oliveri's complaint

about Warren's increasing reliance on gore in general and on the stories "Twisted Medicine" and "Bless Us, Father..." in particular. Price increased to $1.25 and page count increased to 80 pages, probably to pay for having two color sections in this issue.

65. cover: Ken Kelly/back cover: Albert Michini (September 1974)

(1) The Land of Bone [Buddy Saunders/Esteban Maroto, reprinted from *Creepy* #47 (September 1972)] 8p; (2) Star-Slaughter [Rich Margopoulos/Ramon Torrents, reprinted from *Creepy* #51 (March 1973)] 8p; (3) The Men Who Called Him Monster [Don McGregor/Luis Garcia, reprinted from *Creepy* #43 (January 1972)] 14p; (4) Tell-Tale Heart [Archie Goodwin/Reed Crandall, color, reprinted from *Creepy* #3 (June 1965)] 8p; (5) The Quaking Horror [Gardner Fox/Rafael Auraleon, reprinted from *Creepy* #42 (November 1971)] 6p; (6) Bed of Roses [Doug Moench/Felix Mas, reprinted from *Creepy* #51 (March 1973)] 9p; (7) The Accursed Flower [Jose Bea, reprinted from *Creepy* #49 (November 1972)] 10p; (8) A Chronicle! [Steve Skeates/Jorge B. Galvez, reprinted from *Creepy* #42 (November 1971)] 4p; (9) The Third Night of Mourning [Jim Stenstrum/Jaime Brocal, reprinted from *Creepy* #49 (November 1972)] 12p.

Notes: Size increased to 96 pages. Editor: Bill DuBay. The 1974 *Creepy* Annual. This is a particularly good collection of reprints.

66. cover: Ken Kelly (November 1974)

(1) Uncle Creepy's Introduction [Bill DuBay/Berni Wrightson, frontis] 1p; (2) Creepy's Catacombs: Gonazlo Mayo profile/In Defense of a Name!/The Creative Man — Ken Kelly: Doodling Cover Artist! [Bill DuBay/Gonzalo Mayo and Ken Kelly, text articles with photo] 1p; (3) Desecration [Doug Moench/Jose Ortiz] 10p; (4) Portrait of Death [Budd Lewis/Vicente Alcazar] 8p; (5) Solitude! [Archie Goodwin/Martin Salvador] 10p; (6) Pinball Wizard! [Doug Moench/Richard Corben] 7p; (7) Relatively Axe-Cidental [Greg Potter/Adolfo Abellan] 12p; (8) Nightmare! [Gerry Boudreau and Isidro Mones/Isidro Mones] 8p.

Notes: One dollar cover price, with 72 pages. Kelly's clumsy cover depicted an executioner chopping off a head (with an axe movement that would have split the guy's head in half, not chopped off his head), an image for which Kelly forgot to paint the rest of the victim's body! The cover art and the interior story from Potter and Abellan closely resembled (even down to the page count) Jim Stenstrum and Jaime Brocal's much better story "The Third Night of Mourning" from *Creepy* #49, which had just been reprinted the previous issue. Due to scheduling problems Archie Goodwin hadn't had a story of his own appear during his short run as editor. The first of them showed up now and it's a beaut of a Western werewolf story! One of Martin Salvador's best art efforts as well. "Pinball Wizard" by Moench and Corben was also quite good. Jose Ortiz made his Warren debut.

67. cover: Ken Kelly (December 1974)

(1) Uncle Creepy's Introduction [Bill DuBay/ Berni Wrightson, frontis] 1p; (2) Creepy's Catacombs: Once Upon a Time at Warren.../Controversy in the Comics/The Creative Man — Gerry Boudreau: Portrait Artist? [Bill DuBay/ Gerry Boudeau, text articles] 1p; (3) Excerpts from the Year Five! [Budd Lewis/Jose Ortiz] 10p; (4) The Haunted Abbey [Budd Lewis/ Vicente Alcazar] 10p; (5) The Happy Undertaker [Carl Wessler/Martin Salvador] 7p; (6) Edgar Allan Poe's "The Raven" [Richard Corben, color, from the poem by Edgar Allan Poe] 8p; (7) Holy War [Budd Lewis/Adolfo Abellan] 11p; (8) Oil of Dog! [Jack Butterworth/Isidro Mones, from the story by Ambrose Bierce] 8p.

Notes: More scheduling problems. The Ken Kelly cover was supposed to illustrate the interior color section story "Bowser" by Jan Strnad and Richard Corben. However, that story was erroneously dropped during printing (it eventually appeared in *Vampirella*) and was replaced by Corben's solo adaptation of Edgar Allan Poe's "The Raven," which was probably intended for one of the upcoming all–Poe issues. Ironically, the feature page profiled the production staff, including Sherry Berne, future editor Louise Jones (née Simonson), Michele Brand and Bill Mohalley. For all the mixups, however, this is a very good issue. Budd Lewis shows off his writing chops with the excellent "Excerpts from the Year Five!" as well as "The Haunted Abbey." His "Holy War" is an uncredited adaptation of the then-popular anti-war song "One Tin Soldier." Corben's adaptation of "The Raven" was gorgeous, with truly beautiful artwork that

seemed to glow off the page. However, the best work here was Jack Butterworth and Isidro Mones' adaptation of Ambrose Bierce's sly prose masterpiece "Oil of Dog." This was my first encounter with that gleefully savage story of abortion, family ties and salesmanship. I looked everywhere to find the original, but it took me years to finally do so in the pre-internet day. Much to my satisfaction, both the original story and the Butterworth/Mones' adaptation are pure horrific envelope-pushing black humor, watered down nary a bit!

68. cover: Ken Kelly/back cover: Manuel Sanjulian (January 1975)

(1) Uncle Creepy's Introduction [Bill DuBay/ Berni Wrightson, frontis] 1p; (2) Creepy's Catacombs: Berni Wrightson profile/Accept No Substitutes! [Bill DuBay, text articles with photo] 1p; (3) The Stars My Salvation [Doug Moench/John Severin] 11p; (4) Christmas Eve Can Kill You [Gerry Boudreau/Vicente Alcazar] 8p; (5) Reflections in a Golden Spike [Gerry Boudreau/Martin Salvador] 8p; (6) Anti-Christmas [Gerry Boudreau/Richard Corben, color] 8p; (7) A Gentle Takeover [Budd Lewis/ Adolfo Abellan] 8p; (8) Christmas Visit [Budd Lewis/Isidro Mones] 8p; (9) The Christmas Gnome of Timothy Brayle! [Budd Lewis/ Leopold Sanchez] 8p.

Notes: One of *Creepy*'s nastier covers, with a howling Santa and his elves placing chopped off parts of what looked to be a dismembered child into Christmas stockings. Lots of intestines. The back cover wasn't much cheerier — a very long nail is stuck through a bloke's neck — the sharp end covered in blood. Price was $1.25 for 80 pages. This was the first totally Christmas-themed special, or at least it was intended to be. There were yet more scheduling problems as the non-holiday Moench/Severin SF/western story "The Stars My Salvation" was a last-minute substitution for the DuBay/Ortiz Christmas tale "Once Upon a Miracle," which missed the deadline for this issue. That story eventually appeared in *Creepy* #77. The Wrightson art on the frontis was reprinted from an earlier ad for the New York Comicon. Perhaps reflecting on the imminent collapse of Skywald, which was caused by Marvel's flooding the marketplace with its own horror B&W magazines, a marketing tactic which was also hurting Warren, this month's editorial pleaded with readers to stay the course and keep buying Warren magazines. The trouble with a Christmas-themed issue was that the stories tended to cancel each other out. Even if they were good, and most of these were, the repetition of the holiday theme blunted the horror of the situations. Best story and art goes to Boudreau and Corben's "Anti-Christmas" with "Reflections in a Golden Spike" also being quite a good story. More fine art was provided by Vicente Alcazar and Isidro Mones.

69. cover: Ken Kelly (February 1975)

(1) Uncle Creepy's Introduction [Bill DuBay/ Berni Wrightson, frontis] 1p; (2) Everything You Always Wanted to Know ... About the Comics!: The Story [Bill Dubay, text article] 1p; (3) The Pit and the Pendulum [Rich Margopoulos/Jose Ortiz, from the story by Edgar Allan Poe] 10p; (4) Premature Burial [Rich Margopoulos/Vicente Alcazar, from the story by Edgar Allan Poe] 8p; (5) The Fall of the House of Usher [Rich Margopoulos/Martin Salvador, from the story by Edgar Allan Poe] 8p; (6) The Oval Portrait [Rich Margopoulos/Richard Corben, from the story by Edgar Allan Poe] 8p; (7) Ms. Found in a Bottle! [Rich Margopoulos/Leo Summers, from the story by Edgar Allan Poe] 10p; (8) Facts in the Case of M. Valdemar [Rich Margopoulos/Isidro Mones, from the story by Edgar Allan Poe] 8p.

Notes: Back to a $1.00 price and 72-page length. Strnad wrote in to wonder what happened to his cover-featured "Bowser" story for #67. The reply stated that the printer confused the two different color sections—not hard, I suppose, as both were by Corben. This was a special Edgar Allan Poe issue. Since Al Hewetson over at Skywald had mentioned several times that Skywald planned to do a Edgar Allan Poe magazine, perhaps this was Warren's attempt at heading them off, as they had done with *Eerie* Publications in 1965 by rush-publishing the *Eerie* ashcan edition. Whatever, this was a pretty good issue, with interesting adaptations and great art. As noted in the reply to Strnad's letter, Corben's story "The Raven," that had mistakenly appeared in #67, was originally intended as a color section for this issue. As it turned out, no color section appeared. Best art was from Richard Cor-

ben and Leo Summers, with Corben showing a quite subtle blend of airbrush and pen and ink work that really helped the storyline for his Poe tale. All the adaptations were by Margopoulos and he did a fine job. Margopoulos would do more Poe adaptations in the 1980s with Dan and David Day (Gene Day's brothers) and then again in the mid–2000s with Richard Corben for Marvel's revived *Haunt of Horror*. As a whole, this special worked much better than the Christmas special since the original stories had considerable range. The usual feature page was dropped for a four-part series detailing how a Warren magazine is put together.

70. cover: Ken Kelly (April 1975)

(1) Uncle Creepy's Introduction [Bill DuBay/ Berni Wrightson, frontis] 1p; (2) Everything You Always Wanted to Know ... About the Comics!: Lettering [Bill DuBay, text article] 1p; (3) The Murders in the Rue Morgue [Rich Margopoulos/Jose Ortiz, from the story by Edgar Allan Poe] 12p; (4) Man of the Crowd [Rich Margopoulos/Luis Bermejo, from the story by Edgar Allan Poe] 8p; (5) The Cask of Amontillado! [Rich Margopoulos/Martin Salvador, from the story by Edgar Allan Poe] 8p; (6) Shadow [Rich Margopoulos/Richard Corben, from the story by Edgar Allan Poe] 8p; (7) A Descent into the Maelstrom! [Rich Margopoulos/Adolfo Abellan, from the story by Edgar Allan Poe] 10p; (8) Berenice [Rich Margopoulos/Isidro Mones, from the story by Edgar Allan Poe] 8p.

Notes: Another remarkably gory cover, with the orangutan from "Murders in the Rue Morgue" slashing a very deep cut across the largely naked bosom of a young lady. The second and last of the Poe specials, although leftover Poe adaptations would appear over the next year. Wrightson delivered some very nice artwork for the frontis. This issue was even more impressive than the previous one. Sterling adaptations by Margopoulos, particularly on the lesser-known Poe stories "Man of the Crowd," "Shadow" and "Berenice" with great art jobs from all concerned. Bemejo's Warren debut displayed gorgeous and delicate penwork. Just a fine, fine job from all concerned.

71. cover: Ken Kelly (May 1975)

(1) Uncle Creepy's Introduction [Bill DuBay/ Berni Wrightson, frontis] 1p; (2) Room for One

More [Doug Moench/Luis Bermejo] 11p; (3) But When She Was Bad [Gerry Boudreau/Luis Bermejo] 10p; (4) His Name Was John! [Budd Lewis/Luis Bermejo] 12p; (5) The Song of Alan Bane [Gerry Boudreau/Luis Bermejo, poem] 12p; (6) The Minotaur [Rich Margopoulos/Luis Bermejo, from the story by Nathaniel Hawthorne] 10p; (7) Presenting the 1974 Warren Awards [Bill DuBay, text article] 2p.

Notes: Another excellent themed issue! This time the spotlight was on the artist Luis Bermejo and he delivered in all respects. Beautifully rendered artwork enhanced each story. The best was probably "The Song of Alan Bane" or "The Minotaur" but everything here was good. This year's Warren Awards went to Manuel Sanjulian for best covers, Jose Gonzalez for best art on "Sultana's Revenge" (the voters must have been visited by that shrieking Santa from a few issues earlier), Budd Lewis for best story for "Excerpts from the Year Five," Berni Wrightson for best writer/artist, Jose Ortiz for best all-around artist, Budd Lewis for best all around writer and a special award for Ken Kelly.

72. cover: Ken Kelly (July 1975)

(1) Uncle Creepy's Introduction [Bill DuBay/Jose Ortiz, frontis] 1p; (2) Everything You Always Wanted to Know ... About the Comics!: The Art [Bill DuBay, text article] 1p; (3) Vendetta [Rich Margopoulos and Gerry Boudreau/Jose Gual] 12p; (4) Malocchi! [Don McGregor/Jose Gual] 11p; (5) Lick the Sky Red [Doug Moench/Jose Gual] 9p; (6) It: The Terror-Stalked Heiress! [Carl Wessler/Jose Gual] 10p; (7) The Bite [Jeff Rovin/Jose Gual] 7p; (8) Labyrinth [Gerry Boudreau/Jose Gual] 6p.

Notes: Another issue centered around an art-

One of many Poe adaptations that Warren ran, this Rich Margopoulos' adaptation features elegant art by Luis Bermejo. © New Comic Co./used by permission.

ist — this time, Jose Gual. It didn't work as well as the previous issue simply because, while Gual was a good artist, he just wasn't in Bermejo's league. Best story was the two-year-old "Malocchi!" by McGregor. The dead guy called "It" moved back from *Eerie* for his finale. Great, tender cover of a lost-looking robot by Ken Kelly.

73. cover: Ken Kelly (August 1975)

(1) Everything You Always Wanted to Know ... About the Comics!: Production [Bill DuBay, text article] 1p; (2) Uncle Creepy's Introduction [Bill DuBay/Berni Wrightson] 1p; (3) Playpen of a God! [Bill DuBay/Jose Ortiz, framing story for the issue] 4p; (4) The Argo Standing By!

[Budd Lewis/Paul Neary] 10p; (5) A Beast Within! [Budd Lewis/John Severin] 12p; (6) Unprovoked Attack on a Hilton Hotel [Jim Stenstrum/Richard Corben] 8p; (7) Purge! [Bruce Bezaire/Jose Ortiz, color] 8p; (8) Last Light of the Universe [Budd Lewis/Esteban Maroto] 17p.

Notes: Yet another special issue — this time centered on science fiction. Price increased to $1.25 and size increased to 80 pages. The Lewis/Maroto story was a takeoff on Edgar Allan Poe's "The Masque of the Red Death." Stories are pretty much on the grim side, except for the extremely funny and beautifully done "Unprovoked Attack on a Hilton Hotel." Where Stenstrum had been for the last year, I don't know, but his return was much appreciated. Corben's sly artwork was also right on target.

74. cover: montage of interior panels (October 1975)

(1) Vampires Fly at Dusk! [Archie Goodwin/Reed Crandall, reprinted from *Creepy* #1 (January 1965)] 6p; (2) Curse of the Full Moon! [Archie Goodwin/Reed Crandall, reprinted from *Creepy* #4 (August 1965)] 8p; (3) The Cask of Amontillado! [Archie Goodwin/Reed Crandall, from the story by Edgar Allan Poe, reprinted from *Creepy* #6 (December 1965)] 8p; (4) Hot Spell! [Archie Goodwin/Reed Crandall, reprinted from *Creepy* #7 (February 1966)] 8p; (5) The Beast on Bacon Street [Budd Lewis/Reed Crandall, color, art reprinted from *Eerie* #24 (November 1969)] 7p; (6) Hop-Frog! [Archie Goodwin/Reed Crandall, from the story by Edgar Allan Poe, reprinted from *Creepy* #11 (October 1966)] 8p; (7) The Squaw! [Archie Goodwin/Reed Crandall, from the story by Bram Stoker, reprinted from *Creepy* #13 (February 1967)] 8p; (8) Frozen Fear! [Archie Goodwin/Reed Crandall, reprinted from *Creepy* #16 (August 1967)] 6p; (9) Keep Your Spirits Up [Bill Parente/Reed Crandall, reprinted from *Creepy* #25 (February 1969), story miscredited to Archie Goodwin] 7p.

Notes: The 1975 *Creepy* annual and a Reed Crandall special. Budd Lewis wrote a new script for "The Beast on Bacon Street," replacing the original Bill Parente script entitled "Wrong Tenant" from *Eerie* #24. Crandall's 1960s art here was so strong and vibrant that it's somewhat heartbreaking to see the decline that occurred in his work throughout the 1970s.

75. cover: Ken Kelly (November 1975)

(1) Uncle Creepy's Introduction [Bill DuBay/Berni Wrightson, frontis] 1p; (2) The Escape Chronicle [Budd Lewis/Jose Ortiz] 18p; (3) Phantom of Pleasure Island [Gerry Boudreau/Alex Toth] 8p; (4) Snow [Bruce Bezaire/Rich Buckler and Wally Wood] 7p; (5) Death Expression [Jim Stenstrum/John Severin] 10p; (6) Thrillkill [Jim Stenstrum/Neal Adams] 8p.

Notes: Down to 64 pages for $1.00. This was the first issue since #67 not to be a special of some sort. The letters page was cut to one page. The horror magazine wars had concluded with Skywald going out of business and Marvel canceling all of its horror magazines (although they retained a place on the B&W shelves with *The Savage Sword of Conan* and a few other non-horror magazines). Warren had survived, but the cost was steep. The beneficial competition with Skywald was gone, the threat from Marvel was also gone and Warren, for so long the cutting edge of horror comics, began to slowly stagnate. Still, much of that was in the future. Even with cost-cutting measures clearly beginning to show up here, remarkably, this issue was probably the best single issue Warren had published since the heady days of 1967. Alex Toth and Neal Adams returned, along with new work from John Severin and Wally Wood. Rich Buckler and Jose Ortiz provided good work as well. Powerful stories from all concerned. "Snow" had been previewed almost two years earlier on the features page with Buckler then supplying the inks but Wood's inking was a great addition to the story. Paul Kirchner applied screentone to the story. "The Escape Chronicle" was apparently quite popular with readers as a sequel was done for it. A special essay could be written about "Thillkill" all on its own. It is as powerful and influential in its own way as any story ever published in comics. If DuBay's "Bless Us, Father..." was the prototype for parallel storylines in horror comics (although actually, like so many other things, Will Eisner did it first in the pages of the Spirit) then "Thrillkill" was the first fully realized engine. Every writer, every artist who's used that particular story technique owes this story, as well as Jim Stenstrum and Neal Adams, a debt of gratitude. In one storyline, a young man sits on a highrise rooftop, eating an apple and calmly picking off the people in the streets below with a high-powered rifle while the other storyline shows a neighborhood priest, after the murder spree, attempting to explain to a reporter why the "nice young man" would have done such a thing. And it's not just the storytelling technique that's a triumph; the story itself is great. Stenstrum's script is one of the most powerful narratives in comicdom — violent, grim, disturbing, poignant and oddly tender. It provides no clear answers or solutions but will stay, as any great story should, in your memory for years. Adams provided dynamic and shocking art — some of the best of his career. For years I thought the young killer was physically modeled after writer Harlan Ellison but Adams recently confirmed that the model was artist Paul Kirchner, at the time an assistant of Wally Wood's. A beautiful story and a great issue.

76. cover: Manuel Sanjulian (January 1976)

(1) Uncle Creepy's Introduction [Bill DuBay/Walt Simonson and Berni Wrightson, frontis] 1p; (2) Goodbye, Mr. Lincoln [Bill DuBay/Jose Ortiz] 12p; (3) Ensnared [Rich Margopoulos/Alex Toth] 7p; (4) A Flash of Lightning [Gerry Boudreau/John Severin] 9p; (5) My Monster ... My Dad [Jan Strnad/Martin Salvador] 8p; (6) In Darkness It Shall End! [Doug Moench/Vicente Alcazar] 9p; (7) The Imp of the Perverse! [Rich Margopoulos/Luis Bermejo, from the story by Edgar Allan Poe] 8p; (8) 1976 Warren Calendar ad [Manuel Sanjulian, on the inside back cover] 1p.

Notes: Although the issues were smaller, for a time this actually seemed to increase the quality of the stories. Sanjulian delivered a striking cover

STORY: JIM STENSTRUM / ART: NEAL ADAMS

The splash page for what is probably Warren Publications' best single story — Jim Stenstrum and Neal Adams' powerful "Thrillkill." © New Comic Co./used by permission.

of a colonial-clad skeleton galloping on a stallion while holding a headless female corpse. There were no great stories in this issue but no poor ones either. The best art could be split between Alcazar and Severin while the best stories were probably the Poe adaptation and Boudreau's "A Flash of Lightning." Toth completed at least three or four different splash pages for "Ensnared" before he settled on the published version. The Poe adaptation was clearly intended for a possible third all–Poe special. The first Warren calendar, previewed here, consisted of reprinted covers.

77. cover: Manuel Sanjulian (February 1976)

(1) Santa Claus' Introduction [Bill DuBay/Berni Wrightson, frontis] 1p; **(2)** Once Upon a Miracle [Bill DuBay/Jose Ortiz] 10p; **(3)** Tibor Miko [Alex Toth] 6p; **(4)** The Final Christmas of Friar Steel [Budd Lewis/John Severin] 8p; **(5)** Clarice [Bruce Jones/Berni Wrighton, poem] 5p; **(6)** The Believer [Budd Lewis/Richard Corben, color] 8p; **(7)** First Snow, Magic Snow [Budd Lewis/Leopold Sanchez] 6p; **(8)** Final Gift [Bill DuBay/Paul Neary] 8p; **(9)** The Final Christmas [Budd Lewis/Isidro Mones] 8p; **(10)** Uncle Creepy's Catacombs [Louise Jones?, questionnaire] 1p.

Notes: An all–Christmas story special. Face it, there's nothing like seeing Santa shotgunned in half on the roof (in living color!) to build Christmas cheer. This issue cost $1.25 and was 80 pages in length. Future comic artist Brent Anderson sent in a letter. The story "Once Upon a Miracle" was originally intended for *Creepy* #68. The title for "Tibor Miko" does not appear on the actual story. It was on the title page, however. The Jones/Wrightson poem "Clarice" was the most effective narrative here. It's gentle, haunting and a perfectly realized effort.

78. cover: Manuel Sanjulian (March 1976)

(1) The Horseman [Bruce Bezaire/Miguel Quesada] 10p; **(2)** Unreal! [Alex Toth] 6p; **(3)** Creeps [Archie Goodwin/John Severin and Wally Wood] 8p; **(4)** Lord of Lazarus Castle [Gerry Boudreau and Carl Wessler/Jorge Moliterni, miscredited to Claude Moliterni] 6p; **(5)** The Nature of the Beast [Budd Lewis/Martin Salvador] 10p; **(6)** God of Fear [Jeff Rovin/Vicente Alcazar] 7p.

Notes: Back to 64 pages and $1.00. The cover was a little static but all in all, this was a very good issue featuring one great urban paranoia story by the superb team of Goodwin/Severin/Wood. "Creeps" leaves the reader feeling every bit of the urban rot the story dealt with. According to *The Wallace Wood Checklist*, Paul Kirchner supplied layouts and rough pencils for this story. "The Horseman," one of Bezaire's last stories for Warren, was pretty good but the Quesada art doesn't really do it justice. Martin Salvador turned in one of his best jobs for Budd Lewis' "The Nature of the Beast."

The Louise Jones Era

79. cover: Manuel Sanjulian (May 1976)

(1) Uncle Creepy's Introduction [Bill DuBay/Jose Ortiz, frontis] 1p; **(2)** As Ye Sow... [Bruce Jones/Luis Bermejo] 10p; **(3)** Kui [Alex Toth] 6p; **(4)** The Super-Abnormal Phenomena Survival Kit! [Jim Stenstrum/John Severin] 8p; **(5)** The Shadow of the Axe! [Dave Sim/Russ Heath] 6p; **(6)** Visitation at Pliny Marsh [Gerry Boudreau/Martin Salvador] 8p; **(7)** The Pit in the Living Room Floor! [Budd Lewis/Joaquin Blasquez] 8p; **(8)** Presenting the 1975 Warren Awards! [Bill DuBay, text article] 2p.

Notes: The Louise Jones era began with one of *Creepy*'s best single issues! With DuBay gone, there is no actual editor listed. Instead, James Warren was listed as editor-in-chief while Jones was still listed as associate editor. In fact, Warren was nervous about promoting Jones to the editor's position and she challenged him to let her do the job secretly for a time in order to convince him. In reality, she was actually functioning as the editor here. Sanjulian turned in his best cover for Warren Publications, depicting a lovely young blonde standing in front of a gravestone, clutching a bloody, severed hand tightly to her bosom. All the stories are good but two of them are easily ranked among the top twenty Warren stories. "The Super-Abnormal Phenomena Survival Kit!" by Stenstrum and Severin was a very funny spoof of the sort of ads that Warren itself, among many others, ran in the back of their magazines. In fact, this spoof reportedly bothered Jim Warren somewhat for its lampooning of those ads until someone pointed out that readers who enjoyed the spoof might just check out the ads a little more closely. John Severin was the perfect choice to illustrate this story, as he'd done hundreds of comic parodies for the likes of *MAD* and *Cracked*. Stenstrum's script is spot on and actually rather savage in raking the often silly ads over the coals. It must have been a very popular story for both the writer and readers as from this point on, Stenstrum's scripts tended to be more humorous than serious. The other great story, and my personal favorite of all Warren stories, was "The Shadow of the Axe!" Again, the perfect artist was chosen for this grisly tale that centered around a late–nineteenth-century axe murderer, his wife and their young son. The son slowly becomes aware that something is seriously wrong with Daddy, while the beautiful mom appears to be wasting away with the same unspoken knowledge. In a mere six pages, artist Russ Heath rapidly established the locale, characters and living conditions appropriate for the time period, including accurate depictions of the family, the chores, and the daily life of a nineteenth-century farm and town, then artfully brings to the fore the son's slow dawning of awareness regarding the circumstances surrounding a serial killer's rampage, yet all the while still telling a clear story that left no doubt in the reader's mind what was happening, when it was happening and why it was happening. Sim, the future Cerebus writer/artist, was then just starting out (his professional debut had been just the year before in a Skywald magazine) but you'd never know it from the witty, clever script. This, along with "Gamal and the Cockatrice," "Collector's Edition" and "Thrillkill" are probably the best four scripts that Warren ever bought. The last three panels of the story take everything you expected from the story and give them not so much an O. Henry twist as rather a subtle tweak. Delicious and thoroughly satisfying. Too bad Sim never managed to sell a second script to Warren! The 1975 Warren Awards went to Ken Kelly for best covers, Berni Wrightson for best art on "The Muck Monster," best writer/artist to Fernando Fernandez for "Good-Bye, My Love, Good-Bye!" best story to Jim Stenstrum for "Thrillkill," best all-around artist to John Severin, best all-around writer to Bruce Bezaire and special awards

My favorite issue of *Creepy* and one of my favorite covers — this Sanjulian cover is perhaps the best the talented Spaniard delivered to Warren. © New Comic Co./used by permission.

for excellence to Manuel Sanjulian and Alex Toth.

80. cover: Ken Kelly (June 1976)

(1) Benjamin Jones and the Imagineers [Budd Lewis/Luis Bermejo] 6p; (2) Second Genesis [Gerry Boudreau/Esteban Maroto] 8p; (3) The Fable of Bald Sheba and Montebank the Rogue! [Bill DuBay/Jose Bea] 6p; (4) Proof Positive [Alex Toth] 8p; (5) Ain't It Just Like the Night [Doug Moench/Martin Salvador] 8p; (6) The Axe-Man Cometh [Gerry Boudreau and Carl Wessler/Jorge B. Galvez] 5p; (7) The Last Chronicle [Budd Lewis/Jose Ortiz] 8p.

Notes: "The Last Chronicle" was a sequel to "The Escape Chronicles" from *Creepy* #75, but it had none of the impact that story did. The title for Toth's "Proof Positive" is not located on the story itself but is listed on the title page. It was printed sideways on the page and featured the best story and art in the issue. A good cover by Ken Kelly graced this issue but storywise this was somewhat of a disappointment after the previous stellar issue. "Second Genesis" wasted Maroto's skills and he must have agreed as his art seemed phoned in anyway. Bermejo's art was nice but the rest of the contents were rather mediocre. "Benjamin Jones and the Imagineers"

Ken Kelly painted many strong covers for Warren. This one, featuring a demon, a devil and a near-naked woman, is one of his best. © New Comic Co./used by permission.

began a series of unconnected stories from Warren, usually written by DuBay, with rather Victorian sounding titles, although the contents were often not Victorian at all.

81. cover: Ken Kelly (July 1976)

(1) Warren Publishing Company Will Pay a $500 Reward... [James Warren/Jack Davis, frontis, text article] 1p; (2) Brannigan's Gremlins [Bill DuBay/Luis Bermejo] 10p; (3) The Comic Books [Joe Brancatelli, text article] 1p; (4) Wings of Vengeance [Bill DuBay and Esteban Maroto/Esteban Maroto] 8p; (5) The War! [Roger McKenzie/Paul Neary] 8p; (6) Close Shave [Roger McKenzie/Martin Salvador] 6p; (7) Battle Rot [Bill DuBay/John Severin] 6p; (8) Billicar and the Momblywambles of Glass [Steve Clement/Isidro Mones] 8p.

Notes: Louise Jones was listed as senior editor with Bill Du-Bay listed as contributing editor. Joe Brancatelli, a longtime fan writer, began his opinion page on the state of the comic industry. Nice artwork by Severin and Maroto appeared in a rather average issue. The frontispiece article was Jim Warren's response regarding the matter of counterfeit copies of the *Eerie Ashcan* #1 being sold to collectors for big bucks.

82. cover: montage of interior panels (August 1976)

(1) Forgive Us Our Debts [Jim Stenstrum/Esteban Maroto, reprinted from *Creepy* #50 (January 1973)] 18p; (2) The Comic Books [Joe Brancatelli, text article] 1p; (3) A Most Private Terror [Budd Lewis/Esteban Maroto, reprinted from *Creepy* #52 (April 1973)] 12p; (4) Deju Vu [Doug Moench/Esteban Maroto, color, one page edited out, reprinted from *Creepy* #51 (March 1973)] 8p; (5) Relatives! [Bruce Bezaire/Esteban

Maroto, reprinted from *Vampirella* #35 (August 1974)] 6p; (6) A Scream in the Forest [Greg Potter/Esteban Maroto, reprinted from *Creepy* #53 (May 1973)] 12p.

Notes: The 1976 *Creepy* Annual. An Esteban Maroto special issue. It cost $1.25 and had 72 pages. Edited for this issue only by Bill DuBay, perhaps because this issue was put together before his departure from the editor's chair.

83. cover: Frank Frazetta (October 1976), reprinted from *Creepy* #15 (June 1967)

(1) Uncle Creepy's Introduction [Louise Jones/Berni Wrightson, frontis] 1p; (2) The Strange, Incurable Hauntings of Phineas Boggs [Bill DuBay/John Severin] 9p; (3) The Comic Books [Joe Brancatelli, text article] 1p; (4) Process of Elimination [Bruce Jones/Russ Heath] 10p; (5) Country Pie [Bruce Jones/Carmine Infantino and Berni Wrightson] 6p; (6) In Deep [Bruce Jones/Richard Corben, pages 2–9 in color] 10p; (7) Harvey Was a Sharp Cookie [Bill DuBay/Jose Ortiz] 9p; (8) Now You See It... [Bruce Jones/Al Williamson] 8p; (9) The Last Super Hero [Cary Bates/Carmine Infantino] 7p.

Notes: Price increased to $1.50 and size increased to 80 pages. A Richard Corben cover was done to accompany his story "In Deep" but not used, possibly due to deadline problems. It surfaced as the cover to #101 in 1978. The apparent last-minute substitution of Frazetta's cover started a trend of reusing his classic covers over the next several years, presumably to pump up sales at the newsstand. Some fans liked this but a very vocal minority did not. Outside of the old cover, this was a very good issue with strong stories from Bill DuBay and Bruce Jones, along with great art from Severin, Infantino, Heath, Wrightson, Corben, Ortiz and Williamson. Infantino makes his first comics appearances outside the DC books since being fired from his publisher's position there in January 1976. Best story and art here was probably the Jones/Heath tour de force of "Process of Elimination" but Jones also scored with the terrifying "In Deep," graced with beautiful Corben art as well as the fun "Now You See It...," which featured Al Williamson's welcome return to Warren with a story that was originally intended for Marvel's cancelled *Unknown Worlds of Science Fiction*. DuBay's funny "Phineas Boggs" was jauntily illustrated by John Severin, and Jose

Ortiz's work on "Harvey Was a Sharp Cookie" was quite good, although his sharply styled artwork was a bit of a contrast to all the American artists. The Infantino/Wrightson artwork on "Country Pie" was a good combination.

84. cover: Ken Kelly (November 1976)

(1) Hitter's Wind! [Roger McKenzie/Carmine Infantino and Walt Simonson] 8p; (2) The Comic Books: Tarzan's Travails [Joe Brancatelli, text article] 1p; (3) The Mummy's Victory [Roger McKenzie/Richard Corben] 5p; (4) Till Hell Freezes Over! [Steve Englehart/Carmine Infantino and Dick Giordano] 11p; (5) Home Stretch [Roger McKenzie/Leopold Sanchez] 8p; (6) Menace, Anyone...? [David Michelinie/Carmine Infantino and Al Milgrom] 9p; (7) Relic [Roger McKenzie/Carmine Infantino and John Severin] 8p.

Notes: An all-sports special, apparently inspired by DC's *Strange Sports Stories* title. Gene Day sent in a letter rooting for his good buddy Dave Sim's stories. Infantino penciled four out of six stories in this issue. In fact, there have been suggestions that the Spanish artists' domination of Warren magazines began to wane as the direct result of Infantino's speed in completing artwork. Clearly Roger McKenzie was the go-to guy for this issue's stories. This is a good issue, but not great.

85. cover: Ken Kelly (January 1977)

(1) 1977 Warren Calendar ad [Enrich Torres, frontis] 1p; (2) Like Icarus, Quickly Falling [Roger McKenzie/Leopold Sanchez] 8p; (3) The Comics Books: One Down... [Joe Brancatelli, text article] 1p; (4) Hide and Go Mad [Budd Lewis/Carmine Infantino and Walt Simonson] 6p; (5) The Thing in the Well [Roger McKenzie/Leopoldo Duranona] 8p; (6) Orem Ain't Got No Head Cheese! [Bill DuBay/Jose Ortiz] 9p; (7) The Terrible Turnip of Turpin County [Roger McKenzie/Martin Salvador] 9p; (8) A Way in the Woods [Bruce Jones/Luis Bermejo] 10p.

Notes: Billed on the cover as a monster special, although from the stories you'd be hardpressed to notice it since about half the monsters were of the human, psycho kind. I remember back in 1976 when my mom picked up this issue, flipped to "Orem Ain't Got No Head Cheese," started to read it and then asked me with some concern (and a certain amount of fear, I suspect) if I honestly thought reading a story about eating human brains was what I called entertainment. Believe me, there's just no good way to answer a question like that. The Orem story may be the first in an apparent effort by Warren, headed by Bill DuBay in particular, to write extreme gross-out horror stories. Years later, DuBay published a somewhat rewritten version of Orem (with the original artwork) in the *Spooky* fanzine, and said version may have been DuBay's last comic work. The 1977 calendar, like the 1976 one, were reprints of covers. Only this time, the covers were all from, and of, *Vampirella*.

86. cover: Ken Kelly (February 1977)

(1) A Noggin at Mile End [Budd Lewis/Leopold Sanchez] 10p; (2) The Comic Books: Less Is More [Joe Brancatelli, text article] 1p; (3) Dick Swift and His Electric Power Ring! [Bill DuBay/Carmine Infantino and Berni Wrightson] 9p; (4) The Greatest Christmas of All [Roger McKenzie/Leopoldo Duranona] 8p; (5) Mother Knows Best [Bruce Jones/Al Williamson] 8p; (6) Bloodstone Christmas [Gerry Boudreau/Carmine Infantino and John Severin] 8p; (7) Season's Grievings [Bruce Jones/Gonzalo Mayo] 8p; (8) A Gift for Momma [Roger McKenzie/Luis Bermejo] 8p.

Notes: Future writer and artist Fred Hembeck sent in a letter. The third Christmas special was priced at $1.50 and is 80 pages in length. Kelly's cover was noticeably less grisly than in previous years. Although there was no full color section, both "Mother Knows Best" and "Bloodstone Christmas" were colored in red. Best story here was the delightful "Dick Swift and His Electric Power Ring!" from Bill DuBay while best art was from Al Williamson on "Mother Knows Best." Gonzalo Mayo displayed a slightly different, less elaborate, art style on his story which also seemed to enhance, or perhaps better showcase, his storytelling abilities. All the stories were decent and the art was quite nice. A superior issue.

87. cover: montage of interior panels [from Berni Wrightson] (March 1977)

(1) Four Classic Martians [Berni Wrightson] 1p; (2) A Warped Tale [Al Sirois/Gray Morrow] 8p; (3) A Martian Saga [Nicola Cuti/Berni Wrightson, poem] 6p; (4) Those 'Orrible Passions of '78 [Bill DuBay/Carmine Infantino and Dick Giordano] 8p; (5) The Last [Roger McKenzie/John Severin] 8p; (6) They Come Out at Night [Bruce Jones/Martin Salvador] 8p; (7) Warmonger of Mars [Wally Wood/Ralph Reese] 7p.

Notes: This issue was $1.25 and 72 pages. Nicola Cuti guest edited this Science Fiction special issue. "Warmonger of Mars" had been done several years previously and was probably intended for an underground comix. That this was an older story can be seen by the reappearance of Reese's early detailed rendering style — which by this time had been replaced by a more commercial, advertising-friendly version seemingly styled after Dick Giordano's or Win Mortimer's work (his earlier style seemed to be influenced in equal parts by Gil Kane and Wally Wood). Gray Morrow hadn't appeared in a Warren magazine since 1967 yet his return went oddly unheralded. Wrightson's art was quite beautiful; however, the best story and art went to the DuBay/Infantino/Giordano story "Those 'Orrible Passions of '78," which tied in with the then-recent Viking I and II spacecrafts' visits to Mars and the strange, human-looking face formed by hills and shadows that was photographed on the Martian surface. This was, perhaps, the first use of that odd formation or image in a fiction tale.

88. cover: Steve Hickman (May 1977)

(1) Castles Made of Sand [Gerry Boudreau/Jose Ortiz] 8p; (2) The Comic Books [Joe Brancatelli, text article] 1p; (3) Eye for Eye, Fang for Fang [Doug Moench/Carmine Infantino and Ernie Chan] 8p; (4) Do You Believe in Sinsigs! [Gerry Boudreau/Luis Bermejo] 8p; (5) Temple of Seilos [Bruce Jones/Leopold Sanchez] 10p; (6) Iron Man [Bill DuBay/Esteban Maroto] 6p; (7) Second Childhood [Bruce Jones/Ramon Torrents] 8p.

Notes: Hickman's only cover for Warren was quite lovely. Cover was priced at $1.50. Future artist Ken Meyer Jr. sent in a letter. A fairly average issue for this period. Good but not great.

89. cover: Frank Frazetta (June 1977), reprinted from *Blazing Combat* #1 (October 1965)

(1) Blood Brothers [Bruce Jones/Jose Ortiz] 10p; (2) The Comic Books [Joe Brancatelli, text article] 1p; (3) The Windmill [Lou Rossin/Leopoldo Duranona] 5p; (4) Angel of Jaipur [Bill

DuBay/John Severin] 6p; **(5)** The Hungry Dragon [Nicola Cuti/Carmine Infantino and Alex Nino] 8p; **(6)** The Door-Gunner [Larry Hama and Cary Bates/Leopold Sanchez] 8p; **(7)** Coggin's Army [Roger McKenzie/ Martin Salvador] 9p.

Notes: Warren began its irritating use of reprinted covers on a regular basic. Except on *Vampirella*, almost all the reprinted covers were of Frazetta's work. Although fans of the Warren books may dispute it, this policy marked the first real signs of the long decline and fall of the Warren books. This issue was an all-war stories special. It was still $1.50 but the page count dropped to 64 pages. Best story and art here was the nifty "Angel of Jaipur" by DuBay and Severin.

90. cover: Enrich Torres (July 1977)

(1) Warrior on the Edge of Forever [Bill DuBay/Jose Ortiz] 9p; **(2)** The Comic Books [Joe Brancatelli, text article] 1p; **(3)** The Wash Out [Bruce Jones/Leopoldo Duranona] 8p; **(4)** The Search [Roger McKenzie/Carmine Infantino and Gonzalo Mayo] 8p; **(5)** Please ... Save the Children [Bill DuBay/Martin Salvador] 10p; **(6)** The Sacrifice [Jose Toutain/Rafael Auraleon] 4p; **(7)** Dollie [Roger McKenzie/Leopold Sanchez] 10p.

Notes: The first issue not listed as a special of some sort in quite a while. Enrich's cover, depicting a young girl holding a vampire dollie while blood dribbles down the girl's neck, was quite effective. This issue was back up to 72 pages. The story "Warrior on the Edge of Forever" was a leftover for the previous issue's war special. The story "Dollie" was a leftover from the Christmas special. The odd pairing of Infantino and Mayo on "The Search" was surpris-

Warren was just as capable of going for quiet horror as the more extreme, in-your-face efforts. This disturbing image by Erich Torres is a fine example of the power of quiet. © New Comic Co./used by permission.

ingly good and provided the best art for the issue. Best story honors go to Bill DuBay for "Please ... Save the Children."

91. cover: Frank Frazetta (August 1977), reprinted from *Vampirella* #11 (May 1971)

(1) Nightfall [Bill DuBay/Berni Wrightson, reprinted from *Eerie* #60 (September 1974)] 8p; **(2)** The Comic Books: The Worst and the Dullest [Joe Brancatelli, text article] 1p; **(3)** Creeps [Archie Goodwin/John Severin and Wally Wood, reprinted from *Creepy* #78 (March 1976)] 8p; **(4)** Phantom of Pleasure Island [Gerry Boudreau/Alex Toth, reprinted from *Creepy* #75 (November 1975)] 8p; **(5)** Benjamin

Jones and the Imagineers [Budd Lewis/Luis Bermejo, reprinted from *Creepy* #80 (June 1976)] 6p; (6) Cold Cuts [Berni Wrightson/Jeff Jones, reprinted from *Vampirella* #34 (June 1974)] 6p; (7) Thrillkill [Jim Stenstrum/Neal Adams, reprinted from *Creepy* #75 (November 1975)] 8p; (8) Gamal and the Cockatrice [Bruce Bezaire/Rafael Auraleon, reprinted from *Vampirella* #47 (December 1975)] 12p; (9) The Shadow of the Axe! [Dave Sim/Russ Heath, reprinted from *Creepy* #79 (May 1976)] 6p.

Notes: The 1977 *Creepy* Annual. It was $1.50 with 88 pages. If Warren had reserved their use of reprinted covers to the annuals it would have made a great deal more sense. This particular issue is one of the best buys of a Warren magazine you can make. Not a single dud story, exceptionally fine artwork and at least six genuine classics ("Nightfall," "Creeps," "Thrillkill," "Gamal and the Cockatrice," "Cold Cuts" and "The Shadow of the Axe!") appear here. The other two stories are simply very good. Great value for your dollar (and a half)!

92. cover: Frank Frazetta (October 1977), reprinted from *Eerie* #23 (September 1969)

(1) A Toast to No Man's Memory [Len Wein/John Severin] 8p; (2) The Comic Books [Joe Brancatelli, text article] 1p; (3) Mrs. Sludge and the Pickled Octopus Raid [Bill DuBay/Luis Bermejo] 9p; (4) Instinct [Nicola Cuti/Richard Corben] 7p; (5) Towards High Places [Bruce Jones/Ramon Torrents] 10p; (6) The Executioner [Russ Heath and Cary Bates/Russ Heath] 8p; (7) Goddess in a Kingdom of Trolls [Gerry Boudreau/Esteban Maroto] 8p; (8) Everybody and His Sister [Jim Stenstrum/Leopold Sanchez, art miscredited to Jose Sanchez] 8p; (9) The Generations of Noah [Roger McKenzie/Leopoldo Duranona] 9p.

Notes: With this issue, at least, an attempt was made to justify the Frazetta cover reprint, namely by ordering up a new story, "Towards High Places" (and it was a pretty good story, too!), to accompany it. Cover price was $1.75 (just 10 years previously it had been 35 cents!) for 96 pages. The story "Instinct" was an inventory story done in 1970. Since 1975 Warren had been making an effort to insure that the late summer issue of new stories would be a special one. This one was no exception. Very good stories appeared from the teams of Wein/Severin, Jones/Torrents,

Bates/Heath and Boudreau/Maroto but all the stories were of generally high quality.

93. cover: Don Maitz (November 1977)

(1) The Replacement [Roger McKenzie/Carmine Infantino and Dick Giordano] 10p; (2) The Comic Books [Joe Brancatelli, text article] 2p; (3) The Return of Rah [Roger McKenzie/Carmine Infantino and John Severin] 6p; (4) The Great Black Cheese [Bill DuBay/Carmine Infantino and Alfredo Alcala] 9p; (5) Elixer [Roger McKenzie/Leopold Sanchez] 8p; (6) Running Wild [Roger McKenzie/Carmine Infantino and Alex Nino] 9p; (7) Cold Blooded Murder [Bill Mohalley and Nicola Cuti/Leopoldo Duranona] 8p.

Notes: Noted SF and Fantasy artist Don Maitz made his Warren debut. This was the second all-sports special. A third was planned for 1978 but abandoned at some point and the stories were scattered among the three main Warren titles. Price back down to $1.50 with 72 pages. The story "The Return of Rah" was a sequel to "The Mummy's Victory" from *Creepy* #84.

94. cover: Don Maitz (January 1978)

(1) 1978 Warren Calendar ad [Jose Gonzalez, frontis] 1p; (2) Etran to Fulsing [Nicola Cuti/Dick Giordano] 8p; (3) The Comic Books: Superman Versus Soccer [Joe Brancatelli, text article] 1p; (4) Bad Tommy [Roger McKenzie and Nicola Cuti/Martin Salvador] 9p; (5) Bad Ada [Bill Pearson/Alfredo Alcala] 8p; (6) Bessie [Gerry Boudreau/Leopoldo Duranona] 8p; (7) Sacrifice [Roger McKenzie/Luis Bermejo] 8p; (8) Backwaters and Timing Circles [Budd Lewis/Alex Nino] 9p.

Notes: For the first and only time the Warren Calendar featured new artwork from Rafael Auraleon, Luis Bermejo, Richard Corben, Leopoldo Duranona, Jose Gonzalez, Russ Heath, Esteban Maroto, Jose Ortiz, John Severin, Ramon Torrents, Alex Toth and Berni Wrightson. Wrightson's calendar art was from his upcoming *Illustrated Frankenstein* volume. Corben's would later appear as the cover to *The Odd Comic World of Richard Corben*. The Toth and Heath contributions were particularly nice. Nicola Cuti was listed as editor for this issue only, while Jones remains senior editor. This was an all-weird children's special. Maitz's cover was quite attractive. For some reason, at this time, the price of an issue of *Creepy* began to jump all over the place, without apparent reason. In this instance the price dropped down to $1.25. Bill Pearson returned with a story for the first time since the mid–1960s. The best story was "Sacrifice" by McKenzie and Bermejo. When someone pointed out that "Backwaters and Timing Circles" had the same plot as Ray Bradbury's famous "A Sound of Thunder," the editorial response rather lamely explained the story was a "tribute" to Bradbury's original.

95. cover: Don Maitz (February 1978)

(1) The Star Saga of Sirius Sam [Nicola Cuti/John Severin] 8p; (2) The Laughing Man [Bruce Jones/Berni Wrightson] 6p; (3) Murder on the Vine [Cary Bates/Esteban Maroto, color] 8p; (4) The Empire of Chim-Pan-Zee [Nicola Cuti/Luis Bermejo] 8p; (5) The Comic Books: Patent Medicine Profits? [Joe Brancatelli, text article] 1p; (6) The Oasis Inn [Bob Toomey/Jose Ortiz] 10p; (7) The Old Ways [Roger McKenzie/Leopoldo Duranona] 9p.

Notes: An all-apes special. Cuti was now listed as assistant editor. The price was $1.75. "The Laughing Man" was Wrightson's last illustrated story for Warren, although he did do some incidental work for them for future issues. It was also the best story of the lot. "Murder on the Vine" was a decent Tarzan spoof, marred by dreadful coloring. The glory days of the color section were over.

96. cover: Kim McQuaite (March 1978)

(1) Predation [Bruce Jones/Rudy Nebres] 10p; (2) The Comic Books: Kiss and Tell [Joe Brancatelli, text article] 1p; (3) Trilby and the Star Rovers [Budd Lewis and Bill DuBay/Luis Bermejo] 6p; (4) Bonga and Me [Nicola Cuti/Esteban Maroto] 8p; (5) Alien! [Bill DuBay/Martin Salvador] 9p; (6) The Green [Bruce Jones/Luis Bermejo] 6p; (7) Alien Strain [Bill DuBay/Alex Nino] 8p.

Notes: McQuaite's cover looked as if it had wandered over from an issue of *Famous Monsters* or perhaps a Star Wars–style movie magazine. With the horror boom of the early 1970s over and Star Wars mania in full force, Warren began to lean more and more on covers with science fiction themes. This was listed as the *Alien Encounters* special. The cover price was $1.25. The story

"Bonga and Me" was originally intended for *Eerie* #78. Rudy Nebres' art on "Predation" was the best stuff here.

97. cover: Frank Frazetta (May 1978), reprinted from *Eerie* #3 (May 1966)

(1) Momma Is a Vampire [Nicola Cuti/Leopoldo Duranona] 8p; (2) The Comic Books: Safe at Home? [Joe Brancatelli, text article] 1p; (3) The Wax Werewolf [Bob Toomey/Jose Ortiz] 8p; (4) Black Death [Bruce Jones/Leopold Sanchez] 10p; (5) Snaegl or How I Conquered the Snail That Ate Tokyo [Nicola Cuti/Martin Salvador] 8p; (6) Dragon Lady [Bill DuBay/Esteban Maroto] 8p; (7) Sisters [Bill DuBay/Alex Nino] 8p; (8) Presenting the 1977 Warren Awards [Louise Jones/Frank Frazetta, Bruce Jones, Bill DuBay, Alex Nino and Ramon Torrents, text article] 2p.

Notes: This issue was of slightly higher quality than usual. "Momma Is a Vampire" was the best story with Maroto's art on "Dragon Lady" being the highpoint on the illustration front. Duranona had some excellent pages here as well. The 1977 Warren Awards went to Frank Frazetta for best cover on *Eerie* #81; best story and best art went to Bruce Jones and Russ Heath for the story "Yellow Heat," best cover artist to Richard Corben, best all-around writer to Bruce Jones, best all-around artist to Alex Nino and special awards for excellence to Ramon Torrents as well as Bill DuBay and Luis Bermejo for *The Rook*.

98. cover: Attilla Hejje (June 1978)

(1) The Alien Factor [Budd Lewis/Jose Ortiz] 8p; (2) The Comic Books: Classics Illustrated: R.I.P. [Joe Brancatelli, text article] 1p; (3) Helen Horror Hollywood [Gerry Boudreau/Leopoldo Duranona] 8p; (4) Graveyard Shift [Bruce Jones/Leopold Sanchez] 11p; (5) Starlet, Starlet, Burning Bright [Gerry Boudreau/Carmine Infantino and Dick Giordano, art miscredited to Ramon Torrents] 8p; (6) The Image Makers [Nicola Cuti/Jose Ortiz] 8p.

Notes: An all-media horror special. Cover price was $1.50. A run-of-the-mill issue for this time period.

99. cover: Bob Larkin (July 1978)

(1) An Old Game [Nicola Cuti/Pepe Moreno] 8p; (2) The Comic Books: Still More Kiss [Joe Brancatelli, text article] 1p; (3) Ssshh! [Cary

Bates/Joe Vaultz] 8p; (4) Brothers [Bill DuBay/
Jose Ortiz] 10p; (5) A Slight Case of Overkill
[Bill DuBay/Leopold Sanchez] 8p; (6) There
Shall Come a Great Darkness [Bob Toomey/
Alfredo Alcala] 8p; (7) One Hell of a War
[Roger McKenzie/Leopoldo Duranona] 9p.

Notes: Disaster special. The cover price was $1.25.
"A Slight Case of Overkill" was an overflow story
from *Creepy*'s all-ape issue. A rather average issue
with the sole bright spot being the Warren debut
of Pepe Moreno, a fine Spanish artist.

100. cover: Bob Larkin (August 1978)

(1) The Pit at the Center of the Earth! [Gerry
Boudreau/Pablo Marcos] 8p; (2) The Comic
Books: Death by the Numbers [Joe Brancatelli,
text article] 1p; (3) Professor Duffer and the In-
superable Myron Meek! [Bill DuBay/John Sev-
erin] 6p; (4) Tale of a Fox [Nicola Cuti/Jose
Ortiz] 8p; (5) Nobody's Home [Cary Bates/Joe
Vaultz] 5p; (6) Winner Take All! [Len Wein/
Luis Bermejo, color] 8p; (7) Hell Hound [Bruce
Jones/Russ Heath] 10p; (8) Wisper of Dark Eyes
[Gerry Boudreau/Rafael Auraleon] 8p; (9)
They're Going to Be Turning Out the Lights
[Bill DuBay/Alex Nino] 9p.

Notes: Cover price was $1.75 with 88 pages. An
effort was made to make this a very special anniversary issue but, although it's considerably
better than the lackluster #50, most of this issue
seems, well, a bit tired. It's better than the
average issue, but for *Creepy*'s 100th issue, one
might be hoping for something a little more
kickass. From the blah cover to the last story,
there's nothing like that here. The best story was
Cuti's "Tale of a Fox," which became a series
starting with *Vampirella* #95. "Hell Hound" was
beautifully drawn and the story ain't bad but it
seemed a little familiar. The rest of the issue was
simply okay. "They're Going to Be Turning Out
the Lights" was printed sideways.

101. cover: Richard Corben (September 1978)

(1) In Deep [Bruce Jones/Richard Corben, reprinted from *Creepy* #83 (October 1976)] 10p;
(2) In Deep, part 2 [Bruce Jones/Leopoldo Du-
ranona] 9p; (3) A Boy and His Thing [Bill
DuBay/Alex Nino] 10p; (4) Waterbabies [Louise
Jones/Pablo Marcos, color] 8p; (5) The Seven
Sisters of the Sea [Gerry Boudreau/Alfredo Al-
cala] 9p; (6) Alternate Paths [Chris Adames/
Pepe Moreno] 8p.

Notes: The cover price was $1.50. Say you've got
a great cover, a really great cover, that was intended to be the cover for #83. It was meant for
a story so vivid that you couldn't possibly use
that cover to highlight any other issue or story
without it being very apparent that you'd screwed
up two years earlier. What do you do? Well, you
reprint the story, ask the writer to pen a sequel
and cross your fingers that nobody says nothin.'
Unfortunately you picked Leopoldo Duranona
to follow Rich Corben's original artwork. Both
are fine artists but about as incompatible in style
and approach as any two artists you could look
at. So the best art on an original story goes to
Alex Nino for "A Boy and His Thing." Except
for the reprint, the stories are sadly rather lackluster.

102. cover: Patrick Woodroffe (October 1978)

(1) Pantomime at Sea [Cary Bates/Joe Vaultz]
10p; (2) The Comic Books: What Hath Congress Wrought? [Joe Brancatelli, text article] 1p;
(3) Almost Shangri-La [Bruce Jones/Leopoldo
Duranona] 11p; (4) The Thing in the Haunted
Forest [?/Abel Laxamana] 7p; (5) Killer Claw
[Mark Lasky/Walt Simonson and Klaus Janson]
10p; (6) Night Eyes [Bruce Jones/Alfredo Al-
cala] 10p; (7) Fair Prey [Bruce Jones/Isidro
Mones] 10p.

Notes: The price was $2.00. This was an all-
monster issue. Another lackluster issue with the
best work done by Bruce Jones and Alfredo
Alcala on "Night Eyes." Isidro Mones returned
after a long absence with a new art style.

103. cover: Walt Simonson and Kim Mc-
Quaite (November 1978)

(1) Thane: Angel of Doom [Archie Goodwin/
Jeff Jones, reprinted from *Creepy* #16 (August
1967)] 6p; (2) Bookworm [Gerry Conway/
Richard Corben, reprinted from *Eerie* #32
(March 1971)] 7p; (3) The Comic Books: Roll
Over, Brancatelli [Joe Brancatelli, text article]
1p; (4) On Little Cat Feet! [John Jacobson/
Rafael Auraleon, reprinted from *Vampirella* #38
(November 1974)] 11p; (5) Thumbs Down!
[Anne T. Murphy/Al Williamson, reprinted
from *Creepy* #6 (December 1965)] 6p; (6)
Lucky Stiff [Gerry Boudreau and Carl Wessler/
Ramon Torrents, reprinted from *Vampirella* #38
(November 1974)] 5p; (7) The Black Cat [Berni
Wrightson, from the story by Edgar Allan Poe,
reprinted from *Creepy* #62 (May 1974)] 12p.

Notes: The 1978 *Creepy* Annual with a $1.50 cover price. This issue bore all the signs of being assembled by someone just picking up random issues from the file shelves. Not a single story appeared from *Creepy*'s excellent 1976–1977 run. In fact, most of the stories didn't even appear in *Creepy*. This was, at least, the third go-around for both the Williamson story and the Thane tale. Only the reprinting of Wrightson's adaptation of "The Black Cat" was really worthy of an annual placement. Great cover by Simonson and McQuaite, though.

104. cover: Ken Kelly (January 1979), reprinted from the back cover of *Eerie* #63 (February 1975)

(1) The Games [Roger McKenzie/Pablo Marcos] 8p; (2) The Comic Books: Notes on Comix People [Joe Brancatelli, text article] 1p; (3) The Caretaker [Bob Toomey/Alfredo Alcala] 8p; (4) Mother Park [Roger McKenzie/Jose Ortiz] 10p; (5) Wolfer O'Connel: In the City of Gold [Budd Lewis/ Pepe Moreno] 10p; (6) Holocost [Steve Englehart/Terry Austin] 6p; (7) Keep Kool [Bob Toomey/Alex Nino] 8p.

Notes: $1.25 cover price. Kelly's reprinted cover featured Exterminator One. This was an all-robot special. A previous Wolfer O'Connel story had appeared in *Eerie* #76 (August 1976). The O'Connel story and art were also the best one in the issue.

105. cover: Esteban Maroto (February 1979)

(1) Shrivel [Bob Toomey/Val Mayerik] 8p; (2) The Comic Books: The Party [Joe Brancatelli, text article] 1p; (3) Night Life [Bob Toomey/ Rafael Auraleon] 8p; (4) Dime Novel Hero! [Nicola Cuti/Russ Heath] 8p; (5) Always Leave 'em Laughing!

[Len Wein/Alex Nino] 8p; (6) The Sign [Roger McKenzie/Pepe Moreno] 8p; (7) Visit to a Primitive Planet [Bill DuBay/John Severin] 6p; (8) The Summoning [Bruce Jones/Gonzalo Mayo] 11p.

Notes: Great cover from Maroto, which also appeared as the cover years later on an issue of *Heavy Metal*. The cover price was $1.50. This was a very good issue with some great stories in it! "Shrivel," by Toomey and Mayerik, was an amusing little jape. The delightful "Dime Novel Hero!" by Cuti and Heath was a rewrite and expansion of a two-pager Cuti wrote and published in July 1973 for *The Monster Times*. That version,

Esteban Maroto was one of Warren's best artists, illustrating dozens of stories for the company. Here is an example of his rare cover art work. © New Comic Co./used by permission.

entitled "Werewolf Goes West," was illustrated by Frank Brunner. The final page for "Dime Novel Hero!" had a nifty and oh-so-obvious-that-I-should-have-thought-of-it-myself story twist that leaves you with a big grin on your face. About half the horror stories I've read that involve clowns have some variation on the "Always Leave 'em Laughing" title. The title is very much a cliché, but then so is this story itself. "The Sign" was a neat Christmas story and a definite nod to the old Warren Christmas specials. The DuBay/Severin story was a triumph of subtle storytelling while the Jones/Mayo team delivered a fine little shocker. In fact, the Bruce Jones/Gonzalo Mayo story/art team delivered some of Warren's best stories during 1978–1979.

106. cover: Romas Kukalis (March 1979)

(1) Quimby the Barbarian [Bob Toomey/Pablo Marcos] 9p; (2) The Comic Books: Going for the Bucks [Joe Brancatelli, text article] 1p; (3) Fangs [Laurie Sutton/Leopoldo Duranona] 9p; (4) Swords in the World Series [Ken Gale/Jim Starlin and Joe Rubinstein] 8p; (5) Primal Equation [Budd Lewis and Jon Sinsky/Isidro Mones] 6p; (6) Sudden Death Playoff [Bob Toomey/Pepe Moreno] 8p; (7) The Art of Killing [Larry Hama/Val Mayerik] 10p.

Notes: This was cover artist Romas Kukalis' professional debut. Both "Swords in the World Series" and "Sudden Death Playoff" were originally intended to be part of the third all-sports stories special, probably originally intended for *Creepy* #102. That special issue was cancelled and the stories parceled out over different magazines for the next couple of years. The best story here was the Hama/Mayerick samurai story "The Art of Killing," which was clearly inspired by the long-running Japanese series "Lone Wolf and Cub," which hadn't been seen by the general U.S. public at the time this story came out. This was a pretty good tribute, with Mayerick's art appearing to take a giant leap of quality from the often lumpy-looking art he'd been doing for Marvel a few years earlier. The story led to a series for the young samurai warrior that appeared in *Eerie.*

107. cover: Romas Kukalis (May 1979)

(1) The Rubicon [Budd Lewis/Pepe Moreno] 10p; (2) The Comic Books: The Inevitable Su-

perman Story [Joe Brancatelli, text article] 1p; (3) Family Ties [Bruce Jones/Val Mayerik] 10p; (4) Presenting the 1978 Warren Awards [Louise Jones/Ruby Nebres, Leopoldo Duranona, Jordi Penlavi, Kim McQuaite, et al., text article] 2p; (5) The World from Rough Stones [Jean Michel Martin/Joe Vaultz] 4p; (6) Stainless Steel Savior [Len Wein/Leopoldo Duranona] 8p; (7) Quirks [Bob Toomey/Walt Simonson and Terry Austin] 8p; (8) Mindquake [Jim Stenstrum/Garcia Pizarro, story credited to Alabaster Redzone] 9p; (9) The Rook ad [Rudy Nebres, color, on the inside back cover] 1p.

Notes: Due to an editorial error, all credits were missing from the actual stories. The credits were given on the letters page of #110. Best story here probably belonged to Bruce Jones' "Family Ties" while "Quirks" had the best art. The story "Stainless Steel Savior" was overflow from *Creepy* #104's all-robot stories special. The 1978 Warren Awards went to Jordi Penalva for best cover from *Eerie* #96, Bruce Jones for best story for "Hell Hound" from *Creepy* #100, best art to Rudy Nebres for "Predation" from *Creepy* #96, best cover artist to Richard Corben, best all-around writer to Bruce Jones, best all-around artist to Leopoldo Duranona, and special awards of excellence went to Gonzalo Mayo and Kim McQuaite.

108. cover: Terrence Lindall (June 1979)

(1) Hole in the Head [Frank Salvatini/Alex Nino] 9p; (2) The Comic Books: So Much for Traditions [Joe Brancatelli, text article] 1p; (3) Camelot Crosstime [Jean Michel Martin/Val Mayerik] 8p; (4) Sultana [Budd Lewis/Pepe Moreno] 10p; (5) Going by the Book [Kevin Duane/Alfredo Alcala] 8p; (6) House of Magic [Gerry Boudreau/Pablo Marcos] 8p; (7) Hell's Playground [Jean Michel Martin/Leopoldo Duranona] 8p.

Notes: Cover price was $1.75. This was Terrence Lindall's professional debut and his gruesome medieval/primitive–styled art caused quite a bit of controversy when it first appeared. Myself, I quite liked it. Lindall also contributed a self-portrait on the letters page. "Sultana" had very good artwork by the always impressive Pepe Moreno and a fine story by Budd Lewis. In addition, Alex Nino contributed a superior art job and "House of Magic" was also well done.

109. cover: Jim Laurier (July 1979)

(1) Vampire Dawn [Archie Goodwin/Pepe Moreno] 12p; **(2)** The Comic Books: Notes on Comix People [Joe Brancatelli, text article] 1p; **(3)** The Organizer [Bruce Jones/Leopoldo Duranona] 10p; **(4)** The Ravenscroft Affair [Bill DuBay/Paul Neary] 6p; **(5)** Alien Affair [Cary Bates/Val Mayerik] 12p; **(6)** Heart of Darkness [Bill Mantlo/Luis Bermejo] 8p.

Notes: Jim Laurier's spaceship cover looked a lot like either a repainted hair dryer, a flashlight or a lady's pleasure toy. What it didn't look like was an actual working spaceship. Cover price at $1.50. Between editing jobs at Marvel, Archie Goodwin returned to Warren and contributed ten or so stories over the next year and a half. All of them were of high quality with some among his best work. "Vampire Dawn" was a welcome and strong return and easily featured the best story and art for the issue. "The Ravenscroft Affair" was also quite good. Luis Bermejo contributed probably his worst art job for Warren with the dreary and heartless "Heart of Darkness."

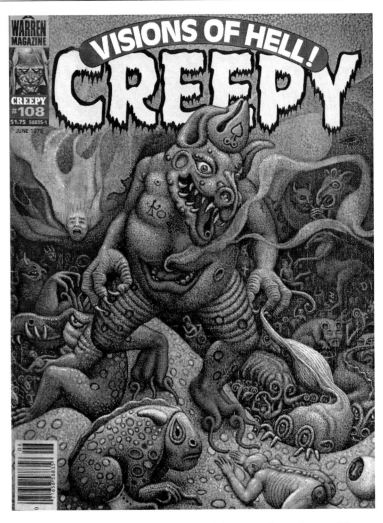

Terrance Lindell's Renaissance approach by way of H. P. Lovecraft's take on horror images was an unusual move by Warren, who usually preferred more stately cover art. Still, it worked and Lindell did a number of fine cover paintings in the late 1970s and early 1980s. © New Comic Co./used by permission.

110. cover: Patrick Woodroffe (August 1979)

(1) Snapper [Bill Kelly/Leopoldo Duranona] 10p; **(2)** The Comic Books: The Corporate Mad [Joe Brancatelli, text article] 1p; **(3)** Sunset Farms [Gerry Boudreau and Alex Southern/Rudy Nebres] 8p; **(4)** Take Your Child, Please! [Cary Bates/Jose Ortiz] 8p; **(5)** The Demon Hater [Nicola Cuti/Rafael Auraleon] 8p; **(6)** Horror Is a Highrise [Archie Goodwin/Leopoldo Duranona] 10p; **(7)** A Knightmare to Remember [Cary Bates/Joe Vaultz] 6p; **(8)** The Clockmaker [Bob Toomey/Jesus Blasco, story credited to Gary Null and the art miscredited to Jesus Blasquez] 9p.

Notes: Patrick Woodroffe's tight closeup of Pan's head was the most striking cover image *Creepy* had seen since Corben's excellent cover to #101. Price bounced up again to $1.75 with 80 pages of story. The rest of the issue didn't hold up to the promise of the great cover but "Snapper" would have fit right in with the stories from the Goodwin era, while Goodwin's own story is quite good. Joe Vaultz's airbrush art was quite crude when he tried to draw human beings but with the right subject matter it was often very effective and "A Knightmare to Remember" is actually well worth remembering. "The Clock-

maker" is an unacknowl-
edged rewrite by Toomey of
a European adaptation of
Edgar Allan Poe's "The Tell-
Tale Heart." This was celebrated European artist Jesus
Blasco's Warren debut but
he would never receive credit
for his work as he was always
miscredited as former Warren artists Jesus Blasquez or
Jaime Brocal. I don't know
why this confusion hap-
pened. Neither of those two
artists' work looks anything
like Blasco's. Perhaps Blasco
was ghosting art for the two?
Toomey would use the pen
name Gary Null for Euro-
pean stories that he provided
rewrites for—perhaps the
same reason Jim Stenstrum
began to use the pen name
Alabaster Redzone.

111. cover: Duane Allen
(September 1979)

(1) Dreams of Grandeur
[Budd Lewis/Val Mayerik
and Klaus Janson] 10p; (2)
The Comic Books: Still
Collecting After All These
Years [Joe Brancatelli, text
article] 1p; (3) A Stiff
Named Sczynsky [Bob
Toomey/Rafael Auraleon]
8p; (4) Heart of the War-
rior [Bill DuBay/Alejandro
Sanchez] 8p; (5) Blood-
Lust [Cary Bates/Leopoldo
Duranona] 12p; (6) Night Wind [Masanabo
Sato and Gary Null/Masanabo Sato] 9p; (7) A
Switch in Dime [Nicola Cuti/Leopoldo Dura-
nona] 11p.

Notes: Another good cover from a newcomer,
although this was Duane Allen's only Warren appearance. This was a fair-to-middlin' issue.
Nothing was particularly notable or awful.

112. cover: Richard Corben (October 1979)

(1) The Homecoming [Archie Goodwin/Al
Williamson] 9p; (2) The Comic Books: The

Richard Corben, another great Warren artist, offers his take on Lon
Chaney's *Phantom of the Opera. Creepy* #112 was perhaps the last of
the great *Creepy* issues, with strong work from Archie Goodwin, John
Severin, Bob Toomey, Al Williamson, John and Val Lakey and Alex
Nino, among others. © New Comic Co./used by permission.

Comic Book Gravevine [Joe Brancatelli, text
article] 1p; (3) Warrior's Ritual [Archie Good-
win/John Severin] 10p; (4) Nobody's Kid [Bob
Toomey/Leopoldo Duranona] 8p; (5) Relic
[Bob Toomey/Walt Simonson] 8p; (6) Beast-
slayer [John Lakey/Val Lakey] 10p; (7) Sunday
Dinner [Larry Hama/Rafael Auraleon] 8p; (8)
The Rook ad [Pablo Marcos] 1p; (9) Thane:
The Last Sorcerer [Archie Goodwin/Alex Nino]
12p.

Notes: There was a $2.00 cover price with
88 pages. A spectacular Corben cover of Lon

Chaney's version of the *Phantom of the Opera* leads off the last truly great issue of *Creepy* that Warren would produce. There'd be some good ones done down the line but none that hit this level of quality. Much of that quality could be attributed to one man — Archie Goodwin, who contributed three stories here, the most he'd had in any one issue since 1967. All three of them were gems. "The Homecoming" had originated from a script by Bruce Jones but Williamson, who had completed the art, decided he didn't like the script and asked Goodwin to write a new one. Jones was (and is) a good writer but Goodwin's SF script is so good that one would have a hard time imagining a better version. The last appearance of Thane (three previous stories had appeared from 1967 to 1969) also graced this issue and it too was a winner, taking the Conan-like Thane and giving him a send-off story that was considerably better than most of the Marvel sword and sorcery adaptations of that time. And I say that despite the fact that I quite enjoyed Roy Thomas' work on Conan. Alex Nino's art was also impressive on this story. The cream of the crop here, however, was the impressive "Warrior's Ritual" with great artwork by John Severin. This French Foreign Legion story was about as good a horror takeoff on Beau Geste as you could ask for. Good as the artwork for all three Goodwin stories was, though, the best art of this issue belongs to Val Lakey's Warren debut with "Beastslayer." Her retouched photos and artwork combo was very impressive. I don't know if John Lakey was her brother or her husband (she later appeared in *Heavy Metal* with a different last name) but his story was quite good as well. "Relic" was a sequel to #107's "Quirks" and it's just as good a tale as the first. I also liked "Nobody's Kid" which had an interesting story and fine artwork by the team of Toomey and Duranona. The only story I didn't like was the rather rancid "Sunday Dinner." Just a fine, fine issue.

113. cover and title page: Berni Wrightson (November 1979)

(1) The Muck Monster [Berni Wrightson, reprinted from *Eerie* #68 (September 1975)] 7p; (2) The Comic Books: Lies Our Forefathers

Told Us [Joe Brancatelli, text article] 1p; (3) The Laughing Man [Bruce Jones/Berni Wrightson, reprinted from *Creepy* #95 (February 1978)] 6p; (4) The Pepper Lake Monster [Berni Wrightson, reprinted from *Eerie* #58 (July 1974)] 10p; (5) Clarice [Bruce Jones/Berni Wrightson, reprinted from *Creepy* #77 (February 1976)] 5p; (6) Cool Air [Berni Wrightson, from the story by H. P. Lovecraft, reprinted from *Eerie* #62 (January 1975)] 7p; (7) Country Pie [Bruce Jones/Carmine Infantino and Berni Wrightson, reprinted from *Creepy* #83 (October 1976)] 6p; (8) A Martian Saga [Nicola Cuti/Berni Wrightson, reprinted from *Creepy* #87 (March 1977)] 6p.

Notes: The 1979 Warren Annual. A Berni Wrightson special. It was $1.50 with 64 pages. This is a top-quality reprint issue well worth looking for, with superb art and very good stories.

114. cover: Kirk Reinhart (January 1980)

(1) Rats [Bob Toomey/Pepe Moreno] 10p; (2) The Comic Books: Notes on Comix People [Joe Brancatelli, text article] 1p; (3) Charnel Combat [Pierce Askegren/Danny Tallerno] 6p; (4) Heat [Gerry Boudreau/Leopoldo Duranona] 8p; (5) Small War [Roger McKenzie/Jim Starlin and Pablo Marcos] 8p; (6) The Reaper [Archie Goodwin/Alex Toth] 10p; (7) An Android Affair [Mark Laskey/Rafael Auraleon] 8p.

Notes: This issue was 72 pages. Nice cover and a nice solid issue that included a chilling story from Archie Goodwin and interesting work from Gerry Boudreau and Bob Toomey. Best art was Pepe Moreno on "Rats" with good work from Alex Toth, Jim Starlin, Pablo Marcos and Leopoldo Duranona.

115. cover: Manuel Sanjulian (February 1980)

(1) Gabriel's Horn [Roger McKenzie/Leopoldo Duranona] 16p; (2) The Comic Books: Some Thoughts on What Has Gone Before [Joe Brancatelli, text article] 1p; (3) 1979 Warren Awards Ballots [Chris Adames, text article] 1p; (4) The Last Labor of Hercules [Budd Lewis/Delando Nino, art credited to A2-120] 10p; (5) Cyrano [Bob Toomey/Michael Saenz] 8p; (6) Rapid Fire Angel [Gerry Boudreau/Axel Laxamana] 8p; (7) Et Tu Brutus [Nicola Cuti/Val Mayerik and Rudy Nebres] 8p; (8) War Children [Gerry Boudreau/Val Mayerik] 8p.

Notes: This one was $1.75 with 80 pages. Sanjulian's first cover since #79 was clearly originally intended to be a "Beastworld" cover for *Eerie*. New Berni Wrightson art adorned the letters page for this issue only. For the first (and possibly only) time, the Warren Awards were open to voting and nominations by the readers. Saenz provided the best art while Roger McKenzie's "Gabriel's Horn" was the best story.

116. cover: Terrence Lindall (March 1980)

(1) Endangered Species [Gerry Boudreau/Fred Carrillo] 10p; (2) The Comic Books: Building a New Marvel [Joe Brancatelli, text article] 1p; (3) The Highway [Nicola Cuti/Val Mayerik and Rudy Nebres] 8p; (4) Day of the Locust [Jordan Black/Masanabu Sato] 6p; (5) The Greatest Editor Alive! [Bill DuBay/Alex Nino and Delano Nino, story is credited to Will Richardson] 11p; (6) Graduation Day [Bruce Jones/Val Mayerik and Jeff Easley] 11p; (7) Never Again [James Warren, text article, on the inside back cover] 1p.

Notes: The issue was 72 pages. For only the second time in Warren history, James Warren penned a political editorial, this time denouncing revolutionary Iran for taking over the U.S. embassy. The accompanying photo showed two Iranians carrying garbage in an American flag. This was the last appearance of Joe Brancatelli's column. At this point Bill DuBay began using the pen name Will Richardson, which would appear for the next year or so. Best story and art goes to "Graduation Day" by the team of Jones/Mayerik/Easley.

The Decline and Fall

117. cover: Ken Kelly (May 1980)

(1) Scream [Bob Toomey/Leopoldo Duranona] 19p; (2) A Noble Gesture [?/Adolfo Abellan] 7p; (3) The Beast [Michael Fleisher/Isidro Mones] 10p; (4) Nightmare Highway [Gerry Boudreau/Carmine Infantino and Steve Leialoha] 10p; (5) The Silkie [Nicola Cuti/Val Mayerik and Jeff Easley] 10p.

Notes: DuBay, as Will Richardson, returned as editor while Louise Jones (nee Simonson) headed off to new frontiers at Marvel. The logo changed to a new, more modern lettering. Kelly's cover originally appeared as a t-shirt design in 1976.

The letters page claimed that Enrich Torres was the uncredited cover artist for *Creepy* #115 but it certainly appeared to be Sanjulian's work. "Scream" seemed to end quite abruptly, without an actual climax. It was originally intended to be one of Bob Toomey's "Gary Null" stories.

118. cover: Enrich Torres (June 1980)

(1) Nursery School [Bob Toomey/Leopoldo Duranona] 15p; (2) Epitaph [Len Wein/Joaquin Blasquez] 7p; (3) The Curse of the Binderwoods [Mark Laidlawith Isidro Mones] 8p; (4) Junior Was a Momma's Boy [Gerry Boudreau/Carmine Infantino and Jorge Benuy] 13p; (5) Process of Elimination [Bob Toomey/Val Mayerik and Pablo Marcos] 10p.

Notes: Enrich's best cover in some time highlighted a solid issue. Good work appeared from just about everybody here. "Nursery School" was intended to be one of Toomey's "Gary Null" stories. Duranona, who wrote the original story, was reportedly astounded at Toomey's rewrite. Best artwork was from the team of Carmine Infantino and Jorge Benuy.

119. cover: Jim Laurier (July 1980)

(1) A Boy and His Thing [Bill DuBay/Alex Nino, reprinted from *Creepy* #101 (September 1978)] 10p; (2) *Eerie* ad [Esteban Maroto] 1p; (3) Keep Kool [Bob Toomey/Alex Nino, reprinted from *Creepy* #104 (January 1979)] 8p; (4) Always Leave 'em Laughing! [Len Wein/Alex Nino, reprinted from *Creepy* #105 (February 1979)] 8p; (5) Sisters [Bill DuBay/Alex Nino, reprinted from *Creepy* #97 (May 1978)] 8p; (6) Backwaters and Timing Circles [Budd Lewis/Alex Nino, reprinted from *Creepy* #94 (January 1978)] 9p; (7) Alien Strain [Bill DuBay/Alex Nino, reprinted from *Creepy* #96 (March 1978)] 8p; (8) The 1979 Warren Awards! [Bill DuBay, text article] 2p.

Notes: Warren began having multiple reprint issues during a given year. Previously, only the annual had featured reprints. For Warren Publications, this was a sure sign of trouble behind the scenes. This issue was an Alex Nino reprint special. The Warren Awards went to Kirk Reinert for best cover on *Creepy* #114 (which was cover dated January 1980), Archie Goodwin for best story for "The Night Willa Jane Gornley Went Home" from *Vampirella* #82, Val Lakey for best art on "Beastslayer" from *Creepy* #112, Patrick

Woodroffe for best cover artist, Bob Toomey for best all-around writer, Abel Laxamana for best all-around artist and special awards for excellence to Terrence Lindall and Lee Elias.

120. cover: Jeff Jones (August 1980)

(1) Uncle Creepy's Introduction [Bill DuBay/Rudy Nebres] 1p; (2) Deathwatch [Roger McKenzie/Leopoldo Duranona] 8p; (3) The Rook ad [Jordi Penalva, B&W reproduction of *The Rook* #3] 1p; (4) Hell House [Jim Stenstrum/Jesus Blasco, story credited to Alabaster Redzone, art miscredited to Jaime Brocal] 6p; (5) Black Rainbow [Budd Lewis/Rueben Yandoc] 8p; (6) One Mind, Closed for Alterations! [Gerry Boudreau/Jess Jodloman] 8p; (7) A Taste for Heroes! [Gerry Boudreau/Carmine Infantino and Pablo Marcos] 10p; (8) Winterbeast [Budd Lewis/Val Mayerik] 8p; (9) Black Snow [Jeff Rovin/Herb Arnold] 8p.

Notes: Jones' cover was done in 1975 and was originally intended for Seaboard/Atlas' horror magazine *Weird Tales of the Macabre*. By this point most of the Spanish artists from S.I. had left the three horror titles, with the notable exceptions of Jose Ortiz, Jose Gonzalez and Rafael Aurleon, and had been replaced by Filipino artists. The Flipino artists tended to be more conservative in story layouts (except for Alex Nino) and in their depictions of nudity. Not to say the Filipino artists didn't use nudity. They actually used it quite a bit, but the S.I. artists from Spain could draw naked women in a sexy manner while the majority of the Filipino artists just drew naked women. There's a difference. That said, this was a darn fine issue, from the snazzy Jones cover to the generally very good stories within. "Death-

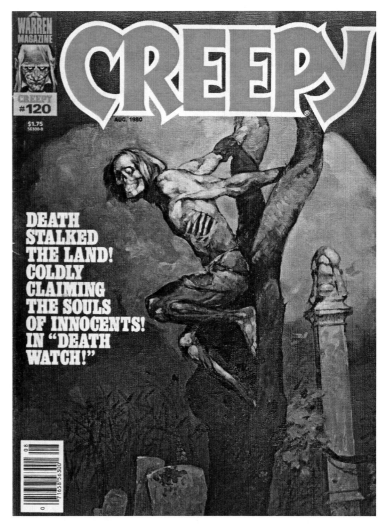

This Jeff Jones effort from 1980 was originally intended as an Atlas/Seaboard cover for either *Weird Tales of the Macabre* or *Devilina*. When Seaboard collapsed, the painting made its way to Warren. © New Comic Co./used by permission.

watch" was the best story, while Duranona, Mayerik and Arnold shared honors for best art. "A Taste for Heroes!" was probably done in 1978 and originally intended for the never-published 3rd all-sports stories special for *Creepy*.

121. cover: Jim Laurier (September 1980)

(1) A Toast to No Man's Memory [Len Wein/John Severin, reprinted from *Creepy* #92 (October 1977)] 8p; (2) The Strange, Incurable Hauntings of Terrible Phinneas Boggs! [Bill DuBay/John Severin, reprinted from *Creepy* #83 (October 1976)] 9p; (3) The Star Saga of Sirius Sam [Nicola Cuti/John Severin, reprinted from

Creepy #95 (February 1978)] 8p; (4) Battle Rot [Bill DuBay/John Severin, reprinted from *Creepy* #81 (July 1976)] 6p; (5) Professor Duffer and the Insuperable Myron Meek! [Bill DuBay/John Severin, reprinted from *Creepy* #100 (August 1978)] 6p; (6) Angel of Jaipur [Bill DuBay/John Severin, reprinted from *Creepy* #89 (June 1977)] 6p; (7) Visit to a Primitive Planet [Bill DuBay/John Severin, reprinted from *Creepy* #105 (February 1979] 6p; (8) Warrior's Ritual [Archie Goodwin/John Severin, reprinted from *Creepy* #112 (October 1979)] 10p.

Notes: The 1980 *Creepy* Annual. A John Severin special. Two of the last three issues had been all reprints. A new Uncle Creepy head by Berni Wrightson appears on the letters page. A great collection of stories.

122. cover: Lee Katz (October 1980)

(1) Uncle Creepy's Introduction [Bill DuBay/Rudy Nebres] 1p; (2) The Killing! [Roger McKenzie/Leopoldo Duranona and Alex Toth] 12p; (3) The Watcher [Bob Toomey/Leopoldo Duranona] 9p; (4) The Perfect Specimen [Budd Lewis/Steve Gan] 5p; (5) Midnight in Chinatown [Gerry Boudreau/Carmine Infantino and Alfredo Alcala] 8p; (6) Routine [Carl Wessler/Martin Salvador] 4p; (7) Magic Man [Gerry Boudreau/Fred Carrillo] 8p; (8) Roomers [Bruce Jones/Mike Zeck, story miscredited to Budd Lewis] 10p.

Notes: Katz's cover had originally been intended for *Eerie*, probably for the "Samurai" serial. Another solid issue. The unexpected art teaming of Duranona and Toth was a surprising success and provided the best art in the issue. "Routine" featured Uncle Creepy actually drawn onto the splash page, something that hadn't happened since 1974 or thereabouts so this story may have been an inventory story from that period. Bruce Jones later wrote a prose version of "Roomers" that appeared in his short story collection "Twisted Tales" (not to be confused with his 1982–1984/1987comic anthologies of the same name), which appeared in 1986 so I believe the Budd Lewis writing credit on that story to be incorrect. "Roomers" is also the best story here although it does have some competition.

123. cover: Ken Kelly (November 1980)

(1) Kiss of the Plague! [Doug Moench/Leo Summers and Alex Toth] 6p; (2) Hands of Fate [Carl Wessler/Martin Salvador] 7p; (3) They Don't Make Movies [Gerry Boudreau/Carmine Infantino and Alfredo Alcala] 10p; (4) The Slave [Jim Stenstrum/Jesus Blasco, story credited to Alabaster Redzone, art miscredited to Jaime Brocal] 5p; (5) Harriman's Monsters! [Greg Potter/Dan Adkins] 8p; (6) Always Leave Them Laughing [Michael Fleisher/Val Mayerik and Rudy Nebres] 8p; (7) Jelly [Nicola Cuti/Herb Arnold] 4p.

Notes: This issue was 64 pages. Best story and art goes to Doug Moench, Carmine Infantino and Alfredo Alcala for "They Don't Make Movies." "Harriman's Monsters!" was written years earlier when writer Potter was a regular at Warren and was to have been illustrated by Alex Toth. Toth either never finished the story and it was finally illustrated by Adkins for its appearance here. "Always Leave 'em Laughing" was another clown story with the same clichéd title. This one, at least, was a bit more original in its storyline.

124. cover: Vicente Segrelles (January 1981)

(1) Uncle Creepy's Introduction [Bill DuBay/Rudy Nebres] 1p; (2) Malphisto's Illusion [Nicola Cuti/Romeo Tanghal and Alex Toth, Tanghal's pencils are credited to Alexis Romeo] 8p; (3) Cult [Archie Goodwin/Martin Salvador] 11p; (4) Paydirt [Roger McKanzie/Carmine Infantino and Alfred Alcala] 8p; (5) Mayhem Museum [Carl Wessler/Aldolpho Buylla] 8p; (6) The Prometheus [Rich Margopoulos/John Garcia and Rudy Nebres] 6p; (7) A Slight Case of Madness! [Bill DuBay/Herb Arnold, story credited to Will Richardson] 10p.

Notes: Segrelles' cover had been done in 1976 as part of the presentation art for the never published magazine *Yesterday, Today ... Tomorrow*. "Mayhem Museum" gives the impression of having been done years earlier. "The Prometheus" has the identical plot and layout to #126's "Hot Bob" story. Although *Creepy* would never reach the dreary levels of boredom that the latterday *Eerie* sank to, the tired stories, even from old established favorites, and the lack of variety in the artwork (the Filipino artists, with the notable exceptions of Alex Nino, Alfredo Alcala, Vic Catan and Nestor Redondo, often tended to lay out and illustrate their stories in very similar fashions) ensured that the glory days of Warren were now behind them.

125. cover: Ken Kelly (February 1981)

(1) Uncle Creepy's Introduction [Bill DuBay/ Rudy Nebres] 1p; (2) Once Upon a Christmas Eve! [Bill DuBay/Martin Salvador, story credited to Will Richardson] 12p; (3) His Own Private Demon! [Roger McKenzie/Anton Caravana] 9p; (4) Top Dog! [Roger McKenzie/Alex Nino] 8p; (5) Jacque Couteau's Circus of the Bizarre [Roger McKenzie/Carmine Infantino and Alex Toth] 5p; (6) The Tempered Sword! [Manuel Auad/Alfredo Alcala] 6p; (7) Living Death Camp! [Roger McKenzie/Rafael Auraleon] 7p; (8) Knight Errant [Roy Kinnard/ Michael Saenz] 8p.

Notes: Kelly's Christmas-themed cover was a shot of nostalgia for the old Christmas specials. However, it's noticeable that the cover is nowhere near as violent or gory as the mid–1970s versions. The best art was from Michael Saenz. The stories, however, were at best so-so.

126. cover: Ken Kelly (March 1981)

(1) Uncle Creepy's Introduction [Bill DuBay/ Rudy Nebres] 1p; (2) Parasite [Budd Lewis/ Martin Salvador] 9p; (3) Nevada Moon [Steven Grant/Bill Draut] 8p; (4) ...And God Created Woman! [Bruce Jones/Anton Caravana] 12p; (5) Ragged Man [Budd Lewis/Romeo Tanghal and Alfredo Alcala, Tanghal's pencils credited to Alexis Romeo] 10p; (6) Dreamer! [Nicola Cuti/ Fred Carrillo] 8p; (7) Hot Bob [Budd Lewis/ Herb Arnold] 6p.

Notes: The cover price was $2.00 cover price for 72 pages. Kelly's cover instantly invoked visual memories of the great DuBay/Wrightson story "Nightfall" from 1975, as well as Windsor McKay's *Little Nemo in Slumberland* comic strip. The accompanying story "Dreamer" was also the best story this issue, although certainly not in either of those stories' league. The best art belonged to Romeo Tanghal and Alfredo Alcala for "Ragged Man." As noted above, "Hot Bob" had the same plot and layout as "The Prometheus" from #124, but this version was both better scripted and drawn.

127. cover: Terrence Lindall (May 1981)

(1) Uncle Creepy's Introduction [Chris Adames/ Rudy Nebres] 1p; (2) Hoodoo the Magnificent! [Bill DuBay/Martin Salvador, story credited to Will Richardson] 6p; (3) Forbidden Fruit! [Bruce Jones/Luis Bermejo] 13p; (4) Prism Second Generation Blues [Gerry Boudreau/Noly Panligan] 9p; (5) Daddy Is a Werewolf [Nicola Cuti/Fred Carrillo] 8p; (6) Wind [Roger McKenzie/Val Mayerik] 8p; (7) Escape [Steven Dietrich/Herb Arnold] 7p.

Notes: Chris Adames became the editor. Lindall's cover was certainly a nasty little torture cover. The best interior story and art was by Roger McKenzie and Val Mayerik for "Wind" although Noly Panligan also delivered a nice job.

128. cover: Frank Frazetta (June 1981), reprinted from *Creepy* #10 (August 1966)

(1) Uncle Creepy's Introduction [Chris Adames/ Rudy Nebres] 1p; (2) Whatever Happened to Orem? [Bill DuBay/Martin Salvador, story credited to Will Richardson] 10p; (3) Outcast of Euthanasia [Bill DuBay/Bill Draut, story credited to Will Richardson] 10p; (4) Old Man at the Morgue [Mark Lasky/Fred Carrillo] 7p; (5) Frankenstein Invades the Universe [Budd Lewis/Romeo Tanghal and Alfredo Alcala, Tanghal's pencils credited to Alexis Romeo] 12p; (6) Abelmar Jones: Lord of the Flies [Bill DuBay/Luis Bermejo, story credited to Will Richardson] 8p.

Notes: "Whatever Happened to Orem?" was a sequel to "Orem Ain't Got No Head Cheese" from *Creepy* #85. Abelmar Jones' series moved over from *Eerie*, where he'd been last seen in *Eerie* #95. An attempt to justify the reprinted cover was made by commissioning the story "Frankenstein Invades the Universe" to link with the Frazetta reprint.

129. cover: Jeff Easley (July 1981)

(1) Uncle Creepy's Introduction [Chris Adames/ Rudy Nebres] 1p; (2) The Terrible Truth About Danny! [Bill DuBay/Martin Salvador, story credited to Will Richardson] 10p; (3) The Saga of Popeye Jackson! [Gerry Boudreau/Paul Neary] 8p; (4) Working Class Hero [Roger McKenzie/Carmine Infantino and Alfredo Alcala] 8p; (5) The Last Voyage of Sinbad [Budd Lewis/Fred Carrillo] 8p; (6) He Who Lives! [Budd Lewis/Danny Bulanadi] 6p; (7) Strategic Retreat [John Ellis Sech/Herb Arnold] 8p.

Notes: Good cover but that's about it.

130. cover: Richard Courtney (August 1981)

(1) Uncle Creepy's Introduction [Chris Adames/ Rudy Nebres] 1p; **(2)** The Vampire on the Hill [John Ellis Sech/Martin Salvador] 7p; **(3)** Dual Nature [Laura Buscemi/John Lakey and Val Lakey, Val Lakey is credited as Artifact] 8p; **(4)** Screaming in the Rain [Don McGregor/Alfredo Alcala] 8p; **(5)** Mythologia [Nicola Cuti/Fred Carrillo] 9p; **(6)** Missing Love [Brian Jacobs/ Pepe Moreno] 7p; **(7)** Small Dreams [Maggie Pierce/Herb Arnold] 8p.

Notes: The original logo returned. Richard Courtney was a good find for Warren, delivering some of the best of their latterday covers. "Dual

Richard Courtney was the last of the great Warren cover artists, delivering often stunning work for the company in the early 1980s. © New Comic Co./used by permission.

Nature" was the best written and illustrated story. Good work was also delivered by Pepe Moreno, Herb Arnold and Don McGregor.

131. cover: Frank Frazetta (September 1981), reprinted from *Creepy* #4 (August 1965)

(1) Uncle Creepy's Introduction [Chris Adames/ Rudy Nebres] 1p; **(2)** The Nut [Budd Lewis/ Delando Nino] 10p; **(3)** Son of the Nut! [Bill DuBay/Martin Salvador, story credited to Will Richardson] 7p; **(4)** Lycanthropist [Budd Lewis/Bill Draut] 8p; **(5)** Possession Is Nine Pounds of the Soul [John Ellis Sech/Danny Bulanadi] 6p; **(6)** Bella Donna [Nicola Cuti/ Fred Carrillo] 8p; **(7)** Mindwar [John Ellis Sech/Noly Panaligan] 13p.

Notes: "The Nut" was an interesting little story but having the rather pointless sequel (by a totally different writer and artist) appear directly after it diminished its effect.

132. cover: Richard Corben (October 1981), reprinted from *Eerie* #90 (February 1978)

(1) A Tangible Hatred [Don McGregor/Richard Corben, reprinted from *Creepy* #41 (September 1971)] 10p; **(2)** Bright Eyes! [Doug Monech/ Richard Corben, reprinted from *Eerie* #43 (November 1972)] 7p; **(3)** A Woman Scorned [Bruce Jones/ Richard Corben, reprinted from *Eerie* #90 (February 1978)] 8p; **(4)** Bowser [Jan Strnad/Richard Corben, reprinted from *Vampirella* #54 (September 1976)] 8p; **(5)** The Pest! [Al Hewetson/ Richard Corben, reprinted from *Eerie* #33 (May 1971)] 8p; **(6)** The Mummy's Victory [Roger McKenzie/ Richard Corben, reprinted from *Creepy* #84 (November 1976)] 5p; **(7)** The Butcher: Forgive Us Our Trespasses [Bill DuBay/Richard Corben, reprinted from *Eerie* #62 (January 1975)] 8p; **(8)** The Butcher: Bye-Bye, Miss

American Dream [Bill DuBay/Richard Corben, reprinted from *Eerie* #64 (March 1975)] 8p.

Notes: The price was $2.25 with 80 pages. The 1981 *Creepy* Annual, a Richard Corben special. Great buy if you're a Corben fan (and who isn't?).

133. cover: Jeff Easley (November 1981)

(1) Uncle Creepy's Introduction [Bill DuBay/ Rudy Nebres] 1p; (2) Junior [Bill DuBay and Timothy Moriarty/Abel Laxamana, DuBay's contribution credited to Will Richardson] 12p; (3) The Dead Remember [Bruce Jones/Martin Salvador] 10p; (4) Kobold [Budd Lewis/Romeo Tanghan and Alfredo Alcala] 8p; (5) Bring on the Clowns! [Michael Fleisher/Fred Carrillo] 9p; (6) Savage Cargo! [Jim Stenstrum/Paul Neary, story credited to Alabaster Redzone] 8p.

Notes: Chris Adames left for Archie Comics and Bill DuBay returned as the editor with Timothy Moriarty as managing editor. It was $2.00 for 72 pages.

134. cover: Ken Kelly (January 1982)

(1) Uncle Creepy's Introduction [Bill DuBay/ Rudy Nebres] 1p; (2) Guardians of the Universe! [Budd Lewis/Delando Nino] 8p; (3) Hear the Organ Grinder Play [Mark Willard/Martin Salvador] 7p; (4) Soul Sucker! [Gerry Boudreau/Fred Carrillo] 8p; (5) Wreck of the Vendigo Shafter! [Rich Margopoulos/Gene Day and Rudy Nebres] 9p; (6) Nefites [Bruce Jones/Jun Lofamia] 10p; (7) Orson Who? [Nicola Cuti/Carmine Infantino and Wayne Howard] 4p; (8) War Is Hell! [Roger McKenzie/Val Mayerik] 6p; (9) The City of God [Budd Lewis/Steve Gan] 4p.

Notes: This was Ken Kelly's last cover for Warren but, like the contents of the magazine itself, it was a pale shadow of his work during Warren's prime. The best story here was probably Bruce Jones' "Nefites," although it revisited themes that he'd explored before. "War Is Hell!" might have been a pretty good story except for a glaring error where McKenzie has the U.S. Marines landing on Omaha Beach. The Marines operated strictly in the Pacific in World War II. The artwork is pretty drab throughout. One wishes that Gene Day had been able to ink his own pencils as Rudy Nebres was not a good match.

135. cover: Richard Courtney (February 1982)

(1) Uncle Creepy's Introduction [Bill DuBay/ Rafael Auraleon] 1p; (2) The Wedding Gift! [Budd Lewis/Fred Carrillo] 10p; (3) ...For We Have Sinned! [Bill DuBay/Martin Salvador] 8p; (4) Angel Hair Wine! [Gerry Boudreau/Jun Lofamia] 8p; (5) Strange in a Stranger Land! [Rich Margopoulos/Peter Hsu] 10p; (6) Morbid Love Story [Michael Fleisher/Rafael Auraleon] 11p; (7) Yonder Star [Budd Lewis/Steve Gan] 7p.

Notes: "...For We Have Sinned!" was a sequel to the far superior Christmas story "Bless Us, Father..." from *Creepy* #59 (January 1974). "Strange in a Stranger Land" copied the opening sequence of the acclaimed children's novel *The Iron Man* (better known by its 1999 movie title, *The Iron Giant*), where the Iron Giant crash-lands out to sea, only to rise up out of the water by a fishing boat.

136. cover: Richard Courtney (March 1982)

(1) Uncle Creepy's Introduction [Timothy Moriarty/Rafael Auraleon] 1p; (2) All the Time in the World! [John Ellis Sech/Fred Carrillo] 8p; (3) Never Say Die! [Gerry Boudreau/Martin Salvador] 9p; (4) The Consumers [Gerry Boudreau/Jun Lofamia] 6p; (5) Day of the Cliché [Greg Potter/Nebot] 9p; (6) Eyewitness News [Gerry Boudreau and Rich Margopoulos/ Carmine Infantino and Pablo Marcos] 8p; (7) Mother Zenobia and the Satan Glass! [Gerry Boudreau and Rich Margopoulos/Gonzalo Mayo] 8p; (8) Daddy's Gone A-Hunting [Steven Grant/Joe Staton] 8p.

Notes: Timothy Moriarty became the magazine's last editor with David Allikas listed as his assistant. Courtney's cover is very colorful. "Never Say Die!" and "Eyewitness News" were both sports/horror stories, probably done in 1978 for the never published third all-sports stories issue of *Creepy*.

137. cover: Rudy Nebres (May 1982)

(1) Al Williamson biography [Timothy Moriarty/Al Williamson, text article, Williamson's art is from interior panels] 1p; (2) H20 World! [Archie Goodwin/Al Williamson and Roy G. Krenkel, reprinted from *Creepy* #1 (January 1965)] 6p; (3) The Success Story [Archie Goodwin/Al Williamson, reprinted from *Creepy* #1 (January 1965)] 6p; (4) Welcome, Stranger [Archie Goodwin/Al Williamson, reprinted from *Creepy* #2 (April 1965)] 7p; (5) Sand Doom [Archie Goodwin/Al Williamson] 6p;

(6) Now You See It... [Bruce Jones/Al Williamson, reprinted from *Creepy* #83 (October 1976)] 8p; (7) Mother Knows Best [Bruce Jones/Al Williamson, reprinted from *Creepy* #86 (February 1977)] 8p; (8) The Homecoming [Archie Goodwin/Al Williamson, reprinted from *Creepy* #112 (October 1979)] 9p.

Notes: For the first time, *Creepy* sported a pen and ink illustrated cover rather than a painted one. An Al Williamson special that was $2.00 for 64 pages. Although *Creepy* was coming out ten times a year at this point, in reality it was largely a bi-monthly, since the additional three or four issues tended to be reprints.

138. cover: Manuel Sanjulian (June 1982)

(1) Uncle Creepy's Introduction [Timothy Moriarty/Berni Wrightson] 1p; (2) Lamb to the Slaughter [John Jacobson/Delando Nino] 13p; (3) Derelict! [Danielle DuBay/Fred Carrillo] 8p; (4) Fools and Kings! [Gerry Boudreau/Martin Salvador] 8p; (5) Dreamworld [Gerry Boudreau/Jun Lofamia] 8p; (6) The Cry of the Glipins [Dan Hallassey/John Garcia and Rudy Nebres] 9p.

Notes: Not much to say here. This is a run-of-the-mill issue. It's pretty bad when the reprint issues are so much better than the original issues.

139. cover: Rudy Nebres (July 1982)

(1) *Creepy*'s Capacious Caucus [Timothy Moriarty, text article] 1p; (2) Daddy and the Pie [Bill DuBay/Alex Toth, reprinted from *Eerie* #64 (Ma. 1975)] 8p; (3) The Monument [Archie Goodwin/Alex Toth, reprinted from *Creepy* #3 (June 1965] 6p; (4) Grave Undertaking [Archie Goodwin/Alex Toth, reprinted from *Creepy* #5 (October 1965)] 6p; (5) Rude Awakening! [Archie Goodwin/Alex Toth, reprinted from *Creepy* #7 (February 1966)] 6p; (6) Survival! [Alex Toth and Archie Goodwin/Alex Toth, reprinted from *Blazing Combat* #3 (April 1966), Toth's original contribution to the story goes uncredited] 6p; (7) Phantom of Pleasure Island [Gerry Boudreau/Alex Toth, reprinted from *Creepy* #75 (November 1975)] 8p; (8) Unreal! [Alex Toth, reprinted from *Creepy* #78 (March 1976)] 6p.

Notes: Another pen and ink cover illustration, this one featuring Pie. An Alex Toth special. The letters page was dropped in favor of a feature page that was identical in all Warren comic magazines.

140. cover: Richard Corben (August 1982)

(1) *Creepy*'s Capacious Caucus [Timothy Moriarty, text article] 1p; (2) Uncle Creepy's Introduction [Timothy Moriarty/Rafael Auraleon] 1p; (3) The Big Itch! [Roger McKenzie/Delando Nino] 9p; (4) The Silver Stallion Conspiracy [Gerry Boudreau/Fred Carrillo] 15p; (5) There Is No Werewolf [Mark Willard/Martin Salvador] 7p; (6) Mummy, Jr. [Gerry Boudreau/Jun Lofamia] 3p; (7) One Good Turn... [Victor de la Fuente] 5p; (8) Spidership Season [Bob Toomey/Peter Hsu] 8p.

Notes: Among other Warren tidbits listed on the feature page, it was announced that *Creepy* would serialize A. E. Van Vogt's story "Space Beagle" in five parts. Unfortunately, that never happened in *Creepy*, although the complete adaptation did appear complete in the final issue of *Eerie*. "The Big Itch!" was a homage to Will Eisner's "The Spirit."

141. cover: Richard Corben (September 1982)

(1) Uncle Creepy's Introduction [Timothy Moriarty/Rafael Auraleon] 1p; (2) I Created the ... Gargoyle! [Danielle DuBay/Delando Nino] 10p; (3) The Puppet Master [John Ellis Sech/Fred Carrillo] 8p; (4) The Check-Out Counter [Timothy Moriarty/Alfonso DeLeon] 7p; (5) Covering All Bases [Kevin Duane/Martin Salvador] 9p; (6) Candle in the Wind [Gerry Boudreau/Jun Lofamia] 9p; (7) Moral Blood [Don McGregor/Al Sanchez] 11p.

Notes: The cost was $2.25 for 72 pages. The letters page returned. McGregor's "Moral Blood" was at least an attempt at forceful storytelling but the bland, cookie-cutter art tended to undercut the story's effectiveness. The story had been written years earlier and sold to Louise Jones when she was the editor.

142. cover: Richard Courtney (October 1982)

(1) *Creepy*'s Capacious Caucus [Timothy Moriarty, text article] 1p; (2) Monster Rally! [Archie Goodwin/Angelo Torres, reprinted from *Creepy* #4 (August 1965)] 8p; (3) One for De-Money [E. Nelson Bridwell/Angelo Torres, reprinted from *Eerie* #2 (March 1966)] 7p; (4) The Duel of the Monsters! [Archie Goodwin/Angelo Torres, reprinted from *Creepy* #7 (February 1966)] 8p; (5) Brain Trust! [Archie Goodwin/Angelo Torres, reprinted from *Creepy* #10 (August 1966)] 6p; (6) The Swamp God! [Archie Goodwin/Angelo Torres, reprinted from *Eerie* #5

(September 1966)] 6p; (7) Howling Success! [Archie Goodwin/Angelo Torres, reprinted from *Creepy* #3 (June 1965)] 7p; (8) Untimely Tomb! [Anne T. Murphy and Archie Goodwin/Angelo Torres, reprinted from *Creepy* #5 (October 1965), Anne T. Murphy's title credit is dropped] 7p; (9) Soul of Horror! [Archie Goodwin/Angelo Torres, reprinted from *Eerie* #3 (May 1966)] 8p; (10) Skeleton Crew! [Archie Goodwin/Angelo Torres, reprinted from *Creepy* #11 (October 1966)] 7p; (11) Night Drop! [Archie Goodwin/Angelo Torres, reprinted from *Blazing Combat* #4 (July 1966)] 7p; (12) Kasserine Pass! [Archie Goodwin/Angelo Torres and Al Williamson, reprinted from *Blazing Combat* #2 (January 1966, Williamson's credit is dropped] 6p.

Notes: Courtney's best cover for Warren graced an excellent reprint issue. The cost was $2.75 for 96 pages. The letters page vanished again. This 1982 *Creepy* Annual was an Angelo Torres special with beautiful art and great stories, most of which were written by Archie Goodwin. Well worth collecting.

143. cover: Tony Roberts (November 1982)

(1) The Spectator Who Wept [Don McGregor/Isidro Mones] 26p; (2) *Creepy*'s Capacious Caucus [Timothy Moriarty, text article] 1p; (3) Moral Blood, part 2 [Don McGregor/Al Sanchez] 10p; (4) Welcome Home Stranger! [Gerry Boudreau/Martin Salvador] 13p; (5) The Continuing Story of H. G. Wells' *The Invisible Man* [Gerry Boudreau/Alex Nino] 8p.

Notes: The price was $2.50 for 72 pages. The "Invisible Man" story was a sequel to the H. G. Wells novel. McGregor's "The Spectator Who Wept" was a good SF tale, told mostly in full page panels and featured both the best story and art.

144. cover: Frank Frazetta (January 1983), reprinted from *Creepy* #5 (October 1965)

(1) The Noxious Newspage [Timothy Moriarty, text article] 1p; (2) Forgotten Flesh [Doug Moench/Vicente Alcarar, reprinted from *Creepy* #64 (August 1974)] 8p; (3) For the Sake of Your Children! [Ed Fedory/Jaime Brocal, reprinted from *Creepy* #45 (May 1972)] 11p; (4) It! [Tom Sutton, reprinted from *Creepy* #53 (May 1973)] 9p; (5) In Darkness It Shall End! [Doug Moench/Vicente Alcazar, reprinted from *Creepy* #76 (January 1976)] 9p; (6) The Ghouls! [Carl Wessler/Martin Salvador, reprinted from *Creepy* #61

(April 1974)] 6p; (7) Berenice [Rich Margopoulos/Isidro Mones, from the story by Edgar Allan Poe, reprinted from *Creepy* #70 (April 1975)] 8p; (8) It: The Terror-Stalked Heiress! [Carl Wessler/Jose Gual, reprinted from *Creepy* #72 (July 1975)] 10p.

Notes: The cost was $2.25 for 80 pages. An all-reprint "Graveyard and Ghosts" special. The feature's page announced the departure of longtime editor Forrest J. Ackerman from *Famous Monsters* and the cancellation of *The Goblin*.

145. cover: Jose Mirelles (February 1983), reprinted from *Nightmare* #9 (October 1972)

(1) The Noxious Newspage [Timothy Moriarty, text article] 1p (2) Uncle Creepy's Introduction [Timothy Moriarty/Rafael Auraleon] 1p; (3) Moral Blood, part 3 [Don McGregor/Al Sanchez] 28p; (4) All of Them Must Die! [Gerry Boudreau and Randy Palmer/Martin Salvador] 10p; (5) The Iceman Killeth [Michael Fleisher/Delando Nino] 8p.

Notes: Final Warren issue, $2.25 for 64 pages. The cover was reprinted from a 1972 Skywald magazine! A number of unpublished stories were discussed on the feature page, including "The Last Recess," a series intended for *Creepy* that was to be written by Carlos Trillo; "Moonstone," a serial by Bill DuBay and Rudy Nebres that was intended for *Vampirella* and "Jan and the Triad," a serial by David Allikas and Pablo Marcos, also intended for *Vampirella*. To my knowledge, none of these stories were published. Based on the feature page announcement, the cancellation of the magazines and Warren's shutdown was a last-minute decision (although it had clearly been in the cards for at least a year). The letters page returned for a final farewell.

146. cover: Richard Corben/title page: Bill Wray/back cover: Frank Frazetta (summer or fall 1985), back cover reprinted from *Vampirella* #11 (May 1971)

(1) Uncle Creepy's Welcome [Tony Dispoto/Bill Wray, frontis] 1p; (2) Sex Kitten [S. K. Pierce/Bill Wray] 9p; (3) Creeps [Archie Goodwin/John Severin and Wally Wood, reprinted from *Creepy* #78 (March 1976)] 8p; (4) Yellow Heat [Bruce Jones/Russ Heath, reprinted from *Vampirella* #58 (March 1977)] 8p; (5) ...The Dump Man [Stephen Perry/Eric Shanower] 8p; (6)

Too Many Termarrows [Timothy Moriarty/Vic Catan, reprinted from *1994* #28 (December 1982)] 9p; (7) Dead Run [Jeff Jones, reprinted from *Vampirella* #32 (April 1974)] 2p; (8) A Base and Nasel Hunger [Stephen Perry/Steve Bissette] 2p; (9) Sacrifice [Roger McKenzie/Luis Bermejo, reprinted from *Creepy* #94 (January 1978)] 8p; (10) Grave Undertaking [Archie Goodwin/Alex Toth, reprinted from *Creepy* #5 (October 1965)] 6p; (11)To Kill a God! [Wally Wood, reprinted from *Vampirella* #12 (January 1971)] 8p; (12) The Super-Abnormal Phenomena Survival Kit! [Jim Stenstrum/John Severin, reprinted from *Creepy* #79 (May 1976)] 8p; (13) Werewolf! [Larry Ivie/Frank Frazetta, reprinted from *Creepy* #1 (January 1965)] 6p; (14) Creepy's Loathsome Lore: Mummy's Curse! [Archie Goodwin/Roy G. Krenkel, reprinted from *Creepy* #6 (December 1965)] 1p; (15) The Machinations of Lust [S. K. Pierce/Mike Harris and Greg Theakston] 10p; (16) No (Horse) Laughing Matter [Doug Moench/Rafael Auraleon, reprinted from *Creepy* #49 (November 1972)] 2p.

Notes: Publisher: Stanley R. Harris. Editor: Tony Dispoto. It was $2.95 for 96 pages. Harris Publications acquired the titles and film from the bankrupt Warren Publishing from an auction in August 1983. They attempted one issue each of *Creepy* and *Vampirella* in the original black and white magazine format, continuing the original numbering. I've included the single issue of *Creepy* they published since it did continue from the original magazine and included a great many Warren stories. Uncle Creepy is featured on both the cover and title page. There was a second issue intended and advertised with at least two original stories mentioned. The first was Alan Moore and Bill Wray's "Come On Down!" which actually appeared in *Taboo* #1 in 1988. On the coming attractions page the title was given as "The Most Shocking Game Show on TV." The second story listed was "Looking for Something Different" by Stephen Perry and Joe Brozowski, which also appeared in 1988 in the Harris Publications' revival of *Vampirella*, numbered #113. Also listed as an intended reprint on the attractions page was the Bruce Jones/Luis Bermejo story "As Ye Sow...."

Eerie Ashcan Edition

1. cover: Jack Davis (September 1965), reprinted from *Creepy* #2 (April 1965)

(1) Image of Bluebeard! [Bill Pearson/Joe Orlando] 7p; (2) Death Plane [Larry Ivie/George Evans] 6p; (3) The Invitation [Larry Englehart, Russ Jones and Maurice Whitman/Manny Stallman] 7p.

Notes: Publisher James Warren. Editor: Archie Goodwin. This is technically the first issue of *Eerie*, rushed into print literally overnight by Warren, Goodwin and letterer Gaspar Saladino to foil *Eerie* Publications from "stealing" the title of Warren's second horror magazine. Only 200 copies were printed. The stories included were all originally intended for either *Creepy* #7 or #8. The magazine was never actually distributed. Copies were dropped off at New York newsstands so that (one would guess) Warren could point them out to lawyers and say, "See, we've already got a magazine called *Eerie* on the stands!" The Jack Davis cover came from an ad that ran in *Creepy*. In 1978, bootleg editions of this issue were released into the fan collector market. Warren ran several ads condemning the practice and offered a $500.00 reward for the arrest of the culprits but they were never caught.

Blazing Combat

1. cover: Frank Frazetta/frontis: John Severin (October 1965)

(1) Viet Cong [Archie Goodwin/Joe Orlando] 7p; (2) Aftermath! [Archie Goodwin/Angelo Torres] 6p; (3) Flying Tigers! [Archie Goodwin/George Evans] 6p; (4) Long View! [Archie Goodwin/Gray Morrow] 6p; (5) Cantigny! [Archie Goodwin/Reed Crandall] 6p; (6) Combat Quiz [Archie Goodwin/Alex Toth] 1p; (7) Mad Anthony! [Archie Goodwin/Russ Jones, Tex Blaisdell and Maurice Whitman] 6p; (8) Enemy! [Archie Goodwin/John Severin] 7p.

Notes: Publisher: James Warren. Editor: Archie Goodwin. The cost was $0.35 for 64 pages. This series was Archie Goodwin's crowning glory. Everything that Harvey Kurtzman's *Two-Fisted Tales* and *Frontline Combat* were in terms of timeliness, art and story, *Blazing Combat* matches and, at times, surpasses. Frazetta's covers were the best of his Warren career. The artists were great and Goodwin's scripts (he wrote almost every story) were inspired. Probably the best war comic ever published. This first issue (along with *Vampirella* #3 and *Eerie* #17) is one of the hardest-to-obtain issues in the Warren canon. Both "Cantigny!" and "Aftermath!" have similar story plots, although both are quite good. The stories are all quite strong but I would rate "Enemy!" as Goodwin's best effort here. The best art belongs to everyone involved. The artwork is outstanding. This was a very controversial series for the times. "Combat Quiz" was exactly what it sounds like, a quiz with spot illustrations.

2. cover: Frank Frazetta/frontis: Gray Morrow (January 1966)

(**1**) Landscape [Archie Goodwin/Joe Orlando] 7p; (**2**) Saratoga [Archie Goodwin/Reed Crandall] 6p; (**3**) Mig Alley [Archie Goodwin/Al McWilliams] 6p; (**4**) Face to Face! [Archie Goodwin/Joe Orlando] 6p; (**5**) Kasserine Pass! [Archie Goodwin/Angelo Torres and Al Williamson] 6p; (**6**) Lone Hawk [Archie Goodwin/Alex Toth] 6p; (**7**) Combat Quiz [Archie Goodwin/Angelo Torres] 1p; (**8**) Holding Action [Archie Goodwin/John Severin] 7p; (**9**) *Eerie* ad [Angelo Torres, on the inside back cover] 1p.

This detail from the Archie Goodwin/Joe Orlando story "Landscape" (*Blazing Combat* #2) highlights Orlando's delicate art approach to this hard-hitting tale. The story's controversial message, however, doomed the magazine.

Notes: "Landscape" was easily the best story to appear in *Blazing Combat*. In fact, if one were to compile a collection of the best stories that comics have ever produced, "Landscape" would be in the top five. (For the record, I'd put Al Feldstein/Bernie Krigstein's "Master Race," Alan Moore/David Lloyd's "V for Vendetta," Jim Steranko's "Who Is Scorpio?" and Will Eisner's "Sand Saref/Bring in Sand Saref" as the other top four. Just my opinion, mind you.) The story concerns an old Vietnamese farmer who finally understands the true economics of war. Goodwin's script, which clearly owed a debt to Kurtzman's EC war stories, still stands on its own two feet and is devastating. Orlando employed a very different art style from his usual approach (so different that letter hacks questioned whether he had actually done the artwork!) and the softness of his pencil work contrasted sharply with the horror that those pencils depicted. However, the story also killed the series. According to Jim Warren, the American Legion began a quiet campaign among distributors, many of whom belonged to the organization, to let the magazine sit on distributor shelves rather than be sent out to the buying public. There were also problems from the armed forces (at the time a major purchaser of B&W comic magazines), who began to refuse to sell *Blazing Combat* on their bases or PXs, due to its perceived "anti-war" stance. Political hawks couldn't have been too thrilled with the rest of the book either. Frazetta's grim cover was one of his most violent. An American soldier bayonets a German, with the bloody bayonet bursting out the German's back, while another American soldier lies dead in the foreground, a bullet hole smoking through his helmet, while blood covers his face and the ground beside him. It's possible that some of the stories within could have appeared anywhere, but "Kasserine Pass" was about an American defeat, "Face to Face!"

used four panels to show a U.S. soldier beating a Spanish soldier to death with a rock, sound effects showing exactly how the head changes from solid to pulp under severe battering, while "Holding Action" was about soldiers who mentally crack under the stress of combat. Hardly the sort of thing military brass would like 18-to-19-year-old recruits reading just before they shipped out to Vietnam. Or the sort of thing members of the Legion might like 16-, 17-, 18-year-olds reading before they considered enlisting. Famed artist Milton Caniff, who knew something about war comics, sent in a complementary letter.

3. cover: Frank Frazetta (April 1966)

(1) Combat Quiz [Archie Goodwin/Angelo Torres, frontis] 1p; (2) Special Forces [Archie Goodwin/Jerry Grandenetti and Joe Orlando, art credited solely to Orlando] 8p; (3) Foragers [Archie Goodwin/Reed Crandall] 6p; (4) U-Boat [Archie Goodwin/Gene Colan] 7p; (5) Survival [Alex Toth and Archie Goodwin/Alex Toth] 6p; (6) The Battle of Britain! [Wally Wood/Dan Adkins and Wally Wood, art credited solely to Wood] 7p; (7) Water Hole! [Archie Goodwin/Gray Morrow] 5p; (8) Souvenirs! [Archie Goodwin/John Severin] 6p.

Notes: Another great Frazetta cover showed a U.S. soldier standing above a pile of dead Viet Cong. Best story and art goes to "Survival" but every story here was well written and illustrated. A fine, fine issue. Publisher and comic fan Richard Kyle appeared on the letters page.

4. cover: Frank Frazetta (July 1966)

(1) Combat Quiz [Archie Goodwin/Dan Adkins, frontis] 1p; (2) Conflict! [Archie Goodwin/Gene Colan] 7p; (3) How It Began! [Archie Goodwin/Gene Evans] 2p; (4) The Edge! [Archie Goodwin/Alex Toth] 6p; (5) Give and Take [Archie Goodwin/Russ Heath] 6p; (6) ME-262! [Archie Goodwin/Ralph Reese, Wally Wood and Dan Adkins, art credited solely to Wood] 7p; (7) The Trench! [Archie Goodwin/John Severin] 6p; (8) Thermopylae! [Reed Crandall and Archie Goodwin/Reed Crandall] 8p; (9) Night Drop! [Archie Goodwin/Angelo Torres] 7p; (10) Easy Way to a Tuff Surfboard! [Archie Goodwin/Frank Frazetta, reprinted from Eerie #3 (May 1966)] ½ p.

Notes: Blazing Combat's final issue showed no compromise with commercial demands. "Conflict," "Give and Take" and "Night Drop" were all powerful, hard-hitting tales. Someone may have noted the dynamic art quality of DC Comics' wash tone "paintings" on their war titles, as five of the stories within are done in total or in part with wash tones. Particularly effective was Torres' work on "Night Drop." However, the best art job was Russ Heath's striking "Give and Take." The American soldiers in that story all look alike because Heath posed for every character in the pictures himself. It may be odd to see so many look-alikes in one squad but in the context of the story it worked quite well. Goodwin's story was inspired by a Bill Mauldin World War II cartoon that appeared in his book "Up Front." The cartoon concerned a rare bottle of wine that a U.S. soldier is willing to protect at any cost. On the letters page, fan Ed Lahmann (who also contributed to the Creepy Fan Club page) warns Warren about the dangers lurking for publishers who depict war too close to real life and reminded him about the controversy that EC endured for publishing similar hard-hitting stories. He was right on the mark but it was too little, too late, as this was the end.

Eerie

2. cover: Frank Frazetta (March 1966)

(1) Welcome to Eerie [Archie Goodwin/Jack Davis, frontis] 1p; (2) Footsteps of Frankenstein [Archie Goodwin/Reed Crandall] 8p; (3) One for De-Money [E. Nelson Bridwell/Angelo Torres] 7p; (4) Eye of the Beholder [Archie Goodwin/Johnny Craig, art credited to Jay Taycee] 6p; (5) Flame Fiend [Otto Binder/Gray Morrow] 7p; (6) Eerie's Monster Gallery No. 1: Werewolf [Archie Goodwin/John Severin] 1p; (7) To Pay the Piper [Larry Ivie/Gene Colan] 6p; (8) Vision of Evil [Archie Goodwin/Alex Toth] 6p; (9) Ahead of the Game [Archie Goodwin/Jerry Grandenetti and Bill Draut, art credited to Joe Orlando] 8p.

Notes: Publisher: James Warren. Editor: Archie Goodwin. The cost was 35 cents. The first actual magazine issue, this was intended to be #1. See the notes for the ashcan issue for total details. Artist Jack Davis did several head illustrations of Cousin Eerie for story introductions. During this time artist Jerry Grandenetti ghosted pencils for several Orlando stories, all of which were credited solely to Orlando. When Grandenetti started receiving his own credits, those ghost pencils stopped. In this case, though, Orlando gets the credit for the story "Ahead of the Game" but appears to have done none of the actual work. There's nothing in this issue to make one sit up and take special notice, but it was competent, solid work that was well written and drawn. The Frazetta cover painting of a wizard and a demon was particularly good.

3. cover: Frank Frazetta (May 1966)

(1) Cousin Eerie's Introduction [Archie Goodwin/Jack Davis, frontis] 1p; (2) Soul of Horror! [Archie Goodwin/Angelo Torres] 8p; (3) The Lighthouse! [Archie Goodwin/Al Williamson] 6p; (4) Room with a View! [Archie Goodwin/Steve Ditko] 6p; (5) Monsterwork! [Archie Goodwin/Rocco Mastroserio] 6p; (6) Under the Skin! [Archie Goodwin/Jerry Grandenetti and Joe Orlando, art credited solely to Orlando] 7p; (7) Eerie's Monster Gallery No. 2: The Vampire! [Archie Goodwin/Johnny Craig, art credited to Jay Taycee] 1p; (8) The Monument [Archie Goodwin/Alex Toth] 6p; (9) Full Fathom Fright [Archie Goodwin/Gene Colan] 8p; (10) Easy Way to a Tuff Surfboard! [Archie Goodwin/Frank Frazetta, anti-smoking ad on the inside back cover] ½ p.

Notes: A strong issue was led off with Frazetta's cover depicting an undersea monster and a diver. All of the art jobs were good but particular note should be given to Angelo Torres, Steve Ditko and Alex Toth. My favorite story here is "Room with a View," partly because when I was a kid, the first Warren comic I read was a coverless *Eerie* #42, which reprinted this story. It was the first story I read in the book and the one that gave me nightmares for several days after. It features sharp art by Ditko with a simple but compelling story by Goodwin. The anti-smoking ad by Goodwin and Frazetta was publisher Jim Warren's reaction to cigarette companies offering him high-paying advertising to target his 14-to-18-year-old readers. It effectively stopped the offers. It should be noted that Warren stuck to his guns on this issue, even during the Dark Age years from 1967 to 1969 when he could have easily caved in and rescued his magazines with cigarette ad revenues.

4. cover: Gray Morrow (July 1966)

(1) Eerie's Monster Gallery No. 3: Zombies! [Archie Goodwin/Roy G. Krenkel, frontis] 1p; (2) House of Evil [Archie Goodwin/Jerry Grandenetti and Joe Orlando, art credited solely to Orlando] 8p; (3) Hatchet Man [Archie Goodwin/Gene Colan] 8p; (4) Gnawing Fear! [Ron Parker/Rocco Mastroserio] 7p; (5) Shrieking Man! [Archie Goodwin/Steve Ditko] 7p; (6) Undying Love! [Archie Goodwin/Donald Norman] 6p; (7) Island at World's End! [Archie Goodwin/Gray Morrow] 10p; (8) Easy Way to a Tuff Surfboard! [Archie Goodwin/Frank Frazetta, reprinted from *Eerie* #3 (May 1966)] ½ p.

Notes: Particularly nice art here from the Grandenetti/Orlando team and from Gray Morrow, but the art highlight was Gene Colan's wash work on "Hatchet Man," a story that foretold Warren's horror slant of the 1970s as there's nary a monster in sight, except for the human serial killer kind. "Shrieking Man" was reprinted in the 1980s as "The Incredible Shrieking Man," which possibly was its original title and thus a title homage to Richard Matheson's 1950s novel *The Incredible Shrinking Man*. Underground cartoonist Jay Lynch wrote in to praise Warren for its anti-smoking ad. Good issue.

5. cover: Frank Frazetta (September 1966)

(1) Eerie's Monster Gallery No. 4: The Mummy! [Archie Goodwin/Dan Adkins and Wally Wood, frontis] 1p; (2) The Mummy Stalks! [Roy G. Krenkel and Archie Goodwin/Reed Crandall] 8p; (3) The Jungle [Archie Goodwin/Al Williamson] 6p; (4) Black Magic [Archie Goodwin/Steve Ditko] 8p; (5) A Matter of Routine! [Archie Goodwin/Gene Colan] 8p; (6) Dr. Griswold's File! [Carl Wessler/Rocco Mastroserio] 7p; (7) The Swamp God! [Archie Goodwin/Angelo Torres] 6p; (8) Vampire Slayer! [Archie Goodwin/Jerry Grandenetti and Joe Orlando, art credited solely to Orlando] 8p.

Notes: Frazetta's dinosaur cover was a nice companion piece to Torres' interior story. Torres' art was not as sharp as usual but was still pretty good. Goodwin and Krenkel's mummy story evoked the style and flavor of the early Universal and Hammer films. Crandall's art was just right. There was also good work from Ditko (a tip of the hat to his "Dr. Strange" style of mystic art) and Mastroserio. Another solid issue.

6. cover: Gray Morrow (November 1966)

(1) Eerie's Monster Gallery No. 5: The Man-Made Monster! [Archie Goodwin/John Severin, frontis] 1p; (2) Cave of the Druids [Archie Goodwin/Reed Crandall] 8p; (3) Deep Ruby! [Archie Goodwin/Steve Ditko] 6p; (4) Running Scared! [Archie Goodwin/Mark Ricton] 8p; (5) The Curse of Kali! [Archie Goodwin/Angelo Torres] 7p; (6) Trial by Fire! [Johnny Craig, story and art credited to Jay Taycee] 6p; (7) Point of View! [Archie Goodwin/Rocco Mastroserio] 6p; (8) The Changeling! [Archie Goodwin/Gene Colan] 8p.

Notes: Morrow delivered a striking cover for the interior story "Cave of the Druids." That story also featured strong artwork by Reed Crandall. Torres' artwork was in the same style of the story in the previous issue. "Druids" and "Deep Ruby" were the best stories. An average issue for this period, which means it was pretty damn good!

7. cover: Frank Frazetta (January 1967)

(1) Eerie's Monster Gallery No. 6: The Hydra! [Archie Goodwin/Gray Morrow, frontis] 1p; (2) Witches' Tide [Archie Goodwin/Gene Colan] 8p; (3) It That Lurks! [Archie Goodwin/Dan Adkins] 6p; (4) Hitchhike Horror! [Archie Goodwin/Hector Castellon] 8p; (5) The Defense Rests! [Johnny Craig] 8p; (6) Fly! [Archie Goodwin/Steve Ditko] 6p; (7) The Quest! [Archie Goodwin/Donald Norman] 6p; (8) Cry Fear, Cry Phantom [Archie Goodwin/Jerry Grandenetti] 7p.

Notes: Frazetta's famous "Sea Witch" painting was the cover here. Roy Krenkel provided layouts for it. At this point, simply by not have any mediocre stories or art jobs, Eerie was actually

surpassing *Creepy* in quality. Craig, Ditko, Grandenetti, Colan and Norman are all well represented here. Castellon went cross-hatch crazy with his art approach! But the best story and art was Goodwin and Adkins' dinosaur tale "It That Lurks."

8. cover: Frank Frazetta (March 1967)

(1) Eerie's Monster Gallery No. 7: Demon! [Archie Goodwin/Angelo Torres, frontis] 1p; (2) Oversight! [Archie Goodwin/Gene Colan] 8p; (3) Dark Rider! [Archie Goodwin/John Severin] 6p; (4) Typecast! [Archie Goodwin/Jerry Grandenetti] 8p; (5) The Day After Doomsday! [Archie Goodwin/Dan Adkins] 8p; (6) The

Frazetti's great cover art for what was supposed to be *Eerie* #1, but ended up as *Eerie* #2. The whole story can be found in the notes for the *Eerie* ashcan edition! © New Comic Co./used by permission.

Covered Bridge! [Archie Goodwin/Bob Jenney] 6p; (7) Wolf Bait! [Buddy Saunders and Archie Goodwin/ Rocco Mastroserio] 8p; (8) Demon Sword! [Archie Goodwin/Steve Ditko] 8p.

Notes: Frazetta's cover of a demon and a swordsman fighting in front of a giant brain was actually rather blah although most artists would be quite happy with it. Filmmaker John Carpenter may have swiped his script for *They Live* from the Goodwin/Colan story herein as it shows a man who is accidentally given a special pair of glasses that lets him see the monsters who live among us, masquerading as humans. Adkins outdid himself with a striking art job on "The Day After Doomsday!" In fact, he's rarely been so good since. This was Texan writer and future comics distributor Buddy Saunders' professional debut. Based on the credits I'd guess that Saunders sent an original script and Goodwin liked it enough to rewrite it into professional form. Regardless of its origins, it was a good story, well rendered by Mastroserio. Ditko turned in his usual work, which, for Warren, was always spectacular. Best story and art here, however, was on "Dark Rider!" by Goodwin and Severin, another story that turned up in that coverless *Eerie* #42. A spooky, macabre and, well, eerie Western tale set in the snowy Rockies that brilliantly evoked that quiet terror that one can experience, for no particular reason, in gray winter woods.

"Dark Rider!" from *Eerie* #7 was the story that got me hooked on Warren magazines. This Western horror tale, by Archie Goodwin and John Severin, puts the reader right in the gloomy, snowy woods, being chased by a nightmarish ... something. © New Comic Co./used by permission.

9. cover: Dan Adkins (May 1967)

(1) Eerie's Monster Gallery No. 8: The Cyclopses! [Archie Goodwin/Roy G. Krenkel, frontis] 1p; (2) Fair Exchange [Archie Goodwin/ Neal Adams] 8p; (3) Rub the Lamp! [Allan Jadro/Jerry Grandenetti] 8p; (4) Terror in the Tomb! [Archie Goodwin/Rocco Mastroserio] 7p; (5) The Wanderer! [Archie Goodwin/Dan Adkins] 8p; (6) Isle of the Beast! [Archie Goodwin/Steve Ditko] 6p; (7) An Occurrence at Owl Creek Bridge! [Archie Goodwin/Bob Jenney, from the story by Ambrose Bierce] 6p; (8) Experiment in Fear! [Archie Goodwin/Gene Colan] 8p.

Notes: Beneath a tame Adkins cover was some

pretty good work. Adams' debut in *Eerie* had him experimenting with a different panel layout for every page. Ditko presented a very good werewolf tale and Gene Colan's tale of a Nazi concentration camp doctor's terrifying end was nerve-wracking. Some letter writers apparently had never heard of Ambrose Bierce and, in later issues, accused Goodwin of ripping off a *Twilight Zone* episode that had also shown an adaptation of Bierce's story. Krenkel's work on the Monster Gallery one-pager was particularly nice.

10. cover: Gray Morrow (July 1967)

(1) Eerie's Monster Gallery No. 9: The Wendigo! [Roy G. Krenkel, frontis] 1p; (2) Warrior of Death! [Archie Goodwin/Steve Ditko] 8p; (3) The Slugs! [Bill Pearson/Joe Orlando] 8p; (4) It! [Archie Goodwin/Dan Adkins] 8p; (5) Voodoo Drum! [Archie Goodwin/Neal Adams] 8p; (6) House of Fiends! [Archie Goodwin/Jerry Grandenetti] 8p; (7) For the Birds! [Archie Goodwin/Gene Colan] 8p.

Notes: The monster in Adkins' story was swiped from the film *Five Million Years to Earth*. Given Ditko's striking work on the sword and sorcery stories that he did for Warren, one wonders why he never got the chance to work on Conan for Marvel. He also did quite nice work on DC's "Stalker" in the 1970s. "Voodoo Drum!" was the art and story fave for this issue. Adams' art, reproduced from his pencils, was very moody and his work was well matched by the Goodwin script. "The Slugs" was also a rather horrible little story (and I mean that in a good way).

11. cover: Joe Orlando (September 1967)

(1) Eerie's Monster Gallery No. 10: The Minotaur [Archie Goodwin/Neal Adams, frontis] 1p; (2) Witch Hunt! [Archie Goodwin/Joe Orlando] 6p; (3) To Slay a Dragon! [Archie Goodwin/Jeff Jones] 6p; (4) The Mummy [Russ Jones/Dan Adkins and Wally Wood, from the 1932 Universal screenplay, reprinted from *Monster World* #1 (November 1964), story and art credited solely to Wood] 7p; (5) Berenice! [Archie Goodwin/Jerry Grandenetti, from the story by Edgar Allan Poe] 6p; (6) The Blood Fruit! [Johnny Craig] 8p; (7) The Monster from One Billion B.C. [Tom Sutton] 8p; (8) Big Change! [Ron Whyte/Larry Woromay] 6p; (9) First Blood [Archie Goodwin/Gene Colan] 6p.

Notes: The money crunch that led to Warren's

Dark Age began to appear with the introduction of reprints in the magazines. Original Warren editor Russ Jones' credit was erased from the reprint of "The Mummy." See notes on *Creepy* #17 as to reasons why. Sutton's story was originally done for *Famous Monsters of Filmland* (and was reprinted very shortly thereafter in those pages) but appeared in *Eerie* first due to a deadline crunch regarding his story "Image in Wax" which ended up in *Creepy* #17. A note here on Sutton. It's my belief that Tom Sutton is probably the most underrated of all the Silver Age artists. He worked for all of the major publishers—Marvel, DC, Charlton, Warren and Skywald—and regularly appeared in fanzines, but never really had a long run on a superhero title, partly because he didn't particularly like superheroes. What he did like was horror and science fiction. He was able to employ a remarkable variety of art styles and was best when left alone to illustrate (and, on occasion, write) the scripts in his own unique way. He was certainly capable of hackwork—his Star Trek work is mind-numbingly average, largely because that's what the studio and the publisher wanted. He technically retired from regular comic work in 1994, although he continued to occasionally work in the field and his final days were spent drawing grotesque porn comics for Fantagraphic's *Eros* line. Yet he was also capable of absolutely breathtaking artwork, as for instance, on Marvel's Future History Chronicles in the B&W *Planet of the Apes* magazine, the many splendid short horror and war tales and covers he did for Charlton, First Comics' eye-opening *Squalor* series, the oddball *Frankenstein* series he did for Skywald and the Warren work recorded in this checklist. He came in at the tail end of the Goodwin era and I suspect if he'd shown up sooner he'd be a good deal better appreciated. His influence shines on every time Bruce Timm draws Frankenstein's Monster or, say, Steve Bissette or John Totleben apply pencil and pen to paper. This was Goodwin's last issue as editor but I've included the next issue in the Goodwin era as he clearly wrote and assembled the artists for much of the contents. Best art here was Jerry Grandenetti's work on the Poe adaptation.

12. cover: Dan Adkins (November 1967)

(1) Eerie's Monster Gallery: Zombies! [Archie Goodwin/Roy G. Krenkel, frontis, reprinted from *Eerie* #4 (July 1966)] 1p; (2) The Masque of the Red Death [Archie Goodwin/Tom Sutton, from the story by Edgar Allan Poe] 6p; (3) Vampyrus! [Archie Goodwin/Jeff Jones] 7p; (4) ...Nor Custom, Stale... [Johnny Craig] 8p; (5) Escape! [Archie Goodwin/Joe Orlando] 7p; (6) Portrait of Satan! [Archie Goodwin/Ric Estrada] 8p; (7) The Past Master [Craig Tennis/Al McWilliams, from the story by Robert Bloch, reprinted from Christopher Lee's Treasury of Terror (September 1966)] 10p.

Notes: Editor: James Warren? According to Clark Dimond, Warren wasn't actually the editor. Instead a friend of Warren's at Gold Key did the actual editing. Goodwin's absence was immediately noticeable as the story credits weren't listed for any story here. This was the last largely original *Eerie* issue for some time as Warren placed a freeze on any new stories or artwork for at least seven months. Including this issue, Goodwin left enough stories in inventory for possibly three issues (and that might be stretching it) so with no new work being produced Warren was forced to resort to all-reprint issues for *Eerie* and largely reprint issues for *Creepy*. He also raided the paperback horror book *Christopher Lee's Treasury of Terror* and its unpublished sequel for stories to print, beginning with this issue. The cover by Dan Adkins was clearly intended for the previous issue's Mummy reprint. Not a bad issue but nowhere close to the strength in story and art that *Eerie* had displayed in the previous 10 issues. Sadly, it was a strength that *Eerie* would never recapture.

Warren's Dark Age

13. cover: Vic Prezio (February 1968)

(1) Wentworth's Day [Russ Jones/Russ Jones and Frank Bolle, from the story by H. P. Lovecraft, reprinted from *Christopher Lee's Treasury of Terror* (September 1966)] 9p; (2) Ogre's Castle [Archie Goodwin/Angelo Torres, reprinted from *Creepy* #2 (April 1965)] 6p; (3) Tell-Tale Heart! [Archie Goodwin/Reed Crandall, from the story "The Tell-Tale Heart" by Edgar Allan Poe, reprinted from *Creepy* #3 (June 1965)] 8p;

(4) Voodoo! [Bill Pearson/Joe Orlando, reprinted from *Creepy* #1 (January 1965)] 6p; (5) Spawn of the Cat People [Archie Goodwin/Reed Crandall, reprinted from *Creepy* #2 (April 1965)] 6p; (6) The Success Story [Archie Goodwin/Al Williamson, reprinted from *Creepy* #1 (January 1965)] 6p.

Notes: There were three months between issues here, reflecting Warren's shaky financial status. Size was reduced to 48 pages. Oddly enough, Russ Jones' name was dropped from "Wentworth's Day" which he did work on but was still included on "Voodoo!" which he did not. An all-reprint issue.

14. cover: Vic Prezio (April 1968)

(1) Eerie's Monster Gallery: The Mummy [Archie Goodwin/Wally Wood and Dan Adkins, frontis, reprinted from *Eerie* #5 (September 1966)] 1p; (2) The Stalkers [Archie Goodwin/Alex Toth, reprinted from *Creepy* #6 (December 1965)] 6p; (3) Pursuit of the Vampire! [Archie Goodwin/Angelo Torres] 6p; (4) Howling Success! [Archie Goodwin/Angelo Torres, reprinted from *Creepy* #3 (June 1965)] 7p; (5) Untimely Tomb! [Anne T. Murphy and Archie Goodwin/Angelo Torres, reprinted from *Creepy* #5 (October 1965)] 7p; (6) Curse of the Full Moon! [Archie Goodwin/Reed Crandall, reprinted from *Creepy* #4 (August 1965)] 8p; (7) Blood and Orchids! [Archie Goodwin/Al McWilliams, reprinted from *Creepy* #4 (August 1965)] 7p.

Notes: All-reprint issue.

15. cover: Vic Prezio (June 1968)

(1) The Graves of Oconoco! [John Benson/Pat Boyette and Rocco Mastroserio] 7p; (2) Wardrobe of Monsters! [Otto Binder/Gray Morrow and Angelo Torres, reprinted from *Creepy* #2 (April 1965)] 8p; (3) The Demon Wakes [Archie Goodwin/Bill Fraccio and Tony Tallarico] 6p; (4) Under the Skin! [Archie Goodwin/Jerry Grandenetti and Joe Orlando, reprinted from *Eerie* #5 (November 1965)] 7p; (5) The Doll Collector! [Dave Kahleer/Gutenberg Mondiero] 8p; (6) A Change in the Moon! [Clark Dimond and Terry Bisson/Jeff Jones, story credited solely to Dimond] 8p.

Notes: The first issue since #12 to feature new stories. The Fraccio/Tallarico (they always used the pen name Tony Williamsune for Warren) art was new but the original Archie Goodwin story was probably a leftover from his tenure. According to Clark Dimond, at this point artist Jeff Jones hadn't been paid for his last three Warren stories and Jones apologized to Dimond for the supposed poor quality of the artwork on "A Change in the Moon!"

16. cover: Barry Rockwell (July 1968)

(1) Eerie's Monster Gallery: The Number 13! [Bill Parente/Bill Fraccio and Tony Tallarico, frontis] 1p; (2) Dracula's Guest [E. Nelson Bridwell/Frank Bolle, from the story by Bram Stoker, reprinted from *Christopher Lee's Treasury of Terror* (September 1966)] 7p; (3) Big-Time Operator [E. Nelson Bridwell/Ric Estrada] 8p; (4) Sara's Forest [Roger Brand/Bill Fraccio and Tony Tallarico] 6p; (5) Evil Spirits! [Archie Goodwin/Johnny Craig] 10p; (6) *Eerie* Fanfare: In Memoriam, Rocco Mastroserio 1927–1968 [Bill Parente/Richard Corben, Rocco Mastroserio and Bruce Jones, text article] 1p; (7) The Monument [Archie Goodwin/Alex Toth, reprinted from *Eerie* #3 (May 1966)] 6p; (8) Ahead of the Game [Archie Goodwin/Jerry Grandenetti and Bill Draut, reprinted from *Eerie* #2 (March 1966)] 8p.

Notes: Editor: Bill Parente. Size increased to 56 pages. A quite good issue! Cousin Eerie's head was obviously pasted over original host Christopher Lee's in the opening story. The Goodwin/Craig story was an unpublished tale from 1967. Richard Corben and Bruce Jones made their comics debut on *Eerie's* first fan page, although Corben may have been working on his first underground work, "Tales from the Plague," prior to this. Today Bruce Jones is known primarily as a writer, but he started off as a quite good artist in the Al Williamson mode. The fan page also announced the death of Warren and Charlton artist Rocco Mastroserio. Best stories are "Evil Spirits" and "Big-Time Operator."

17. cover: Tom Sutton (September 1968) (miscredited to Barry Rockwell)

(1) The Final Solution [Raymond Marais/Bill Fraccio and Tony Tallarico] 8p; (2) The Mummy Stalks! [Archie Goodwin/Reed Crandall, reprinted from *Eerie* #5 (September 1965)] 8p; (3) *Eerie* Fanfare: Tom Sutton profile/Back Pay [Bill Parente and Bill Mantlo/Tom Sutton, Dean Sindork and Mike Whelan, text article, text story] 1p; (4) To Save Face [Bill Parente/Ernie Colon] 6p; (5) Dressed to Kill! [Bill Par-

ente/Tom Sutton] 6p; (6) Demon Sword! [Archie Goodwin/Steve Ditko, reprinted from *Eerie* #8 (March 1967)] 8p; (7) The Death of Halpin Frayser [Craig Tennis/Frank Bolle, from the story by Ambrose Bierce, reprinted from *Christopher Lee's Treasury of Terror* (September 1966)] 7½ p.

Notes: *Eerie* #17 is one of the hardest Warren issues to find, apparently due to a James Warren experiment of non-returnable distribution for this issue. Tony Isabella wrote a letter that revealed who the actual artists behind the Tony Williamsune pen name were. The fan page featured the debut of future comic writer Bill Mantlo and future SF cover artist Michael Whelan.

18. cover: Tom Sutton (November 1968)

(1) Eerie's Monster Gallery: Zombies! [Archie Goodwin/Roy G. Krenkel, frontis, reprinted from *Eerie* #4 (July 1966)] 1p; (2) Hard Luck [Bill Parente/Sal Trapani, story miscredited to James Haggenmiller] 6p; (3) Cry Fear, Cry Phantom [Archie Goodwin/Jerry Grandenetti, reprinted from *Eerie* #7 (January 1967)] 7p; (4) A Change of Pace! [Bill Parente/Tom Sutton] 6p; (5) *Eerie* Fanfare: Barry Rockwell profile/Fish Story [Bill Parente and Thomas Prehoda/Greg Volpert and Gary Meyers, text article/text story with photo] 1p; (6) The Jungle [Archie Goodwin/Al Williamson, reprinted from *Eerie* #5 (September 1966)] 6p; (7) Vampire Slayer! [Archie Goodwin/Jerry Grandenetti and Joe Orlando, reprinted from *Eerie* #5 (September 1966)] 8p; (8) Trial by Fire! [Johnny Craig, reprinted from *Eerie* #6 (November 1966)] 6p; (9) Side Show [Bill Parente/Bill Fraccio and Tony Tallarico] 6p; (10) Uncle Creepy and Cousin Eerie's Cauldron Contest [Bill Parente/Ernie Colon, on the back cover] 1p.

Notes: See the notes for *Creepy* #23 for Cauldron Contest information.

19. cover: Alan Willow (December 1968)

(1) Eerie's Monster Gallery: The Castle of the Frankenstein! [Tom Sutton, frontis] 1p; (2) Tomorrow's Reminder [Bill Parente/Bill Fraccio and Tony Tallarico, title misspelled as "Tommorrow"] 6p; (3) Dark Kingdom! [Archie Goodwin/Gray Morrow, reprinted from *Creepy* #9 (June 1967)] 8p; (4) Dark House of Dreams [Archie Goodwin/Angelo Torres, reprinted from *Creepy* #12 (December 1966)] 6p; (5) Monstrous Mistake [Bill Parente/Barry Rockwell] 6p; (6)

The Squaw! [Archie Goodwin/Reed Crandall, from the story by Bram Stoker, reprinted from *Creepy* #13 (February 1967)] 8p; (7) Unfeeling Heart... [James Haggenmiller/Ernie Colon] 6p; (8) *Eerie* Fanfare: Abracadabra/The Glass Prison [Bill Parente and Roxanne Collier/Bill Black (aka Bill Black) and Brian Clifton, text article/text story] 1p.

Notes: Cover artist Willow was the first European artist to appear in a Warren magazine. Bill Parente started a Satan's Grimoire section on the fan page, beginning with the letter "A," with alternate sections appearing in alternate months in both *Creepy* and *Eerie*. The series was never finished, and it ended with the letter "G." Future artist Bill Black made his second appearance on the fan page.

20. cover: H. B. Harris (March 1969)

(1) Round Trip [Bill Parente/Bill Fraccio and Tony Tallarico] 6p; (2) A Cloak of Darkness [Bill Parente/Reed Crandall] 6p; (3) *Eerie* Fanfare: Candles/A Shrewd Deal [Bill Parente and Gordon Mathews/P. Zimelman and George Meyers, text article/text story] 1p; (4) Cave of the Druids! [Archie Goodwin/Reed Crandall, reprinted from *Eerie* #6 (November 1966)] 8p; (5) The Fall of the House of Usher [Tom Sutton, from the story by Edgar Allan Poe] 11p; (6) Dark Rider! [Archie Goodwin/John Severin, reprinted from *Eerie* #8 (March 1967)] 6p.

Notes: Sutton's Poe adaptation is prose heavy but beautifully drawn.

21. cover: Vic Prezo (May 1969)

(1) Eerie's Monster Gallery: Lucifer's Legions [Tom Sutton, frontis] 1p; (2) Point of View [Archie Goodwin/Rocco Mastroserio, reprinted from *Eerie* #6 (November 1966)] 6p; (3) *Eerie* Fanfare: Cauldron Contest/Once There Was a Planet [Bill Parente and Roger Solberg/Mike Kersey and James King, text article/text story] 1p; (4) Miscalculation [Bill Parente/Bill Fraccio and Tony Tallarico] 7p; (5) Terror in the Tomb! [Archie Goodwin/Rocco Mastroserio, reprinted from *Eerie* #9 (May 1967)] 7p; (6) Fatal Diagnosis [Bill Parente/Ernie Colon] 6p; (7) Warrior of Death! [Archie Goodwin/Steve Ditko, reprinted from *Eerie* #10 (July 1967)] 8p; (8) House of Fiends! [Archie Goodwin/Jerry Grandenetti, reprinted from *Eerie* #10 (July 1967)] 8p.

22. cover: Vic Prezo (July 1969)

(1) Eerie's Monster Gallery: The Minotaur

[Archie Goodwin/Neal Adams, frontis, reprinted from *Eerie* #11 (September 1967)] 1p; (2) H20 World! [Larry Ivie/Al Williamson and Roy G. Krenkel, reprinted from *Creepy* #1 (January 1965)] 6p; (3) Family Curse [T. Casey Brennan/Bill Fraccio and Tony Tallarico] 8p; (4) The Devil to Pay! [Archie Goodwin/Donald Norman, reprinted from *Creepy* #11 (October 1966)] 6p; (5) Permanent Members! [Bill Parente/Tom Sutton] 7p; (6) *Eerie* Fanfare: Familiars/The Finish [Bill Parente and Mike Raab/Len Wein, text article/text story] 1p; (7) Scooped! [Bill Parente/Ernie Colon] 8p; (8) The Spirit of the Thing! [Archie Goodwin/Steve Ditko, reprinted from *Creepy* #9 (June 1967)] 8p; (9) Vampirella Is Coming ad [Bill Parente/Bill Fraccio and Tony Tallarico] 1p.

Notes: Size increased to 56 pages. Prezo's cover of a bikini-clad diver confronted by sea monsters at an undersea wreck was quite good. The story "Permanent Members" appears to have been intended for, or perhaps inspired by, the cover to *Creepy* #22 from a year earlier. T. Casey Brennan made his professional debut here. Future comic writer Len Wein had his comics debut on the fan page as an artist. The *Vampirella* ad featured both Uncle Creepy and Cousin *Eerie*, but not *Vampirella*.

Warren's Rebuilding

23. cover: Frank Frazetta (September 1969)

(1) Beyond Nefera's Tomb [Bill Parente/Ernie Colon] 8p; (2) The Dragon's Tail [Kim Ball/Bill Fraccio and Tony Tallarico] 8p; (3) An Occurrence at Owl Creek Bridge! [Archie Goodwin/Bob Jenney, from the story by Ambrose Bierce, reprinted from *Eerie* #9 (May 1967)] 6p; (4) *Eerie* Fanfare: Hades/Total War/Cauldron Contest Winner: Edward French [Bill Parente and Timothy Boertlein/Bruce Jones, text article/text story with photo] 2p; (5) Soul Pool [Edward R. French/Tom Sutton] 7p; (6) Fair Exchange [Archie Goodwin/Neal Adams, reprinted from *Eerie* #9 (May 1967)] 8p; (7) Space Age Vampire [James Haggenmiller/Mike Royer] 8p; (8) Vampirella Is Coming ad [Bill Parente/Bill Fraccio and Tony Tallarico] 1p; (9) Easy Way to a Tuff Surfboard! [Archie Goodwin/Frank Frazetta, reprinted from *Eerie* #3 (May 1966)] ½ p.

Notes: Although reprints continued for another 8 months or so, this issue, along with *Creepy* #29 and *Vampirella* #1, marked the beginning of Warren's rebuilding from the quality quake of the previous two years. Size increased to 64 pages. Frazetta's cover, "Egyptian Princess," is one of his most famous paintings and justly so. A dynamic use of lighting and shadow (along with some nicely done near-nudity) made this cover a real eye-opener. The accompanying cover story "Beyond Nefera's Tomb" also displayed a remarkable amount of nudity for a 1969 comic. Even a black and white one. Bruce Jones made his second fan page appearance, only a few months before his professional debut in the rival horror magazine *Web of Horror*.

24. cover: Vic Prezo (November 1969)

(1) Eerie's Monster Gallery: ...Perchance to Dream! [Tom Sutton, frontis] 1p; (2) Head for the Lighthouse! [Bill Parente/Mike Royer] 8p; (3) Pursuit of the Vampire! [Archie Goodwin/Angelo Torres, reprinted from *Creepy* #1 (January 1965)] 6p; (4) The Immortality Seeker [James Haggenmiller/Tom Sutton] 7p; (5) *Eerie* Fanfare: Epilogue [Donald Lauzon/Joe Kovacs, text story] 1p; (6) Checkmate [Ron Parker/Bill Fraccio and Tony Tallarico] 8p; (7) Scavenger Hunt [Don Glut/Jerry Grandenetti] 6p; (8) Demon Dictionary [Bill Parente/Bill Fraccio and Tony Tallarico, text article] 1p; (9) Dracula's Guest [E. Nelson Bridwell/Frank Bolle, from the story by Bram Stoker, reprinted from *Christopher Lee's Treasury of Terror* (September 1966)] 7p; (10) Wrong Tennant [Bill Parente/Reed Crandall] 7p.

Notes: Most of the good stories here were reprinted from earlier issues. The reprint of "Dracula's Guest" shows Cousin Eerie's head pasted over the original host, a drawing of actor Christopher Lee.

25. cover: Jim Steranko (January 1970)

(1) Eerie's Monster Gallery: Vampire! [Bill Parente/Bill Fraccio and Tony Tallarico, frontis] 1p; (2) Isle of the Vrukolakas [Don Glut/Ernie Colon] 6p; (3) Mistake! [Buddy Saunders/Bill Black] 6p; (4) Hijack to Horror [R. Michael Rosen/Bill Fraccio and Tony Tallarico] 6p; (5) To Pay the Piper! [Larry Ivie/Gene Colan, reprinted from *Eerie* #2 (March 1966)] 6p; (6) Southern Exposure [Bill Parente/Tom Sutton] 5p; (7) The Thing in the Cave [R. Michael Rosen/Mike Royer] 6p; (8) *Eerie* Fanfare: I Gave Him Life!/To the Ends of Inner Space

[Paul E. King and Tom O'Boyle/David Hubb/text stories] 1p; (9) House of Evil! [Archie Goodwin/Jerry Grandenetti, reprinted from *Eerie* #4 (July 1966)] 8p; (10) Hex Marks the Spot [R. Michael Rosen/William Barry] 6p.

Notes: Steranko's sole contribution to Warren was nice, but gave the appearance of having been originally intended for the gothic paperback lines of the time rather than as an original painting done for the Warren line.

26. cover: Basil Gogos and Vaughn Bode (March 1970)

(1) Eerie's Monster Gallery: The Body Snatchers! [Tom Sutton, frontis] 1p; (2) I Wouldn't Want to Live There! [Bill Parente/Jack Sparling] 7p; (3) Southern Exposure, part 2 [Bill Parente/Tom Sutton] 7p; (4) In the Neck of Time [Al Hewetson/Bill Fraccio and Tony Tallarico] 8p; (5) *Eerie* Fanfare: Al Hewetson profile/Death After Dark/Three Feet from Exit Four/Traitor's Reward [Al Hewetson, Mark Aubry, Mark Hatfield and Dennis Goza/Ernie Colon and Steven Muhmel, text stories with photo] 2p; (6) Spiders Are Revolting! [Bill Warren/Tom Sutton] 9p; (7) The Scarecrow [Nicola Cuti/Frank Bolle] 7p; (8) Tuned In! [Ken Dixon/Dick Piscopo] 7p; (9) Cyked-Out! [Ken Dixon/Jack Sparling] 8p.

Notes: This was the first issue since #10 to have all-original stories. The cover was quite ugly, yet strangely, was selected to be reprinted for an issue in the early 1980s! Future artist Ronn Sutton sent in a letter. Best story and art belonged to the Warren/Sutton story "Spiders Are Revolting!" which did indeed have a truly revolting ending!

27. cover: Vaughn Bode and Jeff Jones (May 1970)

(1) Eerie's Monster Gallery: The Golem! [Tom Sutton, frontis] 1p; (2) Journey into Wonder [Bill Parente/Ken Barr] 10p; (3) Amazonia [Gardner Fox/Miguel Fernandez] 7p; (4) *Eerie* Fanfare: Neal Adams profile/Poetry Corner/-Surprise/The Forewarned [Bill Parente, Brad Linaweaver, Gary Schnoebeden, Cathy Hill, Allen Arnold and Susan Wylie/Dale Stuckert and ?, text article/text stories/poems] 2p; (5) The Machine God's Slave [Buddy Saunders/-Ernie Colon] 6p; (6) Swallowed in Space! [Bill Parente/Tom Sutton] 7p; (7) Enter ... Dr. Laernu! [R. Michael Rosen/Dick Piscopo] 6p; (8) All Sewed Up! [Buddy Saunders/Mike

Royer] 6p; (**9**) Face It! [Nicola Cuti/Jack Sparling] 7p.

Notes: In complete contrast to the previous issue, this Bode/Jones cover was quite lovely. Gardner Fox's character Amazonia reappeared in *Vampirella*, illustrated there by Billy Graham. The best story here was easily Buddy Saunders' "The Machine God's Slave" with art honors shared by Ernie Colon and by Mike Royer for his work on "All Sewed Up!"

28. cover: Pat Boyette (July 1970)

(**1**) Eerie's Monster Gallery: The Saucerians! [Tom Sutton, frontis] 1p; (**2**) The Hidden Evils! [James Haggenmiller/Dan Adkins] 9p; (**3**) The Beast in the Swamp! [Bill Warren/Billy Graham] 8p; (**4**) *Eerie* Fanfare: The Horror of Biscayne Gardens/The Man on the Hill/By The Moon/Who Is in the Shadows?/Poem/A Dragon's Tale [Mike Petit, Jeff Kadish, Peter MacKenzie, Steven Teal, Danny Massoni and Brad Linaweaver/Mike Jasinski, Tony Bishop, Greg Theakston and Arvell Jones, text stories/poems] 2p; (**5**) The Rescue Party! [Buddy Saunders/Jack Sparling] 7p; (**6**) Follow Apollo! [R. Michael Rosen/Tom Sutton] 6p; (**7**) Ice Scream [R. Michael Rosen/Bill DuBay] 7p; (**8**) Pit of Evil [Al Hewetson/Dick Piscopo] 7p; (**9**) The Last Train to Orion! [Pat Boyette] 6p; (**10**) Easy Way to a Tuff Surfboard! [Archie Goodwin/Frank Frazetta, reprinted from *Eerie* #3 (May 1966)] ½ p.

Notes: Editor: James Warren. Interesting cover and story from Pat Boyette but the best story was Bill Warren's and Billy Graham's "The Beast in the Swamp!" This sword and sorcery effort (as well as the Amazonia stories in *Vampirella*) makes one wonder why Graham never got a chance to draw Conan. He'd have been great at it!

29. cover: Ken Kelly (September 1970)

(**1**) An Editorial to the President of the United States and All the Members of Congress [James Warren, text article, frontis] 1p; (**2**) Loophole! [Nicola Cuti/Jack Sparling] 7p; (**3**) The Fiend Planet [Buddy Saunders/Dan Adkins] 6p; (**4**) The Bloodstaff [Rich Buckler] 7p; (**5**) Gallery of Horror [Buddy Saunders/Carlos Garzon] 7p; (**6**) The Vorpal Sword [Nicola Cuti/Tom Sutton] 7p; (**7**) *Eerie* Fanfare: The Tomb of Ankh-Ra/Headsman [Virginia Jenkins and Don Allen/Phillippe Druillet and Frank Frazetta, text stories, Frazetta's art from the

cover of *Creepy* #17] 2p; (**8**) Strange Gateway! [T. Casey Brennan/Jack Sparling] 8p; (**9**) Easy Way to a Tuff Surfboard! [Archie Goodwin/Frank Frazetta, reprinted from *Eerie* #3 (May 1966)] ½ p; (**10**) Snow Job! [Doug Moench/Jack Sparling] 7p.

Notes: Archie Goodwin was listed as associate editor but he was actually selecting the stories and assigning the artwork. Doug Moench made his professional comics debut. Famous French artist Phillippe Druillet made his only Warren appearance, but oddly enough it was on the fan page.

30. cover: Basil Gogos (November 1970)

(**1**) Eerie's Monster Gallery: BEM [Dan Adkins, frontis] 1p; (**2**) The Entail [Pat Boyette] 6p; (**3**) October Weir: Mirror, Mirror [Nicola Cuti/Frank Bolle] 10p; (**4**) Life Species [Bill DuBay] 4p; (**5**) *Eerie* Fanfare: The Prophetic Dream/Escape Claws/Nuts to You!/The Mistake [Carmen Minchella, David O'Dell, Rodney Schroeter, David E. Bruegel/Arthur Suydam and Gray Morrow, text stories] 2p; (**6**) I, Werewolf [Ken Barr] 9p; (**7**) Easy Way to a Tuff Surfboard! [Archie Goodwin/Frank Frazetta, reprinted from *Eerie* #3 (May 1966)] ½ p; (**8**) In Close Pursuit [Gordon Matthews/Jerry Grandenetti] 8p; (**9**) The Return of Amen-Tut! [Don Glut/Jack Sparling] 8p; (**10**) The Creation [Doug Moench/Carlos Garzon] 8p.

Notes: Price increased to 60 cents. Behind a not particularly good cover was a quite good issue! The BEM in Eerie's Monster Gallery is from old science fiction slang for "bug-eyed monster." Future artist Tony Meers sent in a letter. Pat Boyette's story "The Entail" was not only quite good, but quite gruesome as well. Psychic detective October Weir had only two appearances, which was a pity, as his stories were good and Bolle was perfect as the artist. The classic SF tale "Life Species" by DuBay is the kind of story that stays with you all your life. A crackerjack little story. Future artist Arthur Suydam made his comics debut on the fan page.

31. cover: Richard Corben (January 1971)

(**1**) Point of View [Buddy Saunders/Tom Sutton] 9p; (**2**) The Drop [Chris Fellner/Bill Fraccio and Tony Tallarico] 6p; (**3**) The Devil's Hand! [Bill DuBay] 6p; (**4**) The Alien Plague! [Billy Graham] 10p; (**5**) The Oasis [Buddy

Saunders/Carlos Garzon] 8p; (6) October Weir: Lady in Ice [Nicola Cuti/Frank Bolle] 7p; (7) *Eerie* Fanfare: I, The Nightwatchman/Poem/The Pact/Down in Cannery Dough [Ed Fedory/Danny Massoni, Michael Darrah and Craig Hill/Jeff Jones, ?, Greg Theakston and Arvell Jones, text stories/poem] 2p; (8) The Killer Slime [Steve Skeates/Carlos Garzon] 8p; (9) Easy Way to a Tuff Surfboard! [Archie Goodwin/Frank Frazetta, reprinted from *Eerie* #3 (May 1966), on the inside back cover] ½ p.

Notes: Corben's first Warren cover was quite good, featuring hairy, faceless monsters rising up from a dead body and pointing directly at the reader. Bill Fraccio's and Tony Tallarico's art was also good on the drug story "The Drop." At the request of future editor J. R. Cochran, Ed Fedory later reworked his text story from this issue's fan page into a comic script that appeared in *Creepy* #46. The second and final October Weir story appeared.

32. cover: Richard Corben and (in insert) Tom Sutton (March 1971) (Sutton's art is from an interior story)

(1) Eerie's Monster Gallery: The Creature from ... Beyond Ultima Thule! [Clif Jackson, frontis] 1p; (2) Superhero! [Steve Skeates/Tom Sutton] 6p; (3) The Warning of the Hawk! [Gardner Fox/Clif Jackson and Syd Shores] 6p; (4) The Wailing Tower [Larry Herndon/Frank Bolle] 7p; (5) Bookworm [Gerry Conway/Richard Corben] 7p; (6) I Fell for You [John Wolley/Jack Sparling] 7p; (7) *Eerie* Fanfare: The Misunderstanding/Reversal/Ain't It Not Funky Now Brother/Your Last Child Is Leaving [Clayton Fox, Michael Carlisle, Craig Hill and Ken Haubrock/Kevin Schaffer, Craig Hill, Steve Leialoha and Robert Monahan, text stories/poems] 2p; (8) Soul Power! [Don Glut/Mike Royer] 6p; (9) Ice World [Bill DuBay/William Barry, art miscredited to DuBay] 7p.

Notes: While the theme is a mainstay nowadays on such comics as *Astro City*, Steve Skeates' "Superhero!" was the first comic story to link up a nighttime Batman-like superhero with the vampire mythos. Pretty good story, too. Best story and art goes to the Conway/Corben tale "Bookworm." Steve Leialoha made his second appearance on a fan page, along with an odd editorial announcement (that Leialoha assured me was not written by him) to the effect that he was

ready to work for any comic publisher that wants him.

33. cover: Larry Todd (May 1971)

(1) Eerie's Monster Gallery: The Minotaur [Clif Jackson, frontis] 1p; (2) A Trip in Time! [Steve Skeates/Jack Sparling] 6p; (3) 243 Blank Pages! [Steve Skeates/George Roussos] 7p; (4) Whom the Gods Would Destroy [Marv Wolfman/Ken Barr] 11p; (5) Escape into Chaos [Steve Skeates/Ernie Colon] 7p; (6) Starvisions [Larry Todd] 6p; (7) The Pest! [Steve Skeates/Richard Corben, story miscredited to Al Hewetson] 8p; (8) *Eerie* Fanfare: Dave Cockrum profile/The Vampire/Wolf Star/From Beyond the Grave [Dave Cockrum, David Nowicki, Jack L. Bannow and Harry Feinzig/Mike Roberts, R. Goodwin, Pat Broderick, Gerald Colucci, Mark Wallace and Rick Bryant, text stories/poem with photo] 2p; (9) The Painting in the Tower! [Gardner Fox/Pat Boyette] 7p.

Notes: "The Pest!" by Skeates and Corben was the best story although Ernie Colon's experimental art and Pat Boyette's efforts were also worthy of note. Future artists Pat Broderick and Rick Bryant appeared on the fan page.

34. cover: Boris Vallejo (July 1971)

(1) Eerie's Monster Gallery: The Man Who Played God! [Tom Sutton, frontis] 1p; (2) Parting Is Such Sweet Horror! [Tom Sutton] 7p; (3) Eye of Cyclops! [Buddy Saunders/Jaime Brocal] 7p; (4) He Who Laughs Last ... Is Grotesque! [Al Hewetson/Mike Royer] 7p; (5) Food for Thought [Steve Skeates/Bill Fraccio and Tony Tallarico] 5p; (6) The Vow of the Wizard... [Ernie Colon/Ernie Colon and Frank McLaughlin] 7p; (7) The Sound of Wings [F. Paul Wilson/Carlos Garzon] 6p; (8) *Eerie* Fanfare: Oh, to Be a Bat/The Mutant!/The Face of Death! [Edgar Ellington, Robert J. Hurris, Joseph Wiltz/Pat Broderick, Joseph Wiltz, Mitchell Brown and Tony Desensi, poem/text stories] 2p; (9) Lair of the Horned Man [Alan Weiss] 9p.

Notes: Vallejo's second Warren cover (although it was the first bought) got a good deal more respect than his first had when it appeared in *Vampirella*. His barbarian swordsman looked somewhat disjointed, but his harpy was quite terrifying. Vallejo told me he painted this in a single overnight session when he was supposed to be drawing refrigerators for an ad campaign!

The fullscale Spanish invasion of artists began in *Eerie* with the debut of Spanish artist Jaime Brocal. Al Hewetson delivered a story that would have fit right at home in the *Horror-Mood* of Skywald. SF writer F. Paul Wilson made his comics (and perhaps his professional) debut with "The Sound of Wings." Pat Broderick made his second appearance on the fan page.

35. cover: Enrich Torres (September 1971)

(**1**) Eerie's Monster Gallery: Monster Sightings! [John Cornell, frontis] 1p; (**2**) Retribution [Gardner Fox and Steve Englehart/Steve Englehart] 6p; (**3**) The Comet's Curse! [Buddy Saunders/Frank Brunner] 6p; (**4**) The Tower of the Demon Dooms! [Gardner Fox/Mike Ploog] 9p; (**5**) I Am Dead, Egypt, Dead [Doug Moench/Victor de la Fuente] 8p; (**6**) Cats and Dogs [Bill DuBay/Jerry Grandenetti] 7p; (**7**) *Eerie* Fanfare: Sanho Kim profile/ Changing Sands/The Rats/ The End [J. R. Cochran, John D. Warner, John Ayella and David McElmurry/ Robert Putnam, John Ayella, Ken Kelly and Craig Edelblut, text stories] 2p; (**8**) Annual Warren Awards at the New York Comicon... [Martin Greim, text article, reprinted from *Comic Crusader* #10 (1970)] 2p; (**9**) Money [Sanho Kim] 9p; (**10**) Easy Way to a Tuff Surfboard! [Archie Goodwin/Frank Frazetta, reprinted from *Eerie* #3 (May 1966), on the back cover] ½ p.

Notes: Editor: Billy Graham. Enrich Torres made a spectacular cover artist debut with one of the most striking covers of his career. Although it's not generally well known, comic writer Steve Englehart made his debut as an artist and, as is evident from the half dozen or so stories available, wasn't bad at all. Mike Ploog began doing regular comics, after a stint as Will Eisner's as-

This sexy, gory cover from *Eerie* #35 was one *Eerie*'s best, courtesy of Erich Torres. © New Comic Co./used by permission.

sistant on the military magazine, *PS*. The Eisner influence was very apparent in his artwork (and still is today). Sanho Kim's art was impressive, even more so when compared to the often rushed-looking artwork he was doing for Charlton at the time. The Ken Kelly on the fan page (and on the letters page) is not the well known cover artist. A very strong issue.

36. cover: Enrich Torres (November 1971)

(**1**) Eerie's Monster Gallery: Atoms [T. Casey Brennan/Pablo Marcos, frontis] 1p; (**2**) Bad Moon on the Rise [Doug Moench/Tom Sutton] 10p; (**3**) The Silence and the Sleep [Steve Skeates/Rubio] 7p; (**4**) Prototype [Steve Skeates/Bruce Jones] 10p; (**5**) Look What

They've Done! [Steve Skeates/Esteban Maroto] 6p; (6) Crocodile [Don Glut/Mascaro] 6p; (7) The Trap [Greg Potter/L. M. Roca] 4p; (8) *Eerie* Fanfare: Steve Skeates profile/House of Horror/Occupational Hazard [Steve Skeates, Christopher Wolfe and Billie Fowler/Steve Skeates, Steve Lowe and Steve Cassman, text article, text stories] 2p; (9) Oh, Brother! [Steve Skeates/Dave Cockrum] 7p.

Notes: Bruce Jones' art was reproduced from pencils, something only Warren seemed able to do with any degree of care. Marvel's efforts in this regard were usually spotty at best.

37. cover: Enrich Torres (January 1972)

(1) Eerie's Monster Gallery: Air Serpent [Bill DuBay, frontis] 1p; (2) The Other Side of Atlantis [Steve Skeates/Jaime Brocal] 10p; (3) Horror at Hamilton House [Lynn Marron/Ken Barr] 7p; (4) The Ones Who Stole It from You [Don McGregor/Rafael Auraleon] 14p; (5) A Rush of Wings [Larry Herndon/Jaime Brocal] 8p; (6) *Eerie* Fanfare: The Message!/Theory/My, Oh, My!/Final Conqueror/Interchange! [Ted Dasen, Phill Jones, Vernon Shelton, Michael E. Tierney and Steven Taggart/Michael Gilbert, Anthony DeSensi, Solano Lopez and James Kanhard, text stories] 2p; (7) Dethslaker [Doug Moench/Ernie Colon] 11p.

Notes: Nice cover from Enrich. The best story and art was the ghoul story "The Ones Who Stole It from You" by Don McGregor and Rafael Auraleon. McGregor was asked by editor J. R. Cochran to add the first two pages to the story as a prologue. Ernie Colon's lettering for his story's title was so ornate that it is impossible to read! Still, it was one of his best (and sexiest) art jobs for Warren. Brocal's two art jobs clearly show the difference between an artist fully engaged in the story he's illustrating (Atlantis) and one he's just doing for the buck (Wings). Skeates' Atlantis stories were supposedly written from unused Aquaman plots he'd done for DC. A sequel followed this story in #40. Michael Gilbert made his comics debut on the fan page, with a sample from a college comic strip he was drawing. Solano Lopez's sample pages again landed up on the fan page.

38. cover: Ken Kelly (February 1972)

(1) Eerie's Monster Gallery: The Mothman of West Virginia [Doug Moench/Jaime Brocal,

frontis] 1p; (2) Stake in the Game [Doug Moench/Jose Gual] 21p; (3) The Carrier of the Serpent [T. Casey Brennan/Jerry Grandenetti] 10p; (4) 1971 Comicon Awards Go to Frazetta and Goodwin... [J. R. Cochran?/?, text article] 3p; (5) A Stranger in Hell [T. Casey Brennan/Esteban Maroto] 7p; (6) The Night the Snow Spilled Blood! [Don McGregor/Tom Sutton] 12p; (7) *Eerie* Fanfare: Esteban Maroto profile/The Shower!/The Night Desert/See into the Future!/The Brothers/The Farmer's Friend [Bill DuBay, C. D. Stewart, Jim Erskine, Jarry Bradman and M. Joseph Blattberg/Esteban Maroto, Brant Withers, Loper Espi, Manuel Sanjulian and Stephen Stanley, text articles/text stories with photo] 2p.

Notes: Ken Kelly's cover was one of his best! A fanged humanoid struggles with a giant green serpent! Moody and dynamic! Future artist and letterer John Workman sent in a letter pleading for work! "Stake in the Game" was one of the longest (thus far) stories in Warren history but, unfortunately, was none too good. T. Casey Brennan and Jerry Grandenetti turned in another philosophical story (something they were quite good at). Esteban Maroto delivered the best art job with the excellent "A Stranger in Hell" while Don McGregor's "The Night the Snow Spilled Blood!" was the best story. McGregor's story also featured the second appearance of three by police detective Dave Turner, whose first and last adventures appeared in *Creepy*.

39. cover: Ken Kelly (April 1972)

(1) Eerie's Monster Gallery: The Mysterious Men in Black! [Doug Moench/Richard Bassford, frontis] 1p; (2) Head Shop [Don Glut/Jose Bea] 6p; (3) Just Passing Through [Steve Skeates/Rafael Auraleon] 8p; (4) The Disenfranchised [J. R. Cochran/Tom Sutton] 10p; (5) Dax the Warrior [Esteban Maroto and ?/Esteban Maroto, story credited solely to Maroto] 8p; (6) Yesterday Is the Day Before Tomorrow [Doug Moench/Dave Cockrum] 7p; (7) *Eerie* Fanfare: Pity the Stranger/House for Sale/The Coming of Apollo/Welcoming Committee [Greg Balke, Roy Decker, Gary Henry and Marcus Octavious/Steve Monsanto and Jody Clay, text stories] 2p; (8) Ortaa! [Kevin Pagan/Jaime Brocal] 8p.

Notes: Another top-notch Ken Kelly cover! The best story and art was easily J. R. Cochran and Tom Sutton's "The Disenfranchised!" Maroto's

68 ILLUSTRATED PAGES OF TERROR AND SUSPENSE

EERIE

EERIE #38 FEB. 1972

A WARREN MAGAZINE PDC. 60¢

SPECIAL HOLIDAY ISSUE

"CARRIER OF THE SERPENT" BY T. CASEY BRENNAN ILLUSTRATED BY JERRY GRANDENETTI Page 16

—FEATURING: "THE NIGHT THE SNOW SPILLED BLOOD" Page 39

THE BEST IN ILLUSTRATED TERROR AND SUSPENSE!

This striking beastman and python cover was one of Ken Kelly's best efforts. It bridges the borders between quiet and violent horror. © New Comic Co./used by permission.

Dax character began an eleven-chapter run in *Eerie*. These stories had originally been published in Europe a couple of years earlier. For this Warren run, the stories were translated and rewritten by American writers, none of whom were credited. Apparently, each scripter got only one story to adapt so the quality of the scripts would range from quite good to so-so.

40. cover: Manuel Sanjulian (June 1972)

(1) Eerie's Monster Gallery: Dracula's Castle [Fred Ott/Rafael Auraleon, frontis and on the inside back cover] 2p; **(2)** The Story Behind "Stake in the Game." [Doug Moench, text article on the letters page] ⅓ p; **(3)** The Brain of

Frankenstein [Fred Ott/ Mike Ploog] 10p; **(4)** The Once Powerful Prince [Steve Skeates/Jaime Brocal] 13p; **(5)** Dax the Warrior: The Paradise Tree [Esteban Maroto and ?/ Esteban Maroto, story credited solely to Maroto] 8p; **(6)** Deathfall [Sanho Kim] 10p; **(7)** The Prodigy Son [Don Glut/Jose Bea] 6p; **(8)** *Eerie* Fanfare: Buddy Saunders profile/ Kingdom Come/The Grim Spectre/Snowith Puritan's Progress/The Story Behind the Story: "The Night the Snow Spilled Blood!"/ Paradise Lost!/Voice of Doom [Buddy Saunders, James Charles, Rick Cook, Joe Letts, Jerry Bradman, ?, Don McGregor, David Yates and David A. Wasyk/ Bruce Waldman, Tom Sutton and J. A. Williams, text articles/text stories with photo] 2p; **(9)** Pity the Grave Digger! [Buddy Saunders/Rafael Auraleon] 6p.

Notes: Editor: J. R. Cochran. Price increased to 75 cents and size increased to 72 pages. Mike Ploog's final Warren story appeared to be a warm-up for his excellent *Frankenstein* series for Marvel, which appeared about six months later. It was easily the best art in the issue, although Maroto, Kim and Auraleon also do noteworthy jobs. "The Once Powerful Prince" was a sequel to "The Other Side of Atlantis" from *Eerie* #37.

41. cover: Manuel Sanjulian (August 1972)

(1) Eerie's Monster Gallery: The Ghouls of Scotland [Fred Ott/Ken Barr, frontis] 1p; **(2)** Inside 41/The Story Behind the Story: "Head Shop" [J. R. Cochran and Don Glut, text articles on the letters page] ⅓ p; **(3)** Warped [Kevin Pagan/Jerry Grandenetti] 8p; **(4)** West Coast Turnaround [John Wooley/Tom Sutton] 8p; **(5)**

Heir Pollution! [John Wooley/Jose Bea] 9p; (6) The Caterpillars [Fred Ott/Luis Garcia] 8p; (7) Derelict [John Thraxis/Paul Neary] 7p; (8) The Safest Way! [Steve Skeates/Jose Gual] 7p; (9) *Eerie* Fanfare: Tom Sutton profile/The Pet Shop/What's for Supper?/To Save a Witch/Tales from the Crypt Reviewith Cat Fancy [Tom Sutton, Mark Curtis, Jay Richter, Mary Eveland, Jr. R. Cochran, Dave Parker/Tom Sutton and Esteban Maroto, text articles, text stories with photo] 2p; (10) Dax the Warrior: Chess [Esteban Maroto and ?/Esteban Maroto, story credited to Maroto solely] 8p.

Notes: One of Sanjulian's best covers graced this issue. New writer John Wooley wrote several social horror stories with the best being the LSD story "West Coast Turnaround" which also featured good art by Tom Sutton. Englishman Paul Neary made his American debut.

42. cover: Luis Dominguez (October 1972)

(1) The True Story of Eerie ... How to Gain Forty Pounds of Ugly Fat in Six Years! [J. R. Cochran, text article, frontis] 1p; (2) The Mummy Stalks! [Roy G. Krenkel and Archie Goodwin/Reed Crandall, reprinted from *Eerie* #5 (September 1966)] 8p; (3) The Blood Fruit! [Johnny Craig, reprinted from *Eerie* #11 (September 1967)] 8p; (4) It That Lurks! [Archie Goodwin/Dan Adkins, reprinted from *Eerie* #7 (January 1967)] 6p; (5) Dark Rider! [Archie Goodwin/John Severin, reprinted from *Eerie* #8 (March 1967)] 6p; (6) Life Species [Bill DuBay, reprinted from *Eerie* #30 (November 1970)] 4p; (7) Ogre's Castle [Archie Goodwin/Angelo Torres, reprinted from *Creepy* #2 (April 1965)] 6p; (8) Room with a View! [Archie Goodwin/Steve Ditko, reprinted from *Eerie* #3 (May 1966)] 6p; (9) Voodoo Drum! [Archie Goodwin/Neal Adams, reprinted from *Eerie* #10 (July 1967)] 8p; (10) I Am Dead, Egypt, Dead [Doug Moench/Victor de la Fuente, reprinted from *Eerie* #35 (September 1971)] 8p; (11) The Thing in the Alley [Al Hewetson/Berni Wrightson, text story on the back cover] 1p.

Notes: It cost $1.00 and was an 80 page issue. With this issue the *Eerie* yearbook annual became part of the regular numbering. First squarebound issue. I've already mentioned that this was my first Warren purchase. However, even without the rosy glow of nostalgia, this is a pretty great issue, even for a reprint. Great stories and art from all involved. Due to a mix-up at the printer, which Warren and rival publisher Sky-

wald shared for a time, the back cover for Skywald's *Nightmare* #9 (October 1972) was also printed as the back cover for this Warren magazine.

The DuBay Era

43. cover: Luis Dominguez (November 1972)

(1) Eerie's Monster Gallery: Quetzalcoatl, Monster God! [Doug Moench/Luis Garcia, frontis] 1p; (2) Inside 43 [Bill DuBay, text article on the letters page] ⅓ p; (3) Someday [Rich Margopoulos/Jerry Grandenetti] 12p; (4) Musical Chairs [Steve Skeates/Tom Sutton] 8p; (5) Bright Eyes! [Doug Moench/Richard Corben] 7p; (6) *Eerie* Book Reviews: Green Lantern/The Ghouls/Hauntings and Horrors/Tales from the Crypt [Chuck McNaughton, text articles] 1p; (7) The Hunt [Rich Margopoulos/Paul Neary] 8p; (8) Showdown [Steve Skeates/Jesus Suso Rego] 6p; (9) *Eerie* Fanfare: Rich Margopoulos profile/Life's Dream/Encounter with an Artist/Cold Shoulder!/Hate/Black Death [Rich Margopoulos, Richard D. Chase, Jeff Baenen, Bob Hurns, Robert M. Lester and Tim McDonald/Paul Neary, Hidy and Scot Goode, text article/text stories with photo] 2p; (10) Dax the Warrior: Let the Evil One Sleep [Esteban Maroto and ?/Esteban Marato, story credited solely to Maroto] 8p; (11) *Eerie* Monster Gallery: The Mortsafes [Tom Sutton, on the inside back cover] 1p.

Notes: Editor: Bill DuBay. Back to 75 cents and 72 pages. Best art was Rich Corben's "Bright Eyes" although Jesus Suso Rego gives him a run for his money. Suso, whose art seemed perfect for Warren, did only a couple of stories for them but did many more over at Skywald. He also did some work for Seaboard/Atlas before vanishing from the American comic scene.

44. cover: Luis Dominguez (December 1972)

(1) Eerie's Monster Gallery: Werewolf— Fact or Fantasy? [Fred Ott/Jerry Grandenetti, frontis] 1p; (2) Inside 44 [Bill DuBay, text article with photo on the letters page] ⅓ p; (3) Crazy Mazie [J. R. Cochran/Tom Sutton] 10p; (4) Everlasting Mortality [Doug Moench/Jerry Grandenetti] 5p; (5) *Eerie's* Book Reviews: The Time Machine/The Invisible Man/The First Men in the Moon/In the Days of the Comet [Chuck McNaughton, text articles] 1p; (6) The Thrill

of the Hunt [Doug Moench/Martin Salvador] 10p; (7) Hand of the Discarnate [Doug Moench/Bill DuBay] 6p; (8) Mervin's Dead Ringer! [Greg Potter/Luis Dominguez] 4p; (9) Tiller of the Soul [Greg Potter/Rubio] 7p; (10) *Eerie*'s Short-Short Shocker: The Parade! [Doug Moench/Bill DuBay, text story] 2p; (11) *Eerie* Fanfare: Luis Dominguez profile/A Little Farther/Deep Sleep/The Feast/The Fatal Dream/A Touch of Fate/Search for the Sun [Bill DuBay. Harry E. Mongold, Victor Olchowka, Tom Morganti, Mike Weiler, Roberto Tabaldo and Bill Hightower/Luis Dominguez (art from when he was 14!) and Bill MacDonald, text article/text stories with photo] 2p; (12) Dax the Warrior: Lake of Gold! [Esteban Maroto and ?/Esteban Maroto, story credited solely to Maroto] 8p.

Notes: Don McGregor and Jose Gual's "Malocchi" was advertised for the next issue but didn't actually appear until *Creepy* #72 in 1975! "Crazy Mazie" was the best story and art here. A solid and entertaining story, as was the entire issue. Bill DuBay began to experiment with short prose stories, although that didn't last long.

45. cover: Luis Dominguez (February 1973)

(1) Eerie's Monster Gallery: Vlad the Impaler [Fred Ott/Rafael Auraleon, frontis and on the inside back cover] 2p; (2) The Mound [Tom Sutton] 10p; (3) Ri, Master of Men [Hal G. Turner/Martin Salvador] 8p; (4) When Wakes the Dreamer [Don McGregor/Jesus Suso Rego] 8p; (5) A Blade for the Teacher [Bill Warren/Luis Dominguez] 7p; (6) Maneater [Steve Skeates/Rubio] 7p; (7) The Critic's Crypt: King Kong (Radio)/Flash Gordon (Radio)/*The Pan Book of Horror Stories* #4/*The Pan Book of Horror Stories* #5 [Chuck McNaughton, text articles] 1p; (8) *Eerie*'s Short-Short Shocker: Ecology of Death! [Doug Moench/Bill DuBay, text story] 2p; (9) Doug Moench's Confessions: Story of a Ghost Writer!/The Mask Behind the Face! [Doug Moench/Russ Heath, text article with one page strip, comic page reprinted from the *Chicago Sun-Times*' Sunday supplement] 1p; (10) *Eerie* Fanfare: Don McGregor profile/Afterlife/Do Not Step Outside!/What, Me Worry?/Tooth Be or Not Tooth Be [Don McGregor, Frank Christensen, Richard Noel, Steve Clement and Michael Carlisle/Felix Mas, Jose Gual, Moe Romulus and Marshal Rogers, text articles/text stories] 2p; (11) Dax the Warrior: The Witch [Esteban Maroto and ?/Esteban Maroto, story credited solely to Maroto] 8p.

Notes: Marv Wolfman, who worked as the story

editor for Warren for about six months, received his only Warren credit here. A solid issue for story and art. Future writer Steve Clement appeared on the fan page, as did future artist Marshall Rogers. Moench's "Confessions" was an article and one-page story (combined on one page) that he did for the *Chicago Sun-Times*' Sunday supplement about his work as a horror comic writer. Heath's reprinted work was his first appearance in a Warren magazine since 1966. Spectacular art on the Dax story by Maroto.

46. cover: Manuel Sanjulian (March 1973)

(1) Portrait of Dracula [Fred Ott/Bill DuBay, frontis and on inside back cover] 2p; (2) Dracula Prologue and Recap [Bill DuBay] 2p; (3) Dracula [Bill DuBay/Tom Sutton] 10p; (4) The Things in the Dark [Fred Ott/Jimmy Janes] 7p; (5) The Critic's Crypt: Star Trek/Star Trek 2/Star Trek 3/Star Trek 4 [Chuck McNaughton?, text articles] 1p; (6) Garganza! [Bill Warren/Paul Neary] 7p; (7) The Root of Evil [Mike Jennings/Martin Salvador] 8p; (8) Planet of the Werewolves! [Gerry Boudreau/Reed Crandall] 9p; (9) *Eerie* Fanfare: Mike Jennings profile/Twist of Fate/She Has a Cat/The Old Man/Spirits of the Dead [Mike Jennings, Paul E. King, Jr., Terry W. Cloud, Ed J. Pahule and Kathy LaClaire/Jose Bea, Carlos Llerena and Chris Campbell (after Jack Davis), text article/text stories with photo] 2p; (10) Dax the Warrior: The Giant [Esteban Maroto and Steve Englehart/Esteban Maroto, story credited solely to Maroto] 8p.

Notes: Sanjulian's Dracula painting here was one of his best. The Dracula serial here was technically the same dismal Dracula that appeared in *Vampirella*'s strip but, with a reworked character design by Bill DuBay and terrific art by Tom Sutton, this Dracula was improved about 100 percent. The frontispiece series title, "Eerie's Monster Gallery," was dropped, as would be the series itself in another issue. Paul Neary did a nice job channeling the manga style of art, well before it was a common sight in the USA. Crandall's art was shaky but Boudreau's story was quite good on "Planet of the Werewolves." Dax continued his grim storyline. Another solid issue.

47. cover: Manuel Sanjulian (April 1973)

(1) The Story Behind the Story: Mervin's Dead Ringer [Greg Potter, text article on the letters

page] ½ p; (2) Dracula: Enter the Dead-Thing! [Bill DuBay/Tom Sutton] 12p; (3) Lilith [Nicola Cuti/Jaime Brocal] 19p; (4) Snake Man [Greg Potter/Martin Salvador] 11p; (5) The Message Is the Medium [Doug Moench/Paul Neary] 8p; (6) Dax the Warrior: Gemma-5 [Esteban Maroto and Marv Wolfman/Esteban Maroto, story credited solely to Maroto] 8p; (7) *Eerie*'s Delights! [same as the feature's page for *Creepy* #52, text articles] 1p.

Notes: Another Dracula cover by Sanjulian, but this one was downright silly looking, with the cover Dracula looking nothing like the character in the book. In fact, he looked quite a lot like a bad actor with plastic fangs! Was this a cover originally intended for Famous Monsters? Size increased to 72 pages. Both the Dracula and Lilith stories were quite good. The fan page was dropped in favor of a features page, which featured the same content for all Warren horror titles.

48. cover: Manuel Sanjulian (June 1973)

(1) Dracula: The Son of Dracula [Bill DuBay/Rich Buckler and Bill DuBay] 10p; (2) The Mummy Walks: ... and an End! [Steve Skeates/Jaime Brocal] 10p; (3) Think of Me and I'll Be There! [Jack Butterworth/Martin Salvador] 7p; (4) Curse of the Werewolf: On a Stalking Moonlit Night! [Al Milgrom/Rich Buckler and Bill DuBay] 10p; (5) The Resurrection Man [Jack Butterworth/Paul Neary] 7p; (6) Dax the Warrior: The Sacrifice [Esteban Maroto and Len Wein/Esteban Maroto, story credited solely to Maroto] 8p; (7) Eerie's Delights! [same as *Creepy* #53's contents, text articles] 1p.

Notes: *Eerie* began its transformation to a series-dominated magazine. The Dracula story ended abruptly here, unfinished, with the next promised installment to have been entitled "Princess of Bathory Castle!" Both the *Mummy* and *Werewolf* serials started out quite nicely, with Brocal providing perfectly moody art for Steve Skeates' *Mummy* scripts and Al Milgrom, better known today as an artist, delivering a strong script for the *Werewolf*. Both of these series, however, later had sharp declines in quality—crippled by rambling, overlong storylines, idiotic team-ups and writer/artist changes. The Dax story was quite good but the rest of the stories were rather bland.

49. cover: Enrich Torres (July 1973)

(1) A Guest Editorial By Phil Seuling [Phil Seuling, text article on the letters page] ½ p; (2) Marvin, the Dead-Thing: One Is the Loneliest Number [Al Milgrom/Esteban Maroto] 12p; (3) The Mummy Walks: The Death of a Friend! [Steve Skeates/Jaime Brocal] 10p; (4) Curse of the Werewolf: Midnight Prey [Al Milgrom/Rich Buckler and Bill DuBay] 8p; (5) The Alien Nation: Over Population! [Rich Margopoulos/Paul Neary] 12p; (6) Fear Itself! [Steve Skeates/Isidro Mones] 7p; (7) Dax the Warrior: The Vampire [Esteban Maroto and Don McGregor/Esteban Maroto, story credited solely to Maroto] 8p; (8) The *Eerie* Eye! [same as *Creepy* #54's contents, text articles] 1p.

Notes: The cover and interior story "Marvin, the Dead-Thing" spoofed the Swamp Monster craze, particularly DC's Swamp Thing and Marvel's Man-Thing. There's evidence that suggests the author Bill DuBay meant the title as a jab at Marv Wolfman's short editorial stint at Warren. The secondary title had "loneliest" misspelled. The feature page title was changed to "The *Eerie* Eye." The "Alien Nation" story may have been originally intended as a serial.

50. cover: Manuel Sanjulian (August 1973)

(1) Escape from the Creepy-Crawley-Castle Game! [Bill DuBay, game, frontis, interior page and on the inside back cover] 3p; (2) The Mummy Walks: The Mind Within [Steve Skeates/Jaime Brocal] 10p; (3) The *Eerie* Eye! [same as *Creepy* #56's contents, text articles] 1p; (4) Curse of the Werewolf!: This Evil Must Die [Al Milgrom/Martin Salvador] 10p; (5) Satana, Daughter of Satan!: Genesis of Depravity! [Doug Moench/Ramon Torrents] 5p; (6) Monarch's Return [John Jacobson/Paul Neary] 6p; (7) Lord's Wrath [John Jacobson/Aldoma] 8p; (8) The Disciple [Steve Skeates/Isidro Mones] 8p; (9) Dax the Warrior: The Secret of Pursiahz [Esteban Maroto and ?/Esteban Maroto, story credited solely to Maroto] 8p.

Notes: After the harsh criticism of *Creepy*'s fiftieth issue, Warren stepped up to the plate and delivered a much better "special" fiftieth issue for Cousin *Eerie*. Both the *Mummy* and *Werewolf* serials received their official series titles this issue. The new artist on "Curse of the Werewolf," Martin Salvador, was a capable artist but his style was so completely different from Rich Buckler's that it distracted one from the storyline. Months before Marvel unveiled their *Satana, Daughter of Satan* serial in their black and white magazines, Warren issued this one-shot that could almost be regarded a prologue for the Marvel character, so similar were the origins. The same short story also provided an origin for Warren's version of Dracula. Bill DuBay began a series of horror games (later turned into board games for the Captain Company ad pages), that appeared in place of the frontispiece series. This game also appeared in *Creepy* #55.

51. cover: Manuel Sanjulian and cover montage (September 1973)

(**1**) Monster Match [Bill DuBay, game, frontis, interior page and on the inside back cover] 2½ p; (**2**) A Stranger in Hell [T. Casey Brennan/ Esteban Maroto, reprinted from *Eerie* #38 (February 1972)] 7p; (**3**) Pity the Grave Digger! [Buddy Saunders/Rafael Auraleon, reprinted from *Eerie* #40 (June 1972)] 6p; (**4**) The Caterpillars [Fred Ott/Luis Garcia, reprinted from *Eerie* #41 (August 1972] 8p; (**5**) Evil Spirits! [Archie Goodwin/Johnny Craig, reprinted from *Eerie* #16 (July 1968)] 10p; (**6**) *Eerie* #40 and *Creepy* #46 Covers Poster [Manuel Sanjulian, on reproduced cover on each side] 1p; (**7**) Head Shop [Don Glut/Jose Bea] 6p; (**8**) Vision of Evil [Archie Goodwin/Alex Toth, reprinted from *Eerie* #2 (March 1966)] 6p; (**9**) The Curse of Kali! [Archie Goodwin/Angelo Torres, reprinted from *Eerie* #6 (November 1966)] 7p.

Notes: The 1973 *Eerie* annual. Price increased to $1.00, presumably to pay for the double-sided wall poster within. Sanjulian's cover art is lifted from his Cousin Eerie poster, which was sold in the Captain Company ad pages.

52. cover: Manuel Sanjulian (November 1973)

(**1**) Werewolf! [Bill DuBay, game, frontis and on the inside back cover] 2p; (**2**) The *Eerie* Eye! [same as *Creepy* #57's contents, text articles] 1p; (**3**) The Mummy Walks: Ghoulish Encounter [Steve Skeates/Jaime Brocal] 10p; (**4**) Curse of the Werewolf: Darkling Revelation [Al Milgrom/Martin Salvador] 10p; (**5**) Hunter [Rich Margopoulos/Paul Neary] 10p; (**6**) The Beheaded [John Jacobson/Aldoma] 10p; (**7**) The Golden Kris of Hadji Mohammed [George Henderon/Isidro Mones, from the story by Frederick Moore] 8p; (**8**) Dax the Warrior: Death Rides This Night! [Esteban Maroto and Al Milgrom/Esteban Maroto, story credited solely to Maroto] 8p.

Notes: Nice cover from Sanjulian. Future *Batman Animated* director Kevin Altieri sent in a letter. One of *Eerie*'s most popular serials, *Hunter*, debuted. Dax's final appearance set the tone for almost all the Warren serials' endings — dark, depressing and usually hopeless. The stylish adaptation of "The Golden Kris of Hadji Mohammed" had the best story and art for this issue.

53. cover: Manuel Sanjulian (January 1974)

(**1**) Wart Monster of Tennessee [Doug Moench/ Rich Buckler and Bill DuBay, frontis and on the inside back cover] 2p; (**2**) The *Eerie* Eye! [same as *Creepy* #58's contents, text articles] 1p; (**3**) The Mummy Walks: Enter — Mr. Hyde [Steve Skeates/Jaime Brocal] 10p; (**4**) Curse of the Werewolf: To Save a Witch's Soul! [Al Milgrom/Martin Salvador] 10p; (**5**) Hunter, part 2 [Rich Margopoulos/Paul Neary] 10p; (**6**) Schreck: First Night of Terror! [Doug Moench/ Vicente Alcazar and Neal Adams] 12p; (**7**) Fathom Haunt: Spawn of the Dead Thing [Tom Sutton] 9p; (**8**) Two *Vampirella*'s Stun 5,500 at 1973 Comic Art Convention [Garry Boudreau, text article with photo] 1p.

Notes: Nice cover for the *Mummy* series by Sanjulian. Even though *Eerie* was now top heavy with series, this was a pretty good issue. Salvador's artwork for the *Werewolf* serial would have been just fine (it was strongly suggestive of the Universal monster movies from the 1930s) except that his werewolf was noticeably non-scary. One of Sutton's best art and story jobs appears here and seems to have been the direct inspiration for French artist Andreas' much more familiar Rork character, who has appeared in several graphic novels. The two characters are dead ringers for each other, and deal in similar mystic adventures. This Fathom Haunt debut, although clearly intended to be the start of a series, turned out to be his only appearance. It also featured the best story and art for this issue.

54. cover: Manuel Sanjulian (February 1974)

(**1**) A Few Words and Pictures about Our Brand New Comic Magazine [Bill DuBay/Will Eisner and Bill DuBay, text article, frontis and on the inside cover] 2p; (**2**) The *Eerie* Eye: Warren Magazine Questionnaire/Jack Butterworth profile [Bill DuBay/Martin Salvador, text articles with photo] 1p; (**3**) The Mummy Walks:

Stranger in a Village of the Insane! [Steve Skeates/Jaime Brocal] 10p; (4) Curse of the Werewolf: To Cure This Curse! [Steve Skeates/Martin Salvador] 10p; (5) Hunter, part 3 [Rich Margopoulos/Paul Neary] 10p"; (6) The Christmas Spirit of 1947 [Will Eisner, color, reprinted from *The Spirit* (December 21, 1947)] 7p; (7) *The Spirit* ad [Will Eisner, color] 1p; (8) Schreck: Bright Eyes! [Doug Moench/Vicente Alcazar] 12p; (9) Doctor Archaeus: The Evil That Men Do [Gerry Boudreau/Isidro Mones] 9p; (10) Presenting the 1973 Warren Awards [Bill Du Bay, text article] 2p.

Notes: Price increased to $1.00 and size increased to 80 pages. Steve Skeates took over the troubled *Werewolf* serial and promptly turned him into a were-mummy! The upcoming *Spirit* magazine is sampled by a *Spirit* story appearing in the color section. Warren finally came up with a classic horror series that was totally home-grown with the Boudreau/Mones thriller "Doctor Archaeus." Through clearly inspired by Vincent Price's *Dr. Phibes* movie, this series still managed to pack enough punch of its own in relating the tale of the twisted revenge of a hanged man against his jury to be quite memorable.

55. cover: Ken Kelly (March 1974)

(1) The Spirit ad [Will Eisner, frontis] 1p; (2) The *Eerie* Eye [same as *Creepy* #60's content, text articles with photo] 1p; (3) Schreck: Worms in the Mind! [Doug Moench/Vicente Alcazar] 11p; (4) Schreck: No Flies on Schreck! [Doug Moench/Vicente Alcazar] 14p; (5) The Spirit: Bucket of Blood [Will Eisner/John Spranger and Will Eisner, color, reprinted from *The Spirit* (June 16, 1946)] 7p; (6) Dracula ad [Esteban Maroto, color] 1p; (7) Hunter, part 4 [Budd Lewis/Paul Neary] 10p; (8) Doctor Archaeus: The Quest of the Golden Dove [Gerry Boudreau/Isidro Mones] 10p.

Notes: Size decreased to 72 pages. Both *The Mummy Walks* and *Curse of the Werewolf* serials were missing in action so Schreck concluded his run with his final two chapters. Not a great serial but not bad either. The *Mummy* didn't return until #61. Nice cover by Ken Kelly of Hunter with another tasty sampling of the Spirit in the color section. Budd Lewis took over the *Hunter* serial for one episode.

56. cover: Ken Kelly (April 1974)

(1) The Spirit ad [Will Eisner, frontis] 1p; (2)

The *Eerie* Eye [same as *Creepy* #61's content, text articles with photo] 1p; (3) Curse of the Werewolf: ...There Was a Were-Mummy [Steve Skeates/Martin Salvador] 14p; (4) Hunter, part 5 [Bill DuBay/Paul Neary] 10p; (5) Wizard Wagstaff [Jack Butterworth/Richard Corben, color] 8p; (6) It Returns! [Carl Wessler/Enrique Badia Romero] 10p; (7) Doctor Archaeus: The Night of the Red Death [Gerry Boudreau/Isidro Mones] 10p.

Notes: Bill DuBay took over the writing chores on *Hunter*. "It" first appeared in *Creepy* #53, a year earlier. This serial skipped back and forth between *Eerie* and *Creepy* over an extended period of time, making it rather hard to keep track of events. "Wizard Wagstaff" was another humorous fantasy story by Corben.

57. cover: Ken Kelly (June 1974)

(1) Cousin Eerie's Introduction [Bill DuBay/Berni Wrightson, frontis] 1p; (2) The *Eerie* Eye [same as *Creepy* #62's contents, text articles with photo] 1p; (3) The Spook: Stridspider Sponge-Rot [Doug Moench/Esteban Maroto] 10p; (4) Hunter, part 6 [Bill DuBay/Paul Neary] 8p; (5) The Hacker: Hide from the Hacker! [Steve Skeates/Tom Sutton] 10p; (6) Child [Greg Potter/Richard Corben, color] 8p; (7) It: The Terror of Foley Mansion! [Carl Wessler/Jose Gual] 9p; (8) Doctor Archaeus: A Switch in Time... [Gerry Boudreau/Isidro Mones] 10p.

Notes: Great Ken Kelly cover depicting Hunter. Future *Batman Animated* artist and director Kevin Altieri sent in a letter suggesting that Warren revive *Blazing Combat* (possibly because Archie Goodwin was back on board at Warren) but the idea was pooh-poohed in the editorial reply. Doug Moench and Esteban Maroto launched a new serial about a black voodoo man but both were rapidly replaced on the serial. Moench went on record later to state that the serial's title (which could be regarded as a derogatory racial slur) was Bill DuBay's idea and that Moench himself was ignorant of its connotations. Regardless, it wasn't a bad series, with excellent art and generally good stories. This was a superior issue with a strong new serial appearing by Skeates and Tom Sutton and the debut of Child, a sort of Frankenstein's monster in child form, in the color section.

58. cover: Manuel Sanjulian (July 1974)

(1) Cousin Eerie's Introduction [Bill DuBay/Berni Wrightson, frontis] 1p; (2) The *Eerie* Eye [same as the contents of *Creepy* #63 minus the Wrightson illustration, text articles] 1p; (3) Enter: The Exterminator aka They Eat Babies ... Don't They? [Bill DuBay/Esteban Maroto] 8p; (4) The Spook: Webtread's Powercut [Doug Moench/Leopold Sanchez] 8p; (5) The Pepper Lake Monster [Berni Wrightson] 10p; (6) Child: Mind of the Mass! [Greg Potter/Richard Corben, color] 8p; (7) The Spook: Knuckle-bones to Fever Twitch [Doug Moench/Leopold Sanchez] 13p; (8) Doctor Archaeus: Carnage in Costume [Gerry Boudreau/Isidro Mones] 10p.

Notes: The Spook, now illustrated by Leopold Sanchez, was cover-featured and had two stories within. This was Sanchez's American debut. There were more fine episodes of Child and Doctor Archaeus while Bill DuBay began a new series with the Exterminator (sort of—the Exterminator who appears in this story is not the same robot who would appear in the next installment). Best story and art, however, belonged to Berni Wrightson's masterful "The Pepper Lake Monster," with Wrightson at the top of his form.

59. cover: Ken Kelly/back cover: Manuel Sanjulian (August 1974)

(1) Cousin Eerie's Introduction [Bill DuBay/Esteban Maroto and Berni Wrightson, frontis] 1p; (2) Dax the Damned [Esteban Maroto and Budd Lewis/Esteban Maroto, reprinted from *Eerie* #39 (April 1972)] 8p; (3) Dax the Damned: The Paradise Tree [Esteban Maroto and Budd Lewis/Esteban Maroto, reprinted from *Eerie* #40 (June 1972), one page edited out] 7p; (4) Dax the Damned: Chess [Esteban Maroto and Budd Lewis/Esteban Maroto, color, reprinted from *Eerie*

#41 (August 1972)] 8p; (5) Dax the Damned: Let the Evil One Sleep [Esteban Maroto and Budd Lewis/Esteban Maroto, reprinted from *Eerie* #43 (November 1972)] 8p; (6) Dax the Damned: The Golden Lake [Esteban Maroto and Budd Lewis/Esteban Maroto, reprinted from *Eerie* #44 (December 1972) where it was entitled "Lake of Gold"] 8p; (7) Dax the Damned: The Witch ... The Maneater [Esteban Maroto and Budd Lewis/Esteban Maroto, reprinted from *Eerie* #45 (February 1973) where it was entitled "The Witch"] 8p; (8) Dax the Damned: Cyclops [Esteban Maroto and Budd Lewis/Esteban Maroto, reprinted from *Eerie* #46 (March 1973) where it was entitled "The

Even Warren's back covers could have striking artwork. This Manuel Sanjulian effort appeared on the back cover of *Eerie* #59, an all–Dax the Warrior reprint issue. © New Comic Co./used by permission.

Giant"] 8p; (9) Dax the Damned: Starlight [Esteban Maroto and Budd Lewis/Esteban Maroto, reprinted from *Eerie* #47 (April 1973) where it was entitled "Gemma-5"] 8p; (10) Dax the Damned: The Lord's Prayer [Esteban Maroto and Budd Lewis/Esteban Maroto, reprinted from *Eerie* #48 (June 1973) where it was entitled "The Sacrifice"] 8p; (11) Dax the Damned: Death Rides This Night! [Esteban Maroto and Budd Lewis/Esteban Maroto, reprinted from *Eerie* #52 (November 1973)] 8p.

Notes: Price increased to $1.25 and size increased to 96 pages. The 1974 *Eerie* annual. For this reprinting of the Dax stories, all were rewritten and the series retitled by Budd Lewis (sort of making them new all over again), with several receiving new chapter titles as well. One Dax tale, from *Eerie* #50—"The Secret of Pursiahz"—was not reprinted.

60. cover: Ken Kelly/back cover: Berni Wrightson (September 1974)

(1) The *Eerie* Eye: Budd Lewis profile/Child, Archaeus, Exterminator and the Jackassers Are Here but Still No Coffin/The Creative Man — Dube: Inside a Big City Editor [Budd Lewis and Bill DuBay/Bill Dubay, text articles with photo] 1p; (2) Night of the Jackass: 24 Hours of Hell! [Bruce Bezaire/Jose Ortiz] 12p; (3) Nightfall [Bill DuBay/Berni Wrightson] 8p; (4) Exterminator One [Bill DuBay/Paul Neary] 8p; (5) Child: Childhood's End [Budd Lewis/Richard Corbin, color] 8p; (6) The Man Hunters [Gerry Boudreau/Wally Wood, color] 8p; (7) The Unholy Creation [Steve Skeates/Leopold Sanchez] 9p; (8) Doctor Archeaus: Interlude [Gerry Boudreau/Isidro Mones] 10p.

Notes: Back to $1.00 and 72 pages. Ken Kelly's cover was good but the real prize was Berni Wrightson's stunning cover painting, the only cover he did for Warren. For some foolish reason, it ended up on the back cover! The best serial Warren ever ran, *Night of the Jackass*, debuted. This story, which discusses the events following Robert Louis Stevenson's novel *Dr. Jekyll and Mr. Hyde*, details how Jekyll's formula has become a underground drug, which leads to "Jackassing," a sort of rave party in a blocked-off, barricaded apartment building or hotel, with the rape, pillage and murder of the building's unfortunate occupants who serve as the jackassers' party favors. Well thought out and way ahead

of its time, this was an excellent story by Bruce Bezaire and Jose Ortiz that would have made a great movie in the hands of someone like David Cronenberg. The DuBay/Wrightson horror takeoff on Winsor McKay's "Little Nemo" was a delight. *Exterminator One* opened its official series with a strong entry and Child ended on one. Doctor Archeaus delivered a stunning surprise in its penultimate entry. Wally Wood's story, originally entitled "Space Search Seven" was retitled and rewritten on orders of Bill DuBay. Needless to say, Wood was not happy. Still, this is one of *Eerie*'s best issues since the glory days of Archie Goodwin.

61. cover: Ken Kelly (November 1974)

(1) Cousin Eerie's Introduction [Bill DuBay/Berni Wrightson, frontis] 1p; (2) The *Eerie* Eye: Real Heroes Die! Don't They? [same contents as *Creepy* #66 except for a short article by Bill DuBay, text articles with photo] 1p; (3) Coffin: Death Wish! [Budd Lewis/Jose Ortiz] 10p; (4) Killer Hawk [Bill DuBay/Wally Wood and Paul Kirchner, part of the Exterminator series, art credited solely to Wood] 12p; (5) Cotton Boy and Captain Blood! [Gerry Boudreau/Leopold Sanchez] 12p; (6) The Mummies Walk: A Battle of Bandaged Beasts [Steve Skeates/Joaquin Blazquez] 12p; (7) Doctor Archeaus: Foreplay/Penetration [Gerry Boudreau/Isidro Mones] 10p.

Notes: After many delays, the Western serial *Coffin* finally debuted. It was pretty good, too. Future artist Ken Meyer Jr. sent in a letter. Both the Mummy and the Werewolf returned after a long hiatus, teamed up now in a cluttered story with new illustrator Joaquin Blazquez. Doctor Archeaus concluded his run with some rather coy titles. Let's just say the climax wasn't quite as powerful as the foreplay. Still, it was a fine series.

62. cover: Manuel Sanjulian (January 1975)

(1) Cousin Eerie's Introduction [Bill DuBay/Berni Wrightson, frontis] 1p; (2) The *Eerie* Eye [same contents as *Creepy* #67, text articles with photos] 1p; (3) Apocalypse: The War [Budd Lewis/Jose Ortiz] 10p; (4) Cool Air [Berni Wrightson, from the story by H. P. Lovecraft] 7p; (5) The Spook: Crackermeyer's Churchyard [Budd Lewis/Leopold Sanchez] 10p; (6) The Butcher: "Forgive Us Our Trespasses" [Bill

DuBay/Richard Corben, color] 8p; (7) This Unholy Creation: Circus of Pain [Steve Skeates/Leopold Sanchez] 10p; (8) The Mummies Walk: Death Be Proud! [Steve Skeates/Joaquin Blasquez] 10p.

Notes: A great new series by Budd Lewis and Jose Ortiz began. *Apocalypse* was beautifully drawn and well written throughout its run. Along with the *Jackass* series, it's a series crying out for reprinting. Wrightson delivered a tasty adaptation of Lovecraft while Budd Lewis took over the scripting of the *Spook* series. In the *Mummy* series, Arthur Lemming, the Werewolf, finally met his death. DuBay and Corben's "The Butcher" wasn't really a horror story at all, but a 1930s gangland crime melodrama. Quite a good one, too.

63. cover: Manuel Sanjulian/back cover: Ken Kelly (February 1975)

(1) Cousin Eerie's Introduction [Bill DuBay/Berni Wrightson, frontis] 1p; (2) The *Eerie* Eye [same contents as *Creepy* #68, text article with photo] 1p; (3) Night of the Jackass: Storm Before the Calm! [Bruce Bezaire/Jose Ortiz] 10p; (4) Hollow of the Three Hills [Rich Margopoulos/Esteban Maroto, from the story by Nathaniel Hawthorne] 8p; (5) The Spook: Stumpful of Grandaddies! [Budd Lewis/Leopold Sanchez] 10p; (6) Exterminator One, part 2 [Bill DuBay/Paul Neary, color] 8p; (7) The Mummy Walks: Insanity! [Steve Skeates/Joaquin Blasquez] 10p; (8) Apocalypse: The Famine [Budd Lewis/Jose Ortiz] 12p.

Notes: This was $1.25 and an 80-page issue. Nice back cover by Ken Kelly of Exterminator One. An equally fine front cover by Sanjulian featuring *Night of the Jackass*. A very good issue with a beautiful adaptation of a Hawthorne story

This Manuel Sanjulian cover featured the best serial of *Eerie*'s run, the dark but masterful "Night of the Jackass!' by Bruce Bezaire and Jose Ortiz. © New Comic Co./used by permission.

by Margopoulos and Maroto, more fine installments of *Night of the Jackass* and *Apocalypse* and, thankfully, the end of the increasing silly *Mummy* series.

64. cover: Ken Kelly (March 1975)

(1) Cousin Eerie's Introduction [Bill DuBay/Berni Wrightson, frontis] 1p; (2) Night of the Jackass: The Children's Hour [Bruce Bezaire/Jose Ortiz] 10p; (3) Everything You Always Wanted to Know ... About the Comics!: The Story [Bill DuBay, text article] 1p; (4) Exterminator One, part 3 [Bill DuBay/Paul Neary] 8p; (5) The Butcher: Bye-Bye Miss American Dream [Bill DuBay/Richard Corben] 8p; (6)

Daddy and the Pie [Bill DuBay/Alex Toth] 8p; (7) The Spook: The Caul [Budd Lewis/Leopold Sanchez] 12p; (8) Apocalypse: The Plague [Budd Lewis/Jose Ortiz] 10p.

Notes: The Exterminator was cover featured again while the Eerie Eye feature page was dropped. The price reverted to $1.00 and the page count was at 72. Exterminator One and the Butcher concluded their series on high notes but the best story and art was the excellent "Daddy and the Pie," a story tailor-made for Toth's type of art. This 1930s-era story of a visiting alien encountering prejudice and racial hatred was a real winner. It was very popular with readers and a sequel was ordered although neither DuBay nor Toth had a hand in that.

65. Ken Kelly (April 1975)

(1) Cousin Eerie's Introduction [Bill DuBay/ Berni Wrightson, frontis] 1p; (2) Everything You Always Wanted to Know...About the Comics!: Lettering [Bill DuBay, text article] 1p; (3) Night of the Jackass: Endstorm! [Bruce Bezaire/Jose Ortiz] 10p; (4) The Hacker: The Hacker Is Back [Steve Skeates/Alex Toth] 10p; (5) The Spook and Crackermeyer: Coming Storm ... A Killing Rain! [Budd Lewis/Leopold Sanchez] 12p; (6) El Cid and the Troll! [Budd Lewis/Gonzalo Mayo] 8p; (7) Apocalypse: The Death [Budd Lewis/Jose Ortiz] 13p; (8) Presenting the 1974 Warren Awards [Bill DuBay, text article] 2p; (9) El Cid ad [Gonzalo Mayo, on the back cover] 1p.

Notes: The Spook is cover-featured. There was a new letters page logo. Both *Night of the Jackass"* and *Apocalypse* finished their runs. Both of them were great series. *The Hacker* returned in his first appearance since #57 with Toth replacing Sutton as the artist. El Cid, a fantasy look at the legendary character, was previewed with a short story before the next issue's El Cid special.

66. cover: Manuel Sanjulian (June 1975)

(1) Cousin Eerie's Introduction [Bill DuBay/ Berni Wrightson, frontis] 1p; (2) El Cid ... Our Recreated Legend! A Budd Lewis–Gonzalo Mayo First! [Bill DuBay/Gonzalo Mayo and Bill DuBay, text article on the letters page] ½ p; (3) El Cid: The Seven Trials [Bill DuBay and Budd Lewis/Gonzalo Mayo] 28p; (4) El Cid and the Vision [Gerry Boudreau and Budd Lewis/ Gonzalo Mayo] 8p; (5) El Cid: The Lady and

the Lie [Gerry Boudreau and Budd Lewis/ Gonzalo Mayo] 8p; (6) El Cid: The Emir of Aragon [Jeff Rovin and Budd Lewis/Gonzalo Mayo] 10p.

Notes: An El Cid special. Despite the ads telling of a book-length epic, this is actually a series of short stories gathered together. They're not bad stories, just not great. Mayo's artwork at this point was beautiful to look at, but his cluttered panels tended to obstruct the flow of the story.

67. cover: Manuel Sanjulian (August 1975)

(1) Cousin Eerie's Introduction [Bill DuBay/ Berni Wrightson, frontis] 1p; (2) Everything You Always Wanted to Know ... About the Comics!: The Art [Bill DuBay, text article] 1p; (3) Coffin: Death's Dark Curse [Budd Lewis/ Jose Ortiz] 10p; (4) Hunter II [Budd Lewis/Paul Neary] 11p; (5) The Hacker: The Hacker's Last Stand! [Steve Skeates/Alex Toth] 10p; (6) Papa Voodoo: The Man Named Gold! [Budd Lewis/ Leopold Sanchez] 12p; (7) Merlin: The Kingmaker [Budd Lewis/Esteban Maroto] 12p.

Notes: The Western horror hero Coffin returned. *The Hacker* concluded his run — quite nicely, too. "Papa Voodoo" was a sequel of sorts to "The Spook." *Hunter II* and *Merlin* debuted. In my opinion, *Hunter II* was a better serial than the much more popular *Hunter. Merlin* had fine art by Maroto but only appeared once more. Shame really, as it seemed like it had potential.

68. cover: Ken Kelly (September 1975)

(1) Everything You Always Wanted to Know ... About the Comics!: Production [Bill DuBay, text article] 1p; (2) Coffin: Half Walk [Budd Lewis/Jose Ortiz] 12p; (3) Hunter II: Goblin [Budd Lewis/Paul Neary] 10p; (4) Godeye! [Budd Lewis/Leopold Sanchez] 14p; (5) The Muck Monster [Berni Wrightson, color] 7p; (6) Deep Brown and Jorum [Jim Stenstrum/ Esteban Maroto] 12p; (7) Hunter II ad [Paul Neary, on the back cover] 1p.

Notes: The issue was $1.25 and 80 pages long. One of *Eerie's* best issues! A great *Hunter II* cover by Kelly gave a heads up to the great work within. An Exterminator robot popped up in *Hunter II* and remained for the rest of the series. Another good entry of Coffin, but the best stuff was new. A very funny "Godeye!" script managed a literary hat trick by being both cynical and warm-hearted. Wrightson's "The Muck

Monster" was Frankenstein's monster in all but name. Beautifully written and drawn, it's basically a tone poem that foreshadowed the type of work Alan Moore would do so well in *Swamp Thing*. It was supposed to be in B&W but at the last minute became a color section. Normally that would spell doom for the art but here the coloring was quite lovely. The colorist was uncredited but whoever he was did a great job. My favorite story, however, was Jim Stenstrum and Esteban Maroto's lusty, funny, sad and poignant "Deep Brown and Jorum." It told, in one story, the entire careers of a couple of rogues, who are similar to Fritz Leiber's Fafhrd and the Grey Mouser, with the first half of the story detailing their first meeting, then for four pages thereafter featuring two synopses per page of their many adventures together while along the top of each page (ala "Collector's Edition") their last adventure takes place, concluding in the last two pages. I reread it a couple minutes ago and that last page still chokes me up. "And together, they were LEGEND." Damn right.

69. cover: Manuel Sanjulian (October 1975)

(1) Hunter Pin-Up [Paul Neary, with a Berni Wrightson illustration of Cousin Eerie introducing the annual] 1p; (2) Hunter [pgs. 1–30; Rich Margopoulos, pgs 31–40; Budd Lewis, pgs. 41–58; Bill DuBay/Paul Neary; last 8 pages are in color, reprinted from *Eerie* #52–57 (November 1973–June 1974)] 58p.

Notes: The 1975 *Eerie* annual.

70. cover: Manuel Sanjulian (November 1975)

(1) Cousin Eerie's Introduction [Bill DuBay/Berni Wrightson, frontis] 1p; (2) Coffin: The Final Sunrise [Budd Lewis/Jose Ortiz] 14p; (3) Hunter II: Goblin Thrust [Budd Lewis/Paul Neary] 10p; (4) Code Name: Slaughter Five: From the Cradle to the Grave [Gerry Boudreau/Leopold Sanchez] 10p; (5) El Cid: Crooked Mouth [Budd Lewis/Gonzalo Mayo] 10p; (6) Oogie and the Junkers [Bill DuBay/Esteban Maroto] 8p.

Notes: As mentioned in my notes on *Creepy*, at this point Warren began to cut out frills. This issue was reduced to 64 pages and the letters page was cut to one page. Coffin headed into the West (literally) and El Cid made a return visit. "Code Name: Slaughter" would, from the title, seem to

have been intended as a series but from the ending, I've no idea how they could have continued it. Apparently they couldn't either, as this was its only appearance. *Oogie* began a lengthy run. Evidently this series was fairly popular, although I'm not quite sure why. The stories were rather run-of-the-mill SF and, with this story, Maroto departed from his own classic stylings and began using a scratchier, looser art line. This new style wasn't to my taste and, in my opinion, it often seemed to diminish the stories illustrated.

71. cover: Manuel Sanjulian (January 1976)

(1) Cousin Eerie's Introduction [Bill DuBay/Berni Wrightson, frontis] 1p; (2) Goblin [Budd Lewis/Jose Ortiz] 8p; (3) Hunter II: Time in Expansion [Budd Lewis/Paul Neary] 10p; (4) Irving and the Devilpie [Bill DuBay/Leopold Sanchez] 6p; (5) Pooter and the Magic Man [Bill DuBay/Luis Bermejo] 8p; (6) El Cid: Demon's Treasure [Budd Lewis/Gonzalo Mayo] 10p; (7) Mordecai Moondog [Bill DuBay/Esteban Maroto] 9p.

Notes: Not much series action in this issue with only Hunter II and El Cid making an appearance. The Goblin made his first appearance in what was clearly intended as a stand-alone story. The character was revived in 1982 in *The Rook* and received his own short-lived magazine later that year. The best story and art, however, was the DuBay/Maroto story "Mordecai Moondog."

72. cover: Manuel Sanjulian (February 1976)

(1) Cousin Eerie's Introduction [Bill DuBay/Berni Wrightson, frontis] 1p; (2) Cousin Eerie's Crypt [Louise Jones?, questionnaire] 1p; (3) The Demons of Jeremiah Cold aka Daddy Was a Demon Man [Bill DuBay/Jose Ortiz] 15p; (4) Hunter II: The Valley of Armageddon [Budd Lewis/Paul Neary] 10p; (5) Reuben Youngblood: Private Eye!: Beware the Scarlet Combine [Budd Lewis/Howard Chaykin and Berni Wrightson] 10p; (6) The Freaks: A Thin Dime of Pain [Doug Moench/Leopold Sanchez, color] 8p; (7) The Pie and I [Budd Lewis/Luis Bermejo] 9p; (8) Tales of Peter Hypnos: The Incredible People-Making Machines [Jose Bea] 8p.

Notes: This was $1.25 and 80 pages. Hunter II and the Exterminator made the cover. Future artist Ken Meyer Jr. sent in a letter as did future writer Stephen Perry. Reuben Youngblood, like

Chaykin's character Dominic Fortune for Marvel, was clearly a revamping of his Atlas/Seaboard character the Scorpion. All three variations on the character were good. A second Youngblood story was also done at this time but for some reason didn't appear until 1982! The Chaykin/Wrightson art team worked surprisingly well together. After the previous issue's lack of series, this issue made up for it by debuting three new ones. *The Freaks* was uninspired but Bea's *Peter Hypnos* series was quite interesting. "The Pie and I" was a sequel to the DuBay/Toth story "Daddy and the Pie" but wasn't nearly as good.

The Louise Jones Era

73. cover: Ken Kelly (March 1976)

(1) Hunter II: Death of the Phoenix [Budd Lewis/Paul Neary] 8p; (2) The Freaks: Carnival at Midnight [Budd Lewis/Leopold Sanchez] 10p; (3) Day of the Vampire 1992: The Tombspawn [Bill DuBay/Gonzalez Mayo] 10p; (4) It!: A Grave Terror Leads to Death! [Carl Wessler/Jose Gual] 10p; (5) Tales of Peter Hypnos: Voyage to the Final Hole [Jose Bea] 11p.

Notes: Hunter II and the Exterminator were again cover-featured. Back to $1.00 and 64 pages with James Warren listed as editor-in-chief and Louise Jones as assistant editor during her tryout period. Hunter II's series was concluded. It, the Dead Thing, took his final bow. Peter Hypnos again had the best story and art.

74. cover: Ken Kelly (May 1976)

(1) Cousin Eerie's Introduction [Louise Jones/Rafael Auraleon, frontis] 1p; (2) Warren Publishing Company Will Pay a $500 Reward... [James Warren, text article] 1p; (3) The Demons of Jedediah Pan [Bill DuBay/Jose Ortiz] 8p; (4) Father Creator [Bill DuBay/Paul Neary] 8p; (5) Merlin: A Secret King [Budd Lewis/Gonzalo Mayo] 20p; (6) The Expedition! [Budd Lewis/Leopold Sanchez] 10p; (6) Presenting the 1975 Warren Awards! [Bill DuBay, text article] 2p.

Notes: Jedediah Pan was cover featured, with a fine Kelly painting. Merlin made his second and final appearance with an extra-length story. Too bad, as both entries of his series were quite good. With only four stories this issue seemed rather slight.

75. cover: Jose Bea, panel from the interior story "Invasion" (June 1976)

(1) The Demons of Jeremiah Cold [Bill DuBay/Jose Ortiz] 12p; (2) The Freaks: The One Eyed Shall Be King! [Budd Lewis/Leopold Sanchez] 6p; (3) Oogie and the Worm! [Bill DuBay/Esteban Maroto] 10p; (4) Invasion [Esteban Maroto/Jose Bea, reprinted from *Dracula, Book One* (1972), story miscredited to Bea] 5p; (5) Gillian Taxi and the Sky Pirates [Budd Lewis/Luis Bermejo] 16p.

Notes: One of the crappiest-looking covers Warren published. It wasn't so much that Bea's artwork was bad, because it wasn't. It was the bizarre choice of hot pink surrounding the relatively small art panel, which made the cover look like an nasty Valentine card! This was the final appearance of *The Freaks*. Not surprising since, except for Sanchez's art, this series was a snooze. Warren generally had some of the best art reproduction in comics at the time but the reproduction on Bea's "Invasion" was noticeably substandard.

76. cover: Manuel Sanjulian (August 1976)

(1) The Moonweavers: Deliver the Child [Budd Lewis/Leopold Sanchez] 10p; (2) The Comic Books [Joe Brancatelli, text article] 1p; (3) Wolfer O'Connell: Highsong [Budd Lewis/Luis Bermejo] 8p; (4) Oogie and the Scroungers [Bill DuBay/Esteban Maroto] 13p; (5) Tales of Peter Hypnos: The Silver Key [Jose Bea] 9p; (6) Darklon the Mystic! [Jim Starlin] 8p.

Notes: Louise Jones was now listed as Senior Editor while Bill DuBay was listed as a contributing editor. The *Moonweavers* was a greatly improved spinoff from *The Freaks* series, with beautiful art by Sanchez. Wolfer O'Connel was a pretty good character who only appeared in two widely separated stories. The *Oogie* entry continued the downward trend of Maroto's art. Best stories and art would go to Jose Bea's *Peter Hypnos* entry and the debut of Jim Starlin's *Darklon*. *Darklon* was as close to a conventional superhero story as Warren had developed up to now. The company soon, however, made definite motions in that direction.

77. cover: Richard Corben (September 1976)

(1) Within You ... Without You [Bruce Jones/Richard Corben] 10p; (2) The Moonweavers:

The Gift [Budd Lewis/Leopold Sanchez] 10p; (3) Demons of Nob Hill [Bill DuBay/Jose Ortiz] 10p; (4) The Demons of Father Pain [Bill DuBay/Jose Ortiz, color] 8p; (5) The Comic Books [Joe Brancatelli, text article] 1p; (6) Oogie and the Lie [Bill DuBay/Esteban Maroto] 8p; (7) Cronk: Stalker in the Maze [Nicola Cuti/Carmine Infantino and Wayne Howard] 6p.

Notes: Richard Corben delivered a stunningly sexy cover. And it had dinosaurs, too! He and writer Bruce Jones' interior story was the best of a pretty good issue as well. Priced at $1.25 and 72 pages in length. The "Demons of Nob Hill" was apparently originally entitled "The King of Nob Hill!" This was the series finale for Jeremiah and Jedediah Pan. Maroto's art on *Oogie* was improved although the villain in the story appears lifted from a John Buscema villain that appeared in a *Tower of Shadows* story in 1969.

78. cover: montage of interior panels (October 1976)

(1) Cousin Eerie's Introduction [Louise Jones/ Berni Wrightson and Jaime Brocal, frontis, Brocal's art is from story panels] 1p; (2) The Mummy Walks: The Death of a Fiend [Steve Skeates/Jaime Brocal, reprinted from *Eerie* #49 (July 1973)] 10p; (3) The Mummy Walks: The Mind Within [Steve Skeates/Jaime Brocal, reprinted from *Eerie* #50 (August 1973)] 10p; (4) The Mummy Walks: Ghoulish Encounter [Steve Skeates/Jaime Brocal, reprinted from *Eerie* #52 (November 1973)] 10p; (5) The Mummy Walks: Enter Mr. Hyde [Steve Skeates/Jaime Brocal, reprinted from *Eerie* #53 (January 1974)] 10p; (6) The Mummy Walks: Stranger in a Village of the Insane [Steve Skeates/Jaime Brocal, reprinted from *Eerie* #54 (February 1974)] 10p; (7) The Mummy Walks: ...And an End [Steve Skeates/Jaime Brocal, color, two pages deleted, reprinted from *Eerie* #48 (June 1973)] 8p; (8) The Hope of the Future [Doug Moench/Jamie Brocal, reprinted from *Creepy* #57 (November 1973)] 8p; The Comic Books [Joe Brancatelli, text article] 1p.

Notes: The 1976 *Eerie* annual. It was $1.50 and 80 pages. Pretty much a fix-up collection of some of the original *Mummy* stories.

79. cover: Ken Kelly (November 1976)

(1) Time and Time Again [Bruce Jones/Richard Corben] 10p; (2) The Comic Books: Tarzan's Travails [Joe Brancatelli, text article] 1p; (3) The Pea-Green Boat [Budd Lewis/Leopold Sanchez] 8p; (4) Darklon the Mystic: The Price [Jim Starlin] 9p; (5) Third Person Singular [Bruce Jones/Luis Bermejo] 10p; (6) Sam's Son and Delilah! [Bruce Jones/Carmine Infantino and Al Milgrom] 14p.

Notes: This was $1.25 and 72 pages. Somewhat of a companion issue to *Creepy* #84's sports issue, as this one also featured a Ken Kelly sports cover and an interior sports story, both probably overflow from the *Creepy* issue. The Jones/Corben sequel to "Time and Again..." was very good. *The Pea-Green Boat* was a limp new series. "Third Person Singular" was also a rather limp effort, although for other reasons, as Warren explored homosexuality for the first time. Unfortunately, the story (concluded in the next issue) bordered on the idiotic and came with extreme stereotypes.

80. cover: Ken Kelly (January 1977)

(1) Scallywag: The Invisible One [Budd Lewis/ Jose Ortiz] 8p; (2) Darklon the Mystic: Retribution [Jim Starlin] 9p; (3) The Pea Green Boat: On Moonlight Bay [Budd Lewis/Leopold Sanchez] 8p; (4) Tombspawn: Pieces of Hate [Gerry Boudreau/Gonzalo Mayo] 8p; (5) Third Person Singular, part 2 [Bruce Jones/Luis Bermejo] 10p; (6) Cronk: Queen of the Purple Range [Nicola Cuti/Carmine Infantino and Al Milgrom] 8p.

Notes: Steve Perry, future comics and TV writer, and Wayne Faucher, future inker, sent in letters. If one could pick an artist for a strip set in the Orient, Jose Ortiz's name wouldn't be the first (or second or third) to come to mind. However, he did quite a respectable job on *Scallywag*. This was Cronk's last outing, although a third story by Cuti and Infantino was started, pages of which appear in *The Warren Companion*.

81. cover: Frank Frazetta (February 1977)

(1) And Now ... Introducing Exciting *Eerie* No. 81! [Louise Jones/Dick Giordano, Carmine Infantino, Bruce Jones, Leopoldo Duranona, et al., text article, frontis] 1p; (2) Goodbye, Bambi Boone [Cary Bates/Carmine Infantino and Dick Giordano] 8p; (3) The Comic Books: Less Is More [Joe Brancatelli, text article] 1p; (4) Taking of Queen Bovine [Gerry Boudreau/Ramon Torrents] 8p; (5) The Bride of Congo: The

Untold Story [Bill DuBay/Carmine Infantino and Gonzalo Mayo] 10p; (6) You're a Big Girl Now [Bruce Jones/Richard Corben, pages 2–9 in color] 10p; (7) Starchild [Louise Jones and David Michelinie/Jose Ortiz] 5p; (8) The Giant Ape Suit [Roger McKenzie/Luis Bermejo] 8p; (9) Golden Girl [Nicola Cuti/Leopold Sanchez] 8p.

Notes: Frazetta's cover, "Queen Kong," was painted in 1971 and was originally intended for Warren's never-published adult comic magazine, *POW!* Since the cover shows a giant naked woman holding a tiny King Kong on top of the Empire State Building, all the stories deal with a giant naked woman who ends up on top of the Empire State Building. Go ahead, folks, try getting eight good stories out of that concept. This issue was $1.50 and 80 pages in length. The frontis page included a brief bio and art portrait for each of the writers and artists in this issue. Some of the portraits were lifted from the Warren Awards illustrations, some from the old features page profiles and others appear to be new self-portraits. Fred Hembeck sent in a letter. The best story was easily the Jones/Corben "You're a Big Girl Now." The rest are only fair to middlin.'

82. cover: Bill DuBay and Luis Bermejo (March 1977)

(1) The Rook: The Man Whom Time Forgot! [Bill DuBay/Luis Bermejo] 20p; (2) The Comic Books [Joe Brancatelli, text article] 1p; (3) Tombspawn: And Now: The Game Is Afoot [Gerry Boudreau/Carmine Infantino and Gonzalo Mayo] 9p; (4) Scallywag: Castle of the Assassin [Budd Lewis/Jose Ortiz] 8p; (5) The Pea Green Boat: In a Deep Sea Tomb [Budd Lewis/Leopold Sanchez] 10p.

Notes: The cover was a fixup affair, showing DuBay's original presentation art for *The Rook*, along with inserts of interior panel art by Bermejo. Except for *Vampirella*, this was Warren's first open-ended continuing serial. Although *The Rook* was never a great series, it was occasionally quite good, especially in its first three or four episodes here in *Eerie* and the first three or four issues of his own title. Bermejo's art was quite lovely and DuBay's story was interesting, too. Later the silliness that drowned Vampi's series began showing up in this series as well. Although

Tombspawn's ending in this issue clearly signaled another episode, this was actually its finale. The third and concluding entry in the Jones/Corben time travel series was supposed to appear this issue but was a no-show. From this point on horror increasingly began taking a back seat in *Eerie*, with more and more stories being either science fiction or adventure-fantasy (although many of these stories had horror elements).

83. cover: Enrich Torres (May 1977)

(1) The Rook: The Day Before Tomorrow [Bill DuBay/Luis Bermejo] 20p; (2) The Comic Books [Joe Brancatelli, text article] 1p; (3) Hard John's Nuclear Hit Parade: Kansas City Bomber [Jim Stenstrum/Jose Ortiz] 10p; (4) Gaffer: Temptation [Roger McKenzie/Leopoldo Duranona] 9p; (5) Presto the Besto [Jim Stenstrum/Carmine Infantino and Dick Giordano] 8p.

Notes: *The Rook* made his second cover appearance in a row. The *Hard John* series was a continuation of the Hard John Apple story "An Angel Shy of Hell," which had appeared in *Creepy* #64, way back in 1974. The first story was great. The series was fair. Gaffer was another new series and not a bad one at all.

84. cover: Frank Frazetta (June 1977) reprinted from *Eerie* #8 (March 1967)

(1) The Rook Contest [Bill DuBay, contest rules on the letters page] ½ p; (2) The Comic Books [Joe Brancatelli, text article] 1p; (3) The Rook: Yesterday, the Final Day [Bill DuBay/Luis Bermejo] 22p; (4) Hard John's Nuclear Hit Parade: Brass Monkey [Jim Stenstrum/Jose Ortiz] 10p; (5) Godeye: Goodbye, Yellow Brick Rhode [Budd Lewis/Carmine Infantino and Dan Green] 8p; (6) He Who Waits in Shadow [Jim Starlin] 6p; (7) Presenting the 1977 Warren Awards [Louise Jones/Bill DuBay, et al., text article] 2p.

Notes: Page count dropped to 64 pages. *Godeye* returned, but this second story was nowhere near the delight the first one was. "He Who Waits in Shadow" was a gloomy metaphysical explanation by Starlin as to why the last *Darklon* chapter was late. *Darklon* gueststars on the last page and, although this story was included in the Darklon collection put out by Pacific Comics in 1983, this was not actually part of the *Darklon* serial. Rather, it's a tie-in or companion story. The

Warren Awards went to Richard Corben for best cover on *Eerie* #77 and best art on "In Deep"; best story to Bruce Jones for "In Deep," best cover artist to Ken Kelly, best all-around writer to Bill DuBay, best all-around artist to Leopold Sanchez, a special award for excellence to Jose Gonzalez and the Renaissance Man special award to Bill DuBay.

85. cover: Ken Kelly (August 1977)

(1) The Rook: Lost to the Land of Nowhen [Bill DuBay/Luis Bermejo] 14p; (2) The Comic Books [Joe Brancatelli, text article] 1p; (3) Hard John's Nuclear Hit Parade: Gonna Nuke Mankind Right Outa My Hair [Jim Stenstrum/Jose Ortiz] 10p; (4) Gaffer: First Wish [Roger McKenzie/Leopoldo Duranona] 11p; (5) Blackstar and the Night Huntress [Gerry Boudreau/Esteban Marato] 8p; (6) The Pea Green Boat: Dutchman [Budd Lewis/Leopold Sanchez] 8p.

Notes: Nice cover by Kelly of two of the Rook's supporting characters. Decent enough issue, although nothing really stood out. "Blackstar and the Night Huntress" had an extremely tacky sequel appear five years later.

86. cover: Richard Corben (September 1977)

(1) Unprovoked Attack on a Hilton Hotel [Jim Stenstrum/Richard Corben, reprinted from *Creepy* #73 (August 1975)] 8p; (2) The Comic Books: The Worst and the Dullest [Joe Brancatelli, text article] 1p; (3) 1984 ad [Joe Vaultz] 1p; (4)The Oval Portrait [Rich Margopoulos/Richard Corben, from the story by Edgar Allan Poe, reprinted from *Creepy* #69 (February 1975)] 8p; (5) Shadow [Rich Margopoulos/Richard Corben, from the story by Edgar Allan Poe, reprinted from *Creepy* #70 (April 1975)] 8p; (6) Pinball Wizard! [Doug Moench/Richard Corben, reprinted from *Creepy* #66 (November 1974)] 7p; (7) Change ... into Something Comfortable [Doug Moench/Richard Corben, reprinted from *Creepy* #58 (December 1973)] 8p; (8) The Slipped Mickey Click Flip [Doug Moench/Richard Corben, reprinted from *Creepy* #54 (July 1973)] 10p; (9) Friedhelm the Magnificent [Greg Potter/Richard Corben, reprinted from *Creepy* #46 (July 1972)] 8p; (10) Frozen Beauty [Richard Corben, reprinted from *Creepy* #36 (November 1970)] 6p.

Notes: The 1977 *Eerie* annual and a Richard Corben special. Considering all the stories were reprinted from *Creepy*, this probably should have

been a *Creepy* annual. The first *1984* ad appeared, long before the book had a title and almost a year before actual publication. The book was apparently in direct response to the first successful issue of *Heavy Metal*, which was cover-dated April 1977.

87. cover: Frank Frazetta (October 1977), reprinted from *Vampirella* #7 (September 1970)

(1) The Rook: Prisoner in a Chinese Fortune Cookie or: Bad, Bad Granny Gadget! [Bill DuBay/Luis Bermejo] 16p; (2) The Comic Books [Joe Brancatelli, text article] 1p; (3) Scallywag: The Black Demon's Sword [Budd Lewis/Jose Ortiz] 8p; (4) Years and Mind Forever [Bruce Jones/Richard Corben] 10p; (5) Gaffer: Second Wish [Roger McKenzie/Leopoldo Duranona] 14p; (6) The Incredible Illusions of Ira Israel [Roger McKenzie/Leopold Sanchez] 8p; (7) Hunter 3: What Price Oblivion? [Jim Stenstrum/Alex Nino] 8p.

Notes: It was $1.75 and 96 pages. *The Rook*'s story title was based on SF writer C. M. Kornbluth's "Ms. Found in a Chinese Fortune Cookie." The final segment of the Jones/Corbin time travel series appeared six months late. *Hunter 3* was a spoof of *Hunter* and *Hunter II*, not a serious continuation of nor a sequel to the first two series. Although he had contributed inks to several stories penciled by Carmine Infantino, Alex Nino made his solo Warren debut with the *Hunter 3* story, thus beginning the gradual change of the Spanish invasion from Spanish artists to the Filipino artists.

88. cover: Don Maitz (November 1977)

(1) The Rook: Future Shock [Bill DuBay/Luis Bermejo] 12p; (2) Announcing the Grand Prize Winners of the Fabulous Warren Rook Contest! [Louise Jones/Mark Stokes, Gary Goodman and Paul Daly, text article] 1p; (3) The Comic Books: A Matter of Dues [Joe Brancatelli, text article] 2p; (4) Scallywag: The Key [Budd Lewis/Jose Ortiz] 8p; (5) Deathball 2100 A.D. [Bill Mohalley and Nicola Cuti/Dick Giordano] 8p; (6) Boiling Point [Bruce Jones/Leopold Sanchez] 11p; (7) Junkyard Battles or Never Trust an Electric Shaver [Nicola Cuti/Rafael Auraleon] 8p; (8) Runner-Ups and More Finalists! [various, text article] 2p.

Notes: It was $1.50 and 72 pages. As they had done in the previous year, both *Creepy* and *Eerie* sported a sports cover for their final issue of the year, although only *Creepy*'s was completely dedicated to sports. *The Rook* contest had offered readers a chance to create a robot, villain and gadget for *The Rook* and see their creations used in a story. The villain creation — Quarb, by Gary Goodman — became an important part of *The Rook*'s ongoing storyline. For winning the contest, the creators got $100 and a three-year subscription to *Eerie*. Their creations would finally appear over a year later in *Eerie* #98. Future comic pros appearing in the finalist segment of the Rook Contest included Dan Reed, Nancy Collins, Steve Ringgenberg and Gordon Purcell. The *Scallywag* series title was replaced by the title *The Black Demon's Sword* for the duration of the series. I've decided to retain the original series title for clarity's sake.

89. cover: Malcolm McNeill (January 1978)

(1) The Rook: Trouble in the Time Factory [Bill DuBay/Luis Bermejo] 14p; (2) The Comic Books: Superman Versus Soccer [Joe Brancatelli, text article] 1p; (3) Crystabelle! [Bill DuBay/Leopoldo Duranona] 9p; (4) Francesca [Bruce Jones/Gonzalo Mayo] 10p; (5) Scallywag: The Magician's Tower [Budd Lewis/Jose Ortiz] 8p; (6) Boiling Point, part 2 [Bruce Jones/Leopold Sanchez] 10p.

Notes: There was a $1.25 cover price. New cover artist Malcolm McNeill did a number of fine covers for the Marvel B&Ws, particularly on *Planet of the Apes* and *The Deadly Hands of Kung Fu*, all under the name Malcolm McN. This was his only cover for Warren and that's a shame, really, as his dynamic art style and subtle use of shadows would have worked perfectly for the magazines. Bermejo's art began looking more and more rushed and, thus, more generic, probably due to the large number of pages he was doing for Warren. "Francesca" saw a return to the less ornate art style that Mayo had showcased before. It's quite attractive and this two-parter (with the second part skipping an issue) was a superior story. Bruce Jones, who wrote "Francesca," also concluded his "Boiling Point," which was another excellent little story. Looking at Ortiz's artwork here, I wonder why no one at Marvel ever got him to contribute either inks or full artwork to the *Conan* or *Kull* series. His art-

work would have been a welcome change of pace there.

90. cover: Richard Corben (February 1978)

(1) Carrion [Gerry Boudreau/Gonzalo Mayo] 8p; (2) The Show Must Go On! [Roger McKenzie/Leopoldo Duranona] 6p; (3) A Woman Scorned [Bruce Jones/Richard Corben, color] 8p; (4) The Fianchetto Affair or: A Matter of Great Delicacy [Bob Toomey/Jose Ortiz] 8p; (5) The Comic Books: Patent Medicine Profits? [Joe Brancatelli, text article] 1p; (6) The Rook: What Is the Color of Nothingness? [Bill DuBay/Alex Nino] 20p.

Notes: It had a $1.50 cover price. With the exception of the Rook story, all the stories in this issue centered around the Corben cover which featured a girl reclining on a giant gila monster. An additional story on the same idea appeared in *Creepy* at the same time. The Jones/Corben story was the best of that bunch. It's quite a good effort although the coloring, unlike most of the Corben stories done in color, does not appear to have been done by Corben himself. The *Rook* story was probably the best since his first four appearances, with dazzling artwork by Nino and a pretty sharp time travel story by DuBay. The *Rook* story was also printed sideways.

91. cover: Don Maitz (March 1978)

(1) The Rook: The Incredible Sagas of Sludge the Unconquerable, Helga the Damned, and Marmadrake the Magnificent! [Bill DuBay/Luis Bermejo] 20p; (2) The Comic Books: Kiss and Tell [Joe Brancatelli, text article] 1p; (3) Elijah Arnold and the Angel's Egg [Jonathan Thomas/Leopoldo Duranona] 8p; (4) Francesca, Part 2 [Bruce Jones/Gonzalo Mayo] 10p; (5) Moonshadow: Against the Sun [Bob Toomey/Jose Ortiz] 8p; (6) Presenting the 1977 Warren Awards [Louise Jones/Frank Frazetta, Bruce Jones, Bill DuBay, Alex Nino, et al., text article] 2p; (7) 1984 ad [Richard Corben, on the back cover, a reproduction of #1's cover] 1p.

Notes: There was $1.25 cover price. One of Maitz's best covers for Warren featured a giant troll lifting a tiny man to his mouth while a lady, very much in distress, runs for her life. The gothic story "Francesca" concluded, and quite nicely. *Moonshadow*, a fairly decent new series, debuted. Members of the Christian right sent in letters complaining of Warren's use of nudity, a perceived lack of morality, and Warren's continued use of evolution as a plot device. Nothing ever really changes, does it?

92. cover: Kim McQuaite (May 1978) [concept by Bill Mohalley]

(1) Cold Sweat [Bill DuBay/ Jose Ortiz] 8p; (2) The Comic Books: Safe at Home? [Joe Brancatelli], text article 1p; (3) The Rook: Strangers in the Strangest Places! [Bill DuBay/Axel Laxamana] 10p; (4) Let's Hear It for Homo Sapiens [Gerry Boudreau/ Rafael Auraleon] 8p; (5) Moonshadow: Suzanna, Don't You Cry [Bob Toomey/ Jose Ortiz] 8p; (6) Abelmar Jones: Bad Day 'Cross 100th Street [Bill DuBay/Alex Nino] 5p; (7) Gaffer: Final Wish [Roger McKenzie/ Leopoldo Duranona] 9p.

Notes: This sports cover, featuring hockey, and the accompanying story, "Cold Sweat," may have been originally intended for the never-published third all-sports special for *Creepy*. "Let's Hear It for Homo Sapiens" was an overflow story from *Creepy* #95's all-apes special issue. Marvel's Man-Thing made a cameo appearance in one panel on page one of that story. Abelmar Jones made his series debut as Warren tried to get hip with the urban crowd. The Gaffer returned for his finale, after being absent since #87. Bermejo began taking an extended breather from the *Rook* strip, with a series of different artists filling in.

93. cover: Don Maitz (June 1978)

(1) The Rook: Strangers in the Strangest Places, part 2 [Bill DuBay/Alfredo Alcala [pgs 1–2] and Abel Laxamana [pgs 3–11] 12p; (2) The Comic Books: Classics Illustrated R.I.P. [Joe Brancatelli, text article] 1p; (3) Honor and Blood [Nicola Cuti/Leopoldo Duranona] 10p; (4)

This interesting vampire scene is an early effort by acclaimed SF/fantasy artist Don Maitz, from *Eerie* #93. © New Comic Co./ used by permission.

Moonshadow: Kingdom of Ash [Bob Toomey/ Jose Ortiz] 8p; (5) The Einstein Factor [Pepe Moreno and Nicola Cuti/Pepe Moreno] 10p; (6) Abelmar Jones: The Slime Creature of Harlem Avenue [Bill DuBay/Alex Nino] 8p.

Notes: This vampire cover was probably Maitz's best cover for Warren. A very striking image. It illustrated the fine new series *Honor and Blood*, with story by Cuti and art by Duranona. Easily the best work here.

94. cover: Don Maitz (August 1978)

(1) The Rook: The Coming of the Annihilator [Bill DuBay/Luis Bermejo] 12p; (2) The Comic Books: Still More Kiss [Joe Brancatelli, text

article] 1p; (3) Honor and Blood, part 2 [Nicola Cuti/Leopoldo Duranona] 8p; (4) Dead Man's Ship [Nicola Cuti/Isidro Mones] 8p; (5) Divine Wind [Louise Jones and Budd Lewis/Esteban Maroto] 6p; (6) Don't Drink the Water [Gerry Boudreau/Martin Salvador] 8p; (7) Bruce Bloodletter of the IRS [Bill DuBay and Fernando Fernandez/Fernando Fernandez] 8p.

Notes: A good Maitz cover for a better than average issue. Future Eclipse Comics editor Cat Yronwode sent in a letter. *Vampirella* and Pantha guest-starred in the *Rook* story, which took place directly after the Vampi story published six months earlier in *Vampirella* #66. Fernando Fernandez's educational series on taxes featuring Bruce Bloodletter had been done several years previously. Here, Bill DuBay wrote an entirely new script, turning this into a science-fantasy tale. Best story was "Dead Man's Ship," although "Don't Drink the Water" was also good. Best art was Maroto's from "Divine Wind." The writer or writers for that story were not listed. The credits I've given it come from the author list on the title page. I assume that Jones didn't write the story on her own since at this point in her career she usually didn't receive solo writing credits on her stories.

95. cover: Jordi Penalva (September 1978)

(1) The Rook: Warriors from the Stars [Bill DuBay/Luis Bermejo] 12p; (2) The Comic Books: Death by the Numbers [Joe Brancatelli, text article] 1p; (3) Willie's Super-Magic Basketball [Jim Stenstrum/Carmine Infantino and Rudy Nebres] 8p; (4) Abelmar Jones: Faster than a Speeding Whozit [Bill DuBay/Alex Nino] 8p; (5) Nuts! [Nicola Cuti/Pablo Marcos, color] 8p; (6) Harrow House [Bruce Jones/Jose Ortiz] 10p; (7) Mac Tavish: Caucus on Rara Avis [Jim Stenstrum/Pepe Moreno, story credited to Alabaster Redzone] 10p.

Notes: There was a $1.50 cover price. Penalva received a huge amount of praise for his covers but I've never quite seen the reason why. The aura of mystery essential for a horror or mystery title just is not there. Vampi and Pantha again guest-starred in the *Rook* strip. Vampi also shared the cover with the Rook. "Harrow House" was a fine ghost story. Unfortunately, it was split in two with the second half not appearing for another six months! This started to be the norm

for a Warren serial. Two or three or more episodes in a row, then a long wait until the concluding episodes appeared. "Willie's Super-Magic Basketball" was originally intended for the never-published third all-sports stories special for *Creepy*. "Nuts" was a rather cute story but the coloring was simply dreadful. Stenstrum often used the penname "Alabaster Redzone" when he was adapting European stories into English or working from another writer's plot. If that was the case here, the original author is unknown, although it may have been the artist Pepe Moreno's solo work.

96. Cover: Jordi Penalva (October 1978)

(1) Fallen Angels: Revenge [Guillermo Saccomano and Cary Bates/Leopoldo Duranona] 7p; (2) Fallen Angels: The Cutman [Guillermo Saccomano and Cary Bates/Leopoldo Duranona] 9p; (3) Fallen Angels: Explosive Issue [Guillermo Saccomano and Cary Bates/Leopoldo Duranona] 14p; (4) The Comic Books: What Hath Congress Wrought? [Joe Brancatelli, text article] 1p; (5) Mac Tavish: Hero of Zodiac V [Jim Stenstrum/Pepe Moreno] 10p; (6) The Ark [Roger McKenzie/Carmine Infantino and Walt Simonson] 8p; (7) The Shining Sea [Nicola Cuti/Alfredo Alcala] 10p.

Notes: This had a $1.75 cover price with 88 pages. Mac Tavis was cover-featured. All three *Fallen Angels* episodes probably appeared in South America or Europe before their appearance here. The artwork was dated 1976. All three stories were quite good crime tales, reminding one a bit of Frank Miller's *Sin City* stories. Mac Tavish was an average SF serial for the *Star Wars* period. There were no credits for this story but it's safe to assume that Stenstrum would have been billed as Alabaster Redzone again if there were. The Cuti/Alcala story "The Shining Sea" was an okay story but putting a dolphin's head on top of a human body resulted in one of the silliest-looking critters that Warren ever put into print.

97. cover: Val Mayerik (November 1978)

(1) Within You ... Without You [Bruce Jones/Richard Corben, reprinted from *Eerie* #77 (September 1976)] 10p; (2) Time and Time Again [Bruce Jones/Richard Corben, reprinted from *Eerie* #79 (November 1976)] 10p; (3) Years and

Mind Forever [Bruce Jones/Richard Corben, reprinted from *Eerie* #87 (October 1977)] 10p; (4) The Comic Books: Roll Over, Brancatelli [Joe Brancatelli, text article] 1p; (5) The Terror Beyond Time! [Archie Goodwin/Neal Adams, reprinted from *Creepy* #15 (June 1967)] 16p.

Notes: This issue was $1.25 for 64 pages. The 1978 *Eerie* annual. Nicola Cuti replied on the letters page to a previous letter by a Rick Berry, defending the science in one of his stories. The nudity in the Jones/Corben time travel serial had been largely censored since its first appearances. Exactly why is unclear, since Warren was publishing the far more raunchy *1984* at the same time.

98. cover: Patrick Woodroffe (January 1979)

(1) The Rook: Quarb and the Warball [Bill DuBay/Luis Bermejo] 31p; (2) The Comic Books: Notes on Comix People! [Joe Brancatelli, text article] 1p; (3) Got You on My Mind [Bruce Jones/Russ Heath] 12p; (4) Honor and Blood, part 3 [Nicola Cuti/Leopoldo Duranona] 8p.

Notes: *Honor and Blood*, unseen since #94, concluded its run. The *Rook* story uses all of the Rook contest winner creations in a single lengthy story.

99. cover: Jordi Penalva (February 1979)

(1) The Rook: Hickey and the Pirates! [Bill DuBay/Jose Ortiz] 20p; (2) The Comic Books: The Party [Joe Brancatelli, text article] 1p; (3) The Horizon Seekers [Leopoldo Duranona and Cary Bates/Leopoldo Duranona] 11p; (4) The Shining Sea, part 2 [Nicola Cuti/Alfredo Alcala] 10p; (5) Harrow House, part 2 [Bruce Jones/Jose Ortiz] 10p; (6) A Crack in Time [Louise Jones/Pablo Marcos] 8p.

Notes: There was a $1.50 cover price. The *Rook* was cover-featured. An ad for *Eerie* #100 featured art from the various intended stories and appeared on the letters page. A Laura Duranona from Central Islip, NY, sent in a letter praising Leopoldo Duranona's work. Duranona himself began his best serial for Warren with "The Horizon Seekers." "The Shining Sea" was another tale of the goofy-looking dolphin-headed folk. "Harrow House" was a great ghost story, the best in the issue. Louise Jones picks up her first solo writing credit.

100. cover: Jordi Penalva (April 1979)

(1) The Rook: Master of Ti Chi [Bill DuBay/Jimmy Janes and Alfredo Alcala] 30p; (2) The Comic Books: Going for the Bucks [Joe Brancatelli, text article] 1p; (3) Presenting the 1978 Warren Awards [Louise Jones/et al., text article] 2p; (4) Gotterdammerung [Budd Lewis/Isidro Mones] 10p; (5) The Horizon Seekers: In a Strange Land [Leopoldo Duranona and Cary Bates/Leopoldo Duranona] 8p; (6) Darklon the Mystic: Duel [Jim Starlin] 13p.

Notes: It was $2.00 and 88 pages in length. The cover depicted a number of characters who'd starred in serials in *Eerie* including the Rook, Coffin, the Spook, Exterminator One, Darklon, Dax and Hunter II. On the letters page, Bob Toomey replied to a previous Nicola Cuti letter. After not appearing in a story of his own since #80, three years previously, Darklon returned to conclude his serial. Easily the best story here, so it was too bad that it took so long to finish it off. Still, this was a rather lackluster 100th issue, with much of the issue given over to a substandard *Rook* episode.

101. cover: Jim Lauier (June 1979)

(1) The Rook: The Martians Are Coming, The Martians Are Coming! [Bill DuBay/Jim Starlin and Alfredo Alcala] 18p; (2) Gotterdammerung!, part 2 [Budd Lewis/Isidro Mones] 10p; (3) The Horizon Seekers, part 3 [Leopoldo Duranona and Cary Bates/Leopoldo Duranona] 12p; (4) The Comic Books: The Inevitable Superman Story [Joe Brancatelli, text story] 1p; (5) Hunter II: Three Flames of the Phoenix [Budd Lewis/Pepe Moreno] 13p.

Notes: This had a $1.75 cover price and 72 pages. A quite blah cover by Lauier headlined a rather blah issue with only *The Horizon Seekers* episode showing any real spark. Alcala's inks erased any sense of Starlin's pencils on the *Rook* strip. Moreno's artwork on the new standalone *Hunter II* script was quite good but the time or desire for a sequel to the original serial had long since passed.

102. cover: Manuel Sanjulian (July 1979)

(1) The Rook: Terror of the Spaceways! [Bill DuBay/Lee Elias] 12p; (2) The Comic Books: So Much for Traditions [Joe Brancatelli, text article] 1p; (3) The Horizon Seekers: Siege [Leopoldo Duranona and Cary Bates/Leopoldo

Duranona] 9p; (4) The Earthquake Stick [Budd Lewis/Jose Ortiz] 10p; (5) Ophiophobia [Bill DuBay/Martin Salvador] 8p; (6) Tracks [Roger McKenzie/Pepe Moreno] 7p; (7) Neatness Counts [Jean Michel Martin/Joe Vaultz] 4p.

Notes: This issue cost $1.50. Sanjulian returned for his first *Eerie* cover in 3 years but someone appears to have stripped the background out and the cover is an odd combo of Sanjulian's earthy tones in the foreground and a flat white background. *The Horizon Seekers* is cover featured. The best story here is "Tracks" by the team of McKenzie and Moreno. "Ophiophobia" by DuBay and Salvador is a throwback to the old horror-oriented *Eerie* that is quite satisfying as well. The best art is by comics' master Lee Elias on the *Rook* story.

103. cover: Terrence Lindall (August 1979)

(1) The Rook: Terror of the Spaceways!, part 2 [Bill DuBay/Lee Elias] 16p; (2) The Comic Books: The Corporate Mad [Joe Brancatelli, text article] 1p; (3) The Open Sky: Arianne [Bob Toomey/Jose Ortiz] 10p; (4) The Trespasser [Don McGregor/Paul Gulacy] 8p; (5) Samurai: Credentials [Larry Hama/Val Mayerik] 8p; (6) The Horizon Seekers: The Damned and The Dead [Leopoldo Duranona and Cary Bates/Leopoldo Duranona] 17p.

Notes: It had a $1.75 cover price and 80 pages. Terrence Lindall's grisly cover was for *The Horizon Seekers*. Several of the pages in *The Rook* were reprinted from the previous issue. Clearly "Terror of the Spaceways!" had been intended as a single story that had been cut in two for publication. The new serial *The Open Sky* was a prequel to an earlier series, *Moonshadow*. The lead character in "The Trespasser" was based on actor James Coburn. "Credentials" was a sequel to "The Art of Murder" from *Creepy* #106. *The Warren Companion* gave the series the title *Samurai* but that title doesn't actually show up until #108's title page and doesn't appear on a story until #111. After its abrupt, incomplete ending in *Eerie* #111, the series was revived in 1987–1989 (with Chuck Dixon replacing Larry Hama on scripts) for an independent comic publisher under the title *Young Master*. Whatever title you give it, it was a fairly good series, nicely drawn and written and clearly based upon the then

largely unknown Japanese classic, *Lone Wolf and Cub*.

104. cover: Kirk Reinert (September 1979)

(1) The Rook: The Trouble with Tin Men [Bill DuBay/Jimmy Janes and Alfredo Alcala] 11p; (2) The Comic Books: Still Collecting After All These Years [Joe Brancatelli, text article] 1p; (3) The Trespasser: Dusk [Don McGregor/Paul Gulacy] 8p; (4) City of Shadows [Jean Michel Martin/Leopoldo Duranona] 6p; (5) Beastworld [Bruce Jones/Pablo Marcos] 11p; (6) The Rook ad [Rudy Nebres] 2p; (7) The Open Sky: Vladimir [Bob Toomey/Jose Ortiz] 10p; (8) The Horizon Seekers: Temple of the Ravagers [Leopoldo Duranona and Cary Bates/Leopoldo Duranona] 10p.

Notes: The new serial, *Beastworld*, was cover-featured. It was a decent enough, if not profound, battle-of-the-sexes serial. "City of Shadows" was a fumetti strip with Duranona using photos of toys and action figures for the panels.

105. cover: Jordi Penalva (October 1979)

(1) The Rook: Robot Fighters [Bill DuBay/Jimmy Janes and Alfredo Alcala] 16p; (2) The Rook ad [Pablo Marcos and Alfredo Alcala] 1p; (3) The Comic Books: Still Collecting after All These Years [Joe Brancatelli, text article, reprinted from *Eerie* #104 (September 1979)] 1p; (4) The Trespasser: Ruins [Don McGregor/Paul Gulacy] 6p; (5) Beastworld, part 2 [Bruce Jones/Pablo Marcos] 11p; (6) Mac Tavish: Demons of the Zodiac [Gary Null and Jim Stenstrum/Pepe Moreno, Gary Null was Bob Toomey, Strenstrum's contribution credited to Alabaster Redzone] 10p; (7) The Horizon Seekers: Hunger Strike [Leopoldo Duranona and Cary Bates/Leopoldo Duranona] 7p; (8) Samurai: Lair of the Assassins [Larry Hama/Val Mayerik] 8p.

Notes: Following this issue, the Rook moved to his own action-adventure series, which ran from 1979 to 1982. In addition to some fine *Rook* stories, that series featured excellent work by Alex Toth, Alfredo Alcala, Don MacGregor, John Severin, Lee Elias and more. It's a title well worth looking for. In what one would hope was an error, the Brancatelli column for the previous issue was reprinted in this issue. *The Trespasser* concluded its run, with fine art by Gulacy coupled with a somewhat overwrought script by McGregor. Mac Tavis reappeared, with his newest episode coming a full year after his last appearance. To celebrate, he appeared on the cover, with new supporting character Spider Andromeda. *Samurai* continued to ape *Lone Wolf and Cub*, right up to the main villain in this story receiving an arrow wound to the same eye that the main villain in *Lone Wolf* did. They're also dead ringers for each other.

106. cover: Jose Ortiz and Walt Simonson (November 1979)

(**1**) Hard John Apple: An Angel Shy of Hell! [Jim Stenstrum/Richard Corben, reprinted from *Creepy* #64 (August 1974)] 8p; (**2**) The Comic Books: The Comic-Book Grapevine [Joe Brancatelli, text article] 1p; (**3**) Hard John Apple: Kansas City Bomber [Jim Stenstrum/Jose Ortiz, reprinted from *Eerie* #83 (May 1977)] 10p; (**4**) Hard John Apple: Brass Monkey [Jim Stenstrum/Jose Ortiz, reprinted from *Eerie* #84 (June 1977)] 10p; (**5**) Hard John Apple: Gonna Nuke Mankind Right Outa My Hair [Jim Stenstrum/Jose Ortiz, reprinted from *Eerie* #85 (August 1977)] 10p; (**6**) The Super-Abnormal Phenomena Survival Kit [Jim Stenstrum/John Severin, reprinted from *Creepy* #79 (May 1976)] 8p.

Notes: This one cost $1.50 and had 64 pages. The 1979 *Eerie* annual. A Jim Stenstrum special. The cover for this issue was a fix-up job. Jose Ortiz's drawing of Hard John Apple was reprinted from a panel from *Eerie* #83 while Walt Simonson provided a new background.

107. cover: Romas Kukalis (December 1979)

(**1**) The Horizon Seekers: The Last Horizon [Leopoldo Duranona and Cary Bates/Leopoldo Duranona] 14p; (**2**) The Comic Books: Lies Our Forefathers Told Us [Joe Brancatelli, text article] 1p; (**3**) Beastworld, part 3 [Bruce Jones/Pablo Marcos] 11p; (**4**) Mac Tavish: Bad Company [Jim Stenstrum and Alex Sothern/Pepe Moreno, Stenstrum's contribution is credited to Alabaster Redzone] 10p; (**5**) The Prophesy [Bill Kelly/Nestor De Leon] 10p.

Notes: The cost of $1.35 was a rather odd price for 64 pages. For the first and only time in Warren history, a supporting character, Spider Andromeda from the Mac Tavish strip, was cover-featured. Duranona and his wife both guest-star as themselves in the finale of *The Horizon Seekers*. It was a rather nice *Twilight Zone*–style touch.

108. cover: Jim Laurier (January 1980)

(**1**) A Lion in our Midst [Nicola Cuti/Jess Jodloman] 15p; (**2**) The Comic Books: Notes on Comix People [Joe Brancatelli, text article] 1p; (**3**) Beastworld, part 4 [Bruce Jones/Pablo Marcos] 11p; (**4**) Samurai: A Juggler's Tale [Larry Hama/Val Mayerik] 10p; (**5**) Race of the Damned [Norman Mundy and Cary Bates/Joe Vaultz] 7p; (**6**) Growing Pains [Bob Toomey/ Mike Zeck] 8p.

Notes: This had a $1.50 cover price with 72 pages. Lauier's lackluster cover featured "Beastworld." General Walters, a character in "A Lion in Our Midst" was a dead ringer for Marvel's Nick Fury. Mike Zeck provided the best art in this issue, although Val Mayerik and Pablo Marcos were quite good, too. Best story was the *Samurai* episode, "A Juggler's Tale" while "Growing Pains" was a good little horror tale.

109. cover: Kirk Reinert (February 1980)

(**1**) Blood on Black Satin [Doug Moench/Paul Gulacy] 16p; (**2**) 1979 Warren Awards Ballot [Louise Jones, text article] 1p; (**3**) Beastworld, part 5 [Bruce Jones/Pablo Marcos] 11p; (**4**) The Comic Books: Some Thoughts on What Has Gone Before [Joe Brancatelli, text article] 1p; (**5**) Race of the Damned, part 2 [Norman Mundy and Cary Bates/Joe Vaultz] 7p; (**6**) Samurai: Fugue State [Larry Hama/Val Mayerik] 8p; (**7**) Mac Tavish: The End of the Steel Gang [Jim Stenstrum and Alex Southern/Pepe Moreno, Stenstrum's contribution credited to Alabaster Redzone] 12p.

Notes: It had a $2.00 cover price with 80 pages. This month's cover also featured "Beastworld" but, unlike the dreary cover from the issue before, Reinert's effort was quite striking. *Blood on Black Satin* was probably Doug Moench's best effort at Warren and would have made a great Hammer film script. Gulacy's moody artwork was perfect for the story and makes one wish he'd done more horror work. This story was easily the best effort in an issue that had no weak episodes at all.

110. cover: Jim Laurier (April 1980)

(**1**) Blood on Black Satin, part 2 [Doug Moench/Paul Gulacy] 8p; (**2**) The Comic Books: Building a New Marvel [Joe Brancatelli, text article] 1p; (**3**) Beastworld, part 6 [Bruce Jones/Pablo Marcos] 11p; (**4**) The Open Sky:

Francois [Bob Toomey/Jose Ortiz] 10p; (5) Firefly/Starfight [Budd Lewis/Rafael Auraleon] 10p; (6) The Rainmaker [Michael Fleisher/ Leopoldo Duranona] 12p; (7) Never Again [James Warren, editorial, on the back cover] 1p.

Notes: This issue had a $1.75 cover price with 72 pages. The Jim Laurier cover was supposedly for the "Firefly/Starfight" story but the space-ships he painted looked a lot more like Joe Vaultz's earlier designs for the *Race of the Damned* serial's starfighters than anything in the "Firefly"

story. Unseen since #104, *The Open Sky* returned to conclude its storyline. The absence of *Samurai* was due to an injury to Val Mayerik's drawing hand. *Beastworld* concluded. Not a great serial, but at least interesting. Best story here was Michael Fleisher's "The Rainmaker" while best art remained Paul Gulacy's *Blood on Black Satin*.

The Decline and Fall

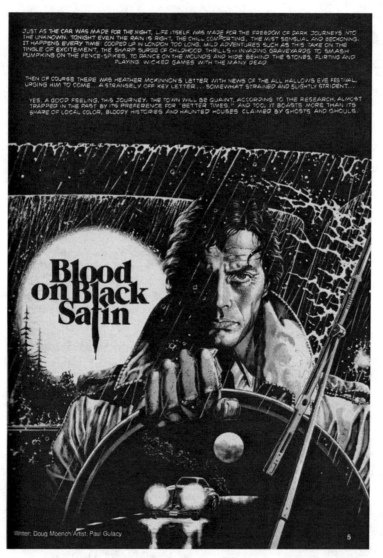

Don Moench and Paul Gulacy's "Blood on Black Satin" was the last great serial to run in *Eerie*. This Hammer Film–like effort featured detailed noir artwork by Gulacy. © New Comic Co./used by permission.

111. cover: Ken Kelly (June 1980)

(1) Blood on Black Satin, part 3 [Doug Moench/Paul Gulacy] 12p; (2) Moto Psycho Cop [Nicola Cuti/John Garcia and Rudy Nebres] 8p; (3) Samurai: The Messenger [Larry Hama/Val Mayerik] 8p; (4) Mac Tavish: 50 Million Spacemen Can't be Wrong [Jim Stenstrum/Pepe Moreno] 12p; (5) Haxtur: Beware of Glahb [Victor de la Fuente] 12p.

Notes: Editor: Bill DuBay as Will Richardson. *Blood on Black Satin* concluded. Along with *Night of the Jackass*, probably the best straight horror serial *Eerie* ever ran. *Samurai* also ended its run quite abruptly (with its ending seemingly telegraphed by the dialogue in the last panel), not to be seen again until 1987 from the team of Chuck Dixon and Val Mayerik. *Mac Tavish*, a solid, if not spectacular, serial also concluded its lengthy run. The sword and sorcery strip *Haxtur* was brought over from *1984/ 1994* after two appearances there. Both Bob Toomey and Don McGregor have mentioned Jim Warren instituting a freeze on the purchase of new stories that began in December 1979 and apparently extended for quite some time. Within weeks after the freeze editor Louise Jones left Warren for Marvel, replaced by Bill DuBay. Later Warren editors complained bitterly of having to use up a massive inventory of stories that Jones had purchased. This story freeze may account for the abrupt ending of the *Samurai* serial. Certainly some of Warren's best writers at the time vanished from its pages.

112. cover: Ken Kelly (July 1980)

(1) The Spook: Stridspider Sponge-Rot [Doug Moench/Esteban Maroto, reprinted from *Eerie* #57 (June 1974)] 10p; (2) Luana [Doug Moench/ Esteban Maroto, reprinted from *Vampirella* #31 (March 1974)] 13p; (3) The Rook ad [Bob Larkin, B&W reproduction of #3's cover] 1p; (4) Enter: The Exterminator — They Shoot Babies, Don't They? [Bill DuBay/Esteban Maroto, reprinted from *Eerie* #58 (July 1974)] 8p; (5) Rusty Bucklers [Bruce Jones/Esteban Maroto, reprinted from *Vampirella* #57 (January 1977)] 8p; (6) Hollow of Three Hills! [Rich Margopoulos/Esteban Maroto, from the story by Nathaniel Hawthorne, reprinted from *Eerie* #63 (February 1975), adaptation miscredited to Bill DuBay] 8p; (7) Fallen Angels [Bill DuBay/ Esteban Maroto, reprinted from *Vampirella* #60 (May 1977)] 8p; (8) The 1979 Warren Awards [Bill DuBay, text article] 2p.

Notes: All-reprint issue. An Esteban Maroto special. *The Spook* was cover-featured. Although the reprints are of high quality, it would probably have been better to use this issue to present all the *Spook* episodes.

113. cover: Jim Laurier (August 1980)

(1) Cousin Eerie's Introduction [Bill DuBay/ Jose Ortiz and Berni Wrightson] 1p; (2) The Manifestation [Budd Lewis and Bill DuBay/ E. R. Cruz, DuBay's contribution credited to Will Richardson] 25p; (3) Code Name: Nova [John Garcia and Bill DuBay/John Garcia and Alfredo Alcala, DuBay's story credited to Will Richardson, with no mention of Garcia's contributions to story or art] 16p; (4) Haxtur and the Slow Death God! [Victor de la Fuente] 12p.

Notes: This issue had a $2.00 cover price with 72 pages. The Cousin Eerie intro page was a fixup effort, with Ortiz's art reprinted from the 1978 Warren Calendar and Wrightson's Cousin Eerie figure coming from one of his stock introduction poses. Although *Creepy* and *Vampirella*

continued as quality publications for some time after DuBay took over for his second stint as editor, *Eerie* almost immediately settled into mediocrity — featuring second-rate artists and writers creating deadly dull stories. Few of the new serials to come in the next three years would generate any excitement. This issue shows exactly why. "The Manifestation" wasn't a bad story, but Cruz's static art robbed it of any real excitement. "Code Name: Nova" was just boring. The *Haxtur* story was okay but its move from sister magazine *1994* meant that many *Eerie* readers hadn't seen the first two episodes and it was hard to get excited about a serial midpoint through its run. In addition, this serial dated from 1971 and while it was a good story and probably provided a lot of excitement in Europe when it first appeared, readers had had the opportunity since then to read hundreds of sword and sorcery stories. By the time *Haxtur* finally appeared in the U.S., he just seemed run of the mill.

114. cover: Manuel Sanjulian (September 1980)

(1) Star Warrior! [David Jacobs/A. L. Sanchez] 31p; (2) The Executioners [Carlos Gimenez] 12p; (3) Haxtur: Panthers, Wolves and Death! [Victor de la Fuente] 12p.

Notes: This issue cost $1.75. Sanjulian delivered a decent *Haxtur* cover while "The Executioners" was a well-written, well-drawn SF thriller. "Star Warrior!," however, was a total dud on all levels. Berni Wrightson provided a new Cousin Eerie illustration for the letters page.

115. cover: Jim Laurier (October 1980)

(1) Night of the Jackass: 24 Hours of Hell! [Bruce Bezaire/Jose Ortiz, reprinted from *Eerie* #60 (September 1974)] 12p; (2) Night of the Jackass: Storm Before the Calm! [Bruce Bezaire/Jose Ortiz, reprinted from *Eerie* #63 (February 1975)] 10p; (3) Night of the Jackass: The Children's Hour [Bruce Bezaire/Jose Ortiz, reprinted from *Eerie* #64 (March 1975)] 10p; (4) Night of the Jackass: Endstorm! [Bruce Bezaire/ Jose Ortiz, reprinted from *Eerie* #65 (April 1975)] 10p; (5) Excerpts from the Year Five! [Budd Lewis/Jose Ortiz, reprinted from *Eerie* #67 (August 1975)] 10p.

Notes: Laurier's cover, depicting the Jackasses, was much better than his usual fare. The 1980

Eerie annual and a Jose Ortiz special. It was nice to see the superior *Night of the Jackass* serial collected in one spot.

116. cover: Enrich Torres (November 1980)

(1) Bishop Dane: Blackjack [Rich Margopoulos/E.R. Cruz] 20p; (2) Star Warriors: Plunderworld [Rich Margopoulos/Fred Redondo] 12p; (3) Cagim: The Marks of Merlin! [Budd Lewis/E. R. Cruz] 12p; (4) Haxtur: Warriors and Friends! [Victor de la Fuente] 6p.

Notes: There was a $1.75 cover price with 64 pages. A dreary sword and sorcery cover by Enrich was supposedly of Haxtur but it looked nothing like the character. "Blackjack" was a story starring the Rook's granddad. The Rook guest-starred in his grandpappy's first but none too interesting solo adventure. The "Star Warriors" story was apparently an attempt at a series but it was extremely lame and led nowhere. It also had nothing to do with the "Star Warrior" story from *Eerie* #114. *Cagim* (read the name backwards) was an okay serial, dealing with an uncredited takeoff on T. H. White's backward living magician (and not the Merlin character that Budd Lewis had written as a serial in the 1970s for *Eerie*). Cruz's artwork was dull on the "Blackjack" story but okay for *Cagim*.

117. cover: Enrich Torres (December 1980), reprinted from *Vampirella* #37's back cover (October 1974)

(1) Cagim: City of Fire [Budd Lewis/E.R. Cruz] 14p; (2) His Brother's Keeper! [Jim Stenstrum/Neil McFeeters] 8p; (3) Bruce Bloodletter: The Jalopy Scam [Cary Bates/Fernando Fernandez] 12p; (4) Haxtur: A Time for Dying [Victor de la Fuente] 17p.

Notes: This 1974 reprint cover was quite lovely and in marked contrast to Enrich's sloppy-looking cover from the previous issue. Cagim became a superhero, complete with costume. The Bruce Bloodletter artwork had again been done years before for a European educational comic called *Space and Adventure*. Here, it was given a completely new script to turn it into a routine science fantasy tale. Haxtur concluded his run with his best story. However, the real delight here is the Stenstrum/McFeeters story "His Brother's Keeper!" While this wasn't Stenstrum's best story for War-

ren, it was head and shoulders better than the low-level material that had been appearing in *Eerie* for the last six months. McFeeters' only art job for Warren was also quite nice.

118. cover: Jordi Penalva (January 1981)

(1) Haggarth: Skull of the Three Snakes [Victor de la Fuente] 18p; (2) Steel Starfire: Tales from the Galactic Inn [Rich Margopoulos/Rudy Nebres] 8p; (3) The Red Shot [Bruce Bezaire/Jess Jodloman] 16p; (4) Space Kids [Fernando Fernandez] 8p.

Notes: Like *Haxtur*, *Haggarth* had been serialized throughout Europe, although this title was from the late, rather than the early, 1970s. Still, it was probably the best serial that *Eerie* published in its last three years. The mysterious Bruce Bezaire returned for one story, but I suspect "The Red Shot" was written years earlier and only illustrated now. Either way, it wasn't a very good story. The so-so Fernandez's effort was an inventory story, done about 1975 or so.

119. cover: Bob Larkin (February 1981)

(1) Zud Kamish: Accept No Substitute! [Jim Stenstrum/E.R. Cruz] 27p; (2) Sindy Starfire [Rich Margopoulos/Rueben Yandoc] 10p; (3) Haggarth: Eyes of the Dead! [Victor de la Fuente] 15p.

Notes: A $1.95 cover price with 72 pages. Bob Larkin delivered a bland cover. *Zud Kamish* was actually a fairly good serial with Stenstrum managing to create some amusement and interest for the reader despite being saddled with E.R. Cruz's artwork. "Sindy Starfire" might have made a fine serial as well, but for some reason, when fans asked for more on the letters page, Warren poohpoohed the idea.

120. cover: Jim Laurier (April 1981)

(1) Zud Kamish: Death of a Cometeer [Jim Stenstrum/E.R. Cruz] 12p; (2) Bishop Dane and Dax the Warrior!: The Warrior and the Gunfighter! [Rich Margopoulos/A. L. Sanchez] 14p; (3) The Mist: A Public and Private Surveillance [Don McGregor/Jun Lofamia] 12p; (4) Haggarth: Sombra the Damned! [Victor de la Fuente] 15p.

Notes: Cover price now $2.00. A better than average issue with three good serial episodes. *Zud* and *Haggarth* continued their winning ways while Don McGregor's fine tale of witchcraft, "The Mist," debuted. It went through three different artists and long gaps in appearances but still managed to tell an effective tale. I suspect this serial was a victim of the story purchase freeze mentioned earlier, with the earliest episodes written before the freeze and the latter after (long after) the freeze ended. Starting with this issue, *Eerie* began a policy of reviving old series stars (even dead ones — in fact, especially the dead ones), without using the original creators, to appear in one-shot stories, often with a guest star. Dax was the first, teamed up with the Rook's granddad. Sanchez, however, was no Maroto and his pudgy Dax looked more like Marvel's Ka-Zar then the thin, wiry Dax of yore.

121. cover: Vaughn Bode and Basil Gogos (June 1981), reprinted from *Eerie* #26 (March 1970)

(1) The Mist: Blood Cycles [Don McGregor/ Jun Lofamia] 15p; (2) Born of Ancient Vision [Robert Morello and Budd Lewis/Robert Morello] 11p; (3) Hunter, Demon Killer and Darklon the Mystic: Ashes to Ashes [Rich Margopoulos/A. L. Sanchez] 14p; (4) Haggarth: Fall of the Death Head! [Victor de la Fuente] 12p.

Notes: Chris Adames becomes the editor. Why the ugliest cover that Vaughn Bode ever did for Warren was the only one of his chosen for reprinting is beyond me. It's really a dog. Robert Morello's decent SF story was visually quite bizarre looking. Sanchez made a real effort this time and his *Darklon* drawings are pretty good. However, combining two characters who have absolutely zero in common with each other is never a good idea.

122. cover: Romas Kukalis (July 1981)

(1) The Beast of Sarnadd-Doom! [Budd Lewis/ Gonzalo Mayo] 11p; (2) The Nu Zud Kamish: The Chameleon Stands Revealed! [Jim Stenstrum/E.R. Cruz, story credited to Alabaster Redzone] 10p; (3) The Mist: Victoria Rode the Subway Last Night! [Don McGregor/Val Mayerik] 14p; (4) Haggarth, Book II [Victor de la Fuente] 14p.

Notes: Romas' cover was quite attractive and the accompanying story "The Beast of Sarnadd-Doom!" was a fine sword and sorcery tale. Zud's series title was slightly changed. The best story

and art belonged to this issue's installment of *The Mist*. Mayerik's art was quite impressive.

123. cover: Manuel Sanjulian (August 1981)

(1) The Mist: Token Resistance [Don McGregor/Val Mayerik] 14p; (2) Born of Ancient Vision: In Sight of Heaven, in Reach of Hell [Budd Lewis/Robert Morello] 15p; (3) Remember All the People [Don McGregor/Leopoldo Duranona] 11p; (4) Harrarth, Book II: Path of the Tempered Soul! [Victor de la Fuente] 12p.

Notes: Sanjulian's cover was done in 1972 and originally intended for *Creepy* #47. See that issue's notes for more details. This would be the last appearance of *The Mist* for a year and a half. Don McGregor's "Remember All the People" was a heartfelt tribute to the slain John Lennon. It also featured Duranona's last art job for Warren. Evidently the freeze on new stories was easing up to some extent as this story had to have been written after John Lennon's December 1980 murder.

124. cover: Frank Frazetta (September 1981), reprinted from *Creepy* #7 (February 1966)

(1) Cagim: The Sea of Red [Budd Lewis/E.R. Cruz] 12p; (2) Pyramid of the Black Sun: Orka [Antonio Segura and Jim Stenstrum/Luis Bermejo, story is credited solely to Alabaster Redzone] 12p; (3) Born of Ancient Vision: God of Light [Budd Lewis/Robert Morello] 17p; (4) Haggarth, Book II: The Sacred Scroll [Victor de la Fuente] 10p.

Notes: "Pyramid of the Black Sun" appeared in Europe in the late 1970s, with a script by Segura and art by Bermejo. It was greatly rewritten here and the art has been rearranged. As *Eerie* issues of this time period go, this was a fairly decent one.

125. cover: Richard Corben (October 1981) reprinted from *Eerie* #77 (September 1976)

(1) Curse of the Vampire! [Archie Goodwin/ Neal Adams, reprinted from *Creepy* #14 (April 1967)] 8p; (2) The Terror beyond Time! [Archie Goodwin/Neal Adams, reprinted from *Creepy* #15 (June 1967)] 16p; (3) Goddess from the Sea [Don Glut/Neal Adams, reprinted from *Vampirella* #1 (October 1969)] 6p; (4) Thrillkill [Jim Stenstrum/Neal Adams, reprinted from *Creepy* #75 (November 1975)] 8p; (5) A Curse of Claws! [Archie Goodwin/Neal Adams, reprinted

from *Creepy* #16 (August 1967)] 6p; (6) Voodoo Drum! [Archie Goodwin/Neal Adams, reprinted from *Eerie* #10 (July 1967)] 8p; (7) Fair Exchange [Archie Goodwin/Neal Adams, reprinted from *Eerie* #9 (May 1967)] 8p.

Notes: A $2.25 cover price and 80 pages. The 1981 *Eerie* annual and a Neal Adams special. There were numerous new Cousin Eerie illustrations by Berni Wrightson used for introductions. A great buy for Adams fans!

126. cover: Richard Corben (November 1981)

(1) The Nu Zud Kamish: Crabs [John Ellis Sech/E.R. Cruz] 14p; (2) Pyramid of the Black Sun: Blekos [Antonio Segura and Jim Stenstrum/Luis Bermejo, story credited solely to Alabaster Redzone] 13p; (3) Korsar [Jim Stenstrum/Esteban Maroto, story credited to Alabaster Redzone] 12p; (4) Haggarth, Book II, part 4 [Victor de la Fuente] 13p.

Notes: A $2.00 cover price for 72 pages. Corben's cover was originally done for a paperback cover. Zud Kamish got a new writer.

127. cover: Nestor Redondo (December 1981)

(1) Justin, King of the Jungle [Bill DuBay and Rich Margopoulos/Rudy Nebres, story credited to Will Richardson] 14p; (2) Reuben Youngblood [Budd Lewis/Howard Chaykin and Lee Elias] 11p; (3) Merlin and the Sorcerer [Budd Lewis/E.R. Cruz] 14p; (4) Haggarth, Book II, part 5 [Victor de la Cruz] 12p.

Notes: Bill DuBay returned as editor with Timothy Moriarty listed as managing editor. The page count was dropped to 64 pages. Future comic artist Alec Stevens sent in a letter complaining about reprint covers while asking for a Wally Wood reprint special. "Justin, King of the Jungle" was an actual horror story, now an unusual happening in *Eerie*, and was quite good, with beautiful Nebres artwork. Reuben Youngblood returned for the first time since #72 back in 1976. This story was obviously done about 1975 as well, except for two new pages that Lee Elias drew, probably to lengthen the story for this appearance. Another inker, possibly Walt Simonson, may have worked on this story back in 1975 as well. "Merlin and the Sorcerer" concerned the Merlin character from the *Cagim* series, not the Budd Lewis penned *Merlin* series from the 1970s.

128. cover: Kirk Reinert (January 1982)

(1) Dr. Coven: Ashes to Ashes! [Rich Margopoulos/Rudy Nebres] 11p; (2) The Demon Queen [Jonathan Thomas/Jose Ortiz] 7p; (3) Zud and Son: Heroes at Large! [John Ellis Sech/E.R. Cruz] 11p; (4) Blackstar and the Night Huntress [Gerry Boudreau/Peter Hsu] 9p; (5) Avenger! [Archie Goodwin/Jim Starlin and Neal Adams] 8p; (6) Haggarth, Book II, part 6 [Victor de la Fuente] 11p.

Notes: A striking Reinert cover highlighted a somewhat better than average issue. "Avenger!" was done in 1974 and was originally intended for *Creepy* #64 (August 1974). The low point was certainly the "Blackstar and the Night Huntress" story, a sequel to the original from *Eerie* #85. Hsu's art was in his "Quandrant" style — awkwardly posed soft-porn cheesecake, with a lot of female model guides and positions taken directly from Playboy centerfold pages. *Haggarth* continued to be the best thing in *Eerie*.

129. cover: Manuel Sanjulian (February 1982)

(1) Marvin, the Dead-Thing: Ode to a Dead Thing! [Bill DuBay/Rudy Nebres] 13p; (2) Ms. Liberty [Rich Margopoulos/Jun Lofamia] 7p; (3) Mercenary! [Nicola Cuti/Pat Boyette] 9p; (4) Space Force: Shipwrecked [Jean-Claude Forest/Paul Gillon, strip credited solely to Gillon] 13p; (5) Haggarth, Book II, part 7 [Victor de la Fuente] 12p.

Notes: The revival of Marvin, the Dead-Thing, a character only done originally as a satirical blast at Marvel and DC's swamp creatures, showed just how far off track Warren had fallen. The original *Marvin* story was funny but this one was played straight and was as run-of-the-mill as you could get. Not to mention the fact that with Nebres doing the art, Marvin looked alarmingly like the Nestor Redondo–illustrated Swamp Thing! "Mercenary!" was a straight action-adventure story with no horror or SF elements at all. I suspect it was originally intended for *The Rook* magazine. "Shipwrecked" was from a French strip that debuted there in 1964. The English translator is unknown. The covers that Sanjulian was supplying Warren with at this point often looked like rejected covers for generic paperback sword and sorcery series, something he was doing quite regularly at the time. They usually had zero to do with the contents of the magazine.

130. cover: Steve Fastner and Rich Larson (April 1982)

(1) *Vampirella* and the Time Force [Rich Margopoulos/E.R. Cruz] 54p.

Notes: Timothy Moriarty became the new (and last) editor. The letters page vanished. This was possibly the most depressing issue of *Eerie* ever produced. It's not so much that the story is bad, because it wasn't that horrible. It's just that the entire concept of this issue trashed so much of *Eerie*'s history. The book-length story borrowed Vampi, along with her supporting cast from a year previous, making one suspect this story was originally intended to be a serial in Vampi's own magazine, then linked her up with a host of *Eerie*'s most recognizable series characters. In addition to Vampi and Pantha, the Pie, Shreck, Child, Exterminator One, Dax the Damned, Hunters I and II, Mac Tavish, the Spook, Coffin, Darklon, Manners the Tin Man, the Rook and his Grandpappy, Bishop Dane, appear. Since, with the exception of the Rook and his supporting cast, most of the characters died at the end of their usually quite grim serials, coupled with the fact that most of their original storylines could not possibly co-exist with each other, the resulting story had a distinct air of desperation that had begun to soak into all of Warren's magazines during this period. Add to that the depressing fact that E.R. Cruz couldn't draw a sexy female if she came up, sat on his lap and twirled widdershins. In addition, all of his men had the exact same facial features and his static layouts tended to make someone looking at a page of his art feel as though they were staring at a blank gray wall and the result was you ended up with an exceedingly dreary issue.

131. cover: Rudy Nebres (June 1982)

(1) Wally Wood, 1927–1981 [Timothy Moriarty?, text article, obituary] 1p; (2) Killer Hawk [Bill DuBay/Wally Wood, reprinted from *Eerie* #61 (November 1974)] 12p; (3) Overworked! [Archie Goodwin/Dan Adkins and Wally Wood, reprinted from *Creepy* #9 (June 1966)] 6p; (4) The Cosmic All [Wally Wood, reprinted from *Creepy* #38 (March 1971)] 8p; (5) The Battle of Britain! [Wally Wood/Dan Adkins and Wally Wood, reprinted from Blazing Combat #3, art credited solely to Wood] 7p; (6) War of the Wizards! [Wally Wood, reprinted from *Vampirella* #10 (March 1971)] 8p; (7) The Manhunters [Gerry Boudreau/Wally Wood, reprinted from *Eerie* #60 (September 1974)] 8p.

Notes: This was $2.00 for 64 pages. An all Wally Wood special. The cover was a pen and ink illustration instead of a painting. From this point on, like *Creepy*, just about every other issue of *Eerie* was a reprint issue.

132. cover: Manuel Sanjulian (July 1982)

(1) The Rook: The Dane Curse! [Budd Lewis/Luis Bermejo] 13p; (2) The Nu Zud Kamish: Hero of the Milky Way [John Ellis Sech/E.R. Cruz] 14p; (3) Space Force: Shipwrecked, part 2 [Jean-Claude Forest/Paul Gillon] 12p; (4) Haggarth, Book II, part 8 [Victor de la Fuente] 12p.

Notes: With the cancellation of his own magazine, the Rook returned to *Eerie*. His story here was the third and concluding part of a serial begun in *The Rook* #13.

133. cover: Manuel Sanjulian (August 1982)

(1) *Eerie*'s Exciting Earful [Timothy Moriarty, text article] 1p; (2) Destiny's Witch [John Jacobson/Ramon Torrents, reprinted from *Creepy* #59 (January 1974)] 12p; (3) Fleur: from the Spain of Legend! [John Jacobson/Ramon Torrents, reprinted from *Vampirella* #34 (June 1974)] 10p; (4) Fleur: Our Tarts Were Young and Gay! [John Jacobson/Ramon Torrents, reprinted from *Vampirella* #35 (August 1974)] 10p; (5) Fleur: Night of the Alleycats [Gerry Boudreau/Ramon Torrents, reprinted from *Vampirella* #68 (April 1978)] 8p; (6) The Quest [Budd Lewis/Ramon Torrents, reprinted from *Vampirella* #67 (March 1978)] 8p; (7) The Goblin ad [Rudy Nebres, on the back cover] 1p.

Notes: An all-reprint Ramon Torrents special. "The Quest" had one page deleted. The features page was revived with a new title.

134. cover: Rudy Nebres (September 1982)

(1) *Eerie*'s Exciting Earful [Timothy Moriarty, text article] 1p; (2) The Rook: The Fallen [Budd Lewis/Luis Bermejo] 9p; (3) Space Force: Shipwrecked, part 3 [Jean-Claude Forest/Paul Gillon] 14p; (4) *Eerie* Showcase: The Fighting Armenian [Bill DuBay/Rudy Nebres, color] 8p; (5) Zud Kamish [John Ellis Sech/

E.R. Cruz] 9p: (**6**) Haggarth, Book II, part 9 [Victor de la Fuente] 10p.

Notes: The cover was a pen and ink illustration, not a painted cover. *The Fighting Armenian* moved over from the cancelled *The Rook* and was cover-featured. Why is a puzzlement, as he was an extremely lame knockoff character to begin with. *The Rook* or *Zud* would have been a much better choice. "Eerie Showcase," a color insert with pages cut in regular color comic size, began. The color and paper resembled a shoddy Charlton comic with really crappy page cutting. It's quite a fall from the glorious Warren color sections of a few years earlier. *Zud Kamish* concluded his series without dying! He only had his arms and legs blown off in a Warren version of a happy ending.

135. cover: Manuel Sanjulian (October 1982)

(**1**) The Spirit of the Thing! [Archie Goodwin/ Steve Ditko, reprinted from *Creepy* #9 (June 1966)] 8p; (**2**) Collector's Edition! [Archie Goodwin/Steve Ditko, reprinted from *Creepy* #10 (August 1966)] 8p; (**3**) Beast Man! [Archie Goodwin/Steve Ditko, reprinted from *Creepy* #11 (October 1966)] 8p; (**4**) Blood of the Werewolf! [Archie Goodwin/Steve Ditko, reprinted from *Creepy* #12 (December 1966)] 8p; (**5**) Second Chance! [Archie Goodwin/Steve Ditko, reprinted from *Creepy* #13 (February 1967)] 6p; (**6**) Where Sorcery Lives! [Archie Goodwin/ Steve Ditko, reprinted from *Creepy* #14 (April 1967)] 8p; (**7**) Thane: City of Doom! [Archie Goodwin/Steve Ditko, reprinted from *Creepy* #15 (June 1967)] 8p; (**8**) The Incredible Shrieking Man! [Archie Goodwin/Steve Ditko, reprinted from *Eerie* #4 (July 1966), originally entitled "Shrieking Man!"] 8p; (**9**) The Fly! [Archie Goodwin/Steve Ditko, reprinted from *Eerie* #7 (January 1967)] 8p; (**10**) Demon Sword! [Archie Goodwin/Steve Ditko, reprinted from *Eerie* #8 (March 1967)] 8p; (**11**) The Goblin ad [Rudy Nebres, on the back cover] 1p.

Notes: It cost $2.75 for 96 pages. An all-reprint Steve Ditko (and Archie Goodwin) special and the 1982 *Eerie* annual. Great collector's issue!

136. cover: Nestor Redondo (November 1982)

(**1**) *Eerie*'s Exciting Earful [Timothy Moriarty, text article] 1p; (**2**) The Rook: The Fallen, part 2 [Budd Lewis/Luis Bermejo] 8p; (**3**) Space Force: Shipwrecked, part 4 [Jean-Claude For-est/Paul Gillon] 15p; (**4**) *Eerie* Showcase: Starlad [Bill DuBay/Vic Catan, color] 8p; (**5**) Haggarth, Book II, part 10 [Victor de la Fuente] 14p; (**6**) The 1981 Warren Awards [Timothy Moriarty, text article] 2p.

Notes: It was $2.25 for 64 pages. Nestor Redondo's cover was quite striking. The Rook made his final appearance. "Space Force: Shipwrecked" did as well, with the serial never being concluded. Haggarth concluded his run and was probably the best serial to run in the latter days of *Eerie*. After a long delay the 1981 Warren Awards were announced with best cover going to Steve Fastner and Rich Larson for *1994* #22, Nicola Cuti winning best writer for his *Fox* serial from *Vampirella*, Victor de la Fuente winning the story of the year for *Haggarth*, Anton Caravana winning best art for "Call It Chaos" from *Vampirella* #100, Luis Bermejo for artist of the year, Nestor Redondo for cover artist of the year and special awards for excellence to Frank Thorne and Rudy Nebres.

137. cover: montage of previous covers (December 1982)

(**1**) *Eerie*'s Exciting Earful [Timothy Moriarty, text article] 1p; (**2**) Darklon the Mystic: The Price [Jim Starlin, reprinted from *Eerie* #76 (August 1976)] 9p; (**3**) Exterminator One [Bill DuBay/Paul Neary, reprinted from *Eerie* #60 (September 1974)] 8p; (**4**) The Mummy: The Mind Within [Steve Skeates/Jaime Brocal, reprinted from *Eerie* #50 (August 1973)] 10p; (**5**) Coffin: Death Wish! [Budd Lewis/Jose Ortiz, reprinted from *Eerie* #61 (November 1974)] 10p; (**6**) *Eerie*'s Greatest Heroes! [Timothy Moriarty, text article with a hero story checklist] 2p; (**7**) Hunter [Rich Margopoulos/ Paul Neary, reprinted from *Eerie* #52 (November 1973)] 10p; (**8**) The Spook: Stridespider Sponge-Rot [Doug Moench/Esteban Maroto, reprinted from *Eerie* #57 (June 1974)] 10p.

Notes: An all-reprint "Origins" special. It was $2.25 for 80 pages. Warren reprinted the opening episodes of various *Eerie* characters without telling their entire story. In my opinion, a good way to frustrate readers, although DC just did the same thing with their 52 issues. The addition of a checklist for back orders was a nice touch. This would have been a great place to collect all the Darklon episodes.

138. cover: Nestor Redondo (January 1983)

(1)The Noxious Newspage [Timothy Moriarty, text article] 1p; (2) The Mist [Don McGregor/ Bill Draut] 13p; (3) The Mist, part 2 [Don Mc-Gregor/Bill Draut] 10p; (4) *Eerie* Showcase: Granny Gutman and the Limbo Men [Rich Margopoulos/Fred Carrillo, color] 8p; (5) Glythis [Timothy Moriarty/E.R. Cruz] 8p; (6) Sherlock Holmes: A Study in Scarlet, part 3 [Rich Margopoulos/Noly Panaligan] 11p.

Notes: A $2.25 cover price for 64 pages. A beautiful Redondo cover heralded the welcome return and conclusion of *The Mist*, unseen since #123, back in August 1981. *Glythis*, a new serial, was

never concluded. *The Sherlock Holmes* strip was the conclusion of a serial begun in the cancelled *The Rook* magazine.

139. cover: Kelly Freas (February 1983)

(1) The Noxious Newspage [Timothy Moriarty, text article] 1p; (2) Voyage of the Space Beagle [Rich Margopoulos/Luis Bermejo, from the story by A. E. Van Vogt] 43p; (3) *Eerie* Showcase: The Infinity Force [Bill DuBay/Rudy Nebres, color] 8p.

Notes: Final issue. Clearly an effort was being made to upgrade the quality of Warren's story offerings as this was a very good adaptation of Van Vogt's classic tale. After the dreariness of the previous two and a half years, this was a nice way for *Eerie* to leave the stage.

Creepy Yearbook

1. cover: montage of previous covers (Summer–Fall 1967)

(1) Uncle Creepy's Introduction [Frank Frazetta, frontis, reprinted from *Creepy* #1 (January 1965)] 1p; (2) The Duel of the Monsters! [Archie Goodwin/Angelo Torres, reprinted from *Creepy* #7 (February 1966)] 8p; (3) Return Trip [Arthur Porges/ Joe Orlando, reprinted from *Creepy* #3 (June 1965)] 8p; (4) Abominable Snowman! [Bill Pearson/John Severin, reprinted from *Creepy* #6 (December 1965)] 6p; (5) Werewolf! [Larry Ivie/Frank Frazetta, reprinted from *Creepy* #1 (January1 965)] 6p; (6) The Thing in the Pit! [Larry Ivie/Gray Morrow, reprinted from *Creepy* #6 (December 1966)] 8p; (7) Vampires Fly at Dusk! [Archie Goodwin/Reed Crandall, reprinted from *Creepy* #1 (January1965)] 6p; (8) Sand Doom [Archie

Nestor Redondo was a much underrated artist, but he delivered great covers and interior art for Warren, as seen in this late cover in *Eerie*'s run. © New Comic Co./used by permission.

Goodwin/Al Williamson, reprinted from *Creepy* #5 (October 1965)] 6p; (9) Hot Spell! [Archie Goodwin/Reed Crandall, reprinted from *Creepy* #7 (February 1966)] 7p.

Notes: It cost $0.50 for 72 pages. Publisher: James Warren. Editor: Archie Goodwin. *Creepy's* yearbook/annuals usually came out sometime during the summer months. The actual title of this issue was *Creepy 1968 Yearbook*, probably designed so that the 1968 date would give it a longer shelflife. The yearbook/annual series always listed the next year as the cover date so a *Creepy 1969 Yearbook*, for example, would come out in 1968.

2. cover: H. B. Harris (1968)

(1) Scream Test! [John Benson and Bhob Stewart/Angelo Torres, reprinted from *Creepy* #13 (February 1967)] 7p; (2) The Doorway! [Archie Goodwin/Dan Adkins, reprinted from *Creepy* #11 (October 1966)] 6p; (3) Monster! [Archie Goodwin/Rocke Mastroserio, reprinted from *Creepy* #10 (August 1966)] 8p; (4) Creepy's Loathsome Lore: Werebeasts! [Archie Goodwin/Frank Frazetta, reprinted from *Creepy* #7 (February 1966)] 1p; (5) Overworked! [Archie Goodwin/-Wally Wood and Dan Adkins, reprinted from *Creepy* #9 (June 1966)] 6p; (6) Curse of the Vampire! [Archie Goodwin/Neal Adams, reprinted from *Creepy* #14 (April 1967)] 8p; (7) The Beckoning Beyond [Archie Goodwin/Dan Adkins, reprinted from *Creepy* #14 (April 1967)] 8p; (8) Midnight Sail [Johnny Craig; reprinted from *Creepy* #10 (August 1966)] 6p.

Notes: The price was $0.50 for 72 pages. The *Creepy 1969 Yearbook*. Editor: Bill Parente.

3. cover: montage of previous covers (1969)

(1) The Body-Snatcher! [Archie Goodwin/Reed Crandall, from the story by Robert Louis Stevenson, reprinted from *Creepy* #7 (February 1966)] 8p; (2) Blood of the Werewolf! [Archie Goodwin/Steve Ditko, reprinted from *Creepy* #12 (December 1966)] 8p; (3) Where Sorcery Lives! [Archie Goodwin/Steve Ditko, reprinted from *Creepy* #14 (April 1967)] 8p; (4) The Terror Beyond Time! [Archie Goodwin/Neal Adams, reprinted from *Creepy* #15 (June 1967)] 16p; (5) Revenge of the Beast! [Archie Goodwin/Gray Morrow, reprinted from *Creepy* #5 (October 1965)] 7p; (6) The Invitation [Larry Englehart, Russ Jones and Maurice Whitman/-Manny Stallman, reprinted from *Creepy* #8 (April 1966)] 7p; (7) Blood of Krylon! [Archie

Goodwin/Gray Morrow, reprinted from *Creepy* #7 (February 1966)] 6p.

Notes: A $0.60 cover price for 72 pages. The *Creepy 1970 Yearbook*.

4. cover: Kenneth Smith (1970)

(1) Beast Man! [Archie Goodwin/Steve Ditko, reprinted from *Creepy* #11 (October 1966)] 8p; (2) A Curse of Claws! [Archie Goodwin/Neal Adams, reprinted from *Creepy* #16 (August 1967)] 6p; (3) The Mountain [Johnny Craig, reprinted from *Creepy* #8 (April 1966)] 6p; (4) Grave Undertaking [Archie Goodwin/Alex Toth, reprinted from *Creepy* #5 (October 1965)] 6p; (5) Castle Carrion! [Archie Goodwin/Reed Crandall, reprinted from *Creepy* #14 (April 1967)] 8p; (6) Image in Wax! [Archie Goodwin/Tom Sutton, reprinted from *Creepy* #17 (October 1967)] 6p; (7) The Rescue of the Morning Maid! [Raymond Marais/Pat Boyette and Rocke Mastroserio, reprinted from *Creepy* #18 (January 1968)] 10p; (8) Skeleton Crew! [Archie Goodwin/Angelo Torres, reprinted from *Creepy* #11 (October 1966)] 7p.

Notes: This cost $0.60 for 64 pages. Editor: James Warren. The title was changed to *Creepy 1971 Annual*.

5. cover: photo of a rubber Zombie mask (1971)

(1) Uncle Creepy's Welcome [Archie Goodwin/-Angelo Torres, frontis, reprinted from *Creepy* #2 (April 1965)] 1p; (2) No Fair! [Bill Parente/Tom Sutton, reprinted from *Creepy* #22 (August 1968)] 6p; (3) Spawn of the Cat People [Archie Goodwin/Reed Crandall, reprinted from *Creepy* #2 (April 1965)] 6p; (4) On the Wings of a Bird [T. Casey Brennan/Jerry Grandenetti, reprinted from *Creepy* #36 (November 1970)] 7p; (5) Tough Customers! [R. Michael Rosen/Tom Sutton, reprinted from *Creepy* #35 (September 1970)] 6p; (6) Creepy's Loathsome Lore: The Body Snatchers Who Stole a Giant! [Tom Sutton, reprinted from *Creepy* #36 (November 1970)] 1p; (7) Pursuit of the Vampire! [Archie Goodwin/Angelo Torres, reprinted from *Creepy* #1 (January 1965)] 6p; (8) The Judge's House! [Archie Goodwin/Reed Crandall, from the story by Bram Stoker, reprinted from *Creepy* #5 (October 1965)] 8p; (9) Grub! [Nicola Cuti/Tom Sutton, reprinted from *Creepy* #28 (August 1969)] 6p; (10) Monster Rally! [Archie Goodwin/Angelo Torres, reprinted from *Creepy* #4 (August 1965)] 8p.

Notes: It was $0.75 for 64 pages. Final issue. James Warren was listed as editor while J. R. Cochran was listed as the managing editor. Retitled *The Creepy Spooktacular 1972 Annual*. Following this issue the annual was incorporated into *Creepy*'s regular numbering.

Eerie Yearbook

1. cover: montage of previous covers (1969)

(1) Cousin Eerie's Welcome [Jack Davis, reprinted from *Eerie* #2 (March 1966)] 1p; (2) Soul of Horror [Archie Goodwin/Angelo Torres, reprinted from *Eerie* #3 (May 1966)] 8p; (3) Shrieking Man! [Archie Goodwin/Steve Ditko, reprinted from *Eerie* #4 (July 1968)] 7p; (4) The Masque of the Red Death [Tom Sutton, from the story by Edgar Allan Poe, reprinted from *Eerie* #12 (November 1967)] 6p; (5) The Wanderer! [Archie Goodwin/Dan Adkins, reprinted from *Eerie* #9 (May 1967)] 8p; (6) A Matter of Routine [Archie Goodwin/Gene Colan, reprinted from *Eerie* #5 (September 1966)] 8p; (7) The Quest [Archie Goodwin/Donald Norman, reprinted from *Eerie* #7 (January 1967)] 6p; (8) One for De-Money [E. Nelson Bridwell/Angelo Torres, reprinted from *Eerie* #2 (March 1966)] 7p; (9) Terror in the Tomb [Archie Goodwin/Rocke Mastroserio, reprinted from *Eerie* #9 (May 1967)] 7p; (10) Easy Way to a Tuff Surfboard! [Archie Goodwin/Frank Frazetta, reprinted from *Eerie* #3 (May 1966)] ½ p

Notes: Publisher: James Warren. Editor: Bill Parente. It was $0.60 for 72 pages.

2. cover: Kenneth Smith plus a montage of previous covers (1970)

(1) Hatchet Man [Archie Goodwin/Gene Colan, reprinted from *Eerie* #4 (July 1966)] 8p; (2) Wolf Bait! [Archie Goodwin/Rocke Mastroserio, reprinted from *Eerie* #8 (March 1967)] 8p; (3) It! [Archie Goodwin/Dan Adkins, reprinted from *Eerie* #10 (July 1967)] 8p; (4) The Defense Rests! [Johnny Craig, reprinted from *Eerie* #7 (January 1967)] 8p; (5) Island at World's End [Archie Goodwin/Gray Morrow, reprinted from *Eerie* #4 (July 1966)] 10p; (6) The Swamp God! [Archie Goodwin/Angelo Torres, reprinted from *Eerie* #5 (September 1966)] 6p; (7) The Changeling [Archie Goodwin/Gene Colan, reprinted from *Eerie* #6 (November 1966)] 8p.

Notes: Editor: James Warren. Title changed to the *Eerie* Annual. It cost $0.60 for 64 pages.

3. cover: John Pederson (1971)

(1) Eerie's Monster Gallery: The Golem! [Tom Sutton, frontis, reprinted from *Eerie* #27 (May 1970)] 1p; (2) Fair Exchange [Archie Goodwin/Neal Adams, reprinted from *Eerie* #9 (May 1967)] 8p; (3) Deep Ruby! [Archie Goodwin/Steve Ditko, reprinted from *Eerie* #6 (November 1966)] 6p; (4) Spiders Are Revolting! [Bill Warren/Tom Sutton, reprinted from *Eerie* #26 (March 1970)] 9p; (5) In Close Pursuit [Gordon Matthews/Jerry Grandenetti, reprinted from *Eerie* #30 (November 1970)] 8p; (6) ...Nor Custom, Stale... [Johnny Craig, reprinted from *Eerie* #12 (November 1967)] 8p; (7) The Monument [Archie Goodwin/Alex Toth, reprinted from *Eerie* #3 (May 1966)] 6p; (8) Eerie's Monster Gallery: The Number 13 [Bill Parente/Tony Tallarico, reprinted from *Eerie* #16 (July 1968)] 1p; (9) Fly! [Archie Goodwin/Steve Ditko, reprinted from *Eerie* #7 (January 1967)] 6p.

Notes: It cost $0.75 for 64 pages. Final issue. James Warren was listed as editor and J. R. Cochran was managing editor. From this point on the annual was incorporated into *Eerie*'s regular numbering.

Vampirella

1. cover: Frank Frazetta (October 1969)

(1) *Vampirella*'s Welcome [Bill Parente/Frank Frazetta, frontis, art reprinted from *Creepy* #29 (September 1969)] 1p; (2) *Vampirella* of Draculon [Forrest J. Ackerman/Tom Sutton] 7p; (3) Death Boat! [Don Glut/Billy Graham] 6p; (4) Two Silver Bullets! [Don Glut/Reed Crandall] 6p; (5) Goddess from the Sea [Don Glut/Neal Adams] 6p; (6) Last Act: October! [Don Glut/Mike Royer] 8p; (7) Spaced-Out Girls! [Don Glut/Bill Fraccio and Tony Tallarico] 6p; (8) Room Full of Changes [Nicola Cuti/Ernie Colon] 6p.

Notes: Publisher: James Warren. Editor: Bill Parente. This was a 64 page issue. This was the first all-original Warren issue since *Eerie* #11 (September 1967). Frazetta's cover of *Vampirella* was a substitute for the original cover by European artist Aslan. That cover also featured *Vampirella*, but was rejected over fears that Vampi looked rather anemic (not good for a vampire, one would guess). That cover was eventually used as the cover for the *Vampirella* 1972 annual. *Vampirella*'s costume and hairstyle was designed by artist Trina Robbins. The first *Vampirella* story was a horror spoof rather than a straight horror tale, as was made obvious by the first two pages being taken up with a sequence of a nude *Vampirella* taking a shower for no particular reason, except for good clean fun. Several years later, this origin tale was greatly rewritten to fit the more horrific manner of her later tales. Best stories are the Graham, Crandall and Adams' stories, all written by Don Glut. Adams' story was in pencils only. The question arises of exactly who edited this first issue. Bill Parente is listed on the masthead but he doesn't appear with a single written story. Unusual for an issue edited by him. Forrest Ackerman created, or at least had a strong hand in creating, *Vampirella* and he clearly had a major influence in shaping the light-hearted bad girl story style of this issue as well. Neal Adams remembered that Archie Goodwin was the person calling up artists for this issue and that this was the main reason a very busy Adams agreed to do his story. That makes sense. Goodwin and Warren had a close relationship and only months later, Goodwin would be back on the masthead as a contributing editor. It's even possible that all three, along with publisher Jim Warren, had an editorial hand in shaping this issue. Regardless, this was a pretty good start. Not up to the later Warren issues from the Goodwin era but a giant step up from the Warren titles published in the previous two years.

2. cover: Bill Hughes (November 1969)

(1) Vampi's Feary Tales: The Bride of Frankenstein [Tom Sutton, frontis] 1p; (2) Evily [Bill Parente/Jerry Grandenetti] 10p; (3) Montezuma's Monster [R. Michael Rosen/Bill Fraccio and Tony Tallarico, story miscredited to Don Glut] 6p; (4) *Vampirella*: Down to Earth! [Forrest J. Ackerman/Mike Royer] 8p; (5) Queen of Horror! [Don Glut/Dick Piscopo] 9p; (6) The Octopus [Nicola Cuti/William Barry] 6p; (7) One, Two, Three [Nicola Cuti/Ernie Colon] 7p; (8) Rhapsody in Red! [Don Glut/Billy Graham] 7p.

Notes: Hughes' cover was quite good, depicting the witch Evily. Evily, who only appeared twice, was listed as *Vampirella*'s cousin, although how that could be, seeing as how they're from different planets, is never unexplained. *Vampirella*

does guest-star in Evily's story. *Vampirella*'s own story (just as much a horror spoof as the previous one) is narrated in a one-shot appearance by *Vampirella*'s twin sister, Draculina. *Vampirella* and Draculina are identical twins except that Draculina is a blonde, rather than a brunette, and her bat birthmark is on the opposite breast from *Vampirella*! "Rhapsody in Red!" was easily the best story/art here, although the Evily story also has some nice Grandenetti art. Otherwise, this issue was a big letdown in quality, both in story and art, from the previous issue.

3. cover: Vaughn Bode and Larry Todd (January 1970)

(1) Vampi's Feary Tales: Queen of Outer Space! [Forrest J. Ackerman/Dick Piscopo, frontis] 1p; (2) Evily: Wicked Is Who Wicked Does! [Bill Parente/Tom Sutton] 7p; (3) Blast Off to a Nightmare! [Al Hewetson/Jack Sparling] 10p; (4) Eleven Footsteps to Lucy Fuhr [Terri Abrahms and Nick Beal/Ed Robbins] 7p; (5) I Wake Up ... Screaming! [Billy Graham] 8p; (6) The Caliegia! [Nicola Cuti/Dick Piscopo] 7p; (7) Didn't I See You on Television? [Billy Graham] 4p; (8) A Slimy Situation! [R. Michael Rosen/Jack Sparling] 6p.

Notes: Although it's not that hard to find, this issue unaccountably is very expensive to acquire! Future comic writer Doug Moench sent in a letter. Billy Graham's "I Wake Up ... Screaming!" featured characters with the likenesses of Frank Sinatra, Dean Martin, John Wayne, Robert Mitchum, Paul Newman, James Dean, David Niven, Kirk Douglas, Sammy Davis, Jr., Bill Cosby, Robert Culp, Robert Vaughn, David McCallum and David Janssen. For all that hoop-dee-doo, the best story here was "Eleven Steps to Lucy Fuhr." With the exceptions of Sutton and Graham's efforts, the artwork is still substandard.

4. cover: Vaughn Bode and Jeff Jones (April 1970)

(1) Vampi's Feary Tales: Burned at the Stake! [Tom Sutton, frontis] 1p; (2) Forgotten Kingdom [Bill Parente/Ernie Colon] 10p; (3) Closer than Sisters [Nicola Cuti/Mike Royer] 7p; (4) Moonshine! [Don Glut/William Barry] 13p; (5) Vampi's Fan Page: Dick Piscopo profile [Dick Piscopo/Alan Weiss, text article with photo] 1p; (6) Come into my Parlor! [R. Michael Rosen/

Dick Piscopo] 6p; (7) Run for Your Wife! [Richard Carnell and Jack Erman/Jack Sparling] 7p.

Notes: Nice SF cover from the team of Bode and Jones. Best art was Mike Royer's snazzy job. Future artist Alan Weiss made his first comics appearance as the as yet untitled fan page debuts. Fans were encouraged to help name that feature.

5. cover: Frank Frazetta (June 1970)

(1) Vampi's Feary Tales: The Satanic Sisterhood of Stonehenge! [Tom Sutton, frontis] 1p; (2) The Craft of a Cat's Eye [Don Glut/Bill Fraccio and Tony Tallarico] 9p; (3) Scaly Death [Don Glut/Billy Graham] 6p; (4) An Axe to Grind [Jeff Jones] 7p; (5) Vampi's Flames: Billy Graham profile/The Sorrowful Hounds/Double Feature/A Pain in the Neck [Billy Graham, John Pitts and James Perry/Richard Charron, text articles/text stories with photo] 2p; (6) Avenged by Aurora [Bill Parente/Tom Sutton] 9p; (7) Ghoul Girl [Don Glut/John Fantucchio] 6p; (8) Escape Route! [T. Casey Brennan/Mike Royer] 6p; (9) Luna [Don Glut/Jack Sparling] 8p.

Notes: Striking Frazetta cover showing a caveman and woman menaced by a T-Rex. Fan page regular Anthony Kowalik named the fan page "Vampi's Flames." Very nice art and story by Jeff Jones. Also good work by Billy Graham, Tom Sutton and John Fantucchio.

6. cover: Ken Kelly (July 1970)

(1) Vampi's Feary Tales: The Centaur [Dan Adkins, frontis] 1p; (2) The Curse of Circe [Gardner Fox/Jerry Grandenetti] 6p; (3) The Brothers Death [Nicola Cuti/Jack Sparling] 7p; (4) Darkworth! [Nicola Cuti/Mike Royer] 7p; (5) New Girl in Town! [Gardner Fox/Dan Adkins] 4p; (6) Victim of the Vampire! [Vern Bennett/Frank Bolle] 7p; (7) Vampi's Flames: Untitled/The Bat [Ron Fisher and Brian O'Malley/Ron Fisher, Ken Christie, Jerry Conessa, Anthony Kowalik, Jack Becker, Toby Caputi, Chris Haug, Richard Cherron and Ed Shea, text stories] 2p; (8) One Way Trip [Larry Herndon/Bill Fraccio and Tony Tallarico] 7p; (9) The Wolf-Man [Buddy Saunders/Frank Bolle] 7p.

Notes: Editor: James Warren. Ken Kelly debuts with his first cover art. The magazine *Comic Book Artist* printed layouts for this cover done by Ken's mentor, Frank Frazetta. Best story and art belonged to "Darkworth!" which featured

some of Mike Royer's best and sexiest renderings. The story revolved around a stripper — always a good subject for a comic strip! Frank Bolle also had two good strips here.

7. cover: Frank Frazetti (September 1970)

(1) An Editorial to the President of the United States and All the Members of Congress [James Warren, text article, frontis] 1p; (2) Why a Witch Trilogy? [Archie Goodwin/Frank Frazetta and Billy Graham, text article] 1p; (3) Prologue: Three Witches [Nicola Cuti/Tom Sutton] 1p; (4) The White Witch! [Nicola Cuti/Tom Sutton] 7p; (5) The Mind Witch [Nicola Cuti/Ernie Colon] 7p; (6) The Black Witch! [Nicola Cuti/Billy Graham] 7p; (7) Epilogue: Three Witches [Nicola Cuti/Tom Sutton] 1p; (8) Plague of the Wolf [Doug Moench/Frank Bolle] 7p; (9) Terror Test! [R. Michael Rosen/Bill Fraccio and Tony Tallarico] 7p; (10) Vampi's Flames: Dan Adkins profile/The Morning Sun/Then Wednesday Afternoon Club [Dan Adkins/Brian Carrick and Ted Dasen/Toby Caputo, text article/text stories] 2p; (11) The Survivor [Buddy Saunders/Ernie Colon] 6p; (12) The Collection Creation [R. Michael Rosen/Jerry Grandenetti, miscredited to Tony Williamsune] 6p.

Notes: An excellent issue! Archie Goodwin became an associate editor although he was actually purchasing the stories and assigning the artwork, which to me means a full editor. Frank Frazetta's corker of a cover showed a witch/shaman with her saber-toothed cat. The *Three Witches* stories by Cuti were all quite good and very well drawn. Grandenetti's work on "The Collection Creation" was worthy of note as well.

8. cover: Ken Kelly (November 1970)

(1) Vampi's Feary Tales: Love! [Tom Sutton, frontis] 1p; (2) *Vampirella*: Who Serves the Cause of Chaos? [Archie Goodwin/Tom Sutton] 21p; (3) Amazonia: The Demon in the Crypt! [Gardner Fox/Billy Graham] 6p; (4) Easy Way to a Tuff Surfboard! [Archie Goodwin/Frank Frazetta, reprinted from *Eerie* #3 (May 1966)] ½ p; (5) Out of the Fog ... and into the Mist! [Steve Skeates/Ken Barr] 5p; (6) Snake Eyes [Nicola Cuti/Jack Sparling] 7p; (7) Vampi's Flames: Do You Want to be a Queen?/Queen of the Night [Steven Teal and Patrick Boles/Robert Thivierge, Toby Caputi, Phillippe Druillet, Peter Sedeky, Tony De Sensi and John Wojick, text stories] 2p; (8) Signs of Sorcery [Don

ILLUSTRATED TALES TO BEWITCH & BEDEVIL YOU

VAMPIRELLA

VAMPI
#7
SEPT

A WARREN MAGAZINE PDC

WHAT WILD
MANNER OF BEING
IS A
WITCH
WOMAN?
READ THIS
TREND-SETTING
23-PAGE
GREAT TRILOGY
ISSUE!

50¢

One of Frazetta's best covers. Frazetta liked to show the contrast between beautiful women and savage beasts and painted a number of covers, for Warren and others, on the same basic theme. *Vampirella* is ® Dynamite Entertainment and © 2012 DFI. All rights reserved/used by permission.

vious appearance in *Eerie*. She was a fairly interesting female sword and sorcery character. Bill Fraccio and Tony Tallarico delivered the best art job they ever did for Warren with "The Gulfer." French master Phillippe Druillet contributed a rendering of *Vampirella* but for some reason it appeared on the fan page. Peter Sedeky's fan page illustration was later reworked into the cult underground comic character Octobriana, who later also appeared in Bryan Talbot's *Luther Arkwright* series. Another solid issue.

9. cover: Boris Vallejo and Wally Wood (January 1971)

(1) Vampi's Feary Tales: Lilith [Nicola Cuti/Jeff Jones, frontis] 1p; (2) *Vampirella*: The Testing! [Archie Goodwin/Tom Sutton] 12p; (3) Monster Bait! [Don Glut/Joe Wehrle] 6p; (4) Fate's Cold Finger! [Doug Moench/Ken Barr] 6p; (5) The Curse [Wally Wood] 8p; (6) Jack the Ripper Strikes Again [Chris Fellner/Jerry Grandenetti] 8p; (7) The Boy Who Loved Trees! [Gardner Fox and Barry Smith/Barry Smith] 6p; (8) Vampi's Flames: Vampi's Vindication/To Die, to Sleep/The Trap [Archie Goodwin?/Michelle Knight and Charles Collins/Bruce Holroyd, Peter Hsu, Carlos Maria Federici, Ronald A. Stringer and Peter Iasillo, text article/text stories] 2p; (9) The Work Orders for the Day! [Alac Justice] 7p.

Glut/George Roussos] 7p; (9) The Gulfer [Nicola Cuti/Bill Fraccio and Tony Tallarico] 6p.

Notes: The first real *Vampirella* story appeared as her character was revamped into a more serious mode. I should go on record here and state I don't think *Vampirella* was ever a strong character. In fact, although generally drawn well, her stories were usually quite bland and often lacking in logic. However, she started up here with a trio of very strong stories from Archie Goodwin and Tom Sutton. In fact, Sutton delivered some of the best art he ever produced for Warren. Amazonia moved here from her pre-

Notes: Vallejo's North American debut cover was shrunk to half the cover size and surrounded by the splash page artwork from Wally Wood's interior story. Not sure why this was done since it was a decent enough, if not particularly strong, cover. This issue was a striking mix between very good and pretty much lousy story and art. Not surprisingly, the best work was by the pros —

Wally Wood, Jeff Jones, Jerry Grandenetti, Archie Goodwin, Tom Sutton, Gardner Fox and Barry Smith (nowadays Barry Windsor-Smith, here making his only Warren appearance). The Fox/Windsor-Smith and Wood stories were the best. Future artist Peter Hsu made his comics debut on the fan page. Goodwin's editorial on the fan page was in regards to a plagiarized story that had appeared on #8's fan page.

10. cover: Bill Hughes (March 1971)

(1) Vampi's Feary Tales: The Face of Medusa [Billy Graham, frontis] 1p; (2) Fiends in the Night! [Buddy Saunders/Tom Sutton] 8p; (3) The Marriage [Steve Skeates/Ralph Reese] 5p; (4) Eye of Newt, Toe of Frog [Gerry Conway/ Frank Brunner] 7p; (5) The Soft, Sweet Lips of Hell! [Denny O'Neil/Neal Adams and Steve Englehart] 10p; (6) War of the Wizards [Wally Wood] 8p; (7) A Thing of Beauty! [Len Wein/ Billy Graham] 7p; (8) Vampi's Flames: The Night/The Protective Father/The Telephone Terror!/Results of the First Miss Vampire Contest! [Diane Reed, Henry C. Brennan, Susan Coakley and ?/Bob Garrison and Kevin Richert, text stories/text article] 2p; (9) Regeneration Gap [Chuck McNaughton/Tom Sutton] 7p.

Notes: Future comics writer Mike Barr sent in a letter. The *Vampirella* story was skipped, presumably due to deadline problems, with two other Tom Sutton–drawn stories put in as replacements. The first of those, "Fiends in the Night," was introduced by Uncle Creepy and was intended for that magazine. When Dynamite issued its second archive volume in 2010, this story was dropped from the book, probably because Dynamite didn't have the rights to publish a story with *Creepy* hosting. This strong issue led with solid artistic strength from Sutton, Ralph Reese, Frank Brunner (although the Conway story was noticeably weak), Wally Wood, Billy Graham and Neal Adams. Top stories came from Len Wein, Steve Skeates, Denny O'Neil and Buddy Saunders. Steve Englehart made his professional debut here working as an artist in combination with Neal Adams. The Conway/ Brunner story was originally intended for Warren rival *Web of Horror*.

11. cover: Frank Frazetta (May 1971)

(1) Vampi's Feary Tales: The Devil's Daughter! [Tom Sutton, frontis] 1p; (2) *Vampirella*:

Carnival of the Damned! [Archie Goodwin/ Tom Sutton] 14p; (3) The Escape! [Larry Herndon/L. M. Roca] 6p; (4) Prisoner in the Pool! [Buddy Saunders/Dave Cockrum] 6p; (5) She'll Never Learn! [Steve Skeates/Ken Barr] 7p; (6) The Green Plague [Nicola Cuti/Jerry Grandenetti] 8p; (7) Vampi's Flames: The Deep/The Elevator [Stephen Darner and ?/Anthony Kowalik, Dave Manak, Pam Presnell, Richard Bassford, Ed Romer and R. Charron, text stories] 2p; (8) Dragon Woman [Sanho Kim] 9p.

Notes: Frazetta's cover "Woman with Scythe" was one of his most popular. *Vampirella* returned, and from here on out, appeared in every issue. Richard Bassford's art on the fan page was a preview for an upcoming six-page story that never appeared. Dave Manak, who did many gag cartoon strips for DC, especially on their *Plop! Humor* title, also appeared on the fan page. Sanho Kim's art and story were particularly impressive.

12. cover: Manuel Sanjulian (July 1971)

(1) Vampi's Feary Tales: The Sirens! [Frank Brunner, frontis] 1p; (2) *Vampirella*: Death's Dark Angel [Archie Goodwin/Jose Gonzalez] 20p; (3) Amazonia and the Eye of Ozirios! [Gardner Fox/Billy Graham] 8p; (4) The Quest [Jeff Jones] 7p; (5) Annual Warren Awards at the New York Comicon... [Martin Greim/Ernie Colon, text article, reprinted from the *Comic Crusader* #10 (1970)] 2p; (6) Vampi's Flames: Join Me!/The Leaking Bath Tub! [David Reiffal and Carl Daigrepont, Jr./J. Haney, Maria Hearley, Hollis Williams, Carlos Federici, James King and Brian Bunick, poem/text story] 2p; (7) To Kill a God! [Wally Wood] 8p.

Notes: Editor: Billy Graham. The Spanish invasion began. Jose Gonzalez debuted on *Vampirella*, and while he was immediately praised, this effort was only so-so, with somewhat scratchy looking art and mediocre storytelling abilities. Same goes for the accompanying cover by Sanjulian. Nice work from Jeff Jones but the real prize here was Wally Wood's "To Kill a God!" Just superb work, with Wood at his awesome best! Gardner Fox's character, Amazonia, made her final appearance. Carlos Federici was a professional artist from South America, stuck side by side with amateur American artists on the fan page. Future comic artist Brian Bunick debuted his work on the fan page.

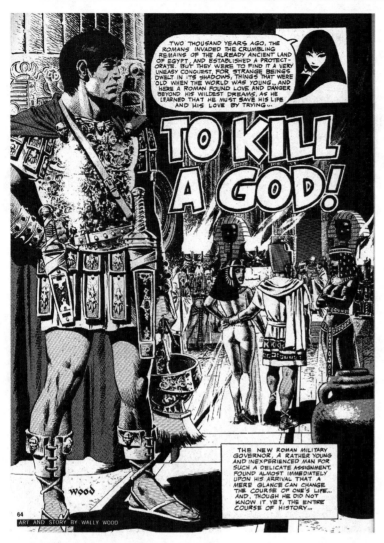

TWO THOUSAND YEARS AGO, THE ROMANS INVADED THE CRUMBLING REMAINS OF THE ALREADY ANCIENT LAND OF EGYPT, AND ESTABLISHED A PROTECTORATE. BUT THEY WERE TO FIND IT A VERY UNEASY CONQUEST, FOR STRANGE BEINGS DWELT IN ITS SHADOWS, THINGS THAT WERE OLD WHEN THE WORLD WAS YOUNG... AND HERE A ROMAN FOUND LOVE AND DANGER BEYOND HIS WILDEST DREAMS, AS HE LEARNED THAT HE MUST SAVE HIS LIFE AND HIS LOVE BY TRYING...

TO KILL A GOD!

THE NEW ROMAN MILITARY GOVERNOR, A RATHER YOUNG AND INEXPERIENCED MAN FOR SUCH A DELICATE ASSIGNMENT, FOUND ALMOST IMMEDIATELY UPON HIS ARRIVAL THAT A MERE GLANCE CAN CHANGE THE COURSE OF ONE'S LIFE... AND, THOUGH HE DID NOT KNOW IT YET, THE ENTIRE COURSE OF HISTORY...

64

ART AND STORY BY WALLY WOOD

Wally Wood's superb effort from *Vampirella* #12 is one of the all-time great Warren stories. *Vampirella* is ® Dynamite Entertainment and © 2012 DFI. All rights reserved/used by permission.

13. cover: Manuel Sanjulian (September 1971)

(1) Vampi's Feary Tales: Lamiae [Gary Kaufman, frontis] 1p; **(2)** *Vampirella*: The Lurker in the Deep! [Archie Goodwin/Jose Gonzalez] 15p; **(3)** From Death's Dark Corner! [Gerry Conway/Steve Hickman] 7p; **(4)** The Silver Thief and the Pharaoh's Daughter [Dean Latimer/Jose Bea] 11p; **(5)** The Frog Prince! [Bill DuBay] 5p; **(6)** Vampi's Flames: Official Contest/Children of the Atom/The Leaking Bath Tub!, part 2 [J. R. Cochran, J. G. Barlow, Carl Daigrepont, Jr./Gregg Davidson, Clyde Caldwell and John Ayella, contest rules, poem/text story] 2p; **(7)** Eye of the Beholder [Gary Kaufman] 7p; **(8)** Easy Way to a Tuff Surfboard! [Archie Good-

win/Frank Frazetta, reprinted from *Eerie* #3 (May 1966)] ½ p.

Notes: Sanjulian's cover was of a much higher quality than the previous issue's. Some good stories and art here but the real prize was the American debut of Jose Bea. Future cover artist Clyde Caldwell also debuted his work on the fan page.

14. cover: Manuel Sanjulian (November 1971)

(1) Vampi's Feary Tales: Ladies of Misfortune [Tom Sutton, frontis] 1p; **(2)** *Vampirella*: Isle of the Huntress! [Archie Goodwin/Jose Gonzalez] 20p; **(3)** The Wedding Gift [Nicola Cuti/Mike Ploog] 7p; **(4)** The Sword of Light [Sam Glanzman] 9p; **(5)** Deadman's Treasure! [Lynn Marron/Tom Sutton] 9p; **(6)** Vampi's Flames: Doug Moench profile/The Crimson Heel!/The Prisoner/The Entity/The Last Blast! [Doug Moench, Fuat Ulus, Ron Lovett, John Kaska and Dan McGee/Cara Shorman, Robert Shugrue, Jose Munoz, Vivian Jane Amick and Glen Abrams, text article/text stories] 2p; **(7)** Wolf Hunt [Joe Wehrle/Esteban Maroto] 7p.

Notes: Great issue! True, the *Vampirella* story was no great shakes (but then, they rarely were) but the rest of the issue was dazzling. Sanjulian's cover was one of the best of the early *Vampirella* run. Esteban Maroto made his first Warren appearance (and it's a beaut!) with "Wolf Hunt." Mike Ploog illustrated a darn good Nic Cuti story. The legendary Sam Glanzman turned in his only Warren work and it's a fine, fine job! Lynn Marron made her professional debut with a solid story and Tom Sutton, who probably illustrated more stories by first-time writers than anyone else at Warren, provided her with an equally solid art job. Another South American pro, this

ILLUSTRATED TALES TO BEWITCH & BEDEVIL YOU

VAMPIRELLA

VAMPI #18 AUG. 1972

A WARREN MAGAZINE PDC 75¢

The Cold Touch of The Conjuress awaits Vampirella -- when she discovers "DRACULA STILL LIVES"

Erich Torres was probably the best artist to grace Vampi's covers and this effort, from #18, is a prime example. *Vampirella* is ® Dynamite Entertainment and © 2012 DFI. All rights reserved/used by permission.

time the great Jose Munoz, saw his sample art stuck on the fan page.

15. cover: Manuel Sanjulian (January 1972)

(1) Vampi's Feary Tales: Metifa! [Bill DuBay/ Richard Corben, frontis] 1p; **(2)** *Vampirella*: The Resurrection of Papa Voudou! [Archie Goodwin/Jose Gonzalez] 20p; **(3)** Quavering Shadows [Doug Moench/Jose Bea] 11p; **(4)** A House Is Not a Home [Dave Mitchell/Nebot] 6p; **(5)** 1971 Comicon Awards Go to Frazetta and Goodwin... [?/?, text article] 3p; **(6)** Vampi's Flames: Bill DuBay profile/Return to Nowhere/Revenge/ Demon's Curse/Final Log

[Bill DuBay, Richard Lysaght, Kenneth Leggett, Jr., Paul E. King and Robb Wilson/Tom Vaughn, T. O. Mears and Andres Bakells, text article/text stories with photo] 2p; **(7)** Welcome to the Witches' Coven [Don McGregor/Luis Garcia] 12p.

Notes: A rather poor issue with "Welcome to the Witches' Coven" and "Quavering Shadows" being the top stories and art. Interesting, if somewhat clumsy looking, airbrush art by Corben appeared on "Creepy's Loathsome Lore." A rather crappy-looking Dracula appeared on the last page of the *Vampirella* strip. The Vampi story was okay, but the artwork was middling to downright poor there. Nebot's poor art in this issue is particularly awful.

16. cover: Manuel Sanjulian (April 1972)

(1) Vampi's Feary Tales: The Gray Women [Jan Strnad/ Rafael Auraleon, frontis] 1p; **(2)** *Vampirella*: ... and Be a Bride of Chaos [Archie Goodwin/Jose Gonzalez] 22p; **(3)** Purification [Nebot] 3p; **(4)** Gorilla My Dreams [Gus St. Anthony/Esteban Maroto] 6p; **(5)** Girl on the Red Asteroid [Don Glut/Bill DuBay] 6p; **(6)** Lover! [Pat Boyette] 6p; **(7)** Vampi's Flames: Jose Gonzlaez profile/Vampire/ Another Night Shot/Spectral Vengeance [J. R. Cochran, Clint Banks, Mary Lou Jurina and Gurn Lee/Jose Gonzalez, Tom Blackshear, Charles L. Pauly and Lloyd Fukuki, text article/ text stories] 1p; **(8)** How Our Artists See Themselves... [J. R. Cochran/Bill DuBay, Dave Cockrum, Richard Corben, Jerry Grandenetti and Billy Graham, a collection of self-portraits] 1p; **(9)** Cilia [Nicola Cuti/Felix Mas] 7p.

Notes: Another sub-standard issue, with only Pat Boyette's tasty "Lover!" rising to the level of a quality story. Future comic writer David

Michelinie sent in a letter. Goodwin's decent script for *Vampirella* was again brought low by inappropriate and awkward art. In fact, Gonzalez's artwork on this issue's fan page was considerably better than what he was producing for the "Vampirella" strip at this point. The lame Dracula appearing in Vampi's story claims to be the same Dracula from the Goodwin/Crandall story "The Coffin of Dracula" from *Creepy* #8 and 9 and, thus, Bram Stoker's Dracula, but he looked and acted nothing like the "Coffin" Dracula. Gonzalez drew him short, paunchy and looking a bit like an aged Italian count. According to J. R. Cochran, in a 1974 letter to the fanzine *Canar* #21–22 (May–June 1974), the feature page effort "How Our Artists See Themselves" was the cause for the departure of editor Billy Graham when Jim Warren strongly objected to the appearance of the finished page, which had been based on a layout Warren himself suggested.

17. cover: Enrich Torres (June 1972)

(1) Vampi's Feary Tales: The Story of Arachne [Jan Strnad/Rafael Auraleon, frontis] 1p; (2) The Story Behind the Story: "Quavering Shadows" [Doug Moench, text article on the letters page] ½ p; (3) *Vampirella*: ... Beware, Dreamers [T. Casey Brennan/Jose Gonzalez] 20p; (4) Tomb of the Gods: Horus [Esteban Maroto] 8p; (5) Death in the Shadows [Doug Moench/Luis Garcia] 8p; (6) A Man's World [Mike Jennings/Jose Bea] 8p; (7) Love of the Bayou [Jan Strnad/L. M. Roca] 8p; (8) Vampi's Flames: Rafael Auraleon profile/Reflections of the Dead/The End!/The Last Room/Revenge of the Dead/The Second Age [J. R. Cochran, Robert R. Arbuthnot, P. R. Seamon, Mark Collins, Doug Moench, Jim Martincie and Bob Siegal/Rafael Auraleon, Dave Carrigan, Thomas J. Golash and Brant Withers, text articles/text stories] 2p; (9) The Wedding Ring [Steve Skeates/Jerry Grandenetti] 7p.

Notes: Editor: J. R. Cochran. Price increased to 75 cents and page increase to 72 pages. Don McGregor sent in a letter complaining about *Vampirella*'s comments at the end of his "Witches' Coven" story from #15. Maroto's "Tomb of the Gods" series was printed in Europe around 1969 or 1970. His artwork had improved a great deal since then, making this series look somewhat undercooked compared with his current work. This

was a much better issue than the previous two with Garcia and Roca providing the best artwork. Strnad's story "Lover of the Bayou" was the best story.

18. cover: Enrich Torres (August 1972)

(1) Vampi's Feary Tales: Nymphs [Kevin Pagan/Luis Garcia, frontis] 1p; (2) Inside 18/The Story behind the Story: "Girl on the Red Asteroid" [J. R. Cochran and Don Glut, text articles on the letters page] ½ p; (3) *Vampirella*: Dracula Still Lives! [T. Casey Brennan/Jose Gonzalez] 20p; (4) Tomb of the Gods: Kali [Esteban Maroto] 8p; (5) Song of a Sad-Eyed Sorceress [Don McGregor/Luis Garcia] 12p; (6) Won't Get Fooled Again [Doug Moench/Rafael Auraleon] 9p; (7) Vampi's Flames: Kevin Pagan profile/Eye of the Skull/Vampire/Hidden Danger/The Assassin/Drink, My Love [Kevin Pagan, Thomas Pallanta, Lloyd M. Auerbach, Eric W. Flesch, Bill Cantey and George Siessel/? Garcia, William Barry, Mike Ploog, Felix Mas, Frank Villano, Jr., Seaward Tuthill, text article/text stories] 2p; (8) The Dorian Gray Syndrome [Don Glut/Felix Mas] 6p.

Notes: One of Enrich's best *Vampirella* covers graced this issue. Gonzalez's artwork finally began to justify his reputation as *the* Vampriella artist. The crappy Dracula was back though. The McGregor/Garcia effort "Song of a Sad-Eyed Sorceress" was the best story in an issue of generally pretty good stories. A Levi's pants ad appears on the fan page, largely because the hippy/stripper chick in the ad wears Levi's, along with a top resembling Vampi's skimpy costume. It should perhaps be noted that Vampi's costume design has become a familiar favorite for those strippers who have the right, eh, attributes for it.

19. cover: Jose Gonzalez and a montage of previous covers (September 1972)

(1) Everything You Always Wanted to Know About *Vampirella* but Nobody Ever Told You... [J. R. Cochran, text article with photo, frontis and on the inside back cover] 2p; (2) *Vampirella*: Shadow of Dracula! [T. Casey Brennan/Jose Gonzalez] 10p; (3) To Kill a God! [Wally Wood, reprinted from *Vampirella* #12 (July 1971)] 8p; (4) Two Silver Bullets! [Don Glut/Reed Crandall, reprinted from *Vampirella* #1 (October 1969)] 6p; (5) Fate's Cold Finger! [Doug Moench/ Ken Barr, reprinted from

Vampirella #9 (January 1971)] 6p; (**6**) Jack the Ripper Strikes Again [Chris Fellner/Jerry Grandenetti, reprinted from *Vampirella* #9 (January 1971), miscredited to Fred Ott] 8p; (**7**) The Survivor [Buddy Saunders/Ernie Colon, reprinted from *Vampirella* #7 (September 1970)] 6p; (**8**) The Soft, Sweet Lips of Hell! [Denny O'Neil/Neal Adams and Steve Englehart, reprinted from *Vampirella* #10 (March 1971)] 10p; (**9**) The Silver Thief and the Pharaoh's Daughter [Dean Latimer/Jose Bea, reprinted from *Vampirella* #10 (March 1971)] 11p.

Notes: Cost increased to $1.00 and size increased to 80 pages. The *Vampirella* annual was now included in *Vampirella*'s regular numbering. Unlike either *Creepy* or *Eerie*'s, *Vampirella*'s annual usually featured a new *Vampirella* story in the early years. The text article revealed that the inspiration for *Vampirella* was Jane Fonda's 1968 movie role depiction of Barbarella. It also disclosed, for the first time, underground cartoonist Trina Robbins' hand in designing *Vampirella*'s costume and look to which Frank Frazetta added the serpentine bracelet and the bat design on the crotch of her costume. Gonzalez's cover art was lifted from his *Vampirella* poster advertised in the back of the magazine's *Captain Company* catalog pages. Manuel Sanjulian painted the *Eerie* and *Creepy* poster versions, which were also advertised there. The *Creepy* poster art was never used in this country (although it was in Europe) for a cover although the *Eerie* poster was. It is this *Vampirella* poster that people often believe actress Barbara Leigh, a dead ringer for Vampi, posed for, but it isn't true.

20. cover: Luis Dominguez (October 1972)

(**1**) Vampi's Feary Tales: The Matrimonial Murderer [Doug Moench/Rafael Auraleon, frontis] 1p; (**2**) Inside 20/The Story behind the Story: "A Man's World!" [Bill DuBay/Mike Jennings, text articles on the letters page] ½ p; (**3**) Vampirella: When Wakes the Dead [T. Casey Brennan/Jose Gonzalez] 14p; (**4**) Tomb of the Gods: Gender Bender [Esteban Maroto] 11p; (**5**) Vampi's Books Reviews: Prince Valiant/A History of the Comic Strip/Ghost Stories/The Phantom [Chuck McNaughton, text articles] 1p; (**6**) Love Is No Game [Steve Skeates/Luis Garcia] 6p; (**7**) Eye Opener! [Martin Pasko/Rafael Auraleon, miscredited to Doug Moench] 7p; (**8**) Vampi's Flames: Greg Potter profile/Spectre of a Goddess/The Time Is Never/The Safe/The Gift/Advance Guard [Greg Potter, Ron Martin, Wendy Crabtree, Richard Pickman, Henry C. Brennan and Douglas W. Justice/L. M. Roca, Richard Corben, Hudson Hill, Cara Sherman and Bill Bryan, text article/text Vampi's Feary Tales: The Headless Hauntress of Shepton Prison [Doug Moench/Rafael Auraleon, on the inside back cover] 1p.

Notes: Editor: James Warren. Back to 75 cents and 72 pages. Dracula appeared again in the *Vampirella* strip.

The DuBay Era

21. cover: Enrich Torres (December 1972)

(**1**) Vampi's Feary Tales: Mind-Benders! [Bill DuBay, frontis and on the inside back cover] 2p; (**2**) Inside 21/The Story Behind the Story: "Song of a Sad-Eyed Sorceress!" [Bill DuBay and Don McGregor, text articles on the letters page] ½ p; (**3**) *Vampirella*: Slithers of the Sand! [Steve Englehart/Jose Gonzalez, story credited to Chad Archer] 23p; (**4**) The Critic's Crypt: Dracula/Dr. Jekyll and Mr. Hyde/The War of the Worlds: Audio Rarities/Themes from Horror Movies [Chuck McNaughton, text articles] 1p; (**5**) Tomb of the Gods: A Legend [Esteban Maroto] 8p; (**6**) Paranoia [Steve Skeates/Luis Garcia] 6p; (**7**) *Vampirella*'s Short-Short Shocker: Puppy Love! [Chuck McNaughton/Rich Buckler, text story] 2p; (**8**) Vampi's Flames: Enrich Torres profile/A Bedtime Story/The Eternal Thirst/And May He Rest in Peace!/Idol of Ualirrma [Bill DuBay, Charles E. Fritch, Wendy Crabtree, Shirley D. Sipe and Michael Benitez/Enrich Torres, Tom Soderberg, Tim Groh and Robert Randall, text article/text stories] 2p; (**9**) The Vampiress Stalks the Castle This Night [Don McGregor/Felix Mas] 12p.

Notes: Enrich provided a pretty cool cover depicting *Vampirella* sweating in the desert beneath a Death's Head sun. Gonzalez's art on *Vampirella* continued to improve. Englehart (who used a pen name because he was employed at the time as a editorial staffer by Marvel) also provided an upswing in the quality of Vampi's stories, although that proved to be short-lived. Still, only the MacGregor/Mas story was anything to really call home about. The rest were just middlin' fare. Maroto's *Tomb of the Gods* serial always suffered since both story and art were several years old

ILLUSTRATED TALES TO BEWITCH & BEDEVIL YOU

VAMPIRELLA

VAMPI #21
DEC. 1972

A WARREN MAGAZINE PDC 75¢   588856

ON THE HOT DESERT SANDS--- VAMPIRELLA AND DRACULA ENCOUNTER THE HORRIBLE GIANT SLUG Page 6

Vampirella's early covers were more illustrative then the later pin-up style efforts. This Torres-illustrated desert scene features the sun as a death mask. *Vampirella* is ® Dynamite Entertainment and © 2012 DFI. All rights reserved/used by permission.

and the new art he was doing for *Creepy* (and even the *Dax* serial then being reprinted in *Eerie*) were of much higher quality.

22. cover: Enrich Torres? (March 1973)

(1) Silent Night, Unholy Night [Bill DuBay, frontis and on the inside back cover] 2p; **(2)** *Vampirella*: Hell from on High [Steve Englehart/Jose Gonzalez] 22p; **(3)** Tomb of the Gods: Orpheus [Esteban Maroto] 7p; **(4)** Dracula ad [Esteban Maroto, color] 1p; **(5)** The Viyi [Esteban Maroto, color] 6p; **(6)** Dracula ad [Esteban Maroto and Jose Bea, color] 1p; **(7)** The Sentence! [Steve Skeates/Jose Bea] 7p; **(8)** The Cry

of the Dhampir [John Jacobson/Rafael Auraleon] 13p; **(9)** Vampi's Flames: Steve Englehart profile/Delayed Payment/Check, Please!/A Fishy Tale/The Challenge [Steve Englehart, Richard Sawyer, Henry Lipput, C. Tye and John Purcell/Kerry Wathen, Ronald Boone and Ira Harmon, Jr., text article/text stories with photo] 2p; **(10)** Minra [Ed Newsome/Felix Mas] 7p.

Notes: For some reason there was a three-month wait between issues. Price increased to $1.00 and size increased to 80 pages. The cover artist was unidentified although he is clearly a Spanish artist. *The Warren Companion* claims it's Enrich Torres, but it just doesn't look like his work to me. Doug Moench sent in a letter correcting a story miscredit in #20. Somewhat of a ripoff occurring here as the color section story was the same as what appeared in *Creepy* #51. However, the issue was redeemed by printing the excellent story "The Cry of the Dhampir." The magazine's frequency was pushed up to 9 issues a year.

23. cover: Manuel Sanjulian (April 1973)

(1) Vampirella: The Blood Queen of Bayou Parish! [Steve Englehart/Jose Gonzalez] 18p; **(2)** Cobra Queen [Don Glut/Esteban Maroto] 7p; **(3)** Call It Companionship! [Steve Skeates/Ramon Torrents] 6p; **(4)** The Accursed! [Kevin Pagan/Jose Bea] 8p; **(5)** The Witch's Promise [Gerry Boudreau/Rafael Auraleon] 8p; **(6)** Won't Eddie Ever Learn? [Jim Stenstrum/Felix Mas] 10p.

Notes: Sanjulian's "Egyptian Princess" cover was somewhat similar to Frazetta's cover from *Eerie* #23, although Sanjulian's princess was considerably skinnier. Price decreased to 75 cents and size decreased to 72 pages. Good issue with superior art from Auraleon and Maroto.

24. cover: Enrich Torres (May 1973)

(1) *Vampirella*: Into the Inferno! [Bill DuBay/Jose Gonzalez] 13p; **(2)** Middle-Am! [Steve Skeates/Esteban Maroto] 6p; **(3)** Homo Superior [R. Michael Rosen/Ramon Torrents] 13p; **(4)** The Choice [Doug Moench/Rafael Auraleon] 10p; **(5)** Changes [Steve Skeates/Felix Mas] 10p; **(6)** Vampi's Vault [same as *Creepy* #53's contents, text articles] 1p.

Notes: Steve Englehart's script for "Into the Inferno!" was lost in the mail with no backup copy available, so Bill DuBay wrote an entirely different story with the same title for *Vampirella*. Vampi's fan page was dropped for a features page that was identical for each horror magazine in the Warren stable.

25. cover: Enrich Torres (June 1973)

(1) A Guest Editorial by Phil Seuling [Phil Seuling, text article on the letters page] ½ p; **(2)** *Vampirella*: What Price Love [Bill DuBay/Jose Gonzalez] 12p; **(3)** The Haunted Child [Nicola Cuti/Rafael Auraleon] 11p; **(4)** Nimrod [Jack L. Bannowith Esteban Maroto, color] 8p; **(5)** Cold Calculation [Doug Moench/Ramon Torrents] 7p; **(6)** The Dead Howl at Midnight! [W. Eaton/Jose Bea] 8p; **(7)** Vampi's Vault [same as *Creepy* #54's contents, text articles] 1p.

Notes: Must have been some last-minute deadline problems, as this issue's "Cold Calculation" was advertised for the next issue on the back cover!

26. cover: montage of interior panels (August 1973)

(1) Death and Doctor Morbidus [George Henderson/Rafael Auraleon, from the story by ?, frontis and on the inside back cover] 2p; **(2)** Vampi's Vault [same as *Creepy* #56's contents, text articles] 1p; **(3)** Vampirella: Demons in the Fog! [Len Wein/Escolano and Jose Gonzalez] 12p; **(4)** Moonspawn [Doug Moench/Esteban Maroto] 10p; **(5)** Fringe Benefits [Doug Moench/Jose Bea, color] 7p; **(6)** Dracula ad [Esteban Maroto, color] 1p; **(7)** Demon Child [James Crawford/Ramon Torrents] 9p; **(8)** Blood Brothers! [Lynn Marron/Isidro Mones] 10p.

Notes: Henderson's effort here may have been an adapted story, since all his other work for Warren consisted of adaptations but I've been unable to verify an original author. "Blood Brothers!" was an interesting story.

27. cover: Enrich Torres (November 1973)

(1) Capture [Bill DuBay, game, frontis, interior page and on the inside back cover] 2½ p; **(2)** Wolf Hunt [Joe Wehrle/Esteban Maroto, reprinted from *Vampirella* #14 (November 1971)] 7p; **(3)** Welcome to the Witches' Coven [Don McGregor/Luis Garcia, reprinted from *Vampirella* #15 (January 1972)] 12p; **(4)** Quavering Shadows [Doug Moench/Jose Bea, reprinted from *Vampirella* #15 (January 1972)] 11p; **(5)** The Frog Prince! [Bill DuBay, reprinted from *Vampirella* #13 (September 1971)] 5p; **(6)** *Vampirella*: Return Trip [Josep Toutain/Jose Gonzalez, color] 8p; **(7)** Cilia [Nicola Cuti/Felix Mas, reprinted from *Vampirella* #16 (April 1972)] 7p; **(8)** Quest [Jeff Jones, reprinted from *Vampirella* #12 (July 1971)] 7p; **(9)** War of the Wizards [Wally Wood, reprinted from *Vampirella* #19 (March 1971)] 8p.

Notes: The 1973 *Vampirella* annual. Good, solid reprint issue with one new story. Price increased to $1.00 and size increased to 80 pages.

28. cover: Enrich Torres (October 1973)

(1) Werewolf! [Bill DuBay, game, frontis and on the inside back cover] 2p; **(2)** Vampi's Vaults [same as *Creepy* #57's contents, text articles] 1p; **(3)** *Vampirella* and the Curse of the Macdaemons! [Mike Butterworth/Jose Gonzalez, story credited to Flaxman Loew] 12p; **(4)** The Clash of Leviathans! [Doug Moench/Ramon Torrents] 9p; **(5)** Blind Man's Guide [Fernando Fernadez] 9p; **(6)** The Power and the Gory! [W. Eaton/Rafael Auraleon, color] 8p; **(7)** Eye Don't Want to Die! [Doug Moench/Ramon Torrents] 6p; **(8)** The Other Side of Heaven! [Jose Bea] 10p; **(9)** Old Texas Road [Bruce Bezaire/Isidro Mones] 7p.

Notes: Good cover by Enrich. Back to normal price and size again. Pretty good issue with Fernando Fernandez taking the honors for best story and art. Fernandez was a great addition to the Warren artist line. His artwork was beautiful and his stories were generally of unusually high quality. Almost all of his stories appeared in *Vampirella*. Jose Bea also delivered a superior story with "The Other Side of Heaven!" Bruce Bezaire (the guy with the best name in horror comics!) made his professional debut. Bezaire didn't write nearly enough for Warren (and he seems to have completely disappeared after his writing stint there) but all his stories were noteworthy for their strong plotting, tight scripts and superior quality. One wishes he had written a good deal more.

29. cover: Enrich Torres (November 1973)

(1) A History of Vampires [Bill DuBay, frontis and on the inside back cover] 2p; (2) Vampi's Vaults [same as *Creepy* #58's contents, text articles] 1p; (3) *Vampirella* and the Undead of the Deep! [Mike Butterworth/Jose Gonzalez, story credited to Flaxman Loew] 12p; (4) The Evil Eye [W. Eaton/Ramon Torrents] 8p; (5) Stairway to Heaven! [Fernando Fernandez] 8p; (6) Last Lunch for Rats! [Doug Moench/Rafael Auraleon] 9p; (7) The Vampires Are Coming! The Vampires Are Coming! [Doug Moench/Isidro Mones] 10p; (8) Two *Vampirellas* Stun 5,500 at 1973 Comic Art Convention [Gerry Boudreau, text article with photos] 1p.

Notes: Odd cover with a very nicely rendered *Vampirella* menaced by a giant toad! A solid, if not spectacular, issue.

30. cover: Enrich Torres (January 1974)

(1) A History of Vampires [Bill DuBay, frontis] 1p; (2) Vampi's Vaults [same as *Eerie* #54's contents, text articles with photo] 1p; (3) *Vampirella*: The God of Blood [Mike Butterworth/Jose Gonzalez, story credited to Flaxman Loew] 12p; (4) Pantha: Re-Birth! [Steve Skeates/Rafael Auraleon] 10p; (5) As Though They Were Living! [Gerry Boudreau/Richard Corben, color] 8p; (6) Memoirs! [Fernando Fernandez] 8p; (7) Captain Death [Carl Wessler/Isidro Mones] 8p; (8) Next issue ad featuring Luana [Neal Adams from Frank Frazetta, color, on the back cover] 1p.

Notes: Nifty cover featuring Vampirella. *Pantha*, a new series about a stripper who turned into a murderous black panther, debuted. Although the series was carried long past its needed expiration date, the first half dozen or so stories (particularly those written by creator Skeates) were quite good. Fernandez delivered the best story and art. The back cover featured a tracing done by Neal Adams of Frazetta's upcoming cover.

31. cover: Frank Frazetta (March 1974) reprinted from the Luana movie poster and novelization

(1) A Few Words and Pictures about Our Brand New Comic Magazine [Bill DuBay/Will Eisner and Bill DuBay, text article, frontis and on the inside back cover] 2p; (2) Vampi's Vault [same as *Creepy* #59's contents, text articles with photos] 1p; (3) *Vampirella*: The Betrothed of the Sun-God! [Mike Butterworth/Jose Gonzalez, story credited to Flaxman Loew] 12p; (4) Pantha: Family Ties! [Steve Skeates/Rafael Auraleon] 10p; (5) The Truth! [Fernando Fernandez] 10p; (6) The Woodlik Inheritance! [Richard Corben, color] 7p; (7) The Strange, Incurable Phobia of Mad Pierre Langlois! [Jose Bea] 8p; (8) Luana [Doug Moench/Esteban Maroto, from the 1974 film] 13p.

Notes: Price increased to $1.00 and size increased to 80 pages. Frazetta's cover was possibly the first time Warren published one of his paintings that they had not originally commissioned. This was a surprisingly good issue with Gonzalez's art on Vampi perhaps his best to date. Pantha delivered a strong episode while Fernando Fernandez and Richard Corben shared honors for best story and art. I don't know how closely the Luana adaptation followed the screenplay but it was quite a lot of fun to read and Maroto's art was very good.

32. cover: Enrich Torres (April 1974)

(1) Vampi's Vault [same as *Creepy* #60's contents, text articles with photo] 1p; (2) *Vampirella*: The Running Red [Mike Butterworth/Jose Gonzalez, story credited to Flaxman Loew] 12p; (3) Pantha: Black on White [Steve Skeates/Rafael Auraleon] 10p; (4) Presenting the 1973 Warren Awards [Bill DuBay, text article] 2p; (5) Harry [Jeff Jones, color] 6p; (6) Dead Run [Jeff Jones, color] 2p; (7) The Man Whose Soul Was Spoiling! [Fernando Fernandez] 12p; (8) Just Like Old Times! [Rich Margopoulos/Ramon Torrents] 10p.

Notes: Back to 72 pages. A bland cover but some good stories. Jones' stories weren't great but the art sure was. *Pantha's* entry was great fun. Best story goes (yet again!) to Fernandez but the Margopoulos/Torrents story was quite nice as well.

33. cover: Enrich Torres (May 1974)

(1) The Believer [Jeff Jones and Berni Wrightson, frontis and on the inside back cover] 2p; (2) Vampi's Vault [same as *Creepy* #61's contents, text articles with photos] 1p; (3) Vampirella and the Sultana's Revenge! [Mike Butter-

ALL NEW STORIES AND ART! PLUS **COLOR!**

VAMPIRELLA

MARCH 1974

LUANA
THE BEAST GIRL!
TRAPPED
IN THE MIDST
OF A
TRIBAL
UPRISING...
Page 55

This effort from #31 was perhaps the only Frazetta cover that wasn't a direct commission from Warren. The jungle princess image doubled as the movie poster for the low-budget film *Luana*. *Vampirella* is ® Dynamite Entertainment and © 2012 DFI. All rights reserved/used by permission.

conclusion to its first story arc. Budd Lewis, Isidro Mones and John Jacobson all contributed strong material but the cream of the crop here was Jack Butterworth and Richard Corben's "Top to Bottom"—a real understated classic. Butterworth's work as a writer for Warren is often overlooked by fans but he was quite good and very consistent in his quality. He may not have written a lot of *great* stories (although his "Oil of Dog" adaptation in *Eerie* is one of the best adaptations Warren ever ran) but there's also not a single story of his you could hold up as an example of a poor story. A steady writer, in the much the same way that Archie Goodwin was a steady writer.

34. cover: Enrich Torres (June 1974)

(1) Extraordinary Verse [William Blake/Jeff Jones, poem, frontis, from the poem "The Tiger" by Blake] 1p; (2) Vampi's Vault [same as *Creepy* #62's contents, text article with photo] 1p; (3) *Vampirella*: The Carnival of Death! [Mike Butterworth/Jose Gonzalez, story credited to Flaxman Loew] 12p; (4) Miranda [Fred Ott/Felix Mas] 6p; (5) Fleur: From the Spain of Legend! [John Jacobson/ Ramon Torrents] 10p; (6) Black and White Vacuum to Blues [Doug Moench/Estevan Maroto, color] 8p; (7) Recurrence! [Steve Skeates/Jose Bea] 8p; (8) Cold Cuts [Berni Wrightson/Jeff Jones] 6p.

worth/Jose Gonzalez, story credited to Flaxman Loew] 12p; (4) Pantha: Childhood Haunt! [Steve Skeates/Rafael Auraleon] 10p; (5) Top to Bottom [Jack Butterworth/Richard Corben, color] 8p; (6) ...Number 37 Is Missing! [Budd Lewis/Isidro Mones] 10p; (7) Barfly! [John Jacobson/Adolfo Abellan] 12p.

Notes: Nice cover with Vampi menaced by a giant spider (just like Conan!). Gonzalez's art continued to improve while *Vampirella*'s stories remained the light, frothy waste of time they usually were. Jeff Jones and Berni Wrightson's two-pager was pretty darn good as was *Pantha*'s

Notes: Editor: Archie Goodwin with Bill DuBay listed as senior editor. Enrich's unusual paneled cover shouldn't have worked but did (plus, Vampi had a nice rump!). Future publisher Mark V. Ziesing sent in a letter begging for a SF magazine. Somebody forgot to change the feature page heading and it went out under *Creepy*'s title. There were a number of *Fleur* stories — most with a raunchy softcore sexual aspect to them. This first one, however, was pretty straight horror and was quite good, with fine work from Torrents. For some reason, Maroto's art never looked as good in color as it did in B&W. This issue's story was no exception. "Recurrance!" was a very well written and drawn story but "Cold Cuts" so perfectly captured the icy northlands that it's set in that it became an instant classic.

35. cover: Enrich Torres (August 1974)

(**1**) Vampi's Vault [same as *Creepy* #63's contents, text articles] 1p; (**2**) *Vampirella*: The Blood-Gulper [Mike Butterworth/Jose Ortiz, story credited to Flaxman Loew] 12p; (**3**) Relatives! [Bruce Bezaire/Esteban Maroto] 6p; (**4**) Fleur: Our Tarts Were Young and Gay! [John Jacobson/Ramon Torrents] 10p; (**5**) Pure as Snow [Jack Butterworth/Felix Mas, color] 8p; (**6**) The Night Ran Red with Gore [Carl Wessler/Rafael Auraleon] 8p; (**7**) Rendezvous! [Fernando Fernandez] 10p.

Notes: Enrich delivered a great cover! One of *Vampirella*'s best! Future *Dr. Watchstop* artist/writer Ken Macklin sent in a letter. Jose Ortiz filled in on Vampi's strip but he seems to be following Gonzalez's style rather than his own. It was a quite good effort, though. Felix Mas' artwork looked even worse displayed in color than Maroto's had the previous issue! Fernandez's story was, once again, the best thing in the issue.

36. cover: Manuel Sanjulian/back cover: Enrich Torres (September 1974)

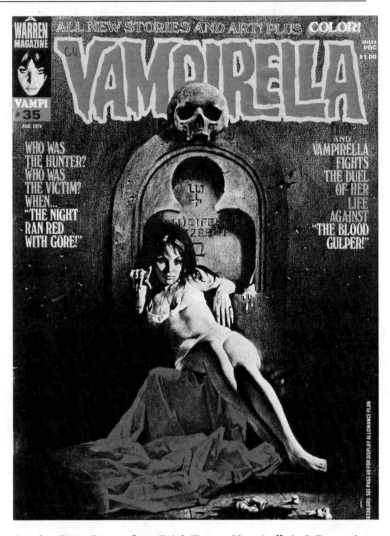

Another "quiet" cover from Erich Torres. *Vampirella* is ® Dynamite Entertainment and © 2012 DFI. All rights reserved/used by permission.

(**1**) *Vampirella*'s Introduction [Bill DuBay/Jose Gonzalez, frontis] 1p; (**2**) Vampi's Vault [same as *Creepy* #64's contents, text articles with photos] 1p; (**3**) Vampirella: The Vampire of the Nile [Mike Butterworth/Jose Ortiz, story credited to Flaxman Loew] 12p; (**4**) A Wonderful Morning! [Fernando Fernandez, color] 8p; (**5**) The Tiara of Dagon! [John Jacobson/Esteban Maroto] 6p; (**6**) Good to the Last Drop! [Martin Pasko/Ramon Torrents] 7p; (**7**) Swordplay [Martin Pasko/Felix Mas] 7p; (**8**) Prey for Me! [Rich Margopoulos/Rafael Auraleon] 12p; (**9**) Puppet-Player! [Jose Bea, color] 8p; (**10**) *Vampirella*'s Farewell [Bill DuBay/Jose Gonzalez, on the inside back cover] 1p.

Notes: Price increased to $1.25 and size increased

to 80 pages. Bill DuBay returned as editor. Sanjulian painted Vampi as the Queen of Hearts for the cover. Ortiz again filled in on Vampi, once again with nice results. Fernandez's artwork looked much better in the color section (especially with Corben's color) than the previous occupants. Jose Bea's color section was quite nice as well. Maroto's art job was nice, although a couple of pages looked like he may have had some help in inking.

37. cover: Manuel Sanjulian/back cover: Enrich Torres (October 1974)

(1) Cobra Queen [Don Glut/Esteban Maroto, reprinted from *Vampirella* #23 (April 1973)] 7p; (2) *Vampirella*: She Who Waits! [Archie Goodwin/Jose Gonzalez, color] 8p; (3) Song of a Sad-Eyed Sorceress [Don McGregor/Luis Garcia, reprinted from *Vampirella* #18 (August 1972)] 12p; (4) The Cry of the Dhampir [John Jacobson/Rafael Auraleon, reprinted from *Vampirella* #22 (March 1973)] 12p; (5) Demon Child [James Crawford/Ramon Torrents, reprinted from *Vampirella* #26 (August 1973)] 9p; (6) The Vampiress Stalks the Castle This Night [Don McGregor/Felix Mas, reprinted from *Vampirella* #21 (December 1972)] 12p; (7) Blood Brothers! [Lynn Marron/Isidro Mones, reprinted from *Vampirella* #26 (August 1973)] 10p; (8) The Accursed! [Kevin Pagan/Jose Bea, reprinted from *Vampirella* #23 (April 1973)] 8p.

Notes: The 1974 *Vampirella* annual. Enrich's back cover was quite good. Goodwin's original *Vampirella* story was a sequel to the reprinted "Cobra Queen" although that story wasn't modified to fit Goodwin's tale. Gonzalez proved once again he can't stage a fight scene.

38. cover: Manuel Sanjulian (November 1974)

(1) Vampi's Vault [same as *Creepy* #66's contents, text articles with photo] 1p; (2) Vampirella: The Mummy's Revenge [Mike Butterworth/Jose Gonzalez, story credited to Flaxman Loew] 12p; (3) Gypsy Curse [Gerry Boudreau and Carl Wessler/Esteban Maroto] 6p; (4) Lucky Stiff [Gerry Boudreau and Carl Wessler/Ramon Torrents] 5p; (5) Out of the Nameless City [John Jacobson/Felix Mas] 12p; (6) On Little Cat Feet! [John Jacobson/Rafael Auraleon] 11p; (7) Trick of the Tide [Jack Butterworth/Isidro Mones] 6p.

Notes: Decent cover by Sanjulian. Size reduction to 72 pages. The story was just okay but the art-

work by Maroto on "Gypsy Curse" was simply beautiful. Best story was "Trick of the Tide."

39. cover: Ken Kelly (January 1975)

(1) *Vampirella*'s Introduction [Bill DuBay/Jose Gonzalez, frontis] 1p; (2) Vampi's Vault [same as *Creepy* #67's contents, text article with photos] 1p; (3) *Vampirella*: The Head-Hunter of London [Mike Butterworth/Leopold Sanchez, story credited to Flaxman Loew] 12p; (4) The Sultan of 42nd Street [Carl Wessler and Gerry Boudreau/Felix Mas] 6p; (5) Snow White and the Deadly Dwarfs [Steve Skeates and Gerry Boudreau/Esteban Maroto] 6p; (6) Dracula: The Circus of King Carnival! [Gerry Boudreau/Esteban Maroto, color] 8p; (7) The Curse of Castle Vlad! [Doug Moench/Rafael Auraleon] 13p; (8) The French Coagulation [Carl Wessler and Gerry Boudreau/Luis Bermejo] 8p; (9) *Vampirella*'s Farewell [Bill DuBay/Jose Gonzalez, on the inside back cover] 1p.

Notes: An interesting Kelly cover showed a silvery, naked woman with coral snakes for fingers, bursting out of a giant skull. It is noticeable that Gonzalez's *Vampirella* pin-ups were considerably better drawn than his actual stories. Maroto delivered two stories this issue and both are among his best, although the poor color marred to some degree his work on the *Dracula* story. That *Dracula* story starred the same Dracula that had previously appeared in the "Vampirella" strip as well as his own never-completed series in *Eerie*. He'd been a moronic joke in the Vampi stories but the *Eerie* series had gone a long way to rehabilitate him, especially with great art by Sutton, Buckler and DuBay, so it was a loss to have it suddenly stop. This three-part series took place a number of years after the aborted earlier series and was quite well written by Boudreau and illustrated by Maroto. Luis Bermejo made his Warren debut with this issue and for the first three years or so, his artwork was just flat-out beautiful, as impressive in its own way as Ortiz's or Maroto's. Afterwards it became much more run of the mill, perhaps reflecting an increasingly heavy workload as he became the regular artist on *The Rook*.

40. cover: Enrich Torres/back cover: Ken Kelly (March 1975)

(1) *Vampirella*'s Introduction [Bill DuBay/Jose Gonzalez, frontis] 1p; (2) Vampi's Vault [same as *Creepy* #68's contents, text articles with

photo] 1p; (3) *Vampirella*: The Nameless Ravisher! [Mike Butterworth/Leopold Sanchez, story credited to Flaxman Loew] 12p; (4) Dracula: The Winged Shaft of Fate [Gerry Boudreau/Esteban Maroto, color] 8p; (5) The Face of Death! [Carl Wessler/Ramon Torrents] 7p; (6) The Man Who Never Was [Fernando Fernandez] 12p; (7) The Time Eater [Jack Butterworth/Paul Neary] 12p; (8) Home for the Holidays [Budd Lewis/Luis Bermeno] 8p.

Notes: It had a $1.25 price and 80-page length. Nice cover by Enrich. Fernandez returned but his scratchy art approach on his story was irritating and distracted from the decent script. "Home for the Holidays" was an overflow story from *Creepy*'s Christmas special. Much like the intended DuBay/Ortiz story that was to have appeared in the Christmas issue, this story must have missed the deadline as it would have made a better substitute for that story than the non-holiday Moench/Severin story that actually appeared there. Best story and art was from "The Face of Death" by Wessler and Torrents. Wessler was an old hand at horror stories, having worked for EC in the 1950s. His stories, at times, seemed rather tame compared to the new style of horror, but he never delivered stories that were less than interesting and, on occasion, they were a good deal more than that. Torrents was a very popular artist at Warren, his near photographic art style lending itself to a wide variety of stories.

41. cover: Enrich Torres (April 1975)

(1) *Vampirella*'s Introduction [Bill DuBay/Jose Gonzalez, frontis] 1p; (2) Everything You Always Wanted to Know ... About the Comics!: The Story [Bill DuBay, text article] 1p; (3) *Vampirella*: The Malignant Morticians [Mike Butterworth/Leopold Sanchez, story credited to Flaxman Loew] 12p; (4) Dracula: Rainy Night in Georgia [Gerry Boudreau/Esteban Maroto] 8p; (5) The House on the Sea [Jim Stenstrum/ Rafael Auraleon] 20p; (6) The Wickford Witches [Gerry Boudreau/Jose Ortiz] 6p; (7) Goodbye, My Love, Goodbye [Fernando Fernandez] 12p.

Notes: Back to $1.00 and 72 pages. Behind a very gothic cover (except for Vampi's costume, of course) were some decent stories and one truly excellent one. Dracula concluded his run with his best story. Its title was lifted from the great song by Tony Joe White. Fernandez again em-

ployed a scratchy art approach but this time it worked in service of the story. However, the great tale here was the Stenstrum/Auraleon effort "The House on the Sea." One of the longest non–*Vampirella* stories to appear in this magazine, it felt anything but padded. It concerned a fog-bound ship, the *HMS Pot-Valiant*, caught in the doldrums and in the midst of a mutiny, which crashes against a huge stone house in the middle of the ocean. The revelations as the captain and crew explore the house and meet the strange occupants therein are perhaps not the freshest of notions, but it was delivered so well that you could easily see this as a great episode of *The Twilight Zone*. Just an excellent, well-told story.

42. cover: Enrich Torres (May 1975)

(1) *Vampirella*'s Introduction [Bill DuBay/Jose Gonzalez, frontis] 1p; (2) Everything You Always Wanted to Know ... About the Comics!: Lettering [Bill DuBay, text article] 1p; (3) *Vampirella*: The Mountain of Skulls [Mike Butterworth/Jose Gonzalez, story credited to Flaxman Loew] 12p; (4) Around the Corner ... Just Beyond Eternity! [Victor Mora and Gerry Boudreau/Luis Garcia, story credited solely to Boudreau] 12p; (5) Laugh, Clown, Laugh! [Shelly Leferman/Ramon Torrents, art miscredited to Esteban Maroto] 8p; (6) Pantha: Straw on the Wind [Budd Lewis/Rafael Auraleon] 10p; (7) The Whitfield Contract [Fernando Fernandez] 12p; (8) Presenting the 1974 Warren Awards [Bill DuBay, text article] 2p.

Notes: Pantha, the were-cat, returned with a new writer. It was a pretty good story, although I'd rate it higher if I didn't know that this sequel to the good first series was merely a lead-in to her dreadful meeting and teamup with *Vampirella*. Shelly Leferman, who wrote "Laugh, Clown, Laugh!" was Warren's longtime letterer. The return of artist Luis Garcia was a welcome sight.

43. cover: Ribas (June 1975)

(1) *Vampirella*'s Introduction [Bill DuBay/Jose Gonzalez, frontis] 1p; (2) *Vampirella* [Bill DuBay/Jose Gonzalez] 12p; (3) The Wolves at War's End! [Victor Mora and Budd Lewis/Luis Garcia, story credited solely to Lewis, art credited to Jose Garcia] 14p; (4) The Easter Bunny Murders [Gerry Boudreau/Ramon Torrents] 9p;

(5) Cult of the Dead! [Gerry Boudreau/Isidro Mones] 8p; (6) The Last Testament of Angus Crow! [Fernando Fernandez] 9p.

Notes: Interesting cover painting by Ribas, who only did this one cover for Warren. Future writer Bob Rodi sent in a letter. The *Vampirella* story was untitled. "The Wolves at War's End!" was a credit to all concerned. Easily the best story in a mediocre issue. Frankly, it would have been the top-notch story in a top-notch issue.

44. cover: Manuel Sanjulian (August 1975)

(1) *Vampirella*'s Introduction [Bill DuBay/Neal Adams, frontis] 1p; (2) Everything You Always Wanted to Know ... About the Comics!: The Art [Bill DuBay, text article] 1p; (3) *Vampirella*: Blood for the Dancing Sorcerer [Bill DuBay and Gerry Boudreau/Jose Gonzalez] 15p; (4) Love Strip [Gerry Boudreau and Victor Mora/Luis Garcia] 18p; (5) Troll [Bruce Bezaire/Ramon Torrents] 10p; (6) Pantha: Changeling [Budd Lewis/Rafael Auraleon] 10p.

Notes: "Love Strip" was not really a horror story, or perhaps it was, just not your usual one. The story concerned a comic artist who specialized in romance strips, just as Garcia did at one point of his career, who appeared to be going crazy from the sheer boredom of it, while his personal life shattered around him. Good art and script. The Pantha story's startling cliffhanger ending would certainly have worked better if the concluding story had ever appeared! As it was, Pantha's solo strip vanished and she resurfaced as a supporting character in *Vampirella*. A big comedown for the stripper catgirl. "Troll" had a decent script by the talented Bezaire that reminded one somewhat of Harlan Ellison's "'Repent, Harlequin!' said the Ticktockman!" but Torrent's photo-realistic artwork undercut its whimsy at every turn.

45. cover: montage of pervious covers (September 1975)

(1) Vampirella: Blood Wager [Len Wein/Gonzalo Mayo] 21p; (2) The Parable of the Hermits of Glastonbury Tor [Gerry Boudreau/Ramon Torrents] 8p; (3) Janis! [Victor Mora and Budd Lewis/Luis Garcia, color] 8p; (4) A Hero Born of Wishes [Gerry Boudreau/Esteban Maroto] 10p; (5) The Winter of Their Discontent [Gerry Boudreau/Isidro Mones] 7p; (6) There Are No

Children in Hungry Hollow, Tennessee [Gerry Boudreau/Jose Ortiz] 9p.

Notes: Bob Rodi sent in yet another letter. Price increased to $1.25 and size increased to 80 pages. For the first time in years "Vampirella" had a quality story to match her usual quality artwork. The best story, however, was "The Winter of Their Discontent." Best art was provided by Estaban Maroto. A superior issue.

46. cover: Ken Kelly (October 1975)

(1) Vampirella: The Origin of Vampirella [J. R. Cochran and Budd Lewis/Jose Gonzalez, plot and art reprinted from *Vampirella* 1972 annual (1972)] 15p; (2) *Vampirella*: Death's Dark Angel [Archie Goodwin/Jose Gonzalez, reprinted from *Vampirella* #12 (July 1971)] 20p; (3) *Vampirella*: Isle of the Huntress [Archie Goodwin/Jose Gonzalez, reprinted from *Vampirella* #14 (November 1971)] 20p; (4) Vampirella: The Monster Called Vampirella [Bill DuBay/Zesar Lopez, color] 8p.

Notes: *Vampirella*'s 1975 annual. "The Origin of Vampirella" reprint had a new script by Budd Lewis, further revamping Vampi's origin. Skywald regular Zesar Lopez made his first Warren appearance.

47. cover: Enrich Torres (December 1975)

(1) *Vampirella*: Mother's Coming Home [Bill DuBay/Gonzalo Mayo] 8p; (2) The Secret Legacy of Gaslight Lil [Victor Mora and Bill DuBay/Luis Garcia, story credited solely to DuBay and art credited to Jose Garcia] 12p; (3) Children of Wrath [Gerry Boudreau/Ramon Torrents] 10p; (4) Gamal and the Cockatrice [Bruce Bezaire/Rafael Auraleon] 12p; (5) The January Man [Gerry Boudreau/Luis Bermejo] 8p.

Notes: Size reduced to 64 pages. Letters page reduced to one page. The lead male character in "Gaslight Lil" was based on Paul Newman. One of the best stories Warren published appeared here. "Gamal and the Cockatrice" was a marvelous story dealing with the art of "grifting." Or was it? In the end neither the reader nor the audience that Gamal tells his story to is sure (or can ever *be* sure) if Gamal ever really fought the cockatrice or not. This was both Bezaire's and Auraleon's best work, and that's saying a lot for both men. A dazzling example of sheer storytelling.

48. cover: Enrich Torres (January 1976)

(1) *Vampirella*: The Wonder World of Amber-gris, Kato and Tonto, too! [Bill DuBay/Zesar Lopez] 10p; (2) The Satan Complex [Bill Du-Bay/Ramon Torrents] 16p; (3) Of Death and Distinction [Gerry Boudreau/Joaquim Blasquez] 8p; (4) The Miracle Hands of Simon Silverstone [Bill DuBay/Luis Bermejo] 7p; (5) Star-Bright Lantern 909 [Gerry Boudreau/Jose Ortiz] 9p.

Notes: Zesar Lopez does a nice job on the Vampi strip. His style was quite a lot like Jose Gonzalez's, but his storytelling and layouts are better (although Gonzalez still draws a prettier Vampi).

49. cover: Enrich Torres (March 1976)

(1) *Vampirella's* Introduction [Bill DuBay/Ramon Torrents and Jose Gonzalez, frontis] 1p; (2) Vampi's Vault [Louise Jones?, questionnaire] 1p; (3) *Vampirella*: The Blood Red Queen of Hearts [Bill DuBay/Esteban Maroto] 12p; (4) The Thing in Jane's Closet [Budd Lewis/Ramon Torrents] 8p; (5) Then One Foggy Christmas Eve [Gerry Boudreau/Joaquin Blasquez] 8p; (6) Jewel in the Mouth of a Snake [Jose Bea] 8p; (7) The Succubus Stone [Gerry Boudreau and Steve Clement/Ramon Torrents, color] 8p; (8) The Oblong Box [Rich Margopoulos/Isidro Mones, from the story by Edgar Allan Poe] 14p.

Notes: Enrich's cover of Vampi in front of a queen of hearts card was very effective. A $1.25 cover price and 80 pages in length. For the first time since the Goodwin/Sutton days, a "Vampirella" story was the best story in the magazine. The introduction of DuBay's Blood Red Queen along with very effective artwork by Maroto combined to present a darn good story. The rest of the issue was decent also. The Boudreau/-Blasquez story was overflow from the *Creepy* Christmas special. The Poe adaptation was also overflow, this time from *Creepy's* Edgar Allan Poe specials. It didn't affect the quality of the issue, however, as both were quite good stories.

50. cover: Manuel Sanjulian (April 1976)

(1) *Vampirella's* Introduction [Bill DuBay/Jose Gonzalez, frontis] 1p; (2) *Vampirella*: Call Me Panther! [Bill DuBay/Jose Gonzalez] 6p; (3) *Vampirella*: The High-Gloss Egyptian Junk Peddler [Bill DuBay/Esteban Maroto] 8p; (4) *Vampirella*: Granny Ghoose and the Baby Dealers [Bill DuBay/Ramon Torrents] 10p; (5) *Vam-*

pirella: The Final Star of Morning [Bill DuBay/Bill DuBay and Jeff Jones] 8p; (6) Pendragon: The Thing in Denny Colt's Grave [Bill DuBay/Jose Ortiz and Will Eisner, Eisner's art appears in only one panel] 8p; (7) Ground Round [Roger McKenzie/Rafael Auraleon] 7p.

Notes: Back to $1.00 and 64 pages. Vampi's "special" fiftieth issue was actually not bad. The four *Vampirella* strips and Pendragon's first solo story form a long book-length story. Pantha (last seen in #44), Fleur (last seen in #35) and the Spirit guest-star. This story tied up the loose ends left over from Pantha's second serial. Nice artwork throughout.

The Louise Jones Era

51. cover: Enrich Torres (May 1976)

(1) Warren Publishing Company Will Pay $500 Reward... [James Warren, text article, frontis] 1p; (2) *Vampirella*: Rise of the Undead [Mike Butterworth/Howard Chaykin and Gonzalo Mayo, story credited to Flaxman Loew] 12p; (3) The Edge of Tomorrow [Gerry Boudreau/Zesar Lopez] 8p; (4) Uncle Wiggly's Magic Box [Bill DuBay/Leopold Sanchez] 8p; (5) Whitechapel [Gerry Boudreau/Rafael Auraleon] 8p; (6) The Castle, the Dungeon and All [Gerry Boudreau/Vicente Alcazar] 8p; (7) Presenting the 1975 Warren Awards [Bill DuBay, text article] 2p.

Notes: Louise Jones was listed as assistant editor and James Warren was listed as editor-in-chief. Mayo's inks totally erased any sense of Chaykin's art in the Vampi segment. An average, decent, unspectacular issue for this period of *Vampirella's* run.

52. cover: Enrich Torres (July 1976)

(1) Warren Publishing Company Will Pay $500 Reward... [James Warren, text article, frontis] 1p; (2) *Vampirella*: Dr. Wrighter's Asylum of Horror [Bill DuBay/Gonzalo Mayo] 12p; (3) *Vampirella*: The Beauty and the Beast [Bill DuBay/Gonzalo Mayo] 12p; (4) The House at Blood Corner [Gerry Boudreau/Ramon Torrents] 9p; (5) Stake-Out! [Gerry Boudreau/Jose Ortiz] 8p; (6) The Segerson Experiment [Gerry Boudreau/Zesar Lopez] 8p.

Notes: One of Enrich's most popular covers of *Vampirella* also began a trend of using Vampi as a pin-up character on the cover rather than doing an illustrative cover dealing with one of her stories. The Boudreau/Torrents story's title was based on a *Winnie the Pooh* title.

53. cover: Enrich Torres (August 1976)

(1) Warren Publishing Company Will Pay $500 Reward... [James Warren, text article, frontis] 1p; (2) *Vampirella*: The Human Marketplace [Gerry Boudreau/Jose Gonzalez] 10p; (3) The Comic Books [Joe Brancatelli, text article] 1p; (4) Opium Is the Religion of the People [Gerry Boudreau/Rafael Auraleon] 8p; (5) The Professional [Bruce Jones/Zesar Lopez] 9p; (6) The Last Man Syndrome [Roger McKenzie/Ramon Torrents] 8p; (7) Jackie and the Leprechaun King [Bill DuBay/Esteban Maroto] 12p.

Notes: Roger McKenzie sent in a letter praising his own Warren debut from #50! Louise Jones was listed as senior editor. Torrents' human skull panel on page 39 was a direct swipe from an earlier Skywald back-cover drawing of the same image by Pablo Marcos. "Jackie and the Leprechaun King" seemed to be a takeoff on the Peter, Paul and Mary song "Puff the Magic Dragon."

54. cover: Enrich Torres (September 1976)

(1) *Vampirella*'s Introduction [Louise Jones/Jose Gonzalez, frontis] 1p; (2) *Vampirella*: The Day the Music Died [Gerry Boudreau/Gonzalo Mayo] 14p; (3) The Comic Books [Joe Brancatelli, text article] 1p; (4) *Vampirella*: Twilight of Blood [Gerry Boudreau/Gonazlo Mayo] 14p; (5) *Vampirella*: Chaos in a Sleepy Suburb [Gerry Boudreau/Gonzalo Mayo] 14p; (6) Bowser [Jan Strnad/Richard Corben, color] 8p.

Notes: It was $1.25 in price and 72 pages in length. As in #50, the *Vampirella* stories were all chapters in a longer tale. The story is overly complicated but it's still better than the average Vampi story. "Bowser" was to have appeared two years earlier in *Creepy* #67, but a mix-up at the printers resulted in another Corben color section being inserted in its place.

55. cover: Manuel Sanjulian (October 1976), reprinted from *Vampirella* #36 (September 1974)

(1) *Vampirella*: The Resurrection of Papa Voodoo! [Archie Goodwin/Jose Gonzalez, reprinted from *Vampirella* #15 (January 1972)] 20p; (2) *Vampirella*: And Be a Bride of Chaos [Archie Goodwin/Jose Gonzalez, reprinted from *Vampirella* #16 (March 1972)] 20p; (3) Vampirella: The Corpse with the Missing Mind [Bill DuBay/Jose Gonzalez, color] 8p; (4) *Vampirella*: The Lurker in the Deep! [Archie Goodwin/Jose Gonzalez, reprinted from *Vampirella* #13 (September 1971)] 15p; (5) The Comic Books [Joe Brancatelli, text article] 1p.

Notes: The 1976 *Vampirella* annual.

56. cover: Enrich Torres (December 1976)

(1) *Vampirella*'s Introduction [Louise Jones/Jose Gonzalez, frontis] 1p; (2) *Vampirella*: The Headless Horseman of All-Hallow's Eve! [Bill DuBay/Jose Gonzalez] 10p; (3) The Comic Books: Tarzan's Travails [Joe Brancatelli, text article] 1p; (4) Mute [Bruce Jones/Luis Bermejo] 10p; (5) Skruffy's Gargoyle! [Bill DuBay/Leopold Sanchez] 10p; (6) Cavalcade of Monsters [Gerry Boudreau/Ramon Torrents] 8p; (7) The Free Lancer [Bruce Jones/Jose Ortiz] 11p.

Notes: Although the story's not much, the artwork on Vampi's story and frontis by Gonzalez was great! "Mute" by Bruce Jones and Luis Bermejo had the best story and art but this was quite a good issue. No real low points at all.

57. cover: Enrich Torres (January 1977)

(1) *Vampirella*: City of Ghosts [Roger McKenzie/Jose Gonzalez] 10p; (2) The Comic Books: One Down... [Joe Brancatelli, text article] 1p; (3) Rusty Bucklers [Bruce Jones/Esteban Maroto] 8p; (4) Stand-In [Bruce Jones/Carmine Infantino and Dick Giordano] 8p; (5) Magnificent Ephemeral [Bruce Jones/Ramon Torrents] 12p; (6) An Insult to Science [Fernando Fernandez/Jose Miralles] 10p.

Notes: I don't know who did the lettering but a number of the Spanish artists' names were misspelled this issue. "Magnificent Ephemeral" presented the best art and story. "Rusty Bucklers" and "An Insult to Science" were also quite good.

58. cover: Enrich Torres (March 1977)

(1) *Vampirella*: Lenore [Roger McKenzie/Jose Gonzalez] 10p; (2) The Comic Books: Less Is More [Joe Brancatelli, text article] 1p; (3) A Matchstick Angel [Budd Lewis/Ramon Torrents] 9p; (4) Yellow Heat [Bruce Jones/Russ Heath] 8p; (5) The Christmas Flower [Budd Lewis/Jose Ortiz] 10p; (6) The Wambaugh [Bruce Jones/Rafael Auraleon] 8p; (7) Little Monster [Roger McKenzie/Carmine Infantino

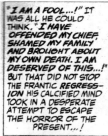

"I AM A FOOL...!" IT WAS ALL HE COULD THINK. "I HAVE OFFENDED MY CHIEF, SHAMED MY FAMILY AND BROUGHT ABOUT MY OWN DEATH. I AM DESERVED OF THIS...!" BUT THAT DID NOT STOP THE FRANTIC REGRESSION HIS CALCIFIED MIND TOOK IN A DESPERATE ATTEMPT TO ESCAPE THE HORROR OF THE PRESENT...!

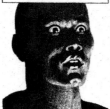

HE HAD BEEN SITTING BENEATH THE SCANT SHADE OF A BAOBAB TREE, WAITING HIS TURN AT THE STRAW TARGET WITH HIS YOUNG WARRIOR PEERS--ANXIOUS TO SHOW HIS PROWESS WITH THE WAR SPEAR--WHEN THEY BROUGHT HER INTO THE CAMP.

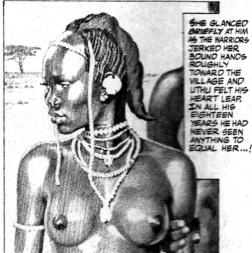

SHE GLANCED BRIEFLY AT HIM AS THE WARRIORS JERKED HER BOUND HANDS ROUGHLY TOWARD THE VILLAGE AND UTHU FELT HIS HEART LEAP. IN ALL HIS EIGHTEEN YEARS HE HAD NEVER SEEN ANYTHING TO EQUAL HER...!

SOMEONE PUNCHED HIS ARM AND HE TURNED NUMBLY TO THE STRAW TARGET. THE SPEAR LEFT HIS HAND OF IT'S OWN ACCORD, FALLING WIDE OF ITS MARK. THE OTHERS LAUGHED HARSHLY. UTHU DIDN'T HEAR. HIS EYES WERE FIXED ONCE MORE ON THE DEPARTING FORM OF THE NATIVE GIRL.

THAT EVENING, UTHU SAT TRANSFIXED BEFORE THE CEREMONIAL FIRE, HIS MIND A MATRIX OF CONFUSION AND LONGING. HE DESPERATELY WANTED WHAT WAS NOT HIS TO DESIRE. FOR AT HIS TENDER AGE, THE MEN OF THE TRIBE HAD LITTLE SAY ABOUT THEIR CHOICE OF WOMAN, PARTICULARLY THE CAPTURED BEAUTY OF AN ENEMY TRIBE.

STILL, THERE WAS HOPE. IF, BY SOME FREAK CHANCE, NONE OF THE OLDER WARRIORS PICKED HER, UTHU WOULD THEN BE WITHIN HIS RIGHTS TO REQUEST PERMISSION FROM THE CHIEF TO BUY THE YOUNG SIREN. IF NO ONE OBJECTED, PERMISSION WOULD PROBABLY BE GRANTED...

Possibly the best story to run in *Vampirella*, "Yellow Heat" featured a gripping script by Bruce Jones and stunning artwork from Russ Heath, all leading to one of the greatest O. Henry–style twists of all time. *Vampirella* is ® Dynamite Entertainment and © 2012 DFI. All rights reserved/used by permission.

and Dick Giordano] 8p; **(8)** The Sleeping Beauty [Bill DuBay and Esteban Maroto/Esteban Maroto] 8p.

Notes: It was $1.50 and 88 pages. One of Warren's best stories ever appeared this issue with the Jones/Heath dazzler "Yellow Heat." Bruce Jones' calm, cool script led you in one direction while setting you up with a honey of a story twist, and the reproduced pencil art of Russ Heath was simply jawdroppingly lovely. The rest of the issue presented us with some pretty good stories and art, particularly by Marato, Torrents, Lewis, McKenzie, Infantino and Giordano. Maroto's "The Sleeping Beauty" was printed sideways. Both "A Matchstick Angel" and "The Christmas Flower" were overflow from the *Creepy* Christmas special.

59. cover: Enrich Torres (April 1977)

(1) *Vampirella*: Pendragon's Last Bow [Bill Du-Bay/Jose Gonzalez] 10p; **(2)** The Comic Books [Joe Brancatelli, text article] 1p; **(3)** Changes [Roger McKenzie/Leopoldo Duranona] 8p; **(4)** Funeral Day [Roger McKenzie/Jose Ortiz] 8p; **(5)** Force-Feed [Cary Bates/Leopold Sanchez] 8p; **(6)** The Plot's the Thing [Roger McKenzie/Martin Salvador] 7p; **(7)** The Beast Is Yet to Come [Nicola Cuti/Carmine Infantino and Alex Nino] 8p.

Notes: Who knew Enrich had an artistic sense of humor? His cover starred Vampi in a spoof of romance comics. This issue's on-sale date must have been around Valentine's Day. Back to $1.25 and 72 pages.

60. cover: Enrich Torres (May 1977)

(1) *Vampirella*: The Return of the Blood Red Queen [Bill DuBay/Jose Gonzalez] 10p; **(2)** The Comic Books [Joe Brancatelli, text article] 1p; **(3)** He Who Laughs Last ... Laughs Best [Bruce Jones/Carmine Infantino and Gonzalo Mayo] 10p; **(4)** Riding Shotgun [Gerry Boudreau/Luis Bermejo] 8p; **(5)** Wish You Were Here [Bill DuBay/Jose Ortiz] 8p; **(6)** Fallen Angels [Bill DuBay/Esteban Maroto] 8p; **(7)** Presenting the 1976 Warren Awards [Louise Jones/Bill DuBay, Bruce Jones and Leopold Sanchez, text article] 2p.

Notes: The Blood Red Queen returned in the first installment of a new *Vampi* serial, following her first appearance in #49. Quite good art here and the serial started off in fine fashion, but soon

the quality was at the same mediocre level as most *Vampi* tales. Best story came from Bruce Jones while the best art was by Esteban Maroto. Marato's story was again printed sideways. There were also good art and stories from DuBay, Boudreau, Bermejo, Infantino and Mayo.

61. cover: Enrich Torres (July 1977)

(1) *Vampirella*: An Eye for an Eye [Bill DuBay/Jose Gonzalez] 10p; **(2)** The Comic Books [Joe Brancatelli, text article] 1p; **(3)** Skimpole's Monsters [Bill DuBay/Ramon Torrents] 13p; **(4)** Brother Hawk [Nicola Cuti/Carmine Infantino and Alex Nino] 8p; **(5)** The Enchanting Fable of Thistlewhite the Bold [Bill DuBay/Russ Heath] 8p; **(6)** Companions to the Sun [Bruce Jones/Leopold Sanchez] 10p.

Notes: A pretty good issue, with the delightful "Thistlewhite the Bold" story taking honors for best story and art. The other stories, even *Vampirella*'s, were quite good as well.

62. cover: Enrich Torres (August 1977)

(1) *Vampirella*: Starpatch, Quark and Mother Blitz [Bill DuBay/Jose Gonzalez] 10p; **(2)** The Comic Books [Joe Brancatelli, text article] 1p; **(3)** U.F.O. [Josep Toutain/Ramon Torrents] 9p; **(4)** Beautiful Screamer [Bruce Jones/Leopold Sanchez] 10p; **(5)** Time Ticket [Gerry Boudreau/Esteban Maroto] 6p; **(6)** Fog [Nicola Cuti/Carmine Infantino and Dick Giordano] 8p; **(7)** By Treason's Knife [Gerry Boudreau/Leopold Sanchez] 8p.

Notes: After an interesting start, the *Vampi/Blood Red Queen* storyline took a turn for the crapper by moving in a poorly drawn and poorly conceived sci-fi direction. "U.F.O." was done in 1976 for the never-published Warren magazine *Yesterday, Today ... Tomorrow.* Several other stories, also done for that magazine, were likewise published in *Vampirella*. "By Treason's Knife" was a leftover from *Creepy's* all-war story special. It was probably the best story here. There were several other good art jobs here but the best art came from Maroto's "Time Ticket."

63. cover: Enrich Torres (September 1977)

(1) *Vampirella* and the Sultana's Revenge [Mike Butterworth/Jose Gonzalez, story credited to Flaxman Loew, reprinted from *Vampirella* #33 (May 1974)] 12p; **(2)** The Comic Books [Joe Brancatelli, text article] 1p; **(3)** Jenifer [Bruce

Jones/Berni Wrightson, reprinted from *Creepy* #63 (July 1974)] 10p; (4) 1984 ad [Joe Vaultz] 1p; (5) Ground Round [Roger McKenzie/Rafael Auraleon, reprinted from *Vampirella* #50 (April 1976)] 7p; (6) As Ye Sow... [Bruce Jones/Luis Bermejo, reprinted from *Creepy* #79 (May 1976)] 10p; (7) The Parable of the Hermits of Glastonbury Tor [Gerry Boudreau/Ramon Torrents, reprinted from *Vampirella* #45 (September 1975)] 8p; (8) The Professional [Bruce Jones/Zesar Lopez, reprinted from *Vampirella* #53 (August 1976)] 9p; (9) Wings of Vengeance [Bill DuBay and Esteban Maroto/Esteban Maroto, reprinted from *Creepy* #81 (July 1976)] 8p.

Notes: This was $1.50 and 80 pages. The 1977 *Vampirella* annual.

64. cover: Enrich Torres (October 1977)

(1) *Vampirella*: The Manipulators [Gerry Boudreau/Carmine Infantino and Gonzalo Mayo] 10p; (2) The Comic Books [Joe Brancatelli, text article] 1p; (3) *Vampirella*: The Eradicators [Gerry Boudreau/Carmine Infantino and Gonzalo Mayo] 10p; (4) *Vampirella*: The Vindicators [Gerry Boudreau/Gonzalo Mayo] 10p; (5) *Vampirella*: The Intruders [Gerry Boudreau/Gonzalo Mayo] 9p; (6) *Vampirella*: The Stalkers [Gerry Boudreau/Gonzalo Mayo] 10p; (7) *Vampirella*: The Iconoclasts [Gerry Boudreau/Gonzalo Mayo] 10p; (8) *Vampirella*: The Survivors [Gerry Boudreau/Gonzalo Mayo] 8p.

Notes: A decent book-length "Vampi" story mercifully interrupted the current inane *Vampi* serial. It was $1.75 and 96 pages.

65. cover: Enrich Torres (December 1977)

(1) To Win $100.00 Plus Starring Role in a Vampi Episode Enter the *Vampirella* Mystery Issue Contest [Louise Jones/Jose Gonzalez, text article, frontis] 1p; (2) *Vampirella*: The Mad King of Drakulon [Bill DuBay/Jose Gonzalez] 10p; (3) The Comic Books: A Matter of Dues [Joe Brancatelli, text article] 2p; (4) A Game of Hide and Seek [Roger McKenzie/Leopoldo Duranona] 8p; (5) Mystery of the Strangled Stockbroker [Gerry Boudreau/Jose Ortiz] 8p; (6) The Pharaoh's Lady [Nicola Cuti/Luis Bermejo] 8p; (7) This Brief Interruption [Bruce Jones/Leopold Sanchez] 8p; (8) Goodbye, Norma Jean [Bill DuBay/Rafael Auraleon] 9p.

Notes: A Mystery Contest special. The last pages were dropped from all the stories except Vampi's and the reader was encouraged to guess the

actual ending. The endings themselves were held for the next issue. The first person to get all six correct would win the contest. As it turned out, only one person actually guessed correctly. It was an interesting, if somewhat irritating, idea, although only Bruce Jones' story really made effective use of the gimmick.

66. cover: Enrich Torres (January 1978)

(1) *Vampirella*: To Be a Bride in Death [Bill DuBay/Jose Gonzalez] 12p; (2) The Comic Books: Superman Versus Soccer [Joe Brancatelli, text article] 1p; (3) Down Under [Bruce Jones/Luis Bermejo] 11p; (4) Picture Complete [Bruce Jones/Gonzalo Mayo] 10p; (5) The Blazer [Bruce Jones/Jose Ortiz] 10p; (6) Here Are the Solutions... [Louise Jones, text article] 1p; (7) Mystery Contest Solution Pages [Roger McKenzie, Gerry Boudreau, Nicola Cuti, Bruce Jones, and Bill DuBay/Leopoldo Duranona, Jose Ortiz, Luis Bermejo, Leopold Sanchez and Rafael Auraleon] 5p.

Notes: Pantha, unseen since #50, became a regular member of Vampi's strip. The endings of the previous issue's stories were published. Bruce Jones provided three good stories with the best probably being "Picture Perfect." That story was a sequel of sorts to *Creepy* #92's "Toward High Places" and used Frazetta's cover for *Eerie* #23 as a direct story element.

67. cover: photo of Barbara Leigh in *Vampirella* costume (March 1978)

(1) *Vampirella*: The Glorious Return of Sweet Baby Theda [Bill DuBay/Jose Gonzalez] 15p; (2) The Quest [Budd Lewis/Ramon Torrents] 9p; (3) The Comic Books: Patent Medicine Profits? [Joe Brancatelli, text article] 1p; (4) Fish Bait [Nicola Cuti/Alex Nino] 8p; (5) Announcing the *Vampirella* Mystery Contest Grand Prize Winner: Jim Elkins [Louise Jones, text article] 2p; (6) Home Sweet Horologium [Nicola Cuti/Paul Neary] 8p; (7) Choice Cuts [Cary Bates/Russ Heath] 3p; (8) The Last Dragon King [Roger McKenzie/Esteban Maroto, color] 8p.

Notes: A $1.50 cover price. A photo of actress Barbara Leigh appeared on the first of many covers she did while costumed as *Vampirella*. At the time, there were efforts being made to bring *Vampirella* to the silver screen and Leigh was apparently the choice of Hammer Films and

Warren Publications to portray her, although a later letters page answer would deny this. Leigh was a beautiful woman and she certainly had the physical attributes to play the part. In her story, Vampi gave Pantha a new outfit, which, since Pantha is a former stripper, looked exactly like a stripper's outfit. As, of course, does Vampi's, come to think of it. Pantha then tells everyone she feels like a movie star. She's right — if she's in a porn film!!! Future Warren writer John Ellis Sech was one of the runner-ups to the Mystery Contest. The three-pager "Choice Cuts," had the best story and art. It was a nifty little horror tale that will make you squirm. Alex Nino had some particularly disturbing visuals on the last page of his story. Downright creepy.

68. cover: Enrich Torres (April 1978)

(1) *Vampirella*: Orphee, Poor Orphee [Bill DuBay/Jose Ortiz] 12p; **(2)** The Comic Books: Kiss and Tell [Joe Brancatelli, text article] 1p; **(3)** October Man [Bruce Jones/Leopold Sanchez] 10p; **(4)** Fleur: Night of the Alleycats [Gerry Boudreau/Ramon Torrents] 8p; **(5)** By Degrees [Bruce Jones/Jose Ortiz] 10p; **(6)** The Munificent Ali Addan and Son! [Bill DuBay and Esteban Maroto/Esteban Maroto] 8p; **(7)** Presenting the 1977 Warren Awards [Louise Jones/Frank Frazetta, Bruce Jones, Bill DuBay, Alex Nino, et al, text article] 2p.

Notes: A $1.25 cover price. Jose Gonzalez made Orphee, the monster in the Vampi strip, look as silly as any critter Tony Williamsune ever drew. Fleur made her first appearance since #50. She was starting to look a little jaded, worse for wear and tear. Bruce Jones' story "By Degrees," was later turned into a prose story for his 1986 short story collection *Twisted Tales* (which shouldn't be confused with the three different comic anthologies bearing the same title which were published by Pacific, Eclipse and Blackthorne respectively — this particular Blackthorne collection contained actual short stories). "Ali Addan" was printed sideways.

69. cover: photo of Barbara Leigh (May 1978)

(1) *Vampirella*: The Saga of Frick and Frack Freckles [Bill DuBay/Gonzalo Mayo] 12p; **(2)** The Comic Books: Safe at Home? [Joe Brancatelli, text article] 1p; **(3)** Hit Six [Bruce Jones/Luis Bermejo] 10p; **(4)** Off the Beaten Empath

[Gerry Boudreau/Leopoldo Duranona] 8p; **(5)** Reagan Redux [Bruce Jones/Jose Ortiz] 10p; **(6)** Jessie's Friend [Bruce Jones/Gonzalo Mayo] 10p.

70. cover: Ken Kelly (July 1978)

(1) Vampirella: Ghostly Granny Gearloose [Bill DuBay/Gonzalo Mayo] 9p; **(2)** The Comic Books: Classics Illustrated R.I.P. [Joe Brancatelli, text article] 1p; **(3)** Mask of Ugin [Nicola Cuti and Gerry Boudreau/Jose Ortiz] 8p; **(4)** Swamp Lover [Bill DuBay/Leopoldo Duranona] 12p; **(5)** Reality Twice Removed [Gerry Boudeau/Ramon Torrents] 8p; **(6)** The Terrible Exorcism of Adriennes Pompereau! [Luis Vigil and Bill DuBay/Rafael Auraleon] 8p.

Notes: Ken Kelly delivered a very attractive cover. "Swamp Lover" was the best written and illustrated story here. "The Terrible Exorcism of Adriennes Pompereau!" was done in 1976 for the never published-magazine *Yesterday, Today ... Tomorrow*. Its original title was simply "Exorcism" and this version was heavily rewritten by Bill DuBay.

71. cover: photo of Barbara Leigh (August 1978)

(1) *Vampirella*: The Case of the Connected Clowns and the Collector! [Bill DuBay/Jose Gonzalez] 12p; **(2)** The Comic Books: Still More Kiss [Joe Brancatelli, text article] 1p; **(3)** Trial of the Sorceress [Bill DuBay and Esteban Maroto/Esteban Maroto] 8p; **(4)** Night of the Chicken [Michael Fleisher/Jess Jodloman] 12p; **(5)** Machu Picchu: The Treasure of the Incas [Josep Toutain and Nicola Cuti/Luis Bermejo] 6p; **(6)** Australopithicus [Bruce Jones/Leopoldo Duranona] 11p; **(7)** The Odd Comic World of Richard Corben ad [illustrated: Richard Corben, on the back cover] 1p.

Notes: The Fleisher/Jodloman story "Night of the Chicken" featured an extremely bizarre sex/fetish outfit, worn by the young leading lady of the tale. Pretty grisly little story, too. Like "Adriennes Pompereau" from the issue before, "Machu Picchu" was done in 1976 for the never-published Warren magazine *Yesterday, Today ... Tomorrow* and the story had again been rewritten from the original script, this time by Cuti.

72. cover: Enrich Torres (September 1978)

(1) *Vampirella*: The Beauty and the Behemoth [Bill DuBay/Jose Gonzalez] 12p; **(2)** The Comic

Books: Death by the Numbers [Joe Brancatelli, text article] 1p; (3) The Eyes Have It [Rafael Auraleon] 7p; (4) Fruitcake [Bill DuBay/Az-pini] 8p; (5) Scheherazade [Bill DuBay?/Esteban Maroto, color] 8p; (6) Invasion of the Cyclops Monsters [Nicola Cuti/Jose Ortiz] 9p; (7) A Nightmare for Mrs. Agatha [Guillermo Saccomanno; illustrated: Leopoldo Duranona] 9p; (8) 1984 ad [illustrated: Richard Corben, on the back cover] 1p.

Notes: After a series of tired-looking cover paintings that gave the appearance that he was running out of inspiration, Enrich came up with a winner. In fact, it was his best cover since #58. A $1.50 cover price. The best story and art here belonged to "A Nightmare for Mrs. Agatha" by Saccomanno and Duranona. This story, like the *Fallen Angels* series by the same team that appeared in *Eerie*, was dated 1976 and probably was printed in South America at that time. The cover of *1984* #2 used in the ad on the back cover was the first version of the cover by Corben, before Bill DuBay altered some details on the lady depicted.

73. cover: Bob Larkin (October 1978)

(1) *Vampirella*: A Gathering of Demons [Bill DuBay/Gonzalo Mayo] 71p; (2) The Comic Books: What Hath Congress Wrought? [Joe Brancatelli, text article] 1p.

Notes: A $1.75 cover price and 88 pages.

74. cover: photo of Barbara Leigh (December 1978)

(1) *Vampirella*: Hell from on High [Steve Englehart/Jose Gonzalez, reprinted from *Vampirella* #22 (March 1973)] 22p; (2) The Comic Books: Roll Over, Brancatelli [Joe Brancatelli, text article] 1p; (3) Vampirella: The Blood Queen of Bayou Parish! [Steve Englehart/Jose Gonzalez, reprinted from *Vampirella* #23 (April 1973)] 18p; (4) Wolf Hunt [Joe Wehrle/Esteban Maroto, reprinted from *Vampirella* #14 (November 1971)] 7p.

Notes: The 1978 *Vampirella* annual. A $1.25 cover price and 64 pages.

75. cover: Jose Gonzalez and Kim McQuaite (January 1979)

(1) *Vampirella*: The Blob Beast of Blighter's Bog [Bill DuBay/Jose Gonzalez] 12p; (2) The Comic Books: Notes on Comix People [Joe Brancatelli,

text article] 1p; (3) Peter, Peter [Gerry Souter/Leopoldo Duranona] 10p; (4) Sasquatch Love [Cary Bates/Jose Ortiz] 9p; (5) Business Is Booming [Bob Black/Isidro Mones] 10p; (6) A Matter of Principle [Budd Lewis and Len Wein/Azpiri] 7p.

Notes: The issue had 72 pages. Kim McQuaite applied paint tones and a background to an original Gonzalez drawing of Vampi for the cover. It looks quite nice. "Peter, Peter" had the best story and art here, although "Sasquatch Love" was quite good as well.

76. cover: photo of Barbara Leigh (March 1979)

(1) *Vampirella*: Curse of the Pasha's Princess [Bill DuBay/Jose Gonzalez] 16p; (2) The Almost Anything Goes Fan Page [Ray Woycitzky/George Kozman, Ti Christa and Pedro Pereira, crossword puzzle] 1p; (3) The Comic Books: The Party [Joe Brancatelli, text article] 1p; (4) Gravity Field [Bob Toomey/Pepe Moreno] 8p; (5) The Games of Sharn [Bruce Jones/Ramon Torrents] 10p; (6) Swift Sculpture [Bob Toomey/Val Mayerik] 8p; (7) Time for a Change [Nicola Cuti/Alex Nino] 5p; (8) The Haunted [Bruce Jones/Russ Heath] 11p.

Notes: A $1.50 cover price and 80 pages. A short-lived revival of the fan page debuted this issue. Ramon Torrents delivered his last original Warren story. Best story and art (lots of naked and near-naked Heath babes!) by Bruce Jones and Russ Heath on "The Haunted." "Swift Sculpture" was also of high quality.

77. cover: photo of Barbara Leigh (April 1979)

(1) *Vampirella*: Shadow of the Dragon [Bill DuBay/Gonzalo Mayo] 10p; (2) The Almost Anything Goes Fan Page [Mike Roucheleau, Lori Anderson and Bill Sharp/Scott Cassman, Ingrid Neilson, George Kozman and Pedro Pereira, poems] 1p; (3) The Comic Books: Going for the Bucks [Joe Brancatelli, text article] 1p; (4) The Night of the Yeti! [Michael Fleisher/Russ Heath] 10p; (5) The Night the Birds Fell [Nicola Cuti/Pepe Moreno] 9p; (6) Siren of the Seekonk [Jonathan Thomas/Rafael Auraleon] 8p; (7) Presenting the 1978 Warren Awards [Louise Jones/et al., text article] 2p; (8) Weird Wolf [Gerry Boudreau/Jeff Easley] 3p; (9) Futura House Is not a Home [Nicola Cuti/Isidro Mones] 8p.

Notes: A $1.50 cover price and 72 pages. George Kozman's art on the fan page was of exceptionally high quality. Heath again took best art honors although Moreno and newcomer Easley provided great art as well. Best story was probably Cuti's "The Night the Birds Fell." All in all, a pretty good issue.

78. cover: photo of Barbara Leigh (May 1979)

(1) The Rook ad [Rudy Nebres, frontis] 1p; (2) *Vampirella*: Kiss of the Dragon Queen! [Bill Du-Bay/Gonzalo Mayo] 12p; (3) Little Guy [Nicola Cuti/Rafael Auraleon] 8p; (4) The Comic Books: The Inevitable Superman Story [Joe Brancatelli, text story] 1p; (5) Passion [Steve Englehart/Jose Ortiz] 10p; (6) The Service [Bruce Jones/Jim Starlin and Alfredo Alcala] 11p; (7) "Zooner or Later" [Bruce Jones/Russ Heath] 12p; (8) The Almost Anything Goes Fan Page [Louise Jones/Gonzalo Mayo, trivia quiz] 1p.

Notes: A $1.75 cover price. A better than average issue with fine work appearing from Steve Englehart, Jose Ortiz, Jim Starlin and Alfredo Alcala, although the best story here was the Bruce Jones/Russ Heath gutbuster "Zooner or Later." I defy anyone to read this story, get to the last page and not end up with a big grin on their face.

79. cover: Jordi Penalva (July 1979)

(1) *Vampirella*: Shanghaied [Bill DuBay/Gonzalo Mayo] 12p; (2) The Comic Books: So Much for Tradition [Joe Brancatelli, text article] 1p; (3) The Almost Anything Goes Fan Page [Louise Jones/John Schettino, Randall Foster, Joel Repp and George Kozmon, pin-ups] 1p; (4) Edward and Griselda [Cary Bates/Val Mayerik and Joe Rubenstein] 10p; (5) I Think I'll Keep Her [Cary Bates/Rafael Auraleon] 8p; (6) Night of the Squid [Michael Fleisher/Jose Ortiz] 9p; (7) Fungus [Archie Goodwin/Leopoldo Duranona; photos by Duranona and Hilda Lizarazu] 11p.

Notes: Penalva's cover painting of a dragon seemed squarely based on those very common Chinese dragon candlestick holders. "Fungus" is a fumetti strip with the monster drawn in with pen and ink. A solid issue, but there's nothing special here.

80. cover: Esteban Maroto (August 1979)

(1) *Vampirella*: Slaves of the Alien Amazon [Bill DuBay/Pablo Marcos] 12p; (2) The Comic

Books: Notes on Comix People [Joe Brancatelli, text article] 1p; (3) Like Father, Like Son [Cary Bates/Leopoldo Duranona] 8p; (4) Transference [Bruce Jones/Jose Ortiz] 10p; (5) The Eternal Triangle [Cary Bates/Martin Salvador] 9p; (6) John Donne and the Asteroid Pirates! [Chris Adames/Pablo Marcos] 12p.

Notes: Due to a deadline problem, the concluding chapter of the latest *Vampi* serial was held back until the next issue with the "Alien Amazon" story moved up to take its place. Both stories were concluded in the next issue. Although *Vampirella*'s covers had generally dropped the illustrative approach some time back and either concentrated on photo covers or Playboy style pin-up paintings, the last two issues had happily brought back the illustrative covers. This issue was certainly the better of the two, with Maroto's moody barbarian queen saluting a departing space ship. "Transference" was an interesting sex change story.

81. cover: Manuel Sanjulian (September 1979), reprinted from *Vampirella* #16 (April 1972)

(1) *Vampirella* and the Alien Amazon [Bill DuBay/Pablo Marcos] 13p; (2) *Vampirella*: Scourge of the Dragon Queen [Bill DuBay/Gonzalo Mayo] 13p; (3) The Comic Books: ? [Joe Brancatelli, text article] 1p; (4) *Vampirella*: ... and Be a Bride of Chaos! [Archie Goodwin/Jose Gonzalez, reprinted from *Vampirella* #16 (April 1972)] 20p; (5) *Vampirella*: Dracula Still Lives [T. Casey Brennan/Jose Gonzalez, reprinted from *Vampirella* #18 (August 1972)] 13p.

Notes: An all–Vampi issue that is mostly reprints or the last parts of two different serials.

82. cover: Jose Gonzalez (October 1979)

(1) *Vampirella*: The Lost Soul of Adam Van Helsing [Bill DuBay/Jose Gonzalez] 16p; (2) The Comic Books: Still Collecting After All These Years [Joe Brancatelli, text article] 1p; (3) Blind Justice [Bruce Jones/Leopoldo Duranona] 11p; (4) Prey for the Wolf [Cary Bates/Brian Lewis] 6p; (5) Fever [Roger McKenzie/Val Mayerik] 10p; (6) Deep Love [Cary Bates/Joe Vaultz] 6p; (7) The Night Willa Jane Gornley Went Home [Archie Goodwin/Val Mayerik and Jeff Easley] 10p; (8) The Rook ad [Pablo Marcos and Alfredo Alcala] 1p.

Notes: Jose Gonzalez delivered a rare cover painting. It had a $2.00 cover price with 80 pages. "Blind Justice" was a combination of mostly foreground drawings and fumetti backgrounds. Brian Lewis, *House of Hammer's* longtime cover artist, did his only strip for Warren. Sadly, he died shortly after completing it. It's the best art in the issue. The best story was easily Archie Goodwin's tearjerker "The Night Willa Jane Gornley Went Home." A tender and very sad story that was one of Goodwin's best and, thus, one of Warren's best. That story alone makes this issue well worth collecting.

83. cover: Jose Gonzalez and Kim McQuaite (December 1979)

(1) *Vampirella*: The God of Blood [Mike Butterworth/ Jose Gonzalez, story credited to Flaxman Loew, reprinted from *Vampirella* #30 (January 1974)] 12p; (2) *Vampirella*: The Betrothed of the Sun-God! [Mike Butterworth/Jose Gonzalez, story credited to Flaxman Loew, reprinted from *Vampirella* #31 (March 1974)] 12p; (3) The Comic Books: Lies Our Forefathers Told Us [Joe Brancatelli, text article] 1p; (4) Second Childhood [Bruce Jones/Ramon Torrents, reprinted from *Creepy* #88 (May 1977)] 8p; (5) Yellow Heat [Bruce Jones/Russ Heath, reprinted from *Vampirella* #58 (March 1977)] 8p; (6) Harry [Jeff Jones, reprinted from *Vampirella* #32 (April 1974)] 6p.

Notes: Like the cover for #75, this cover consisted of an original Vampi drawing by Gonzalez with painted tones and backgrounds by Kim McQuaite. If anything, this sexy cover was better than #75's. The 1979 *Vampirella* annual. It was 64 pages for $1.75.

84. cover: Steve Harris (January 1980)

Jose Gonzalez was the all-time best artist for *Vampirella's* own series. This rare cover effort, with fellow artist Kim McQuaite, shows why. *Vampirella* is ® Dynamite Entertainment and © 2012 DFI. All rights reserved/used by permission.

(1) *Vampirella*: Phantasmagoria of Terror [Bill DuBay/Jimmy Janes and Rudy Nebres] 17p; (2) The Comic Books: Notes on Comix People [Joe Brancatelli, text article] 1p; (3) Vampire Bite [Nicola Cuti/Rafael Auraleon, art miscredited to Jose Ortiz] 8p; (4) Steak-Out [Jean Michel Martin/Abel Laxamana] 6p; (5) Final Act [Pierce Askegren/Garcia Pizarro] 9p; (6) Native Strain [Marc Laidlaw/Val Mayerik and Jeff Easley] 8p.

Notes: A new cover artist appeared but this cover was particularly awful with Vampi looking like someone squashed her face in a vise. This was Harris' only Warren appearance. It was always hard to tell what Jimmy Janes' pencil work actually looked like since he was always paired with strong inkers like Nebres or Alfredo Alcala who had a tendency to make all pencilers look like them. (Steve Leialoha and John Severin are also known for this.) "Native Strain" was the best story and art here.

85. cover: Paul Gulacy/title page: Jose Gonzalez (March 1980)

(**1**) *Vampirella*: Flame Spirit [Bob Toomey/John Lakey and Val Lakey] 19p; (**2**) The Comic Books: Some Thoughts on What Has Gone Before [Joe Brancatelli, text article] 1p; (**3**) The Conscience of the King [Budd Lewis/Rafael Auraleon] 10p; (**4**) 1979 Warren Awards Ballot [Louise Jones, text article] 1p; (**5**) Curly's Gold [Michael Fleisher/Leopoldo Duranona] 10p; (**6**) A Green Phoenix [Laurie Sutton/Noly Zamora] 11p; (**7**) Lilywhite and Lavender [Gerry Boudreau/Alex Nino] 8p.

Notes: A $2.00 cover price with 80 pages. A beautiful cover by Paul Gulacy of Vampi and equally beautiful artwork on her episode by the Lakey team make this one of *Vampirella*'s best appearances. The delicate pencilwork on "Flame Spirit" was not only striking in its own right but it did something that had never been done before (nor was it done afterwards), namely, eliminate entirely Vampi's cheesecake factor from consideration in the art by dressing her in normal clothes. She still was strikingly beautiful and, in my opinion, this approach worked, giving Toomey's decent script a seriousness it might not otherwise have obtained. However, the fans, God bless their pointed little heads, complained extensively and the experiment was never again tried. Too bad, as this was a really good story and art. "Curly's Gold" had foreground art and photographed backgrounds, which, in the context of the script (an excellent job by Fleisher) worked very well. "Lilywhite and Lavender," judging by the number of naked bodies displayed, may have originally been intended for *1994*. Jose Gonzalez' title-page Vampi illustration was also of high quality. A strong issue.

86. cover: Terrence Lindall/title page: Gonzalo Mayo (April 1980)

(**1**) Vampirella: Revenge of the Renegade Wizard [Bill DuBay/Gonzalo Mayo, story credited to Will Richardson] 21p; (**2**) The Comic Books: Building a New Marvel [Joe Brancatelli, text article] 1p; (**3**) Snarking Down [Bruce Jones/Rafael Auraleon] 12p; (**4**) Brain Food [Michael Fleisher/Jun Lofomia] 10p; (**5**) The Pygmalion Effect [Nicola Cuti/Val Mayerik and Jeff Easley] 9p; (**6**) Never Again [James Warren, editorial, on the back cover] 1p.

Notes: A $1.75 cover price with 72 pages. Lindall's Vampi had fingers that were entirely too long (but then, everyone on the cover had fingers of an odd exaggerated length) but was otherwise quite good. A decent issue for Louise Jones' last Warren issue.

The Decline and Fall

87. cover: Enrich Torres (May 1980), reprinted, with an edited background, from *Vampirella* #52 (July 1976)

(**1**) *Vampirella*: The Return of the Blood Red Queen [Bill DuBay/Jose Gonzalez, reprinted from *Vampirella* #60–62 and 65–67 (May–August 1977 and December 1977–March 1978] 54p.

Notes: An all-reprint issue with some changes to the story and art. Of the original 57 pages this story covered, three were edited out. Word balloons were rearranged, one page is flipped or reversed and the last three pages (the only ones from *Vampirella* #67) were rewritten and somewhat redrawn with Pantha's costume changed. Louise Jones had left for Marvel and Bill DuBay was now the editor under his pen name Will Richardson.

88. cover: Enrich Torres (July 1980)

(**1**) *Vampirella*: Night of the Hell Dream [Bill DuBay/Rudy Nebres] 22p; (**2**) The Rook ad [Bob Larkin, B&W reproduction of #3's cover] 1p; (**3**) Night Walk! [Archie Goodwin/Rafael Auraleon] 17p; (**4**) The Talent of Michael Crawley [Bruce Jones/Jose Ortiz] 12p; (**5**) The 1979 Warren Awards [Bill DuBay, text article] 2p.

Notes: One of Enrich's best covers ever graced this issue. After a lengthy fallow period of uninspired Vampi portraits, Enrich seemed to become excited about doing the covers again and some of his best work appeared from here until the end of the magazine's run. Former Warren writer John Jacobson sent in a letter. Rudy Nebres became the new Vampi artist and promptly gave her a weight gain, mostly around the hips, of about 10–15 pounds. With only three stories, this issue might have felt somewhat slight but the Vampi story was readable, and the remaining two were quite good, with both Goodwin and Jones delivering excellent tales. A very strong issue.

89. cover: Enrich Torres (August 1980)

(1) *Vampirella*: A Gathering of Wizards! [Bill DuBay/Rudy Nebres, story credited to Will Richardson] 23p; (2) Over the Edge! [Bruce Jones/Rafael Auraleon] 12p; (3) The Rook ad [Nestor Redondo, B&W reproduction of #4's cover] 1p; (4) Sight Unseen [Bruce Jones/Jose Ortiz] 20p.

Notes: Enrich's cover was quite good but it was a reprint from one of the *Vampirella* paperbacks that had appeared in the late 1970s. Again, only three stories but, yet again, high-quality ones. The best was Bruce Jones and Jose Ortiz's excellent gothic "Sight Unseen," one of the best, and longest, non–Vampi stories to appear in this title.

90. cover: Enrich Torres (September 1980)

(1) *Vampirella*: The Insane Alchemist [Rich Margopoulos/Pablo Marcos and Rudy Nebres] 16p; (2) Pantha: Eye of Anubis [Rich Margopoulos/Leopoldo Duranona and Alex Toth, Toth's inking is credited to Atoz] 12p; (3) Devil Woman! [Don Glut/Alfredo Alcala] 10p; (4) Dead Ringer [Gerry Boudreau/Rafael Auraleon] 7p; (5) Revenge, Inc. [Gerry Boudreau/Anton Caravana] 8p.

Notes: Enrich's attractive pin-up cover of Vampi had her stretched out in a position no human being (although Vampi's not actually human) could achieve, but it still looked good. Pantha, who had been a regular in Vampi's strip since #66, was spun back into her own serial with some of Vampi's supporting cast moving with her. She also appeared in this issue's "Vampi" episode for the last time as a regular.

91. cover: Enrich Torres and a montage of past covers/title page: Jose Gonzalez (October 1980)

(1) *Vampirella*: The Carnival of Death! [Mike Butterworth/Jose Gonzalez, story credited to Flaxman Loew, reprinted from *Vampirella* #34 (June 1974)] 12p; (2) *Vampirella*: The Human Market-Place [Gerry Boudreau/Jose Gonzalez, reprinted from Vampriella #53 (August 1976)] 10p; (3) *Vampirella*: City of Ghosts [Roger McKenzie/Jose Gonzalez, reprinted from *Vampirella* #57 (January 1977)] 10p; (4) *Vampirella*: The Headless Horseman of All-Hallow's Eve! [Bill DuBay/Jose Gonzelez, reprinted from *Vampirella* #56 (December 1976)] 10p; (5) *Vampirella*: Pendragon's Last Bow! [Bill DuBay/Jose Gonzalez, reprinted from *Vampirella* #59 (April 1977)] 10p.

Notes: The 1980 *Vampirella* annual.

92. cover: Enrich Torres (December 1980)

(1) *Vampirella*: Bracelets, Demons, and Death! [Rich Margopoulos/Rudy Nebres] 25p; (2) That Future Long Ago [Bruce Jones/Rafael Auraleon] 18p; (3) Second Coming! [Bill DuBay/Jose Ortiz, story credited to Will Richardson] 11p.

Notes: Great cover by Enrich and generally strong stories from all involved. "Second Coming!" was the best although it is unclear if the hypnotist in the first storyline and the husband in the second storyline are the same men. The script seems to indicate that they are not while the art gives them near identical features (although different clothing).

93. cover: Enrich Torres (January 1981)

(1) *Vampirella*: Apocalypse Inc. [Rich Margopoulos/Rudy Nebres] 20p; (2) Cassandra St. Knight: The Psychic Assault [Rich Margopoulos/Rafael Auraleon, art miscredited to Rudy Nebres] 8p; (3) Pantha: Encore for Anubis [Rich Margopoulos/Leopoldo Duranona and Alfredo Alcala] 12p; (4) Cobra Goddess [Esteban Maroto] 11p.

Notes: Sixty-four pages for $1.75. Enrich's cover was quite sexual and quite lovely. From this point on *Vampirella* (the magazine) assumed *Eerie*'s old role as the host for Warren's horror serials. Jedediah Pan, who'd had his own series in *Eerie*, guest-starred in Vampi's strip. The new serial, *Cassandra St. Knight*, was okay, although Cassandra herself was a rather dour little witch.

94. cover: Enrich Torres and a montage of covers (March 1981)

(1) *Vampirella*: Death Machine! [Rich Margopoulos/Rudy Nebres] 12p; **(2)** Cassandra St. Knight: The Psychic Assault, part 2 [Rich Margopoulos/Rafael Auraleon] 8p; **(3)** Pantha: Druids on 54th Street! [Rich Margopoulos/Jose Ortiz] 10p; **(4)** The Big Shot! [Michael Fleischer/Delando Nino] 10p; **(5)** The Last Gift! [Roger McKenzie/Esteban Maroto] 9p; **(6)** Gunplay [John Lakey, Val Lakey and Laura Buscemi, story and art credited to Artifact] 7p.

Notes: It had 72 pages for $1.95. All in all, a pretty good issue with a nice Christmas story by McKenzie and Maroto, the start of a promising storyline in *Pantha* and two decent stand-alone stories by the Artifact team and Fleischer/Nino.

95. cover: Ken Kelly (April 1981)

(1) *Vampirella*: Plague of Vampires [Rich Margopoulos/Rudy Nebres] 22p; **(2)** Cassandra St. Knight: The Initiation [Rich Margopoulos/Rafael Auraleon] 16p; **(3)** Pantha: Reflections in Blood! [Rich Margopoulos/Jose Ortiz] 12p; **(4)** The Fox [Nicola Cuti/Luis Bermejo] 8p.

Notes: Cover price at $2.00. Ken Kelly's last cover for *Vampirella* was quite good. *The Fox* serial was a sequel to the story "Tale of a Fox" from *Creepy* #100 (August 1978). An all-series issue with *The Fox* being the best written and drawn.

96. cover: Enrich Torres (May 1981)

(1) *Vampirella*: The Hound of Hell [Rich Margopoulos/Rudy Nebres] 17p; **(2)** Cassandra St. Knight: A Matter of Karma [Rich Margopoulos/Rafael Auraleon] 13p; **(3)** Pantha: Night of the Cat Goddess [Rich Margopoulos/Jose Ortiz] 14p; **(4)** Armistice [Jim Stenstrum/Masanabu Sato, story credited to Alabaster Redzone] 6p.

Notes: Chris Adames became editor.

97. cover: Enrich Torres/title page: Jose Gonzalez (July 1981), reprinted from *Vampirella* #58 (March 1977)

(1) *Vampirella*: Army of the Dead! [Rich Margopoulos/Gonzalo Mayo] 10p; **(2)** Cassandra St. Knight: Many Faces of God [Rich Margopoulos/Rafael Auraleon] 10p; **(3)** Pantha: A Night Full of Zombies! [Rich Margopoulos/Jose Ortiz] 12p; **(4)** Hershey's Rock [Kevin Duane/Felix Santos] 9p; **(5)** Wormbrand [Bruce Jones/Rafael Auraleon] 8p.

98. cover: Enrich Torres/title page: Gonzalo Mayo (August 1981), reprinted from *Vampirella* #53 (August 1976)/title page reprinted from *Vampirella* #97 (July 1981).

(1) *Vampirella*: Army of the Dead!, part 2 [Rich Margopoulos/Gonzalo Mayo] 12p; **(2)** Cassandra St. Knight: Mindwars [Rich Margopoulos/Rafael Auraleon] 12p; **(3)** Pantha: The Haitian Connection [Rich Margopoulos/Jose Ortiz] 10p; **(4)** Dragon [Esteban Maroto] 8p; **(5)** The Fox, part 2 [Nicola Cuti/Luis Bermejo] 9p.

Notes: Although Maroto's careful not to name him, the hero of his story "Dragon" appears to be Dax the Warrior.

99. cover: Manuel Sanjulian/title page: Jose Gonzalez (September 1981), reprinted from *Vampirella* #23 (April 1972)/title page reprinted from *Vampirella* #24's cover (June 1972)

(1) *Vampirella*: Spell of Laughter [Rich Margopoulos/Gonzalo Mayo] 14p; **(2)** Missing You [Bruce Jones/Leopold Sanchez] 10p; **(3)** Friends [Val Lakey/John Lakey, Val Lakey and Laura Buscemi, art credited to Artifact] 10p; **(4)** Pantha: The Lair of Dr. Rictus [Rich Margopoulos/Jose Ortiz] 12p; **(5)** Salome [Esteban Maroto] 8p.

Notes: A good issue with the beautifully drawn "Friends" taking the art honors and the first half of "Missing You" the honors for best story. "Salome" by Maroto was also very good.

100. cover: montage of previous covers/title page: Jose Gonzalez (October 1981)

(1) Vampirella: Call It Chaos! [Archie Goodwin/Anton Caravana] 21p; **(2)** In Memoriam: Anton Caravana [Chris Adames, text article] 1p; **(3)** Vampirella: The Origin of Vampirella [Budd Lewis/Jose Gonzalez, reprinted from *Vampirella* #46 (October 1975)] 15p; **(4)** Vampirella: Shadow of Dracula [T. Casey Brennan/Jose Gonzalez, reprinted from *Vampirella* #19 (September 1972)] 10p; **(5)** Vampirella: When Wakes The Dead [T. Casey Brennan/Jose Gonzalez, reprinted from *Vampirella* #20 (November 1972)] 13p.

Notes: The 1981 *Vampirella* annual and a very disappointing 100th issue. Yes, Archie Goodwin returned to *Vampi* (and Warren) for the last time and delivered a good story but the rest of the stories were reprints and not great ones at that. Even the cover intended for this issue was bounced to the next issue, prompting the fourth non-original cover in a row. A $2.25 cover price for 80 pages and a load of disappointment. This was Caravana's only *Vampi* story as he was struck by a jeepney (a European passenger vehicle) and killed while bicycling shortly after completing this story, as was revealed in the obituary in this issue.

101. cover: Noly Panaligan/title page: Jose Gonzalez (December 1981)

(**1**) *Vampirella*: Attack of the Star Beast [Rich Margopoulos/Gonzalo Mayo] 14p; (**2**) Pantha: A Night Full of Zombies, Chapter Four [Rich Margopoulos/Jose Ortiz] 8p; (**3**) Cassandra St. Knight: Hell on Earth [Rich Margopoulos/Rafael Auraleon] 14p; (**4**) The Fox: Dynasty of Evil [Nicola Cuti/Luis Bermejo] 9p; (**5**) Victims! [Scott Hampton] 3p.

Notes: It was $2.00 for 72 pages. As stated above, this cover was clearly intended for #100's only original story. *The Fox* serial was updated to 1910 with the descendent of the original Fox-woman now appearing. This was Scott Hampton's professional debut. His story is quite short but very good. Bill DuBay again became the editor, with Timothy Moriarty as the managing editor.

102. cover: Enrich Torres/title page: Jose Gonzalez (January 1982), cover miscredited to Manuel Sanjulian

(**1**) *Vampirella*: Return of the Blood-Red Queen! [Rich Margopoulos/Gonzalo Mayo] 16p; (**2**) Pantha: A Night Full of Zombies, part 5 [Rich Margopoulos/Jose Ortiz] 7p; (**3**) Cassandra St. Knight: Kill Quake! [Rich Margopoulos/Rafael Auraleon] 10p; (**4**) The Fox: Night of the Devil-dogs! [Nicola Cuti/Luis Bermejo] 8p; (**5**) Perseus [Timothy Moriarty/Esteban Maroto] 6p; (**6**) Alicia [Carl Wessler/Alphonso Font] 8p.

Notes: The Blood-Red Queen in this issue's "Vampi" tale was actually the ill-fated sister of the original queen. *Vampirella* was the only Warren magazine in 1982 that consistently tried to hold up the standards of the glory days of Warren. As a result, this issue was actually quite good, with strong artwork and decent story-telling, even in the "Vampirella" story. The covers also reverted from the pin-up style of recent years to a more illustrative approach. "Alicia" appeared to have been done years earlier, probably in the mid–1970s.

103. cover: Enrich Torres/title page: Jose Gonzalez (March 1982)

(**1**) *Vampirella*: The Last Prince! [Rich Margopoulos/Jose Gonzalez] 8p; (**2**) Cassandra St. Knight: The Mephisto List! [Rich Margopoulos/Rafael Auraleon] 8p; (**3**) Pantha: The Final Solution! [Richard Margopoulos/Jose Ortiz] 9p; (**4**) The Fox: Terror in the Tomb! [Nicola Cuti/Luis Bermejo] 10p; (**5**) Pentesilea [Timothy Moriarty/Esteban Maroto] 7p; (**6**) Lover [John Lakey/John Lakey, Val Lakey and Laura Buscemi, art credited to Artifact] 12p.

Notes: Editor: Timothy Moriarty. Best art belonged to the Artifact team for "Lover" although Esteban Maroto also delivered a superior job. Best story was either "Lover" or the installment of *The Fox*. Beautiful, peaceful cover by Enrich.

104. cover: Enrich Torres/title page: Jose Gonzalez (April 1982)

(**1**) Vampirella: The Wax House! [Rich Margopoulos/Jose Gonzalez] 8p; (**2**) Pantha: Death Snare! [Rich Margopoulos/Jose Ortiz] 12p; (**3**) The Fox: Jaded [Nicola Cuti/Luis Bermejo] 6p; (**4**) Jeremy [Paul Gillon/Paul Gillon and Rudy Nebres] 12p; (**5**) Missing You!, part 2 [Bruce Jones/Leopold Sanchez] 10p.

Notes: It was $2.25 for 64 pages. Gonzalez did a particularly nice job on the "Vampi" strip. *Jeremy* was originally published in Europe in 1971. For its Warren publication, Rudy Nebres provided a new splash page. The Jones/Sanchez "Missing You" was finally completed five issues after the first half appeared.

105. cover: Enrich Torres (May 1982)

(**1**) *Vampirella*: Horrors of Heartache City [Bill DuBay/Jose Gonzalez, reprinted from Vampriella #67–68 (January–March 1978), #71 (August 1978) and #75 (January 1979)] 48p.

Notes: A fix-up issue with a book-length tale cobbled together from separate "Vampi" stories. The story from #67 had three pages dropped. The scripts were extensively rewritten and there were numerous art changes including re-inking Pantha's costume.

106. cover: Enrich Torres/title page: Jose Gonzalez (July 1982)

(**1**) *Vampirella*: A Love Blessed in Hell [Rich Margopoulos/Jose Gonzalez] 8p; (**2**) Sweetwater

Nessie [Don McGregor/Rafael Auraleon] 12p; (3) Pantha: On the Trail of the Cat [David Allikas/Jose Ortiz] 8p; (4) The Fox and the Deer [Nicola Cuti/Luis Bermejo] 6p; (5) Jeremy, part 2 [Paul Gillon] 9p; (6) Safari [David Allikas/Esteban Maroto] 8p.

Notes: Lots of nudity and sex scenes in the "Vampi" strip along with very attractive art by Gonzalez. The best art, however, belonged to Auraleon for his superb job on the first installment of *Sweetwater Nessie.* The credits were left off all the strips by mistake. Cuti's "The Fox and the Deer" was a rewrite of his Charlton story "Orion" from 1975. That version, illustrated by Don Newton, was set in Greece with the woman changing into a deer. Good story in both versions.

107. cover: Manuel Sanjulian/title page: Jose Gonzalez (August 1982)

(1) *Vampirella*: The Blood Red Queen of Hearts [Bill DuBay/Esteban Maroto, reprinted from *Vampirella* #49 (March 1976)] 12p; (2) Moonspawn [Doug Moench/Esteban Maroto, reprinted from *Vampirella* #26 (August 1973)] 10p; (3) Black and White Vacuum Blues [Doug Moench/Esteban Maroto, reprinted from *Vampirella* #34 (June 1974)] 8p; (4) Dracula: The Circus of King Carnival [Gerry Boudreau/Esteban Maroto, reprinted from *Vampirella* #39 (January 1975)] 8p; (5) Look What They've Done! [Steve Skeates/Esteban Maroto, reprinted from *Eerie* #36 (November 1971)] 6p.

Notes: An all-reprint Esteban Maroto special.

108. cover: Enrich Torres/title page: Jose Gonzalez (September 1982)

(1) *Vampi's Vivacious Vignettes* [Timothy Moriarty, text article] 1p; (2) *Vampirella*: Spawn of the Star Beast [Rich Margopoulos/Jose Gonzalez] 8p; (3) Sweetwater Nessie, part 2 [Don McGregor/Rafael Auraleon] 13p; (4) Pantha: Circus Monstrous [David Allikas/Jose Ortiz] 8p; (5) The Fox: The Beast Lies Sleeping [Nicola Cuti/Luis Bermejo] 9p; (6) Jeremy, part 3 [Paul Gillon/Paul Gillon and Rudy Nebres] 12p; (7) Torpedo, 1936: I'm Luca [E. Sanchez Abuli/Alex Toth] 8p; (8) The 1981 Warren Awards! [Timothy Moriarty, text article] 2p.

Notes: It was $2.50 for 80 pages with a new features page replacing the letters page. Although the rest of the strip was an average Vampi strip,

the splash page has a striking gray-toned portrait of a nude *Vampirella.* The *Sweetwater Nessie* strip appeared for the last time, and its storyline was never concluded. Too bad as it was pretty good. Rudy Nebres once again provided a new splash page for the *Jeremy* strip. Any magazine that featured Alex Toth's version of *Torpedo* (published at nearly the same time in the Spanish/European version of *Creepy*) was worth buying.

109. cover: Manuel Sanjulian/frontis: Jose Gonzalez (October 1982)

(1) Vampirella: The Corpse with the Missing Mind [Bill DuBay/Jose Gonzalez, reprinted from *Vampirella* #55 (October 1976)] 8p; (2) The Sultan of 42nd Street [Carl Wessler and Gerry Boudreau/Felix Mas, reprinted from *Vampirella* #39 (January 1975)] 6p; (3) Dungeons of the Soul [T. Casey Brennan/Felix Mas, reprinted from *Creepy* #45 (May 1972)] 8p; (4) Out of the Nameless City [John Jacobson/Felix Mas, reprinted from *Vampirella* #38 (November 1974)] 12p; (5) The Climbers of the Tower [T. Casey Brennan/Felix Mas, reprinted from *Creepy* #50 (January 1973)] 7p; (6) Miranda [Fred Ott/Felix Mas, reprinted from *Vampirella* #34 (June 1974)] 6p; (7) The Dorian Gray Syndrome [Don Glut/Felix Mas, reprinted from *Vampirella* #18 (August 1972)] 6p; (8) The Killer [Steve Skeates/Felix Mas, reprinted from *Creepy* #52 (April 1973)] 8p; (9) Minra [Ed Newsome/Felix Mas, reprinted from *Vampirella* #22 (March 1973)] 7p; (10) Changes [Steve Skeates/Felix Mas, reprinted from *Vampirella* #24 (May 1973)] 10p.

Notes: It was $2.75 for 96 pages. The 1982 *Vampirella* annual and, with the exception of the "Vampirella" strip, a Felix Mas special.

110. cover: Enrich Torres/title page: Jose Gonzalez (December 1982)

(1) *Vampi's Vivacious Vignettes* [Timothy Moriarty, text article] 1p; (2) *Vampirella*: A Feast of Fear [Rich Margopoulos/Jose Gonzalez] 8p; (3) The Masque of the Red Death! [Rich Margopoulos/Rafael Auraleon, from the story by Edgar Allan Poe] 10p; (4) Jeremy, part 4 [Paul Gillon] 11p; (5) Torpedo, 1936: The Judas Job! [E. Sanchez Abuli/Alex Toth] 8p; (6) Nightwind [Gerry Boudreau/Rafael Auraleon] 8p; (7) Queen of Souls! [Bill DuBay/Esteban Maroto] 7p; (8) *Vampirella*: Tales of Lost Drakulon! [Bill DuBay/Gonzalo Mayo] 6p.

Notes: Enrich's last Warren cover. It was $2.50 for 80 pages. The features page advertised the never-published *Goblin* #4 with stories of the Goblin, the Micro-Buccaneers, the Hobgoblin and the Troll Patrol (the latter probably a color insert) scheduled for it. Best story and art belonged to the *Torpedo* strip.

111. cover: Pujolar/title page: Jose Gonzalez (January 1983), reprinted from *Devilina* #1 (January 1975)

(1) The Noxious Newspage [Timothy Moriarty, text article] 1p; (2) *Vampirella*: The Curse of the MacDaemons [Mike Butterworth/Jose Gonzalez, story credited to Flaxman Loew, reprinted from *Vampirella* #28 (October 1973)] 12p; (3) *Vampirella*: The Undead of the Deep! [Mike Butterworth/Jose Gonzalez, story credited to Flaxman Loew, reprinted from *Vampirella* #29 (November 1973)] 12p; (4) The Time Eater! [Jack Butterworth/Paul Neary, reprinted from *Vampirella* #40 (March 1975)] 12p; (5) Ali Addan and Son! [Esteban Maroto and Bill DuBay/Esteban Maroto, reprinted from *Vampirella* #68 (April 1978)] 8p; (6) Force-Feed [Cary Bates/Leopoldo Sanchez. reprinted from *Vampirella* #59 (April 1977)] 8p; (7) Fog [Nicola Cuti/Carmine Infantino and Dick Giordano, reprinted from *Vampirella* #62 (August 1977)] 8p; (8) The French Coagulation [Carl Wessler and Gerry Boudreau/Luis Bermejo, reprinted from *Vampirella* #39 (January 1975)] 8p.

Notes: An all-reprint issue. The cover was reprinted from the Atlas/Seaboard's copycat magazine *Devilina* instead of a *Vampirella* issue!

112. cover: Martin Hoffman/title page: Jose Gonzalez (March 1983)

(1) The Noxious Newspage [Timothy Moriarty, text article] 1p; (2) *Vampirella*: The Walker of Worlds [Rich Margopoulos/Jose Gonzalez] 8p; (3) The Fox: Shadows of the Mind [John Ellis

Sech/Luis Bermejo] 7p; (4) Torpedo, 1936: Frankie [E. Sahchez Abuli/Jordi Bernet] 8p; (5) The Ransom [Michael Fleisher/Rafael Auraleon] 7p; (6) Limbo [Bill DuBay/Esteban Maroto] 8p; (7) Vampirella and Pantha: Feeding Frenzy [Rich Margopoulos/Gonzalo Mayo] 20p.

Notes: Final Warren issue and their final published comic magazine. A striking cover by newcomer Martin Hoffman and decent stories and art throughout gave *Vampirella* a decent farewell.

113. cover: Erich Torres/frontis and title page: Jose Gonzalez (April 1988)

(1) Vampirella and the Sultana's Revenge! [Mike Butterworth/Jose Gonzalez, story credited to Flaxman Loew, reprinted from *Vampirella* #33 (May 1974)] 12p; (2) Vampi's Feary Tales: The

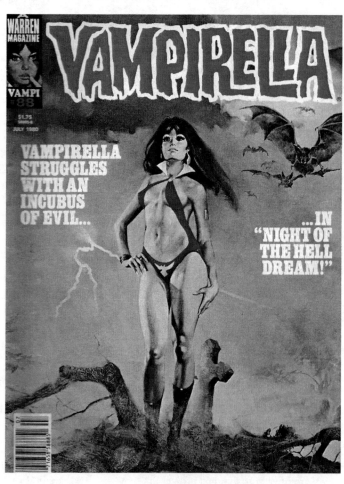

One of the last of the really great Vampi covers, this Torres effort shows that, just standing still, *Vampirella* was both authoritative and sexy. *Vampirella* is ® Dynamite Entertainment and © 2012 DFI. All rights reserved/used by permission.

Sirens! [Frank Brunner, reprinted from *Vampirella* #12 (July 1971)] 1p; (3) Vampirella: The Vampire of the Nile [Mike Butterworth/Jose Ortiz, story credited to Flaxman Loew, reprinted from Vampriella #36 (September 1974)] 12p; (4) Vampi's Feary Tales: The Face of Medusa [Billy Graham, reprinted from *Vampirella* #10 (March 1971)] 1p; (5) Vampirella: The Mummy's Revenge [Mike Butterworth/Jose Gonzalez, story credited to Flaxman Loew, reprinted from *Vampirella* #38 (November 1974)] 12p; (6) ...Looking for Something Different? [Steve Perry/J. J. Brozowski] 10p; (7) Vampirella and Pantha: Feeding Frenzy [Rich Margopoulos/Gonzalo Mayo, reprinted from *Vampirella* #112 (March 1983)] 20p; (8) *Vampirella*: The Walker of Worlds [Rich Margopoulos/Jose Gonzalez, reprinted from *Vampirella* #112 (March 1983)] 8p; (9) Vampi's Feary Tales: The Gray Women [Jan Strnad/Rafael Auraleon, reprinted from *Vampirella* #16 (April 1972)] 1p; (10) Pantha: Druids on 54th Street! [Rich Margopoulos/Jose Ortiz, reprinted from *Vampirella* #94 (March 1981)] 10p; (11) Vampirella: The Wax House! [Rich Margopoulos/Jose Gonzalez, reprinted from *Vampirella* #104 (April 1982)] 8p; (12) Vampi's Feary Tales: Nymphs [Kevin Pagan/Luis Garcia, on the inside back cover, reprinted from *Vampirella* #18 (August 1972)] 1p.

Notes: It cost $3.95 for 96 pages. Publisher: Stanley Harris. Editor: Tony Dispoto. With one exception this entire issue reprinted Warren stories. The exception was "...Looking for Something Different?" done in 1985 and originally intended for Harris Publications' never-published *Creepy* #147. A number of faces in the new story appeared to have been inked by Neal Adams.

Vampirella Annual

1. cover: Aslan (1971)

(1) Vampi's Feary Tales: The Bride of Frankenstein [Tom Sutton, reprinted from *Vampirella* #2 (November 1969)] 1p; (2) Vampirella: The Origin of Vampirella [J. R. Cochran/Jose Gonzalez] 15p; (3) The Curse of Circe [Gardner Fox/Jerry Grandenetti, reprinted from *Vampirella* #6 (July 1970)] 6p; (4) Goddess from the Sea [Don Glut/Neal Adams, reprinted from *Vampirella* #1 (October 1969)] 6p; (5) The Curse [Wally Wood, reprinted from *Vampirella* #9 (January 1971)] 8p; (6) Snake Eyes [Nicola Cuti/Jack Sparling, reprinted from Vampriella #8 (November 1970)] 7p; (7) Vampi's Feary Tales: Love! [Tom Sutton, reprinted from *Vampirella* #8 (November 1970)] 1p; (8) Forgotten Kingdom [Bill Parente/Ernie Colon, reprinted from *Vampirella* #4 (April 1970)] 10p; (9) Vampi's Feary Tales: Lilith [Nicola Cuti/Jeff Jones, reprinted from *Vampirella* #9 (January 1971)] 1p.

Notes: Publisher: James Warren. Editor: J. R. Cochran. It was $0.75 for 64 pages. The cover by Aslan was done in 1969 and originally intended for *Vampirella* #1. This was the only *Vampi* annual issue as, beginning in 1972, the annual was incorporated into *Vampirella*'s regular numbering. Unlike either *Creepy* or *Eerie*'s annuals, *Vampi*'s usually had an original "Vampirella" story included. This one retold Vampi's origin, revamping it from the rather silly Ackerman/Sutton origin story from #1, to reflect the more serious approach the "Vampi" strip was taking. It was later rewritten by Budd Lewis, although the same art was used, to further revamp Vampi's origin.

Comix International

1. cover: montage of interior panels (July 1974)

(1) Terror Tomb [Richard Corben, reprinted from *Creepy* #61 (April 1974)] 8p; (2) Lycanklutz [Richard Corben, reprinted from *Creepy* #56 (September 1973)] 8p; (3) The Hero Within [Steve Skeates/Richard Corben, reprinted from *Creepy* #60 (February 1974)] 8p; (4) The Low Spark of High Heeled Noise! [Doug Moench/Richard Corben, reprinted from *Creepy* #57 (November 1973)] 8p; (5) Bless Us, Father... [Bill DuBay/Richard Corben, reprinted from *Creepy* #59 (January1974)] 7p; (6) Judas [Rich Margopoulos/Richard Corben, reprinted from *Creepy* #62 (May 1974)] 8p; (7) Child [Greg Potter/Richard Corben, reprinted from *Eerie* #57 (June 1974)] 8p; (8) As Though They Were Living [Gerry Boudreau/Richard Corben, reprinted from *Vampirella* #30 (January 1974)] 8p; (9) Top to Bottom [Jack Butterworth/Richard Corben, reprinted from *Vampirella* #33 (May 1974)] 8p; (10) Demon in the Cockpit [Rich Margopoulos/Richard Corben, reprinted from *Creepy* #63 (July 1974)] 8p.

Notes: The cost was $2.00 for 80 pages. Publisher: James Warren. An all-reprint, all-color magazine which sold almost exclusively via mail order from the Captain Company back pages of the Warren line. The title was originally intended for a proposed underground book put together by Keith Green for Warren but it never progressed very far. Outside of the cover, no publishing or editorial information appeared in the magazine itself, although it was probably edited by Bill DuBay. This first issue was an all–Richard Corben special, which was notable for the speed in which the color sections were reprinted, some within only weeks of their original appearance. Fairly expensive to obtain but a beautiful book.

2. cover: montage of interior panels (1975)

(**1**) The Raven [Richard Corben, from the poem by Edgar Allan Poe, reprinted from *Creepy* #67 (December 1974)] 8p; (**2**) Anti-Christmas [Budd Lewis/Richard Corben, reprinted from *Creepy* #68 (January 1975)] 8p; (**3**) The Butcher: Forgive Us Our Trespasses [Bill DuBay/Richard Corben, reprinted from *Eerie* #62 (January 1975)] 8p; (**4**) Dracula: The Circus of King Carnival [Gerry Boudreau/Esteban Maroto, reprinted from *Vampirella* #39 (January 1975)] 8p; (**5**) Dracula: The Winged Shaft of Fate [Gerry Boudreau/Esteban Maroto, reprinted from *Vampirella* #40 (March 1975)] 8p; (**6**) The Manhunters [Gerry Boudreau/Wally Wood, reprinted from *Eerie* #60 (September 1974)] 8p; (**7**) Purge! [Bruce Bezaire/Jose Ortiz, reprinted from *Creepy* #73 (August 1975)] 8p; (**8**) Janis! [Victor Mora/Luis Garcia, reprinted from *Vampirella* #45 (September 1975)] 8p; (**9**) The Beast on Bacon Street [Budd Lewis/Reed Crandall, reprinted from *Creepy* #74 (October 1975)] 7p; (**10**) The Muck Monster [Berni Wrightson; reprinted from *Eerie* #65 (September 1975)] 7p; (**11**) Artist profiles: Richard Corben/Reed Crandall/Luis Garcia/Esteban Maroto/Jose Ortiz/Wally Wood/Berni Wrightson [Bill DuBay, text article] ?p

Notes: Edited by Bill DuBay. Both this and #3 were published at the same time in late 1975.

3. cover: montage of interior panels (1975)

(**1**) Child: Mind of the Mass! [Greg Potter/Richard Corben, reprinted from *Eerie* #58 (July 1974)] 8p; (**2**) Child: Childhood's End [Budd Lewis/Richard Corben, reprinted from *Eerie* #60 (September 1974)] 8p; (**3**) Wizard Wagstaff [Jack Butterworth/Richard Corben, reprinted from *Eerie* #56 (April 1974)] 8p; (**4**) Hard John Apple: An Angel Shy of Hell [Jim Stenstrum/Richard Corben, reprinted from *Creepy* #64 (August 1974)] 8p; (**5**) Harry [Jeff Jones, reprinted from *Vampirella* #32 (April 1974)] 6p;

(**6**) Dead Run [Jeff Jones, reprinted from *Vampirella* #32 (April 1974)] 2p; (**7**) A Wonderful Morning [Fernando Fernandez, reprinted from *Vampirella* #36 (September 1974)] 8p; (**8**) Puppet-Player [Jose Bea, reprinted from *Vampirella* #36 (September 1974)] 8p; (**9**) Dax the Damned: Chess [Esteban Maroto and ?/Esteban Maroto, reprinted from *Eerie* #41 (August 1972)] 8p; (**10**) Mates [Doug Moench/Esteban Maroto, reprinted from *Creepy* #64 (August 1974)] 8p; (**11**) *Vampirella*: Return Trip [Josep Toutain/Jose Gonzalez, reprinted from *Vampirella* #27 (September 1973)] 8p; (**12**) Artist profiles: Jose Bea/Richard Corben/Fernando Fernandez/Jeff Jones/Esteban Maroto [Bill DuBay, text article] ?p

Notes: The *Dax* story included here was the only *Dax* tale that did not appear in *Eerie* #59's reprinting of the *Dax* saga and it is also the only story reprinted here (in color) that was not originally printed as a color section.

4. cover: montage of interior panels (1976)

(**1**) The Believer! [Budd Lewis/Richard Corben, reprinted from *Creepy* #77 (February 1976)] 8p; (**2**) The Power and the Gory [W. Eaton/Rafael Auraleon, reprinted from *Vampirella* #28 (October 1973)] 8p; (**3**) The Freaks: A Thin Dime of Pain [Doug Moench/Leopold Sanchez, reprinted from *Eerie* #72 (February 1976)] 8p; (**4**) Child [Greg Potter/Richard Corben, reprinted from *Eerie* #57 (June 1974)] 8p; (**5**) Tell-Tale Heart [Archie Goodwin/Reed Crandall, from the story "The Tell-Tale Heart" by Edgar Allan Poe, reprinted (the color version) from *Creepy* #65 (September 1975)] 8p; (**6**) Exterminator One [Bill DuBay/Paul Neary, reprinted from *Eerie* #63 (February 1975)] 8p; (**7**) Hunter [Bill DuBay/Paul Neary, reprinted (the color version) from *Eerie* #69 (October 1975)] 8p; (**8**) Vampirella: The Monster Called Vampirella [Bill DuBay/Zesar Lopez, reprinted from *Vampirella* #46 (October 1975)] 8p; (**9**) Artist profiles: Rafael Auraleon/Richard Corben/Reed Crandall/Felix Mas/Paul Neary/Leopold Sanchez/Zesar Lopez [Louise Jones?, text article] ?p.

Notes: Size reduced to 68 pages. I don't have a copy of this magazine but if Felix Mas is listed in the profile section it's possible that a story is missing from this listing. The editor was Louise Jones. "Child" was reprinted for the second time in this series, as it also appeared in #1. *The Overstreet Price Guide* cites a second printing with an additional Richard Corben story.

5. cover: montage of interior panels (1977)

(1) Bowser [Jan Strnad/Richard Corben, reprinted from *Vampirella* #54 (September 1976)] 8p; **(2)** The Succubus Stone [Gerry Boudreau and Carl Wessler/Ramon Torrents, reprinted from *Vampirella* #49 (March 1976)] 8p; **(3)** Vampirella: The Corpse with the Missing Mind [Bill DuBay/Jose Gonzalez, reprinted from *Vampirella* #55 (October 1976)] 8p; **(4)** The Mummy: ... and an End [Steve Skeates/Jaime Brocal, reprinted (the color version) from *Eerie* #78 (October 1976)] 8p; **(5)** Déjà Vu [Doug Moench/Esteban Maroto, reprinted (the color version) from *Creepy* #82 (August 1976)] 8p; **(6)** Demons of Father Pain [Bill DuBay/Jose Ortiz, reprinted from *Eerie* #77 (September 1976)] 8p; **(7)** The Spirit: The Origin of the Spirit [Will Eisner/Will Eisner and Chuck Kramer, reprinted from *The Spirit* #6 (February 1975)] 8p; **(8)** In Deep [Bruce Jones/Richard Corben, reprinted from *Creepy* #83 (October 1976)] 10p.

Notes: Final issue. Like its previous reprinting, the story "Déjà Vu" had one page dropped from its original appearance.

Warren Presents

1. cover: Kim McQuaite and James Warren (October–November? 1977)

(1) U.F.O. [Josep Toutain/Ramon Torrents, reprinted from *Vampirella* #62 (August 1977)] 9p; **(2)** Daddy and the Pie [Bill DuBay/Alex Toth, reprinted from *Eerie* #64 (March 1975)] 8p; **(3)** The Pie and I [Budd Lewis/Luis Bermejo, reprinted from *Eerie* #72 (February 1976)] 9p; **(4)** Companions to the Sun [Bruce Jones/Leopold Sanchez, reprinted from *Vampirella* #61 (July 1977)] 10p; **(5)** The Generations of Noah [Roger McKenzie/Leopoldo Duranona, reprinted from *Creepy* #92 (October 1977)] 9p; **(6)** Visitation at Pliny Marsh [Gerry Boudreau/Martin Salvador, reprinted from *Creepy* #79 (May 1976)] 8p; **(7)** The Stars My Salvation [Doug Moench/John Severin] 11p.

Notes: Publisher: James Warren. Editor: Nicola Cuti, with Louise Jones listed as senior editor. This issue was subtitled *UFO and Alien Comix.* This series was, at least initially, inspired by the *Star Wars* phenomenon, where every comic that had the word "Star" in its title sold well. The *Warren Presents* umbrella title had a very convoluted history with four issues appearing as one-shot "specials" before the *Warren Presents* tag ap-

peared. Twelve of the issues were composed of reprinted comics with each issue having a separate, unique title but the remaining two were composed of text reprints from *Famous Monsters.* The magazine followed no regular schedule, sometimes appearing annually, sometimes with two issues at once and sometimes a full year or more between issues. The irony was that in the latter issues these reprint magazines (due to cherry-picking good stories) were often better than any of the regular magazines' runs at the time. Based on the 1977 original publication dates for three of the stories contained within, this debut issue probably came out in October or November 1977.

2. cover: Larry Todd (September 1978), reprinted from *Eerie* #33 (May 1971)

(1) Starvisions [Larry Todd, reprinted from *Eerie* #33 (May 1971)] 6p; **(2)** Mates [Doug Moench/Esteban Maroto, reprinted from *Creepy* #64 (August 1974)] 8p; **(3)** Incident in the Beyond! [Archie Goodwin/Gray Morrow, reprinted from *Creepy* #3 (June 1965)] 6p; **(4)** Behold the Cybernite! [Rich Margopoulos/Tom Sutton, reprinted from *Creepy* #46 (July 1972)] 8p; **(5)** Taking of Queen Bovine [Gerry Boudreau/Ramon Torrents, reprinted from *Eerie* #81 (February 1977)] 8p; **(6)** Hunter 3 [Jim Stenstrum/Alex Nino, reprinted from *Eerie* #87 (October 1977)] 8p; **(7)** Within You ... Without You [Bruce Jones/Richard Corben, reprinted from *Eerie* #77 (September 1976)] 10p; **(8)** The Argo Standing By! [Budd Lewis/Paul Neary, reprinted from *Creepy* #73 (August 1975)] 10p.

Notes: Titled *Future World Comix.* Editor: Louise Jones.

3. cover: Ken Kelly (October 1978), reprinted from *Creepy* #73 (August 1975)

(1) Last Light of the Universe [Budd Lewis/Esteban Maroto, reprinted from *Creepy* #73 (August 1975)] 17p; **(2)** Epilogue [Bill DuBay/Jose Ortiz, reprinted from *Creepy* #73 (August 1975)] 1p; **(3)** Stars Wars Revisited [Kis Stulken, Deb Thomston and Ann Wilson, text article, reprinted from *Famous Monsters of Filmland* #? (? 1977)] 10p; **(4)** The Last Hero [Steve Skeates/Ramon Torrents, reprinted from *Creepy* #52 (April 1973)] 10p; **(5)** Unprovoked Attack on a Hilton Hotel [Jim Stenstrum/Richard Corben, reprinted from *Creepy* #73 (August 1975)] 8p; **(6)** Judas [Rich Margopoulos/Richard Corben, reprinted from *Creepy* #62 (May 1974)] 8p; (7) The War [Roger McKenzie/Paul Neary, reprinted from *Creepy* #81 (July 1976)] 8p.

Notes: Titled *Starquest Comix.*

4. cover: Patrick Woodroffe (December 1978)

(1) Killer Hawk [Bill DuBay/Wally Wood, reprinted from *Eerie* #61 (November 1974)] 12p; (2) Battlestar Galactica [Terry Pinckard, text article, reprinted from *Famous Monsters of Filmland* #149? (November? 1978)] 10p; (3) Star-Slaughter [Rich Margopoulos/Ramon Torrents, reprinted from *Creepy* #51 (March 1973)] 8p; (4) Starbright Lantern [Gerry Boudreau/Jose Ortiz, reprinted from *Vampirella* #48 (January 1976)] 9p; (5) The Time Eater! [Jack Butterworth/Paul Neary, reprinted from *Vampirella* #40 (March 1975)] 12p; (6) Mother Knows Best [Bruce Jones/Al Williamson, reprinted from *Creepy* #86 (February 1977)] 8p; (7) Now You See It... [Bruce Jones/Al Williamson, reprinted from *Creepy* #83 (October 1976)] 8p.

Notes: Titled *Galactic War Comix.*

5. cover: Manuel Sanjulian (January 1979), reprinted from *Eerie* #41 (August 1972)

(1) The Curse [Wally Wood, reprinted from *Vampirella* #9 (January 1971)] 8p; (2) The Last Dragon King [Roger McKenzie/Esteban Maroto, reprinted from *Vampirella* #67 (March 1978)] 8p; (3) Jackie and the Leprechaun King [Bill DuBay/Esteban Maroto, reprinted from *Vampirella* #53 (August 1976)] 12p; (4) Prelude to Armageddon [Nicola Cuti and Wally Wood/Wally Wood, reprinted from *Creepy* #41 (September 1971)] 12p; (5) Merlin: The King [Budd Lewis/Gonzalo Mayo, reprinted from *Eerie* #74 (May 1976)] 20p; (6) Dax the Damned: Chess [Esteban Maroto and Budd Lewis/Esteban Maroto, reprinted from *Eerie* #59 (August 1974)] 8p.

Notes: The first issue to carry the title *Warren Presents.* Subtitled *Ring of the Warlords.*

6. cover: Paul Gulacy (May 1979)

(1) The Making of a Comic Book Hero [Bill DuBay, text article] 2p; (2) The Rook: The Man Whom Time Forgot [Bill DuBay/Luis Bermejo, reprinted from *Eerie* #82 (March 1977)] 20p; (3) The Rook: The Day Before Tomorrow [Bill DuBay/Luis Bermejo, reprinted from *Eerie* #83 (May 1977)] 20p; (4) The Rook: Yesterday, the Final Day [Bill DuBay/Luis Bermejo, reprinted from *Eerie* #84 (June

1977)] 22p; (5) The Rook: Lost to the Land of Nowhen [Bill DuBay/Luis Bermejo, reprinted from *Eerie* #85 (August 1977)] 14p.

Notes: Subtitled *Wanted: The Rook.* Editor: Bill DuBay. The Gulacy cover originally had an elaborate background identifying the stories as taking place at the Alamo, but the background was dropped with only the foreground figure of the Rook remaining, while the background was solid white. This special was a preview with promo/pilot for the upcoming *Rook* magazine.

7. cover: Kim McQuaite (August 1979)

(1) The Beast Is Yet to Come [Nicola Cuti/Carmine Infantino and Alex Nino, reprinted from *Vampirella* #59 (April 1977)] 8p; (2) It! [Archie Goodwin/Dan Adkins, reprinted from *Eerie* #7 (January 1967)] 8p; (3) The Mound [Tom Sutton, reprinted from *Eerie* #45 (February 1973)] 8p; (4) Alien [Forrest J. Ackerman, text article, reprinted from *Famous Monster of Filmland* #? (? 1979)] 8p; (5) The Man Hunters [Gerry Boudreau/Wally Wood, reprinted from *Eerie* #69 (September 1974)] 8p; (6) The Star Saga of Sirius Sam [Nicola Cuti/John Severin, reprinted from *Creepy* #95 (February 1978)] 8p; (7) Tibor Miko's Christmas [Alex Toth, reprinted from *Creepy* #77 (February 1976), originally entitled "Tibor Miko"] 6p.

Notes: Subtitled Alien Invasion Comix.

8. cover: John Stone (September 1979), photo collage

(1) This issue is made up entirely of reprinted articles from *Famous Monsters of Filmland.*

Notes: Subtitled *Movie Aliens Illustrated.*

9. cover: Basil Gogos (September 1979), reprinted from *Famous Monsters of Filmland* #105 (March 1974)

(1) Pursuit of the Vampire! [Archie Goodwin/Angelo Torres, reprinted from *Creepy* #1 (January 1965)] 6p.

Notes: Subtitled *Dracula.* Except for the single comic reprint, this entire issue was made up of reprinted articles from *Famous Monsters of Filmland.*

10. cover: Manuel Sanjulian (October 1979), reprinted from *Eerie* #46 (March 1973)

(1) Curse of the Vampire! [Archie Goodwin/Neal Adams, reprinted from *Creepy* #14 (April

1967)] 8p; (2) A Flash of Lightning [Gerry Boudreau/John Severin, reprinted from *Creepy* #76 (January 1976)] 9p; (3) Like Icarus, Quickly Falling [Roger McKenzie/Leopold Sanchez, reprinted from *Creepy* #85 (January 1977)] 8p; (4) A Game of Hide and Seek [Roger McKenzie/Leopoldo Duranona, reprinted from *Vampirella* #65 (December 1977)] 9p; (5) Swamped! [Archie Goodwin/Angelo Torres, reprinted from *Creepy* #3 (June 1965)] 8p; (6) Day of the Vampire 1992: The Tombspawn [Bill DuBay/Gonzalo Mayo, reprinted from *Eerie* #73 (March 1976)] 10p.

Notes: Subtitled *Strange Stories of Vampires Comix*. This is the first time that the story "A Game of Hide and Seek" was printed complete in one issue.

11. cover: Bob Larkin (October 1980)

(1) Pantha: Re-Birth [Steve Skeates/Rafael Auraleon, reprinted from *Vampirella* #30 (January 1974)] 10p; (2) Pantha: Family Ties! [Steve Skeates/Rafael Auraleon, reprinted from *Vampirella* #31 (March 1974)] 9p; (3) Pantha: Black on White [Steve Skeates/Rafael Auraleon, reprinted from *Vampirella* #32 (April 1974)] 10p; (4) Pantha: Childhood Haunt! [Steve Skeates/Rafael Auraleon, reprinted from Vampriella #33 (May 1974)] 10p; (5) Pantha: Straw on the Wind [Budd Lewis/Rafael Auraleon, reprinted from *Vampirella* #42 (May 1975)] 10p.

Notes: Subtitled *Pantha*. Editor: Bill DuBay as Will Richardson.

12. cover: Jim Laurier (November 1980)

(1) The Rubicon [Budd Lewis/Pepe Moreno, reprinted from *Creepy* #107 (May 1979)] 10p; (2) The Empire Strikes Gold! [?, text article, reprinted from *Famous Monsters of Filmland* #166 (August 1980)] 8p; (3) Gotterdammerung, parts 1 and 2 [Budd Lewis/Isidro Mones, reprinted from *Eerie* #100 and 101 (April and June 1979] 20p; (4) The Green [Bruce Jones/Luis Bermejo, reprinted from *Creepy* #96 (March 1978)] 6p; (5) Gravity Field [Bob Toomey/Pepe Moreno, reprinted from *Vampirella* #76 (March 1979)] 8p.

Notes: Editor: Chris Adames. Subtitled *Empire Encounters Comix*.

13. cover: Manuel Sanjulian (October 1981)

(1) A Scream in the Forest [Greg Potter/Esteban Maroto, reprinted from *Creepy* #53 (May 1973)] 12p; (2) Spotlight on Dragonslayer [Forrest J.

Ackerman, text article, reprinted from *Famous Monsters of Filmland* #? (? 1981) 6p; (3) Merlin: The Kingmaker [Budd Lewis/Esteban Maroto, reprinted from *Eerie* #67 (August 1975)] 11p; (4) Goddess in a Kingdom of Trolls [Gerry Boudreau/Esteban Maroto, reprinted from *Creepy* #92 (October 1977)] 8p; (5) Scheherazade [Bill DuBay/Esteban Maroto, reprinted from *Vampirella* #72 (September 1978)] 8p; (6) The Sleeping Beauty [Bill DuBay/Esteban Maroto, reprinted from *Vampirella* #58 (March 1977)] 8p.

Notes: An Esteban Maroto special. Subtitled *Sword and Sorcery Comix*.

14. cover: Bob Larkin/frontis: Rudy Nebres (November 1981)

(1) Rex Havoc [Jim Stenstrum/Abel Laxamana, reprinted from *1984* #4 (October 1978)] 10p; (2) Rex Havoc: She Who-Must-Be-Okay! [Jim Stenstrum/Abel Laxamana, reprinted from *1984* #6 (June 1979)] 22p; (3) Rex Havoc: Humungus [Jim Stenstrum/Abel Laxamana, reprinted from *1984* #9 (October 1979)] 20p.

Notes: Final issue. These stories were slightly edited for content and Rex's group, the Asskickers of the Fantastic, was renamed the Raiders of the Fantastic. One supposes this editorial softening was to make "Rex Havoc" appeal to a broader group than the fans of the raunchy *1984*. Still, Asskickers of the Fantastic is a damn funny name.

Vampirella Special

1. cover: montage of interior panels (1977)

(1) Meet Pepe Gonzalez [Bill DuBay/Jose Gonzalez, frontis, text article] 1p; (2) *Vampirella*: Death's Dark Angel [Archie Goodwin/Jose Gonzalez, reprinted from *Vampirella* #12 (July 1971)] 20p; (3) *Vampirella*: The Lurker in the Deep [Archie Goodwin/Jose Gonzalez, reprinted from Vampriella #13 (September 1971)] 15p; (4) *Vampirella*: Isle of the Huntress! [Archie Goodwin/Jose Gonzalez, reprinted from *Vampirella* #14 (November 1971)] 20p; (5) Vampirella: The Mummy's Revenge [Mike Butterworth/Jose Gonzalez, story credited to Flaxman Loew, reprinted from *Vampirella* #38 (November 1974)] 12p; (6) *Vampirella*: The Mountain of Skulls [Mike Butterworth/Jose Gonzalez, story credited to Flaxman Loew, reprinted from *Vampirella* #42 (May 1975)] 12p.

Notes: Editor: Louise Jones and Josep Toutain. All of the *Vampi* strips were colored for this appearance. A hardcover edition, signed by Jose Gonzalez, was also offered at $12.50.

1984/1994

1. cover: Richard Corben (June 1978)

(1) Remember the Good Old Days? Who Would Have Thought They'd Return ... in 1984? [Bill DuBay/Joe Vaultz, frontis, text article] 1p; (2) Last of the Really Great, All-American Joy Juice [Bill DuBay/Jose Ortiz] 12p; (3) The Saga of Honey Dew Melons [Nicola Cuti/ Esteban Maroto] 8p; (4) Once Upon Clarissa [Bill DuBay/Alex Nino] 8p; (5) Quick Cut [Wally Wood and Bill DuBay/Wally Wood, story credited solely to Wood] 6p; (6) The Saga of Xatz and Xotz [Bill DuBay/Alfredo Alcala] 1p; (7) Bugs! [Bill DuBay/Joe Vaultz] 4p; (8) Mutant World [Richard Corben, color] 8p; (9) Faster-Than-Light Interstellar Travel [Jim Stenstrum/Luis Bermejo] 12p; (10) Angel! [Bill DuBay/Rudy Nebres] 12p; (11) Momma, Can You Hear Me? [Nicola Cuti/Alex Nino] 8p; (12) 1984 ad [Joe Vaultz, on the inside back cover] 1p; (13) Next issue cover ad [Richard Corben, on the back cover] 1p.

Notes: Publisher: James Warren. Editor: Bill DuBay. A $1.50 cover price with 80 pages. No ads. Ahhh, what can you say about *1984*? Put into the publishing pipeline when Jim Warren apparently panicked over the successful debut of *Heavy Metal* in 1977, this single magazine set out to pretty much confirm every parent, feminist, African American, Native American, liberal, conservative, and just plain ol' American Joe or Jane's worst fears about comics. Juvenile, sleazy, scatalogical, racist, demeaning to women, heavy handed in its treatment of violence and lame in its sense of humor — all aptly describe *1984*. And that's just the stories. Behind the scenes, DuBay apparently rewrote other writers' stories so that straight SF stories written for *Eerie* or *Creepy* would conform to *1984's* more adult "standards" and to make stories written directly for *1984* even more sleazy than they originally were. A lawsuit was prompted when writer Harlan Ellison sued over an unauthorized (and disguised) adaptation of his award winning story "A Boy and His Dog," a suit that may have been a major factor in killing the entire Warren publishing company.

At least one stellar writer/artist swore never to work for Warren again after his work's treatment in the pages of *1984*. The George Orwell estate supposedly pressured Warren into changing the title midway through the run. Buying an issue of *1984* or *1994* in 1978–1982 gave one about the same feeling as buying a *Hustler*. You might like comics, you might like skin magazines, but liking these two magazines was akin to admitting that maybe you were a little bit of a sleazy dumbass, too. Even today, I cringe a little, just knowing a complete set of *1984/1994* is stored in my closet. However, in its defense, *1984* published the best art (often quite spectacular art) of any Warren magazine during its run and *DID* publish some pretty decent stories.

Now, as to this issue in particular, when you lead off with a story about collecting semen, the reader might get a negative idea of where the issue was going to go. That negative idea would be pretty much right on target, but there are some definite hightlights here. Rich Corben's "Mutant World" starts off a serial that any adult (not porn, but adult — there's a *difference*) magazine in 1978 would have been proud to publish. Nicola Cuti managed to write a couple of worthwhile stories, even as they were nearly buried in silly sexual antics. Jim Stenstrum delivered the best story of the bunch, a charming, silly, and adult story that managed to lightly tapdance its way past the open sewer that many of the other stories leaped into somewhat cheerfully. The artwork was very good, with Maroto, Corben, Nino and Bermejo providing great jobs. Good work was also seen from Alcala and Vaultz. However, Rudy Nebres, usually a very dependable artist, turned in one ugly set of pages while Ortiz's work was just run of the mill. The Wally Wood story was another matter. Wood's original story was entitled "The End" and was 12 pages long. It was a part of or a sequel to his *Wizard King* series. Bill DuBay, without Wood's permission or knowledge, split the story in two, rearranged pages and panels, rewrote Wood's original script and presented the greatly altered work as two separate stories, changing Wood's original rather charming adult-oriented tale into shorter pieces that leaned heavily on the scenes (which were also in Wood's original but not nearly so highlighted there as their appearance here) of naked women in bondage being whipped and brutalized. Understandably, Wood was outraged and never worked for Warren again. He published the original version himself in his newsletter *The Wood Gazette* and that original version again appeared in the *Wallace Woods* series of reprinted work that Eclipse published in 1985 or 1986. Even today, it's hard to understand why this happened. It's easy to imagine a newcomer to comics being treated in such a fashion but in 1978 Wood was a major star in the comic field. He had worked on *The Spirit*, was one of the original EC artists, and had done stellar work throughout most of his career. His original story would have looked just fine in *Creepy* or *Eerie*. Yes, it was somewhat tame according to the lights of *1984* but to see the original story and compare it to the two tawdry six-page stories that appeared here is quite depressing. The ad on the back cover shows the original version of #2 cover before it was altered by DuBay.

2. cover: Richard Corben and Bill DuBay (August 1978)

(1) The Last of the Red Hot Lovers [Bill Du-Bay/Jose Ortiz] 8p; (2) Scourge of the Spaceway [Bill DuBay/Esteban Maroto] 8p; (3) ...Sure-Fire Quick-Carnage Self-Decimation Kit! [Bill DuBay/Alex Nino] 8p; (4) One Night, Down on the Funny Farm! [Wally Wood and Bill DuBay/Wally Wood] 6p; (5) The Janitor [Bill DuBay/Nebot] 9p; (6) Mutant World, part 2 [Richard Corben, color] 8p; (7) Messiah [Bill DuBay/Rudy Nebres] 11p; (8) Don't Call Me ... Maneater! [Bill DuBay/Alfredo Alcala and Jim Janes] 7p; (9) The Microbe Patrol [Nicola Cuti/Abel Laxamana] 14p.

Notes: For some reason, the brunette on Corben's original cover was turned into a blonde by Bill DuBay. It doesn't seem to have affected the thrust of the cover in any particular way. Best story and art here is the DuBay/Nino effort, which read a bit like a more violent version of the Jim Stenstrum/John Severin story "The Super-Abnormal Phenomena Survival Kit" from 1976. "The Janitor" was somewhat amusing, with the art and storyline looking like it would fit right into a modern-day sex magazine like *Sizzle*. Nebres' art is much better than in the previous issue. "Don't Call Me ... Maneater!" was a

spoof of Marvel's version of Conan, with Alcala (who did a great deal of work on Marvel's Conan character) making the leading oaf in the story look like the dumb and dumber twin of the Robert E. Howard creation.

3. cover: Patrick Woodroffe (September 1978)

(1) Squeezin's [Bill DuBay/Jose Ortiz] 14p; (2) Whatever Happened to Idi Amin? [Bill DuBay/ Esteban Maroto] 11p; (3) In the Beginning...! [Bill DuBay/Alex Nino] 12p; (4) Mutant World, part 3 [Jan Strnad/Richard Corben, color] 8p; (5) Bring Me the Head of Omar Barsidian! [Bill DuBay/Jim Janes and Rudy Nebres] 6p; (6) The Strange Adventures of Doctor Jerkyll [Nebot] 5p; (7) Scourge of All Disneyspace [Bill DuBay/Alfredo Alcala] 6p; (8) Commfu [Jim Stenstrum/Abel Laxamana, story credited to Alabaster Redzone] 7p; (9) The Harvest [Bill DuBay/Jose Ortiz] 8p; (10) The Quickie Adventures of Happy Jim Sunblaster [Jim Stenstrum and Bill DuBay/Herb Arnold, color, on the inside back cover, Stenstrum's contribution credited to Alabaster Redzone] 1p.

Notes: Patrick Woodroffe was one of Warren's best cover artists during this period and this cover is one of the reasons why. Striking and eerie. "Squeezin's" was a quite good story by the team of DuBay and Ortiz, while Corben's "Mutant World" picked up even more steam by adding scripter Jan Strnad. The *Idi Amin* story boasted some of Maroto's best art for Warren, unfortunately in service to a very dumb serial. The *Happy Jim Sunblaster* stories were a combo of a new one-page serial that always doubled as a *1984* ad. Any good will that DuBay and Ortiz had acquired by "Squeezin's" was totally destroyed by the vile "The Harvest" which related the happy adventures of a (white) father and son in a world where blacks were regarded as hunting animals. After they track down and kill a near-term pregnant black woman, we're treated to the lovely sight of them ripping her baby from her womb, holding the fetus above their heads in a spray of blood, while commenting on how they're going to have "some prime veal!" Absolutely disgusting and something I have no problem placing in that section of "literature" called "violent and unnecessary pornography."

4. cover: Patrick Woodroffe (October 1978), wraparound cover

(1) The Last War ... of the Worlds! [Bill DuBay/ Jose Ortiz] 16p; (2) Idi and Me [Bill DuBay/ Esteban Maroto] 10p; (3) Mondo Megillah [Jim Stenstrum/Alex Nino, story credited to Alabaster Redzone] 12p; (4) Mutant World, part 4 [Jan Strnad/Richard Corben, color] 8p; (5) The Stunning Downfall of Muhammad Reptillicus! [Jim Janes and Bill DuBay/Jim Janes and Rudy Nebres] 8p; (6) Ogre [Jan Strnad/Richard Corben, color] 8p; (7) Lullaby [Jim Stenstrum/Jose Gonzalez, story credited to Alabaster Redzone] 6p; (8) Boys' Camp [Jim Stenstrum/Herb Arnold, story credited to Alabaster Redzone] 8p; (9) Rex Havoc and the Asskickers of the Fantastic [Jim Stenstrum/Abel Laxamana] 10p; (10) Happy Jim Sunblaster Rides Again! [Bill DuBay/Herb Arnold, color, on the inside back cover] 1p.

Notes: It was $1.75 for 88 pages. "The Last War ... of the Worlds!" was a sequel to H. G. Wells' novel, "War of the Worlds." Two color sections appeared this issue, with the "Ogre" story's art being composed of enhanced photos and clay models by Corben. Very nicely done. A sequel to this story, "Ogre II," appeared in *Fantagor* #5 in 1983. "Mondo Megillah" was the story Harlan Ellison considered a ripoff of his award-winning story "A Boy and His Dog." The story goes that Warren Publishing was attempting to obtain the rights to the Ellison story and, in anticipation of getting them, Bill DuBay plotted and had Nino illustrate an actual adaptation. However, Ellison refused to allow the adaptation, so, after Nino changed his art to feature a monster instead of a dog and a girl instead of a guy (and some monster/girl humping, just for kicks), the actual scripting of the story was then handed off to Stenstrum, who may or may not have been aware of the Ellison connection. Ellison spotted the adaptation's source material immediately and sued Warren Publications. He won his case and, within months of the win, Warren Publications went out of business. Whether the two events are related are unknown, although Ellison has claimed there is a direct connection. Outside of this embarrassment, Stenstrum had a pretty good time in this issue, with the debut of his funny serial *Rex Havoc*, and the fine stories of "Lullaby" and "Boys' Camp." "Lullaby" featured the best artwork Gonzalez ever did for Warren and "Boys' Camp" featured some interesting

work by Herb Arnold. Arnold's artwork was often mistaken for Corben, although I've never been sure why. Their art is similar but certainly not an exact match. It's easy to tell the two apart.

5. cover: Patrick Woodroffe (February 1979)

(1) The Odd Comic World of Richard Corben ad [Richard Corben, frontis] 1p; (2) The Greatest Hero of Time and Space! [Jim Stenstrum and Bill Dubay/Jose Ortiz, Stenstrum's contribution credited to Alabaster Redzone and DuBay's to Strontium Whitehead] 8p; (3) Idi and the Ratmen of Hunger Hollow [Bill DuBay/Esteban Maroto, story credited to Strontium Whitehead] 8p; (4) Timothy Sternbach and the Multi-Colored Sunrise! [Gerry Boudreau/Alex Nino] 8p; (5) I Wonder Who's Squeezing Her Now? [Nicola Cuti/Ernie Colon and Wally Wood] 7p; (6) Luke the Nuke Brings It In! [Jim Stenstrum/Rudy Nebres] 6p; (7) Mutant World, part 5 [Jan Strnad/Richard Corben, color] 8p; (8) The Box! [Len Wein/Mike Nassar and Alfredo Alcala] 8p; (9) Killman One [Jim Stenstrum/Herb Arnold, story credited to Alabaster Redzone] 8p; (10) Rex Havoc and the Asskickers of the Fantastic: The Spud from Another World! or: Who Goes There? [Jim Stenstrum/Abel Laxamana] 14p; (11) The Quickie Adventures of Happy Jim Sunblaster Again! [Bill DuBay/Herb Arnold, color, on the inside back cover] 1p.

Notes: Back to $1.50 for 80 pages. There was a five-month gap between #4 and 5, possibly to gauge how sales were going. Woodroffe's cool, subtle cover also appeared as the cover to Jack Vance's novel *The Gray Prince*. The letters page was four pages long with fantasy/SF artist Rick Berry and fan writer R. Fiore sending in highly critical letters. The Cuti/Wood tale "I Wonder Who's Squeezing Her Now?" was done in 1971 and was originally intended for the never published *POW!* #1, under the title "Incident at Laurelhurst." The *Rex Havoc* story, also the best story in this issue, spoofed John W. Campbell's famous original story "The Thing from Another World" and the equally famous Howard Hawks' movie adaptation. All of Stenstrum's stories, with the exception of "The Greatest Hero of Time and Space!" were quite good. The Boudreau/Nino story was also good. Best art honors go to Richard Corben.

6. cover: Jim Lauier (June 1979)

(1) The Warhawks [Bill DuBay/Jose Ortiz] 17p; **(2)** The Final Days of Idi Amin! [Bill DuBay/ Esteban Maroto] 11p; **(3)** Liaison Aboard a Skylab [Jeff Rovin/Alex Nino] 9p; **(4)** Mutant World, part 6 [Jan Strnad/Richard Corben, color] 8p; **(5)** Twilight's End! [Jim Stenstrum/ Rudy Nebres, story credited to Alabaster Redzone] 9p; **(6)** Rex Havoc and the Asskickers of the Fantastic: She Who-Must-Be-Okay! [Jim Stenstrum/Abel Laxamana] 22p.

Notes: Another long wait between issues. "The Warhawks" was a rather harsh spoof on Quality and DC's Blackhawks. Oddly enough, DuBay went on to write an unpublished Blackhawks mini series in the mid–1980s for DC, with art by Carmine Infantino and Bob McLeod. I wonder if DC ever saw this mean-spirited take on the World War II vets. Frank Thorne's "Ghita of Alizarr" was previewed on the letters page. Best story and art in this issue goes to the *Rex Havoc* tale.

7. cover: Patrick Woodroffe (August 1979)

(1) Teleport 2010 [Budd Lewis/Alex Nino] 14p; **(2)** Freeze a Jolly Good Fellow! [Budd Lewis/ Jose Ortiz] 6p; **(3)** Kaiser Warduke and the Indispensable Jasper Gemstone! [Rich Margopoulos/Jimmy Janes and Alfredo Alcala] 9p; **(4)** Mutant World, part 7 [Jan Strnad/Richard Corben, color] 8p; **(5)** Twilight's End!, part 2 [Jim Stenstrum/Rudy Nebres, story credited to Alabaster Redzone] 9p; **(6)** Ghita of Alizarr: Alizarr [Frank Thorne] 15p; **(7)** Zincor and the Fempire [Gerry Boudreau/Alex Nino] 14p; **(8)** The Quickie Adventures of Happy Jim Sunblaster [Bill DuBay/Herb Arnold, color, on the inside back cover] 1p.

Notes: A $1.75 cover price. Beneath a rather bizarre, although striking, cover painting of an alien by Woodroffe was a fairly interesting issue with "Teleport 2010" and the latest installment of *Mutant World* being the best stories. This issue featured the debut of Frank Thorne's soft-porn reworking of his *Red Sonja* series from Marvel, *Ghita of Alizarr*. Alex Nino delivered the best artwork here.

8. cover: Jim Laurier (September 1979)

(1) Painter's Mountain [Bill DuBay and Budd Lewis/Alex Nino] 16p; **(2)** Herma: All You Need Is Love [Bill DuBay/Jose Gonzalez] 8p;

(3) Twilight's End, part 3 [Jim Stenstrum/Rudy Nebres, story credited to Alabaster Redzone] 13p; **(4)** Mutant World, part 8 [Jan Strnad/ Richard Corben, color] 8p; **(5)** Ghita of Alizarr, part 2 [Frank Thorne] 11p; **(6)** Madmen and Messiahs [Bill DuBay/Abel Laxamana] 9p; **(7)** The Rook ad [Rudy Nebres et al.] 2p; **(8)** Once Upon a Holocaust! [Nicola Cuti and Bill DuBay/Alex Nino] 8p; **(9)** The Miniscule Adventures of Happy Jim Sunblaster! [Bill DuBay/ Herb Arnold] 1p.

Notes: With the conclusion of "Mutant World" Corben ceased working for Warren, except for the occasional cover. He did leave on a high note. As a whole, "Mutant World" was one of the best stories he'd ever done for Warren. The best single story here was "Painter's Mountain," which was surprisingly thoughtful and beautifully drawn. "Herma" was drawn in 1974 but remained unpublished until it appeared in a European publication shortly before its North American printing here. It was greatly rewritten by DuBay and the art adjusted to meet the larger dimensions of a magazine.

9. cover: Patrick Woodroffe (October 1979)

(1) Break Even [Kevin Duane/Alex Nino] 18p; **(2)** Herma [Bill DuBay/Jose Gonzalez] 8p; **(3)** The Rook ad [Rudy Nebres et al.] 2p; **(4)** A Clear and Present Danger! [Gerry Boudreau/Jess Jodloman] 9p; **(5)** Starfire [Bill DuBay/Frank Springer and Herb Arnold, color] 8p; **(6)** Rex Havoc and the Asskickers of the Fantastic: Humungus [Jim Stenstrum/Abel Laxamana] 20p; **(7)** The Schmoo Connection [Bill DuBay?/Alex Nino] 8p.

Notes: For the first time ads began to appear on interior pages of this title. The *Rex Havoc* story spoofed the Godzilla movies. Schmoos were the creation of Al Capp in his comic strip *Li'l Abner* and were extraordinarily popular in the 1950s.

10. cover: Patrick Woodroffe (December 1979)

(1) The Whatever Shop! [Jim Stenstrum/Alex Nino] 12p; **(2)** Herma [Bill DuBay/Jose Gonzalez] 8p; **(3)** The Little Spaceship That Could! [John Ellis Sech/Jose Ortiz] 7p; **(4)** The Klanks Are Coming! The Klanks Are Coming! [Rich Margopoulos/Vic Catan] 10p; **(5)** The Starfire Saga, part 2 [Bill DuBay/Rudy Nebres, color] 8p; **(6)** Ghita of Alizarr, part 3 [Frank Thorne] 12p; **(7)** Haxtur [Victor de la Fuente] 11p; **(8)** Thinking of You! [Nicola Cuti/Abel Laxamana] 9p.

Notes: Comic artist Ronn Sutton sent in a letter. *Haxtur* was done in 1971 and appeared all over Europe before being serialized here. Both "The Whatever Shop" and "Thinking of You!" were superior stories. The artwork was generally fine throughout.

11. cover: Alex Nino (February 1980), cover credited to A2-120

(1) 1984 Magazine: A Eulogy! [Bill DuBay, text article, on the letters page] ⅓ p; (2) East of Euthanasia [Bill DuBay/Alex Nino, story credited to Will Richardson] 10p; (3) The Jewels of Araknid [Rich Margopoulos/Jose Ortiz] 8p; (4) Outpost 1017 [Rich Margopoulos/Michael Saentz] 8p; (5) Live Large [John Ellis Sech/E.R. Cruz] 9p; (6) The Starfire Saga, part 3 [Bill DuBay/Rudy Nebres, color] 8p; (7) Ghita of Alizarr, part 4 [Frank Thorne] 15p; (8) Haxtur, part 2 [Victor de la Fuente] 12p; (9) Once There Was a ... Masher! [Alex Nino] 3p.

Notes: Editor Bill DuBay reinvented himself as Will Richardson for the next year or so. *1984* changed its name, according to the letters page explanation so that newsstand readers wouldn't confuse it with George Orwell's novel *1984*. To the more cynical, possibly so that the George Orwell estate wouldn't sue Warren's sleaziest title while Warren was already embroiled in a lawsuit with Harlan Ellison. Orwell's novel was also given a strong plug in the title change essay. Other than the title switch, not much of anything changed about the magazine, at least for now. After this issue, *Haxtur* moved to *Eerie* for the remainder of his run.

12. cover: Manuel Sanjulian (April 1980)

(1) The Seed! [Bill DuBay/Alex Nino, story credited to Will Richardson] 15p; (2) Jailbreak ... on Channel 69! [Bob Toomey/Jose Gonzalez] 4p; (3) Over Four Billion Served [Kevin Duane/Delando Nino] 9p; (4) The Starfire Saga, part 4 [Bill DuBay/Rudy Nebres, story credited to Will Richardson] 10p; (5) Ghita of Alizarr, part 5 [Frank Thorne] 10p; (6) Baby Makes Three! [Kevin Duane/Abel Laxamana] 16p.

Notes: Size reduced to 72 pages. *Baby Makes Three!* was a good serial. The color section was dropped.

13. cover: Jose Bea (June 1980)

(1) Imaginary Lover! [John Ellis Sech/Alex

Nino] 11p; (2) Cyberman [Rich Margopoulos/Delando Nino] 12p; (3) The Crop! [Bill DuBay/Jose Ortiz, story credited to Will Richardson] 12p; (4) The Starfire Saga, part 5 [Bill DuBay/Rudy Nebres, story credited to Will Richardson] 6p; (5) Ghita of Alizarr, part 6 [Frank Thorne] 12p; (6) Voyage to the Bottom of the Barrel [Budd Lewis/Abel Laxamana] 11p.

Notes: Bea, not seen on the Warren stage for some years, made a welcome return with a cover that recalled his excellent *Eerie* serial *Tales of Peter Hypnos.*" Comics artist Carl Potts sent in a letter. "The Crop!" was just as offensive as #3's "The Harvest," while "Voyage to the Bottom of the Barrel" was a dumbass, jive-talking turkey of a story that was summed up in its own title quite accurately.

14. cover: Manuel Sanjulian (August 1980), wraparound cover

(1) Womb with a View! [Nicola Cuti/Alex Nino] 10p; (2) The Benevolence! [Jim Stenstrum/Jose Ortiz] 22p; (3) The Galaxy Grand Prix [Jim Stenstrum/Vic Catan, story credited to Alabaster Redzone] 10p; (4) Ghita of Alizarr, part 7 [Frank Thorne] 16p; (5) Baby Makes Three, part 2 [Kevin Duane/Abel Laxamana] 6p.

Notes: *Ghita* was cover-featured in one of Sanjulian's better covers. "The Benevolence!" was such a good story that it stuck out like a healthy thumb in this issue. ad pages now appeared on a regular basis.

15. cover: Alex Nino (October 1980), cover credited to A2–120

(1) Spearchucker Spade, Intergalactic Eye! [Bill DuBay/Alex Nino, story credited to Will Richardson] 21p; (2) Coming Out Party [Rich Margopoulos/Delando Nino] 8p; (3) The Missionary [Carlos Gimenez] 8p; (4) The Starfire Saga, part 6 [Bill DuBay/Rudy Nebres, story credited to Will Richardson] 7p; (5) Baby Makes Three!, part 3 [Kevin Duane/Abel Laxamana] 9p; (6) 1894 [Budd Lewis/Alex Nino] 6p.

Notes: As had happened with *Eerie*'s The Spook, DuBay again used a racial slur (actually two slurs) against blacks to name an African American character. Future comic artist Chas Truog sent in a letter.

16. cover: Jordi Penalva (December 1980)

(1) Sci-Fi Writer [Kevin Duane/Alex Nino] 9p; (2) Dog Star [Bill DuBay/Delando Nino, story credited to Will Richardson] 8p; (3) Agony [Carlos Gimenez, from a passage in the novel *The Stellar Diaries* by Stanislaw Lem] 8p; (4) The Day after Dooms Day! [John Ellis Sech/ Luis Bermejo] 12p; (5) The Starfire Saga, part 7 [Bill DuBay/Rudy Nebres] 7p; (6) Baby Makes Three!, part 4 [Kevin Duane/Abel Laxamana] 12p; (7) Fruit of the Grape! [Kevin Duane/Alex Nino] 8p.

Notes: The cover was one of Penalva's best for Warren. Duane's humorous little "Sci-Fi Writer" and the equally funny "Fruit of the Grape!" indicated that he was one of the better of the latterday Warren writers. Bermejo's art was surprisingly quite poor on his story. "Baby Makes Three!" concluded in fine fashion. The adaptation of "Agony" had the best story and art here.

17. cover: Jim Stenstrum and Bill DuBay (February 1981), DuBay's art credited to Will Richardson

(1) Asshole of the Universe! [Bill DuBay/Alex Nino, story credited to Will Richardson] 10p; (2) Mad Amy [Bill DuBay and Kevin Duane/ Jose Ortiz, DuBay's contribution credited to Will Richardson] 14p; (3) Ghita of Alizarr, part 8 [Frank Thorne] 16p; (4) Kid Rust [Bill Du-Bay?/Jose Ortiz, color] 8p; (5) The Big Cerebration [Jim Stenstrum/Abel Laxamana] 4p; (6) Man Is God! [John Ellis Sech/Alex Nino] 2p.

Notes: *1994* joined the ranks of the regular Warren magazines with $1.95 cover price for 64 pages. The Stenstrum/DuBay cover was quite colorful but otherwise this is a rather hoohum issue.

18. cover: H. R. Giger (April 1981)

(1) The Lost Loves of Cranfranz P. Thitwacker [Bill DuBay/Alex Nino, story credited to Will Richardson] 10p; (2) Lone Wolf [John Ellis Sech/Delando Nino] 16p; (3) The Mad Planet [Gerry Boudreau and Bill DuBay/Vic Catan, DuBay's contribution credited to Will Richardson] 8p; (4) Ghita of Alizarr, part 9 [Frank Thorne] 16p; (5) The Starfire Saga, part 8 [Bill DuBay/Rudy Nebres, story credited to Will Richardson] 10p.

Notes: A $2.00 cover price for 72 pages. H. R. Giger, famed for his alien designs for the movie *Alien*, contributed a typically creepy cover. From this point on, *1994* had pretty much the same story-to-ad ratio as the other magazines in the Warren line. One John Hiatt (was the singer a comic fan?) sent in a letter.

19. cover: Jordi Penalva (June 1981)

(1) Young Sigmund Pavlov, Psychoanalytic Itinerant Extraordinaire! [Bill DuBay/Alex Nino, story credited to Will Richardson] 11p; (2) Fugue for a Ferrite Fugitive [Kevin Duane and Bill DuBay/Vic Catan, DuBay's contribution credited to Will Richardson] 9p; (3) The Holy Warrior! [John Ellis Sech and Bill DuBay/ Delando Nino, DuBay's contribution credited to Will Richardson] 8p; (4) Ghita of Alizarr, part 10 [Frank Thorne] 16p; (5) Et Tu Casey! [Kevin Duane/Abel Laxamana, poem] 7p; (6) Exterminator: Steele! [Budd Lewis and Bill DuBay/Alex Nino] 12p.

Notes: Penalva's cover was quite good. Nino's art was getting increasingly more bizarre. It was beautiful but often hard to read. The *Young Sigmund* stories were generally of a somewhat higher quality then the usual raunchy fare. "Et Tu Casey!" was a parody of the baseball poem "Casey at the Bat." The "Steele" story, printed sideways, told the tale of the first *Exterminator* and guest-starred Hunter. Different *Exterminator* stories had originally appeared in *Eerie*.

20. cover: Nestor Redondo (August 1981)

(1) Young Sigmund Pavlov! [Bill DuBay/Alex Nino, story credited to Will Richardson] 16p; (2) Diana Jacklighter, Manhuntress! [Jim Stenstrum/Esteban Maroto, story credited to Alabaster Redzone] 8p; (3) Little Beaver [Bill DuBay/Vic Catan, story credited to Will Richardson] 11p; (4) Ghita of Alizarr, part 11 [Frank Thorne] 8p; (5) Spearchucker Spade: Intergalactic Eye!, part 2 [Jim Stenstrum and Bill DuBay/Alex Nino, Stenstrum's contribution credited to Alabaster Redzone and DuBay's to Will Richardson] 18p.

Notes: Redondo's cover was a beauty and so was all the interior art. One wishes one could say the same about the stories. *Diana Jacklighter* is a pretty decent serial, if you mentally edited the juvenile style of profanity out as you read it.

21. cover: Alex Nino (October 1981)

(1) Lord Machina! [Bill DuBay?/Alex Nino] 12p; (2) Diana Jacklighter, Manhuntress!, part 2

[Jim Stenstrum/Esteban Maroto] 8p; (3) Love Is a Many Tentacled Thing [Bill DuBay?/Delando Nino] 8p; (4) Ghita of Alizarr, part 12 [Frank Thorne] 8p; (5) Angel! [Bill DuBay/Rudy Nebres] 15p; (6) Mars Bar: Tales of the Red Planet Saloon [Gerry Boudreau?/Redondo Studio] 6p; (7) Freefall! [Bill DuBay?/Alex Nino] 6p.

Notes: Credits were left off the stories themselves and never identified in later issues so the writers' credits here are largely a matter of guessing and logic (such as DuBay usually wrote Nino's stories in *1994*, etc.). The *Angel* series was not connected with the "Angel" story in #1. Jim Stenstrum was listed as co-editor along with DuBay for this issue only. This is his last credited work for Warren. Nowadays he works in animation, mostly on the *Scooby-Doo* cartoons.

22. cover: Steve Fastner and Rich Larson (December 1981)

(1) Young Sigmund Pavlov! [Bill DuBay/Alex Nino] 14p; (2) Love among the Ruins! [Bill DuBay and Timothy Moriarty/Delando Nino] 12p; (3) Ariel Hart: Bringing Up Baby! [Bill DuBay/Peter Hsu] 8p; (4) Angel, part 2 [Bill DuBay/Rudy Nebres] 10p; (5) Mike Marauder: Knight Errant of the Spaceways! [Rich Margopoulos/Rueben Yandoc] 8p.

Notes: Fastner and Larson were credited with the cover on the title page but on the cover itself an additional credit entitled Egge can be seen below Fastner and Larson's names. Larson and Fastner are best known today for their cheesecake pin-up books for SPQ Publications but Larson, at least, started out as a horror artist in the Steve Ditko vein for Charlton. He was good, too. This issue's *Sigmund Pavlov* pages created a long, dazzling and obscene single panel if laid end to end. Pun intended. In fact, this was probably the most explicit artwork that *1984* or *1994* ever produced. Open, shaved vulva, semi-erect penises and sex acts abound. Hsu's art looked a lot like the covers from a porn paperback series issued by Greenleaf Press in the early to mid–1970s. Perhaps he had a hand in working on them?

23. cover: Alex Nino (February 1982), credited to A2-120

(1) Break Even [Kevin Duane/Alex Nino, reprinted from *1984* #9 (October 1979)] 18p;

(2) Painter's Mountain [Bill DuBay and Budd Lewis/Alex Nino, reprinted from *1984* #8 (September 1979)] 16p; (3) Teleport: 2010 [Budd Lewis/Alex Nino, reprinted from *1984* #7 (August 1979)] 14p; (4) Zincor and the Fempire [Gerry Boudreau/Alex Nino, reprinted from *1984* #7 (August 1979)] 14p.

Notes: All-reprint Alex Nino special. It was $2.00 for 64 pages.

24. cover: Steve Fastner and Rich Larson (April 1982)

(1) The Ugliest Woman in Creation! [Bill DuBay/Vic Catan] 10p; (2) Diana Jacklighter, Manhuntress!, part 3 [Bruce Jones/Esteban Maroto] 8p; (3) The Star Queen [John Ellis Sech/Delando Nino] 12p; (4) Ghita of Alizarr, Book II [Frank Thorne] 12p; (5) Coming of Age! [Bill DuBay/Alex Nino] 10p.

Notes: Editor: Timothy Moriarty. Writer/artists credits were left off the stories so the credits for writers are, again, an educated guess.

25. cover: Lloyd Garrison (June 1982)

(1) The God of the Month Club [Kevin Duane/Alex Nino] 10p; (2) The God of the Month Club Poster [Alex Nino] ½ p; (3) Diana Jacklighter, Manhuntress!, part 4 [Bruce Jones/Esteban Maroto] 12p; (4) Ghita of Alizarr, Book II, part 2 [Frank Thorne] 13p; (5) Angel, part 3 [Bill DuBay, Rudy Nebres] 13p; (6) Small World, Isn't It? [Timothy Moriarty/Delando Nino] 8p.

Notes: Nino goes crazy! The pages of "The God of the Month Club" form a single giant panel that can expand infinitely in space and, one would think, in time.

26. cover: Richard Corben (August 1982)

(1) Young Sigmund, Sr. [Bill DuBay/Alex Nino] 10p; (2) Paper Your Walls with Psychedelic Schizophrenia! [Timothy Moriarty/Alex Nino, text article] 1p; (3) Diana Jacklighter, Manhuntress!, part 5 [Don Hallassey and Bruce Jones/Esteban Maroto] 12p; (4) Ghita of Alizarr, Book II, part 3 [Frank Thorne] 7p; (5) Little Beaver [Dan Hallassey/Vic Catan] 9p; (6) The Trials and Tribulations of Ariel Hart! [Bill DuBay/Peter Hsu] 7p; (7) Retard [John Ellis Sech/Alex Nino] 10p.

Notes: Corben's cover was done in 1977. Nino's art for "Young Sigmund, Sr." was another infinitely expanding panel. *Ghita of Alizarr* was cover-featured. "Ariel Hart" was almost straight porn.

27. cover: Terry Oates (October 1982)

(1) 94's Nebulous Newspage [Timothy Moriarty, text article] 1p; (2) The Big Dollhouse of Space! [John Ellis Sech/Delando Nino] 12p; (3) Diana Jacklighter, Manhuntress!, part 6 [Dan Hallassey and Bruce Jones/Esteban Maroto] 12p; (4) The Trials and Tribulations of Ariel Hart!, part 2 [Bill DuBay/Peter Hsu] 11p; (5) The Warhawks! [Bill DuBay/Abel Laxamana] 7p; (6) Annabel Lee! [Rich Margopoulos/Jose Matucenio, from the poem by Edgar Allan Poe] 8p; (7) Vehicle 2315 [Rich Margopoulos/Joe Vaultz] 3p.

Notes: While Rich Margopoulos' Poe adaptations are always a welcome sight, this one leaves something to be desired. "Diane Jacklighter" features the best story and art.

28. cover: Steve Fastner and Rich Larson (December 1982)

(1) Young Sigmund Pavlov! [Bill DuBay/Alex Nino] 11p; (2) Too Many Termarrows [Timothy Moriarty/Vic Catan] 9p; (3) Ghita of Alizarr, book II, part 4 [Frank Thorne] 8p; (4) Angel, part 4 [Bill DuBay/Rudy Nebres] 13p; (5) Diana Jacklighter, Manhuntress!, part 7 [Dan Hallassey and Bruce Jones/Esteban Maroto] 14p.

Notes: Both *Angel* and *Diana Jacklighter* concluded their runs this issue. If you excused the juvenile cursing and sniggering sex jokes that ran through almost all *1984/1994* stories, *Diana Jacklighter* was a decent enough serial.

29. cover: John Berkey (February 1983)

(1) Grandmother Running Box [Bill DuBay/Vic Catan] 11p; (2) The Noxious Newspage [Timothy Moriarty, text article] 1p; (3) Goddess [Timothy Moriarty/Peter Hsu] 13p; (4) Ghita of Alizarr, book II, part 5 [Frank Thorne] 10p; (5) Farmed Out [John Ellis Sech/Delando Nino] 14p; (6) The Warhawks, part 2 [Bill DuBay/Abel Laxamana] 8p.

Notes: Final issue. It was $2.25 for 64 pages. John Berkey was a major SF cover artist of the 1960s and 1970s. "Grandmother Running Box" was a supporting character from the *Little Beaver* strip and Little Beaver has a cameo in this start for a never-completed serial. Vic Catan's art was

absolutely gorgeous for both of these strips and it's a shame the stories were so dreadful. In fact, considering all the stories presented here, this is a pretty crappy issue to go out on.

Odds and Ends

THE MONSTER WORLD COMICS

(1) The Mummy [Russ Jones/Dan Adkins and Wally Wood, from *Monster World* #1 (November 1964)] 6p; (2) The Mummy's Hand [Russ Jones/Joe Orlando, from *Monster World* #2 (January 1965)] 7p; (3) Curse of Frankenstein [Russ Jones/Joe Orlando and Angelo Torres, from *Monster World* #3 (April 1965)] 7p.

Notes: These were adaptations of Universal monster films from the 1930s and are actually Warren's first horror comics. The first two adaptations actually predated the first appearance of *Creepy*. Both of these were reprinted in either *Creepy* or *Eerie* in 1967. The third story was reprinted in *Famous Monsters of Filmland* but never appeared in the main horror titles.

The Odd Comic World of Richard Corben

1. cover: Richard Corben (1977)

(1) Introduction [Will Eisner/Richard Corben, text article, Corben's art from interior panels] 4p; (2) Horrilor's Introduction [Richard Corben, reprinted from *Grim Wit* #2 (September 1973)] 1p; (3) The Dweller in the Dark [Herb Arnold/Richard Corben, reprinted from *Hot Stuf'* #3 (Winter 1976)] 11p; (4) Horrilor's Introduction [Richard Corben, reprinted from *Grim Wit* #1 (1972)] 1p; (5) Razar the Unhero [Starr Armitage/Richard Corben, reprinted from *Fantagor* #1 (1970)] 8p; (6) Mangle, Robot Mangler [Richard Corben, reprinted from *Slow Death* #4 (November 1972)] 6p; (7) How Howie Made It in the Real World [Richard Corben, reprinted from *Slow Death* #2 (December 1970)] 8p; (8) For the Love of a Daemon [Richard Corben, color, reprinted from *Fantagor* #4 (1972)] 7p; (9) Damsel in Dragon Dress [Doug Moench/Richard Corben, color, reprinted from *Grim Wit* #2 (September 1973)] 6p; (10) C-Dopey [Richard Corben, color, reprinted from *Up from the Deep* #1 (May 1971)] 8p; (11) Space Jacked [Richard Corben, color, reprinted from *Fantagor* #4 (1972)] 10p; (12) Going Home [Richard Corben, color, reprinted from *Up from the Deep* #1 (May 1971)] 8p.

Notes: Publisher: James Warren. Editor: Josep Toutain? The cover and title page listed the book as a Warren Adult Fantasy Publication. It was printed in Spain and sold in the U.S. via mail order from the Captain Company pages in the back of the Warren magazines. This trade paperback collected a number of Corben's underground stories, none of which had previously appeared in a Warren magazine.

The Best of Blazing Combat

1. cover: Frank Frazetta (1978) reprinted from *Blazing Combat* #4 (July 1966)

(1) Introduction [James Warren, text article] 1p; (2) Give and Take [Archie Goodwin/Russ Heath, reprinted from *Blazing Combat* #4 (July 1966)] 6p; (3) U-Boat [Archie Goodwin/Gene Colan, reprinted from *Blazing Combat* #3 (April 1966)] 7p; (4) Landscape! [Archie Goodwin/Joe Orlando, reprinted from *Blazing Combat* #2 (January 1966)] 7p; (5) Foragers [Archie Goodwin/Reed Crandall, reprinted from *Blazing Combat* #3 (April 1966)] 6p; (6) The Edge! [Archie Goodwin/Alex Toth, reprinted from *Blazing Combat* #4 (July 1966)] 6p; (7) Holding Action [Archie Goodwin/John Severin, reprinted from *Blazing Combat* #2 (January 1966)] 7p; (8) Water Hole! [Archie Goodwin/Gray Morrow, reprinted from *Blazing Combat* #3 (April 1966)] 5p; (9) Conflict! [Archie Goodwin/Gene Colan, reprinted from *Blazing Combat* #4 (July 1966)] 7p; (10) Special Forces! [Archie Goodwin/Jerry Grandenetti and Joe Orlando, art credited solely to Joe Orlando, reprinted from *Blazing Combat* #3 (April 1966)] 7p; (11) Saratoga [Archie Goodwin/Reed Crandall, reprinted from *Blazing Combat* #2 (January 1966)] 6p; (12) The Trench! [Archie Goodwin/John Severin, reprinted from *Blazing Combat* #4 (July 1966)] 6p; (13) Viet Cong [Archie Goodwin/Joe Orlando, reprinted from *Blazing Combat* #1 (October 1965)] 7p; (14) The Battle of Britain! [Wally Wood/Dan Adkins and Wally Wood, art credited solely to Wood, reprinted from *Blazing Combat* #3 (April 1966)] 7p; (15) Flying Tigers! [Archie Goodwin/George Evans, reprinted from *Blazing Combat* #1 (October 1965)] 6p; (16) Long View! [Archie Goodwin/Gray Morrow, reprinted from *Blazing Combat* #1 (October 1965)] 6p; (17) MIG Alley [Archie Goodwin/Al McWilliams, reprinted from *Blazing Combat* #2 (January 1966)] 6p; (18) Enemy! [Archie Goodwin/John Severin, reprinted from *Blazing Combat* #1 (October 1965)] 7p; (19) Cover Gallery [Frank Frazetta,

color, reprinted from *Blazing Combat* #1–4 (October 1965–July 1966)] 4p.

Notes: Editor: Louise Jones. Not a magazine, but an actual early trade paperback. This book is fairly rare, possibly due to the binding which was the sort that split, cracked and fell apart almost upon opening. Excellent collection of stories, though, if you can find it.

Unpublished Magazines

Comix International was originally to be Warren's entry into underground comix. Keith Green was to be the editor but as far as I know nothing was produced for it. The title was later used for the color section reprint magazine.

POW!, from 1971, was to be Warren's initial entry into a more adult-oriented (read — lots of nudity) magazine. Edited by Nicola Cuti, a cover by Frazetta ("Queen Kong," printed as the cover to *Eerie* #81 in 1978) and one story were actually completed. That story, "Incident at Laurenhurst," was published as "I Wonder Who's Squeezing Her Now?" in *1984* #5 in 1979. Another story, "Mother Earth" — two pages of which appear in *The Warren Companion* — was started but not completed by Archie Goodwin and Jeff Jones.

Yesterday ... Today, Tomorrow, from 1976, was developed by Josef Toutain as a magazine that would put as much emphasis on science fiction as horror. Two presentation pieces and two covers were done for the magazine as well as a full slate of stories for the first issue. One of the presentation pieces, by Vicente Segrelles, appeared as the cover to *Creepy* #124, with the original vision of a destroyed Eiffel Tower in the background replaced by a New York City skyline. Three of the stories: "Macchu Picchu," "U.F.O." and "Exorcism" (as "The Terrible Exorcism of Adriennes Pompereau") appeared, heavily rewritten, in *Vampirella* in 1977. Three more stories were listed — "The Sprinx" (credited to S.I. artists), "Too Many..." (credited to Josep Toutin and Jose Gonzalez) and "The Awakening" (uncredited, but possibly a Richard Corben story) — but did not appear in a Warren magazine, at least not under those titles. Whether they appeared elsewhere is unknown. The two covers

I've seen are both science fiction in nature — the first is by Manuel Sanjulian and depicts a rather awkward-looking man and a naked woman in a devastated New York, confronting a giant rat coming up the steps of the 8th Avenue subway entrance. The second cover (also possibly by Sanjulian) shows an astronaut on one of Saturn's moons with giant Easter Island heads around him. With an awkward title and run-of-the-mill stories, it's probably a good thing this magazine never saw the light of day.

Published Magazines Not Included

Warren published three titles that were not horror and so are excluded from full coverage here. The first is *The Spirit*, published for 16 issues between April 1974 and October 1976. One of Warren's best efforts revived Will Eisner's 1940s–1950s character the Spirit and presented his stories for a new generation (including myself). My first issue discovered and purchased was #5 and I loved the stories and art so much that it prompted me to order the earlier issues from the back issues ad in the back of the magazine. This was the first (although far from the last) time I did that. Outside of the covers almost all of the stories are reprints from 1945–1950 but

they are great stories and worth the time to locate simply for the beautiful B&W reproduction. B&W, in my opinion, is the best way to read and view these stories. A great series that was continued from #17 to #41 by Kitchen Sink Press after Warren had to reluctantly cancel the magazine. There was also a color reprint magazine — *The Spirit Special*— that came out in the summer of 1975 and copied the style of the *Comix International* color titles.

The second title was *The Rook*, which ran for 14 issues from October 1979 to April 1982. The Rook was, naturally enough, the lead character and the stories were of generally higher quality than his appearances in the previous year or so in *Eerie*. In addition to the Rook, impressive work appeared from Alfredo Alcala (Voltar), Alex Toth (Bravo for Adventure), Lee Elias (Kronos), Jim Stenstrum (Joe Guy), Don McGregor (Dagger) and John Severin (Eagle). There are some very good stories here.

The third and least was *The Goblin*, which ran for three issues (and advertised a never-published fourth) from June to November 1982. Not much here to get excited about although the Goblin had some decent artwork and fair to middling stories. The back-up stories were none too good.

The Complete Skywald Checklist

The origin of Skywald Publications is shrouded, to some degree, in mystery. Israel Waldman was the publisher, with business affairs handled by his son Herschal. Waldman had prior experience as a comic book publisher. In 1958 he started IW Publications (later renamed Super Comics). IW was a reprint only company (except for new covers), which collected its stories from the companies that had collapsed or gone out of the comics business since the advent of the Comics Code in 1955. Waldman purchased either the original artwork or the printing plates that the defunct companies had left behind them, printed the stories with new covers and titles, then repackaged them in the then–innovative "three comics for a quarter" plastic bags. Waldman probably never obtained the necessary copyrights for these reprintings, which included former Quality Comics titles such as *Plastic Man* or *Doll Man* that DC had acquired rights to as well as several issues of creator Will Eisher's *The Spirit*. It appears that he was rarely, if ever, challenged by the actual copyright holders. Perhaps this was because his titles never appeared on the newsstands or spinner racks, but instead, because of their bagged nature, they only appeared in either the toy or novelty sections of discount stores.

IW/Super Comics closed up shop in 1964. Skywald was begun in 1970, with Waldman as publisher and former Atlas/Marvel production head and all-around Renaissance man Sol Brodsky as the editor. The initial issues of both *Nightmare* and *Psycho* featured a few new stories but the majority of those issues were heavily reworked reprints, many from the old Avon comics line. They also started up a twenty-five-cent series of color titles, mostly Westerns, although there were also a romance title and a single issue of *The Heap*. The lead story in these color comics was usually only 14–16 pages long and the remainer of the title featured 1950s-era reprints. Some of the reprints, particularly those featuring Jack Kirby's Bullseye character, were actually better than the rather boring title characters. The color line lasted less than a year, and its failure nearly caused the collapse of the B&W titles as well. There were six-month gaps between B&W issues in late 1971 and mid–1972.

When the reprints were eased out for the B&W titles and the books went all original, the Brodsky-edited books acted almost as an alternate issue of the Warren books. The stories were of a similar nature. The artists were often the same artists, although they occasionally used pen names so Jim Warren wouldn't get upset. And those artists who weren't Warren veterans had long histories at either Marvel or DC. The cover artists were ones that Warren readers would have seen before. If they weren't quite up to the quality of Warren's best, the early Skywald stories weren't that far below them either. Jim Warren noticed this and issued a mocking ad in the trade papers, awarding Skywald the fictious "Xerox" Award for so thoroughly copying the Warren style.

However, after the collapse of the color line and with nearly two years of Skywald publishing under his belt, Brodsky went back to Marvel in mid–1972, this time as the vice president of operations, a newly created title that allowed Brodsky back in the larger company at a similar position and salary to his old job, which had been ably filled by John Verpooten.

As his replacement, Brodsky recommended Al Hewetson, a Canadian writer who'd worked as Stan Lee's assistant in the late 1960s and early 1970s (and where he and Brodsky met), then had written a number of stories for Jim Warren and Warren Publishing before getting a job as Brodsky's assistant editor at Skywald.

Hewetson immediately went about putting his stamp on the Skywald magazines, creating an editorial and story stance that he called the Horror-Mood. What exactly the Horror-Mood was, even Hewetson couldn't really explain, even years later, but the end result of the advent of the Horror-Mood were B&W magazines that oozed mood, even more than story integrity. In 1972 Warren had moved past the traditional monsters that they'd focused on during their early years, and its then current stories were beginning to focus strongly on serial killers, urban blight, grim science fiction and continuing characters who weren't likely to have a happy ending. Still, each Warren story or serial was expected to stand on its own.

Skywald, under Hewetson, featured stories that were expected to build and expand on those stories that had previously appeared, even though the stories were often, or even usually, unrelated to each other. In addition, Hewetson—who wrote 80 percent of the stories from 1972 to 1975—leaned his own stories upon the works and worldviews of horror masters Edgar Allan

Poe and H. P. Lovecraft. There were numerous Poe stories adapted for Skywald and, if Hewetson had been able to afford the literary rights, Lovecraft would have had many of his stories adapted as well.

In that regard, Hewetson treated each separate issue of a Skywald magazine, regardless of the title, as another issue of a single entity. Skywald's horror titles, particularly under Hewetson's reign, should best be read in order of publication of *all* the titles, not in the more standard way of issue by issue of a particular title. This is further necessitated by the way that serials flitted from title to title. If you want to read those serialized tales in order, you must put the Skywald magazines in publishing order, not title order. Following the various magazines checklists, there is a preferred reading guide provided.

Hewetson also applied some of the editorial lessons he'd learned at Marvel, giving himself and his two main fellow writers—Ed Fedory and Augustine Funnell—company nicknames that resembled horror host names. Hewetson's was Archaic Al.

Thus, the Skywald stories often resembled fever dreams that drifted above, below and around horror motifs rather than traditional horror stories. If a story's character wasn't particularly well-defined, if his motivations appeared to be slightly crazed, be assured that the circumstances that surrounded him and his story were both crazed *and* well-defined. Under Hewetson, there was no difficulty telling a Warren and Skywald story apart.

This aspect of the horror-mood even

Left: Sol Brodsky, the "Sky" in Skywald, was a Renaissance man, accomplished as an artist, publisher, production head, promoter and editor. *Right:* Al Hewetson was the second editor of the Skywald magazines. He created a unified and unique approach to Skywald horror and wrote most of the stories himself, using dozens of pseudonyms to disguise the fact.

appeared in the letters pages, which didn't resemble any other company's letters page, as the Skywald version not only featured reader comments but mixed Hewetson's editorial comments and Skywald news into a textual stew.

In addition, under Hewetson's reign, there was no apparent connection between Skywald artists and Warren artists. Although both used mainly Spanish artists from the S.I. Studio, with rare exceptions (Jesus Suso Rego, Zesar Lopez, Ramon Torrents) most of the artists appeared exclusively at one company or the other. It was possible to see a Skywald artist at Marvel (Pablo Marcos) or DC (Ricardo Villamonte) but not all that many.

As competitors and rivals, both Skywald and Warren shared the marketplace and the newsstands without really doing damage to each other. In fact, a strong argument could be made that their rivalry was *good* for both companies. Skywald's demise, according to an interview Hewetson and I did in December 2003, came about because of Marvel's full-fledged 1973 move into the B&W market. Both Warren and Skywald were hammered by the flood of Marvel magazines, many of whom used Warren and Skywald artists who'd never appeared in a Marvel comic up to that point. The Marvel magazines also featured fan favorites doing the art, even if those art pages were often less than half the number of pages that either a Warren or Skywald magazine had traditionally featured. Unlike Warren (however Warren may have wished otherwise) or Skywald, Marvel wasn't out to share the marketplace but dominate it. Its powerful distributor eventually forced Skywald's B&W magazines off the newsstands. According to Hewetson, it wasn't that people were bored with the Skywald magazines, it was that they couldn't find them for sale. By 1975, Marvel's onslaught had crushed Skywald and damaged Warren to such an extent that the latter never fully recovered.

Marvel had also flooded the horror market to such an extent, both in their B&W and color lines, that the once robust horror revival that had begun in 1964 largely collapsed by the end of 1975. Only Warren and, in the color comics field, DC continued to focus a large number of magazines in the horror genre.

As with Warren, a number of Skywald B&W titles were not horror titles. Two of them were released in 1971— the first, *The Crime Machine*, lasted for two issues. It was a reprint-only title featuring pre-code crime stories largely gathered from the St. John or Avon publishing companies. *Hell-Rider*, on the other hand, featured new stories and art revolving around the title character, a black-leather-clad and masked motorcycle rider who solved crimes in some of the wide open sections of the United States. Written by Gary Friedrich, *Hell-Rider* appeared to be a non-supernatural prototype version of his more famous *Ghost Rider*, which he set up at Marvel the following year. Secondary characters in the *Hell-Rider* title were the costumed superhero the Butterfly and the benign motorcycle gang, the Wild Bunch. Like *The Crime Machine*, *Hell-Rider* only lasted two issues, although a third issue was advertised. One issue of a science fiction title —*Science Fiction Odyssey*— was completed but never printed or released. Waldman blocked the title just before it was to be sent to the printers, citing the then common belief that science fiction (SF) titles didn't sell. It may also have been a victim of Skywald's color comic failure. After waiting a full year for a publishing change of heart, Hewetson split the SF stories between the three horror titles where they saw publication (often under more horrorific titles than they had originally had).

This Skywald index/commentary is as complete as possible given Skywald's custom of often dropping credits off stories, hiding credits in the art of the story (mostly under Hewetson's reign — where they appeared in windowsills, gables, panel borders, as debris, etc.), the heavy use of pseudonyms, the Spanish habit of using single names instead of full names and the frequent miscrediting of stories to the wrong artist. Even in 2003, Hewetson often confused the credits of the Spanish artists Cesar Lopez's and Zesar Lopez's work, although, as Hewetson well knew, their artwork looked nothing alike.

Many of the mysteries regarding credits have been solved thanks to access to Al Hewetson's notes and checklists as well as the aid of Christos N. Gage, David Kerekes and Stephen Sennitt. An earlier, less complete version of this index, done by me, appeared in the appendix of *The Illustrated History of the Skywald Horror-Mood*. Elements of that version that appear in this updated version are used with permission.

Nightmare

1. cover: Brendan Lynch (December 1970)

(1) The Pollution Monsters [Mike Friedrich/ Don Heck and Mike Esposito] 10p; (2) Master of the Dead! [?/Norman Nodell and Vince Alascia, reprinted from *Eerie* #14, Avon (February 1954)] 6p; (3) Dance Macabre [?/? and Bill Everett?, reprinted from the 1950s] 6p; (4) Orgy of Blood [Ross Andru and Mike Esposito/Ross Andru and Mike Esposito] 8p; (5) A Nightmare Pin-Up [Bill Everett] 1p; (6) The Skeletons of Doom! [Art Stampler/Bill Everett, text story] 3p; (7) Help Us to Die! [?/?, reprinted from the 1950s] 6p; (8) The Thing from the Sea! [?/Wally Wood and Mike Esposito?, reprinted from *Eerie* #2, Avon (September 1951)] 7p; (9) The Creature Within! [?/?, reprinted from the 1950s] 3p; (10) The Deadly Mark of the Beast! [Len Wein/ Syd Shores and Tom Palmer] 8p; (11) Nightmares's Nightmail [letters page] 1p.

Notes: Publisher: Sol Brodsky and Israel Waldman. Editor: Sol Brodsky with Herschel Waldman listed as associate editor. It cost $0.50 for 64 pages. Much of the first two issues featured 1950s-era reprints. The artwork on these reprints is heavily retouched. There are no direct credits for individual stories but authors listed on the title page include Wayne Benedict, Marv Wolfman, Mike Friedrich, Noel Haven, Ross Andru and Mike Esposito while artists listed include Don Heck, Mike Esposito, Syd Shores, David Hadley, Bill Everett, Tom Palmer and Dick Richards. Some of these, most likely Benedict, Haven, Hadley and Richards, are almost certainly house names. While there are only three new stories and a new text story in this issue, some of the 1950s-era art appears to have been re-inked by Bill Everett, especially noticeable in the story "Dance Macabre," which also may have 1950s-era pencils or modern 1970s inks by Syd Shores. Best new story here is Len Wein's "The Deadly Mark of the Beast!" while Bill Everett's pin-up has the best art. Wally Wood's "The Thing from the Sea!" has been so heavily reworked, probably by Mike Esposito, so that

the art looks nothing like Wood whatsoever! The presence of a letters page is also suspect, since it featured letters written before the first issue appeared! Al Hewetson's personal checklist listed Mike Esposito as the cover artist but it is clearly Brendan Lynch's work.

2. cover: Boris Vallejo (February 1971)

(1) Children of the Cold Gods! [Ross Andru and Mike Esposito/Ross Andru and Mike Esposito] 10p; (2) The Phantom of Philip Hawks [?/A. C. Hollingsworth, reprinted from *Diary of Horror* #1 (December 1952)] 6p; (3) The Mirror of Death [?/?, reprinted from *Diary of Horror* #1 (December 1952)] 6p; (4) The Circle of Circe! [Gardner Fox/Syd Shores and Mike Esposito] 8p; (5) Nightmare Pin-Up #2 [Bill Everett] 1p; (6) Time Stop [Art Stampler, text story] 3p; (7) Blood for the Vampire [?/Norman Nodel and Vince Alascia, reprinted from *Eerie* #7, Avon (July 1952)] 8p; (8) The Massacre of Mankind! [?/?, reprinted from the 1950s] 8p; (9) Pressed for Time [Marv Wolfman/Dan Adkins] 8p.

Notes: Again there are no individual story credits but the authors' list includes Wayne Benedict, Marv Wolfman, Mike Friedrich, Noel Haven, Ross Andru and Mike Esposito, Gardner Fox and Phil Seuling. There are no artists' credits. Again, there are three new stories and a new pin-up. Best art and story go to the intriguing little witchcraft tale "Pressed for Time." "Children of the Cold Gods!" is a *very* odd and grotesque story. Gardner Fox also wrote another story dealing with Circe for Warren's *Vampirella* around this same time period. A letter to readers promises all new stories beginning in the next issue.

3. cover: Boris Vallejo (April 1971)

(1) The Inner Man [Tom Sutton/Tom Sutton and Dan Adkins, Sutton's story is credited to Sinclair Rich, while his art is credited to Sean Todd] 10p; (2) The Victims [Gerry Conway/ Rich Buckler] 6p; (3) Vault of a Vampire [Al Hewetson/Serg Moren] 8p; (4) When the Dawn Gods War! [Gardner Fox/Paul Reinman and Mike Esposito] 8p; (5) A Rottin' Deal [Bruce Jones, story and art credited to Philip Roland] 9p; (6) Horror Man [Art Stampler, text story] 2p; (7) Nightmare Pin-Up #2 [Chic Stone] 1p; (8) Soul of the Warlock [Chic Stone] 8p; (9) Beware Small Evils! [Jack Katz and Frank Giacoia/Jack Katz and Frank Giacoia, story credited to Frank Voltaire] 10p; (10) ad for

Psycho #2 and The Crime Machine #1 [on the inside back cover].

Notes: All new stories begin. Many of the Warren artists appearing here, mindful of Jim Warren's 1969 edict that they couldn't work for Warren and his B&W competitors at the same time, used pseudonyms to hide their identities. That might have worked for writers but for artists such as Sutton or Ernie Colon's, their art styles were so distinctive that it's hard to see how Warren could have not known it was them. This was a fairly decent issue with the best story and

art going to Bruce Jones (hiding behind the name Philip Roland) for his delightfully disturbed "A Rottin' Deal" while good work also appeared from Tom Sutton, Al Hewetson, Serg Moren, Jack Katz and Frank Giacoia and Chic Stone. The pin-up by Chic Stone is listed as "Nightmare Pin-Up" #2 but it is actually #3 and one of the corpses bursting out of their graves in that pin-up is clearly Warren's Uncle Creepy! "Vault of a Vampire" is future editor Al Hewetson's first story for Skywald.

4. cover: Harry Rosenbaum (June 1971), cover is miscredited to Boris Vallejo

(1) Phantom of the Rock Era [Chuck McNaughton/Ralph Reese] 8p; (2) Shoot-Out at Satan's Coffin [Mike Jennings/Jack Abel] 10p; (3) The Mad Mind Doctor! [Chuck McNaughton/Dick Ayers and Mike Esposito] 6p; (4) A Nightmare Pin-Up [Bill Everett] 1p; (5) Hag of the Blood Basket! [Al Hewetson/Tom Sutton, Sutton's art credited to Sean Todd] 16p; (6) A Living Death! [Gary Friedrich/Tom Palmer] 10p; (7) The Horror on the Chapel Wall [Gardner Fox/Serg Moren] 9p.

Notes: It was $0.60 for 64 pages with the issues now squarebound. Ads for the never-published *Science Fiction Odyssey* #1 appear. The delirious "Hag of the Blood Basket," a clear forerunner of the Skywald Horror-Mood, featured the best story and art. The lead character in that story greatly resembled EC's Old Witch! There's also good work from Chuck McNaughton, Ralph Reese, Bill Everett and Tom Palmer. The actual letters page begins. This is a pretty good issue hidden behind a relatively unimpressive cover.

This Chic Stone–illustrated pin-up page from *Nightmare* #3 features Warren's Uncle *Creepy* (the bald fellow in the lower right corner) as one of the zombies bursting from the grave.

5. cover: Boris Vallejo (August 1971)

(1) The Man Who Became ... Frankenstein! [Allan Asherman/Harold Shull, frontis] 1p; **(2)** Slime World [Chuck McNaughton/Ralph Reese] 10p; **(3)** Whence Stalks the Werewolf [Len Brown/Carlos Garzon] 6p; **(4)** Nightmare's Nightmail [letter's page; short bio and photo of Boris Vallejo appears] 2p; **(5)** The Doom Star! [Chuck McNaughton/Tom Sutton, Dan Adkins and Ralph Reese, Sutton's pencils credited to Sean Todd] 10p; **(6)** Great Men of the Horror Films: Boris Karloff [Allan Asherman, text article with photos] 4p; **(7)** Creature of the Deep [Chuck McNaughton/Jack Katz and Jack Abel] 12p; **(8)** Nazi Death Rattle [Al Hewetson/Serg Moren] 9p; **(9)** Within the Torture Chamber [Kevin Pagan/Doug Wildey] 8p; **(10)** back cover ads for Hell-Rider #1; The Crime Machine #2 and the never-published Science Fiction Odyssey #1] 1p.

Notes: More ads appear for the aborted *Science Fiction Odyssey*. Best story and art go to the excellent Parisian sewer tale, "Slime World," by Chuck McNaughton and Ralph Reese. Other good work was done by Tom Sutton, Al Hewetson, Kevin Pagan, Doug Wildey and Serg Moren. The Pagan/Wildey story "Within the Torture Chamber" is a bondage/torture tale of exactly the sort that the Comics Code was established to suppress.

6. cover: Jeff Jones (December 1971)

(1) Medea [Michael Kaluta, frontis] 1p; **(2)** Nightmare's Nightmail [letter's page; features an interview with Jeff Jones] 2p; **(3)** Love Witch and the Battle of the Living Dead [Marv Wolfman/Ernie Colon and Jack Abel] 15p; **(4)** The Living Gargoyle [Jerry Siegal/Carlos Garzon] 6p; **(5)** Broken Sparrow [Larry Todd] 6p; **(6)** Great Men of the Horror Films: Boris Karloff, part 2 [Allan Asherman, text article with photos] 4p; **(7)** Corpse by Computer! [Robert Kanigher/Doug Wildey] 11p; **(8)** The Cosmos Strain [Michael Kaluta, story credited to Steve Stern] 6p; **(9)** The Geek! [Pat Boyette] 6p.

Notes: "The Love Witch" is continued from *Psycho* #3 and has several pages of its story printed out of sequence. "The Living Gargoyle," written by Superman creator Jerry Siegal, has nothing to do with the later *Human Gargoyles'* series, although the gargoyles are identical. Steve Stern was a fan writer of the time but in subsequent reprinting "The Cosmos Strain" is credited to

Michael Kaluta for both story and art. The Stern credit appears only twice for Skywald, both times for artists — Kaluta and Jeff Jones — known for their close relationship in both fanzines and professional magazines. It's my belief that Steve Stern as used here is a house name. Best art and story belong to Pat Boyette's "The Geek!" with other good stories appearing from Kaluta and Larry Todd. Jeff Rovin interviews cover artist Jeff Jones on the letters page.

7. cover: Pujolar (June 1972)

(1) The Haunted Strangler [Al Hewetson/Pablo Marcos, frontis] 1p; **(2)** The Penitent [Ed Fedory/Ferran Sostres] 7p; **(3)** Group Jeopardy [S. F. Starr/Amador Garcia] 6p; **(4)** The Giant Death Rat [Al Hewetson/Serg Moren, story credited to Howie Anderson] 7p; **(5)** Gasp! [Donald Brown] 3p; **(6)** FANtasia [Jeff Rovin, text article] 1p; **(7)** Dracula [Allan Asherman, text article with photos] 6p; **(8)** The Altar of Blood [Bob Kirschen/Pablo Marcos] 7p; **(9)** A Father's Lament [Ed Fedory/Francisco Cueto] 9p; **(10)** Artifacts [Dennis Fujitake] 4p; **(11)** The Essential Horror [Al Hewetson/Ramon Torrents] 8p; **(12)** Mummy Pin-Up [Pablo Marcos, on the back cover] 1p.

Notes: After a publishing hiatus of several months, brought on by the collapse of Skywald's color comic line, the magazines returned with some changes. Herschel Waldman was now listed as business manager. The issue number appears for the first time on the cover. A reader's contest is announced with the prize being the original art to Bill Everett's pin-up from #1. Best story is Al Hewetson's "The Giant Death Rat" while the best art belongs to Ferran Sostres' "The Penitent." A contract with the Spanish art agency S.I. to provide artwork begins to push the more expensive American artists out of the Skywald pages. S. F. Starr is probably a pseudonym for an unknown writer.

8. cover: Vicente Segrelles (August 1972)

(1) Andras: The Grand Marquis of Hell! [Al Hewetson/Pablo Marcos, frontis] 1p; **(2)** Snow-Bound! [Ed Fedory/Felipe Dela Rosa] 8p; **(3)** Hey Creep: Play the Macabre Waltz [Al Hewetson/Ferran Sostres] 6p; **(4)** Rot, Robin, Rot! [Al Hewetson/Dan Sevilla, story credited to Jay Wood] 3p; **(5)** The Tunnels of Horror [Al Hewetson/Pablo Marcos] 8p; **(6)** Satan's Grave-

This snappy Tom Sutton artwork from *Nightmare* #4 appears to feature EC Comics' Old Witch as the protagonist.

yard [Al Hewetson/Syd Shores and Dan Adkins, Shores' pencils credited to Jim Elder] 7p; (7) Nightmare Movie Review: Tales from the Crypt [Al Hewetson, text article with photos] 4p; (8) Hung Up [Bruce Jones] 10p; (9) The Sting of Death [Chic Stone] 8p; (10) The Weird and the Undead [Al Hewetson/Ferran Sostres, story credited to Howie Anderson] 7p; (11) Phantom of the Opera Pin-Up [Pablo Marcos, on the back cover] 1p.

Notes: Al Hewetson is now listed as asso-

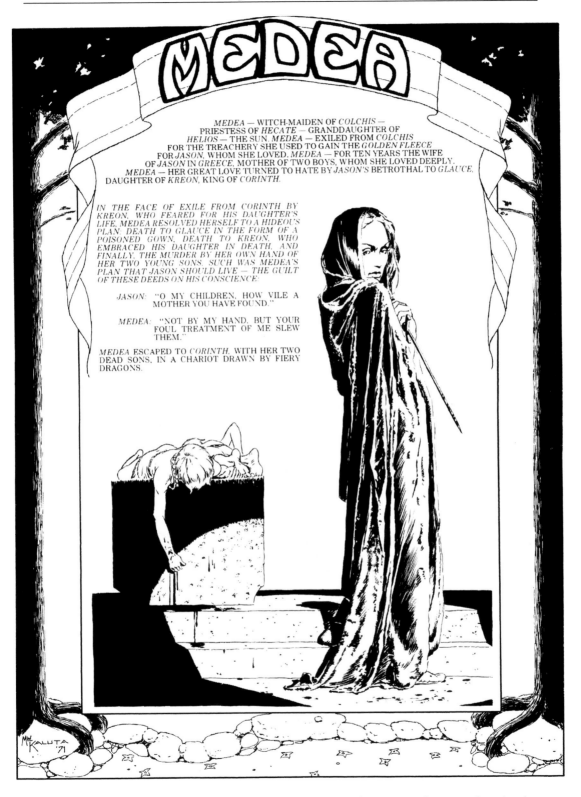

Frontispiece artwork by Michael Kaluta depicting the Greek character Medea, just after she slays her children. From *Nightmare* #6.

ciate editor. Best art is provided by Bruce Jones on "Hung Up" although Felipe Dela Rosa and Pablo Marcos also deliver high quality work. Best story is Hewetson's "The Tunnels of Horror," which, like a number of early Skywald stories, takes place in the sewers of Paris. Julie (Mrs. Al) Hewetson sends in a letter complaining about Al biting her neck at night! *The Tales from the Crypt* movie review reprints two EC comic panels. The photos used as background art in the story "Satan's Graveyard" were taken by Al Hewetson. This story also caused a falling out between friends Hewetson and Shores when Shores became angered over what he regarded as a vindictive inking job on his pencil work by Ad-

kins, who was apparently angry over Skywald's low pay rates. Shores demanded a house name (Jim Elder) be used instead of his and announced that he'd never work for Skywald again. Hewetson spent two years rebuilding bridges with Shores until in early/mid–1973, Shores agreed to do another Skywald tale. Unfortunately, Shores died before actually beginning the artwork.

9. cover: Jose Mirelles (October 1972)

(1) Mr. Pook's Introduction [Al Hewetson/ Pablo Marcos, frontis and title page] 2p; **(2)** Markheim [Al Hewetson/Jesus Duran, from the story by Robert Louis Stevenson, art credited to D. Duran] 7p; **(3)** The Nightmare World of James Edgar: Call Them Ghouls, Call Them Trolls, Call Them Things [Al Hewetson/Pablo Marcos, from a dream by James Edgar] 3p; **(4)** The Guillotine [Al Hewetson/ Felipe Dela Rosa] 1p; **(5)** Zoo for the Beasts of the Universe [Al Hewetson/Maelo Cintron] 2p; **(6)** Lunatic Letters page/Editorial [Al Hewetson, text article] 2p; **(7)** The Shoggoths: The Skull Forest of Old Earth [Al Hewetson/ Zesar Lopez] 7p; **(8)** The Abominable Dr. Phibes [Al Hewetson, text article with photos] 4p; **(9)** The 300th Birth Day Party [Al Hewetson/Ramon Torrents] 5p; **(10)** The Gargoyle Trilogy [Al Hewetson/Felipe Dela Rosa] 11p; **(11)** The Night in the Wax Museum [Al Hewetson/Xavier Villanova] 8p; **(12)** Dracula [Al Hewetson/ Pablo Marcos] 1p; **(13)** The Beast Within [Al Hewetson/ Amador Garcia] 9p; **(14)** Next issue ad [Al Hewetson/ Pablo Marcos] 1p; **(15)** The Thing in the Alley [Al Hewetson/Berni Wrightson, text story, on the back cover] 1p.

THE ULTIMATE IN SPINE-TINGLING TERROR!

NIGHTMARE

NO 8 AUGUST 1972 60¢

A SKYWALD PUBLICATION

TUNNELS OF HORROR!

INCREDIBLE MIND-BENDING FANTASIES OF FEAR!

Many of the early Skywald stories take place in the vast Parisian sewer systems. "Tunnels of Horror" from *Nightmare* #8 was one of the best.

Notes: Al Hewetson was now the full editor and it immediately shows in the many series debuts amid full-blown horror-mood themes. Mirelles' cover is a striking image. Hewetson introduces a short-lived horror host for *Nightmare*, who was later named Mr. Pook. Hewetson later described this introduction of a kid host as "disastrous." The contents page features the first mention of the term "horror-mood" in this title. Maelo Cintron, one of the mainstays of the latter-day Skyward artists, makes his professional debut. *Nightmare World* began a semi-regular series in which readers sent in their nightmares, which were then adapted into stories. Although the gargoyles in the story "The Gargoyle Trilogy" are drawn identically to those of the *Human Gargoyle* series, this story was not a part of that series. The *Human Gargoyle*s, whose first chapter was also drawn by Dela Rosa, did, however, appear in *Psycho* #8 at almost the same time as this story. The *Shoggoth*s series begins, with Hewetson using H. P. Lovecraft's Shoggoths as villains. The stories themselves are new tales, not adaptations of Lovecraft originals. Hewetson's Shoggoths also didn't physically resemble Lovecraft's descriptions. Spanish artist Xavier Villanova's name was variously spelled with one or two Ls throughout his Skywald run. Since his work for Seaboard/Atlas Publishing was spelled with two Ls, I've followed that custom. This was also the first appearance for the Darkos Mansion (sometimes called Darkkos Manse, or other similar variations). Darkos Mansion was the setting for stand-alone stories tied together by the mythology of the location, a rotting mansion in a swamp. By a printer's error, the back cover text story and the inside back cover ad for this issue also appeared on the back and inside back cover for Warren's *Eerie* #42, which came out the same month! This was apparently due to the fact that, for a time, both Skywald and Warren shared the same printer. The Wrightson artwork that appeared in that text story was originally intended as a spot illustration for the aborted *Science Fiction Odyssey* #1. The letters page mentions a script submission by future Marvel writer Roger McKenzie, although apparently it was not purchased as it never appeared. For all the innovation taking place, this isn't a particularly good issue, with the stories being somewhat weak. The best story and art was for the Stevenson adaptation by Hewetson and

Duran. The all-original 1972 *Nightmare* annual appeared between this issue and #10.

10. cover: Ken Kelly (December 1972)

(**1**) Mr. Pook's Introduction [Al Hewetson/ Pablo Marcos, frontis and title page] 2p; (**2**) Princess of Earth! [Al Hewetson/Pablo Marcos] 7p; (**3**) Nightmare Movie Review: Frogs [Al Hewetson/Berni Wrightson and Pablo Marcos, text article] 3p; (**4**) The Funeral Barge [Al Hewetson/Juez Xirinus] 7p; (**5**) Satan's Cellar [Al Hewetson/Ferrer Maitz] 6p; (**6**) The Proverbial Killer [Doug Moench/Xavier Villanova] 7p; (**7**) A Macabre Fact of Life: Demonic Possession [Al Hewetson/Pablo Marcos] 4p; (**8**) Game of Skill [Joan Cintron/Maelo Cintron, story credited to Kinsman] 1p; (**9**) The Nightmare World of Trisha Hamlin of Livingston, Kentucky: They Crawled Out of the Crater [Al Hewetson/Lara, from a dream by Trisha Hamlin] 4p; (**10**) Black Communion [Ed Fedory/Felipe Dela Rosa] 8p; (**11**) ...Slither into the Concocted Lunacy of the Astonishing Horror-Mood within This Noxious Nightmare Number 10... [Al Hewetson/Ernie Colon, Berni Wrightson and Basil Wolverton, text article/editorial] 2p; (**12**) The Human Gargoyles, part 2: 1 And 1 Equals 3 [Al Hewetson/Maelo Cintron] 9p; (**13**) ad for Psycho #10 [Al Hewetson, on the inside back cover] 1p.

Notes: Herschel Waldman now listed as co-publisher. The Horror-Mood phase made its first cover appearance. The letters page featured illustrations by Basil Wolverton, who Hewetson said inspired his signature use of alliteration, and Ernie Colon. The *Human Gargoyles* serial, which had debuted in *Psycho* #8, moved to *Nightmare*, with Maelo Cintron now the artist. The lead character's looks and his dialogue in "The Proverbial Killer" were clearly modeled on those of director Woody Allen! Wrightson's art for the movie review was originally intended as a spot illustration for the aborted *Science Fiction Odyssey* #1. The Cintron one-pager "Game of Skill" was Cintron's sample page, which was one of Al Hewetson's first purchases after becoming editor. Best story was Ed Fedory's "Black Communion" while the best art belonged to Juez Xirinius' dynamic, moody art for "The Funeral Barge." Good work was also supplied by Maelo Cintron, Felipe Dela Rosa, Al Hewetson, Doug Moench and Pablo Marcos.

11. cover: Jose Antonio Domingo (February 1973), credited to JAD

(1) Mr. Pook's Introduction [Al Hewetson/ Pablo Marcos, frontis and title page] 2p; (2) The Wetness in the Pit [Al Hewetson/Pablo Marcos] 5p; (3) Taw!!! [Ed Fedory/Antonio Borrell] 6p; (4) Lon Chaney, Sr. in the Phantom of the Opera [Al Hewetson/Pablo Marcos] 1p; (5) Nightmare World: The Beasts of Tomb Beach! [Al Hewetson/Wayne Howard, from a dream by Mike Black] 4p; (6) Where Gods Once Stood [T. Casey Brennan/Carlos Garzon] 6p; (7) Corridors of Caricature [Al Hewetson/ Jesus Duran] 7p; (8) Man-Bat [Al Hewetson/ Pablo Marcos] 1p; (9) Letters-Editorial Page: Doug Moench profile [Al Hewetson/Jay Lynch, text article with photos] 2p; (10) The Shoggoths: Where Are the Inhabitants of Earth? [Al Hewetson/Zesar Lopez] 10p; (11) Titan Weep [Al Hewetson/Pablo Marcos] 3p; (12) Nightmare Movie Macabre Reviews: The Classics [Al Hewetson, text article with photos] 5p; (13) The Horror War [Al Hewetson/Antonio Borrell] 9p; (14) ad for Psycho #11 [on the inside back cover, the Heap is featured] 1p.

Notes: Pablo Marcos was listed as art director for this issue only. The lead character in "The Wetness in the Pit" is based on Skywald business manager/co-publisher Herschel Waldman. "The Horror War" included Richard Nixon as a character and featured a photo of Nixon taken by Hewetson himself. The Man-Bat in the one-pager looks exactly like DC's famous Man-Bat. This was neither a particularly good issue, nor a particularly bad one. The all-original *Nightmare* 1973 winter special appeared between this issue and #12.

12. cover: Vicente Segrelles (April 1973)

(1) Nightmare in the House of Poe [Al Hewetson/Ferran Sostres] 13p; (2) Premature Burial [Al Hewetson/Juez Xirinius, from the story by Edgar Allan Poe] 8p; (3) Kiss of the Vampires [Chic Stone] 9p; (4) I Am Dead: I Am Buried! [Al Hewetson/Xavier Villanova] 10p; (5) The Night of the Corpse-Bride [Doug Moench/ Xavier Villanova] 7p; (6) Screaming Scrawlings: Editorial Letters page: Herschel Waldman profile [Al Hewetson, text article] 2p; (7) The Assassin-Bug [Al Hewetson/Antonio Borrell] 9p; (8) Monster, Monster on the Wall! [Augustine Funnell/Pablo Marcos] 4p.

Notes: Augustine Funnell makes his professional debut with "Monster, Monster on the Wall."

That story was originally intended as a stand-alone story but Hewetson persuaded Funnell to continue it as a series. Chic Stone's "Kiss of the Vampires" was probably done in 1971. "Nightmare in the House of Poe" featured the best art, by Ferran Sostres, although Pablo Marcos, Juez Xirinius and Antonio Borrell also delivered good work. Best story is Hewetson's adaptation of Poe's classic "Premature Burial."

13. cover: Vicente Segrelles (June 1973)

(1) ...The Corpse-Feast! [Ed Fedory/Juez Xirinius, frontis] 1p; (2) At Mind's Edge [Ed Fedory/Jesus Duran] 6p; (3) Curse of the Werewolf [Ed Fedory/Xavier Villanova] 1p; (4) ...Die Little Spider! [Al Hewetson/Fernando Rubio, story credited to Stuart Williams] 4p; (5) The Mad Nightmare World of H. P. Lovecraft [Al Hewetson/Felipe Dela Rosa] 2p; (6) ...Only the Wretched Die Young... [Al Hewetson/Ricardo Villamonte, story credited to Ricardo Villamonte] 9p; (7) Editorial Page: Syd Shores profile [Al Hewetson, text article] 2p; (8) The Corpse [Al Hewetson/Francisco Cueto, story credited to Howie Anderson] 10p; (9) Frankenstein 1973 [Al Hewetson/Xavier Villanova, story credited to Earle Leroy] 9p; (10) Nightmare Movie Review: Ben and Willard [Al Hewetson, text article with photos] 5p; (11) The Human Gargoyles, part 3: Only the Strong Shall Survive [Al Hewetson/Maelo Cintron] 9p; (12) Psycho ad [various, on the inside back cover] 1p; (13) Scream ad [?, on the back cover] 1p.

Notes: Segrelles' cover is particularly dynamic and is probably the best single cover that Skywald ever published. The letters page features a photo of Syd Shores, who was planning to return to the Skywald fold, as well a letter from future artist Gene Day. Hewetson also mentions a story that Shores was to illustrate but, as mentioned earlier, Shores died before the story was drawn. Reader feedback is requested in a "Bigger Bunch of Questions" section. The Frankenstein story is continued from *Psycho* #6 and is a continuation of Tom Sutton's *Frankenstein, Book II* series. That series concluded in *Scream* #6 a year later. Ricardo Villamonte delivered the best art while the *Human Gargoyles* chapter featured the best story.

14. cover: Xavier Villanova (August 1973)

(1) The Easter Island Things [Al Hewetson/ Maelo Cintron, frontis] 1p; (2) The Diary of an

Absolute Lunatic [Al Hewetson/Felipe Dela Rosa] 10p; (3) A Wretched Bunch of Letters/Editorial [Al Hewetson, text article] 2p; (4) The Plastic Plague [Jack Katz] 8p; (5) Death of the 80th Victim! [Doug Moench/Ricardo Villamonte] 8p; (6) ...Werewolf... [Ed Fedory/Juez Xirinius] 1p; (7) ...And the Corrupt Shall Dine! [Ed Fedory/Fernando Rubio] 5p; (8) Charles Laughton: Scream Screen Scenes [Al Hewetson/Domingo Gomez] 2p; (9) Starchild [Bruce Jones] 6p; (10) The Creature from the Black Lagoon [Al Hewetson/Ricardo Villamonte] 2p; (11) The Butchered at Earth's Core! [Ed Fedory/Jesus Suso Rego] 7p; (12) The Human Gargoyles, part 4: And They Did Battle with the Thing from Underneath [Al Hewetson/Maelo Cintron] 9p.

Notes: It cost $0.75 for 64 pages. Villanova's cover is rather noteworthy as it is in paneled comic form and actually is a separate story in its own right. Bruce Jones' story "Starchild" was done in 1971 and originally intended for the aborted *Science Fiction Odyssey*. It features the best art in this issue and is also a very good story. Jack Katz's story may also date from 1971 when he did the majority of his Skywald work. Best story goes to Al Hewetson's great "The Diary of an Absolute Lunatic," which could almost be a poster child template for the Horror-Mood. Good work also appears from Maelo Cintron, Felipe Dela Rosa, Ricardo Villamonte, Doug Moench, Jesus Suso Rego, Ed Fedory and Fernando Rubio. A photo of Ricardo Villamonte appears on the letters page.

15. cover: Ken Kelly (October 1973)

(1) How They Killed the Chicago Vampiress [Ed Fedory/Emilio Bernardo, frontis] 1p; (2) Dracula Did Not Die! [Al Hewetson/Antonio Borrell] 9p; (3) The Gargoyle Who Went to War [Al Hewetson/Fernando Rubio] 2p; (4) Nightmare Movie Review: Theatre of Blood [Al Hewetson, text article with photos] 4p; (5) The Truth Behind the Myths About Bats ... Particularly Vampire Bats [Al Hewetson/Domingo Gomez] 2p; (6) The Kid and the Killer and the Bum Rap [Al Hewetson/Francisco Cueto, story credited to Joe Westmuller] 6p; (7) Tapestry of Blood! [Ed Fedory/Fernando Rubio] 7p; (8) A Wretched Bunch of Letters/Editorial: Felipe Dela Rosa profile [Al Hewetson, text article with photos] 2p; (9) The Shoggoths: The Grotesque Green Earth [Al Hewetson/Zesar Lopez] 11p; (10) ...Ravings of the Damned! [Ed Fedory/Juez Xirinius]

The most striking cover Skywald published, this Vicente Segrelles effort is a minor masterpiece of horror.

8p; (11) The Human Gargoyles, part 5: Once Upon a Time in Alabama: A Horror [Al Hewetson/Maelo Cintron] 9p; (12) Psycho ad [various, on the inside back cover] 1p.

Notes: Al Hewetson and Zesar Lopez appear as protagonists in the *Shoggoth* story. Best story is Hewetson's "The Kid and the Killer and the Bum Rap" while the best art is Rubio's "Tapestry of Blood!"

16. cover: Jose Antonio Domingo (December 1973), credited to JAD

(1) The Voodoo Dead [Al Hewetson/Ricardo Villamonte, story credited to Joe Dentyn] 7p; (2) The Werewolf Macabre: The Birth of a Beast [Al Hewetson/Fernando Rubio] 9p; (3) The Werewolf Macabre: Dragnet: Werewolf [Al Hewetson/Jesus Suso Rego] 9p; (4) When the Devil Sent Us Death! [Augustine Funnell/Maro Nava] 5p; (5) The Ghoul Out of Hell [Al Hewetson/MaeloCintron, text story] 2p; (6) A Wretched Bunch of Letters: Editorial: Antonio Borrell profile [Al Hewetson/Antonio Borrell, text article] 2p; (7) The Roots of Evil [Al Hewetson/Antonio Borrell, story credited to Howie Anderson] 10p; (8) I Am Legend Review [Augustine Funnell/Gene Day, text article] 2p; (9) The Vampyre! [Ed Fedory/Pablo Marcos] 9p; (10) Hell Hath No Face [Al Hewetson/Ricardo Villamonte, story credited to Harvey Lazarus] 6p; (11) Human Gargoyles ad [Vicente Segrelles] 1p.

Notes: "The Roots of Evil" was originally intended as the cover story for *Scream* #1. Ed Fedory's story "The Vampyre" was originally entitled "Nosferatu" but was changed due to the *Nosferatu* serial that had begun running in *Scream.* The back cover advertises a special *Human Gargoyles* magazine (with a Vicente Segrelles cover) that was never published. It was intended to be a one-shot magazine that would reprint all the *Gargoyle* chapters that had appeared thus far. Best artwork here belongs to Suso Rego's work on the second half of "The Werewolf Macabre." Best story is "Hell Hath No Face."

17. cover: Sebastia Boada (February 1974)

(1) The End of All Vampires [Al Hewetson/Jesus Suso Rego, story credited to Howie Anderson] 10p; (2) Wretched Nightmare Letters/Editorial [Al Hewetson, text article] 2p; (3) The

Vampire out of Hell [Al Hewetson/Ricardo Villamonte, story credited to Edward Farthing] 10p; (4) The Night in the Horror-Hotel [Al Hewetson/Jesus Duran, story credited to Stuart Williams] 7p; (5) An Exclusive Interview with Christopher "Dracula" Lee [Christopher Lee and Al Hewetson, text article with photos] 8p; (6) The Psycho [Al Hewetson/Ruben Sosa] 10p; (7) The Inquisition [Al Hewetson/Lombardia, story credited to Joe Dentyn] 4p; (8) The Autobiography of a Vampire, Chapter 1 [Al Hewetson/Ricardo Villamonte] 10p; (9) The Lunatic Creations of Edgar Allan Poe [Al Hewetson/Domingo Gomez, on the back cover] 1p.

Notes: Sebastia Boada's makes his Skywald debut with a strikingly erotic cover which is also one of Skywald's best. The letters page promised an upcoming interview with Vincent Price that never appeared. "Autobiography of a Vampire" continued in *Scream* #5.

18. cover: Jose Antonio Domingo (April 1974), credited to JAD. This was a special issue featuring *The 7 Tales of the Man-Macabre.*

(1) The Vampire [Al Hewetson/Zesar Lopez, art is miscredited to Cesar Lopez] 8p; (2) The Werewolf [Al Hewetson/Jesus Suso Rego, story credited to Howie Anderson] 11p; (3) The Archaic Horror Mailbag [Al Hewetson, text article] 2p; (4) The Creep [Al Hewetson/Jesus Duran] 10p; (5) The Dead Things [Al Hewetson/Ricardo Villamonte, story credited to Stuart Williams] 2p; (6) The Vulture [Al Hewetson/Jose Cardona; story credited to Joe Dentyn] 12p; (7) The Ancient One [Al Hewetson/Ricardo Villamonte, story credited to Howie Anderson] 7p; (8) The Thing in the Space [Al Hewetson/Emilio Bernardo, story credited to Harvey Lazarus] 10p.

Notes: Domingo's cover is particularly good. With the exception of "The Ancient One," all the stories in this issue were grouped together as part of *The 7 Tales of the Man-Macabre.* Al Hewetson introduces the first story and the issue as a whole. "The Thing in the Space" is a takeoff on Lewis Carroll's *Alice in Wonderland.* Jesus Suso Rego was probably the best single artist that Skywald had during Hewetson's tenure (although Maelo Cintron was a strong presence as well). It's strange he didn't achieve more fame here in the States. His women were beautiful but realistic, his pacing and storytelling top notch, and his pages looked great. His artwork again is the best in this issue. Although the use of the multiple pseudonyms tried to mask it, this was an all–Hewetson-authored issue and the stories are all generally quite good.

19. cover: Sebastia Boada (June 1974)

(**1**) Horror Fragments: The Hell Hounds of the Baskervilles [Al Hewetson/Ferran Sostres, frontis] 1p; (**2**) What the Hell Is Dracula Doing Alive and Well in 1974? [Al Hewetson/Jesus Duran, story credited to Howie Anderson] 9p; (**3**) Horror Preview Contest [Ricardo Villamonte, a fill in the word balloons contest] 1p; (**4**) The Archaic Horror Mailbag [Al Hewetson, text article] 2p; (**5**) William Wilson [Al Heweston/Alphonso Font, from the story by Edgar Allan Poe] 8p; (**6**) The Shoggoths: The Vault [Al Hewetson/Jose Cardona, story credited to Howie Anderson] 10p; (**7**) The Great Classic Monster-Men [Al Hewetson, text article] 2p; (**8**) Tales Out of Hell: The Kingdom of the Dead [Al Hewetson/Jesus Duran] 10p; (**9**) The Autobiography of a Vampire, part 3: My Tomb Is My Castle [Al Hewetson/Ricardo Villamonte] 10p; (**10**) The Human Gargoyles, part 6: The Human Gargoyles vs. the United States of America [Al Hewetson/Maelo Cintron] 9p.

Jose Antonio Domingo, always credited as JAD, did many covers for both Skywald and Marvel. His distinctive, slick approach to horror is quite memorable.

Scream #5. Best art is from Maelo Cintron. Best story is the *Shoggoth* tale.

Notes: A voice balloon contest was begun, in which readers were encouraged to fill in empty dialogue balloons from a Ricardo Villamonte-illustrated page. Al Hewetson and Jose Cardona appeared in the *Shoggoth* story, despite the fact that "Howie Anderson" supposedly wrote the story. "Howie Anderson" was one of Hewetson's many pseudonyms and was so popular with readers that he got his own fan mail. "Tales out of Hell" continued in *Scream* #10. "The Autobiography of a Vampire" is continued from

20. cover: Sebastia Boada (August 1974)

(**1**) Horror Fragments: The Demon Whale [Al Hewetson/Ferran Sostres, frontis] 1p; (**2**) The Shoggoths: The Scream and the Nightmare [Al Hewetson/Jose Cardona] 20p; (**3**) The Archaic Horror Mailbag [Al Hewetson, text article] 2p; (**4**) Wanted: ...More Dead Than Alive... [Al Hewetson/Emilio Bernardo, story credited to Howie Anderson] 12p; (**5**) A Tale of Horror [Al Hewetson/Luis Collado] 10p; (**6**) The Black Cat [Al Hewetson/Ricardo Villamonte, from the story by Edgar Allan Poe] 5p; (**7**) The Castle [Al Hewetson/John Byrne and Duffy Vohland] 2p; (**8**) The Human Gargoyles, part 8: I,

The World War II effort, "A Tale of Horror" by Al Hewetson and Luis Collado, was one of the best written and illustrated stories from Skywald's run. It originally appeared in *Nightmare* #20.

Gargoyle [Alan Hewetson/Maelo Cintron] 9p; **(9)** ad for Psycho 1974 yearbook [Steve Hickman, on the inside back cover, art reprinted from *Psycho* #2 (March 1971)] 1p.

Notes: At the end of the *Shoggoth* story, Hewetson announces the start of a planned expedition to travel beneath the Earth to locate and battle the Shoggoths. The reader was encouraged to send in 15 cents to receive a Shoggoth Crusade certificate, signed by Hewetson and others, making the reader a member of the expedition! Both Hewetson and Cardona appear in the story, while publisher Herschel Waldman has a cameo. The letters page included a new reader's questionnaire. It also announces that *The Heap* would be returning with story and art by Duffy Vohland and Don Maitz. That plan was abandoned. The first page of "Wanted: More Dead than Alive" featured a wanted poster that was a photo of Al Hewetson in a sombrero. John Byrne made his professional debut on "The Castle." During the *Human Gargoyles'* story, the Gargoyles appear on the *Tonight Show* with Johnny Carson and Ed McMahon! Best story and art is for Al Hewetson and Luis Collado's superb World War II horror story, "A Tale of Horror," one of the best Horror-Mood stories published. Collado's beautiful penciled artwork is particularly noteworthy.

21. cover: Jose Mirelles (October 1974)

(1) Let Her Rot in Hell [Al Hewetson/Jose Cardona] 10p; **(2)** The Slither Slime Letters page/Editorial [Al Hewetson, text article] 2p; **(3)** Valley of Blood [Charles McNaughton/Jack Katz and Frank Giacoia, reprinted from *Psycho* #2 (March 1971)] 8p; **(4)** The Cosmos Strain [Michael Kaluta, reprinted from *Nightmare* #6 (December 1971)] 6p; **(5)** Comes the Stalking Monster! [Tom Sutton/Tom Sutton and Syd Shores, reprinted from *Psycho* #4 (September 1971)] 5p; **(6)** Sleep [Jeff Jones, reprinted from *Psycho* #6 (May 1972)] 5p; **(7)** Corpse by Computer [Robert Kanigher/Doug Wildey, reprinted from *Nightmare* #6 (December 1971)] 11p; Sand Castles [Ed Fedory/Pablo Marcos, reprinted from *Psycho* #6 (May 1972)] 14p.

Notes: The cover states that this is the 1974 *Nightmare* summer special. Only the title page states that this is also #21. This is largely a reprint issue with only one new story, "Let Her Rot in Hell," but it is a good one. Cardona delivered

what was probably his best art job for Skywald. The letters page mentions several never published stories that Jesus Suso Rego was to illustrate, including "Screaming Bloody Murder" and "Killer Fu Manchu" (a 20-page story to feature Fu Manchu vs. Dracula) as well as the news that Suso would be taking over the *Darkkos Mansion* serial.

22. cover: Salvador Faba (December 1974)

(1) The Mood-Team Undertakers [Al Hewetson/Maelo Cintron, frontis, portrays Maelo Cintron, Zesar Lopez, Ed Fedory, Cesar Lopez, Jesus Duran, Al Hewetson and Augustine Funnell] 1p; **(2)** Tomb of Horror Introduction [Al Hewetson/Domingo Gomez] 2p; **(3)** The Tales of the Vulture: The Bat — Mercy, Mercy Cries the Monster [Al Hewetson/Jose Martin Sauri] 10p; **(4)** Tomb of Horror editorial page [Al Hewetson/Ernie Puchades, text article with photos] 2p; **(5)** When I Was a Boy I Watched the Blood-Wolves! [Augustine Funnell/Jose Cardona] 6p; **(6)** Kill, Kill, Kill, and Kill Again [Al Hewetson/Ferran Sostres] 7p; **(7)** My Soul Is in Hell [Al Hewetson/Gene Day, text article] 2p; **(8)** The War of the Hell-Damned! [Al Hewetson/Jesus Duran] 10p; **(9)** The Coxsackie-Axe Murder [Ed Fedory/John Agras] 9p; **(10)** Daughter of Darkness ad [Al Hewetson/Maelo Cintron, advertises a Cintron husband/wife teamup on an upcoming story] 1p; **(11)** Tales of Evil ad [?, ad for an upcoming special or series] 1p; **(12)** The Mummy Khafre: The Funeral [Al Hewetson/Cesar Lopez] 10p; **(13)** Learn to Die in the Tomb of Horror [Al Hewetson/Zesar Lopez, on the back cover] 1p.

Notes: Misdated October 1974. It should be the December 1974 issue. The error probably occurred when this issue was intended to be #21 and was bumped back for the special reprint issue. In 1974, Skywald had planned a new magazine — *The Tomb of Horror* — but it was decided that the stands were too crowded to launch a new book at the time, so the contents were repackaged as this issue, which was billed as the *Tomb of Horror* special edition. However, Hewetson makes it clear to the readers that this is a "pilot" issue, meaning that if the demand was there, *Tomb of Horror* could still see the light of day. The question was rendered moot as the entire Skywald line folded with a couple of months. *Tomb of Horror'*s kick was to have the authors and artists introduce the stories, instead of the

The books in the bookstore window feature many of Skywald's serials as titles. Artwork by Maelo Cintron and script by Al Hewetson from *Nightmare* #20 and featuring *The Human Gargoyles*.

usual EC/Warren/*Web of Horror*–type horror hosts. The editorial page featured photos of Hewetson, Augustine Funnell, Ed Fedory and Maelo Cintron as well as art by Ernie Puchades. The artist Jose Martin Sauri has created a bit of confusion over the last few years. He was always listed in the Skywald magazines as either Robert or Bob Martin. One of his splash pages was signed Martin Sauri and when I did the first version of this checklist years ago, that was the name I listed for him. When Al Hewetson sent me his personal checklist shortly before his death, he had his name listed as Roberto Martinez and, assuming that Al would know his name, I changed my listings. Later, the *Warren Companion* listed him as Josep Martin Sauri and mentioned that he was listed as Paul Martin in the Skywald books, which was incorrect as well. I finally tracked down a modern art listing for him (including new comic pages) where his name was listed as Jose Martin Sauri and that is the name I am currently listing. Best story here is Ed Fedory's "The Coxsackie-Axe Murders." Coxsackie was his hometown at the time. Best artwork is Ferran Sostres' work on "Kill, Kill, Kill, And Kill Again," by Hewetson (besides the great story, that title was a great *Horror-Mood* title!).

23. cover: Maelo Cintron and Vicente Segrelles/frontis: Gene Day (February 1975)

(1) The Human Gargoyles, part 9: The Human Gargoyles vs. the Human Dead [Al Hewetson/Maelo Cintron, story never concluded] 9p; **(2)** The Human Gargoyles cover [Vicente Segrelles, B&W reproduction of a future [never published] cover featuring the Human Gargoyles] 1p; **(3)** Nightmare Mailbag [Jose Martin Sauri, text article and letters page] 1p; **(4)** The Fiend of Changsha! ad [Sanho Kim, promo for Kim's story in *Psycho* #24] 1p; **(5)** Tradition of the Wolf [Ed Fedory/Jose Martin Sauri] 8p; **(6)** Death Walk! [Ed Fedory/Jose Cardona, art credited to Andy Crandon] 8p; **(7)** Time for Living, Time for Dying [Al Hewetson/Gene Day, text story] 2p; **(8)** The Vampire Freaks [Al Hewetson/Paul Pueyo, story credited to William Davie, art credited to Stan Connerty] 6p; **(9)** The Thing in the Ragged Mountains [Al Hewetson/Amador Garcia, story credited to Ted Freeman, art credited to Walter Fortiss] 7p; **(10)** Fistful of Flesh [Al Hewetson/Folsengo Cabrerizo, story credited to Leslie Jerome, art credited

to Denis Ford] 5p; **(11)** Snakewizard! [Augustine Funnell/Jose Cardona] 8p; **(12)** Werewolf graphic novel ad [Jose Martin Sauri, on the back cover] 1p.

Notes: Final issue. It was $1.00 for 64 pages. The cover identifies this as the 1975 *Nightmare* winter special. Only the title page identifies it as #23. Segrelles painted the actual cover while Citron painted a cover insert. The *Human Gargoyles* story was originally intended for the *Human Gargoyles* special title advertised in the notes for *Nightmare* #16. A house ad again shows the Segrelles cover advertised for that special, but that cover was now planned for use on a special *Human Gargoyles* issue of *Nightmare* (obviously never released). Two more chapters in the *Human Gargoyles* series were written and penciled but never completed. One of the chapters featured the Gargoyles interacting with the lead characters of the TV show *Dragnet*, as portrayed by the actors Jack Webb and Harry Morgan. The letters page announced that Hewetson and Sanho Kim's "The Fiend of Changsha" would continue in *Psycho* #24, thanks to reader demand. The *Werewolf* ad on the back cover advertised a graphic novel that never appeared. "Tradition of the Wolf" is remarkable largely for the extraordinary number of art swipes in it. Backgrounds appear to be lifted wholescale from various Esteban Maroto stories, while foreground characters are lifted from Maroto and Frazetta stories done for Warren Publications, especially Frazetta's "Werewolf" from *Creepy* #1. The back pages had the debut of a five-page ad section called "The Little Horror-Mood Shop of Horrors"—a catalog of novelty items similar to Warren's Captain Company ads. A quite striking cover was done for the intended next issue (the art is unidentified but could be by either Sebastia Boada, the mysterious Martin Poll or Salvador Faba) which was to feature the *Town of Evil* set of stories, a review of the Kolchak TV series and a Frankenstein contest. A cover by Warren cover artist Enrich Torres was intended for #25.

Psycho

1. cover: Brendan Lynch (January 1971)

(1) The Skin and Bones Syndrome! [Roger Elwood/Gray Morrow] 8p; **(2)** The Glistening

Death [?/Martin Nodell and Vince Alascia, reprinted from *City of the Living Dead* #1 (1952)] 6p; (3) I Painted Only Terror! [?/?, reprinted from *Eerie* #5, Avon (March 1952)] 6p; (4) Psycho's Gruesome Gallery No. 1: The Mirror [Steve Hickman, a pin-up] 1p; (5) The Thing in the Mirror [?/Everett Raymond Kinstler, reprinted from *The Phantom Witch Doctor* #1 (1952)] 6p; (6) The Steps in the Cellar! [Art Stampler/?, text story] 4p; (7) ...and Then There's Cicero! [Gardner Fox/Paul Reinman] 6p; (8) Anatomical Monster [?/A. C. Hollingsworth, reprinted from *Eerie* #13, Avon (? 1953)] 7p; (9) The Hands of Death! [?/Norman Nodel and Vince Alascia, reprinted from *Eerie* #9, Avon (November 1952)] 7p; The Gruesome Faces of Mr. Cliff! [Len Wein?/Mario Acquaviva?] 8p.

Notes: Publisher: Sol Brodsky and Israel Waldman. Editor: Sol Brodsky, with associate editor listed as Herschel Waldman. It cost $0.50 for 64 pages. There are no credits on the stories themselves, but the title page lists the authors as Gardner Fox, Roger Elwood, Art Stampler and Wayne Benedict, while the artists are listed as David Haldey, Paul Reinman, Gray Morrow and Mario Acquaviva. I have credited individual stories only where the contributor's identity has been confirmed. Like *Nightmare*'s first two issues, many of the stories were 1950s-era reprints, probably from Waldman's IW/Super Comics stock, many of which have retouched artwork. There were three new stories and a pin-up. Best story was "The Gruesome Faces of Mr. Cliff!" while the best art was Gray Morrow's for "The Skin and Bones Syndrome!" which, alas, was a terrible story. Lynch's cover is quite horrific and much in the style of the pre-code 1950s horror covers. The 1950s reprint "Anatomical Monster" has a great splash page. There is a Horror House ad (for rubber shrunken heads and the like) illustrated by John Severin which takes great care to point out that it is a real ad! Did Severin do a lot of fake ads for *Cracked*?

2. cover: Hector Varella (March 1971)

(1) The Heap [Chuck McNaughton/Ross Andru and Mike Esposito] 10p; (2) To Laugh ... Perchance to Live! [Chuck McNaughton/Jack Katz and Rich Buckler] 9p; (3) Death's Stranger [Marv Wolfman/Tom Palmer] 8p; (4) Psycho's Gruesome Gallery #2: The Vampire [Steve

Hickman, a pin-up] 1p; (5) Revolution! [Rich Margopoulos/Tom Sutton and Dan Adkins, story credited to Rick Poulos, penciling credited to Sean Todd] 8p; (6) The Quest! [Rich Margopoulos/Chic Stone, story credited to Rick Poulos] 8p; (7) Dream Planet [Phil Seuling/Serg Moren] 8p; (8) Valley of Blood [Chuck McNaughton/Jack Katz and Frank Giacoia] 8p.

Notes: The start of all new stories. Skywald's first series, *The Heap*, began, featuring the origin and first appearance of Skywald's most popular continuing character — among readers, anyway. Future editor Al Hewetson himself hated the character. One issue of a color comic featuring the character was also produced by Skywald, with Robert Kanigher scripting and the team of Tom Sutton and Jack Abel illustrating. This Heap is not the same character that Hillman published in the 1940s–1950s or which Eclipse revived in the 1980s, although some similarities exist. Skywald's Heap is particularly gross looking, often resembling a blob of phlegm. The best story here would probably be either "To Laugh ... Perchance to Live!" or "Valley of Blood," both written by Chuck McNaughton. Best art is Jack Katz and Rich Buckler's on "To Laugh ... Perchance to Live!" There's also good art from Chic Stone and Serg Moren.

3. cover: Boris Vallejo (May 1971)

(1) Frankenstein, Book II: Chapter One [Tom Sutton/Tom Sutton and Dan Adkins, story and penciling credited to Sean Todd] 12p; (2) A Coffin for Captain Cutlass [Gardner Fox/Serg Moren] 9p; (3) The Heap: The Heap Meets the Horror Master! [Chuck McNaughton and Ross Andru/Ross Andru and Mike Esposito] 15p; (4) Gruesome Crewcut! [Chic Stone] 3p; (5) The Man Who Stole Eternity [Gardner Fox/Bill Everett] 10p; (6) The Love Witch [Marv Wolfman/Ernie Colon, art is credited to Jack Purcell] 11p.

Notes: Skywald's continuation of Mary Shelly's novel *Frankenstein* began, with Sutton's storyline taking place directly after the events in her novel. The Frankenstein monster is also cover-featured, with a striking cover by Vallejo. The letters page begins under the title "Psycho Delivery." The short-lived *Love Witch* debuted, with her next and last appearance showing up in *Nightmare* #6. Best artwork and story easily goes to the superb Fox/Everett tale "The Man Who Stole Eternity."

4. cover: Ken Kelly (September 1971)

(1) The Innsmouth Apparition [Larry Todd, frontis] 1p; **(2)** The Heap: Night of Evil! [Ross Andru/Ross Andru and Mike Esposito] 10p; **(3)** Out of Chaos ... A New Beginning [Marv Wolfman/Rich Buckler] 10p; **(4)** Museum Piece [Len Wein/Serg Moren] 7p; **(5)** Comes the Stalking Monster! [Tom Sutton/Tom Sutton and Syd Shores, story credited to Larry Todd, art credited to David Cook] 5p; **(6)** Behind the Planet of the Apes [Allan Asherman/?, text article with storyboard art] 4p; **(7)** Escape [Dennis Fujitake] 2p; **(8)** Plague of Jewels [Bruce Jones] 10p; **(9)** Frankenstein, Book II: Freaks of Fear! [Tom Sutton/Tom Sutton and Jack Abel, story and pencils credited to Sean Todd] 10p; **(10)** The Heap Pin-Up [Bill Everett, on the back cover] 1p.

Notes: First squarebound issue. Editorial assistant: Helen Rudin. Tom Sutton, who wrote and penciled "Comes the Stalking Monster," often used pseudonyms, presumably to avoid getting into trouble with Jim Warren, for whom Sutton also worked, and who was legendary for unleashing his wrath on freelancers who worked for the "enemy." In this case, for penciling, Sutton used the name "David Cook." For writing it is likely he meant to use his old standby "Sean Todd" but a mix-up credited the story to Larry Todd, who was (and is) a real, separate writer-artist who mostly appeared in underground comics. The Wolfman/Buckler "Out of Chaos..." was a two-parter (concluded in the next issue) that was particularly good and provides the best story and art this issue, although Sutton's work on *Frankenstein, Book II* and Bruce Jones' on "Plague of Jewels"

also delivered very good stories and art. Dennis Fujitake made his professional debut here and was warmly received. Everett's rendering of Skywald's version of the Heap was probably the best rendition that character ever received.

5. cover: Boris Vallejo (November 1971)

(1) A Psycho Scene [Bill Everett, frontis, a pin-up] 1p; **(2)** Let the Dreamer Beware [Jerry Siegel/Ralph Reese] 7p; **(3)** Power of the Pen! [Doug Moench/Doug Wildey] 9p; **(4)** The Psycho-Analyst [Jeff Rovin, text article with photo] ½ p; **(5)** The Heap: Cavern of Doom [Ross Andru/Ross Andru and Mike Esposito] 10p; **(6)** The Vampire [Allan Asherman, text article with photos] 4p; **(7)** The Unholy Satanists [Al Hewetson/Serg Moren] 8p; **(8)** Out of Chaos ... A

This early Boris Vallejo cover painting from *Psycho* #5 demonstrates his talent in horror composition.

New Beginning, part 2 [Marv Wolfman/Rich Buckler] 10p; (9) Frankenstein, Book II: The Sewer Tomb of Le Suub! [Tom Sutton/Tom Sutton and Jack Abel, story and pencils credited to Sean Todd] 10p; (10) ad for Nightmare #6 [Jeff Jones, on the inside back cover, B&W reproduction of the next issue's cover] 1p; (11) ad for Hell-Rider #3 [Gray Morrow, on back cover, this magazine was never published] 1p.

Notes: It was $0.60 for 64 pages. Helen Rudin's last issue as editorial assistant. Boris Vallejo turned in his last and best Skywald cover. A pencil sketch by Vallejo of the cover to #3 appeared on the letters page. Future artists John Workman and Duffy Vohland send in letters. Jeff Rovin's column "The Psycho-Analyst" interviewed Al Hewetson. In the story "Power of the Pen," the lead characters appear to be modeled on Warren editor Archie Goodwin and Marvel editor Stan Lee! Best artwork is Ralph Reese's great job on Jerry Siegel's "Let the Dreamer Beware." Best story is Tom Sutton's nutty, but great "The Sewer Tomb of Le Suub!," yet another Parisian sewer tale. Other good stories and art were delivered by Doug Moench, Doug Wildey, Jerry Siegal, Marv Wolfman and Rich Buckler.

6. cover: Vicente Segrelles (May 1972)

(1) Psycho's Supernatural Series: Abrasax [Al Hewetson/Pablo Marcos, frontis] 1p; (2) The Vow! [Pat Boyette] 7p; (3) The Midnight Slasher [Doug Moench/Pablo Marcos] 6p; Sleep [Jeff Jones, story credited to Steve Stern] 5p; (4) The Psycho-Analyst [Jeff Rovin, text article with photo] ½ p; (5) The Heap: Dark Victory [Ross Andru/Ross Andru and Pablo Marcos] 8p; (6) The Seventh Voyage of Sinbad [Jeff Rovin/photos: Allan Asherman, text article with photos] 2p; (7) Of a Sudden Is Thy Death! [Gus St. Anthony] 2p; (8) Frankenstein, Book II: The Phantom of the Opera [Tom Sutton, story and art credited to Sean Todd] 10p; (9) Sand Castles [Ed Fedory/Pablo Marcos] 14p; (10) Werewolf Pin-Up [Bill Everett, on the back cover] 1p.

Notes: A six-month gap occurred between #5 and #6. Herschel Waldman was now business manager. Jeff Rovin was listed as assistant editor for this issue only. This was the last *Frankenstein, Book II* story by Tom Sutton. The storyline was continued by Al Hewetson and Cesar Lopez a year later in *Nightmare* #13. Best story here is Ed

Fedory's grisly "Sand Castles." Best art was for Pat Boyette's "The Vow!" Other good stories and art appeared from Doug Moench, Pablo Marcos, Tom Sutton, Jeff Jones and Gus St. Anthony.

7. cover: Vicente Segrelles (July 1972)

(1) Edgar Allan Poe's Pit and Pendulum [Al Hewetson/Pablo Marcos, frontis] 1p; (2) Kerene [David Anthony Kraft/Domingo Gomez] 5p; (3) Horror Has 1 Thousand Faces! [Al Hewetson/Domingo Gomez] 8p; (4) The Family Jewels! [Dennis Fujitake] 5p; (5) guest column [Ed Fedory, text article] 1p; (6) The Heap: A Spawn of Satan [Al Hewetson/Pablo Marcos] 9p; (7) The Terrible Tragedy of the Tormented One! [Marv Wolfman/Pablo Marcos, art credited to Jim Elder] 5p; (8) The Masters of Blood [Al Hewetson, text article with photos] 4p; (9) I Am Demona: The Feastings of Prince Yamm [Gardner Fox/Steve Englehart and Vince Colletta (figures only), art credited solely to Englehart] 10p; (10) The Asylum of Frozen Hell [Al Hewetson/Pablo Marcos] 8p; (11) Forewarned Is Forearmed! [Jim Pinkoski] 2p; (12) The Discombobulated Hand [Al Hewetson/Ramon Torrents, story credited to Jay Wood] 3p; (13) Skeleton Pin-Up [Pablo Marcos, on the back cover] 1p.

Notes: Al Hewetson was now listed as associate editor. Dennis Fujitake must have had a good laugh over that title for his story! This was Steve Englehart's last outing as an artist, although he's had a long and celebrated career as a comics writer. David Anthony Kraft delivers the best story here with "Kerene" while Pablo Marcos has the best art for "The Terrible Tragedy of the Tomented One!" That story was by Marv Wolfman although the title certainly seems like Al Hewetson must have had a hand in it.

8. cover: Erich Torres (September 1972)

(1) The Theater of Horror [Al Hewetson/Domingo Gomez, frontis] 1p; (2) The Human Gargoyles, part 1: A Gargoyle — A Man [Al Hewetson/Felipe Dela Rosa] 10p; (3) Scream Screen: Lon Chaney: A Thousand Faces of Ultimate Horror [Al Hewetson/Pablo Marcos, text article with photos] 4p; (4) Devil's Woman [Marv Wolfman/Ross Andru and Mike Esposito] 10p; (5) The Psycho-Analyst [Al Hewetson, text article] 2p; (6) Have You Ever Seen the Black Rain? [Al Hewetson/Juez Xirinius] 9p; (7) The Filthy Little House of Voodoo [Al Hewetson/Ramon Torrents] 9p; (8) Bad Choke

[Don Glut/Juez Xirinius] 6p; (9) City of Crypts [Al Hewetson/Xavier Villanova] 10p; (10) Ghoul Pin-Up [Pablo Marcos, on the back cover] 1p.

Notes: Publisher: Israel Waldman; business manager: Herschel Waldman; editor: Al Hewetson. For years I credited this beautiful cover to Jose Mirelles but while researching European horror covers, this painting rolled up, and that version clearly carried the very familiar signature of Erich Torres in the lower lefthand corner! The first mention in this title regarding the Horror-Mood appears inside the magazine. The *Human Gargoyles* serial made its debut, illustrated by

This rare non–Warren appearance by Erich Torres was one of the best of the early Skywald covers only identified as his when a check of European covers revealed a magazine version that didn't crop off his name.

Dela Rosa for this episode only. After this appearance, the serial moved to *Nightmare*, where it was drawn by Maelo Cintron. *The Psycho-Analyst* makes its final appearance. *Scream Screen* began a regular horror movie review column. The 1972 *Psycho* annual appeared between this issue and #9. Definite reflections of the Horror-Mood are present in Hewetson's "Have You Seen the Black Rain?" and "The Filthy Little House of Voodoo," which were the best stories in this issue. Best art goes to Ramon Torrents with good work from Juez Xirinius and Felipe Dela Rosa.

9. cover: Domingo Gomez (November 1972)

(1) Horror-Mood Introduction [Al Hewetson/Pablo Marcos, the intro is by the Slither-Slime Man, frontis and title page] 2p; (2) The Slither-Slime Man [Al Hewetson/Pablo Marcos] 7p; (3) Ghastly Reunion [Doug Moench/Ramon Torrents] 6p; (4) Psycho Scribblings [Al Hewetson/Pablo Marcos and Ernie Colon, text article with spot illustrations] 2p; (5) ...Suffer the Little Children [Al Hewetson/Xavier Villanova, sequel to Henry James' *The Turn of the Screw*] 8p; (6) Ghouls of the Cinema! [Al Hewetson/Pablo Marcos, text article with photos] 4p; (7) A Plot of Dirt [Doug Moench/Felipe Dela Rosa] 10p; (8) A Question of Identity!!! [Ed Fedory/Zesar Lopez] 8p; (9) Voodoo Initation [Al Hewetson/Pablo Marcos] 1p; (10) The Graveyard Jungle [Al Hewetson/Juez Xirinius] 8p; (11) All the Ways and Means to Die [Jeff Jones, from the story "All the Myriad Ways" by Larry Niven] 8p; 12) ad for Nightmare #10 [Al Hewetson/Berni Wrightson, on the inside back cover] 1p.

Notes: The Slither-Slime Man is cover-featured. Hewetson must have loved the Slither-Slime Man as he used him as a quasi-mascot representing the Horror-Mood and in various cameos, although he would only appear in one additional story. The Horror-Mood declaration was now a permanent part of the cover. Herschel Waldman listed as co-publisher. The letters page mentions a script submission from future comic writer Roger McKenzie. It also includes a favorable mention of the French magazine *Pilote* with a picture of a recent cover. Also on the letters page, Al Hewetson responded to Jim Warren's Xerox Award insult, which had been aimed directly at Skywald. Best story here is Hewetson's "The Slither-Slime Man," although Doug Moench and Ed Fedory also turned in good stories. Best art is by Zesar Lopez, making his Skywald debut on "A Question of Identity!!!" Larry Niven's SF story was also adapted by Doug Moench and Vicente Alcazar for Marvel's *Unknown Worlds of Science Fiction* title in 1975. This version, by Jeff Jones, was done in 1971 and originally intended for the aborted *Science Fiction Odyssey* #1. The inside back cover ad not only identified *Nightmare*'s new child vampire host as Mr. Pook for the first time, but it was also the only time the name was mentioned in any Skywald book.

10. cover: Pablo Marcos and Fernando Fernandez (January 1973)

(1) Introduction [Al Hewetson/Pablo Marcos, frontis and title page] 2p; (2) The Suicide Werewolf [Al Hewetson/Pablo Marcos] 10p; (3) The Legend of the Man-Macabre [Al Hewetson/Xavier Villanova] 9p; (4) ...Peter Piper Picked a Peck of Pickled Corpses... [Al Hewetson/Maelo Cintron] 6p; (5) The Legend of an 18th Century Gentleman: H. P. Lovecraft [Al Hewetson, text article with photos] 3p; (6) This Is the Slither-Slime Page [Al Hewetson, mini bio of Ed Fedory, text article with photo] 2p; (7) The Heap: Even a Heap Can Die! [Al Hewetson/Pablo Marcos] 9p; (8) The Transplant!! [Ed Fedory/Fernando Rubio] 7p; (9) Scream Screen: A Leering Look at the Frankenstein Monster ... Karloff [Al Hewetson, text article with photos] 2p; (10) Tightrope to Nowhere [Al Hewetson/Juez Xirinius] 9p; (11) Re-Write: Frankenstein [Al Hewetson/Maelo Cintron, this was not a part of the Frankenstein serial, but a joke story] 2p; (12) ...It... [Al Hewetson/Maelo Cintron, text story, on the back cover] 1p.

Notes: Hewetson writes a fine little text feature on H. P. Lovecraft, who, along with Edgar Allan Poe, Hewetson credited with the inspiration for the Horror-Mood. The article contains photos of HPL's home and neighborhood in Providence, RI, taken by Hewetson, who was a former newspaper photographer. During his trip, Hewetson was inspired to write the back cover story, "It." The letters page announces a contest in which the prizes are "gargoyle eggs," which were actually smooth, round stones that Hewetson and Fedory picked up along the beach! This was doubly odd as the *Human Gargoyles* themselves delivered their baby the old-fashioned mammalian way. "Re-Write" was intended as a regular feature in which classic horror films were to be parodied. Apparently it was poorly received as it never appeared again. Best story and art belong to the Hewetson/Villanova story "The Legend of the Man-Macabre" with good work also appearing from Maelo Cintron, Ed Fedory and Fernando Rubio.

11. cover: Fernando Fernandez (March 1973), reprinted in B&W on the frontis

(1) ...And It Whispered ... And It Wept ... And It Did Shudder ... And It Did Die... [Al Hewetson/Felipe Dela Rosa] 7p; (2) Scream Screen Movie Review: Blacula [Al Hewetson, text article with photos] 3p; (3) ...Make Mephisto's Child Burn... [Ed Fedory/Felipe Dela Rosa] 2p; (4) The Heap: A Ship of Fiends [Al Hewetson/Pablo Marcos] 9p; (5) ...Roast Their Evil Bones... [Ed Fedory/Antonio Borrell] 1p; (6) Her Majesty — The Corpse [Ed Fedory/Juez Xirinius] 1p; (7) Hit and Run: Miss and Die [Doug Moench/Xavier Villanova] 9p; (8) A Bunch of Answers: Pablo Marcos profile [letters page and text article with photos] 2p; (9) Don't Die Up There, Stanley [Al Hewetson/Jesus Suso Rego] 9p; (10) Tales of Darkos Manse: The Thing in Horror-Swamp! [Al Hewetson/Pablo rcos] 10p; (11) A Bag of Fleas [Al Hewetson/Jose Gual] 8p.

Notes: Hewetson announces the start of phase two of the Horror-Mood. The second part of the *Heap* story also features the werewolf who had originally appeared in the *Darkos Mansion* story from *Nightmare* #9. The letters page had a photo of Pablo Marcos as well as a photo of Al Hewetson, Ed Fedory and their wives having a picnic in a graveyard. That picnic directly inspired the story "The Lunatic Picnic" that appeared in #12. The little two-pager "...Make Mephisto's Child Burn..." is one of the most disturbing and horrific stories Skywald published. Best story and art belong to "Don't Die Up There, Stanley" by Hewetson and Suso Rego, which was based on a real comedian who was a friend of Hewetson's. Dela Rosa, Xirinius, Borrell and Marcos also delivered high-quality art.

12. cover: Jeff Jones (May 1973)

(1) The Mad-Doll Man [Al Hewetson/Jose Gual] 8p; (2) Lunatic Picnic [Al Hewetson/Zesar Lopez] 6p; (3) The Truth Behind the Horrors of Salem [Al Hewetson, text article with photos] 3p; (4) Studies in Horror [Al Hewetson/Felipe Dela Rosa] 2p; (5) The Weird Way It Was [Al Hewetson/Pablo Marcos] 12p; (6) The Swordsman of Sarn [Gardner Fox/Jack Katz and Vince Colletta] 12p; (7) Scream Screen Scene: Asylum [Al Hewetson, text article with photos] 2p; (8) The Lunatic Page: Gary Friedrich profile [letters page and text article with photo] 2p; (9) The Heap: And the World Shall Shudder [Al Hewetson/Xavier Villanova] 9p; (10) Welcome to My Asylum [Al Hewetson/Xavier Villanova] 4p.

Notes: Both Jones' cover and the story "The Swordsman of Sarn" were done in 1971 and originally intended for the aborted *Science Fiction Odyssey* #1. This was a rather poor issue with only "The Mad-Doll Man" and "Welcome to My Asylum" managing to rise above mediocrity. "The Weird Way It Was" was another takeoff on Lewis Carroll's *Alice's Adventures in Wonderland*. The letters page featured a photo of Gary Friedrich, who hadn't written a story for Skywald in two years.

13. cover: Vincente Segrelles (July 1973)

(1) Prologue to Horror [Al Hewetson/Domingo Gomez, frontis] 1p; (2) The Day Satan Died [Al Hewetson/Felipe Dela Rosa] 8p; (3) The Slither-Slime Pages: Maelo Cintron profile [Al Hewetson/Letters page, text article with photo] 2p; (4) Monster, Monster in the Grave! [Augustine Funnell/Pablo Marcos] 6p; (5) Macabre Movie Review: Dracula A.D. 1972 [Al Hewetson, text article with photos] 3p; (6) Let's All Drink to the Death of a Clown [Doug Moench/Fernando Rubio] 8p; (7) The Heap: When Dies a Lunatic ... So Dies a Heap [Al

Hewetson/Xavier Villanova] 11p; (8) A Taste of Human Flesh... [Ed Fedory/Ferran Sostres] 2p; (9) The Horror Within and Without [Rich Buckler and Chuck McNaughton/Michael Kaluta, from the story "City of Yesterday" by Terry Carr] 8p; (10) The Raven [Al Hewetson/Manuel ?, story credited to Jessica Vogel] 2p; (11) The Taste of Carrion [Ed Fedory/Pablo Marcos] 7p; (12) Scream Screen Scene: The Mummy [Al Hewetson/Maelo Cintron] 2p.

Notes: The cover for this issue was intended to highlight the story "The 13 Dead Things" which didn't actually appear until #15. The story "The Horror Within and Without" was done in 1971 and originally intended for the aborted *Science Fiction Odyssey* #1. A photo of Maelo Cintron graced the letters page, where it was revealed that former news photographer Al Hewetson took all contributor photos. The *Heap* series ended with an uncharacteristic happy ending (the Heap is taken in by his parents to live as normal a life as a horrific-looking snot monster can), and a question was asked of the readers: Did they want more of the Heap? The answer was a resounding "Yes!" Much to Hewetson's chagrin, as he hated the character. Plans were made to relaunch the series as soon as an artist could come up with a suitable reconception of the character. After Hewetson rejected four different proposals, eventually Gene Day came up with a suitable design, and a relaunch of the series was announced—although the Skywald line folded before it could see print. *Scream Screen Scene* was not a movie review, but a brief retelling of a particular film in comic form. Best story here was Ed Fedory's "The Taste of Carrion" and the best art was Michael Kaluta's work on "The Horror Within and Without." Good work also appeared from Hewetson, Dela Rosa, Marcos, Rubio, Funnell and Moench.

14. cover: Ken Kelly (September 1973)

(1) The Dead [Al Hewetson/Maelo Cintron, text story, frontis] 1p; (2) The Classic Creeps [Al Hewetson/Francisco Cueto] 13p; (3) The Monstrosity ... Strikes! [Augustine Funnell/Ricardo Villamonte] 5p; (4) The Slither-Slime Page: Augustine Funnell profile [letters page, Bob Burros/Jay Lynch, text article] 2p; (5) Scream Screen Reviews: Vault of Horror and Who Slew Auntie Roo? [Al Hewetson, text article with

photos] 4p; (6) The Artist's Other Hand [Al Hewetson/Jesus Suso Rego] 7p; (7) The Horror That's Not as It Seems [Al Hewetson/Antonio Borrell] 1p; (8) A Man Who Dare Not Sleep! [Ed Fedory/Felipe Dela Rosa] 5p; (9) Cassandra ... Sorceress of the Seventh Wind [Marv Wolfman/Don Heck and Mike Esposito] 10p; (10) The Hippy-Criters Are Comin' [Al Hewetson/Fernando Rubio] 5p; (11) I Battle the Vicious Vampire Bats of Transylvania and I Lived to Tell It [Al Hewetson/Maro Nava, story credited to Maro Nava] 8p.

Notes: It cost $0.75 for 64 pages. The letters page featured a cartoon by Jay Lynch and a text story by Bob Burros. In the story "The Artist's Other Hand" the main character was drawn to look like Al Hewetson. Kelly's cover, which depicted classic movie monsters, could just as easily have graced a magazine like *Famous Monsters of Filmland*. Best story is Hewetson's "The Artist's Other Hand" while the best art goes to newcomer Maro Nava. Other good work appeared from Francisco Cueto, Jesus Suso Rego and Augustine Funnell. Bit of a sloppy title for the last story, as it mixes present and past tense verbs.

15. cover: Vicente Segrelles (November 1973)

(1) How to Make a Mummy [Al Hewetson/Maelo Cintron, frontis] 1p; (2) The 13 Dead Things [Al Hewetson/Jesus Duran, art credited to D. Duran] 12p; (3) Letters page: Jose Gual profile [Al Hewetson/Jose Gual and Maro Nava, text article] 2p; (4) When the Bad Moon Rises ... I Am a Ghoul! [Rodion Eis/Mario Nava, the author is possibly Al Hewetson] 9p; (5) The Ghoul [Al Hewetson/Ferran Sostres, story credited to Howie Anderson] 8p; (6) The House of Demons [Chic Stone/Amador Garcia] 11p; (7) Scream Screen: All Girl-Ghoul Movies of the Macabre [Al Hewetson, text article with photos] 5p; (8) Ghouls Walk Among Us [Augustine Funnell/Ferran Sostres] 7p; (9) The Town That Crumbled [Al Hewetson/Jesus Suso Rego] 1p; (10) I Laugh the Laugh of the Graceful Dead! [Al Hewetson/Felipe Dela Rosa] 5p; (11) Scream ad [Zesar Lopez, on the back cover] 1p.

Notes: The letters page featured a photo of Jose Gual. A voice balloon contest appeared this issue. "The 13 Dead Things" was originally intended as the cover story for #13. It was the best story in this issue. Best art went to Maro Nava for "When the Bad Moon Rises ... I Am a Ghoul!"

with more fine art from Jesus Suso Rego, Ferran Sostres and Amador Garcia.

16. cover: Domingo Gomez (January 1974)

(1) The Old Vampire Lady [Al Hewetson/Jesus Duran] 10p; (2) The Archaic Horror Mailbag/Editorial: Christopher Lee's Comic Opinion [Al Hewetson and Christopher Lee, text article with photos] 2p; (3) Monster, Monster Rise from Thy Crypt [Augustine Funnell/Ricardo Villamonte] 8p; (4) Darkkos Manse: They Lived in Darkkos Manse! [Al Hewetson/Maro Nava, story credited to Joe Dentyn] 10p; (5) The Thing with the Red Ribbon in Its Hair [Al Hewetson/Domingo Gomez, story credited to Domingo Gomez] 1p; (6) Dead — But Not Yet Buried: Edgar Allan Poe [Al Hewetson, text article with photos] 4p; (7) The Thing in the Box [Al Hewetson/Fernando Rubio, story credited to Harvey Lazarus] 6p; (8) Hunger of the Slaughter-Sludge Beasts! [Doug Moench/Jesus Suso Rego] 11p; (9) A Tale in Old Egypt: The Premature Burial [Al Hewetson/Felipe Dela Rosa] 2p; (10) Movie Reviews: Nosferatu [Ed Fedory, text article with photos] 1p; (11) Greed [Al Hewetson/Ricardo Villamonte, story credited to Edward Farthing] 8p.

Notes: The letters page featured a guest "Comics Opinion" by Christopher Lee, which was actually an unused segment of the interview with Lee that appeared in *Nightmare* #17. In a classic comment, Lee ventures that comic characters, like the Human Gargoyles, wouldn't work in the context of films as there was no way (at the time) to depict them realistically. There was also a plug for future Cerebus writer/artist Dave Sim's fanzine *Now and Then Times*. A back cover ad touts Skywald's Edgar Allan Poe adaptations. The monster in the story "Greed" is identical to the monster depicted on the cover for #18. The best story here is Hewetson's delightful "The Old Vampire Lady" while the best art would be Ricardo Villamonte's work on the *Monster, Monster* segment and "Greed."

17. cover: Salvador Faba (March 1974)

(1) The Death Pit [Al Hewetson/Domingo Gomez, frontis] 1p; (2) The Black Sculpture of the Pharaohs [Al Hewetson/Ricardo Villamonte] 7p; (3) Horror Preview Contest [Ricardo Villamonte, a fill in the word balloon contest section] 1p; (4) Slither-Slime Previews for '74 [Al Hewetson/various, text article] 2p;

(5) This Is Your Life, Sam Hammer, This Is Your Death! [Al Hewetson/Jose Cardona] 7p; (6) This Is the Vault of the Living Dead! [Al Hewetson/Maro Nava, story credited to Harvey Lazarus] 8p; (7) These Are the Things That Are Dead [Al Hewetson/Felipe Dela Rosa, story credited to Howie Anderson] 8p; (8) The Crime in Satan's Crypt! [Ed Fedory/Antonio Borrell] 8p; (9) The Lunatic Class of '64 [Jane Lynch/Emilio Bernardo] 4p; (10) The Narrative of Skut [Al Hewetson/Luis Collado] 7p; (11) Monster, Monster, Heed Death's Call [Augustine Funnell/Ricardo Villamonte] 8p.

Notes: A Horror Preview Contest segment appeared. "Horror Previews for '74" featured a montage of panels from upcoming stories. Jane Lynch, writer of "The Lunatic Class of '64," was the wife of underground cartoonist Jay Lynch. The inside back cover proclaims an imminent return of the Heap, although the announcement proved overly optimistic. The best art again was Villamonte's, on both "The Black Sculpture of the Pharaohs" and the *Monster, Monster* segments. Good work also appeared from Maro Nava and Felipe Dela Rosa. Best story was Hewetson's "The Black Sculpture of the Pharoahs," although Ed Fedory, Gus Funnell and Jane Lynch's stories were also good.

18. cover: Xavier Villanova (May 1974)

(1) The Macabre [Al Hewetson/Ricardo Villamonte] 10p; (2) The Archaic Horror Mailbag: Jose Maria Cardona profile [Al Hewetson/Jesus Suso Rego, text article] 1p; (3) Lady Satan Sketch [Pablo Marcos, a pin-up] 1p; (4) The Rats [Al Hewetson/Felipe Dela Rosa] 10p; (5) The Saga of the Victims Promo [Al Hewetson/Jesus Suso Rego] 1p; (6) A Descent into the

Xavier Villanova did a lot of interior artwork for Skywald. This cover effort, showing rats devouring a man's face, was done in the style of a jigsaw puzzle.

Maelstrom [Al Hewetson/Cesar Lopez, from the story by Edgar Allan Poe] 10p; (7) Horror Preview Contest [Ricardo Villamonte, a fill-in-the-word-balloon contest] 1p; (8) Now ... Another Maniac! [Al Hewetson/Maelo Cintron, story credited to Howie Anderson] 6p; (9) Uncle Ed's Grave [Al Hewetson/Alphonso Font, story credited to Howie Anderson] 7p; (10) Horror Books-Music-Movies [Ed Fedory, Augustine Funnell and Al Hewetson, text article] 2p; (11) The Boutique Macabre [Al Hewetson/Antonio Borrell, story credited to Edward Farthing] 3p; (12) Monster, Monster, Watch Them Die [Augustine Funnell/Ricardo Villamonte] 8p.

Notes: Villanova's cover of a man being attacked by rats was done in the form of a puzzle and was one of *Psycho*'s most striking (and gruesome) covers. Hewetson's Poe adaptations were often some of the best work he did and this issue's effort on "A Descent into the Maelstrom" was no exception, easily having the best story and art here. "The Boutique Macabre" was originally intended for the *Town of Evil* special that was to have run in the never-published *Nightmare* #24. A photo of Jose Cardona appears on the letters page. Lady Satan's new costume is previewed in a pencil sketch by Pablo Marcos.

19. cover: Sebastia Boada (July 1974)

(1) Old Horrors [Al Hewetson/Domingo Gomez, frontis] 1p; (2) Lady Satan: The Son of Lord Lucifer [Al Hewetson/Pablo Marcos] 9p; (3) Like a Bat Outta Hell [Al Hewetson/Ricardo Villamonte, story credited to Edward Farthing] 7p; (4) The Yeti [Al Hewetson/Alphonso Font, story credited to Howie Anderson] 7p; (5) Ligeia [Al Hewetson/Jesus Duran, from the story by Edgar Allan Poe] 5p; (6) Horror-Mood Artist of the Month: Ricardo Villamonte [Al Hewetson/ Ricardo Villamonte, text article] 2p; (7) Psychotic Psycho Mailbag: Luis Collado profile [Al Hewetson/Jesus Suso Rego, text article, art from *The Saga of the Victims*] 2p; (8) The Revenge of Dracula: Hell Is on Earth! [Al Hewetson/Emilio Bernardo] 9p; (9) Horror Preview Contest [Jose Martin Sauri] 1p; (10) Scenes from the Great Classic Horror Movies [Al Hewetson/photos and art from various stories] 11p; (11) Monster, Monster: And in This Land ... A Monster [Augustine Funnell/Ricardo Villamonte] 8p.

Notes: Lady Satan's series moved over from *Scream* for its last Skywald appearance. This character, as well as Skywald's version of *The Heap*, was revived in 2003 in John Gallagher's *Bedlam* fanzine from Great Britain. The letters page featured a photo of Luis Collado and a letter from Christopher Lee reacting favorably to the interview with him that appeared in *Nightmare* #17. Best story and art are from the *Lady Satan* segment.

20. cover: Savador Faba (August 1974)

(1) Nosferatu ad [Zesar Lopez, frontis] 1p; (2) The Dead and the Superdead [Al Hewetson/Jose Cardona] 15p; (3) The Horror Film Vault [Al Hewetson, text article with photos] 3p; (4) ad for 1974 Nightmare yearbook [Jose Martin Sauri] 1p; (5) The Burial Vault of Primal Eld!!! [Ed Fedory/Antonio Borrell] 8p; (6) Horror-Mood Artist of the Month: Maelo Cintron [Al Hewetson/Maelo Cintron, text article] 2p; (7) The

This rebooted version of Lady Satan from *Psycho* #19 was illustrated by Pablo Marcos and written by Al Hewetson. It was probably her best Skywald appearance.

Masque of the Red Death [Al Hewetson/Ricardo Villamonte, from the story by Edgar Allan Poe] 9p; (8) Tomorrow the Snowman Will Kill You! [Augustine Funnell/Luis Collado] 5p; (9) Requiem for a Human Being [Al Hewetson/Antonio Borrell, story credited to Howie Anderson] 8p; (10) The Human Gargoyles, part 7: The Freaks [Al Hewetson/Maelo Cintron] 9p; (11) ad for 1974 Nightmare yearbook [?, on the inside cover] 1p; (12) ad for Tomb of Horror [?, on the back cover, ad for a never-published magazine] 1p.

Notes: The letters page revealed that subscriptions for Skywald magazines were no longer currently available, reflecting Skywald's uncertain future as Marvel B&W magazines and Marvel's distributor ate up valuable shelf space on the magazine stands. Al Hewetson and Maelo Cintron appeared incognito in the *Human Gargoyles* story, which moved to *Psycho* for this issue only, probably due to the concurrent *Nightmare* issue being a reprint special. Best story was Hewetson's superb adaptation of Poe's "The Masque of the Red Death" while best art honors went to both Villamonte for that story and Cintron for the *Human Gargoyles* segment. "The Burial Vault of Primal Eld!!!" was another good story by Ed Fedory.

21. cover: Prieto Muriana (October 1974)

(1) The Fiend of Changsha! [Al Hewetson/Sanho Kim] 8p; (2) Psychotic Psycho Mailbag [Al Hewetson/Zesar Lopez, letters page and text article] 2p; (3) The Facts in the Case of M. Valdemar [Al Hewetson/Jose Cardona, from the story by Edgar Allan Poe] 7pp; (4) 1974 Nightmare yearbook ad [Jose Martin Sauri] 1p; (5) The Gloomb Bomb [Jack Katz] 12p; (6) The Cadaver [Al Hewetson/Gene Day, text story] 2p; (7) The Ghost of the Corpse [Al Hewetson/Luis Collado, story credited to Edward Farthing] 8p; (8) Maxwell's Blood Hammer [Al Hewetson/Jose Cardona, story credited to Joe Dentyn] 10p; (9) The Claws of Death! [Ed Fedory/Folsengo Cabrerizo] 8p; (10) Scream #9 ad [Salvador Faba, B&W reproduction of cover, on the inside back cover] 1p.

Notes: Hewetson presents a new reader survey, entitled "Behemoth Bunch of Questions." "The Gloomb Bomb" was done in 1971 and originally intended for the aborted *Science Fiction Odyssey* #1. "The Fiend of Changsha!" had a request for

readers to write in if they'd like another episode. Evidently the response was positive as it would return in the final issue of *Psycho*. Best story here was Ed Fedory's "The Claws of Death" while the best art honors go to Sanho Kim's "The Fiend of Changsha!." "Maxwell's Bloody Hammer" was clearly a takeoff on the Beatles' song "Maxwell's Silver Hammer." There's something about the title "The Ghost of the Corpse" that bothers me. What other kind of ghost is there?

22. cover: Prieto Muriana (November 1974)

(1) The Saga of the Frankenstein Monster: Die, Frankenstein's Monster! [Al Hewetson/Cesar Lopez] 10p; (2) Psychotic Psycho editorial page [Al Hewetson/Virgil Finley; H. P. Lovecraft and Zesar Lopez, text article with spot illustrations] 2p; (3) Revolution! [Tom Sutton/Tom Sutton and Dan Adkins, reprinted from *Psycho* #2 (March 1971)] 8p; (4) The Vow! [Pat Boyette, reprinted from *Psycho* #6 (May 1972)] 7p; (5) Birth Announcement! [Al Hewetson/Ramon Torrents, reprinted from *Psycho* 1972 annual (October 1972)] 4p; (6) Phantom of the Rock Era [Chuck McNaughton/Ralph Reese, reprinted from *Nightmare* #4 (June 1971)] 8p; (7) The Midnight Slasher [Doug Moench/Pablo Marcos, reprinted from *Psycho* #6 (May 1972)] 6p; (8) Within the Torture Chamber [Kevin Pagen/Doug Wildey, reprinted from *Nightmare* #5 (August 1971)] 8p; (9) Vault of a Vampire [Al Hewetson/Serg Moren, reprinted from *Nightmare* #3 (April 1971)] 8p; (10) Nightmare Pin-Up [Gene Day, on the back cover] 1p.

Notes: The 1974 *Psycho* fall special is also *Psycho* #22, although it doesn't say so anywhere in the issue itself. There was also a 1974 *Psycho* yearbook that came out the same month, further confusing the matter. "The Saga of the Frankenstein Monster" is not a continuation of Skywald's earlier *Frankenstein, Book II* (although the writer/artist team are the same people who concluded that series) but rather a continuation of Hewetson's personal take on the character, which had begun in *Scream* #7. The letters'/editorial page was all about H. P. Lovecraft and the *Shoggoth* series. It contained a Virgil Finley portrait of Lovecraft, a concept sketch of Cthulhu by HPL himself, a checklist of Skywald's *Shoggoth* stories, and an offer for a *Shoggoth* crusade certificate, signed by Hewetson and others, making the reader a part of Skywald's crusade against the

This *Human Gargoyles* page from *Psycho* #20, features doppelgangers of both writer Al Hewetson (the bearded reporter) and artist Maelo Cintron (the man with glasses).

Shoggoths (playing off the fact that Hewetson and other Skywald creators had been featured as protagonists in the earlier Shoggoth stories).

23. cover: Sebastia Boada (January 1975)

(1) People of the Dark [Robert E. Howard/Gene Day, frontis] 1p; (2) The Phantom of the Dead: Midnight in Wax [Al Hewetson/Jose Martin Sauri] 10p; (3) Psycho Mailbag: Gene Day/Augustine Funnell profiles [letters page, text article] 2p; (4) The Curse of the Snake Goddess [Ed Fedory/Jose Cardona] 7p; (5) Portfolio of the Master Criminal, The Vampire [Gene Day, Ricardo Villamonte, Ferran Sostres, Zesar Lopez, Paul Puigagut, Jesus Duran, Pablo Marcos text article with photos — with the exception of Day's work, all art is from previous stories] 3p; (6) A Garden of Hellish Delight [Al Hewetson/Cesar Lopez, story credited to Edward Farthing] 4p; (7) Killerclown [Augustine Funnell/Gene Day, text story] 2p; (8) The Werevampirewolf [Al Hewetson/Jose Cardona, story credited to Jose Cardona] 5p; (9) The Man of the Crowd [Al Hewetson/Ferran Sostres, from the story by Edgar Allan Poe] 5p; (10) The 300th Birth Day Party! [Al Hewetson/Ramon Torrents, reprinted from *Nightmare* #9 (October 1972)] 5p; (11) The Mummy Khafre, part 2: The Murderess [Al Hewetson/Cesar Lopez] 10p; (12) Pin-Up [Maelo Cintron, on the inside back cover] 1p; (13) Zombie Pin-Up [Gene Day, on the back cover] 1p.

Notes: Gene Day's frontis work consisted of a brief bit of prose from a horror writer (in this case, Robert E. Howard) and a full-page illustration for that bit. At least 12 of these pages were completed but only two saw print. A "Horror-Mood Character Vote" in which readers could vote on their favorite continuing character was included in the letters page/editorial section. "The Little Horror-Mood Shop of Horrors"— a 5-page catalog of novelty items similar to Warren's Captain Company — began appearing this issue. "The Werevampirewolf" story was a wordless tale. Best story was Fedory's "The Curse of the Snake Goddess." Best art was Jose Martin Sauri's "Midnight in Wax." Otherwise, this issue is not too good.

24. cover: Sebastia Boada/frontis: Gene Day (March 1975)

(1) A Fragment in the Life of Dracula: Within the Walls of Castle Dracula! [Al Hewetson/Jose Martin Sauri, story credited to Howie Anderson] 10p; (2) Monster, Monster, chapter 7: Visions of Bloody Death [Augustine Funnell/Paul Puigagut] 8p; (3) Daughter of Darkness [Joan Cintron/Maelo Cintron] 6p; (4) The Book of the Dead! [Al Hewetson/Domingo Gomez, story credited to Hugh Lasky] 2p; (5) From Hell to Eternity! [Ed Fedory/Jose Cardona, art credited to Andy Crandon] 8p; (6) The Cry of the White Wolf [Dave Sim/Luis Collado, art credited to Stan Connerty] 6p; (7) Psycho Mailbag [letters page/editorial, text article] 2p; (8) ...If I Should Die Before I Wake... [Al Hewetson/Jose Cardona, story credited to Victor Buckley, art credited to Andy Crandon] 5p; (9) The Fiend of Changsha, part 2: Dead by Day, Fiend by Night [Al Hewetson/Sanho Kim, this serial was never finished] 8p; (10) Werewolf ad [Jose Martin Sauri, on the inside back cover, same ad appears in *Nightmare* #23, advertising an upcoming original graphic novel, which was never published] 1p; (11) Psycho next issue ad [Gene Day; on back cover, same art as *Nightmare* #23's frontispiece] 1p.

Notes: Final issue, and the last Skywald magazine released. Now $1.00 for 64 pages. The cover stated this was the 1975 *Psycho* winter special. Only the title page identified it as #24. Dave Sim made his professional debut with the story of "The Cry of the White Wolf," which featured a photo of Sim on the splash page, along with the note that Skywald was "pleased to introduce demented Dave Sim for the first time in the comic medium." The letters page mentioned Basil Wolverton's *Barflyze* book, previewed a pencil sketch for a never-published cover by Sebastia Boada and mentioned that upcoming stories (never published, naturally) would be written by former EC writer Carl Wessler and former Warren editor/writer J. R. Cochran. Cochran's story eventually appeared in one of Bruce Hamilton's trio of B&W horror titles in 1990–1991. Augustine Funnell's *Monster Monster* serial also had one more segment that went unpublished. "The Fiend of Changsha!" returned with an extremely good segment that was the best of this issue. It's a pity that we'll never know how it was to end. Best art was shared by Sanho Kim, Maelo Cintron and Jose Martin Sauri. A cover was produced for the never published 25th issue, cover-dated May 1975, which stated that another episode of "The Fiend of Changsha!" and seven more stories would have appeared there.

Scream

1. cover: Vicentes Segrelles (August 1973)

(1) Prologue to a Scream [Al Hewetson/Zesar Lopez, text article, frontis] 1p; (2) Welcome to Scream #1 [Al Hewetson, text article with photos] 1p; (3) I, Slime [Al Hewetson/Jose Gual] 6p; (4) Weird Count, Black Vampire Bats and Lunatic Horrors [Al Hewetson/Felipe Dela Rosa] 5p; (5) The Sloggoths: This Archaic Breeding Ground... [Al Hewetson/Jose Gual] 10p; (6) ...Hickory Dickory Dock... [Al Hewetson/Ferran Sostres] 10p; (7) Nosferatu: Where Lunatics Live [Al Hewetson/Zesar Lopez] 10p; (8) The Skeleton in the Desert [Al Hewetson/Maelo Cintron, text article] 2p; (9) The Tale of the Perfect Crime [Al Hewetson/Fernando Rubio] 6p; (10) The Comics Macabre [Al Hewetson/Maelo Cintron] 6p; (11) The Strange Painting of Jay Crumb [Al Hewetson/Felipe Dela Rosa] 5p; (12) Scream [Al Hewetson/Zesar Lopez, on the back cover] 1p.

Notes: Publisher: Israel and Herschel Waldman. Editor: Al Hewetson. It was $0.75 for 64 pages. Most stories from #1–4 do not list a writer but Hewetson told me before his death that he wrote all of them. According to Hewetson's introduction, *Scream* #1 was put together in response to readers' opinions as expressed in the "Bunch of Questions" survey and was phase three of the Horror-Mood. The best story and art was for the Hewetson/Cintron story "The Comics Macabre," which featured lead characters based on *Seduction of the Innocent* author Fredric Wertham and then Comics Code Authority president Leonard Darvin as well as Al Hewetson, Herschel Waldman, Maelo Cintron, Jane Lynch and possibly other Skywald staffers and artists. In the story the dopplegangers of Darvin and Wertham visit the Skywald offices to complain about the gruesome horror comics being published by the company, get into an argument and kill Hewetson whereupon tiny versions of Skywald's Heap, Frankenstein's Monster and others come off the comic pages lying about in the Skywald offices and kill Wertham and Darvin! Hewetson sent a copy of the story to Wertham, with whom he corresponded for a number of years but, according to Hewetson, Wertham claimed not to get the point. That would not be the first time Wertham claimed to misunderstand what others saw as obvious. "The Strange Painting of Jay Crumb" was a spoof/takeoff on underground cartoonists Jay Lynch and Robert Crumb. This is a pretty good first issue.

2. cover: Jose Miralles (October 1973)

(1) Editorial [Al Hewetson/Ricardo Villamonte, text article] 1p; (2) Lady Satan: The Macabre Beginning [Al Hewetson/Ricardo Villamonte] 9p; (3) I Was a Vampire for Hire [Al Hewetson/Felipe Dela Rosa] 10p; (4) Gothic Fairy Tales: The Thing in the Black Dress [Al Hewetson/Jesus Suso Rego] 5p; (5) The Pit and the Pendulum [Al Hewetson/Ricardo Villamonte, from the story by Edgar Allan Poe] 6p; (6) The Phantom of the Opera [Al Hewetson/Maro Nava] 2p; (7) The Vampire Hunters [Al Hewetson/Domingo Gomez] 1p; (8) The Vampire Letters [Al Hewetson/Emilo Bernardo] 8p; (9) The Thing That Left No Fingerprints [Al Hewetson/Ferran Sostres] 1p; (10) The Fetid Belle of the Mississippi [Al Hewetson/Jesus Suso Rego] 8p; (11) Mailbag: Jesus Suso Rego profile [Al Hewetson/Jesus Suso Rego, text article] 2p; (12) Nosferatu: The Name Is Sinner Cane ... And the Name Means Evil! [Al Hewetson/Zesar Lopez] 9p; (13) A Gothic Fairy Tale: A Tale of 2 Macabre Snakes [Al Hewetson/Felipe Dela Rosa, on the back cover] 1p.

Notes: Lady Satan was a rare (for the 1970s) female African-American horror character that was generally well written and illustrated. Best story here was Hewetson's "The Thing in the Black Dress" while the best artwork came from Jesus Suso Rego, although the stories and art are generally quite good throughout this issue.

3. cover: Xavier Villanova/frontis: Jesus Duran (December 1973), wraparound cover

(1) The Phantom of the Opera [Al Hewetson/Jesus Duran, from the novel by Gaston Leroux] 18p; (2) Lunatic Letters from the Macabre Scream Mailbag/Editorial [Al Hewetson, text article with photos] 2p; (3) Lady Satan, part 2: What Is Evil and What Is Not [Al Hewetson/Ricardo Villamonte] 9p; (4) The Fall of the House of Usher [Al Hewetson/Maro Nava, from the story by Edgar Allan Poe] 12p; (5) Messers. Crypts and Graves: Undertakers [Al Hewetson/Ruben Sosa, story credited to Joe Dentyn] 8p; Nosferatu: The Tale of Another [Al Hewetson/Zesar Lopez] 10p; (7) Nightmare ad [Ricardo Villamonte, on the inside back cover] 1p.

Notes: The issue number doesn't appear until page 22. Dave Sim sends in a letter. The letters page also featured a bio and photo of Domingo Gomez. Hewetson and Nava's adaptation of "The Fall of the House of Usher" featured the best story and art but the "Phantom of the Opera" adaptation was also very good as was the latest installment of Lady Satan.

4. cover: Xavier Villanova (February 1974) [Wraparound cover.]

(1) Lady Satan, part 3: Satan Wants a Child [Al Hewetson/ Ricardo Villamonte, story credited to Howie Anderson] 9p; (2) Edgar Allan Poe in the Movies [Al Hewetson, text article with photos] 4p; (4) The Oblong Box [Al Hewetson/Maro Nava, from the story by Edgar Allan Poe] 7p; (4) Archaic Scream Announcements: Ed Fedory profile/Comics Opinion [Al Hewetson and Dave Sim/Jose Gual and Jack Davis, text article with photo and spot illustrations] 2p; (5) The Skull of the Ghoul [Al Hewetson/ Ferran Sostres] 10p; (6) The Legend of the Cannibal Were-Wolf [Ed Fedory/Ricardo Villamonte] 8p; (7) The Lunatic Mummy [Al Hewetson/Cesar Lopez] 10p; (8) The Vampire Kingdom [Al Hewetson/Domingo Lopez] 2p; (9) Nosferatu: When the Dusk Falls ... So Does Death... [Al Hewetson/Zesar Lopez] 9p.

Notes: An ad appeared for Russ Cochran's EC color reprints. The letters page had a photo of Ed Fedory. *Lady Satan* was continued in *Psycho* #19. *Lady Satan* also had the best story and art in this issue, although I also quite liked the Hewetson/Sostres's tale, "The Skull of the Ghoul."

5. cover and back cover: Fernando Fernandez (April 1974)

(1) The Autobiography of a Vampire, Chapter 2 [Al Hewetson/Ricardo Villamonte] 10p; (2) The Macabre Scream Mailbag/The Comics Opinion

A SKYWALD HORROR-MOOD PUBLICATION

SCREAM

ZOMBIE— RISE OUT OF THY TOMB AND DIE AGAIN

75¢
47821
NO. 5
APRIL
1974
T.M.

This cover art from *Scream* #5 shows why Skywald's 1973–1975 horror-mood approach to covers couldn't be mistaken for a Warren effort from the same time period, even if the actual artist, Fernando Fernandez, was more familiar as a *Vampirella* artist.

[Augustine Funnell, text article] 2p; (3) Darkkos Manse: Get Up and Die Again [Al Hewetson/Alphonso Font, story credited to Howie Anderson] 8p; (4) The Cask of Amontillado [Al Hewetson/Maro Nava, from the story by Edgar Allan Poe] 7p; (5) The Black Orchids and the Tale of Anne [Al Hewetson/Jose Cardona, story credited to Stuart Williams] 7p; (6) The Conqueror Worm and the Haunted Palace [Al Hewetson/Domingo Gomez, from the poems by Edgar Allan Poe] 2p; (7) Are You Dead Yet? [Al Hewetson/Ricardo Villamonte] 10p; (8) Shift: Vampire [Augustine Funnell/Emilo Bernardo] 6p; (9) The Picture of Dorian Gray [Al Hewetson/Zesar Lopez, from the novel by Oscar Wilde] 9p.

Notes: The back cover featured a pen and ink version of the cover, used as an ad for the proposed *Tomb of Horror* title. Pages 4 and 5 of the story "Are You Dead Yet?" are out of order. "The Autobiography of a Vampire" was continued from *Nightmare* #17. I didn't really like much of anything about this issue. It's not a terrible issue, just not too interesting.

6. cover: Salvador Faba (June 1974)

(1) The Vampire of the Opera [Al Hewetson/Ricardo Villamonte] 15p; (2) Ms. Found in a Bottle [Al Hewetson/Alphonso Font, from the story by Edgar Allan Poe] 6p; (3) Frankenstein 2073: The Death of the Monster [Al Hewetson/Cesar Lopez, story credited to Henry Bergman] 9p; (4) The Archaic Horror Mailbag/Editorial: Zesar Lopez profile [Al Hewetson, text article with photo] 2p; (4) Nosferatu: ...and the Gutters Ran with Blood... [Al Hewetson/Zesar Lopez] 9p; (6) The Saga of the Victims: What Is Horror? No, Who Is Horror? [Al Hewetson/Jesus Suso Rego] 20p; (7) Psycho ad [Sebastia Boada, on the inside back cover, B&W repo of #19's cover] 1p.

Notes: "Frankenstein 2073" featured the death of Frankenstein's Monster and the end of the *Frankenstein, Book II* serial that had begun in *Psycho* #3 with Tom Sutton as writer and penciller and was continued from *Nightmare* #13. The letters page featured Zesar Lopez's bio and photo. The scarred man on the cover was modeled on actor Peter Cushing. The big news this issue was the debut of what may be considered to be one of the first modern graphic novels. Hewetson and Suso's *The Saga of the Victims* featured two college-aged girls, one white and one black, who ventured into the basement of their school only to discover a nightmare world of pain, madness and degradation. Sounds like a BDSM novel but it wasn't. For five giddy episodes the girls went on a nightmarish roller-coaster ride through virtually every horror cliché one could imagine. Hewetson stated that his goal was to write a horror story that nobody could figure out the ending to ahead of time. Then *Scream* was cancelled with a single episode left unpublished and fans spent years wondering how Hewetson had planned (or even if he could have planned) to tie it all up. Finally, in the spring of 2004, British small press publisher John Gal-

lagher of Chimera Arts, with the permission of the late Al Hewetson and artist Jesus Suso Rego, published the entire saga, including the previously unpublished 17-page final chapter (with Gallagher himself filling in a few missing panels). Lo and behold, Hewetson and Suso had come up with an ending that actually worked ... and fulfilled Hewetson's desire to lead the reader down unfamiliar paths. If you're interested, both Headpress in Great Britain (also the publisher of Al Hewetson's *The Illustrated History of the Skywald Horror-Mood*) and Bud Plant in the USA carry the book, which is damned good. (Pun intended.)

7. cover: Manuel Brea Rodriguez (July 1974)

(1) Horror Fragments: The Headless Horseman [Al Hewetson/Ferran Sostres, frontis] 1p; (2) The Man with No Face [Al Hewetson/Jose Cardona, story credited to Howie Anderson] 10p; (3) The Archaic Horror Mailbag/editorial [Al Hewetson/Jose Martin Sauri, text article] 1p; (4) Nosferatu: Satan's Third Reich [Al Hewetson/Zesar Lopez] 9p; (5) Berenice [Al Hewetson/Ricardo Villamonte, from the story by Edgar Allan Poe] 7p; (6) Horror-Mood Artist of the Month: Zesar Lopez [Al Hewetson/Zesar Lopez, text article] 2p; (7) The Saga of the Frankenstein Monster: The Descent into Hell! [Al Hewetson/Cesar Lopez] 9p; (8) Tomb of Horror ad [Zesar Lopez, ad for never-published magazine] 1p; (9) The Saga of the Victims: I Am Horror [Al Hewetson/Jesus Suso Rego] 20p.

Notes: The "Saga of the Frankenstein Monster" was not a continuation of the *Frankenstein, Book II* serial that concluded in the previous issue but Hewetson's own interpretation of the Frankenstein saga. It continued in the *Psycho* 1974 fall special. Best story and art are from *The Saga of the Victims*.

8. cover: Salvador Faba (August 1974)

(1) Psycho 1974 yearbook ad [Steve Hickman, frontis, art reprinted from *Psycho* #2 (March 1971)] 1p; (2) The Tell-Tale Heart [Al Hewetson/Ricardo Villamonte, from the story by Edgar Allan Poe] 8p; (3) The Archaic Horror Mailbag/Augustine Funnell profile [Al Hewetson, text article] 2p; (4) Nosferatu: My Prison in Hell [Al Hewetson/Zesar Lopez, art miscredited to Cesar Lopez] 9p; (5) The Slither-Slime Man Rises Again [Al Hewetson/Jose Cardona, story credited to Howie Anderson] 8p; (6) Jesus

Manuel Brea Rodriguez, a Spanish artist, did a number of distinctive covers for Skywald. This one was for *Scream* #7.

Suso Rego: Horror-Mood Artist of the Month [Al Hewetson/Jesus Suso Rego, text article] 2p; (7) The Mechanical Cannibals [Rich Buckler/ Rich Buckler and Chic Stone, from the story "From Fanaticism or for Reward" by Harry Harrison] 11p; (8) The Saga of the Victims: I ... Am Torment [Al Hewetson/Jesus Suso Rego] 20p; (9) Nightmare ad [Sebastia Boada, on the inside back cover, B&W reproduction of #20's cover] 1p.

Notes: The letters page offered readers a chance to join the Shoggoth Crusade (see the *Psycho* 1974 fall special). "The Mechanical Cannibals" was originally done in 1971 and had been intended to appear as a 10 page story for the aborted *Science Fiction Odyssey* #1. It was expanded to 11 pages by inserting a pin-up page

taken from what was intended to be the frontispiece. The adapted author, Harry Harrison, was one of the original EC horror artists. Frankly, any issue the *Saga of the Victims* appeared in tended to be dominated in both story and art by that chapter and this issue was no exception.

9. cover: Salvador Faba (September 1974)

(1) Psycho ad for The Fiend of Changsha! [Sanho Kim, frontis] 1p; (2) Down to Hades ... to Die! [Augustine Funnell/Paul Puigagut] 7p; (3) The Archaic Scream Mailbag/Editorial [Al Hewetson, text article] 2p; (4) Metzengerstein [Al Hewetson/Luis Collado, from the story by Edgar Allan Poe] 6p; (5) Nosferatu: Who Killed the Shark? [Al Hewetson/Zesar Lopez] 10p; (6) Horror-Mood Artist of the Month: Pablo Marcos [Al Hewetson/ Pablo Marcos, text article] 2p; (7) The Asylum [Al Hewetson/John Agras, story credited to Howie Anderson] 5p; (8) Gothic Fairy Tales: I Never Heard of a Ghost Actually Killing Anyone! [Al Hewetson/Antonio Borrell] 6p; (9) The Saga of the Victims: I Am Treachery ... I Am Horror [Al Hewetson/Jesus Suso Rego] 20p; (10) Nightmare ad [Gene Day, on the back cover] 1p.

Notes: Hewetson" adaptation of Poe's "Mezengerstein" was the best story this issue while Suso's latest chapter of *The Saga of the Victims* continued to offer the best artwork. "Down to Hades ... to Die!" by Gus Funnell was also a good story.

10. cover: Sebastia Boada (October 1974)

(1) The Narrative of Arthur Gordon Pym of Nantucket preview [Cesar Lopez, frontis] 1p; (2) My Flesh Crawls [Al Hewetson/Jose Martin Sauri] 10p; (3) The Archaic Scream Mailbag/editorial [Al Hewetson, text article] 2p; (4) A

Fragment in the Life of Dracula: Creatures in the Night [Al Hewetson/Jose Cardona] 9p; (5) The Murders in the Rue Morgue [Al Hewetson/Cesar Lopez, from the story by Edgar Allan Poe] 12p; (6) The Art of Killing Human Monsters [Al Hewetson, text article] 3p; (7) The Stranger Is the Vampire [Al Hewetson/Paul Pueyo, story is miscredited to Paul Pueyo] 10p; (8) Tales Out of Hell, part 2: In His Master's Blood [Al Hewetson/Jesus Duran, story credited to Howie Anderson] 10p.

Notes: The frontispiece carries an ad for an upcoming 25-page Poe adaptation by Hewetson and artist Cesar Lopez. At least part of it was drawn, since a page is reproduced here (see also *The Horror-Mood Odyssey*) but if completed, it never saw print. *Tales out of Hell* was continued from *Nightmare* #19. *The Saga of the Victims* skipped an issue to allow Suso to catch up on his deadlines. Best story would be "The Stranger Is the Vampire" although it is hampered by lackluster art, while Jose Martin Sauri has the best art honors in "My Flesh Crawls."

11. cover: Ballestar (March 1975)

(1) Werewolf Illustrated novel ad [Jose Martin Sauri, frontis] 1p; (2) Nosferatu: I Kill to Live [Al Hewetson/Zesar Lopez] 10p; (3) Scream Mailbag and previews [Al Hewetson/Cesar Lopez and Paul Puigagut, text article and an ad for the never-published *Psycho* #25 which describes the intended ten linked stories about a single town snatched from hell planned for that issue] 2p; (4) You Can't Judge a Killer by the Corpse! [Augustine Funnell/Jose Cardona, art credited to Andy Crandon] 9p; (5) Who Are They? The Breeders! [Ed Fedory/Luis Collado] 7p; (6) The Exorcist Reviews [Ed Fedory, Augustine Funnell and Al Hewetson/Gene Day, text article with photos] 4p; (7) The Raven [Al Hewetson/Peter Cappiello, from the poem by Edgar Allan Poe, story credited to Peter Cappiello, while the art was credited to Denis Ford] 5p; (8) The Saga of the Victims: I Am a Proud Monstrosity [Al Hewetson/Jesus Suso Rego, the *Saga* story was finally concluded in 2004 and published as a graphic novel by England's John Gallagher for his Chimera Arts Books. See the notes for #6] 20p; (9) Psycho #25 ad [?, on the back cover] 1p.

Notes: Final issue. It was $1.00 for 64 pages. Cover announces this as the 1975 winter special. There was a six months' hiatus between #10 and #11. The title page lists the cover artist Ballestar's

first name as Ed but Hewetson confirmed that he made up that name because he was so tired of Spanish artists without surnames. He also changed Spanish names to Anglo-Saxon ones so it would appear that he had American artists working on the magazines. The editorial page explains why *The Heap* hadn't reappeared (see notes for *Nightmare* #20). The editorial page also mentions that *Psycho* #25 was to be a *Tales of Evil* special edition and that the *Monster, Monster* series would end with part 9. None of those stories saw print. "The Little Horror-Mood Shop of Horrors" — a five-page catalog of novelty items similar to Warren's Captain Company — appeared. The frontispiece advertises a never-published graphic novel by Hewetson and Martin Sauri.

Psycho 1972 Annual

1. cover: Pujolar (August 1972)

(1) Psycho's Supernatural Series: The Horned Goat of Satan [Al Hewetson/Pablo Marcos, frontis] 1p; (2) Lucifer Awaits You! [David Anthony Kraft/Xavier Villanova] 6p; (3) Burn, Baby, Burn [Len Brown/Carlos Garzon] 6p; (4) The Heap: What Hath Hell Wrought? [Al Hewetson/Pablo Marcos] 8p; (5) The Myth of Dracula [Al Hewetson/Ramon de la Fuente] 7p; (6) ...Blind Fate [Ed Fedory/Francisco Cueto] 7p; (7) The Cursing of Captain Skull [Gardner Fox/Steve Hickman] 10p; (8) The Furnace of Hell [Robert Kanigher/Amador Garcia] 12p; (9) Birth Announcement [Al Hewetson/Ramon Torrents] 4p; (10) Pin-Up [Pablo Marcos, on the back cover] 1p.

Notes: It was $0.75 for 64 pages. Editor: Al Hewetson. Skywald was unique among the B&W publishers in having summer specials or annuals that featured all new stories. Ramon de la Fuente was the brother of the much better known (in the States anyway) Spanish artist Victor de la Fuente. The best story here is Hewetson's "The Myth of Dracula" while Francisco Cueto provided the best art. Good work also appeared from Robert Kanigher, Steve Hickman, Ramon Torrents (his American debut), Carlos Garzon and Xavier Villanova.

Nightmare 1972 Special

1. cover: Fernando Fernandez (November 1972)

(1) The Truth Behind the Myth of the Bride of Dracula [Al Hewetson/Juez Xirinius, frontis] 1p; (2) The Strange Case of Dr. Jekyll and Mr. Hyde [Al Hewetson/Juez Xirinius, from the novel by Robert Louis Stevenson] 10p; (3) A Macabre Fact of Life: The Indian Rope Trick [Al Hewetson/Ricardo Villamonte] 2p; (4) Beauty Is Only Skin Deep [Doug Moench/Fred Carrillo] 9p; (5) Limb from Limb from Death [Al Hewetson/Pablo Marcos] 7p; (6) The Nightmare World: A Grave Beneath the Sea! [Al Hewetson/Bill Payne, from a dream by Joseph Elliott] 4p; (7) Alone [Bruce Jones] 12p; (8) And If A Fiend Should Come A-Callin' [Al Hewetson/Luis M. Roca] 6p; (9) The Day the Earth Will Die! [Al Hewetson/Ferran Sostres] 10p.

Notes: It cost $0.75 for 64 pages. Editor: Al Hewetson. Both my online checklist and the Headpress edition of *The Illustrated Horror-Mood* (which I provided credits for) originally credited this cover to Vincente Segrelles but Skywald fan James Fletcher pointed out that on a European horror magazine website, a more complete version of this cover is seen and there is a faint backward signature in the sunlight on the lower left side of the cover that reads Fernando. The signature is very small and hard to read when the cover is normal sized but is just visible when a scanned cover image is blown up on the computer screen. Thanks to jpegs, another mystery is solved! This new knowledge means the cover image was flipped or reversed during production for both the Euro and U.S. covers and that the true cover artist is Fernando Fernandez. This was the last squarebound issue of the Skywald line. This is a very good issue with strong stories throughout. Best story was Hewetson's "Limb from Limb from Death," which was possibly the goriest story that Skywald ever published. Best art belongs to Bruce Jones' "Alone," which also had a very good story. Other fine work appeared from Juez Xirinius, Ricardo Villamonte, Doug Moench, Luis Roca and Ferran Sostres.

The 1973 Nightmare Winter Special

1. cover: Ken Kelly (March 1973)

(1) Die Mummy! [Al Hewetson/Jesus Duran] 8p; (2) Nightmare Movie Review: Dr. Phibes Rises Again [Al Hewetson, text article with photos] 3p; (3) I Left My Heart in the Burial Pit, I Had No Choice [Al Hewetson/Jose Gual] 7p; (4) Beyond the Walls!!! [Ed Fedory/Xavier Villanova] 1p; (5) Mephisto's Brand [Ed Fedory/Jesus Suso Rego] 1p; (6) The Horror Tub [Al Hewetson/Fernando Rubio] 8p; (7) The Event in the Night? [Al Hewetson/Pablo Marcos] 7p; (8) Beware It ... Fear It ... It Screams! [Al Hewetson/Antonio Borrell] 9p; (9) The Night of the Mutant-Eaters [Al Hewetson/Dennis Fujitake] 8p; (10) The Last Witch! [Ed Fedory/Antonio Borrell] 1p; (11) Special Awards Page [Al Hewetson/Gahan Wilson, text article with spot illustrations] 2p; (12) Whether Man or Scarecrow [Al Hewetson/Felipe Dela Rosa] 7p.

Notes: It was $0.75 for 64 pages. Editor: Al Hewetson. The letters page featured a previously unpublished Gahan Wilson cartoon. Kelly's cover is quite good. Fine work appears here from Suso, Ed Fedory, Rubio and Pablo Marcos but the best story and art go to the Hewetson/Borrell psycho-sexual drama "Beware It ... Fear It ... It Screams!"

The 1974 Psycho Yearbook

1. cover: montage of *Psycho* covers #1, 3, 7, 8, 9 and 13/frontis: Paul Pueyo (April 1974)

(1) The Saga of the Frankenstein's Monster: The Brides of Frankenstein [Al Hewetson/Cesar Lopez] 9p; (2) Horror-Mood ad [Bill Everett, art reprinted from the prose story in *Nightmare* #1 (December 1970) 1p; (3) Psychotic Psycho Mailbag [letters page, tributes to Syd Shores and Bill Everett, text article] 1p; (4) Slime World [Chuck McNaughton/Ralph Reese, reprinted from *Nightmare* #5 (August 1971)] 10p; (5) The Man Who Stole Eternity [Gardner Fox/Bill Everett, reprinted from *Psycho* #3 (May 1971)] 10p; (6) Beware Small Evils! [Jack Katz and Frank Giacoia, reprinted from *Nightmare* #3 (April 1971)] 10p; (7) The Inner Man [Tom Sutton/Tom Sutton and Dan Adkins, reprinted from *Nightmare* #3 (April 1971)] 10p; (8) The Deadly Mark of the Beast! [Len Wein/Syd Shores and Tom Palmer, reprinted from *Nightmare* #1 (December 1970)] 8p.

Notes: It was $0.75 for 64 pages. Editor: Al Hewetson. With this issue, the Skywald annuals began to resemble the Warren annuals, becoming mostly reprint books with one new story. Good stories throughout, though.

The 1974 Nightmare Yearbook

1. cover: Vicente Segrelles plus previous covers including #3, 7, 11 and 13 (October 1974)

(1) Dracula: The God of the Dead [Al Hewetson/Jose Martin Sauri] 9p; (2) Dracula Is Alive (?) and Evil in This 1974 *Nightmare* Yearbook [Al Hewetson, text article] 2p; (3) A Rottin' Deal [Bruce Jones, reprinted from *Nightmare* #3 (April 1971)] 11p; (4) Let the Dreamer Beware [Jerry Siegal/Ralph Reese, reprinted from *Psycho* #5 (November 1971)] 7p; (5) Escape [Dennis Fujitake, reprinted from *Psycho* #4 (September 1971)] 2p; (6) Whence Stalked the Werewolf [Len Brown/Carlos Garzon, reprinted from *Nightmare* #5 (August 1971)] 6p; (7) Power of the Pen! [Doug Moench/Doug Wildey, reprinted from *Psycho* #5 (November 1971)] 11p; (8) Hag of the Blood Basket! [Al Hewetson/Tom Sutton, reprinted from *Nightmare* #4 (June 1971)] 16p; (9) *Psycho* #20 ad [Vicente Segrelles, on the inside back cover, B&W reproduction of cover] 1p; (10) *Scream* ad [Jesus Suso Rego, on the back cover] 1p.

Notes: It cost $0.75 for 64 pages. Editor: Al Hewetson. Another good reprint collection, with the sole new story also being quite a good little story.

The Contents of the Never-Published Science Fiction Odyssey

1. cover: Jeff Jones/frontis: Rich Buckler (unpublished — intended for September 1971, Jones' cover appeared as the cover to *Psycho* #12)

(1) Introduction [Sol Brodsky?, text article] 1p; (2) From Fanaticism or for Reward [Rich Buckler/Rich Buckler and Chic Stone, from the story by Harry Harrison, published in *Scream* #7 as "The Mechanical Cannibals"] 10p; (3) All the Myriad Ways [Jeff Jones, from the story by Larry Niven, published in *Psycho* #9 as "All the Ways and Means to Die"] 6p; (4) The Swordsman of Sarn [Gardner Fox/Jack Katz and Vince Colletta, published in *Psycho* #12] 12p; (5) Author's Space [bios of Terry Carr, Gardner Fox, Harry Harrison, Larry Niven and Don Thompson, text article] 2p; (6) City of Yesterday [Rich Buckler and Chuck McNaughton/Michael Kaluta, from the story by Terry Carr, published in *Psycho* #13 as "The Horror Within and Without"] 8p; (7) The Weapon Within Us [Jack Katz/Jack Katz and Jack Abel, published in *Psy-*

cho #21 as "The Gloomb Bomb"] 12p; (8) The New Science [Don Thompson/Berni Wrightson, text article, art was published as spot illustrations for the text story "The Thing in the Alley" and for a movie review of *Frogs*] 2p; (9) Starchild [Bruce Jones] 6p.

Notes: Story listings and order came from Al Hewetson before his death. Skywald's famous aborted magazine would have been the first adult SF comic since EC's *Incredible Science Fiction* in 1956, but in the wake of the color line's collapse and the Waldmans' belief that SF didn't sell, the magazine was withdrawn, after film had been shot of the pages and just before delivery to the printers. Publisher: Israel Waldman and Sol Brodsky. Editors: Rich Buckler, Chuck McNaughton and Sol Brodsky. From the first issue's intended contents, it would have been a pretty good magazine.

Related Magazines

The Horror-Mood Rap

1. cover (April 1973)

Seven-page in-house newsletter sent to Augustine Funnell, Ed Fedory, Jane Lynch and Maelo Cintron [Al Hewetson]

Notes: This in-house newsletter was limited in copies to the people it was sent and editor Hewetson to so this issue had only five copies. This series of newsletters is extremely rare and, to my knowledge, there is only one complete set still in existence.

2. cover (October 1973)

Twenty-four-page in-house newsletter sent to Augustine Funnell, Ed Fedory, Jane Lynch and Maelo Cintron [Al Hewetson]

3. cover (May 1974)

Fifty-nine-page in-house newsletter sent to Augustine Funnell, Ed Fedroy, Maelo Cintron, Sanho Kim and Gene Day [Al Hewetson]

The Horror-Mood Odyssey

1. cover: Maelo Cintron and Al Hewetson (? 1975), edited: Harry Kramer — never published

Notes: Intended publisher and editor: Harry Kramer. The cover would have featured *The Human Gargoyles*. This fanzine effort was finished and intended for publication in 1975. The contents were to include checklists for *Nightmare*, *Psycho* and *Scream*, articles on such topics as the Skywald team and various series, an previously unpublished six-page story entitled "Gulliver's Island" by Hewetson and Dennis Fujitake, several leftover covers, a large piece of art by Gene Day, at least some segments of the unpublished "Arthur Gordon Pym" Poe adaptation by Hewetson and Cesar Lopez and more. Canadian comic shop owner Kramer didn't have the money to go to print and, after his death in 2003, the intended contents were auctioned off on eBay. Much, although by no means all, of this material finally appeared in either *The Illustrated History of the Skywald Horror-Mood* or in this book.

Other Skywald Titles of Interest

In 1971 Skywald published *Hell-Rider*, a two-issue experiment in creating a pre–*Ghost Rider* motorcycle "hero," written by the man,

Gary Friedrich, who later had a hand in co-creating that Marvel character a year later. There was also the 1971 title *The Crime Machine*, a crime comics title that reprinted 1950s pre–Code tales. There's some nice early Joe Kubert tales reprinted there.

The Preferred Skywald Magazine Reading Order

As mentioned earlier, Skywald magazines are best read in order of publication. Here is a preferred reading list covering *Nightmare* (N), *Psycho* (P), *Nightmare* 1972 annual (N1972A), *Psycho* 1972 annual (P1972A), 1973 *Nightmare* winter special (1973NWS), *Scream* (S), 1974 *Nightmare* yearbook (1974NY) and 1974 *Psycho* yearbook (1974PY):

N1, P1, N2, P2, N3, P3, N4, N5, P4, P5, N6, P6, N7, P7, N8, P8, P1972A, N9, P9, N1972A, N10, P10, N11, P11, 1973NWS, N12, P12, N13, P13, N14, S1, P14, N15, S2, P15, N16, S3, P16, N17, S4, P17, N18, S5, P18, N19, S6, P19, S7, P20, N20, 1974NY, 1974PY, S8, N21, P21, S10, P22, N22, P23, N23, S11, P24.

Marvel's Black and White Horror Magazines Checklist

This checklist is intended to provide information on Marvel Comics black and white *horror* magazines from 1971 to 1983 only. Thus, the adventure oriented titles such as *The Savage Sword of Conan, Doc Savage, The Deadly Hands of Kung Fu, Planet of the Apes*, etc., are not included here. One-off issues of a regular series, such as *Savage Tales* #1 or various issues of *Marvel Preview Bizarre Adventures*, which were primarily horror, will be. In addition, science fiction magazines, which in the comics field have always displayed a large amount of horror, are also included in this checklist.

After Warren's success (as well as the success of the pre–Code reprint magazines from *Eerie* and Stanley Publications) on the newsstands, Marvel had made a tryout effort in the field with a *Spider-Man* black and white magazine in 1968. It had only limited, if that, success. A second attempt occurred with *Savage Tales* in 1971, with similar results. However, by 1973 it was clear that, while superheroes and adventure magazines were an unproven topic in black and white, horror was quite successful. Marvel launched four black and white horror magazines in 1973 as well as a prose horror digest. A fifth horror title was added in 1974. In addition to these horror titles, Marvel also released anywhere from two to three action adventure, humor, superhero and movie-related titles a year from 1973 through 1978 or so.

By launching so many titles in a short period, Marvel essentially flooded the marketplace in 1973–1975, the results of which can be read in the intros to both the Warren and Skywald sections.

Still, the horror magazines that Marvel produced were of generally high quality, with many of the best of the Marvel bullpen artists contributing as well as a healthy selection from the European, Filipino and South American contingent of artists from the so-called "Spanish Invasion" of the early to mid–1970s. There were strong stories from the likes of Steve Gerber, Roy Thomas, Marv Wolfman, Don McGregor, Stephen Perry and others as well as memorable art from artists such as Mike Ploog, Gene Colan, Michael Kaluta, Neal Adams, John Buscema, Pablo Marcos, Tom Sutton, Alex Nino, Steve Bissette and others, many of whom had also contributed to the Warren or Skywald magazines.

The sheer extent of what Marvel considered workable in the B&W field was also impressive. The sword and sorcery, action and science fiction titles were often quite impressive while the humor and superhero titles usually were decent, if not superior, entertainment. One noticeable difference between the Marvel and the Warren/Skywald camps was that Marvel's printing process was often inferior to that used by either Warren or Skywald. Marvel's process couldn't easily accommodate artwork done in pencil, for example, and ink and wash pages occasionally lost their sharpness in reproduction.

Marvel's horror work could also be seen as generally distinct from the Warren or Skywald brands. Marvel, which had built much of its company and reputation on the never-ending story serials of the superhero genre, had difficulty with the notion that horror stories not only needed an ending but, in particular, that horrific ending needed to stand out. Many of their horror titles were based on the continuing adventures of a particular character — Dracula in *Dracula Lives!*, Simon Garth in *Tales of the Zombie*, Moebius in *Vampire Tales*, the monster of Frankenstein in *Monsters Unleashed* and many more. Knowing that a character was intended to be ongoing meant nothing too horrible was going to happen to that character and often undercut any real tension in the storyline, no matter how good the writer and artist were.

To Marvel's credit, they tried to work around that obstacle. Many of Dracula's stories were set in historical times, rather than the present times being chronicled in his companion color comic *Tomb of Dracula*, and in those tales he was often a full-fledged monster. Don McGregor wrote some striking horror tales revolving around Moebius, even while the color comics' version of the character was mired in mediocre science fiction trappings. Zombie Simon Garth's saga actually had a satisfying ending although Marvel fully intended to revive him. Luckily his revival story was lost in the mail and his magazine was cancelled before the story was recovered (if it ever was).

There were one-off stories, both original and adapted, from the likes of Gerry Conway, Ralph Reese, Steve Gerber, Pablo Marcos, Tom Sutton, Tony Isabella, Esteban Maroto, Stephen Perry and Steve Bissette, among others, that were every bit as hard hitting and haunting as anything Warren or Skywald produced.

And that's another thing, Marvel had the financial resources, unlike Warren and Skywald, to regularly pay for and adapt contemporary copyrighted fiction. Works by Harlan Ellison, Larry Niven, August Derleth, H. P. Lovecraft, Robert E. Howard, Thomas M. Disch, Michael Moorcock and others were adapted for the first time into comic form, often with spectacular results.

Although Marvel's other B&W titles certainly deserve a book of their own, these horror offerings are well written and illustrated and well worth taking a look at, particularly if you can locate the original B&W magazines. While Marvel has done a decent job of reprinting their lead characters' stories, those reprints are often edited

to eliminate the generally mild nudity that occasionally appeared in the original printings. I had a great time revisiting these titles and stories. I think you will, too.

Enjoy!

Savage Tales

1. cover: John Buscema (May 1971)

(1) Conan the Barbarian: The Frost Giant's Daughter [Roy Thomas/Barry Smith, from the story by Robert E. Howard] 11p; (2) The Fury of the Femizons [Stan Lee/John Romita] 10p; (3) The Story Behind the Scenes [Roy Thomas, text article] 1p; (4) Man-Thing! [Gerry Conway and Roy Thomas/Gray Morrow] 11p; (5) Black Brother! [Denny O'Neil/Gene Colan and Tom Palmer, O'Neil's story credited to Sergius O'Shaughnessy] 11p; (6) Next issue ad [John Romita, Ka-Zar, Conan and Kull are featured] 1p; (7) Ka-Zar: The Night of the Looter! [Stan Lee/John Buscema] 15p; (8) Next issue ad [John Romita, Conan and Lyra of the Femizons are featured] 1p.

Notes: It was $0.50 for 64 pages. Publisher and editor: Stan Lee. Roy Thomas listed as associate editor. Two science fantasy stories, one sword and sorcery classic and two horror tales make up this issue. The *Conan* story is one of Thomas/Smith team's best efforts. This version features nudity, which was censored when the story was reprinted in the regular *Conan* comic. That version also acquired a new splash page, bringing the page count up to 12, which has remained constant for subsequent reprinting. With one exception, the censored version is the version usually reprinted. The exception occurred in 1974 when a 12-page version of the original art plus the added splash page appeared in *The Savage Sword of Conan* #1 (August 1974). The long-running Marvel swamp monster, *Man-Thing*, also debuted in this issue. "The Femizons" and the *Conan* adaptation had the best art (from John Romita and Barry Windsor-Smith) while Conan also had the best story. This was Marvel's second B&W magazine attempt, following a one-issue Spider-Man effort in 1968. According to legend, distribution problems ensured a poor sell-through and this was the single issue published at this time. Although a second issue of *Savage Tales* was clearly planned, it didn't actually appear until November 1973, with almost totally different contents than the original version of #2! Those original contents were parceled out in Marvel color books. The second *Man-Thing* story (featuring beautiful artwork by Neal Adams) appeared in *Astonishing Tales*, shoehorned into a Ka-Zar tale! The *Conan* story intended for #2 appeared (again, with the original nudity censored) in *Conan the Barbarian* #12. A *Kull* story was also promised but I'm not sure if it ever appeared. A science fiction story, "Dark Tomorrow," actually did appear 2½ years later in the revived *Savage Tales* #2. It was two more years before Marvel attempted another black and white magazine venture

Dracula Lives!

1. cover: Boris Vallejo (June 1973)

(1) Dracula, 1973: A Poison of the Blood [Gerry Conway/Gene Colan and Tom Palmer] 13p; **(2)** Dracula, 1691: Suffer Not a Witch! [Roy Thomas/Alan Weiss and Dick Giordano] 12p; **(3)** Dracula Is Alive and Living on Madison Avenue [Roy Thomas, text article] 1½ p; **(4)** Monsters Unleashed ad [Pablo Marcos] ½ p; **(5)** Zombie! [?/Tony DiPreta, reprinted from *Journey into Mystery* #5 (February 1953)] 6p; **(6)** Ghost of a Chance! [?/Bill LaCava, reprinted from *Adventures into Terror* #8, originally entitled "The Miracle"] 2p; **(7)** What Can You Say About a Five-Hundred Year Old Vampire Who Refuses to Die? [Marv Wolfman, text article with photos] 6p; **(8)** Fright! [Stan Lee?/Russ Heath, reprinted from *Journey into Mystery* #5 (February 1953)] 7p; **(9)** Dracula, 1890s: To Walk Again in Daylight! [Steve Gerber/Rich Buckler and Pablo Marcos] 10p; **(10)** Next issue ad [Neal Adams] 1p.

Notes: Publisher: Stan Lee. Editor: Roy Thomas. Sol Brodsky, who had been the first editor for the Skywald line of B&W horror magazines, was the production manager for the Marvel line. It cost $0.75 for 72 pages. The magazine's only date is 1973 but this issue was actually the June 1973 issue. This time Marvel launched a full-scale assault on the B&W magazine market, essentially flooding the market with four horror magazines, a humor magazine, a revived and reformatted *Savage Tales* and a gag photo movie magazine in 1973 alone. *Dracula Lives!* was the first of these titles and it features one of Boris

Vallejo's best covers for the B&W market (not to mention it being his Marvel debut). Nowadays, Vallejo's work seems somewhat overrated, with his heavy reliance on posed models producing artwork that can often look stiff and lifeless. Yet between 1971 and 1977 he produced some of the most striking covers in the field for Warren, Skywald, Atlas and Marvel as well as some superb paperback covers (check out the 1976 Ballantine edition of Edgar Pangborn's *Davy* or the 1979 Ballantine edition of Theodore Sturgeon's *E Pluribus Unicorn*). This Dracula Lives! cover is a symbolic painting featuring a vampire bat with Dracula's head floating above a cobra, a female vampire, a caveman, a skull and assorted demons. It's quite dynamic. To avoid problems with the continuing modern-day storylines from *The Tomb of Dracula*, this magazine's stories tended to take place during different time periods ranging from 1459 though 1973. One thing one should note about the Marvel books is that, although the cover price was generally less than a Warren title, you actually paid a lot more for fewer comic pages. This issue has only 35 new pages of story and art. The rest of the magazine consists of pre–Code 1950s era reprints and text articles. One of the reasons Marvel claimed for this practice was that it was paying its writers and artists more than either Warren or Skywald, their main rivals in the B&W horror market. This was not strictly true, as Warren paid its top artists more than either Marvel or DC, although the going rate for their writers was considerably less. The other reason offered was that it was very expensive to launch a full line of magazines (especially with only three magazines' worth of material) and cost-cutting was absolutely required. That said, if you didn't like *Famous Monsters of Filmland* or articles of that sort (I can see my teenaged self wildly waving his hand here — couldn't stand 'em) then the articles were not only clearly padding but a snooze as well. The pre–Code reprints were often awful, with corny stories and lame artwork. This wasn't always true, however, and this issue's "Fright!" is a standout story, reprint or not, with great Heath artwork highlighting a nasty little tale concerning a brutal overseer of an insane asylum. The best of the new material is the Thomas/

Weiss tale of Dracula influencing the Salem Witch Trials. The other two stories are decent enough also. For some reason five of the pages have panel borders or details in the panels colored in red. Each of the stories had a one-page introduction with photos from old movies used as artwork. The next issue ad reprinted Neal Adams' art from the cover of the color comic *The Tomb of Dracula* #1, with the art reversed or flipped. A fair first issue.

2. cover: Jordi Penalva (August 1973)

(1) Dracula, 1459: That Dracula May Live Again! [Marv Wolfman/Neal Adams] 13p; (2) An Editorial [Roy Thomas, text article] ½ p; (3) Tales of the Zombie ad [John Romita over Bill Everett?] ½ p; (4) Vampires Drink Deep! [?/Joe Sinnott, reprinted from *Strange Tales* #9 (August 1952, originally entitled "Drink Deep, Vampire!"] 6p; (5) Who Is Bram Stoker and Why Is He Saying Those Terrible Things About Me! [Chris Claremont, text story with photos] 5p; (6) Dracula, 1944: The Terror That Stalked Castle Dracula! [Steve Gerber and Tony Isabella/Jim Starlin and Syd Shores] 11p; (7) Vampire Tales ad [Gil Kane, Moebius, the Living Vampire is featured] 1p; (8) One Corpse ... One Vote! [Stan Lee/Fred Kida, reprinted from ?] 6p; (9) Dracula, 1973: The Voodoo Queen of New Orleans [Roy Thomas/Gene Colan and Dick Giordano] 14p; (10) Next issue ad [Tom Palmer] 1p.

Notes: Penalva's cover started a gothic cover tradition that lasted through #12. On each cover, a beautiful blonde girl, usually clad in a frilly nightgown (although for this cover she's dressed in only bra and panties) was menaced by Dracula, who was usually dressed in what looks like an 1890s opera costume (basically, his standard costume for the color comics). Marv Wolfman, Gerry Conway, Don McGregor and Tony Isabella are listed as editorial staff. Marvel's version of Dracula gets a terrific origin tale, courtesy of Wolfman and Adams. Jim Starlin does only the layouts for the 1944 Dracula tale. The majority of the artwork is by Syd Shores. Simon Garth, the Zombie (from the B&W magazine *Tales of the Zombie*), has a one-panel cameo in "The Voodoo Queen of New Orleans." As in the first issue, occasional pages have the color red in certain panel's backgrounds, often for less than obvious reasons. Thirty-nine pages of original art and story.

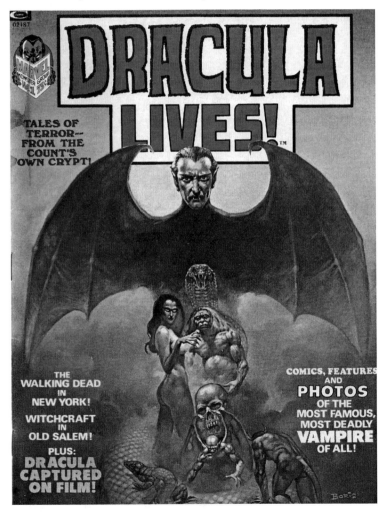

Cover artist **Boris Vallejo** starts the Marvel B&W explosion of horror titles with a symbolic painting for the premiere issue of *Dracula Lives!* © Marvel Worldwide/used by permission.

3. cover: Neal Adams/title page: Pablo Marcos (October 1973)

(**1**) Dracula, 1459: Lord of Death ... Lord of Hell! [Marv Wolfman/John Buscema and Syd Shores] 12p; (**2**) The Haunt of Horror/Savage Tales ad [Kelly Freas and Barry Smith] 1p; (**3**) The Vampire-Man [?/?, reprinted from ?] 5p; (**4**) Doc Savage/Tales of the Zombie ad [Rich Bucker and Pablo Marcos] 1p; (**5**) Bela Lugosi: Dracula of Stage, Screen and Coffin [Doug Moench, text article with photos] 6p; (**6**) Solomon Kane and Dracula, 1553: Castle of the Undead [Roy Thomas/Alan Weiss and The Crusty Bunkers] 12p; (**7**) Vampire Tales ad [John Romita, Satana is featured] 1p; (**8**) I Was Once a Gentle Man... [Chris Claremont, text story with photos] 6p; (**9**) Strange Tales/Marvel Spotlight ad [John Romita and Herb Trimpe, Brother Voodoo and the Son of Satan are featured] 1p; (**10**) Fire Burn and Cauldron Bubble [?/C. A. Winter, reprinted from ?] 5p; (**11**) Crazy ad [Marie Severin] ½ p; (**12**) Dracula, 1973: Shadow in the City of Light! [Gerry Conway/Alphonso Font] 11p; (**13**) Dracula Lives! Feature Page: Stan Lee profile/Dracula Returns book review [Roy Thomas? and Don Thompson, text article with photos] 1p; (**14**) Next issue ad [Pablo Marcos] 1p.

Notes: Adams' terrific painting of Dracula standing on a rain-swept cathedral in Paris (holding the blonde in the nightgown) is the best cover to appear on an issue of *Dracula Lives!* Marv Wolfman is listed as the associate editor and is actually the de facto editor at this point. "Lord of Death ... Lord of Hell" is a sequel and continuation of Dracula's origin tale. The last page in the reprint story "The Vampire-Man" has an obvious Jack Davis swipe on page 5, panel 2. Solomon Kane was a Puritan adventurer created by Robert E. Howard, the creator of *Conan* and *Kull*, among many others. This story (a Roy Thomas original, although based on an unpublished fragment by Howard) details the clash between Stoker's Dracula and Howard's Kane. It's a terrific tale with beautiful art by Weiss and the Bunkers. The Crusty Bunkers were a loose, constantly shifting collection of artists headed by Neal Adams. Adams clearly inked a lot of this story. Other Bunkers included Russ Heath, Dick Giordano, Vicente Alcazar, Terry Austin, Joe Rubenstein, Pat Broderick, Dan Green, Weiss himself and many more. Several of those mentioned could have worked on this story as well. The *Vampire Tales* ad features Romita's original costume design for Satana, although she never actually wore this costume in a B&W magazine. She may have done so in the color comics. *The Haunt of Horror* ad was for the digest prose magazine, not the later B&W comic magazine. The "Fire Burn and Cauldron Bubble" reprint is a comic retelling of the death of Macbeth and has nothing to do with vampires. It's rather nicely done, though. The letters page debuts with an illustration of Dracula by Pablo Marcos. Thirty-six pages of new story and art.

4. cover: Earl Norem/title page: Rich Buckler and Pablo Marcos (January 1974)

(**1**) Marvel Magazines ad [various, frontis] 1p; (**2**) Dracula, 1973: Fear Stalker [Marv Wolfman/Mike Ploog and Ernie Chan, Chan's art credited to Ernie Chua] 14p; (**3**) Tales of the Zombie ad [Boris Vallejo, a B&W reproduction of #3's cover] 1p; (**4**) In Search of Dracula: A True History of Dracula and Vampire Legends [Chris Claremont, text article 2/photos] 6p; (**5**) Transylvania: Vacation Spot of Europe? [Dwight R. Decker/Pablo Marcos, text article] 1p; (**6**) When Calls the Vampire! [?/Joe Maneely, reprinted from *Adventure into Terror* #10 (June 1952)] 6p; (**7**) Dracula, 1606: This Blood Is Mine! [Gardner Fox/Dick Ayers] 12p; (**8**) Dracula Lives! Feature Page: Yes, Marv Wolfman Is His Real Name! [Marv Wolfman, text article with photos] 1p; (**9**) Film Review: The Horror of Dracula [Gerry Boudreau, text article with photos] 6p; (**10**) Of Royal Blood [?/Tony Mortellaro, reprinted from *Journey into Unknown Worlds* #29 (July 1954)] 4p; (**11**) Marvel Magazines ad [Pablo Marcos, Esteban Maroto, John Buscema? and Mike Ploog, Morbius, the Living Vampire, Satana, Gulliver Jones of Mars and Frankenstein's Monster are featured] 2p; (**12**) Dracula, 1459: Look Homeward, Vampire [Gerry Conway/Vicente Alcazar] 11p; (**13**) Next issue ad [Pablo Marcos] 1p.

Notes: Our cover blonde is wearing a pink dress and heels. Ploog's pencil art is sadly buried beneath Chan's inks. Dick Ayers did a lot of work for the schlocky, gory *Eerie* Publications and, unfortunately, his work on "This Blood Is Mine!" looks more like work for that company than his usual work for Marvel. The story concerns Dracula's fictional encounter with the real-life Baroness Bathory, who really did drain the blood of virgins into her bathtub, since she believed that bathing in virgin blood would help preserve her youth. The vampire in the reprint story "Of Royal Blood" appears to have had his head redrawn to look more like Marvel's version of Dracula. The story "Look Homeward, Vampire!" is the third part of Dracula's origin tale and is easily the best written and illustrated story here. Thirty-seven pages of story and art.

5. cover: Luis Dominguez/frontis and inside back cover: Gene Colan (March 1974)

(1) Dracula [Roy Thomas/Dick Giordano, from the novel by Bram Stoker] 12p; (2) Transylvania on a Budget [Doug Moench, text article with photo] 2p; (3) Movie review: Dracula, Prince of Darkness [Doug Moench, text article with photos] 5p; (4) Crazy ad [Marie Severin] 1p; (5) Dracula, 1785: A Duel of Demons [Gerry Conway/Frank Springer] 10p; (6) Dracula: Demons in Darkness [Gerry Conway/Pablo Marcos, text story, additional art from *The Tomb of Dracula* color comic] 6p; (7) Coffin Chronicles [Carla Joseph/?, text article] 2p; (8) When a Vampire Dies... [Stan Lee/?, reprinted from *Marvel Tales* #128 (November 1954)] 5p; (9) Book review: The Dracula Archives [Chris Claremont, text article with photos] 3p (10) Dracula, 1974: Night Flight to Terror! [Marv Wolfman and Tony Isabella/Gene Colan and Pablo Marcos] 10p; (11) The Deadly Hands of Kung Fu ad [John Romita] 1p; (12) The Boyhood of Dracula [Tony Isabella/Val Mayerik] 1p; (13) Next issue ad [Pablo Marcos, on back cover] 1p.

Notes: Size reduced to 64 pages. This issue featured the beginning of Roy Thomas and Dick Giordano's superb adaptation of Bram Stoker's *Dracula*, an adaptation that would not be concluded until 2005, with a gap between episodes of 29 years! Regardless, this is an extremely impressive adaptation, with a faithful script by Thomas and what is probably Giordano's finest artwork. A rare example of Gene Colan inking his own 1970s work (at least at Marvel) appears with his two-page pin-up. Pablo Marcos is all over this issue with ad work, inking, text story illustrations and whatnot—makes one wonder why he wasn't given an opportunity to helm a solo story. He would have done a great job! Only 33 pages of original art and story this issue, if you don't count (and I don't and won't) the text story.

6. cover: Luis Dominguez (May 1974)

(1) Dracula, 1974: A Death in the Chapel [Steve Gerber/Gene Colan and Ernie Chan, Chan's art is credited to Ernie Chua] 10p; (2) Yes, Virginia, There Is a Real Dracula (Undead and Well in Wallachia) [Doug Moench/text article with photos] 8p; (3) The Mark of a Vampire! [?/Mac Pakula, reprinted from *Spellbound* #22 (May 1954) with one page dropped from the story] 4p; (4) Dracula: Blood Moon [Thompson O'Rourke/Ernie Chan, text story, Chan's art credited to Ernie Chua] 6p; (5) Dracula, 1789: Shadow Over Versailles [Tony Isabella/John Buscema and Pablo Marcos] 11p; (6) Dracula Has Risen from the Grave [Tony Isabella, text article with photos] 5p; (7) The Haunt of Horror ad [Ralph Reese] 1p; (8) Dracula, part 2: Into the Spider's Web [Roy Thomas/Dick Giordano, from the novel by Bram Stoker] 12p; (9) Next issue ad [Pablo Marcos, on the inside back cover] 1p.

Notes: Two good original stories and the great Stoker adaptation made this one of the better Dracula Lives! For some reason, Chan's inking on Gene Colan's pencils was much better than his earlier heavy-handed inking on Mike Ploog's. "Shadow Over Versailles" is an excellent story with a great ending. The second adapted chapter of Dracula has a two-page rehash of the previous chapter with reformatted art from that chapter, something that Thomas and Giordano would do throughout the 1974–1975 appearances of this adaptation series. The actual adaptation is only 10 pages long. Only 31 pages of new art and story here.

7. cover: Luis Dominguez (July 1974)

(1) Dracula, 1974: Here Comes the Death Man [Gerry Conway/Vicente Alcazar] 10p; (2) Crazy ad [Kelly Freas] 1p; (3) Dracula: Blood Moon, part 2 [Thompson O'Rourke/Ernie Chan, text story, Chan's art credited to Ernie Chua] 7p; (4) The Deadly Hands of Kung Fu ad [Paul Gulacy] 1p; (5) Dracula, 1690: Assault of the She-Pirate! [Mike Friedrich/George Evans] 12p; (6) Marvel Magazines ad [John Buscema and Ernie Chan] 1p; (7) Movie review: Taste the Blood of Dracula [Tony Isabella, text article with photos] 6p; (8) Dracula, part 3: The Female of the Species [Roy Thomas/Dick Giordano, from the novel by Bram Stoker] 12p; (9) Giant-Size Master of Kung Fu ad [Ernie Chan] ½ p; (10) Coffin Chronicles [Carla Joseph, text article with photos] 3p.

Notes: Although the story's only so-so, Alcazar's art on "Here Comes the Death Man" is the best in the issue, with Evans and Giordano also delivering fine art jobs. Best story is the Stoker adaptation by Thomas with Friedrich's pirate tale also being quite good. From this point on the 1950s–era reprints are dropped from the magazine. Thirty-two pages of new story and art.

8. cover: Luis Dominguez/frontis and title page: Pablo Marcos (September 1974)

(1) Dracula, 1974: Last Walk on the Night Side [Doug Moench/Tony DeZuniga] 11p; (2) Dracula, 1926: Black Hand ... Black Death! [Len Wein/Gene Colan and Ernie Chan, Chan's art credited to Ernie Chua] 10p; (3) Crazy ad [Fumetti photo art, Stan Lee is featured] 1p; (4) Dracula: Child of the Sun [Chris Claremont/Pablo Marcos, text story] 11p; (5) Marvel Magazines ad [Alfredo Alcala, Frankenstein's Monster, Werewolf by Night, Conan, Simon Garth the Zombie, Dracula, Gulliver Jones and Satana are featured in a "l'il kids"–style illustration] 1p; (6) Coffin Chronicles [Carla Joseph, text article with photos] 2p; (7) Dracula, part 4: "And in That Sleep...!" [Roy Thomas/Dick Giordano, from the novel by Bram Stoker] 14p; (8) The Deadly Hands of Kung Fu [Neal Adams, B&W reproduction of #3's cover] ½ p.

Notes: A striking splash page on the Stoker adaptation as Giordano continues to impress. Thomas' script is darn good, too. Tony DeZuniga also delivers a superior art job on the first half of Moench's serial. Too bad he couldn't do both parts. Marv Wolfman is now listed as editor (a job he'd been doing since at least #3) with Thomas as editor-in-chief and Tony Isabella as consulting editor. Thirty-three new pages of art and story.

9. cover: Luis Dominguez (November 1974)

(1) How to Ward Off Vampires [Tony Isabella/Ernie Chan, frontis, Chan's art credited to Ernie Chua] 1p; (2) Dracula, 1974: The Lady Who Collected Dracula [Doug Moench/Frank Robbins and Frank Springer, part 2 of "Last Night on the Wild Side" from the previous issue] 10p; (3) Dracula, 1600s: Scarlet in Glory! [Doug Moench/Paul Gulacy and Mike Esposito] 10p; (4) Crazy ad [Marie Severin] 1p; (5) Movie review: The Scars of Dracula [Gerry Boudreau, text article with photos] 6p; (6) Dracula, 1934:

A Night in the Unlife! [Gerry Conway/Alfredo Alcala] 10p; (7) Dracula, 1903: Twice Dies the Vampire! [Gerry Conway/Sonny Trinidad] 10p; (8) Planet of the Apes ad [Bob Larkin, B&W reproduction of #2's cover] 1p; (9) Next issue ad [Dave Cockrum, Lilith, Daughter of Dracula is featured] 1p.

Notes: The cover blonde has switched to a green nightie. There are more ads in this issue but there is also an increase of comic pages with 40 pages of new art and story. The Robbins/Springer art on the second half of "Last Night on the Wild Side" is so completely unlike DeZuniga's from the previous issue that it looks bad by comparison. Robbins would have been great doing a 1930s–1940s era Dracula story, so this is really a bit of a shame. Sonny Trinidad provides the best artwork here while Doug Moench's "Scarlet in Glory!" is the best story.

10. cover: Luis Dominguez/frontis: Don Maitz and Duffy Vohland (January 1975)

(1) The Marvel Bullpen Page Goes Black and White and Read All Over [Marv Wolfman, text article] 1p; (2) Dracula, 1809: The Pit of Death [Doug Moench/Tony DeZuniga] 10p; (3) Crazy ad [photo, Stan Lee, wearing an Uncle Sam suit, is featured] 1p; (4) Movie Review: Dracula A.D. 1972 [Gary Gerani, text article with photos] 6p; (5) Dracula, part 5: Ship of Death [Roy Thomas/Dick Giordano, from the novel by Bram Stoker] 10p; (6) Lilith, Daughter of Dracula: The Blood Book [Steve Gerber/Bob Brown and the Crusty Bunkers] 16p; (7) A Vampire Stalks Melrose Abbey [Doug Moench/Winslow Mortimer] 2p; (8) Savage Tales ad [John Romita, Ka-Zar and Shanna, the She-Devil are featured] 1p.

Notes: The first half of the Moench/DeZuniga's serial *The Pit of Death* is quite good and features the best story and art for the issue. Lilith's story is continued from her appearance in *Vampire Tales* #6. As mentioned earlier, the Crusty Bunkers were a loose group of various inkers operating out of Neal Adams' studio. Adams almost always had a hand in the inking and certainly does here. The Moench/Mortimer two-pagers were originally intended as frontispiece/inside back cover pieces, although it was rare that they were actually used for that. Thirty-eight pages of original art and story. Don McGregor and Len Wein are now listed as assistant or associate editors.

11. cover: Steve Fabian/frontis: Bob Hall (March 1975)

(1) Dracula, 1809: Pit of Death, part 2: Agent of Hell [Doug Moench/Tony DeZuniga] 11p; (2) The Vampire of Mednegna [Doug Moench/ Winslow Mortimer] 2p; (3) Dracula, part 6: If Madness Be Thy Master...! [Roy Thomas/Dick Giordano, from the novel by Bram Stoker] 12p; (4) Lilith, Daughter of Dracula: Nobody Anybody Knows [Steve Gerber/Bob Brown, Frank Chiramonte and Pablo Marcos] 21p; (5) Next issue ad [Ken Bald, B&W reproduction of next issue's cover] 1p; (6) Tales of the Zombie ad [Earl Norem, B&W reproduction of #10's cover] 1p.

Notes: SF and fantasy great Steve Fabian contributes a cover, putting the blonde girl in a purple nightie. Future Eclipse publisher Dean Mullaney sent in a letter, revealing that he was a pretty intense Marvel fanboy in the day. Moench's *Pit of Death* serial concluded in fine fashion. The new chapter of Bram Stoker's *Dracula* was pretty good too. With an almost equal number of pages as Dracula, Lilith almost took over the magazine. Forty-six pages of new story and art, which was nearly equal to a Warren 64-pager.

12. cover: Ken Bald/frontis: photo of Christopher Lee reading *Dracula Lives!* #4 (May 1975)

(1) Fearsome Features, Far-Out Fabrications, and Fictional Configurations! [?, text listing of Marvel magazines] 1p; (2) Dracula, 1597: Parchments of the Damned! [Doug Moench/ Sonny Trinidad] 10p; (3) Dracula, 1597: Parchments of the Damned, part 2: The Stealer of Dracula's Soul [Doug Moench/Yong Montano] 10p; (4) Dracula, 1597: Parchments of the Damned, part 3: Paper Blood [Doug Moench/ Steve Gan] 11p; (5) Christopher Lee: Hammer's Hero of Horror [Doug Moench, text article with photos] 8p; (6) Dracula, 1465: The Sins of the Fathers [Gerry Conway/Tom Sutton] 10p.

Notes: All three parts of a serial appear with the most effective art showing up in the chapter by Sonny Trinidad and Steve Gan. The best art and story, however, go to the Conway/Sutton effort, "The Sins of the Fathers." Sutton drew versions of Dracula for both Warren and Marvel and both versions are great. It's worth buying this issue just for his work alone.

13. cover: Earl Norem/frontis: Vicente Alcazar (July 1975)

(1) Factful Features and Fantastic Frivolity Formed and Fermented from Frugal-Minded Armadillos! [?, listing of Marvel comics then on sale] 1p; (2) Dracula, 1885: Bounty for a Vampire [Tony Isabella/Tony DeZuniga] 12p; (3) Kull and The Barbarians/Unknown Worlds of Science Fiction ad [Michael Whelan and Frank Brunner, B&W repos of #2 and #4 respectively] 1p; (4) Dracula, 1974: Bloody Mary [Rich Margopoulos/George Tuska and Virgilio Redondo] 10p; (5) Doc Savage ad [movie poster art] 1p; (6) Unknown Worlds of Science Fiction ad [Robert L. Kline] 1p; (7) The Toad [Tom Sutton] 7p; (8) A Dracula Portfolio [Russ Heath] 3p; (9) Dracula, 1471: Blood of My Blood! [Gerry Conway/Steve Gan] 11p; (10) Marvel Preview ad [Tony DeZuniga, the Punisher is featured] 1p; (11) Marvel Movie preview ad [Earl Norem, B&W reproduction of #1's cover] 1p; (12) Marvel Magazines ad [various] 2p.

Notes: Final issue. The blonde babe has vanished from the cover. Archie Goodwin is listed as a consulting editor. Dean Mullaney and future Marvel writer Ralph Macchio send in letters. "Blood of My Blood" is the best Dracula story although "Bounty for a Vampire" is also good. The latter story seems inspired by DC's Jonah Hex comic, which DeZuniga also drew. Perhaps it could be considered an unofficial intercompany crossover? Best art honors go to Russ Heath's gory portfolio pieces. So good that one wishes that Heath could have done a Lilith or Dracula story for Marvel. Sutton's excellent "The Toad" was the only non–Dracula or Lilith original story ever published in *Dracula Lives!* It was a beautiful job on both story and art. This issue also featured a rare non–Warren appearance for writer Rich Margopoulos. *A Dracula Lives!* annual appeared in place of a 14th issue.

The Haunt of Horror (Digest Version)

1. cover: Gray Morrow (June 1973)

(1) The Unspoken Invitation [Gerry Conway, text article] 2p; (2) Conjure Wife [Fritz Leiber/ John Romita and Gene Colan, reprinted from *Unknown Worlds* (April 1943)] 69p; (3) Dr. Warm: The First Step [George Alec Effinger/ Frank Brunner, story credited to John K.

Diomede] 20p; (4) Neon [Harlan Ellison/Walt Simonson] 10p; (5) Loup Garou [A. A. Attansio/Mike Ploog] 11p; (6) In the Wind [Gerry Conway, text article] 1p; (7) Seeing Stingy Ed [David R. Bunch] 3p; (8) The Lurker in the Family Room [Denny O'Neil, text article] 5p; (9) A Nice Home [Beverly Goldberg/?] 3p; (10) Ghost in the Corn Crib [R. A. Lafferty/Dan Green] 6p; (11) Nightbeat [Ramsey Campbell/Frank Brunner] 5p; (12) Boo Kreview: The Book of Skulls/Dying Inside/The Dreaming City/The Sleeping Sorceress [Baird Searles, text article] 4p; (13) Author's Page [Gerry Conway, text article] 2p; (14) Usurp the Night [Robert E. Howard/?, reprinted from ?, (? 1970)] 17p.

Notes: Publisher: Stan Lee. Editor: Gerry Conway. Associate editor: George Alec Effinger. $0.75 for 160 pages. This is not a comic magazine but an actual prose digest, like the *Magazine of Fantasy and Science Fiction*, etc. It's included here strictly because Marvel later used the title for a B&W comic magazine and I didn't want people to get confused. All stories are prose unless otherwise indicated. That said, this is a really good little magazine. Leiber's novel is a genuine classic (you can find it today in an edition published by Tor entitled *Dark Ladies*) and many of the other stories are quite good reading, especially the Lafferty and Howard pieces. Ellison had the last two pages of his story switched in editing and the story was printed out of sequence. That mistake was corrected in the next issue. The title of the book review section is accurate—that's how it's spelled in both issues. The artwork is quite nice with special mention going to Ploog's and Brunner's contributions.

2. cover: Kelly Freas (August 1973)

(1) Conditional Terror [Gerry Conway/Walt Simonson, text article] 2p; (2) Devil Night [Denny O'Neil/John Buscema] 13p; (3) Pelican's Claws [Arthur Byron Cover/Dan Green] 6p; (4) Dr. Warm: The Jewel in the Ash [George Alec Effinger/Walt Simonson, story credited to John K. Diomede] 20p; (5) Conjure Wife, part 2 [Fritz Leiber/Walt Simonson, reprinted from *Unknown Worlds* (April 1943)] 69p; (6) Kilbride [Ron Goulart/Frank Brunner] 10p; (7) In the Wind [Gerry Conway, text article] 1p; (8) Finders Keepers [Anne McCafferty/Billy Graham] 10p; (9) Digging Up Atlantis [Lin Carter/?, text article] 6p; (10) Special Feature [Gerry Conway, text article] 1p; (11) Neon [Harlan Ellison/Kelly

Freas, reprinted from *The Haunt of Horror* #1 (June 1973)] 8p; (12) Author's Page [Gerry Conway, text article] 1½ p; (13) Mono No Aware [Howard Waldrop/?] 5½ p

Notes: Final issue. Ellison's story was reprinted with the ending pages corrected. Each story had the same ending illustration provided by Walt Simonson. The next issue section, "In The Wind" listed a number of stories intended for the third issue, including John Jakes' "The Running of Ladyhound," George Zebrowski's "Fire of Spring," R. A. Lafferty's "Goldfish," Alan Brennert's "The Night People," Ramsey Campbell's "Writer's Curse," a new Dr. Warm story by George Alec Effinger (aka John K. Diomede) and non-fiction articles by Lin Carter and Denny O'Neil. The intended cover, by Kelly Freas, could be seen in ads in the various B&W magazines as well as the additional information that the non-fiction article by Carter was to have been called "The New Witchcraft." That cover, and several of the stories mentioned, never saw print, to my knowledge. The story "The Running of the Ladyhound" would appear as "The Running of the Demonhound" in an issue of *Savage Tales*.

Monsters Unleashed!

1. cover: Gray Morrow (July 1973)

(1) The Man Who Cried Werewolf! [Gerry Conway/Pablo Marcos, from the story "The Man Who Cried Wolf" by Robert Bloch] 10p; (2) Ghosties and Ghoulies and Things That Go Bump in the Brain... [Roy Thomas, text article with photos] 1p; (3) The Thing in the Freezer [Marv Wolfman/Syd Shores] 5p; (4) Vampire Tale [Stan Lee/Doug Wildey, reprinted from *Journey into Mystery* #16 (June 1954)] 5p; (5) The Haunt of Horror ad [Kelly Freas] 1p; (6) Solomon Kane: Skulls in the Stars [Roy Thomas/Ralph Reese, from the story by Robert E. Howard] 10p; (7) Portrait of the Werewolf as a Young Man: The Odyssey of Larry Talbot [Tony Isabella, text article with photos] 4p; (8) One Foot in the Grave [Stan Lee/Tony DiPreta, reprinted from *Journey into Mystery* #1 (June 1952)] 4p; (9) The Fake! [Stan Lee/?, reprinted from ?] 5p; (10) World of Warlocks! [Gardner Fox and Roy Thomas/Gene Colan] 10p; (11) Next issue ad [Mike Ploog] 1p.

Notes: Publisher: Stan Lee. Editor: Roy Thomas. It was $0.75 for 72 pages. Like their other horror

B&Ws, photos from old movies were used to provide introductions to each story. *Monsters Unleashed* not only had an awkward title but was also the most unfocused and downright poor B&W that Marvel published. It never seemed to be sure what it was really about. *Dracula Lives!* featured Dracula. *Vampire Tales* featured, well, vampires. *Tales of the Zombie* was headlined by the zombie Simon Garth and was also accompanied by various voodoo stories. Even the latter version of *The Haunt of Horror* seemed more focused, even as that particular title did 180-degree spins in intent and content. Thomas promises in the editorial that the focus would be on monsters of all stripes. Okay, so based on this issue you'd think that this book was intended as a home for the literary horror adaptations that the color books *Journey into Mystery* and *Chamber of Chills* had been delivering. Not a bad idea at all but that approach never continued past this issue. Two of the stories herein were actually sword and sorcery tales that would have fit right in at *Savage Tales*. Not really straight monster stories at all, although the Solomon Kane adaptation certainly straddles both genres. With the second issue, Marvel took a different direction, attempting to do B&W versions of some of their color comic monsters but those efforts were beset with deadline problems, hampered by stories that made no sense unless you read the color books and cursed with embarrassingly poor serials. The magazine often seemed padded, even more so than Marvel's other B&Ws. That's not to say that good material didn't appear here. This first issue is not bad at all. The Bloch adaptation is quite acceptable and the Howard adaptation is great. "World of Warlocks!" seems stodgy and old-fashioned but Colan's pencils and inks are fun to see. Thirty-two pages of new art and story.

2. cover: Boris Vallejo (September 1973)

(1) Frankenstein 1973 [Gary Friedrich/John Buscema and Syd Shores] 13p; (2) Vampire Tales ad [Gil Kane] 1p; (3) Monster Rally [Roy Thomas, text article with photos] 1p; (4) Book review: Karloff: The Man, the Monster, the Movies [Tony Isabella, text article with photos] 6p; (5) Lifeboat! [Gerry Conway/Jesus Blasco] 8p; (6) Tales of the Zombie ad [Pablo Marcos] ½ p; (7) The Madman [Stan Lee/Bill Everett, reprinted from *Menace* #4 (June 1953)] 7p; (8) Monster Madness/Dracula Lives! ad [photo/Neal Adams] 1p; (9) The World's Most Wanted Monster: The Saga of the Karloff Frankenstein [Martin Pasko, text article with photos] 6p; (10) Strange Tales/Marvel Spotlight/Savage Tales Ads [John Romita, Herb Trimpe, Barry Smith, Brother Voodoo, the Son of Satan and Conan are featured] 2p; (11) Sword of Dragonus [Frank Brunner and Chuck Robinson/Frank Brunner, reprinted from *Phase* #1 (September 1971)]; (12) Crazy ad [Marie Severin] ½ p; (13) The Roaches! [Gerry Conway/Ralph Reese, from the story by Thomas M. Disch] 10p.

Notes: Great cover by Vallejo featuring Frankenstein's monster. Thomas announces a new direction in the second issue, this time concentrating on serials, with the first being the monster of Frankenstein. The best horror work Marvel ever produced was featured in the first six issues of the color comic *The Monster of Frankenstein*, which initially adapted Mary Shelley's novel, coupled with a new wraparound story. Gary Friedrich's adaptation and expansion of the novel was top notch and it was beautifully complemented by Mike Ploog's artwork (you can find those stories in stunning B&W in *The Essential Monster of Frankenstein*— in fact, those six issues are the only reason to buy that book). However the storyline was set in the 1890s or thereabouts and Marvel wanted a more contemporary series. So Friedrich, with artists Buscema and Shores, bumped the monster up to 1973, leaving how he got there a bit of a mystery. It's a good start for this series, with a strong script and excellent artwork. John Buscema does such a good job, in fact, that one wonders why his artwork for the color book (he took over with #7) was so dreadful. Maybe this issue's art is so good simply due to Shores' strong inking. "Sword of Dragonus" is a reprint from a fanzine and is very good, with the best art of the issue. It was done in 1970 and originally intended to appear in *Web of Horror*. A sequel to this story would appear in Mike Friedrich's independent magazine *Star*Reach* #3 (1976). Best script goes to Gerry Conway's excellent adaptation of "The Roaches!" Thirty-one pages of new story and art.

3. cover: Neal Adams (November 1973)

(1) Man-Thing! [Roy Thomas and Gerry Conway/Gray Morrow, reprinted from *Savage Tales*

#1 (May 1971)] 11p; **(2)** Monsters Unleashed! ad [Neal Adams] 1p; **(3)** The Cyclops [Stan Lee/ Jack Davis, reprinted from *Journey into Unknown Worlds* #50 (October 1956)] 4p; **(4)** Frankenstein A.K. (After Karloff) [Martin Pasko, text article with photos] 4p; **(5)** The Death-Dealing Mannikin [Kit Pearson and Tony Isabella/Winslow Mortimer] 8p; **(6)** Crazy ad [Kelly Freas] 1p; **(7)** Contact! [Tom Sutton, reprinted from *Tower of Shadows* #6 (July 1970)] 2p; **(8)** Swamp Girl [?/Vic Carabotta, reprinted from *Mystic* #19 (June 1953)] 5p; **(9)** Preview: The Son of Satan [Carla Joseph/Herb Trimpe, art from various Son of Satan stories] 4p; **(10)** The Cold of the Uncaring Moon [Steve Skeates/ George Tuska and Klaus Janson] 7p; **(11)** Birthright! [Roy Thomas/Gil Kane and the Crusty Bunkers] 13p; **(12)** Monsters Unleashed! Feature Page: Playboy's Gahan Wilson/The Story Behind the Swamp [Don Thompson and Roy Thomas/Gahan Wilson and Neal Adams, text articles] 1p; **(13)** Next issue ad [Pablo Marcos, Gullivar Jones of Mars is featured] 1p.

Notes: *Man-Thing* is cover featured. Marv Wolfman is now listed as associate editor, although he actually functions as the editor. The second offering of *Frankenstein 1973* was delayed when Syd Shores suddenly died in the midst of inking the story. The *Man-Thing* reprint was undoubtedly rushed in as a replacement. "Birthright!" was completed by Neal Adams' Crusty Bunkers when the original inker (who appears to be Ralph Reese, based on pages 1–3) got caught short for time. Al Williamson was listed in fanzine records at the time as an artist for a SF/fantasy story that was to appear in *Monsters Unleashed*! His contribution never appeared and I suspect that "Birthright" was intended to be that story. Best story and art goes to "The Cold of the Uncaring Moon," a decent little werewolf tale. Twenty-eight pages of new art and story. The letters page debuts.

4. cover: Jordi Penalva and Luis Dominguez (February 1974)

(1) They Might Be Monsters [Tony Isabella/ Pablo Marcos, frontis] 1p; **(2)** Frankenstein 1973: The Classic Monster! [Gary Friedrich/ John Buscema, Syd Shores and Winslow Mortimer] 10p; **(3)** Crazy ad [Marie Severin] 1p; **(4)** The Hands! [Stan Lee/Gene Colan, reprinted from *Adventures into Terror* #14 (Winter 1952)] 5p; **(5)** Our Martian Heritage: An Excursion

into Fantasy [Chris Claremont, text article with photos] 4p; **(6)** Gullivar Jones, Warrior of Mars: Web of Hate [Tony Isabella/Dave Cockrum] 11p; **(7)** Gullivar Jones: First Man on Mars [The Bullpen/Jim Steranko, test article, details the history of Gullivar Jones] 1p; **(8)** A Monster Reborn [Steve Gerber/Pablo Marcos] 5p; **(9)** Dracula Lives! ad [Pablo Marcos] 1p; **(10)** Book review: The Monster Maker — A Review of Ray Harryhausen's Film Fantasy Scrapbook [Tony Isabella, text article with photos] 7p; **(11)** Vampire Tales/Werewolf by Night ads [Esteban Maroto/Mike Ploog] 1p; **(12)** The Killers [?/Bernie Krigstein, reprinted from *Adventure into Weird Worlds* #10 (September 1952)] 5p; **(13)** To Love, Honor, Cherish ... 'Til Death [Chris Claremont/Don Perlin] 8p; **(14)** In Memoriam: Lon Chaney, Jr. [Martin Pasko, text article with photos] 1p.

Notes: A four-month gap separated #3 and #4. The cover (thanks to Jeff Clem for the info!) was a rare combo painting by Warren cover artist Jordi Penalva and DC cover artist Luis Dominguez. Syd Shores had inked the first seven pages of the *Frankenstein 1973* episode when he died unexpectedly and Win Mortimer finished the inking, also re-inking the head of the monster throughout. Gullivar Jones was a science fantasy strip, based on a novel by Edwin L. Arnold that predated Edgar Rice Burroughs' John Carter of Mars novels. It had previously appeared in the color comic *Creatures on the Loose* #16–21. Bernie Krigstein has a large and justly earned reputation as an artist but his reprint appearance here is just standard 1950s art. Nothing special. The story was somewhat marred by page 2 appearing as page 4 with pages 3 and 4 moved forward to fill the gap. For all the ballyhoo of the return of Frankenstein's monster (after six months who really remembered the first episode?) and the B&W debut of Gullivar Jones, the best story here (and it's a little gem!) is Steve Gerber and Pablo Marcos' oddly tender tale of a lonely rabbi's restoration of faith by way of a golem. One of Marvel's best stand-alone stories. Thirty-five pages of new art and story.

5. cover: Bob Larkin/frontis and inside back cover: Frank Brunner (April 1974), Brunner's art is a reprint from *Man-Thing* #1's cover

(1) Man-Thing: all The Faces of Fear! [Tony Isabella/Vicente Alcazar] 11p; **(2)** Movie review:

The Golden Voyage of Sindbad or What to Do Till the Genie Comes [Gerry Conway, text article with photos] 6p; (2) Peter Snubb: Werewolf [Tony Isabella/Ron Wilson] 1p; (4) Crazy ad [Marie Severin] 1p; (5) The Dark Passage [Stan Lee/Ogden Whitney, reprinted from *Adventures into Terror* #10 (June 1952)] 5p; (6) Glenn Strange, Frankenstein: Monster of Dodge City [Don Glut, text article with photos] 2p; (7) Demon of Slaughter Mansion! [Don McGregor/Juan Boix] 10p; (8) Monsters Unleashed! ad [Pablo Marcos, Frankenstein's Monster is featured] 1p; (9) Monsters in the Media [Carla Joseph, text article with photos] 5p; (10) The Haunt of Horror ad [Ralph Reese, art from an interior story] 1p; (11) Werewolf Tale to End All Werewolf Tales! [?/Paul Hodge, reprinted from *Journey into Unknown Worlds* #29 (July 1954)] 4p; (12) Frankenstein 1974: Once a Monster...! [Gary Friedrich/John Buscema and Winslow Mortimer] 10p.

Notes: *Man-Thing* returns with a cover appearance and a new story. It's not too bad, and Alcazar's art is darn good. Pages 8 and 9 of "Demon of Slaughter Mansion!" are printed out of order. The *Frankenstein 1974* episode lists John Buscema as penciler and you can see his work on occasion but 90 percent of this story appears to be Mortimer's art. Buscema probably did the layouts or thumbnail sketches. From an excellent first episode and a decent second, this serial had begun to lurch about, appearing in this issue with an overly complicated plot about mind swapping that barely made sense at all. Friedrich appeared burnt out completely. It would only get worse. Thirty-two pages of new story and art. Size reduction to 64 pages.

6. cover: Boris Vallejo (June 1974)

(1) Thunderbird [Tony Isabella/Ernie Chan, frontis, Chan's art credited to Ernie Chua] 1p; (2) Frankenstein 1974: Always a Monster! [Doug Moench/Val Mayerik] 12p; (3) Monsters in the Media [Carla Joseph, text article with photos] 3p; (4) Crazy ad [Kelly Freas] 1p; (5) The Strange Children! [?/Sam Kweskin, reprinted from *Adventures into Terror* #19 (May 1953)] 5p; (6) Dracula Lives! ad [Pablo Marcos] 1p; (7) Book review: The Dinosaur Dictionary [Alan Gold, text article with photos] 6p; (8) Darkflame! [Gerry Conway/Carlo Freixas] 7p; (9) Vampire Tales [Luis Dominguez, B&W reproduction of #4's cover] 1p; (10) Werewolf by Night: Panic by Moonlight [Gerry Conway/

Mike Ploog, text story] 6p; (11) Giant-Size Spiderman/The Deadly Hands of Kung Fu ads [Gil Kane and John Romita/Paul Gulacy, Spider-Man, Dracula and Shang Chi are featured] 2p; (12) The Maggots! [?/Hy Rosen, reprinted from *Adventures into Terror* #19 (May 1953)] 3p; (13) The Waters of Werewolves [Doug Moench/Winslow Mortimer] 2p; (14) The Scrimshaw Serpent [Doug Moench/Alphonso Font] 10p.

Notes: A dismal issue! Vallejo delivers a blah cover for Frankenstein's monster. Moench and Mayerik take over the *Frankenstein* serial, reviving (without explanation) characters who had clearly died in earlier stories, dealing in more mindless mind swapping and, in general, mucking the place up. Maybe Friedrich's bizarre previous tale would have been hard to follow but ye gods!!! Moench was, and is, a pretty decent writer but he clearly had no grasp on how to handle the monster. Mayerik's art was an improvement over the Buscema/Mortimer team but he was still in his early, lumpy stage of art, with most of the characters appearing to be constructed of gobs of clay thrown rather randomly into the shapes of humans. The worst of it, though, was that as bad as this story was (and believe me, it stinks!) the regular color comic (which Moench and Mayerik had also taken over) was even worse! From premiering as the best of Marvel's horror attempts to crumbling to the worst by far in less than a year was the most horrifying thing about the monster's strips. With the lead story being such a disaster, the back-ups for this magazine needed to be pretty good. No luck here. The reprints, usually pretty bad anyways, are even worse this issue. They appear to have been chosen by the always handy method of picking a comic off the shelf (in this case, *Adventures into Terror* #19) and reprinting anything that looks vaguely useable. "Darkflame!" could easily be mistaken for one of the 1950s reprints since the art was so bad. The "Werewolf by Night" text story has a great two-page Ploog splash but the rest of the art is badly reproduced Ploog work from the color comic. Only "The Scrimshaw Serpent" is worth reading here and it's, at best, an average tale. Just a lousy issue, although *Monsters Unleashed!* hadn't hit bottom yet. Future comic artist Ken Meyer Jr. sends in a rather critical letter dealing with issue 4.

7. cover: Richard Hescox/title page: ? (August 1974)

(1) The Burning Man [Tony Isabella/Ernie Chan, frontis, Chan's art is credited to Ernie Chua] 1p; (2) Frankenstein 1974: A Tale of Two Monsters! [Doug Moench/Val Mayerik] 14p; (3) Marvel Magazines ad [Alfredo Alcala] 1p; (4) The Monster in the Mist! [?/Al Williamson, reprinted from *Astonishing* #60 (April 1957)] 4p; (5) The Frankenstein Legend [Alan Gold, text article with photos] 4p; (6) Bleeding Stones [Doug Moench/Vicente Alcazar] 10p; (7) Werewolf by Night: Panic by Moonlight, part 2: Madness Under a Mid-Summer Moon [Gerry Conway/Pat Broderick and Klaus Janson, text story] 8p; (8) The Savage Sword of Conan ad [Boris Vallejo, B&W reproduction of #1's cover] 1p; (9) Blind Man's Bluff! [Gerry Conway/Carlos Freixas] 7p; (10) Planet of the Apes ad [Bob Larkin, B&W reproduction of #1's cover] 1p; (11) Monsters in the Media [Carla Joseph, text article with photos] 2p; (12) Next issue ad [George Perez and Frank Giacoia, Gullivar Jones is featured] 1p.

Notes: Editor: Tony Isabella. Moench and Mayerik continue to flail about, trying to dig themselves out of the chasm they leaped into the previous issue. They also attempt a blatant rip-off of the *Swamp Thing*'s character Arcane. Bizarrely enough, the 1950s reprint has the best art here, with a nice clean effort by Al Williamson. Best story is probably "Bleeding Stones." Twenty-eight pages of new art and story.

8. cover: Earl Norem (October 1974)

(1) Monsters from the Sea [Tony Isabella/Ernie Chan, frontis, Chan's art is credited to Ernie Chua] 1p; (2) Monsters Confidential [Tony Isabella, text article] 1p; (3) Frankenstein 1974: Fever in the Freak House [Doug Moench/Val Mayerik] 15p; (4) Monsters Unleashed ad [? and Duffy Vohland, Frankenstein's Monster is featured] 1p; (5) Man-Thing: Several Meaningless Deaths [Steve Gerber/Pat Broderick and Al Milgrom, text story] 7p; (6) Swamp Stars of the Silver Screen [Don Glut, text article with photos] 6p; (7) One Hungers [Neal Adams/Neal Adams and Dan Adkins, reprinted from *Tower of Shadows* #2 (November 1969)] 7p; (8) Gullivar Jones — Warrior of Mars: A Martian Genesis! [Tony Isabella and Doug Moench/George Perez, Duffy Vohland and Rich Buckler] 14p; (9) Next issue ad [Herb Trimpe, the Wendigo is featured with art reprinted from *The Incredible Hulk* #181] 1p.

Notes: If anything, this issue is worse than #6, with Moench and Mayerik delivering a lame, boring story inspired (if that's the word) in equal parts by DC's *Swamp Thing* and Marvel's own origin of *Doctor Doom*. At least the "Always a Monster!" episode from #6 had delivered the horrid interest that a plane wreck or car crash had. This story, however, is simply dreary. *Gullivar Jones* featured artwork by a very young George Perez, with results that look rushed and very uneven. This was Gullivar's last episode and deservedly so. The only quality story here is the five-year-old Neal Adams tale which displayed a respectable amount of mystery and great art. Thirty pages of new art and story, none of it worth a damn.

9. cover: Earl Norem/title page: Dave Cockrum (December 1974)

(1) The Atomic Monster [Tony Isabella/Arvell Jones and Duffy Vohland, frontis] 1p; (2) Monsters Confidential [Tony Isabella, text article] 1p; (3) Frankenstein 1974: The Conscience of the Creature [Doug Moench/Val Mayerik] 16p; (4) Monsters of the Movies ad [Bob Larkin, B&W reproduction of #4's cover] ½ p; (5) The Jewel That Snarled at Slight Greed [Don Perlin and Doug Moench/Don Perlin] 10p; (6) Man-Thing: Several Meaningless Deaths, part 2 [Steve Gerber/Pat Broderick and Al Milgrom, text story] 6p; (7) Crazy ad [Marie Severin] 1p; (8) The Wendigo: Snowbird in Hell [Chris Claremont/Yong Montano] 11p; (9) Savage Tales ad [John Buscema, Ka-Zar is featured] 1p; (10) Next issue ad [Marie Severin and Duffy Vohland, Tigra is featured] 1p.

Notes: The Wendigo is cover-featured while *Man-Thing* appears on the title page. Future Marvel writer Ralph Macchio sends in a letter. The *Frankenstein* story is rather pointless but it did have Mayerik delivering his best art to date on the strip. The improving artwork doesn't save the story but it's at least nice to look at. The cute little Moench/Perlin fantasy "The Jewel That Snarled at Slight Greed" seems out of place in this magazine. It's the best story here, though. The Wendigo had originally appeared as a Hulk villain in *The Incredible Hulk* #181 but largely misfired as the lead of his own story. Thirty-eight pages of new art and story.

10. cover: Jose Antonio Domingo? (February 1975), credited to JAD, see below

(1) They Might Be Monsters [Tony Isabella/Pablo Marcos, frontis, reprinted from *Monsters Unleashed* #4 (February 1974)] 1p; **(2)** The Marvel Bullpen Page Goes Black and White and Read All Over [Marv Wolfman; text article] 1p; **(3)** The Frankenstein Monster: The 11:10 to Murder [Doug Moench/Val Mayerik] 19p; **(4)** Beauty's Vengeance [Doug Moench/Sanho Kim] 8p; **(5)** Vampire Tales/The Deadly Hands of Kung Fu Ads [Jose Antonio Domingo?/Earl Norem, B&W repos of #9 and #7's covers] 1p; **(6)** Tigra, The Were-Woman: The Serenity Stealers [Tony Isabella and Chris Claremont/Tony DeZuniga] 15p; **(7)** Next issue ad [Sanho Kim] 1p.

Notes: Editor: Don McGregor. The cover art, credited to JAD, doesn't really look like Domingo's slick style of artwork. It may be Sebastia Boada's work but I'm simply not sure. Domingo had another cover credited to him for *Vampire Tales* that also doesn't look like his work (and looks nothing like the cover art here either). Future Marvel writer Peter B. Gillis sends in a letter. The *Frankenstein* episode would have you believe that a train carrying the president of the United States would also have a freight car with an open door, and could be hopped on by a cute blonde and a seven-foot-tall monster with no one noticing. "Beauty's Vengeance" is a quite lovely tale with delicate artwork by Kim, a greatly underrated artist from Korea. The Tigra story dates from her early brief horror appearances, before she became a superhero and joined the Avengers. The next issue ad featured art for a never-published Doug Moench/Sanho Kim story entitled "Overload." It also advertised the next installment of The *Frankenstein* serial, which wouldn't actually appear until *The Legion of Monsters* #1.

11. cover: Frank Brunner (April 1975)

(1) The Creature from the Black Lagoon! [Scott Edelman/Dave Cockrum, frontis] 1p; **(2)** An Editorial Felled [Don McGregor, text article] 1p; **(3)** Gabriel, Devil-Hunter: An Angel Felled [Doug Moench/Sonny Trinidad] 22p; **(4)** The Empire [Gerry Conway/Rico Rival] 10p; **(5)** This Is the Valiant One, Signing Out! [Don McGregor/Billy Graham] 12p.

Notes: Final issue. This is pretty much a fix-up issue, with the unexpected appearance of the *Gabriel, Devil-Hunter* story that was probably intended for the never-published The Haunt of Horror #6 while "This Is The Valiant One, Signing Out!" was originally done in 1971 and intended for a Warren magazine. Even with all that, this is the best issue of this title since #4. Dean Mullaney, future publisher of Eclipse Comics, sent in a letter. A *Monsters Unleashed!* annual appeared in the late summer/early fall of 1975.

Tales of the Zombie

1. cover: Boris Vallejo (August 1973)

(1) Simon Garth: The Altar of the Damned! [Roy Thomas and Steve Gerber/John Buscema and Tom Palmer] 13p; **(2)** Vampire Tales ad [Gil Kane] 1p; **(3)** Simon Garth: Zombie! [Stan Lee/Bill Everett, reprinted from *Menace* #5 (July 1953)] 7p; **(4)** Iron-Head [?/Dick Ayers, reprinted from *Journey into Mystery* #1 (June 1952)] 5p; **(5)** The Sensuous Zombie [Tony Isabella, text article with photos] 6p; **(6)** Back to Back and Belly to Belly at the Zombie Jamboree Ball! [Roy Thomas, text article] 1p; **(7)** Monsters Unleashed! ad [Pablo Marcos] ½ p; **(8)** The Thing from the Bog! [Kit Pearson and Marv Wolfman/Pablo Marcos] 10p; **(9)** The Mastermind [Tom Sutton, reprinted from *Chamber of Darkness* #7 (October 1970)] 2p; **(10)** Simon Garth: Night of the Walking Dead [Steve Gerber/John Buscema and Syd Shores] 11p.

Notes: Publisher: Stan Lee. Editor: Roy Thomas. The cost was $0.75 for 72 pages. Vallejo's best cover for a comic magazine graces this issue. There isn't much that's new or trendsetting on the cover, just a bold striking image that perfectly captures the drama and mystery of the Simon Garth (aka The Zombie) strip. This book is worth buying just for the cover. Simon Garth was Marvel's best B&W serial, largely because it actually had a satisfying ending. Most of Marvel's serials were open-ended. You couldn't do anything too drastic with Dracula, or Morbius or Man-Thing because their stories were never intended to end. However, Simon Garth was already dead and his spiritual quest to find final peace was the main theme behind almost all of his adventures. He was lucky to have great scripts from Steve Gerber and Tony Isabella and equally great artwork from a variety of artists, but mainly Pablo Marcos. His origin tale is quite interesting as it was based on a 19-year-old pre–Code story by Stan Lee and Bill Everett, reprinted in this issue. For this appearance this superior reprint story was slightly rewritten and redrawn with Garth's Zombie persona given long hair via art touchups. For the new parts John Buscema provided layouts and Tom Palmer and Syd Shores' the finished art. It was an impressive debut. Like all of the Marvel horror mags, photos from old movies were used to provide story introductions. Simon Garth appeared on the cover for all ten issues. 34 pages of new art and story.

Vallejo's best effort for the horror titles is this painting of Simon Garth, the zombie for the premiere issue of *Tales of the Zombie*. © Marvel Worldwide/used by permission.

2. cover: Boris Vallejo/title page: Pablo Marcos (October 1973)

(1) Simon Garth: Voodoo Island! [Steve Gerber/Pablo Marcos] 12p; (2) Vampire Tales ad [Jose Antonio Domingo, B&W reproduction of #2's cover] 1p; (3) In Memoriam: Bill Everett [Jim Steranko, text article with photos] 1p; (4) Voodoo Unto Others [Tony Isabella/Winslow Mortimer] 6p; (5) Vampire Tales ad [John Romita, Satana is featured] 1p; (6) Acid Test! [Stan Lee/George Tuska, reprinted from *Menace* #5 (July 1953)] 5p; (7) Introducing Brother Voodoo! [Tony Isabella/John Romita, Gene Colan and Dan Adkins, text article] 4p; (8) Twin Burial [Nicola Cuti/Ralph Reese, story credited to Chuck Robinson] 10p; (9) From Out of the Grave! [?/Gene Colan, reprinted from *Adventures into Terror* #29 (March 1954)] 5p; (10) Monsters Unleashed!/ Savage Tales ads [Boris Vallejo/Barry Smith, Vallejo's art is a B&W reproduction of #2's cover] 1p; (11) Voodoo: What's It All About, Alfred? [Chris Claremont, text article with photos] 5p; (12) Crazy ad [Marie Severin] ½ p; (13) Simon Garth: Night of the Spider! [Steve Gerber/Pablo Marcos] 10p; (14) Next issue ad [Pablo Marcos, Simon Garth is featured] 1p.

Notes: Another great Vallejo cover and two great Simon Garth tales. The *Brother Voodoo* text piece gave the color comic history of the Marvel character. Cuti was an editor at Charlton at this time and he used fan writer Chuck Robinson's name to hide the fact that he was writing for another company. Thirty-eight pages of new art and story. Steranko's eulogy for Bill Everett is an excellent model for anyone needing to write one.

3. cover: Boris Vallejo (January 1974)

(1) Simon Garth: When the

Gods Crave Flesh! [Steve Gerber/Pablo Marcos] 22p; (**2**) With the Dawn Comes ... Death! [Chris Claremont, text story with photos] 6p; (**3**) Net Result! [?/Tony DiPreta, reprinted from ?] 5p; (**4**) Savage Tales/Dracula Lives! ads [Barry Smith/Jordi Penalva and Luis Dominguez, the Penalva and Dominguez's art is a B&W reproduction of #4's cover] 2p; (**5**) Warrior's Burden [Tony Isabella/Vicente Alcazar] 6p; (**6**) Movie Review: Night of the Living Dead [Don Mc-Gregor, text article with photos] 6p; (**7**) I Won't Stay Dead! [?/Bill Walton, reprinted from *Journey into Mystery* #10 (July 1953), originally entitled "He Wouldn't Stay Dead!"] 5p; (**8**) Jilimbi's Word [Doug Moench/Enrique Romeo Badia] 9p; (**9**) Zombie Feature Page: Steve Gerber profile/Code Name: Trixie [Steve Gerber and Gerry Boudreau, text article with photos] 1p; (**10**) Next issue ad [Pablo Marcos, Simon Garth is featured] 1p.

Notes: Three-month gap between issues. Marv Wolfman is listed as associate editor and probably is the actual editor. This is a pretty good issue, despite a rather weak cover by Vallejo, with a dandy Simon Garth episode and two very good stand-alone stories. "Warrior's Burden" (a new script by Isabella for a story that first appeared in Europe) is a fine samurai tale while "Jilimbi's Word" has very good artwork by Badia. Thirty-five pages of new art and story. The letters page begins with a new illustration by Pablo Marcos.

4. cover: Boris Vallejo/frontis and on inside back cover: Pablo Marcos (March 1974)

(**1**) Simon Garth: The Law and Phillip Bliss! [Steve Gerber/Pablo Marcos] 11p; (**2**) Movie review: James Bond Meets Baron Samedi or Live and Let Die Revisited [Don McGregor/Frank Springer and Pablo Marcos, text article with photos] 7p; (**3**) The Drums of Doom! [Gerry Conway/Rich Buckler, Vic Martin and Winslow Mortimer] 5p; (**4**) Neo Witch Craft [Lin Carter, text article with photos] 5p; (**5**) Courtship by Voodoo [Tony Isabella/Ron Wilson] 1p; (**6**) Nightfilth Rising [Doug Moench/Winslow Mortimer] 7p; (**7**) Four Daughters of Satan [John Albano/Ernie Chan, Chan's art credited to Ernie Chau] 8p; (**8**) Simon Garth: Dead Man's Judgement!, The Law and Phillip Bliss, part 2 [Steve Gerber/Pablo Marcos] 12p; (**9**) Zombie Feature Page: Pablo Marcos profile [Marv Wolfman, text article with photos] 1p; (**10**) Dracula Lives! ad [Luis Dominguez, B&W reproduction of #5's cover] 1p.

Notes: Another striking cover (his last for this title) by Boris Vallejo, although Simon Garth's feet are huge compared to the rest of his body. He must be a very lucky dead guy. For some reason, *Tales of the Zombie* had its allotment of new art and story increased months before any of Marvel's other B&W magazines did. This issue has 46 new pages. Rich Buckler provides only layouts for "The Drums of Doom!" with Win Mortimer appearing to do the bulk of the artwork. As usual, the best story and art is from the Simon Garth two-parter but "Four Daughters of Satan" is also quite good. The extra-large pin-up on the frontispiece and inside back cover features Simon Garth. The magazine size was reduced to 64 pages.

5. cover: Earl Norem/frontis and on inside back cover: Pablo Marcos (May 1974)

(**1**) Simon Garth: Palace of Black Magic! [Steve Gerber/Pablo Marcos] 22p; (**2**) Crazy ad [Kelly Freas] 1p; (**3**) Movie Review: White Zombie: Faithful Unto Death [Doug Moench, text article with photos] 6p; (**4**) Who Walks with a Zombie! [?/Russ Heath, reprinted from ?] 4p; (**5**) With the Dawn Comes Death, part 2 [Chris Claremont, text story with photos and artwork from "The Cold of the Uncaring Moon" by George Tuska and Klaus Janson, reprinted from *Monsters Unleashed* #3 (November 1973)] 5p; (**6**) Brother Voodoo Lives Again [Doug Moench/Gene Colan and Dan Adkins, text article with artwork from a *Strange Tales* story] 3p; (**7**) Voodoo War! [Tony Isabella/Syd Shores, Dick Ayers and Mike Esposito] 8p; (**8**) Death's Bleak Birth! [Doug Moench/Frank Springer] 9p; (**9**) Next issue ad [Earl Norem, B&W reproduction of next issue's cover] 1p.

Notes: Earl Norem, Marvel's go-to cover artist for this period, became the regular cover artist from here on out. Art Stampler, who wrote prose stories for the Skywald B&Ws, sent in a letter. Simon Garth was featured in a large pin-up on the frontispiece and the inside back cover. Dick Ayers finished the "Voodoo War" pencils after initial artist Syd Shores died. Shores penciled only the first two pages of the story. Chris Claremont's text story was concluded after skipping an issue. "Death's Bleak Birth!" had the best story and art here. Thirty-nine pages of new story and art.

6. cover: Earl Norem/frontis and title page: Pablo Marcos (July 1974)

(1) Tales of the Zombie Prologue [Steve Gerber/Pablo Marcos, text synopsis of previous issues with reformatted art from those issues] 1p; (2) Simon Garth: Child of Darkness! [Steve Gerber/Pablo Marcos] 19p; (3) Dracula Lives! ad [Gene Colan] 1p; (4) The Plague of the Zombies [Gerry Boudreau, text article with photos] 6p; (5) The Savage Sword of Conan ad [John Buscema and Ernie Chan] 1p; (6) Movie review: Sugar Hill [Jim Harmon, text article with photos] 3p; (7) The Compleat Voodoo Man [Chris Claremont, text article with photos and art for a Brother Voodoo story] 4p; (8) Brother Voodoo: End of a Legend! [Len Wein and Doug Moench/Gene Colan and Frank Chiaramonte] 17p; (9) The Voodoo Beat [Carla Joseph, text article with photos] 3p.

Notes: Future Marvel writer Ralph Macchio sent in a letter. The *Brother Voodoo* story was almost certainly intended for the never published *Strange Tales* #174 and displays all the overwrought melodrama of a typical Marvel color comic of that period. Thirty-six pages of new art and story but only the Simon Garth story is really worth reading.

7. cover: Earl Norem/frontis: Alfredo Alcala/ title page: Pat Broderick (September 1974), Alcala and Broderick's artwork is from interior panels

(1) Simon Garth: Prologue/Epilogue [Steve Gerber/Pablo Marcos] 2p; (2) Simon Garth: The Blood-Testament of Brian Collier [Doug Moench/Alfredo Alcala] 30p; (3) Marvel Magazines ad [Alfredo Alcala] 1p; (4) Voodoo in the Park [Kenneth Dreyfack/Dan Green, text article] 3p; (5) Haiti's Walking Dead [Doug Moench/Winslow Mortimer] 2p; (6) Book review: Inside "Inside Voodoo" [Chris Claremont/Pat Broderick, text article] 4p; (7) A Second Chance to Die [Carl Wessler/Alfredo Alcala] 7p; (8) Crazy ad [fumetti strip, starring Stan Lee] 1p; (9) Next issue ad [Pablo Marcos] 1p.

Notes: Editor: Tony Isabella. Moench and Alcala deliver a 30-page fill-in to give the regular Simon Garth team a breather. It's a pretty good effort. Alcala also illustrates another story by former EC writer Carl Wessler. It's not bad, either. All in all, a solid issue with 41 pages of new art and story.

8. cover: Earl Norem (November 1974)

(1) Voodoo Killers [Tony Isabella/Michael Kaluta, frontis] 1p; (2) The Happy Hougan Speaks [Tony Isabella] 1p; (3) Simon Garth: A Death Made Out of Ticky-Tacky! [Steve Gerber/Pablo Marcos] 22p; (4) The Haunt of Horror ad [Enrique Romeo Badia, Satana is featured] ½ p; (5) Jimmy Doesn't Live Here Anymore [David Anthony Kraft/Michael Kaluta, text story] 4p; (6) Night of the Hunted! [Larry Lieber/Ron Wilson, Mike Esposito and Frank Giacoia] 8p; (7) Tales of the Happy Humfo [Chris Claremont/ Michael Kaluta, text article] 4p; (8) Makao's Vengeance [David Anthony Kraft/Alfredo Alcala] 6p; (9) Crazy ad [Marie Severin] 1p; (10) The Deadly Hands of Kung Fu/Planet of the Apes ads [Ron Wilson and Mike Ploog] 1p; (11) Savage Tales ad [John Buscema, Ka-Zar is featured] 1p.

Notes: The installation of Tony Isabella as editor last issue must have been a late decision as his editorial introduction appears here. He was evidently determined to shake this magazine up a bit as his first order of business was to announce the replacement of Pablo Marcos on the Simon Garth serial. He promised that Steve Gerber would remain as writer but that proved to be incorrect. He also mentioned dropping the text pieces for actual prose stories, beginning with this issue's "Jimmy Doesn't Live Here Anymore," bringing back *Brother Voodoo* (outside of the Living Mummy, one of the dullest of Marvel supernatural characters) and, in #11, debuting a new serial entitled *Voodoo Island*, which was to be written by Isabella and Moench. In the midst of all that, Gerber and Marcos deliver their best Simon Garth story, Michael Kaluta graces the issue with spot illustrations as well as a one-pager and Alfredo Alcala spices up Dave Kraft's "Makao's Vengeance." A good, solid issue.

9. cover: Earl Norem (January 1975)

(1) Was He a Voodoo-Man? [Tony Isabella/ Winslow Mortimer, frontis] 1p; (2) The Marvel Bullpen Page Goes Black and White and Read All Over [Marv Wolfman, text article] 1p; (3) Simon Garth: Simon Garth Lives Again [Tony Isabella/Virgilio Redondo and Alfredo Alcala] 13p; (4) Simon Garth: A Day in the Life of a Dead Man [Tony Isabella and Chris Claremont/Yong Montano and Alfredo Alcala] 12p; (5) Simon Garth: The 2nd Death Around!

[Tony Isabella/Ron Wilson and Pablo Marcos] 11p; (**6**) Savage Tales ad [John Romita, Shanna, the She-Devil and Ka-Zar are featured] 1p; (**7**) Herbie the Liar Said It Wouldn't Hurt [Doug Moench/Alfredo Alcala] 7p.

Notes: Dean Mullaney sent in a letter. *Simon Garth*'s serial did what all the best Warren B&W hero serials had done. It ended! Best of all, it was an ending that made sense and remained true to the character that the reader had been following for the last nine issues. The magazine was actually intended for cancellation with this issue, but got a last-minute reprieve. In true Marvel tradition, the powers that be not only revived the magazine but fully intended to revive Simon Garth in the very next issue, but (thank God!) it didn't happen and since the magazine actually was cancelled with #10, this fine finale wasn't undercut. Before we got to the last page, however, a lot of turmoil took place. First, although it was his title and possibly his plot, Gerber didn't script this story. According to editor Tony Isabella, Gerber's heavy workload forced him to leave the strip. Isabella himself filled in on at least the scripting, with some help from newcomer Chris Claremont. The script for the third episode was lost so Isabella rewrote the final chapter over a weekend, feeding the pages to the artists. Second, the artwork for the issue was clearly done in a bit of a rush. Alcala (a fine artist) didn't do the complete art job. He inked the first two chapters while all three chapters were penciled by different artists. Who would ink the third chapter? Why, only the guy who was bumped off the strip in the first place — Pablo Marcos! Still, for all the backstage drama that was going on, *Simon Garth* got a fine sendoff. "Herbie the Liar..." is also a pretty good story. A fine issue.

10. cover: Earl Norem/frontis: Tom Sutton (March 1975)

> (**1**) The Partial Resurrection of a Voodoo-Haunted Editorial [Don McGregor, text article] 1p; (**2**) Brother Voodoo: The Resurrection of Papa Jambo [Doug Moench/Tony DeZuniga] 21p; (**3**) Next issue ad [Rico Rival, Simon Garth is featured] 1p; (**4**) Eye for an Eye, Tooth for a Tooth [Gerry Conway/Virgilio Redondo and Rudy Nebres] 9p; (**5**) Malaka's Curse! [Carl Wessler and John Warner/Vicente Alcazar] 7p; (**6**) Grave Business [Tom Sutton] 10p.

Notes: Final issue. Although Simon Garth appears on the cover, he doesn't have a story inside. Tom Sutton's frontispiece illustration was painted in gray tones and both the illustration and the story it was intended for may have originally been intended for a Charlton comic. Ralph Macchio sends in a letter. David Anthony Kraft and Don McGregor take over as co-editors. Caught 30 pages short for this issue with the disappearance in the mail of the intended Simon Garth story (was it ever found?), the new editors scrambled to come up with voodoo-style stories to accompany the return of *Brother Voodoo*. John Warner rapidly scripted a story that the editors apparently didn't have time to send back to plotter Carl Wessler while Sutton's Lovecraftian tale (which at least featured dead guys) was probably drafted into service by Don McGregor, who was a major Sutton fan. As for the *Brother Voodoo* story they were to accompany? When you've got a crap character, you usually get a crap story, although Moench and DeZuniga make a real effort here. Still, the best story and art easily belong to Tom Sutton's effort, which was both stylish and well-crafted. The next issue ad promised the return of *Simon Garth* in "The Partial Resurrection of Simon Garth!." They even promised that "this time, nothing can stop him!" Except, of course, having your magazine canceled out from under you. In addition to the *Simon Garth* story, a tale called "A Fire Within" by Bill Mantlo, Don Heck and Bob McLeod was expected. To my knowledge, neither of these stories ever appeared. Outside of *Dracula Lives!*, *Tales of the Zombie* was probably the most satisfying read of all the Marvel B&W horror mags and its absence was a real loss. A *Tales of the Zombie* annual came out in the late summer of 1975.

Vampire Tales

1. cover: Esteban Maroto (August 1973)

> (**1**) Morbius [Steve Gerber/Pablo Marcos] 14p; (**2**) Blood Is Thicker... [Roy Thomas, text article with photo] 1½ p; (**3**) Savage Tales ad [Barry Smith] ½ p; (**4**) To Kill a Werewolf! [Stan Lee/ Bill Everett, reprinted from *Menace* #9 (January 1954), originally entitled "The Fangs of the Wolf!"] 5p; (**5**) The Vampire: His Kith and Kin; an Analysis in Five Parts of the Book by Montague Summers [Chris Claremont, text

article with photos] 4p; (6) Crazy/Tales of the Zombie ad [Marie Severin/Bill Everett and John Romita?] 1p; (7) The Vampyre! [Ron Goulart and Roy Thomas/Winslow Mortimer, from the story by John Polidori] 13p; (8) Satan Can Wait! [?/Paul Reinman, reprinted from *Journey into Mystery* #15 (April 1954)] 5p; (9) The Worst (No Kiddin'!) Vampire Films Ever Made! [Mark Evanier, text article with photos] 4p; (10) Dracula Lives!/The Haunt of Horror ad [Neal Adams] 1p; (11) Revenge of the Unliving! [Gardner Fox/Jordi Bernet] 8p; (12) Next issue ad [Pablo Marcos] 1p.

Notes: Publisher: Stan Lee. Editor: Roy Thomas. It was $0.75 for 72 pages. Marvel had a curious habit of limiting the scope and range of their horror magazines. This one featured stories based solely on vampires although they couldn't use Dracula as he already has his own color comic and B&W magazine. This should have caused the magazine to suffer, but this was actually one of Marvel's better B&Ws. As in the other horror magazines, photos from old movies introduced each story. Morbius was not a supernatural vampire, but one created by science (in the pages of *Spider-Man*). Thus he *was* actually living and not one of the undead. The irony here is that, unlike most of Marvel's vampires, who fit right in with the human crowd, Morbius looked dead, with corpse-white skin and a half-decayed nose, somewhat resembling the latter-day Michael Jackson. The adaptation of the Polidori story is interesting as the original story is one of the first English language fiction tales featuring vampires, predating Dracula by 78 years. Polidori was the fourth writer — the other three were Lord Byron, Percy Bysshe Shelley and Mary Wollstonecraft Shelley — attending the reading of horror stories at Lake Geneva that gave birth to Mary Shelley's novel *Frankenstein*. The four were so enthralled with the horror tales that they all promised to write one of their own. Polidori's contribution was this tale. The Bill Everett art on the *Menace* reprint is actually quite nice. As with all the Marvel monster magazines, pre–Code reprints and text pieces take up a large percentage of the pages. Thirty-five pages of new story and art.

2. cover: Jose Antonio Domingo (October 1973), credited to JAD

(1) Morbius: The Blood Sacrifice of Amanda Saint! [Don McGregor/Rich Bucker and Pablo Marcos] 11p; (2) V Is for Vampire! [Roy Thomas, text article with photo] 1p; (3) Dracula Lives! ad [Neal Adams, B&W reproduction of #3's cover] 1p; (4) Witch Hunt! [?/Mannie Banks, reprinted from *Journey into Mystery* #15 (April 1954)] 4p; (5) Crazy ad [Kelly Freas] 1p; (6) The Haunt of Horror/Monsters Unleashed! ad [Kelly Freas/Mike Ploog] 1p; (7) A Vampire by Any Other Name: A Look at Lugosi's Non-Dracula Roles [Doug Moench, text article with photos] 6p; (8) Five Claws to Tryphon [Gardner Fox/Jesus Blasco and John Romita] 10p; (9) A Generation of Vampires: Part Two of a Five-Part Study of Montague Summers' The Vampire — His Kith and Kin [Chris Claremont, text article with photos, art from issues of *The Tomb of Dracula*] 4p; (10) Satana [Roy Thomas/John Romita] 4p; (11) Tales of the Zombie ad [Pablo Marcos] 1p; (12) At the Stroke of Midnight [Jim Steranko, reprinted from *Tower of Shadows* #1 (September 1969)] 7p; (13) Savage Tales ad [Barry Smith] ½ p; (14) Hodiah Twist: The Praying Mantis Principle [Don McGregor/Rich Buckler, Carlos Garzon and Klaus Janson] 11p.

Notes: Marv Wolfman is listed as the associate editor and probably became the de facto editor around this time. A very good issue with Don McGregor taking over the scripting chores on Morbius and moving him firmly in a horror direction that was much more satisfying than the lame SF stories that his color series was giving him. Nice art here from Buckler and Marcos as well. McGregor also debuted his Sherlock Holmes clone, Hodiah Twist, in an interesting adventure. Twist was originally conceived as a character for a never-published Warren magazine. Again, Buckler provided the pencils with the help of fine inking from Garzon and Janson. Satana debuted in a little vignette that was actually better than any of her regular adventures (with the exception of her appearance in *Marvel Preview*). A tight script by Thomas and exceptionally good art from Romita highlighted a good little mystery tale. A deadline problem was probably the reason Jesus Blasco didn't complete "Five Claws to Tryphon." John Romita stepped in to finish the last four pages but their art styles didn't really mesh and the story certainly suffered from it. Surprisingly, the best story and art go to a reprint! Jim Steranko's classic "At the Stroke of Midnight!" was only four years old and one wonders why Marvel didn't chuck out most of their lame 1950s reprints and just use the decent reprints that were available from Marvel's short-lived venture into color horror anthologies. Only three or four of the 40 or so quite decent stories produced during 1969–1971 and some 20–30 more produced in 1972–1973 were reprinted. Steranko's tale looked even better in black and white than it did in its color comics' debut. Thirty-six pages of new story and art.

3. cover: Luis Dominguez (February 1974)

(**1**) Satana: The Kiss of Death [Gerry Conway/ Esteban Maroto] 10p; (**2**) The Collection [Russ Jones and Bhob Stewart/Paul Reinman] 4p; (**3**) Vampire Hunting for Fear and Profit: The Vampire — His Kith and Kin, part 3 [Chris Claremont, text article with photos] 6p; (**4**) Don't Try to Outsmart the Devil! [Stan Lee/Carmine Infantino, reprinted from *Adventures into Terror* #13 (December 1952)] 8p; (**5**) Everything You Always Wanted to Know About Satana (But Were Too Awestruck to Ask) [Carla Joseph/Esteban Maroto and John Romita, text article] 5p; (**6**) Crazy ad [Kelly Freas] 1p; (**7**) Bat's Belfry [Don McGregor/Vicente Ibanez, from the story by August Derleth] 9p; (**8**) Marvel Comics ad [various] 1p; (**9**) Savage Tales ad [Pablo Marcos, B&W repro of #3's cover] 1p; (**10**) Vampires in Time and Space [Tony Isabella/Pablo Marcos] 1p; (**11**) Morbius: Demon Fire! [Don McGregor/Rich Buckler and Klaus Janson] 12p; (**12**) Next issue ad [Esteban Maroto, art from an upcoming story] 1p; (**13**) Vampire Tales Feature Page: Support Your Local Short Auto-Biographer [Don McGregor/Marie Severin, text article] 1p; (**14**) Monsters Unleashed!/Crazy/Dracula Lives! ad [Frank Brunner, Kelly Freas and Pablo Marcos, Brunner's art is a B&W reproduction of #4's cover] 2p.

Notes: Four months passed between #2 and #3's appearances. Morbius is cover featured. Warren star Esteban Maroto moved over to Marvel for a short period. His art here is quite good, with a very sexy Satana. *Satana* moved after this appearance to the new B&W magazine *The Haunt of Horror*. The letters page debuts with an illustration of a vampire bat as the masthead. Best story and art here are split between the *Satana* and *Morbius* episodes, although I'm tempted to include the *Satana* tryout illustrations from Maroto and Romita as well. They are

quite striking. Thirty-two pages of new art and story.

4. cover: Boris Vallejo (April 1974)

(**1**) Morbius, the Living Vampire: Lighthouse of the Possessed [Don McGregor/Tom Sutton] 13p; (**2**) Everything You Wanted to Know About Vampires (But Were Afraid to Ask), Part 4 of a Five-part Series Based on the Vampire — His Kith and Kin by Montague Summers [Chris Claremont, text article with photos] 6p; (**3**) Vampire Tales Feature Page: Notes on a Piece I Don't Want to Write [Gerry Conway, text article, profile] 1p; (**4**) Somewhere Waits the Vampire [?/Paul Reinman, reprinted from *Journey into Unknown Worlds* #27 (December 1952)] 5p; (**5**) A Vampire's Home Is His Castle [Doug Moench/Lombardia] 9p; (**6**) Movie Review: Hell House Is Dying [Don McGregor, text article with photos] 5p; (**7**) Crazy ad [Marie Severin] 1p; (**8**) The Vampire's Coffin! [?/Tony DiPreta, reprinted from *Mystery Tales* #15 (September 1953)] 5p; (**9**) The Drifting Snow [Tony Isabella/Esteban Maroto, from the story by August Derleth] 11p; (**10**) Lilith: The First Vampire [Tony Isabella/Ernie Chan, on the inside back cover, Chan's art credited to Ernie Chua] 1p; (**11**) Next issue ad [Pablo Marcos, on back cover, Moebius and Satana are featured] 1p.

Notes: Size reduction to 64 pages. McGregor's *Morbius* story was originally intended as a *Vampirella* story for Warren. McGregor changed Vampi and her supporting cast to Morbius and his crew, but the story is otherwise unchanged. Tom Sutton does the art honors on the *Morbius* strip and demonstrates why he was the definitive artist for our living vampire. It's a standout effort on Sutton's part but the best art and story honors here go to Tony Isabella and Esteban Maroto's superb adaptation of Derleth's "The Drifting Snow." This is one of the most impressive stories (and one of the best adaptations) that the Marvel B&Ws published. Excellent work. Only 34 pages of new story and art but a top issue.

5. cover: Esteban Maroto (June 1974)

(**1**) The Vampire Viscount of France [Doug Moench/Winslow Mortimer, frontis and on the inside back cover] 2p; (**2**) Morbius, the Living Vampire: Blood Tide! [Don McGregor/Rich Buckler and Ernie Chan, Chan's inking credited to Ernie Chua] 14p; (**3**) Movie Review: Count Yorga — Vampire of the Year [Don Glut, text article with photos] 6p; (**4**) The Living Dead

[Roy Thomas/Alan Kupperberg and Dick Giordano] 8p; (5) Devil's Den [Carla Joseph, text article with photos] 5p; (6) Morbius, the Living Vampire: ...The Way It Began! [Roy Thomas/Gil Kane and Frank Giacoia, reprinted and edited down from the original 35-page story in *Spider-Man* #102 (November 1971)] 11p; (7) The Vampire Wants Blood! [Doug Moench/Val Mayerik] 9p; (8)The Haunt of Horror ad [Ralph Reese] 1p; (9) Dracula Lives! ad [Pablo Marcos] 1p.

Notes: Future Marvel writer Ralph Macchio sends in a letter. "The Living Dead" is an interesting story but the stiff artwork cripples it. Likewise, the artwork again diminishes the story on "The Vampire Wants Blood!" Mayerik's art soon vastly improved over his lumpy, claylike effort here. Best story here is "Blood Tide" but the best art is from the reprinted Kane/Giacoia artwork on Morbius' origin. Thirty-three pages of new art and story.

6. cover: Boris Vallejo/frontis and title page: Pablo Marcos (August 1974)

(1) Lilith, Daughter of Dracula [Marv Wolfman and Steve Gerber/Bob Brown and Tom Palmer] 10p; (2) Marvel Magazines ad [Alfredo Alcala] 1p; (3) Crazy ad [Kelly Freas] 1p; (4) A Novel Way to Die!: Part 5 of a Series Based on the Vampire — His Kith and Kin by Montague Summers [Chris Claremont/Pablo Marcos and a B&W reproduction of *Dracula Lives!* #3's cover by Neal Adams, text article] 6p; (5) Angie's Soul [Chris Claremont/Barcells] 8p; (6) Blood Death [Doug Moench/Alfredo Alcala] 8p; (7) TV Review: Dark Shadows [Gerry Boudreau, text article with photos] 5p; (8) The Color of Crimson Gold [Doug Moench/Vicenta Alcazar] 11p; (9) Devil's Den [Carla Joseph, text article with photos] 3p; (10) Tales of the Zombie ad [Pablo Marcos] 1p.

Notes: There are considerable signs of artistic touchups on Vallejo's cover, with the culprit appearing to be John Romita. Lilith is featured on the cover and the title page while Morbius is featured on the frontispiece. Marv Wolfman is now listed as full editor although he'd probably been doing the actual editing since #3. Ralph Macchio sends in another letter. Lilith previously appeared in the color comic *Giant-Size Chillers* #1 (June 1974). She had only one appearance here in *Vampire Tales*, soon transferring over to *Drac-*

ula Lives! Brown and Palmer made a good artist teamup. Best story here is "Angie's Soul" by Chris Claremont. Thirty-seven new pages of art and story.

7. cover: Jose Antonio Domingo/frontis and title page: ? (October 1974), credited to JAD

(1) Morbius, the Living Vampire: Where Is Gallows Bend and What the Hell Am I Doing There? [Don McGregor/Tom Sutton] 18p; (2) Crazy ad [Marie Severin] 1p; (3) Sip the Sweet Poison [Doug Moench/Billy Graham] 9p; (4) Marvel Magazines ad [Alfredo Alcala] 1p; (5) The Devil's Den [Carla Joseph, text article with photos] 2p; (6) Bats [Doug Moench/Paul Gulacy and Duffy Vohland] 7p; (7) Iron Fist ad [Gil Kane and ?] 1p; (8) Agents of the High Road [Doug Moench/Howard Chaykin] 9p.

Notes: The unknown artist doing the frontispiece and title-page art is probably one of the Filipino artists. Ralph Macchio sends in another letter. "Bats" is a wordless story. Best art and story is the superb *Morbius* episode. Probably the best *Morbius* story ever. The Moench/Chaykin "Agents of the High Road" is also quite good. Forty-three pages of new art and story, bringing the magazine closer to the story content of a Warren 64-page comic.

8. cover: Jose Antonio Domingo (December 1974), credited to JAD

(1) The Heart Devourer [Tony Isabella/Ernie Chan, frontis, Chan's art is credited to Ernie Chua] 1p; (2) Morbius, the Living Vampire: High Midnight [Don McGregor/Mike Vosburg and Frank Chiarmonte] 19p; (3) Tales of the Zombie ad [Alfredo Alcala] ½ p; (4) The Vendetta [Carla Conway (aka Carla Joseph) and Gerry Conway/Joe Staton] 6p; (5) The Inheritance [Carla Conway and Gerry Conway/Alfredo Alcala] 10p; (6) Blade, the Vampire Slayer: Beware the Legions! [Marv Wolfman/Tony DeZuniga] 11p.

Notes: Ralph Macchio sends in another letter. Vosburg and Chiarmonte's art on *Morbius* was in a Tom Sutton mode. Nice try but they'd have done better to follow their own styles. "The Vendetta" had snappy Staton art. Blade was a *Tomb of Dracula* villain (or hero, actually, since Dracula was such a rotter) from the color comic.

9. cover: Marti Ripoll (February 1975), credited to Jose Antonio Domingo, aka JAD

Another JAD effort, this time for Marvel's *Vampire Tales*. Domingo's paintings were often quite beautiful in spite of the subject matter. © Marvel Worldwide/used by permission.

(1) The Vampire of the Inn [Tony Isabella/Ernie Chan, frontis] 1p; (2) The Marvel Bullpen Page Goes Black and White and Read All Over [Marv Wolfman, text article] 1p; (3) Blade, the Vampire Slayer: Bloodmoon [Marv Wolfman and Chris Claremont/Tony DeZuniga] 12p; (4) Monsters Unleashed/The Haunt of Horror ad [Sebastia Boada?/Dick Giordano, B&W repos of #10 and #5's covers] 1p; (5) Blood Lunge [Doug Moench/Russ Heath] 5p; (6) The Bleeding Time [Gerry Conway and Carla Conway/ Virgilio Redondo, Alfredo Alcala and Tony DeZuniga] 10p; (7) Unknown Worlds of Science Fiction ad [Rick Bryant] 1p; (8) Blood Stalker! [Larry Leiber/Jesus Blasco] 9p; (9) Planet of the Apes/Monsters of the Movies ad [Bob Larkin, B&W repos of #4 and #7's covers]

1p; (10) Shards of a Crystal Rainbow [Doug Moench/ Tony DeZuniga] 7p; (11) Next issue ad [Sonny Trinidad, Moebius is featured] 1p; (12) Marvel Magazines ad [Alfredo Alcala, caricatures of Dracula, Conan, Werewolf by Night, Frankenstein's Monster, Gulliver Jones, Simon Garth, Satana and Moebius are featured] 1p.

Notes: Although Jose Antonio Domingo, aka JAD, is listed as the cover artist, this cover looks nothing like his usual sleek work. A perusal of the *Dossier Negro* Archives website revealed that the artist is Marti Ripoll who painted this cover for Spain's *Dossier Negro* #4 in either 1968 or 1969. Another cover attributed around this time to JAD (*Monsters Unleashed!* #10, which can be glimpsed in an ad in this book) also looks nothing like JAD's normal work. The artist for the *Monsters Unleashed!* book, however, looks more like Sebastia Boada's work. In that case, Boada, like JAD, was also a Skywald cover artist so it's possible that Marvel simply got the credits wrong. Both this and the *Monsters Unleashed!* covers are pretty good, by the way. Future Eclipse publisher Dean Mullaney sends in a letter. Doug Moench's "Shards of a Crystal Rainbow" is the best story here with Russ Heath's "Blood Lunge" providing the best artwork. The *Blade* serial was continued in *Marvel Preview* #3.

10. cover: Richard Hescox/frontis: Paul Gulacy and Duffy Vohland (April 1975)

(1) Exposed at Last! The Munificent Marvel Maniacs!: Stan Lee, Marv Wolfman, Don McGregor, David Anthony Kraft, John Warner, Roy Thomas, Len Wein and John Romita

mini-profiles [Marv Wolfman, text article] 1p; (2) Morbius, the Living Vampire: A Taste of Crimson Life [Doug Moench/Sonny Trinidad] 25p; (3) Monsters of the Movies/Planet of the Apes ad [Sebastia Boada? and Bob Larkin, B&W repos of #7 and #6's covers] 1p; (4) A House of Pleasure, The House of Death [Doug Moench/Mike Vosburg and Howard Nostrand] 10p; (5) Blindspot! [Gerry Conway/Virgilio Redondo and Alfredo Alcala] 9p; (6) The Savage Sword of Conan/The Deadly Hands of Kung Fu ad [Boris Vallejo/Neal Adams, B&W repos of $5 and #$11's covers] 1p.

Notes: *Morbius* is featured on both the cover and frontispiece. Dean Mullaney and Ralph Macchio both send in letters. The lengthy *Morbius* story is split up into three chapters subtitled "Fast of Blood," "Temptation" and "Feast of Blood" respectively. It also has the best story and art here, although Moench takes the Living Vampire in a much more familiar Marvel-style action adventure path than McGregor had been doing.

11. cover: Richard Hexcox/frontis: Pete Lijauco (June 1975)

(1) Fearsome Features, Far-Out Fabrications, and Fictional Configurations! [Archie Goodwin, a listing of Marvel Magazines and Comics on sale] 1p; (2) Morbius, the Living Vampire: Death Kiss [Doug Moench/Sonny Trinidad] 34p; (3) Hobo's Lullaby [John Warner/Yong Montano] 9p; (4) Next issue ad [Tony DeZuniga, Blade is featured.] 1p; (5) Marvel preview ad [John Romita and Tony DeZuniga, the Punisher is featured] 1p.

Notes: Final issue. Archie Goodwin is the editor. A 12th issue is promised but the story intended for that issue, a full-length *Blade* story, appeared in *Marvel Preview* #3 instead. A *Vampire Tales* annual appeared in place of the 12th issue.

The Haunt of Horror

1. cover: Bob Larkin/frontis and title page: Alfredo Alcala (April 1974)

(1) The Rats! [Gerry Conway/Ralph Reese] 8p; (2) Crazy ad [Marie Severin] 1p; (3) The Deadly Hands of Kung Fu ad [Dick Giordano] 1p; (4) Crazy ad [Kelly Freas] 1p; (5) The Hint of Horror [Roy Thomas/Alfredo Alcala, text article, art is a negative image of the frontispiece art] 1p; (6) Heartstop [George Alec Effinger/Walt Simonson, text story] 21p; (7) The Last Man!

[?/Russ Heath, reprinted from ?] 5p; (8) His Own Kind! [Roy Thomas/Val Mayerik and Mike Esposito, from the story by Thomas M. Disch] 9p; (9) Dracula Lives! ad [Pablo Marcos] 1p; (10) The Nightmare Patrol [Gerry Conway/Ernie Chan, Chan's art credited to Ernie Chua] 8p; (11) In the Shadows of the City [Steve Gerber/Vicente Alcazar] 7p.

Notes: Publisher: Stan Lee. Editor: Roy Thomas with Marv Wolfman listed as associate editor. It was $0.75 for 64 pages. This magazine reused the cancelled digest magazine's title. The stated intent of this magazine was to present a "quieter" brand of horror. That approach lasted for just this single issue, even though some of Marvel's best B&W horror tales appeared in this issue. Bob Larkin's werewolf cover is one of the best he did for either Marvel or Warren comics. The prose story "Heartstop" was originally intended for the digest *Haunt of Horror*. Most of Marvel's horror stories weren't very scary. That's not too surprising, considering that Marvel made its reputation on providing strong serial adventures. Thus, most of the horror material were really action-adventure yarns with an underpinning of horror. This issue, however, had some stories that went straight after horror, with the Gerber/Alcazar offering, "In the Shadows of the City" being downright creepy. In fact, I'd go so far as to say that this story was Marvel's best achievement in short-form horror (*The Monster of Frankenstein* #1–6 being the best long-form horror achievement). Gerber's excellent, yet uncomfortable, first-person script depicts a serial killer's nocturnal hunt for victims with the reader himself as the ultimate victim. That was bad enough, but Alcazar's disquieting artwork and character design only intensified the horror by stripping away much of the sense of fantasy or fiction from the tale. The bleak urban portrait puts one in mind of the Warren story, "Creeps," by Archie Goodwin, John Severin and Wally Wood, which had a unbalanced man so thoroughly appalled by the "creeps" he saw everyday that he eventually became one himself. This story may be even more bleak. It's not just the idea that urban blight and the creatures that dwell within that blight are there and menacing you, it's that they're targeting you directly that is the most horrifying aspect of this story. Thirty-two pages of new art and story.

2. cover: Earl Norem/frontis and title page: Pablo Marcos (July 1974)

(**1**) Gabriel, Devil-Hunter [Doug Moench/Billy Graham] 14p; (**2**) "Something Wicked!" [Chris Claremont, text article with photos] 5p; (**3**) The Hint of Horror [Roy Thomas] 1p; (**4**) The Exorcist Tapes [Chris Claremont, Marv Wolfman, Gerry Conway, Carla Joseph, Steve Gerber, Don McGregor, Sandy McGregor, Glynis Wein, Len Wein and Michele Wolfman, text article with photos] 13p; (**5**) Crazy ad [Kelly Freas] 1p; (**6**) Gran'ma Died Last Year [Doug Moench/Gene Colan and Frank Chiarmonte] 10p; (**7**) Satana: A Fire in Hell [Gerry Conway/Pablo Marcos, text story] 8p; (**8**) Satana: Bloody Is the Path to Hell! [Gerry Conway/Enrique Romeo Badia] 10p.

Notes: The "quiet" approach to horror is chucked right out the window as *Haunt of Horror* debuts the delirious and hell-haunted *Gabriel, Devil-Hunter* series while moving *Satana* over from *Vampire Tales*. The Moench/Graham Gabriel tale, which was certainly inspired by the then-recent film *The Exorcist*, is just fine and easily the best story here. The prose *Satana* story is an adaptation of Conway's original script which Esteban Maroto was supposed to have illustrated. Due to some miscommunications between Europe and the U.S., it had to be rapidly converted into a prose story to bridge the gap between *Satana*'s first full-length story, which appeared in *Vampire Tales*, and her third story, debuting here. "The Exorcist Tapes" is probably the most boring and idiotic non-fiction article that Marvel published. Thirteen loooong pages of a transcript of the Marvel bullpenners sitting around chatting about the movie *The Exorcist*. *Gabriel* is featured on the cover and title page while *Satana* is featured on the frontispiece. Thirty-four pages of new art and story.

3. cover: Jose Antonio Domingo (August 1974), credited to JAD

(**1**) Gabriel, Devil-Hunter: House of Brimstone [Doug Moench/Billy Graham, Pablo Marcos, Frank Giacoia and Mike Esposito] 17p; (**2**) The Restless Coffin! [Doug Moench/Pat Broderick and Al Milgrom] 3p; (**3**) The Exorcist Tapes, part 2 [Chris Claremont, Gerry Conway, Steve Gerber, Carla Joseph, Don McGregor, Sandy McGregor, Glynis Wein, Len Wein, Marv Wolfman and Michele Wolfman, text article with photos] 12p; (**4**) Flirting with Mr. D. [Doug Moench/Billy Graham and Marie Severin, text article, Graham's artwork from the first episode of Gabriel, Devil-Hunter] 4p; (**5**) Crazy ad [photos, fumetti strip starring Stan Lee] 1p; (**6**) Marvel Magazines ad [Alfredo Alcala] 1p; (**7**) The Swamp Stalkers [Larry Lieber/Larry Lieber and Winslow Mortimer] 8p; (**8**) Tales of the Zombie/Savage Tales ad [Boris Vallejo and John Buscema, the Vallejo art is a line drawing of #1's cover] 1p; (**9**) They Wait Below [?/Bernie Krigstein, reprinted from *Uncanny Tales* (April 1956)] 4p; (**10**) Last Descent to Hell [Doug Moench/Frank Springer, the last page is on the inside back cover] 8p.

Notes: Editor: Tony Isabella. The concluding three pages for the *Gabriel* story were destroyed when Billy Graham spilled coffee all over them, so Pablo Marcos, with inkers Frank Giacoia and Mike Esposito, illustrated the concluding pages (now stretched out to seven) of the story over a very long weekend. Moench's article on the Gabriel series mentions the unintentional sick joke aspect of having an artist with the same name as evangelist Billy Graham working on a series where demons and Hell itself is regularly invoked. Outside of the excellent cover, this is a rather mediocre issue, with the pointless "The Exorcist Tapes" making (thank God!) its final appearance. Thirty-six pages of new art and story.

4. cover: Bob Larkin/frontis and inside back cover: Neal Adams (November 1974)

(**1**) Satana: This Side of Hell [Tony Isabella/Enrique Romero Badia] 12p; (**2**) Marvel Magazine ad [Alfredo Alcala] 1p; (**3**) The Hint of Horror [Tony Isabella, text article with photos] 1p; (**4**) Savage Tales ad [John Buscema, Ka-Zar is featured] 1p; (**5**) Fright Pattern! [Jack Younger/Syd Shores and Wayne Howard] 5p; (**6**) Satana: Doorway to Dark Destiny [Chris Claremont/Pat Broderick and the Crusty Bunkers, text story] 12p; (**7**) The Deadly Hands of Kung Fu/Tales of the Zombie Ads [Ron Wilson/Pablo Marcos] 1p; (**8**) Deathwatch! [Gerry Conway/Yong Montano] 8p; (**9**) Crazy ad [Marie Severin] 1p; (**10**) Gabriel, Devil-Hunter: To Worship the Damned [Doug Moench/Sonny Trinidad] 15p; (**11**) Next issue ad [Bob Hall and Duffy Vohland, on back cover, *Gabriel, Devil-Hunter* is featured] 1p.

Notes: *Gabriel* is cover- and frontispiece-featured with the frontispiece reproduced from Neal Adams' pencils. Future Eclipse publisher Dean Mullaney and future comic writer Peter Gillis send in letters. Forty pages of new art and story.

5. cover: Dick Giordano/frontis: Pablo Marcos (January 1975)

(1) The Marvel Bullpen Page Goes Black and White and Read All Over [Marv Wolfman, text article] 1p; (2) Gabriel, Devil-Hunter: The Possession of Jenny Christopher [Doug Moench/Sonny Trinidad] 20p; (3) Three Spiders on Gooseflesh [Doug Moench/George Evans] 9p; (4) Marvel Magazines ad [Alfredo Alcala] 1p; (5) Destiny: Oblivion [David Anthony Kraft/Paul Kirchner and Rudy Nebres] 7p; (6) Satana: If This Be Hell...? [Chris Claremont/George Evans] 13p; (7) Unknown Worlds of Science Fiction ad [Rick Bryant and Kelly Freas, Freas' art is a B&W reproduction of #1's cover] 1p; (8) Savage Tales ad [John Romita, Ka-Zar is featured] 1p; (9) Next issue ad [Pablo Marcos and George Evans, on the back cover] 1p.

Notes: Final issue. *Satana* is cover- and frontispiece-featured. Too bad Giordano didn't do more covers for Marvel. This one is quite good. The *Gabriel* story is also a solid effort. A sixth issue is promised but never appears. The next issue ad promised a *Gabriel* story entitled "Messenger of the Devil" by Moench and Marcos that never appeared, at least under that title. Another *Gabriel* story entitled "An Angel Felled" by Moench and Trinidad did appear in *Monsters Unleashed!* #11. In addition, a *Satana* story by Chris Claremont and George Evans entitled "Return of the Elder Gods" is promised. This is probably the same story promised for *The Legion of Monsters* #2, although there it was titled "Night of the Demon — Night of the Damned." In either case, the story has never been published although it appears to have been completed. Claremont mentions it in his introduction to *Satana*'s appearance in *Marvel Preview* #7 and both ads show different pages of Evans' art. All in all, *The Haunt of Horror* was a decent magazine that never really got a chance to hit its stride.

Unknown Worlds of Science Fiction

1. cover: Kelly Freas and John Romita/frontis: Esteban Maroto (January 1975)

(1) 1975: A Space Odyssey [Roy Thomas, text article] 1p; (2) Slow Glass Prologue/Epilogue [Tony Isabella/Gene Colan and Tom Palmer, from the "Slow Glass" concept created by Bob Shaw] 5p; (3) The Day of the Triffids [Gerry Conway/Ross Andru and Ernie Chan, from the novel by John Wyndham, Chan's art credited to Ernie Chua] 15p; (4) A View from Without... [Neal Adams, reprinted from *Phase* #1 (September 1971)] 8p; (5) The Bradbury Chronicles [Shel Dorf and Ray Bradbury, text article — interview] 10p; (6) Marvel Magazine ad [Alfredo Alcala] 1p; (7) Smash Gordon: A Funny Thing Happened on the Way to Mongo! [Frank Brunner, reprinted from *Heritage 1A* (1972)] 4p; (8) Savage World [Wally Wood/Al Williamson, Frank Frazetta, Angelo Torres and Roy G. Krenkel, reprinted from *witzend* #1 (July 1966)] 8p; (9) Past and Present Master: An Interview with Kelly Freas [Gerry Conway and Kelly Freas/Kelly Freas, text article — interview] 4p; (10) Hey Buddy, Can You Lend Me a... [Michael Kaluta, reprinted from *Scream Door* #1 (1971)] 5p; (11) Light of Other Days [Tony Isabella/Gene Colan and Mike Esposito, from the story by Bob Shaw] 7p; (12) Next issue ad [Rick Bryant] 1p.

Notes: Publisher: Stan Lee. Editor: Roy Thomas. It was $1.00 for 80 pages. After hiring famed SF artist Kelly Freas to do the cover and provide an interview, Marvel manages to screw it up by having John Romita repaint the two young people on the cover. Why I don't know. Freas' original artwork, which was reprinted in a later issue, looked just fine to me. As to the question of why I'm including Marvel's science fiction magazine but not including their sword and sorcery entries, the reason is this: Marvel's S&S books were action adventure books. Yes, they did have monsters in the giant spider or gila monster vein but they were never intended to scare anyone. Nor did they. However, this magazine, which presented adaptations of actual science fiction stories and novels as well as original stories, did provide chills. To be honest, probably more actual chills than the four or five regular horror magazines Marvel published. Hence its inclusion here. That said, this magazine is a direct descendent of the color comic *Worlds Unknown* which ran from May 1973 to April 1974 (the relevant issues, anyway. Two more issues were produced which adapted the George Pal movie *The Golden Voyage of Sindbad*, a fantasy film). That color comic adapted stories by Theodore Sturgeon, Keith Laumer, Frederik Pohl and Fredric Brown, among others, and did quite a good job of it but was hampered by restrictions from the Comics Code and was ultimately killed off by the difficulty of adapting anything meaningful when the color books' story page counts kept dropping. *Unknown Worlds of Science Fiction* was the ideal solution, since the Comics Code didn't apply and story pages weren't mandated by the strict 15- or 17-page count the color comics had. This first issue is quite good, especially considering how much of it consists of reprints (but not lame 1950s-era SF stories — thank God!). The lead adaptation, "The Day of the Triffids," was, based on page count, clearly intended to be the original occupant of *Worlds Unknown #7–8*. In fact, the only story that was probably done specifically for this issue was the fine "Slow Glass" adaptation and the prologue/epilogue sections, which also used the "Slow Glass" concept. The best story and art here is Neal Adams' powerful "A View from Without..." which was written and illustrated in the late 1960s. One of Adams' best and most innovative art jobs, the controversial story concerned an alien's observations regarding an U.S.–led attack on a Vietnamese village and the horrifying aftermath. It also has one of the most chilling endings, aimed directly at the male comic reader between the ages of 14–18, that comics have ever produced. The story is a towering achievement that is finally back in print, after years of neglect, in the Adams retrospective volume *The Art of Neal Adams*. Other reprints include a cute Flash Gordon parody by Frank Brunner and a fine early effort by Michael Kaluta that was left over from *Web of Horror* [see "The Best of the Rest!" section], and ended up in a fanzine, as well as a couple of interesting interviews. The "Savage World" story's art was done in 1954 for Buster Crabb Comics but it was unused. In 1966 Wally Wood wrote a new script (the original had been lost) for the artwork and published the story in

the first issue of his landmark fanzine *witzend*. Judging by the care in production, the excellent selection of worthy science fiction stories and the matching of strong artist/writer teams for those stories, this must have been a project quite close to editor Roy Thomas' heart.

2. cover: Michael Kaluta/frontis: Alex Nino (March 1975) Nino's frontispiece art is reprinted from *The Hannes Bok Memorial Showcase of Fantasy Art* (1974)

(**1**) The Shape of Things That Came [Roy Thomas/Rick Bryant, text article] 1p; (**2**) Slow Glass Prologue/Epilogue [Tony Isabella/Frank Brunner and Klaus Janson] 5p; (**3**) War Toy [Tony Isabella/George Perez and Rico Rival] 12p; (**4**) Unknown Worlds ad [Rick Bryant] 1p; (**5**) There Are No Yesterdays: A Conversation with Alfred Bester, Author of *The Demolished Man* [Denny O'Neil and Alfred Bester/Rick Bryant and Stanley Pitt, text article — interview with photo] 5p; (**6**) Adam ... and No Eve [Denny O'Neil/Frank Robbins and Jim Mooney, from the story by Alfred Bester] 6p; (**7**) The Hunter and the Hunted [Michael Kaluta, reprinted from *Abyss* #1 (November 1970)] 4p; (**8**) Science Fiction, Fans, and the Hugo (Not Necessarily in That Order) [Don Thompson, text article with photos] 4p; (**9**) Specimen [Bruce Jones, reprinted from *Abyss* #1 (November 1970)] 8p; (**10**) The Day of the Triffids, part 2 [Gerry Conway/Rico Rival, from the novel by John Wyndham] 20p; (**11**) Next issue ad [Alex Nino] 1p; (**12**) Monsters of the Movies/The Savage Sword of Conan Ads [Bob Larkin/Boris Vallejo, B&W repos of #5 and #4's covers] 1p.

Notes: Kaluta's original version of this cover did not include the robot, which was also featured in the story "War Toy." Either way, it was a pretty nifty cover with three soldiers and a robot in the classic "raising the flag on Iwo Jima" stance. The Bester interview included a full page of Australian artist Stanley Pitt's adaptation of Bester's acclaimed novel *The Stars My Destination*. An adaptation of Harlan Ellison's classic story "Repent, Harlequin!" Said the Ticktockman" was supposed to appear this issue but was delayed until the next. "War Toy" was a good story, although the only way you could detect George Perez's artwork here was in his distinctive shaping of the panel borders. Rival's inking completely covered any penciling traces. The best story here is again a fanzine reprint, this time Kaluta's odd little space war tale "The Hunter and the Hunted." Don Thompson's article related the history of Science Fiction's fan-based awards, the Hugos. A solid issue.

3. cover: Michael Whelan/frontis: Gray Morrow (May 1975)

(1) A Night at the Space Opera [Roy Thomas/ Rick Bryant and Kelly Freas, text article] 1p; (2) Slow Glass Prologue/Epilogue: The Star-Magi [Tony Isabella/Gene Colan and Frank Chiarmonte] 6p; (3) Occupation Force [Gerry Conway/George Perez and Klaus Janson] 5p; (4) Unknown Worlds ad [Robert L. Kline] 1p; (5) ...Not Long Before the End [Doug Moench/Vicente Alcazar, from the story by Larry Niven] 15p; (6) Conan the Barbarian Treasury Edition ad [Barry Smith, B&W reproduction of #4's cover] 1p; (7) Marvel Preview ad [John Romita and Tony DeZuniga, the Punisher is featured] 1p; (8) Sandworms and Saviors: A Conversation with Frank Herbert, Author of Dune [Ed Leimbacher and Frank Herbert/Rick Bryant, Ed Hannigan and ?, text article — interview with photos] 7p; (9) Kull and The Barbarians/Marvel Preview Ads [Michael Whelan/Neal Adams, B&W repos of both #1/s covers] 1p; (10) Gestation [Bruce Jones] 7p; (11) Next issue ad [Rick Bryant] 1p; (12) SFWA: The Thing That Spawned Nebulas [Don Thompson/Rick Bryant, text article with photos] 4p; (13) "Repent, Harlequin!" Said the Ticktockman [Roy Thomas/Alex Nino, from the story by Harlan Ellison] 17p.

Notes: Thomas' editorial includes a B&W reproduction of Kelly Freas' un-retouched cover for #1. Whelan's cover artwork is from very early in his professional career and is pretty much a generic space scene. Still, this is an excellent issue with two great adaptations. "...Not Long Before the End" is a marvelous Niven tale and it is done up proudly by Moench and Alcazar. It's ironic that Niven's tale, which relates the harm that can come when the oafish barbarian swordsmen take over the world, was done by Marvel, the comic home of the premiere (and often oafish-looking) barbarian swordsman, Conan. Ellison's on record that he dislikes this adaptation of his award-winning story but I think it's beautifully done, preserving Ellison's thoughtful story with a carefully considered script by Thomas and wild (and, in my opinion, wildly appropriate) artwork by the

gonzo madman himself, Alex Nino. The "Ticktockman" is the best story in this issue, although it had stiff competition. The "Slow Glass" prologue and epilogue is a futuristic (and uncredited) takeoff on O. Henry's "The Gift of the Magi." The letters page debuts with letters from Robert Bloch, Dean Mullaney, Bob Shaw and Ray Bradbury. The letters page also promises an adaptation of Bloch's classic tale "A Toy for Juliette" although it never happens. Bloch's story was later adapted beautifully by Rick Geary for an independent comic in the mid–1980s. This time, the SFWA article relates the history of Science Fiction's professionals-based awards, the Nebulas.

4. cover: Frank Brunner/frontis: Robert L. Kline (July 1975)

(1) The Savage Sword of Conan/Kull and the Barbarians ads [Alex Nino/Michael Whelan, B&W repros of #6 and #2's covers] 1p; (2) Slow Glass Prologue/Epilogue: An Official Inquiry [Tony Isabella/Don Heck and Frank Chiaramonte] 6p; (3) The Enchanted Village [Don Thompson and Maggie Thompson/Dick Giordano, from the story by A. E. Van Vogt] 11p; (4) Doc Savage ad [Roger Kastel, B&W reproduction of #1's cover] 1p; (5) The Dreaming Kind: A Conversation with SF Master Author A. E. Van Vogt [Alan Brennert and A. E. Van Vogt/ Rick Bryant, text article — interview with photos] 6p; (6) Otis Adelbert Kline: Visionary of Venus [David Anthony Kraft, text article with photo] 1p; (7) A Vision of Venus [Tim Conrad, from the story by Otis Adelbert Kline] 5p; (8) Unknown Worlds ad [Robert L. Kline] 1p; (9) FANtastic Worlds [Don Thompson and Maggie Thompson/Steve Harper, Kelly Freas and Rick Bryant, text article with photo] 4p; (10) Good News from the Vatican [Gerry Conway/Ading Gonzales, from the story by Robert Silverberg] 7p; (11) Encounter at War [Jan Strnad/Richard Corben, reprinted from *Anomaly* #4 (1972)] 13p; (12) Kick the Can [Bruce Jones] 8p; (13) Next issue ad [Frank Brunner and Duffy Vohland] 1p.

Notes: The adaptations aren't quite as stunning this issue (although all three are quite good) but the originals and reprints rise up to their level, making this a very satisfactory issue. The best story here is the Strnad/Corben reprint, although it would have been nice if someone had bothered to redo the original shaky lettering. "Good News from the Vatican" was the best adaptation. Not much in the way of action but a very sly and sneaky spoof. "The Enchanted Village" and "Kick the Can" were also very good. Brunner's cover, with minor modifications, could have fit easily on a horror magazine and appears to be a tribute to the old EC science fiction covers. The next issue ad featured Brunner's pencil study for what became #6's cover, with somewhat amateurish-looking inking by Duffy Vohland. The letters page includes an obituary for longtime Marvel letterer Artie Simek along with a letter from future artist Ken Meyer, Jr. It also promises several stories written by Bruce Jones and illustrated by the likes of Al Williamson, Gray Morrow and Berni Wrightson. Only the Morrow one would actually appear in *Unknown Worlds*. The Williamson story appeared in an issue of Warren's *Creepy* in 1976 and I suspect the Wrightson story was never actually started or, at least, finished.

5. cover: Sebastia Bodia/frontis: Howard Chaykin (September 1975), Bodia's cover art is credited to one of his middle names — Puigdomenech!

(1) Unknown Worlds ad [Robert L. Kline] 1p; (2) Slow Glass Prologue/Epilogue [Roy Thomas/ Gene Colan and Frank Chiarmonte] 3p; (3) Paradise Found [Bruce Jones/Gray Morrow] 14p; (4) The Many Many Worlds of Larry Niven: A Conversation with the Award-Winning "Hard" SF Author [Alan Brennert and Larry Niven/John Allison, ? and Rick Bryant, text article — interview with photo] 6p; (5) All the Myriad Ways [Howard Chaykin, from the story by Larry Niven] 10p; (6) FANtastic Worlds [Don Thompson and Maggie Thompson/Michael Kaluta, text article] 3p; (7) Addict [Don Glut/Virgilio Redondo] 9p; (8) Half Life [John Allison, reprinted from *Orb* #2 (1974)] 10p.

Notes: Size reduced to 72 pages. The superior adaptation of Larry Niven's "All the Myriad Ways" included here was preceded by an earlier adaptation done by Jeff Jones in 1971. The Jones' adaptation was intended for the never-published *Science Fiction Odyssey*, a SF magazine developed by Skywald Publications, but ended up appearing in *Psycho* #12 under the new title "All the Ways and Means to Die." It was probably re-

titled because someone at Skywald didn't think readers would know what the word "myriad" meant. Allison's reprinted story was accompanied on the letters page by a plug for the Canadian fanzine *Orb*, where it originally appeared. Several pencil sketches of Boada's cover can be seen in his recent artbook *Fatal Visions*.

6. cover: Frank Brunner/frontis: Pat Broderick (November 1975)

(1) Foreword Is Forearmed [Roy Thomas/Rick Bryant, text article] 1p; (2) Slow Glass Prologue/Epilogue [Roy Thomas/Gene Colan and Dan Adkins] 3p; (3) Behold the Man [Doug Moench/Alex Nino, from the novella by Michael Moorcock] 23p; (4) Thru a Glass Slowly: An Article About (and by) SF Author Bob Shaw [Roy Thomas and Bob Shaw with Gary Brodsky and Brian Moore, text article — interview with photo] 4p; (5) Old Soldier [Bruce Jones] 7p; (6) Mind Games [John Allison] 10p; (7) Visitation [Don Glut/Reuben Yandoc] 10p.

Notes: Final issue. Thomas's nervous editorial cautions the reader to enjoy Moorcock's story (which concerns a time traveler who goes back in time to observe the death of Jesus Christ but then accidentally becomes Christ on the cross) but not to take it too much to heart. The letters page at the end of the issue announces the magazine's cancellation. In between appears the superb adaptation of Moorcock's powerful classic. A beautiful script by Moench and stunning artwork from Nino don't soften Moorcock's bitter rage from the original story one iota. Next to this stunning adaptation, the Marvel-created stories appear a little old hat but they are actually well done and entertaining. A seventh issue did appear, although it was called a special, showing up in the late fall or early winter of 1976. You'll find the particulars farther down this checklist. For my money, this was Marvel's best B&W magazine, period.

Masters of Terror

1. cover: Gray Morrow/frontis: Gil Kane and Tom Palmer (May 1975), frontispiece reprinted from the cover of *Journey into Mystery* #2 (December 1972)

(1) "I Hate Horror Comics" [Tony Isabella, text article] 1p; (2) It [Roy Thomas/Marie Severin

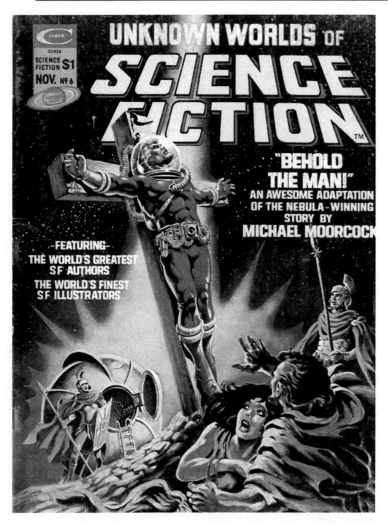

Frank Brunner's crucified spaceman wasn't the subject of the interior story, Michael Moorcock's "Behold the Man." Still the controversial story and cover art were edgy fare for the 1970s. © Marvel Worldwide/used by permission.

from the Stars! [Ron Goulart/Jim Starlin and Tom Palmer, from the story by Robert E. Howard, reprinted from *Journey into Mystery* #3 (February 1973)] 8p; **(8)** Time Out for Terror [Don Thompson and Maggie Thompson/Wayne Howard, text article] 2p; **(9)** Terror Toons [Stu Schwartzberg, cartoons] 1p; **(10)** Yours Truly, Jack the Ripper! [Ron Goulart and Roy Thomas/Gil Kane, Ralph Reese and Neal Adams, from the story by Robert Bloch, reprinted from *Journey into Mystery* #2 (December 1972)] 10p; **(11)** Next Issue ad [Jim Steranko, art reprinted from the cover of *Supernatural Thrillers* #2 (February 1973)] 1p.

Notes: Publisher: Stan Lee. Editor: Tony Isabella. It was $1.00 for 72 pages. This was a reprint magazine but very much a superior one. One thing Marvel did, probably better than any other comic publisher at the time, was to adapt famous horror stories with care, craft and precision. This magazine reprinted the best of these so one got very good value for their dollar. The cover is painted by Morrow but based solidly on the cover by Jim Steranko for *Supernatural Thrillers* #1. The adaptation by Thomas and Marie Severin (artist John Severin's sister and one of the most accomplished female artists in the comics field, having done stellar work for EC Comics, Marvel Comics and more) of Theodore Sturgeon's classic swamp monster tale, "It" is damn near as good as the 1940 original, and the original is one of the all-time horror classics. Sturgeon's "It" has also been hugely influential to the comic field, directly or indirectly spawning such characters as Solomon Grundy, the Hulk, the Glob, the Heap, Swamp Thing and Man-Thing. Beautiful job and one unlikely to be reprinted anytime

and Frank Giacoia, from the story by Theodore Sturgeon, reprinted from *Supernatural Thrillers* #1 (December 1972)] 21p; **(3)** The Horror from the Mound! [Gardner Fox/Frank Brunner, from the story by Robert E. Howard, reprinted from *Chamber of Chills* #2 (January 1973); original color comic version entitled "The Monster from the Mound"] 8p; **(4)** The Terrible Old Man [Roy Thomas/Barry Smith, Dan Adkins and John Verpoorten, from the story by H. P. Lovecraft, reprinted from *Tower of Shadows* #3 (January 1970)] 7p; **(5)** Master-Pieces [Tony Isabella, text article] 2p; **(6)** The Drifting Snow [Tony Isabella/Esteban Maroto, from the story by August Derleth, reprinted from *Vampire Tales* #4 (April 1974)] 11p; **(7)** The Shambler

This Gray Morrow effort was based on Jim Steranko's color comic art for the 1971 comic *Supernatural Thrillers* #1. Both efforts were based on famed SF/fantasy writer Theodore Sturgeon's classic swamp monster "It." © Marvel Worldwide/used by permission.

and the back cover (a B&W reproduction) is reprinted from the cover of *Monsters Unleashed!* #1 (July 1973)

(1) What's a Nice Editor Like You Doing in a Magazine Like This? [Tony Isabella, text article] 1p; (2) The Invisible Man [Ron Goulart, Val Mayerik and Dan Adkins, from the novel by H. G. Wells, reprinted from *Supernatural Thrillers* #2 (February 1973)] 21p; (3) The Man Who Cried Werewolf! [Gerry Conway/Pablo Marcos, from the story "The Man Who Cried Wolf" by Robert Bloch, reprinted from *Monsters Unleashed!* #1 (July 1973)] 10p; (4) Master-Pieces [Tony Isabella, text article] 2p; (5) Unknown Worlds of Science Fiction/The Legion of Monsters ads [Frank Brunner and Duffy Vohland/Neal Adams, The Legion of Monsters is a B&W reproduction of #1's cover] 1p; (6) Dig Me No Grave! [Roy Thomas/Gil Kane and Tom Palmer, from the story by Robert E. Howard, reprinted from *Journey into Mystery* #1 (October 1972)] 8p; (7) Terror Toons [Stu Schwartzberg, cartoons] 1p; (8) The Music of Erich Zann! [Roy Thomas/Johnny Craig, from the story by H. P. Lovecraft, reprinted from *Chamber of Darkness* #5 (June 1970), originally entitled "The Music from Beyond!"] 8p; (9) Pickman's Model [Roy Thomas/Tom Palmer, from the story by H. P. Lovecraft, reprinted from *Tower of Shadows* #9 (January 1971)] 7p; (10) Time Out for Terror [Don Thompson and Maggie Thompson, text article] 2p; (11) The Roaches! [Gerry Conway/Ralph Reese, from the story by Thomas M. Disch, reprinted from *Monsters Unleashed!* #2 (September 1973)] 10p; (12) Reader's Poll [Tony Isabella] 1p.

Notes: Final issue. As before, the cover painting is based on a Jim Steranko cover, this time for

soon as Marvel appears to have lost or misplaced the original contracts for most of their literary adaptations of the 1970s, which would have specified the manner in which those stories could be reprinted. I've already mentioned my admiration for "The Drifting Snow" in the *Vampire Tales* notes. "Yours Truly, Jack the Ripper!" is a gem also. In fact, there's not a poor story here. Just top-notch entertainment.

2. cover: Dan Adkins/frontis: Gil Kane and Tom Palmer/back cover: Gray Morrow (September 1975), the frontispiece is reprinted from the cover of *Journey into Mystery* #1 (October 1972)

Supernatural Thrillers #2. Another fine issue, with "The Roaches!" probably being the best adaptation, although all of the stories are quite good. Two fine magazines to search for in back-issue bins as none of these stories are likely to be reprinted soon.

Vampire Tales Annual

1. cover: Bob Larkin (Summer 1975)

(1) Vampires in Time and Space [Tony Isabella/ Pablo Marcos, frontis, reprinted from *Vampire Tales* #3 (February 1974)] 1p; (2) Morbius: Lighthouse of the Possessed! [Don McGregor/ Tom Sutton, reprinted from *Vampire Tales* #4 (April 1974)] 13p; (3) Blood Death [Doug Moench/Alfredo Alcala, reprinted from *Vampire Tales* #6 (August 1974)] 8p; (4) Hodiah Twist: The Praying Mantis Principle! [Don McGregor/Rich Buckler, Carlos Garzon and Klaus Janson, reprinted from *Vampire Tales* #2 (October 1973)] 11p; (5) Satana Pin-Up [Esteban Maroto, reprinted from *Vampire Tales* #3 (February 1974)] 1p; (6) Satana: The Kiss of Death [Gerry Conway/Esteban Maroto, reprinted from *Vampire Tales* #3 (February 1974)] 10p; (7) Blood Lunge [Doug Moench/Russ Heath, reprinted from *Vampire Tales* #9 (February 1975)] 5p; (8)The Vampire Wants Blood! [Doug Moench/Val Mayerik, reprinted from *Vampire Tales* #5 (June 1974)] 9p; (9) Morbius: Blood Tide! [Don McGregor/Rich Buckler and Ernie Chan, reprinted from *Vampire Tales* #5 (June 1974)] 14p.

Notes: An announcement on the letters page confirms that this is the final issue of the regular *Vampire Tales* although it has new numbering and volume numbers. It was $1.25 for 88 pages. "Blood Lunge" has pages printed out of order.

Monsters Unleashed! Annual

1. cover: Ken Bald (Summer 1975)

(1) Thunderbird [Tony Isabella/Ernie Chan, frontis, reprinted from *Monsters Unleashed!* #6 (June 1974)] 1p; (2) The Cold of the Uncaring Moon [Steve Skeates/George Tuska and Klaus Janson, reprinted from *Monsters Unleashed!* #3 (November 1973)] 7p; (3) They Might Be Monsters [Tony Isabella/Pablo Marcos, reprinted from *Monsters Unleashed!* #4 (February 1974)] 1p; (4) World of Warlocks [Gardner Fox and Roy Thomas/Gene Colan, reprinted from *Monsters Unleashed!* #1 (July 1973)] 10p; (5) Lifeboat! [Gerry Conway/Jesus Blasco] 8p; (6) Savage

Sword of Conan ad [Gil Kane] 1p; (7) Demon of Slaughter Mansion [Don McGregor/Juan Boix, reprinted from *Monsters Unleashed!* #5 (April 1974)] 10p; (8) Birthright! [Roy Thomas/Gil Kane and the Crusty Bunkers, reprinted from *Monsters Unleashed!* #3 (November 1973)] 13p; (9) To Love, Honor, Cherish ... 'Til Death! [Chris Claremont/Don Perlin, reprinted from *Monsters Unleashed!* #4 (February 1974)] 8p; (10) Man-Thing: All the Faces of Fear [Tony Isabella/Vicente Alcazar, reprinted from *Monsters Unleashed!* #5 (April 1974)] 11p; (11) Marvel Preview ad [Dan Adkins, Sherlock Holmes is featured] 1p; (12) Thunderbird [Tony Isabella/ Ernie Chan, reprinted from *Monsters Unleashed!* #6 (June 1974)] 1p; (13) Monsters from the Sea [Tony Isabella/Ernie Chan, reprinted from *Monsters Unleashed!* #8 (October 1974)] 1p.

Notes: It was $1.25 for 88 pages. An announcement on the letters page confirms the magazine's cancellation. Keeping pace with the general sloppiness of the regular *Monsters Unleashed!* title, the "Thunderbird" filler page appears twice in the same issue while "Demon of Slaughter Mansion" still has pages 8 and 9 reversed!

Tales of the Zombie Annual

1. cover: Earl Norem/frontis: Pablo Marcos (Summer 1975), frontispiece reprinted from *Tales of the Zombie* #6's Simon Garth story's splash-page (July 1974)

(1) Simon Garth: The Altar of the Damned! [Roy Thomas and Steve Gerber/John Buscema and Tom Palmer, reprinted from *Tales of the Zombie* #1 (August 1973)] 13p; (2) Simon Garth: Zombie! [Stan Lee/Bill Everett, reprinted from *Menace* #5 (August 1954)] 7p; (3) Simon Garth: Night of the Walking Dead! [Steve Gerber/John Buscema and Syd Shores, reprinted from *Tales of the Zombie* #1 (August 1973)] 11p; (4) Twin Burial [Nicola Cuti/Ralph Reese, reprinted from *Tales of the Zombie* #2 (October 1973)] 10p; (5) Warrior's Burden [Tony Isabella/Vicente Alcazar, reprinted from *Tales of the Zombie* #3 (January 1974)] 6p; (6) Jilimbi's Word [Doug Moench/Enrique Badia Romero, reprinted from *Tales of the Zombie* #3 (January 1974), page one is deleted from the original printing] 8p; (7) Death's Bleak Birth! [Doug Moench/Frank Springer, reprinted from *Tales of the Zombie* #5 (May 1974)] 9p; (8) A Second Chance to Die [Carl Wessler/Alfredo Alcala, reprinted from *Tales of the Zombie* #7 (September 1974)] 7p.

Notes: It was $1.25 for 88 pages.

Dracula Lives! Annual

1. cover: Gray Morrow (Summer 1975)

(1) How to Ward Off Vampires [Tony Isabella/ Ernie Chan, frontis, reprinted from *Dracula Lives!* #9 (November 1974)] 1p; (2) Factful Features and Fantastic Frivolity Formed and Fermented from Frugal-Minded Armadilloes! [Marv Wolfman, text article] 1p; (3) That Dracula May Live Again! [Marv Wolfman/Neal Adams, reprinted from *Dracula Lives!* #2 (August 1973)] 13p; (4) Lord of Death, Lord of Hell [Marv Wolfman/John Buscema and Syd Shores, reprinted from *Dracula Lives!* #3 (October 1973)] 12p; (5) Doc Savage ad [Tony DeZuniga?, pencil sketches] 1p; (6) Look Homeward, Vampire! [Gerry Conway/Vicente Alcazar, reprinted from *Dracula Lives!* #4 (January 1974)] 11p; (7) Solomon Kane and Dracula: Castle of the Undead [Roy Thomas/Alan Weiss and the Crusty Bunkers, reprinted from *Dracula Lives!* #3 (October 1973)] 12p; (8) A Duel of Demons [Gerry Conway/Frank Springer, reprinted from *Dracula Lives!* #5 (March 1974)] 10p; (9) Shadow over Versailles [Tony Isabella/ John Buscema and Pablo Marcos, reprinted from *Dracula Lives!* #6 (May 1974)] 11p.

Notes: It cost $1.25 for 88 pages. There's an announcement on the letters page stating that this is the last issue of *Dracula Lives!* (thus it probably came out in either August or September 1975) while also advertising the first issue of *The Legion of Monsters*.

The Legion of Monsters

1. cover: Neal Adams/frontis: Pablo Marcos (September 1975), Dracula, the Manphibian and Frankenstein's Monster are cover featured while Frankenstein's Monster is featured on the frontispiece

(1) Support Your Local Monster [Tony Isabella/ Marie Severin, text article] 1p; (2) Frankenstein's Monster: The Monster and the Masque [Doug Moench/Val Mayerik, Dan Adkins and Pablo Marcos] 15p; (3) Manphibian: Vengeance Crude [Marv Wolfman and Tony Isabella/Dave Cockrum and Sam Grainger] 10p; (4) The Legion Report [Don Thompson and Maggie Thompson/Sandy Plunkett, text article with photos] 4p; (5) The Flies! [Paul Kirschner, Ralph Reese and Gerry Conway/Paul Kirschner and Ralph Reese] 9p; (6) Monster Madness [Stu Schwartzberg, cartoons] 1p; (7) Dracula, part 7: Death Be Thou Proud! [Roy Thomas/Dick Giordano, from the novel by Bram Stoker, the first five pages are rehashed story and art from previous episodes] 15p; (8) Monster Gallery [Hermoso D. Pancho, Pete Lijauco and Gray Morrow, pin-ups] 3p; (9) Next issue ad [Pablo Marcos, Satana and Dracula are featured] 1p; (10) Masters of Terror ad [Jim Steranko, art reprinted from the cover of *Supernatural Thrillers* #2 (February 1973)] 1p.

Notes: A very short-lived attempt (this is the only issue) to keep the headliners alive (as it were) from the various cancelled Marvel B&W horror magazines. Publisher: Stan Lee. Editor: Tony Isabella, with Archie Goodwin listed as the editor-in-chief. It was $1.00 for 72 pages. The Frankenstein's Monster story was originally intended for *Monsters Unleashed!* #11. The *Dracula* adaptation is continued from *Dracula Lives!* This was Manphibian's only B&W appearance, I believe, which was probably just as well as he was an awful character. The Stoker adaptation has the best script and art but "The Flies" is a good, grisly story also. The next issue ad promised a *Morbius* story, which eventually appeared in *Marvel Preview*, a *Satana* story by Chris Claremont and George Evans, "Night of the Demon—Night of the Damned," originally intended for the never-published *The Haunt of Horror* #6 (this story has never appeared although it was described as completed in a recounting of Satana's career that appeared in *Marvel Preview* #7) and the next installment of the Dracula adaptation, which actually didn't appear until *Stoker's Dracula* #2 in December 2004!

Marvel Preview/ Bizarre Adventures

3. cover: Gray Morrow with frontis: Gene Colan (October 1975)

(1) Blade: The Night Josie Harper Died! [Chris Claremont/Tony DeZuniga] 56p; (2) A Short Picto-History of Blade [Scott Edelman, text article with art reprinted from Blade's various appearances] 2p; (3) Next issue ad [Rich Buckler] 1p.

Notes: *Marvel Preview* was a B&W magazine in the vein of DC's *Showcase*. Each issue featured a different concept or character. Sometimes the story was in the form of a pilot, testing the waters for a possible series; others were definite stand-alone stories. I'm including only those issues of this title that were solidly horror issues or predominately horror. This issue, edited by Marv Wolfman, presents the contents of what was supposed to be *Vampire Tales* #12. After *Vampire Tales* was cancelled earlier in the year, the entire issue was simply printed here.

7. cover: Bob Larkin/Vicente Alcazar (July 1976)

(1) Why a Devil's Daughter...? [John Warner, text article] 1p; (2) Satana: The Damnation Waltz [Chris Claremont/Vicente Alcazar] 15p; (3) Satana: La Dimphonie Diable (The Devil's Symphony) [Chris Claremont/Vicente Alcazar] 16p; (4) From the Devil, a Daughter [Chris Claremont/Mike Nasser and Esteban Maroto, text article, Maroto's art reprinted from *Vampire Tales* #3 (February 1974)] 4p; (5) Just a Little over a Year Ago Today... [Bill Mantlo/Terry Austin, text article] 2p; (6) The Sword in the Star! Part 2: Witch World! [Bill Mantlo/Keith Giffen] 18p.

Notes: John Warner is the editor. The *Satana* stories were originally intended for *The Haunt of Horror* and were essentially a rebooting of the character. Alcazar's art is just beautiful and Claremont's story is strong enough to make one wish this version had continued on. "The Sword in the Star" is a science fantasy story and was the second episode in a proposed 12-part backup series for the aborted Star Lord SF magazine. The first episode had appeared in an earlier issue of *Marvel Preview*. I remember, as a kid, quite liking this story. I believe only the first two episodes ever appeared.

8. cover: Ken Barr/frontis: Vicente Alcazar (October 1976)

(1) The Man-God Conspiracy: A Marvel Apologia [John Warner/?, text article] 1p; (2) Morbius: The Madman of Mansion Slade [Doug Moench/Sonny Trinidad] 21p; (3) Monsters Unleashed ... Again [Ralph Macchio/Dave Cockrum, Vicente Alcazar, Alfredo Alcala, Gray Morrow, ? and Sandy Plunkett, text article, Morbius and Simon Garth appear in spot illustrations] 5p; (4) Blade: Into the House of Terror [Marv Wolfman/Gene Colan] 6p; (5) The Reality Manipulators [Don McGregor/Mike Ploog, Marie Severin is credited with the gray

tones on this story — a first for Marvel (or any other B&W book I can think of)] 11p; (6) Curse of Anubis! [Russ Jones and John Warner/Val Mayerik] 10p.

Notes: *Blade* and *Morbius, the Living Vampire* are cover-featured while *Man-Thing* appears on the frontispiece. This was a collection of stories left over from the horror magazines that had been cancelled in 1975. They were published only because *Marvel Preview* had a hole in its schedule when the Man-God story intended for this issue didn't appear. The issue was subtitled *The Legion of Monsters*. The *Morbius* story was originally intended for *The Legion of Monsters* #2. Bob Rodi sent in a letter. The best art here is the work by Mike Ploog. The best story is the *Morbius* tale by Doug Moench. Macchio's article is a history of Marvel's earlier horror effort and is worthwhile reading for a complier like myself. The artist who provided the *Man-Thing* illustration in that article is unknown to me.

12. cover: Earl Norem/frontis and title page: John Buscema and Ernie Chan (October 1977)

(1) Editorial [Roger Slifer/Tom Sutton, text article] 2p; (2) Lilith, Daughter of Dracula Prologue [Steve Gerber/George Perez and Pablo Marcos] 2p; (3) Lilith: Profits Are Plunging! [Steve Gerber/Bob Brown and Frank Springer] 14p; (4) The Rampaging Hulk ad [Jack Kirby and Jim Starlin] 1p; (5) Slinking Through the Psycho-Ward [Doug Moench/Michael Kaluta] 7p; (6) Death of the Living Dead! [David Anthony Kraft/Bob Brown and Pablo Marcos] 8p; (7) Dracula, Lord of Vampires Pin-Up [John Buscema] 1p; (8) Dracula, 1975: Picture of Andrea [Doug Moench/Sonny Trinidad] 20p; (9) Marvel Bullpen Bulletins [Stan Lee et al., text article] 2p.

Notes: Edited by Roger Slifer and subtitled *The Haunt of Horror*, this was Slifer's attempt to revive that title. It was supposed to have a tryout issue here and then come out as a quarterly but the quarterly never appeared. All of the stories included here were inventory from 1975, with both the Lilith and Dracula stories probably intended for the never published *Dracula Lives!* #14, while "Death of the Living Dead!" was clearly intended for *Tales of the Zombie*, and "Slinking through the Psycho-Ward" was probably aimed at the original *Haunt of Horror* B&W

magazine. Sutton's artwork (the only original art in the book) for Slifer's editorial is a nice pin-up of the Marvel horror crew, including Lilith, Dracula, Morbius, Frankenstein's Monster, Werewolf by Night, the Living Mummy and Man-Thing, along with editors Roger Slifer and Ralph Macchio. Lilith is cover-featured while Dracula appears on the frontispiece.

16. cover: Gene Colan and Tom Palmer/ frontis: John Buscema (October 1978)

(**1**) Out of the Dark [Richard Marschall, text article] 1p; (**2**) Hodiah Twist: The Hero-Killer Principle! [Don McGregor/Gene Colan and Tony DeZuniga, story miscredited to Richard Marschall] 23p; (**3**) Voices! [Marv Wolfman/ Gene Colan and Tom Palmer] 8p; (**4**) The Rise of the Private Eye [Ron Goulart, text article] 2p; (**5**) Lilith: Death by Disco! [Steve Gerber/Gene Colan and Tony DeZuniga] 22p; (**6**) Robin Hood Portfolio ad [Howard Chaykin] 1p; (**7**) Scenes from the Magic Planet Portfolio ad [Richard Corben] 1p; (**8**) Next Issue ad [Gil Kane, Blackmark is featured] 1p; (**9**) Cody Starbuck Portfolio ad [Howard Chaykin, on the back cover] 1p.

Notes: Edited by Richard Marschall. This is a rather odd issue. Subtitled *Masters of Terror*, all of the stories are horror while Goulart's article and Buscema's frontispiece art were clearly intended for some sort of crime magazine. I've never heard anything about such a title from Marvel, however. *Hodiah Twist* was a *Sherlock Holmes* homage who'd previously appeared in *Vampire Tales* #2 (October 1973) and in a cameo in a Killraven story in the color comic *Amazing Adventures*. This new *Hodiah Twist* story had been in the works since at least 1973 when McGregor began mentioning it as the followup story to *Twist*'s original outing. The story itself is uncredited. On the title page, Richard Marschall is credited as the author but Marschall himself credits Mc-Gregor in his editorial. It is McGre-

gor's work, with his credit deleted by the powers-that-be as punishment for not signing Marvel's controversial work-for-hire contract. Twist had battled a vampire in his debut and this time out battles a werewolf. Unlike the previous horror outings in *Marvel Preview*, all of the actual stories appear to have been done especially for this issue.

29. cover: Walt Simonson (December 1981)

(**1**) Editorial [Denny O'Neil, text sentence] 1p; (**2**) The Lawnmower Man [Stephen King/Walt Simonson, from the story by Stephen King] 21p; (**3**) Greenberg the Vampire [J. M. DeMatteis/ Steve Leialoha] 25p; (**4**) Epic Illustrated ad [John Bolton, Marada, the She-Wolf is featured] 1p; (**5**) Mirror, Mirror [Bruce Jones/John

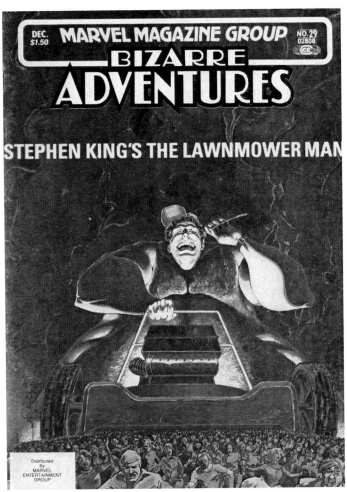

Walt Simonson's cover effort for his and writer Stephen King's adaptation of King's "The Lawnmower Man." © Marvel Worldwide/used by permission.

Buscema and Bob Wiacek] 8p; (6) Next issue ad [Val Mayerik and ?, Paradox and Silhouette are featured] 1p; (7) Bucky Bizarrre! [Steve Skeates/Steve Smallwood] 2p.

Notes: Edited by Denny O'Neil. *Marvel Preview* had been re-titled *Bizarre Adventures* with its 23rd issue, to my mind a much better title. It had been three years since the last horror appearance in this magazine but the long wait was over. This is one of the best horror issues that Marvel produced. Stephen King and Walt Simonson do a spectacular job adapting and illustrating King's story while J. M. DeMatteis displays for the first time the writing chops that would lead to such stories as *Moonshadow* and *Abadazad*. Greenberg may be the first Jewish, homosexual vampire in history. In fact, he may be the only one. The online Grand Comicbook Database lists the title of this story as "My Uncle, the Vampire" but that title doesn't appear on either the story itself or the title page, just "Greenberg the Vampire." The only poor story here was "Mirror, Mirror." Jones' script was fair enough but the stiff, awkward Buscema/Wiacek artwork sank the story completely. Bucky Bizarre appeared in most of the *Bizarre Adventures* issues. He was a comical space traveler who often had little to do with the theme of the issue. Okay effort, if you like that sort of thing.

31. cover: Joe Jusko (April 1982)

(1) From the Warp of Dennis O'Neil: Slaughter thy Neighbor? [Denny O'Neil, text article] 1p; (2) The Philistine [Denny O'Neil/Frank Miller] 8p; (3) Dr. Deth with Kip and Muffy [Larry Hama] 10p; (4) The Hangman [Mark Gruenwald/Bill Sienkiewicz] 12p; (5) Violence Wears Many Faces [John Byrne] 2p; (6) Recondo Rabbit [Larry Hama/Mark Armstrong] 8p; (7) Let There Be Life! [Tom DeFalco/Herb Trimpe] 5p; (8) Pacific Comics ad [Jack Kirby and Mike Grell, B&W repos of the covers of *Captain Victory* #2 and *Starslayer* #1] 1p; (9) A Frog Is a Frog [Stephen Perry/Steve Bissette] 10p; (10) Bucky Bizarre! [Steve Skeates/Steve Smallwood] 3p.

Notes: This was probably *Bizarre Adventures*' (or for that matter, *Marvel Preview*'s) best issue. A beautiful and controversial cover by Joe Jusko depicts a pretty blonde hooker opening up her trenchcoat to reveal not only her scantily clad body but an overwhelming load of guns, knives and grenades. The independent publisher, Renegade Press, did a takeoff (illustrated by Paul Smith) of this cover for an equally controversial ad campaign in the mid–1980s. With the exception of the lame "Let There Be Life!," every story was good and at least two were exceptional. Sienkiewicz was still operating as a Neal Adams clone but his gory story here was still quite good. Larry Hama either worked as one of Wally Wood's assistants or was heavily influenced by him — his *Dr. Deth* strip could have easily fit into *witzend*. "The Philistine" had a good Denny O'Neil script, coupled with excellent Frank Miller artwork. Since this issue was a violence-themed issue, all of the stories mentioned had heavy doses of explicit violence; however, the best stories were the quieter ones. John Byrne's wordless vignette deals with a religious group invading the town library and hauling books off the shelves to burn them in the street. The only book identified is Darwin's *Origin of the Species* but any book would clearly do for the smiling throng depicted in the last panel. Short but chilling. "A Frog Is a Frog" is the second best B&W horror story (following "In the Silence of the City" from *The Haunt of Horror* #1) Marvel ever published. A young boy, wrapped up in gory fantasies (including this very issue of *Bizarre Adventures*), gradually realizes that his best friend is a budding serial killer. Bissette was only a few months away from taking over *Swamp Thing* and his dark, creepy artwork is absolutely perfect here. Perry's thoughtful, dense script is equally fine, expertly detailing that love that all boys undergoing puberty have of the perverse, which can be just as easily depicted in comics as it can be in books, movies or video games, and then paralleling that oddly normal and understandable love of the imagined perverse that the good kid has with the truly perverse sickness and bloodlust of his pal. There's also a twist ending that manages to be gentle, right, comforting and chilling at one and the same time. This story is a genuine horror and comic classic and well worth seeking out for the true horror fan.

33. cover: Michael Sullivan/back cover: Steve Bissette (December 1982)

MARVEL MAGAZINE GROUP

APR. $1.50

NO. 31 02808

BIZARRE ADVENTURES

A HARD LOOK AT VIOLENCE

Distributed By MARVEL ENTERTAINMENT GROUP

A young Joe Jusko painted this controversial cover for *Bizarre Adventures* #31's violence-themed issue. Jusko's mom posed with the trench coat so he could get the folds right, but she doesn't serve as the model. © Marvel Worldwide/used by permission.

tale, *The Haunt of Horror* for the DeMatteis story, and *The Tomb of Dracula* for, naturally, the *Dracula* story. The odd one was the Bruce Jones story, which appeared under the heading of the *Vault of Evil*, which wasn't a B&W title, but one of their pre–Code reprint titles and a title uncomfortably close to EC's *Vault of Horror*. The *Simon Garth* story was not a revival of the character. The story takes place between adventures in the original serial. This is a good solid issue with no clunkers in the lot. Particularly noteworthy was the Perry/Bissette/Totleban effort on the *Dracula* story, which was woven around the origin story [by Wolfman and Adams] of Marvel's *Dracula* that had appeared in *Dracula Lives!* #2. This Bissette/Totleban art effort was done just before their acclaimed *Swamp Thing* debut and is worth seeing simply for the strong graphics. However, the story is pretty damn solid as well and features a extremely unsettling villain.

(1) From the Warp of Dennis O'Neil [Denny O'Neil, text article] 1p; (2) Simon Garth: Damballah's Deeds [Doug Moench/Dave Simons] 16p; (3) Slayride! [Bruce Jones/Bob Hall] 10p; (4) The Survivor [J. M. DeMatteis/Geoff Isherwood, Ian Akin and Brian Garvey] 9p; (5) Dracula, 1459: The Blood Bequest [Stephen Perry/Steve Bissette and John Totleban] 25p; (6) Bucky Bizarre! [Steve Skeates/Steve Smallwood] 3p; (7) Next issue ad [Larry Hama, on the inside back cover] 1p.

Notes: Yet another effort by Marvel to revive their horror titles. Each of the four stories here are sectioned off under previous Marvel horror titles — *Tales of the Zombie* for the *Simon Garth*

Unknown Worlds of Science Fiction Special

1. cover: Don Newton/Rick Bryant (November 1976)

(1) Interrupted Journey [Roy Thomas/Michael Kaluta, text article] 1p; (2) A Martian Odyssey [Don Glut/Reuben Yandoc, from the story by Stanley Weinbaum] 13p; (3) The Last Horizon: A Conversation with Theodore Sturgeon [Alan Brennert and Theodore Sturgeon, text article — interview with photo] 5p; (4) Journey's End! [Bruce Jones/Alex Nino] 8p; (5) The Forest for the Trees [Bruce Jones/Vicente Alcazar] 10p; (6) FANtastic Worlds [Don Thompson and Maggie

Thompson/Michael Kaluta, text article with photos] 4p; (7) Clete [Bruce Jones] 13p; (8) Preservation of the Species [Bruce Jones/Reuben Yandoc, miscredited to Redondo] 13p; (9) Sinner [Archie Goodwin, reprinted from *witzend* #1 (July 1966)] 4p; (10) Arena [Gerry Conway/John Buscema and Dick Giordano, from the story by Fredric Brown, reprinted from the color comic *Worlds Unknown* #4 (November 1973)] 15p; (11) Threads [Mat Warrick/Ading Gonzales, story may actually be by Mal Warrick, a fanzine and science fiction writer of the day] 3p.

Notes: Publisher: Stan Lee. Editor: Roy Thomas. It was $1.25 for 96 pages. This came out almost a year after the last regular issue of *Unknown Worlds*. The inking for the story "Preservation of the Species" is clearly Reuben Yandoc's. It's possible the pencils were by one of the Redondo brothers and, if that's the case, the penciler was probably Virgilio Redondo but until someone can tell me different, I'm going to award sole credits to Mr. Yandoc. How was this as an issue? Well, not bad, not great. The reprints were high-quality picks. The new adaptation of Weinbaum's classic tale was well done. I enjoyed the Sturgeon interview and most of the new stories are decent if not spectacular. "Clete" is very well done, as is "Threads." I suspect the John Allison adaptation of James Tiptree, Jr.'s story "The Man Who Walked Home" which was completed and published in the fanzine *Andromeda* #1 in 1977, was originally intended for *Unknown Worlds*. Other than that story, however, this issue seems to have picked up all the loose ends and leftover stories.

The Tomb of Dracula

1. cover: Bob Larkin and photos/frontis: Gene Colan and Bob McLeod (October 1979)

(1) "Welcome to My House! Enter Freely and of Your Own Will!" [Marv Wolfman/Gene Colan, text article] 1p; (2) Dracula, 1979: Black Genesis [Marv Wolfman/Gene Colan and Bob McLeod] 43p; (2) The Newest Dracula [Jason Thomas, text article with photos] 5p; (4) The Hulk! ad [Marie Severin] 1p; (5) Movie Review: Love at First Bite! [Tom Rogers, text article with photos] 3p; (6) Howard the Duck ad [Gene Colan, et al.] 1p; (7) Legend: According to the Movies [Tom Rogers, text article with photos] 6p; (8) Marvel Magazine Notes [?, text article] 1p; (9)

Next issue ad [Gene Colan and Tom Palmer] 1p; (10) The Savage Sword of Conan/Epic Illustrated ads [John Buscema/Peter Ledger] 2p.

Notes: Publisher: Stan Lee. Editors: Richard Marschall and Marv Wolfman. It was $1.25 for 64 pages. This magazine combined the concepts of the old B&W, *Dracula Lives!*, and the then recently cancelled color comic, which had also been titled *The Tomb of Dracula*. In the last issue of the color comic, the long-time creative team of Wolfman, Colan and Palmer had killed off Dracula, so the first order of business was to revive him. This was done in fine fashion, although Marvel's habit of reviving characters previously declared dead was and is always irritating. Unfortunately, the color book inker, Tom Palmer, was not present. Apparently, a backstage editorial feud was taking place, with then editor-in-chief Jim Shooter attempting to break up the mini-fiefdoms that longtime editor/writers like Roy Thomas and Marv Wolfman had obtained during the course of the 1970s at Marvel. Shooter's directive was apparently that no writer could have himself as an editor. Both Wolfman's and Thomas' contract renewals were coming up and Shooter was flexing his power as editor-in-chief, in this case to deny the revived *Dracula* strip its regular inker. The short-term result of that pressure was that in less than a year both Thomas and Wolfman departed Marvel for the friendlier pastures of DC Comics, along with a host of other 1970s Marvel creators, including Gene Colan, Jim Mooney, Doug Moench and more. At this point in time, the horror boom of 1971–1975 was long over and while Marvel maintained a presence in the B&W magazine field, this title was the first regular horror title since the cancellation of *The Legion of Monsters* in 1975. As such there was a lot riding on it and, sadly, as good as this book was, it really showed fans nothing new. Not enough of the color comic's fans followed along for Dracula's B&W revival and the B&W readers just didn't pick up the book. Part of that, in my opinion, was the dreadful editorial idea of having the cover layout for the first three issues look like a movie magazine's. Larkin painted a great cover, but it was reduced to less than the size of a digest magazine's cover while photos of Frank Langella and George Hamilton (both of whom were appearing in vampire movies at the time) floated along beside. It just looked much more like one of those quickie one-shot, unauthorized movie tie-in magazines that Myron Fass put out than a horror magazine from Marvel Comics.

2. cover: Bob Larkin and photos/frontis: Tom Palmer (December 1979)

(1) The Savage Sword of Conan ad [John Buscema] 1p; (2) Dracula, 1979: The Dimensional Man [Marv Wolfman/Steve Ditko] 36p; (3) Howard the Duck ad [Gene Colan and Dave Simons] 1p; (4) "Dracula" Director John Badham: The Making of the Movie [Steve Swires, text article with photo] 2p; (5) Movie Review: Nosferatu, the Vampyre [Tom Rogers, text article with photos] 5p; (6) Dracula, 1459: Court of the Dead! [Marv Wolfman/Frank Robbins, John Romita and John Tartaglione] 15p; (7) Next issue ad [Gene Colan and ?] 1p; (8) Meteor/Warriors of the Shadow Realm [Gene Colan and Tom Palmer/John Buscema, the last ad appeared on the inside back cover] 2p.

Notes: Rick Marschall was gone and Lynne Graeme was in as the new co-editor. A bold move by Wolfman as he hired Steve Ditko to illustrate the second adventure of the revived *Dracula*. Ditko had long since ceased to be a fan favorite but somebody must have been remembering those beautiful B&W stories he had done for Warren Publications in 1966–1967. Ditko certainly attempted to deliver the goods! His artwork looked nothing like any previous Marvel representation of Dracula but it was still very good, possibly his best work since the late 1960s. Unfortunately, Marvel's reproduction methods were far below the quality that Warren had employed for Ditko's work in 1966–67 and his delicate gray tones appeared to be washed out, giving the artwork a bland, grayish appearance rather than the somber, moody effect obviously intended. Fans reacted badly (something they might have done, anyway, since Ditko and Colan's styles were so far apart) and there were no further artistic experiments of that sort attempted again. Frank Robbins' artwork was also not to the fans' liking, although his story didn't come in for the criticism that Ditko's had. It was a shame, really. Both artists delivered good work, but their art styles were so out of tune with the times that I

suspect that any work they might have done would have been raked over the coals. The letters page debuts, with letters commenting on the last issue of the color comic as well as the first issue of the new magazine.

3. cover: Bob Larkin/frontis: Jerry Bingham (February 1980)

(1) Dracula, 1980: And from Order, There Will Come — Chaos! [Marv Wolfman/Gene Colan and Tom Palmer] 36p; (2) Bloodline: A Probable Outline of the Career of Count Vlad Dracula [Peter Gillis/Gene Colan and Tom Palmer, text article, the artwork is reprinted from various issues of the color comic, also called *The Tomb of Dracula*.] 6p; (3) Next issue ad [Joe Jusko] 1p; (4) Metamorphosis of a Vampire [Lynn Graeme/Gene Colan and John Romita, Frank Miller, text article] 3p; (5) Lilith, Daughter of Dracula: One Curse, with Love [Lora Byrne, text article] 2p; (6) Dracula, 1980: Soul of an Artist [Marv Wolfman/Gene Colan and Tom Palmer] 14p; (7) A Memo from Marv [Marv Wolfman, text article, on letters page] ½ p.

Notes: The photos on the cover are dropped but the cover art is only slightly increased in size. Both *Dracula* stories are well written and illustrated. It was especially nice to see the return of Tom Palmer as Colan's inker. However, this was the last teamup of the Wolfman/Colan/Palmer Dracula crew as Wolfman announced his leaving beginning with the next issue. The "Metamorphosis of a Vampire" article concerns a revamping of *Lilith, Dracula's Daughter* with new costumes designs by Gene Colan/John Romita and Frank Miller. Miller's version is quite striking but, to my knowledge, was never used.

4. cover: Gene Colan and Tom Palmer/frontis: Freff (April 1980)

(1) Dracula, 1980: Angelica [Roger McKenzie/Gene Colan and Tom Palmer] 37p; (2) The Dark Beyond the Door: Walking (Nervously) into Stephen King's World [Freff and Stephen King, text article — interview with photos] 4p; (3) Dracula, 1823: Death Vow! [Roger McKenzie/John Buscema and Klaus Janson] 20p; (4) Next issue ad [Gene Colan and Freff, on the inside back cover] 1p.

Notes: Lynn Graeme was now sole editor. Palmer painted the cover over Gene Colan's pencils. The cover painting took up the full cover. Roger

McKenzie took over the writing chores and, based on this issue, was superbly suited to write this series. "Angelica" is quite good and "Death Vow" is even better. Both have tight plot turns and Dracula himself is given a nasty edge to his evil that matches and, in some respects, surpasses Wolfman's version of the character. How McKenzie would have done long term on this character we'll never know, as he lasted only one more issue, but it's certainly an impressive debut. Good as Colan and Palmer's art on "Angelica" is, the art honors here go to a striking art job by John Buscema and Klaus Janson on "Death Vow!" The interview with Stephen King is from quite early in his career, taking place shortly after the publication of *The Shining*. King's three children pose with him for photos, which is a pretty good clue that he wasn't in a security conscious mode yet. The next issue ad features a Gene Colan illustration taken from a splash page from the color *Tomb of Dracula*, with new inking by Freff, whose full name is Connor Freff Cochran.

5. cover: Howard Chaykin/frontis: Freff (June 1980)

(1) Dracula, 1980: Sanctuary [Roger McKenzie/Gene Colan and Dave Simons] 15p; (2) Lilith, Daughter of Death! [Ralph Macchio and Lynn Graeme/Gene Colan and Tom Palmer] 25p; (3) P. Craig Russell's The Curse of the Ring Portfolio ad [Craig Russell] 1p; (4) Dracula, 1980: Pavane for an Undead Princess! [Peter Gillis/John Buscema and Bob McLeod] 13p; (5) The Tomb of Dracula ad [John Romita] 1p; (6) The Dark Beyond the Door, part II: Smack in the Middle of Stephen King's World [Freff and Stephen King,

text article — interview with photos] 4p; (7) In a Literary Vein...: Hotel Transylvania/The Palace/Blood Games [Gil Fitzgerald, text article] 1p; (8) Shadow Shows [Tom Rogers, text article] 1p; (9) Next issue ad [Gene Colan and ?, on the back cover] 1p.

Notes: Howard Chaykin debuts as the cover artist and he's quite good, too. I don't usually mention frontispiece artwork but Freff's work here is quite distinctive. McKenzie's "Sanctuary" is quite good but certainly suffers from being only a lead in to the *Lilith/Dracula* story. This was McKenzie's final shot at *Dracula* and that's a shame, as I think he could have really done

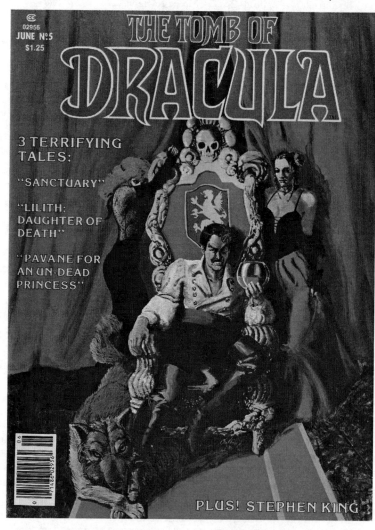

Howard Chaykin provided two nicely stylized covers featuring Vlad Dracul for the 1979–1980 B&W magazine *The Tomb of Dracula*. This is one of them. © Marvel Worldwide/used by permission.

something with this strip. Lilith returns in a tacky costume that looks nothing like either version spotlighted in #3. This one gives her the usual cape, along with a bat-symbol bra, bikini panties topped by a slit-to-the-waist transparent skirt, and finished off with pirate boots. Pretty much as awful looking as it sounds. "Pavane" was a decent enough story and a real effort was made to make the art special but all it really did was point out the fact that Buscema needed an inker (like the previous issue's Klaus Janson) who understood horror and its needs. McLeod's inking would have been perfect for a SF or fantasy tale but it didn't really work here. The next issue ad features Colan's splash page art for the next issue but the unknown inker is not Dave Simons, who actually inked the published page.

6. cover: Howard Chaykin/frontis: Haim Kano (August 1980)

> **(1)** Editorial [Lynn Graeme/Dave Simons, text article] 1p; **(2)** Dracula, 1862: A House Divided [Jim Shooter/Gene Colan and Dave Simons] 30p; **(3)** The Hulk ad [Ron Wilson] 1p; **(4)** Lilith: Violets for a Vampire [Lynn Graeme and Ralph Macchio/Bill Sienkiewicz and Eric Von Krupp] 14p; **(5)** Vampires 'Round the World [Tom Rogers/Marie Severin, text article] 4p; **(6)** Epic Illustrated/Bizarre Adventures ads [Paul Gulacy/Joe Jusko] 2p; **(7)** Chelsea Quinn Yarbo: An Alternate Reality [Lora Byrne and Chelsea Quinn Yarbo/John Tartaglione, text article — interview] 4p; **(8)** Marvel Magazine ad [Rudy Nebres, Red Sonya is featured] 1p; **(9)** Marvel Preview ad [Michael Golden] 1p; **(9)** In

a Literary Vein...: The Dead Zone [Gil Fitzgerald, text article with photo] 1p; **(10)** Shadow Shows: The Fog [Tom Rogers, text article with photo] 1p; **(11)** Dracula Pin-Ups [Gene Colan, Joe Rubinstein and Tom Palmer, the last pin-up is on the inside back cover] 2p.

Notes: Final issue. At least *Drac* went out in style. For all the controversy and drama that accompanies Jim Shooter's every move in comics, the one thing he's usually had going for him is his storytelling ability. From his work as a teenager on the *Legion of Superheroes* to his two abortive efforts at starting his own companies in the 1990s, he's usually been able to tell a good story. He does so here with a fine *Dracula* tale set during the American Civil War. Bill Sienkiewicz, still in his Neal Adams clone mode, does the *Lilith* entry for this issue and has the smarts to put her in regular, everyday clothes. Not a trace of the idiotic costume she was wearing only an issue earlier. The Yarbo interview has a nicely done pencil portrait of the author by longtime Marvel inker John Tartaglione. Gene Colan and Dave Simons provide the best art. The final pin-up has Dracula promising, "I Will Return!" He never really did but it was a very nice way to end his series. One final *Dracula* story appeared, as previously mentioned, in *Bizarre Adventures* in 1983 and that was it until Marvel revived *The Tomb of Dracula* for a color mini-series in 2004, apparently after a highly successful reprinting of the original *Dracula* stories in their *Essential* B&W volumes.

The Best of the Rest!
Web of Horror, Atlas/Seaboard, and Others

Some of the titles in this section were direct competitors of Warren's B&W magazines. All of them were certainly inspired in some manner or degree by the presence of Warren's books. Some were full-fledged assaults for space on the marketplace magazine racks, others simply half-hearted efforts done to placate enthusiastic editors or writer/artists. Some of these titles were so promising it's a real loss to the field that they didn't make it.

The best of these would be *Taboo*, *Web of Horror* and *Warrior*. However, all of these titles provided some good and, occasionally, more than good stories and art.

Major Publications

Web of Horror

Web of Horror was published by Major Publications (also publishers of *Cracked* and a host of men's adventure magazines) and was the first serious rival to the Warren B&W line of the 1960s. It showcased many young professionals who soon rose to prominence in the 1970s and, for that alone, should be remembered.

1. cover: Jeff Jones (December 1969)

(1) Webster's Welcome [Terry Bisson/Berni Wrightson, frontis] 1p; (2) Growth [Nicola Cuti/Wayne Howard] 6p; (3) Blood Thirst! [Terry Bisson/Syd Shores] 7p; (4) The Game That Plays You! [Dick Kenson/Berni Wright-

son] 6p; (5) Web of Horror Comic Artist Contest [Terry Bisson/Ralph Reese] 2p; (6) Dead Letter [Terry Bisson?/Donald Norman] 6p; (7) The Skin-Eaters [Terry Bisson/Ralph Reese] 4p; (8) Island of the Walking Dead [Carl Dimond/Donald Norman] 11p.

Notes: Publisher: Robert Sproul. Editor: Terry Bisson. $0.35 for 64 pages. The magazine's host and mascot was a rather cute spider named Webster. At this point in time, at least a third of the contents of Warren's *Creepy* and *Eerie* magazines consisted of reprints. *Web of Horror* had all new stories, many from a group of young artists called the "young turks," who would shortly usher in a new level of excitement to both Marvel and DC, creating a treasure trove of art and comics for collectors. *WOH*'s all-new-stories approach (combined with no internal ads, something that Jim Warren must have *hated*) probably prompted Warren to discontinue its own reprints. The competition threat also caused Jim Warren to issue his "them or us" letter to his freelancers, bluntly stating that you could work for Warren or you could work for other B&W horror comic publishers, but you couldn't work for both. Of the youngsters appearing here, Berni Wrightson was likely the most notable, having made his professional debut less than a year earlier. Ralph Reese had been an assistant to Wally Wood, but his story here is the earliest I've seen him credited with a solo effort so it may well be his professional solo debut. Cuti had made his professional debut only a couple of months earlier in a Warren magazine. The old pro here is Syd Shores, who illustrated *Captain America* back in the 1940s. Editor Terry Bisson went on to become a major SF writer, winning many awards. The comic art contest consisted of an elaborate two-page spread with an open space for budding artists to add their own art and dialogue. The intended prize was apparently for the winner to get his or her first publication credit but the magazine ended before the first winner could be announced. The best story here, "Island of the Walking Dead" reads as though it were intended as a series, although this was the main characters' only appearance. It's somewhat hampered by an

uninspired art job. The script was originally 15 pages in length. Best art is Reese's effort. Throughout the run of this series, the cover art was reprinted on the back without copy, thus, for all intents and purposes, appearing as a color pin-up. According to a Berni Wrightson interview that appeared in *Infinity* #2, *Web of Horror* pay rates were $40 a page for pencils and ink with a $5 boost if the artist lettered the page as well. Stories paid scripters $13 a page while the painted covers went for $250.

2. cover: Jeff Jones (February 1970)

(1) Webster's Welcome [Terry Bisson/Ralph Reese, frontis] 1p; (2) Mother Toad [Terry Bisson/Berni Wrightson] 5p; (3) Ashes to Ashes! [Ron Barlowith Roger Brand] 6p; (4) Sea of Graves [Otto Binder/Michael Kaluta] 7p; (5) Web of Horror Comic Artist Contest [Terry Bisson/Michael Kaluta] 2p; (6) Breathless! [Marv Wolfman/Berni Wrightson] 7p; (7) The Unmasking! [Wilson Shard/Bill Fraccio and Tony Tallarico, art credited to Alfred Payan] 6p; (8) Man-Plant from the Tomb [Otto Binder/Ralph Reese] 6p.

Notes: The title logo was in a different font and style for all three *Web* issues as well as for the unpublished fourth issue, with the best published version appearing on #3. The letters page debuts with an original illustration by Berni Wrightson and Jeff Jones. "Sea of Graves" was Kaluta's second published professional appearance, following a war story for Charlton that appeared in *Flash Gordon* #18, dated January 1970. The writer's name, Wilson Shard, on the Fraccio/Tallarico–drawn story,

Jeff Jones does the premiere issue cover art for Warren's first serious rival — *Web of Horror*. For the short life of the magazine, the cover art was always repeated on the back without copy.

sounds like a pen name. Best story and art goes to the Binder/Reese combo on "Man-Plant from the Tomb."

3. cover: Berni Wrightson (April 1970)

(1) Webster's Welcome [Terry Bisson/Frank Brunner, frontis] 1p; **(2)** Dead End [Otto Binder/Michael Kaluta] 6p; **(3)** Curse of the Yeti [Otto Binder/Ralph Reese] 7p; **(4)** Santa's Claws [Frank Brunner] 7p; **(5)** Web of Horror Comic Artist Contest [Terry Bisson/Berni Wrightson] 2p; **(6)** Strangers! [Syd Shores] 7p; **(7)** Point of View [Bruce Jones] 6p; **(8)** Feed It! [Mike Friedrich/Berni Wrightson] 6p.

Notes: Final issue. The comic artist contest featured here was to be the last of the tryout pages. The winner of the first contest was to be announced in the never-published fourth issue. The second letters page appears, with several fans definitely disliking Kaluta's artwork (don't know why; it looked quite nice to me). For some reason, the letters page from the previous issue was reprinted as well. Best story and art for this issue (and best story and art that appeared in this title, period) belongs to the excellent little chiller "Feed It!" by Friedrich and Wrightson. Bruce Jones makes his professional debut. Nowadays better known for his scripts on the likes of the Hulk and Batman, Jones began his career as a writer/artist. His artwork was quite good, too, somewhat in the style of Al Williamson and Roy Krenkel. This was Frank Brunner's professional comics debut as well, although he'd had strips appearing in the movie magazine *Castle of Frankenstein* and in numerous fanzines. Following this issue, Bisson quit as editor to join a commune (well, it was the 1970s) and, later, established a career as an award-winning science fiction writer. With Bisson gone, Berni Wrightson and Bruce Jones convinced Robert Sproul to let them become the new editors. They had assembled a fourth issue when one weekend they went out to Long Island to meet with Sproul for a conference, only to discover him gone to Florida (or possibly simply across town) along with a large quantity of the art and stories intended for future issues of *Web of Horror*. Not all of the stories disappeared, however, as sometime during these events Frank Brunner, suspecting the magazine was going under, bluffed

his way into the Sproul's offices and, claiming that *he* was the new editor, rescued a goodly amount of stories, all of which ended up getting published in various fanzines of the time. The following items were intended for the never-published Wrightson/Jones–edited issues of *Web of Horror*.

4. cover: Berni Wrightson, layout cover (all that survived) that was published in *Scream Door* #1

(1) Webster's Welcome [Michael Kaluta, published in *Reality* #2] 1p; **(2)** Quasar! [Steve Hickman, published in *Reality* #1] 7p; **(3)** Death Is the Sailor [Len Wein/Michael Kaluta, published in *Reality* #1 and 2] 7p; **(4)** Eye of Newt, Toe of Frog [Gerry Conway/Frank Brunner, published in *Vampirella* #10] 7p; **(5)** Outside-In [Bruce Jones, published in *Reality* #2] 7p; **(6)** Rat! [Tom Sutton, credited to Sean Todd (see the reference to Warren's "them or us" letter above), published in *Scream Door* #1] 7p; **(7)** Out on a Limb [Berni Wrightson, published in *I'll Be Damned* #4] 6p; **(8)** Hey, Buddy, Can You Lend Me a...? [Michael Kaluta, published in *Scream Door* #1] 5p; **(9)** Sword of Dragonus [Chuck Robinson and Frank Brunner/Frank Brunner, published in *Phase* #1] 8p.

Stories that vanished included the following:

(1) A SF story by Clark Dimond and Ralph Reese featuring pirates and galleons in outer space; **(2)** a Berni Wrightson story entitled "The Monster Jar"; **(3)** two Michael Kaluta stories.

Frank Brunner has long stated that the first *Dragonus* story, "Sword of Dragonus" was intended for a future issue of *Web of Horror*. After *Web* collapsed, Warren offered to publish it as they did, "Eye of Newt, Toe of Frog," but Brunner wanted to retain the rights to this because he believed *Dragonus* would make a good continuing series. Thus, "Sword of Dragonus" ended up in the only issue of the fanzine *Phase*. A second *Dragonus* story appeared in the early independent comic *Star*Reach* #3.

DC Comics

Spirit World

1. cover: Neal Adams via Jack Kirby (fall 1971)

(1) The President Must Die! [Jack Kirby/Jack Kirby and Vince Colletta] 10p; (2) House of Horror! [Jack Kirby/Jack Kirby and Vince Colletta] 12p; (3) Children of the Flaming Wheel! [Jack Kirby?, text article] 3p; (4) The Screaming Woman [Jack Kirby/Jack Kirby and Vince Colletta] 10p; (5) Spirit of Vengeance! [Steve Sherman and Mark Evanier/Jack Kirby and Vince Colletta] 3p; (6) Amazing Predictions [Jack Kirby/Jack Kirby and Vince Colletta] 9p; (7) Weird Humor [Sergio Aragones] 1p.

Notes: Publisher: Carmine Infantino. Editor: Jack Kirby, Steve Sherman and Mark Evanier. It was $0.50 for 48 pages. One of two titles comprising DC's short-lived entry into publishing B&W comics magazines. The other title was *Tales of the Mob*, also edited, written and drawn by Jack Kirby. Kirby's original cover for this title was part artwork and part collage, something that he did a lot of in the early 1970s. DC apparently didn't like it and had Neal Adams completely redo the cover but it was based squarely on Kirby's original de-

Neal Adams based his cover painting here squarely on the original Jack Kirby effort, which DC management had rejected.

sign. The magazine came accompanied by a large pull-out poster called "Souls." Most copies of the magazine being offered for sale don't have the poster any longer. Some of these stories remind one of Joe Simon and Kirby's 1950s horror comic *Black Magic*. Colletta's the wrong inker for a horror book but the art is nice and the stories aren't bad. I quite liked "The President Must Die!," which dealt with predicting John F. Kennedy's assassination and "Amazing Predictions" which covered Michel De Nostradamus' predictions. According to Kirby (and many of the Nostradamus code readers/writers in the 1970s) Nostradamus' predictions were to be completely fulfilled in 1993. It's two decades later

and Nostradamus "scholars" keep pushing back the deadline. A second issue was completed, with inking this time by Mike Royer, but it never appeared. Many of the stories intended for that issue ended up in some of DC's color "mystery" titles.

The Atlas/Seaboard Titles

Weird Tales of the Macabre

1. cover: Jeff Jones (January 1975)

(1) Macabre Mails [written: Jeff Rovin, text article] 1p; (2) The Demon Is Dying! [Pat Boyette] 8p; (3) Tales of the Sorceress ad [Ric

Estrada, Devilina is featured] 1p; (4) Time Lapse [Augustine Funnell/Leopoldo Duranona] 7p; (5) Atlas Magazines ad [Ernie Colon] ½ p; (6) The Many Horrors of Dan Curtis [Gary Gerani, text article with photos] 7p; (7) Atlas Comics ad [Ernie Colon] 1p; (8) A Second Life [Ramon Torrents] 8p; (9) The Cheese Is for the Rats [Villanova] 8p; (10) Tour de Force [Martin Pasko/Leo Summers] 8p; (11) Speed Demon [Ernie Colon] 8p.

Notes: Publishers: Martin and Charles "Chip" Goodman. Editor: Jeff Rovin. It was $0.75 for 64 pages. Rovin dedicated this issue to Warren Publishing's editor Bill DuBay (!) and mentions that DuBay would be doing a color comic for Atlas. The comic was *Wonderworld* but it was never published, reportedly due to James Warren being unhappy that his editor would be working for competitors. The editorial and an accompanying ad also stated the *Weird Tales'* sister magazine was to have been entitled *Tales of the Sorceress* but it actually was published under the title *Devilina*. All in all, this is a pretty good issue. Jones' cover isn't one of his best but there is fine interior work from Torrents, Summers, Colon, Boyette and Pasko. Best story is the Funnell/Duranona "Time Lapse" with best art going to Ramon Torrents' "A Second Life." None of the stories are credited but the credits were given in the next issue's letters page. While the color comics were issued under the company heading of Atlas, all the B&W magazines appeared under the actual company name of Seaboard Periodicals.

2. cover: Boris Vallejo (March 1975)

(1) The Bog Beast [Gabriel Levy/Enrique Badia Romero] 9p; (2) Dr. Mercurio's Diary [Al Moniz/Juez Xirinius] 8p; (3) Carrion of the Gods [Pat Boyette] 8p; (4) The Films of Edgar Allan Poe [Karl Macek, text article with photos] 8p; (5) Who Toys with Terror! [George Kashdan/John Severin] 7p; (6) The Staff of Death [Leo Summers] 8p.

Notes: Final issue. If anything, this was better than the premiere issue. Vallejo's cover of a witch burning at the stake is striking and one of his best horror covers. The accompanying story, "The Staff of Death" by Leo Summers, had a surprisingly strong sexual content. It also had the best story and art in the magazine. Still, there

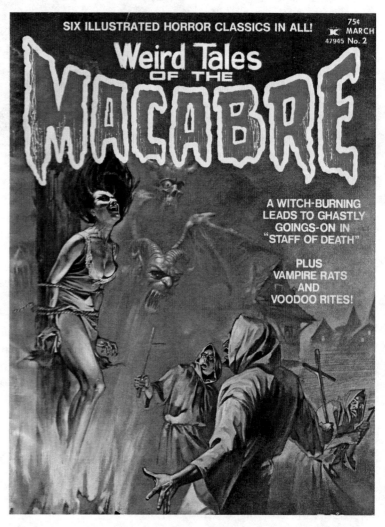

One of Vallejo's last efforts in the horror field is this dynamic witch burning, done for the short-lived Atlas/Seaboard magazines. © Nemesis Group, Inc./used by permission.

are no weak stories here. "The Bog Beast" was a preview of the upcoming color comic, with considerably better art than what actually appeared in that color book. A letters page debuted with future Eclipse publisher Dean Mullaney sending in a letter. A next issue blurb on the letters page also revealed the intended contents of the never-published third issue, which would have included "Man of Magic," written by John Albano and illustrated by Dan Adkins, an untitled SF story by Skywald artist Jesus Suso Rego, "Monster X," written by Gabriel Levy and illustrated by Howard Nostrand — intended to be the first segment of a series entitled *The Monster Saga* (another segment, written by Levy and illustrated by Walt Simonson, was also produced), "Night Jury" written and illustrated by Mexican artist Juan Berger and, finally, "The Were-Hound," written by George Kashdan and illustrated by Jack Sparling. To my knowledge, none of the stories ever appeared. There were also at least two leftover Jeff Jones covers, one of which appeared as a *Creepy* cover in 1980. Both of those covers can be seen in the coffee table artbook *The Art of Jeff Jones.*

Devilina

1. cover: Pulojar (January 1975)

(1) The Devil's Dungeon [Jeff Rovin, text article] 1p; (2) Devilina: Satan's Domain [Ric Estrada] 11p; (3) The Lost Tomb of Nefertiri [Gabriel Levy/Pablo Marcos] 8p; (4) Atlas Comics ad [Ernie Colon, most of the Atlas/Seaboard color and B&W characters appear] 2p; (5) Lay of the Sea [Gabriel Levy/Leopoldo Duranona] 8p; (6) Midnight Muse [Michael Cahlin/Ralph Reese] 2p; (7) Merchants of Evil! [John Albano/Jack Sparling] 8p; (8) Filmdom's Vampire Lovers [Gary Gerani, text article with photos] 6p; (9) William Shakespeare's The Tempest [Martin Pasko/Leo Summers] 10p; (10) Devilina ad [Ric Estrada] 1p.

Notes: Publishers: Martin and Charles "Chip" Goodman. Editor: Jeff Rovin with Richard Meyers as assistant editor. It cost $0.75 for 64 pages. Rovin's editorial is the same one used for *Weird Tales of the Macabre* #1. This is basically a knock-off of Warren Publications' *Vampirella* magazine. And like *Vampirella*, the weakest segment belongs to the lead character. However, there are

some excellent backup stories, including "Lay of the Sea" and "Midnight Muse." Pablo Marcos delivers beautiful artwork for "The Lost Tomb of Nefertiri" and the team of Pasko and Summers render a striking adaptation of Shakespeare's "Tempest." Pulojar's quite good cover was reprinted in 1982 as the penultimate cover for the Warren run of *Vampirella*!

2. cover: George Torjussen (May 1975)

(1) Devilina: Curse of the Ra Scarab [Ric Estrada] 12p; (2) Vendetta [John Albano/Frank Thorne] 8p; (3) The Devil's Procuress! [Carl Macek/Jack Sparling] 8p; (4) Flesh Gordon: The Perils of Flesh [Gary Gerani?, text article with photos] 6p; (5) The Prophesy [Jesus Suso Rego] 8p; (6) Night Creature [Leo Summers] 8p.

Notes: Final issue. Torjussen's cover is, at best, only fair. Devilina's story is downright poor. However, the remaining stories are very good. A much stronger sexual content appears in this issue, especially in "The Devil's Procuress!" (where the letters of the title were inhabited by naked women striking poses) and "Night Creature," which featured a fairly explicit rape in a barn. Even the movie review article discussed the X-rated *Flesh Gordon*, a 1970s spoof of the more famous *Flash Gordon*. If you don't mind the sex content, this is a pretty good issue. Best art is by Jesus Suso Rego on his own story "The Prophesy" while the best story is Leo Summers' "Night Creature."

A Myron Fass Publication

GASM

1. cover: Terry Pastor (November 1977)

(1) Editorial [Jeffrey Goodman, text article] 1p; (2) Diana [Raoul Vezina] 4p; (3) Baby [Gene Day] 15p; (4) Easily Amused [Buzz Dixon/Judy Hunt] 3p; (5) Gasm [Mark Wheatley, color] 12p; (6) Corny and Zorn [Buzz Dixon] 9p; (7) The Hunter [Arvell Jones and Connie Harold] 6p; (8) untitled [Seaton "Chuck" Hancock] 7p; (9) Visit [John Workman] 1p; (10) The Mere Fact of an Atmosphere [Ben Katchor] 4p.

Notes: Publisher: Myron Fass and Irving Fass. Editor: Jeffrey Goodman. It was $1.50 for 64 pages. Myron Fass was a Golden Age artist who became a publisher in 1956 with the *MAD Magazine* knockoff *Lunatickle*. By the 1970s he was publishing about 50 different pulp magazines, generally of the lowest common denominator, including the schlocky *Eerie* Publications' refried horror magazines as well as magazines focusing on UFOs, skin pictures, gun collectors, men's sweat books, movie and TV tie-ins and more. If you want an idea of how classy Fass' product was, this magazine's title is short for "orgasm." This magazine was almost certainly inspired by *Heavy Metal's* unexpected success the year before, as was Warren's adult SF magazine *1984*. Unlike the *Eerie* product, which featured a lot of re-touched or redrawn 1950s reprints, *GASM* was an effort to produce an all-original (or at least mostly so) comic magazine. Like *Web of Horror*, it used many artists just stepping out of the fanzines and into the professional arena. Like both Warren and *Heavy Metal*, it also featured a decently done color section. The back cover featured an ad with Ken Kelly's artwork for the Kiss album *Love Gun*. As for the artists, Raoul Vezina had worked on Michael Gilbert's fanzine *New Paltz Comics*. Gene Day had done work for Sky-wald and *Star*Reach* as well as apparently dozens of Canadian fanzines, some of which he self-published. John Workman had previously appeared in *Star*Reach* and had just joined or was about to join the staff at *Heavy Metal*. Buzz Dixon (who is not the same guy as writer Chuck Dixon) made his professional debut as both a writer and artist. His artwork looks somewhat similar to Phil Foglio. The editor, Jeffrey Goodman, had started out writing porn novels and graduated to editing dozens of Fass' magazines. Arvell Jones' story contains no dialogue or captions. Best art here goes to his story as well as the artwork by Gene Day and John Workman. Best story is Gene Day's "Baby" although I rather liked Ben Katchor's odd little tale as well. There is an extremely funny ad on the inside back cover for a bong and some "perfectly legal" imitation hashish and opium mixtures made from wild lettuce that was apparently supposed to help your sex drive. The fake stuff was called Lettucene. As the ad slogan goes — "Relax ... Smoke Lettucene with your lover and feel your

bodies smile at each other." What a horrific image!

2. cover: Terry Pastor (December 1977)

(1) Or... [Jeffrey Goodman, text article] 1p; (2) Pin-Up [?] 1p; (3) Rogue World [Gary Winnick, reprinted from *Venture* #5 (1976)] 11p; (4) Gasm, part 2 [Mark Wheatley, color] 8p; (5) Killing Time with Speedy, Flip ... and Duke [Buzz Dixon] 12p; (6) War Mind [Matt Howarth] 6p; (7) Nymphs [Fred Bobb] 2p; (8) The Jar [Buzz Dixon/Judy Hunt] 5p; (9) The Arrival of a Guest from Another Solar System Will Long Go Unnoticed [Ben Katchor, color] 4p; (10) Le Valise [Jeff Goodman/Ned Sonntag, first four pages are in color] 9p; (11) Girl Named Sexx ... the Original Belle Baldwin [John Workman] 2p.

Notes: A better issue than the first with "Rogue World," "The Jar," "War Mind" and "Le Valise" providing solid entertainment. "Rogue War" was a reprint from Frank Cirocco and Brent Anderson's fanzine *Venture*. Best art came from John Workman with the best story honors going to Ben Katchor.

3. cover: Steve Hickman/back cover: Bob Aull (February 1978)

(1) Gasm Comics [Jeffrey Goodman/Ned Sonntag, text article] 1p; (2) B. J. Butterfly [John Workman] 1p; (3) The Triad [Horizon Zero Graphiques/Frank Cirocco and Steve Leialoha, reprinted from Venture #5 (1976)] 11p; (4) Terminal Geeks [Jeff Goodman/Ned Sonntag, color on the first eight pages] 10p; (5) The Adjutant [Gene Day] 10p; (6) Cyborg 28-H [Don Lomax] 9p; (7) Piece of Cake [Buzz Dixon] 6p; (8) The Cotillion Borealis [Ben Katchor] 4p; (9) Black Hole [?, signature on the last page appears to read Lamont] 3p; (10) Gasm, part 3 [Mark Wheatley, color] 8p.

Notes: Like "Rogue World" in the previous issue, "The Triad" was a reprint from Brent Anderson and Frank Cirocco's fanzine *Venture*. The author for that story listed himself (or themselves) as Horizon Zero Graphiques. The magazine continued to improve, with a much better cover than the previous two issues and decent stories and art throughout the book. The story "Black Hole" is uncredited and has a strong sexual content. The title page lists Judy Hunt as a contributor but she is not credited for anything on the actual pages. Perhaps she had a hand in inking "Black Hole." Best story and art go to Gene Day's "The Adjutant," despite the fact that the title is so ornately lettered that you can't read it. Good issue.

4. cover: Jim Burns/back cover: Richard Corben (April 1978)

(1) Editorial [Jeffrey Goodman, text article] 1p; (2) The Buy [Don Lomax] 10p; (3) Gasm, part 4 [Mark Wheatley, color] 8p; (4) Incident on Planetoid 7 [James O'Barr] 9p; (5) Twilight of the Dogs [Richard Corben, reprinted from *Fantagor* #1 (December 1971)] 10p; (6) The Long Goodbye to Everything! [Gene Day] 13p; (7) Horrible Harvey's House! [Richard Corben, pages 4–11 in color, reprinted from *Skull* #3 (November 1971)] 11p; (8) Passions [John Workman] 2p.

Notes: It cost $1.95 for 64 pages. The cover says this is a "special super Corben issue." Both Corben stories, however, are reprinted from 1971. James O'Barr makes his professional debut here with some very crude artwork. John Workman's story is set in SF author Edgar Pangborn's "Davy's World" storyline and is dedicated to the (then) recently deceased writer. The positioning of the color pages forced some odd splits between pages in the B&W stories. Best art and story goes to Gene Day's excellent SF tale. Good work also appeared from Workman, Lomax, the Corben reprints and Mark Wheatley. Jim Burns' cover was also quite striking. The classic Corben artwork for recording artist Meat Loaf's album *Bat out of Hell* appears on the back cover.

5. cover: Ned Sonntag (June 1978)

(1) Editorial [Jeffrey Goodman, text article] 1p; (2) Downed... [Don Lomax] 5p; (3) Gasm, part 5 [Mark Wheatley, color, except on page one] 9p; (4) Ah Rilly Ount Nuh! [Marc Hempel] 1p; (5) City Ship [Gene Day] 18p; (6) To Meet the Faces You Meet [Jan Strnad/Richard Corben, reprinted from *Fever Dreams* #1 (1972)] 16p; (7) Bondlord [Gary Winnick, color] 8p; (8) Heads Up in Bugtown [Matt Howarth with Mark Kernes] 4p.

Notes: Final issue. As in the previous issue, Corben's artwork for recording artist Meat Loaf's album *Bat out of Hell* appears on the back cover. "City Ship" is printed sideways. Another good issue with fine artwork. Luckily for readers,

Mark Wheatley concludes the *Gasm* serial. Best art and story go to the Strnad/Corben reprint.

Quality Communications

Warrior

1. cover: Steve Dillon/frontis: Garry Leach (March 1982)

(1) Freedom's Road [Dez Skinn, text article] 1p; (2) Marvelman: ...a Dream of Flying [Alan Moore/Garry Leach] 8p; (3) Marvelman, Mightiest Man in the Universe [Dez Skinn/Mike Angelo Studios, text article] 3½ p; (4) Next issue ad [Paul Neary] ½ p; (5) The Spiral Path: Prologue [Steve Parkhouse] 5p; (6) A True Story? [Steve Moore/Dave Gibbons] 2p; (7) The Legend of Prester John [Steve Moore/John Bolton] 7p; (8) V for Vendetta: The Villain [Alan Moore/David Lloyd] 6p; (9) Father Shandor, Demon Stalker: Spawn from Hell's Pit! [Steve Moore/John Bolton, reprinted from *House of Hammer* #8 (April 1977)] 6p; (10) Laser Eraser and Pressbutton [Steve Moore/Steve Dillon, story credited to Pedro Henry] 6p; (11) Warriors All!: John Bolton, Steve Dillon, Dave Gibbons, Garry Leach, David Lloyd, Alan Moore, Steve Moore, Steve Parkhouse and Dez Skinn profiles [various, text articles with photos, the last page is on the inside back cover] 2p; (12) Forbidden Planet ad [Brian Bolland, on the back cover] 1p.

Notes: Publishers: Graham Marsh and Dez Skinn. Editor: Dez Skinn. 50p or $2.00 for 48 pages. Alex Pressbutton and Mysta Mystalis (the Laser Eraser) were cover-featured while Mysta was also featured on the frontispiece. *Warrior* occupied the same position in the UK as Mike Friedrich's *Star*Reach* did in the 1970s in the U.S. It provided a place for established pros and up "n" comers to display their work in a manner unfettered by the constraints of the more commercial British comic companies. It was also the first (and possibly only) British magazine to be easily available in the U.S. (I bought all my own copies in Idaho, so it had to have been well distributed). If that was all that this magazine accomplished, it would still have been an important addition to the B&W horror magazines, but, again, like what *Star*Reach* did for independent comics and publishers in the early

1980s, this title also provided the groundwork for what much of the comics field looked like in the latter part of the 1980s and early 1990s. It launched Alan Moore's career in the U.S., giving him a platform to step over to *Swamp Thing*, whose stories gave birth to the *Vertigo* line, as well as establishing the dark tone applied to classic characters that Frank Miller employed so successfully on the original *Dark Knight* series. Moore wasn't alone, of course. *Warrior* also gave at least a half dozen British artists worldwide exposure, largely creating the British invasion of comics, not only for veterans of *Warrior*, but for an apparent host of British writers and artists, who, to this day, are the major driving force behind mainstream comics. As for this issue, it featured the debuts of Moore's early serials *Marvelman* and *V for Vendetta*— neither strictly horror, but both featuring strong horror overtones— along with Steve Parkhouse's serial *The Spiral Path* and the respective returns of two Steve Moore' serials: *Laser Eraser and Pressbutton* and the excellent *Father Shandor*, the latter of which stands firmly in the horror field. I distinctly remember reading Moore's version of *Marvelman* for the first time in 1982 and feeling a sharp tang of electricity shoot through my mind. *Marvelman* had all the familiar superhero trappings but there was something new and strange there as well. It was more the startling fact that this character had had apparently a long and successful career in the UK, yet was totally unknown in the U.S. It was, I suspect, the sneaky feeling I had that, as a reader, I was in on the ground floor of something big, something really new in comics. Moore's tight script and Leach's masterful artwork were bold and striking, quite unlike the stuck-in-a-rut American comics of the time. For one thing, the printing was clear and bold, whereas most American comics, even from the big companies, appeared to have been printed on toilet paper, with the artwork looking like a muddy, garish, off-centered mess. The *Marvelman* content seemed adult in nature, yet it appeared without the blatant, over-the-top sexuality or violence that often passes for adult in comics, although there was strong violence and sexuality in the stories. There was a feeling, with this first story, that the reader was in the same situation as Mike Moran, caught just between the uttering of the "magic" transformation word and the actual transformation itself. Then, improbably, Moore's second serial, *V for Vendetta*, was even better. Moore's script of a mysterious Guy Fawkes look-alike was as creepy as you could ask for. Lloyd's artwork was even more than one could ask for. Excellent as Leach's work was on *Marvelman*, his work was somewhat familiar, since I'd seen thousands of pages of superhero art by 1982. Lloyd's artwork was much different, quite unlike anything being produced at the time. His use of heavy blacks and the charcoal sooty appearance of the characters meshed perfectly with Moore's script and seemed tailor-made for B&W reproduction. At the time, it seemed impossible that this style of artwork could ever be colored adequately (although DC and Lloyd proved me wrong in 1988–1989 when the entire story came out in color). Good as *Marvelman* was, *V for Vendetta* was simply better, deeper, richer. Even today, the collected work stands as one of Moore's best graphic novels. This in no way slights the other excellent work that appeared in this first issue. Parkhouse's "Spiral Path" is a moody evocation of druid days while the Moore/Bolton "Legend of Prester John" story is an excellent stand-alone tale with great artwork. The *Father Shandor* strip consisted of reprints for its first three appearances here, before appearing with new episodes (and a new artist) in #4, but over time it developed into an excellent graphic novel, with intriguing, often grisly twists and a real feel for the horror genre. The revival of the Axel Pressbutton character (originally an underground comix, written by Steve Moore as Pedro Henry, illustrated by Alan Moore as Curt Vile and published in *Sounds* magazine) with a new partner, Mysta Mystalis, might have seemed somewhat commonplace if only because it was in such stellar company. It actually was a pretty decent little SF thriller, with lively twists, good to great supporting characters (especially Zirk!) and colorful settings. An excellent start to an excellent magazine.

2. cover: Garry Leach/frontis: Jim Baikie (April 1982)

(1) Marvelman [Alan Moore/Garry Leach] 6p;

(2) Comics Showcase ad [Marshall Rogers, the Joker is featured] 1p; (3) The Life, Death and Earlier Days of Axel Pressbutton, Esquire [Dez Skinn/Steve Dillon and Alan Moore, text article, Moore's art is credited to Curt Vile] 4½ p; (4) V for Vendetta: The Voice [Alan Moore/David Lloyd] 8p; (5) Father Shandor, Demon Stalker: River of Corpses ... Tower of Death [Steve Moore/John Bolton, reprinted from *Halls of Horror* #21 (June 1978)] 6p; (6) Madman [Paul Neary] 6p; (7) The Spiral Path: The Lord of Death! [Steve Parkhouse] 5p; (8) Laser Eraser and Pressbutton, part 2 [Steve Moore/Steve Dillon, story credited to Pedro Henry] 9p; (9) Dispatches [Dez Skinn/David Lloyd, text article, Lloyd's artwork is a sample from a comic strip adaptation of a movie called Roar] 2p.

Notes: *Marvelman* was cover-featured with a standard superhero-style cover. Paul Neary's odd little horror strip, *Madman*, debuted. Otherwise, all of the stories that debuted in the issue before continued, with *V for Vendetta* having a particularly strong outing. Kid Marvelman made his debut in the *Marvelman* strip with a one-panel cameo.

3. cover: Paul Neary (July 1982)

(1) Marvelman: "When Johnny Comes Marching Home..." [Alan Moore/Garry Leach] 6p; (2) The Spiral Path: The Birth of a Warrior! [Steve Parkhouse/Steve Parkhouse and Geoff Senior] 6p; (3) Madman, part 2 [Paul Neary] 6p; (4) Father Shandor, Demon Stalker: The Devil's Dark Destiny [Steve Moore and Dez Skinn/John Bolton, reprinted from ?] 6p; (5) Zirk, Silver Sweater of the Spaceways [Steve Moore/Brian Bolland, story credited to Pedro Henry] 4p; (6) V for Vendetta: Victims [Alan Moore/David Lloyd] 8p; (7) Laser Eraser and Pressbutton, part 3 [Steve Moore/Steve Dillon] 8p.

Notes: The letters page debuted while *Madman* was cover-featured. The back cover was a preview of #4's cover. *Laser Eraser and Pressbutton*'s weird little pig-like, slime-covered, football-shaped alien, Zirk, got his own fun (and often near-pornographic) strip, beautifully illustrated by Brian Bolland. The *Marvelman* strip was an excellent example of how to build mounting tension in a comic strip. It's beautifully rendered by Garry Leach.

4. cover: Steve Dillon (August 1982)

(1) Marvelman: The Yesterday Gambit [Alan Moore/Steve Dillon, Paul Neary and Alan

Davis] 10p; (2) The Spiral Path: The Dark Dreamer! [Steve Parkhouse] 4p; (3) V for Vendetta: Vaudeville [Alan Moore/David Lloyd] 7p; (4) Madman, part 3 [Paul Neary] 6p; (5) Father Shandor, Demon Stalker: City of the Tombs [Steve Moore/David Jackson] 6p; (6) Golden Amazon [David Lloyd, from the stories by John Russell Fearn] 7p; (7) Laser Eraser and Pressbutton [Steve Moore/David Jackson, last page on the inside back cover] 5p.

Notes: The cover served as a showcase both for current and future strips, featuring *Marvelman*, V, Caed from *The Spiral Path*, *Warpsmith*, Big Ben, Laser Eraser, Pressbutton and a samurai warrior. Much of the contents of this issue, including the cover, were originally intended for a *Warrior* summer special, where the intent was to present the characters from the regular Warrior series in one-off stories while their serials continued in *Warrior*. That idea was abandoned at the last minute and the one-off stories were spread out over a period of time in the regular issues. The title page still lists this as the summer special 1982 although it should be considered the August issue. The *Marvelman* story was not a part of the ongoing serial (at least not yet) but a summer special story designed as a tryout for potential artists to replace Garry Leach. Dillon didn't seem really comfortable with the superhero format; Neary's art was a bit cartoony and perhaps gave Marvelman too much of the Uber-Man appearance, while Davis' art seemed a bit more on target (although it's rather crude by Davis' later standards). The Warpsmiths debuted in this time travel story that previewed future Marvelman developments, much of it years before it would actually see print. The story itself has never been reprinted, making this issue one of the more valuable of the *Warrior* run. Both the "Golden Amazon" adaptation and the tale of Axel Pressbutton's first meeting with Mysta Mystralis were originally intended for the summer special as well. Future comic writer Warren Ellis sent in a letter complementing both Alan Moore's and Steve Moore's writing efforts in #1.

5. cover: photo cover by Dez Skinn (September 1982)

(1) Marvelman: Dragons [Alan Moore/Garry Leach] 6p; (2) V for Vendetta: Versions [Alan

Moore/David Lloyd] 6p; (3) All Change [Dez Skinn/Jim Baike, Steve Parkhouse, Alan Davis, text article] 2p; (4) Father Shandor, Demon Stalker: The Empire of Sin [Steve Moore/David Jackson] 5p; (5) Madman: Mk1 [Paul Neary/Mick Austin] 2p; (6) The Spiral Path: The Drowning Woman [Steve Parkhouse] 5p; (7) Laser Eraser and Pressbutton, part 4 [Steve Moore/Steve Dillon, story credited to Pedro Henry] 8p; (8) V for Vendetta: Vertigo [Alan Moore/David Lloyd] 5p.

Notes: *V* is featured on a unique and nicely done photo cover. Alan Moore's script for this installment of *Marvelman* is terrifying while the *V for Vendetta* script gives a first glimpse into the mysterious V's obsessions. Both are brilliantly done. The "All Change" segment provided a preview of Marvelman's new artist, Alan Davis's, pencils as well as previews of two upcoming series — *Twilight World* and *The Bojeffries Saga*. This issue's segment of *Father Shandor*'s continuing saga had the title only on the title page. It does not appear on the story. The *Madman* and *Spiral Path* segments as well as the extra *V for Vendetta* stories were originally intended for the summer special and were not part of the ongoing serials. Alan Moore's "Vertigo" story employs a literary device in which V forces a man to walk around a skyscraper on a ledge, hundreds of feet off the ground. The same basic story idea was used by Stephen King in *The Ledge* and by Joe Lansdale in *Steel Valentine*. Probably used by a lot of other writers as well. Skinn begins using a part of the letters page for mini-editorials.

6. cover: Steve Parkhouse (October 1982)

(1) Marvelman: Fallen Angels, Forgotten Thunder [Alan Moore/Alan Davis and Garry Leach] 7p; (2) The Spiral Path: The Valley of the Shadow [Steve Parkhouse] 5p; (3) Madman, part 4 [Paul Neary/Mick Austin] 4p; (4) Van Helsing's Terror Tales: Mrs. Murphy's Murders [Steve Moore/Dave Gibbons, reprinted from ?] 4p; (5) Father Shandor, Demon Stalker [Steve Moore/David Jackson] 6p; (6) V for Vendetta: The Vision [Alan Moore/David Lloyd] 6p; (7)

The British magazine *Warrior* actually sold more copies in the U.S. than in Great Britain. This Mick Austin cover for #7 shows Alan Moore and Garry Leach's revival of Marvelman, whose storyline gradually became one of the most horrific superhero tales ever written. © Quality Communications/used by permission.

Laser Eraser and Pressbutton, part 5: Oasis [Steve Moore/Steve Dillon, story credited to Pedro Henry] 7p.

Notes: Davis debuted as the new *Marvelman* artist, helped in the transition by Leach's inks on his first two episodes. Caed and *The Spiral Path* were cover-featured. Strong stories from everyone involved.

7. cover: Mick Austin (November 1982)

(1) Marvelman: Secret Identity [Alan Moore/ Alan Davis/Garry Leach] 8p; **(2)** The Spiral Path: The Oracle Speaks [Steve Parkhouse] 5p; **(3)** Madman, part 5 [Paul Neary/Mick Austin] 4p; **(4)** Father Shandor, Demon Stalker: The Hordes of Hell [Steve Moore/David Jackson] 6p; **(5)** V for Vendetta: Virtue Victorious [Alan Moore/David Lloyd] 6p; **(6)** Laser Eraser and Pressbutton, part 6 [Steve Moore/Steve Dillon] 7p.

Notes: Austin provided an iconic image for his first *Marvelman* cover. It was repeated sans copy on the back cover. It's a truly beautiful cover. If Marvel does ever get around to reprinting the Moore/Gaiman series of *Marvelman* stories, this would make a great first trade paperback cover. Is letter writer Bambos Georgiou the same guy as the artist Bambos? Although the *Madman* episode promised a conclusion for the next issue, it never appeared, apparently due to Neary's busy schedule, and the strip was dropped.

8. cover: David Jackson (December 1982)

(1) Marvelman: Blue Murder [Alan Moore/Alan Davis] 7p; **(2)** The Spiral Path, part 7 [Steve Parkhouse] 5p; **(3)** Stir Crazy [Hunt Emerson] 5p; **(4)** Father Shandor, Demon Stalker: Hand of Glory [Steve Moore/David Jackson] 6p; **(5)** V for Vendetta: The Valley [Alan Moore/David Lloyd] 8p; **(6)** Laser Eraser and Pressbutton, part 7 [Steve Moore/Steve Dillon, story credited to Pedro Henry] 4p.

Notes: With this issue, editor Dez Skinn began writing a regular mini-editorial that ran on the letters page. Future ACG publisher Roger Broughton sent in a letter, with a good third of the letters page given over to letters from the U.S. or Canada. "Stir Crazy" was apparently a last-minute substitute for the missing *Madman* segment. *Father Shandor* was cover-featured (and it was quite a nice illustration, too!). With Davis

assuming full art chores on *Marvelman*, while also illustrating the Alan Moore–written *Captain Britain* for Marvel, this brought up the rather unique situation of the same writer/artist team doing the best two superhero sagas in Great Britain (and probably the U.S. as well) at one and the same time for different publishers.

9. cover: Mick Austin (January 1983)

(1) Marvelman: Out of the Dark [Alan Moore/ Alan Davis] 7p; **(2)** The Spiral Path [Steve Parkhouse/Steve Parkhouse and John Ridgway] 6p; **(3)** Warpsmith: Cold War, Cold Warrior [Alan Moore/Garry Leach] 4p; **(4)** Father Shandor, Demon Stalker: Angel of Death [Steve Moore/David Jackson] 6p; **(5)** V for Vendetta: Violence [Alan Moore/David Lloyd] 8p; **(6)** Laser Eraser and Pressbutton, part 8 [Steve Moore/Steve Dillon, story credited to Pedro Henry] 5p.

Notes: Axel Pressbutton was cover-featured and, like Austin's previous *Marvelman* cover, this portrait was again reprinted sans copy on the back cover. Big Ben made his debut in the *Marvelman* strip. The Warpsmiths also debuted in the first of a two-part story. Supposedly this story was considerably longer in the original script. Leach's company Atomika is reportedly going to (someday!) print the complete version. *Father Shandor* concluded his first serial in fine fashion. This was a superior horror strip and deserves to be collected into a graphic novel someday. Bambos Georgiou sent in another letter.

10. cover: Garry Leach (April–May 1983)

(1) Marvelman: Inside Story [Alan Moore/Alan Davis] 7p; **(2)** V for Vendetta: Venom [Alan Moore/David Lloyd] 8p; **(3)** Camelot 3000 ad [Brian Bolland] 1p; **(4)** Warpsmith: Cold War, Cold Warrior, part 2 [Alan Moore/Garry Leach] 6p; **(5)** Father Shandor, Demon Stalker: The Quick and the Dead [Steve Moore/David Jackson] 6p; **(6)** The Spiral Path [Steve Parkhouse/ Steve Parkhouse and John Ridgway] 5p; **(7)** Laser Eraser and Pressbutton, part 9 [Steve Moore/Steve Dillon, story credited to Pedro Henry] 6p.

Notes: With this issue, *Warrior* became a bi-monthly. Although Skinn tries to put a good face on it, the reality is that slowing your publication rate is usually a sign of trouble. He did promise to go monthly again with #12. He also mentioned ongoing negotiations to turn the British strips into color comics for the U.S. Americomics publisher Bill Black sent in a letter. *Warpsmith* was cover-featured with the cover repeated sans copy on the back cover. The U.S. price for the magazine remained the same but the British price went to 60p.

11. cover: Garry Leach (July 1983)

(1) Marvelman: Zarathustra [Alan Moore/Alan Davis] 8p; (2) Marvelman Special ad [Mike Angelo Studios?] ½ p; (3) The Spiral Path: Dark Dreamer, White Giant! [Steve Parkhouse/Steve Parkhouse and John Ridgway] 5p; (4) The Legend of Prester John [Steve Moore/John Stokes and John Bolton, Bolton's art reprinted from *Warrior* #1 (March 1982)] 10p; (5) V for Vendetta: The Vortex [Alan Moore/David Lloyd] 8p; (6) Jeremy Brood ad [Richard Corben] 1p; (7) Comic Tales ad [Angus McKie] 1p; (8) Creepshow ad [Jack Kamen] 1p; (9) Laser Eraser and Pressbutton, part 10 [Steve Moore/Steve Dillon, story credited to Pedro Henry] 5p; (10) Halls of Horror ad [Garry Leach, on the back cover] 1p.

Notes: *V* was cover-featured. Three serials, *Marvelman*, *V for Vendetta* and *Laser Eraser and Pressbutton*, finished off their first story arcs, all on a high note. *The Legend of Prester John* sequel featured two pages that rehashed the first story, using reworked Bolton art for illustrations. The actual story segment is only eight pages long. The *Marvelman* special advertised here featured four pages of new Moore/Davis Marvelman linking work as well as a number of 1950s–

1960s stories from the Mick Angelo Studios, along with a new cover by Mick Austin of the Marvelman family. Its publication (in Great Britain, I don't believe it was ever distributed here in the States) caused Mighty Marvel to lean legally on little Quality Communications, eventually resulting in the *Marvelman* strip being pulled from *Warrior* and Marvelman's name being changed to Miracleman for its publication here in the States. Ironically, the first mention of *Miracleman* occurred in Marvel's own *Captain Britain* strip, also done by Moore and Davis,

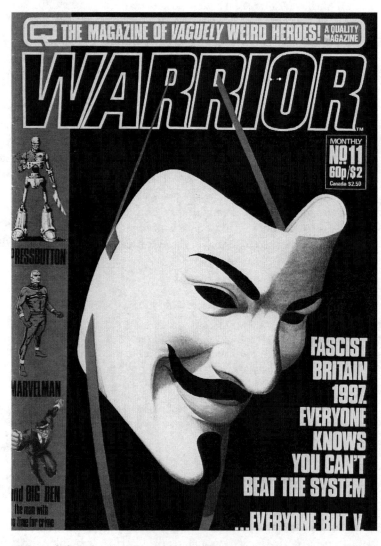

The mask for Alan Moore and David Lloyd's lead character in "V for Vendetta" has become a symbol of political protest worldwide in the years since its first cover appearance in 1983. © Quality Communications/used by permission.

when Marvel/Miracleman cameoed in an unau-
thorized intercompany crossover. Alan Moore
personally answered a reader's complaint about
the amount of profane language in *Marvelman*
and *V for Vendetta*. *Warrior* resumed a monthly
schedule.

12. cover: Steve Parkhouse (August 1983)

(1) The Bojeffries Saga: The Rentman Cometh
[Alan Moore/Steve Parkhouse] 8p; (2) The Spi-
ral Path: Black Phoenix [Steve Parkhouse/Steve
Parkhouse and John Ridgway] 5p; (3) The Leg-
end of Prester John, part 2 [Steve Moore/John
Stokes] 7p; (4) V for Vendetta: This Vicious
Cabaret [Alan Moore and David Jay/David
Lloyd, song] 5p; (5) Young Marvelman [Alan
Moore/John Ridgway] 5p; (6) Laser Eraser and
Pressbutton [Steve Moore/Mick Austin, story
credited to Pedro Henry] 4p.

Notes: The Moore/Parkhouse laughfest *The Bojeffries Saga* made its debut. *The Spiral Path* concluded its run. There's a brief note at the end
that a sequel, "The Silver Circle," might appear
at some point but I don't believe it ever did. All
three of the serials that finished their first story
arcs in the previous issue took a breather from
their regular ongoing storylines and served up
one-shot appearances. The *V for Vendetta* story
was an adaptation of an Alan Moore–David Jay
song, complete with a score, that served as a prologue to the second *V for Vendetta* story arc.
Young Marvelman was a charming wordless strip
that plays out like a 1950s romance comic. Ridgway's artwork appeared heavily influenced by
John Severin's work. David Lloyd replied to a
reader's request for more Golden Amazon stories.
Dez Skinn mentioned that former *Star*Reach*
publisher Mike Friedrich was acting as the U.S.
syndication agent for *Warrior* strips. Twenty-
four Quality badges were advertised on the back
cover, with images from the *Marvelman, V for
Vendetta, Laser Eraser and Pressbutton, Bojeffries
Saga* and *Zirk* strips.

13. cover: Garry Leach (September 1983)

(1) Marvelman, Book Two: Catgames [Alan
Moore/Alan Davis] 6p; (2) Twilight World Pre-
view [Steve Moore/Jim Baikie, text article] 4p;
(3) The Bojeffries Saga: One of Our Rentmen Is
Missing [Alan Moore/Steve Parkhouse] 6p; (4)
Father Shandor, Demon Stalker: Lords of the
Abyss [Steve Moore/David Jackson] 6p; (5) The
Shroud, the Spire and the Stars [Steve Park-
house/John Ridgway] 4p; (6) V for Vendetta,
Book Two: The Vanishing [Alan Moore/David
Lloyd] 7p; (7) Judge Dredd ad [Brian Bolland]
1p; (8) Zirk: The All-Girl Amazon Attack Bat-
talion [Steve Moore/Garry Leach, story credited
to Pedro Henry] 5p.

Notes: Leach's cover, featuring *Zirk*, was reprinted sans copy on the back cover. A new title
logo was tried out. Both *Marvelman* and *V for
Vendetta* began their new story arcs. *Father Shandor*, missing in action since #10, returned. Bambos Georgiou sent in another letter. Dez Skinn's
mini-editorial mentioned that *Warrior* sold
better in the U.S. and Canada than it did in
Great Britain. He also made an interesting ob-
servation that the comics industry had gone
through a radical sea change in previous couple
of years over the types of magazines available.
From the 1940s through the early 1980s, comics
were aimed at the general public. Those comics
most favored by the rabid comic fan were generally failures because they tended to be too edgy
or not entry-level friendly enough for the mainstream buying public, i.e., teenage boys. With
the advent of the then relatively new and more
profitable direct market, titles aimed at the fan
market were thriving and comics aimed solely at
the ever-shrinking newsstand market were becoming steadily unprofitable. Skinn warned that
such instant-cash, higher-priced comics, which
could often be understood only by fans who im-
mersed themselves in comic trivia, may wreck
the market for comics as a whole. Sound familiar? He also mentioned pressure to convert
Warrior into a traditional American 32-page
color comic, which would theoretically increase
sales fivefold or more in the States.

14. cover: Jim Baikie and Garry Leach (October 1983)

(1) Marvelman, Book Two: One of Those Quiet
Moments [Alan Moore/Alan Davis] 6p; (2)
Dreams of Empire, Nightmares of Pressbutton
[Dez Skinn and Steve Moore/Jim Baikie, Steve
Dillon and Cam Kennedy, text article] 4p; (3)
Twilight World [Steve Moore/Jim Baikie] 6p;
(4) Father Shandor, Demon Stalker: How Hard
the Heart... [Steve Moore/David Jackson] 6p;
(5) V for Vendetta, Book Two: The Veil [Alan

Moore/David Lloyd] 6p; (6) Ektryn [Steve Moore/Cam Kennedy] 5p.

Notes: One of Marvelman's best segments appeared as the superhero meets a young rough London lad. Neil Gaiman later wrote a sequel of sorts to this particular tale. The text article tied together the histories of Laser Eraser, Pressbutton, Ektryn and *Twilight World* into one Quality universe. *Twilight World* was cover-featured.

15. cover: Mick Austin (November 1983)

(1) Marvelman, Book Two: Nightmares [Alan Moore/Alan Davis] 6p; (2) Sweatshop Talk [Steve Moore/David Jackson, Jim Baikie and John Bolton, text article, most of the art is reprinted from previous stories] 9p; (3) Twilight World, part 2 [Steve Moore/Jim Baikie] 6p; (4) Father Shandor, Demon Stalker: Ordeal by Fire [Steve Moore/David Jackson] 6p; (5) V for Vendetta: Video [Alan Moore/David Lloyd] 6p; (6) Laser Eraser and Pressbutton, Book Two [Steve Moore/Steve Dillon, story credited to Pedro Henry] 6p.

Notes: *Laser Eraser and Pressbutton* were cover-featured. Austin's cover was again reprinted sans copy on the back cover. The new *Laser Eraser and Pressbutton* strip begun this issue disappeared following its appearance here and would not be finished until late 1985 when the complete story finally appeared in *Axel Pressbutton* #6 (December 1985). In the new text feature *Sweatshop Talk,*" Pedro Henry, Steve Moore's pseudonym, interviewed Steve Moore! Garry Leach filled in as editor while Dez Skinn went to the U.S. for the San Diego Comic Con.

16. cover: Mick Austin (December 1983)

(1) Zirk: Sweat Dreams Are Made of This [Garry Leach, a Christmas card greeting] 1p; (2) Marvelman, Book Two: The Approaching Light [Alan Moore/Alan Davis] 6p; (3) Sweatshop Talk II: 'Ey Up [Steve Moore and Dez Skinn/John Bolton, Bill Titcombe, Angus McKie, Steve Dillon and more, text article] 8p; (4) Twilight World, part 3 [Steve Moore/Jim Baikie] 6p; (5) Father Shandor, Demon Stalker: The Depths [Steve Moore/David Jackson] 6p; (6) V for Vendetta, Book Two: A Vocational Viewpoint [Alan Moore/David Lloyd] 6p; (7) Axel Pressbutton: Christmas on Depravity [Steve Moore/Alan Moore, story credited to Pedro Henry, art credited to Curt Vile, reprinted from

Sounds (December 26, 1981) while one panel reprints Steve Dillon's art from *Warrior* #1] 8p.

Notes: *Marvelman* was cover-featured, graced with a sparkly Paul Newman head. The cover art was reprinted sans copy on the back cover. Skinn's editorial gloomily noted the changeover by former B&W magazines' *Bizarre Adventures*, *Nexus* and *Eclipse Magazine* to regular-sized 32-page comic books, while further noting that Warren Publishing and their magazines, *Creepy*, *Eerie*, *Vampirella* and *1994*, which hadn't converted over to the more commercial format, had gone out of business. Steve Parkhouse sent in a letter dealing with, well, letters. Skinn made mention of Alan Moore assuming the writing reins on DC Comics' *Saga of the Swamp Thing*. The *Axel Pressbutton* reprint was printed sideways.

17. cover: David Jackson (March 1984)

1) Marvelman Family: The Red King Syndrome [Alan Moore/John Ridgway] 12p; (2) Sweatshop Talk III: Behind the Painted Smile [Steve Moore and Alan Moore/David Lloyd, text article] 8p; (3) Jaramsheela [Steve Moore/David Jackson, story credited to both Moore and his alter-ego, Pedro Henry] 6p; (4) Twilight World, part 4 [Steve Moore/Jim Baikie] 6p; (5) Home Is the Sailor [Steve Parkhouse/John Ridgway] 5p.

Notes: Jaramsheela, the popular villainess in the *Father Shandor* strip, was cover-featured with the cover reprinted sans copy on the back cover. She also got a stand-alone strip of her own. *Marvelman*'s regular strip took a vacation while a new Marvelman family story, which had major implications for the future of the *Marvelman* saga, appeared. Both *V for Vendetta* and *Father Shandor* also went on vacation. As in the previous winter, *Warrior* reverted to a bi-monthly schedule. Segments of Lloyd's artwork on the Marvel U.K. *Nightraven* strip accompanied the very informative *V for Vendetta* interview with Alan Moore. *Twilight World* ended rather abruptly. The Parkhouse/Ridgway "Home Is the Sailor" is an excellent war tale. The letters page skipped letters for this issue in favor of announcing *Warrior*'s big wins at the annual Eagle awards. Many photos were included, featuring Alan Moore, Brian Bolland, Steve Moore, Garry Leach, Dez Skinn, Dave Gibbons, Mick Austin and David Lloyd.

This version of *Warrior* #17's cover by David Jackson is actually the back cover of the same magazine. Like *Web of Horror*, *Warrior* often presented its cover art sans copy on the back. © Quality Communications/used by permission.

18. cover: Steve Parkhouse (April 1984)

(1) Marvelman, Book Two: "I Heard Woodrow Wilson's Guns..." [Alan Moore/Alan Davis] 6p; (2) Sweatshop Talk IV: Garry Leach on Line Art Techniques [Steve Moore and Garry Leach/ Garry Leach, text article] 7p; (3) Father Shandor, Demon Stalker: A Day in the Life ... A Day in the Death [Steve Moore/David Jackson] 6p; (4) V for Vendetta, Book Two: The Vacation [Alan Moore/David Lloyd and Tony Weare] 6p; (5) The Demon at the Gates of Dawn [Steve Parkhouse, reprinted from *House of Hammer* #12 (September 1977), originally entitled "Ter-

ror at the Gates of Dawn."] 4p; (6) Zee-Zee's Terror Zone: One Man's Meat [Martin Asbury, reprinted from *House of Hammer* #5 (August 1977)] 5p.

Notes: The title logo previewed in #13 begins alternating every other issue with the original logo. *Zee-Zee's Terror Zone* reprinted stories from the 1970s version of the British movie magazine *House of Hammer*, which usually ran a comic adaptation of a movie and an original comic tale every issue, along with the usual horror film articles. The former host, a drawing of Peter Cushing as Van Helsing, was removed and replaced by Garry Leach's Zee-Zee. Parkhouse's cover-featured samurai story had evidently been intended to be reprinted in the aborted *Warrior* Summer Special in 1982, as the main character appears on the cover intended for that special. Somewhere around this time, Skinn entered into an agreement with the independent American comic publisher, Pacific Comics, to publish both *Marvelman* and *Laser Eraser and Pressbutton* as regular color comics. Other Warrior serials, such as *Ektryn*, *Twilight World*, *Zirk* and various stand-alone stories were also included as backup features. Pacific went under before any of that could happen but Eclipse Comics picked up the rights and began both titles (under the new titles *Miracleman* and *Axel Pressbutton*) in 1985. *Warrior*'s price for Brit customers went up to 70p; U.S. price stayed the same.

19. cover: Garry Leach/back cover: Mick Austin (June 1984), back cover reprinted from *Warrior* #7 (November 1982)

(1) The Bojeffries Saga: Raoul's Night Out [Alan Moore/Steve Parkhouse] 6p; (2) Sweatshop Talk V: From Axes to Axel [Dez Skinn and Mick Austin/Mick Austin, text article] 5p; (3) Father Shandor, Demon Stalker: Dealing with Devils [Steve Moore/David Jackson] 6p; (4) V for Vendetta. Book Two: Variety [Alan Moore/David Lloyd] 6p; (5) Dracula Comics special ad [Paul Neary and John Bolton] 1p; (6) Marvelman special ad [Mick Austin, B&W reproduction of #1's cover] 1p; (7) Big Ben, the Man with No Time for Crime [Garry Leach and Dez Skinn/William Simpson] 7p; (8) Judgment of the Trinity [Alan Booth/David Jackson] 6p.

Notes: The Dracula ad featured 1970s era artwork from Neary and Bolton. Big Ben finally got his own strip — except the strip was set entirely within his doctored mind! V for Vendetta was cover-featured. The Marvelman special featuring Mick Angelo's old stories that was mentioned in earlier notes was published in June 1984. It featured a new four-page strip by Moore and Davis. The remainder of the special consisted of reprints from the original British comic book.

20. cover: Garry Leach and photos (July 1984)

1) Marvelman, Book Two: A Little Piece of Heaven [Alan Moore/Alan Davis] 6p; (2) Sweatshop Talk VI: Getting in on the Act — Hints and Tips on Starting Out [Steve Parkhouse, Steve Moore, John Bolton, Hunt Emerson, Dave Gibbons, Bryan Talbot, Brian Bolland, David Lloyd, Dez Skinn/ various, text article, all art from previous Warrior issues] 5p; (3) The Bojeffries Saga: Raoul's Night Out, part 2 [Alan Moore/Steve Parkhouse] 6p; (4) Father Shandor, Demon Stalker: Revelations [Steve Moore/David Jackson] 6p; (5) V for Vendetta: Vincent [Alan Moore and David Lloyd/Tony Weare] 4p; (6) Big Ben, part 2 [Dez Skinn/William Simpson] 7p.

Notes: Leach's cover features Big Ben and is backed by a photo collage of various British TV spies including Patrick McGoohan's Prisoner, Robert Vaughn and David McCallum's men from U.N.C.L.E., Sean Connery's James Bond and Diana Rigg and Patrick McNee's Avengers. The cover was reprinted on the back cover sans copy. This issue's installment of Sweatshop Talk consisted of pros giving their advice or personal history on how to break into the comics business.

The V for Vendetta segment was a stand-alone segment and not part of Book Two's continuity. Skinn mentioned the proposed Alan Moore/Bryon Talbot Nightjar strip on the letters page. He also mentioned that it's not going to be coming out any time soon.

21. cover: Mick Austin/back cover: Garry Leach (August 1984), back cover reprinted from Warrior #20 (July 1984)

(1) Marvelman, Book Two: ...and Every Dog Its Day [Alan Moore/Alan Davis] 6p; (2) Terror Zone: The Mirror [E. Sanchez Abuli and Garry Leach/John Boix] 6p; (3) Father Shandor, Demon Stalker: The Kingdom of the Mad [Steve Moore/David Jackson] 6p; (4) Big Ben vs the Gnomes of General Zurich [Dez Skinn/William Simpson] 6p; (5) V for Vendetta, Book Two: Visitors [Alan Moore/David Lloyd] 6p; (6) Laser Eraser and Pressbutton: Brides of the Sluzzgeep [Steve Moore/Alan Davis, story credited to Pedro Henry] 6p.

Notes: This was the last Marvelman strip to appear in Warrior, partly due to a falling out between Moore and Skinn and partly due to a squeeze play on the character by Marvel Comics. See the notes for #25 for additional information. Axel Pressbutton was cover-featured.

22. cover: Geoff Senior (September 1984)

(1) The Liberators: Death Run [Dez Skinn/John Ridgway] 5p; (2) Sweatshop Talk VII: The Frank Bellamy Interview [Dez Skinn, Dave Gibbons and Frank Bellamy/Frank Bellamy, text article] 6p; (3) Bogey: Only You [Antonio Segura and Dez Skinn/Leopold Sanchez] 14p; (4) V for Vendetta, Book Two: Vengeance [Alan Moore/David Lloyd] 6p; (5) Big Ben: Dai The Death! [Dez Skinn/William Simpson] 5p; (6) A Mystery Uncovered [Dixie, on the letters page, fan art] 1p.

Notes: Two new series debuted, one (The Liberators) set in the Quality universe while the other was an import from Spain. Leopold Sanchez was a Warren Comics veteran. The Liberators were cover-featured, while the cover itself was reprinted sans copy on the back cover. Bogey was a pretty good detective yarn.

23. cover: Jim Baikie and Garry Leach (October 1984)

(1) Editorial [Dez Skinn/Steve Dillon and Brian

Bolland, text article, Dillon's art reprinted from *Warrior* #1 (March 1982)] 1p; (2) Bogey: For Old Times Sake [Antonis Segura and Dez Skinn/Leopold Sanchez] 9p; (3) Sweatshop Talk VIII: The Life of Brian [Dez Skinn and Brian Bolland/Brian Bolland, text article] 10p; (4) Father Shandor, Demon Stalker: The Triumph of the Goat [Steve Moore/David Jackson] 6p; (5) V for Vendetta, Book Two: Vicissitude [Alan Moore/David Lloyd] 6p; (6) Big Ben [Dez Skinn/William Simpson] 7p.

Notes: *Bogey* was cover-featured. Skinn's editorial shows the cover for the first *Axel Pressbutton* issue, at that time to be published by Pacific Comics.

24. cover: John Bolton (November 1984)

(1) Laser Eraser and Pressbutton: One of Those Days in Downtown Delta Five [Steve Moore/Alan Davis, story credited to Pedro Henry] 7p; (2) Much More Red Than Dredd: Axel Slashes Out! [Dez Skinn/Brian Bolland, text article] 2p; (3) Father Shandor, Demon Stalker: Queen of Sin [Steve Moore/David Jackson] 6p; (4) Sweatshop Talk IX: John Bolton's Heroes and Horrors [Dez Skinn and John Bolton/John Bolton, text article] 10p; (5) V for Vendetta, Book Two: Vermin [Alan Moore/David Lloyd] 6p; (6) Big Ben: The Reality [Dez Skinn/William Simpson] 5p; (7) Cold Warrior, Cold Storage [Mike Poole, on the letters page, fan art] 1p; (8) How to Make a Zirk [Terry Jones and Steve Moore/Garry Leach, color, text article, on the back cover] 1p.

Notes: Great Bolton cover. The *Axel Pressbutton* text article discussed the American color comic, which, due to Pacific Comics' collapse, ended up not being published for over a year. *Father Shandor* concluded his second and last story arc. Great, if grim, story. The fallout between Dez Skinn and Alan Moore had apparently taken place as Skinn mentions that Moore would no longer be producing *Bojeffries Saga* stories for *Warrior*. Marv Wolfman sent in a letter. Skinn also gave a rather vague explanation of *Marvelman*'s absence from *Warrior*'s pages as having to do with the "uncertain syndication side."

25. cover: Garry Leach (December 1984)

(1) Editorial [Dez Skinn, text article] 1p; (2) Walls of Warrior?/By Any Other Name/Viva/And on the Third Day/Quality Expansion/Is It a Bird ... ?/Eagle Awards Ballot [Dez Skinn and

David Reeder/various, text articles] 5p; (3) Ektryn: The Poet and the Flowers [Steve Moore/Cam Kennedy, story credited to Pedro Henry] 6p; (4) Laser Eraser and Pressbutton: One of Those Days in Downtown Delta Five, part 2 [Steve Moore/Alan Davis, story credited to Pedro Henry] 8p; (5) Father Shandor, Demon Stalker [Steve Moore/John Stokes and John Bolton, first two pages are rehashed and reprinted pages from the first Father Shandor story from 1977] 10p; (6) Sweatshop Talk X: From Comics to Cannibals [Dave Reeder, text article, art from EC Comics stories] 3p; (7) The Many Worlds of Cyril Tompkins, Chartered Accountant [Carlos Trillo/Horacio Altuna] 5p; (8) V for Vendetta, Book Two: Valerie [Alan Moore/David Lloyd and Tony Weare] 6p; (9) Big Ben [Dez Skinn/William Simpson and Dave Hine] 8p.

Notes: It was 90p for 64 pages. No U.S. price listed but presumably $2.50. *Ektryn* was cover-featured with the cover reprinted sans copy on the back cover. The brief text article "By Any Other Name" printed Marvel's legal department's letter threat to sue if *Warrior* and Quality Publications did not cease publication of any *Marvelman* titles or stories, based on copyright infringement. That it was a nonsense bully-tactic suit was clear. Marvel Comics didn't even come into existence until six years after the first publication of *Marvelman* in 1955. Nonetheless, Skinn also printed his reply, stating that *Marvelman* had been pulled from *Warrior*, as of #21 and his hope that the matter could be settled amicably. *Father Shandor* had been pretty effectively dealt with in his final episode in the previous issue. The new story, done in 1982, took place directly after the very first *Shandor* story from 1977 and tied in with the Hammer Film, *Dracula, Prince of Darkness*. It may well have been done in 1977 as well. Peter Cushing's image as Van Helsing from the film was used in the story. One of Alan Moore's best chapters of *V for Vendetta*, "Valerie" was a moving, poetic, beautifully done chronicle of hope in the face of near-overwhelming odds.

26. cover: Steve Moore and Garry Leach (February 1985) [Wraparound cover]

(1) Zirk: Devo of the Future [Steve Moore/Garry Leach, color, a wraparound story cover appearing on the front and back covers] 2p; (2)

Editorial/Zirk Makes Penthouse/Taste What?/ Who and Crewith Eagle Comics/By Any Other Name: Part the Second/Colonel Canuck?/Britain Strikes Back! [Dez Skinn/Dave Gibbons, Richard Starkings, Brian Bolland and Alan Davis, text articles] 6p; (3) Worrier [Kev F., a comic strip run along the bottom of the text articles] ½ p; (4) The Liberators: Night Moves [Dez Skinn/John Ridgway, the story is never concluded] 5p; (5) Bogey: The Money Go Round [Antonio Segura and Dez Skinn/Leopold Sanchez] 12p; (6) Sweatshop Talk XI: Tainted Meat: The Horror Comic [Dave Reeder/Berni Wrightson, text article, additional art from EC Comics stories] 4p; (7) The Many Worlds of Cyril Tompkins, Chartered Accountant [Carlos Trillo/Horacio Altuna] 5p; (8) V for Vendetta, Book Two: The Verdict [Alan Moore/David Lloyd] 6p; (9) The Black Currant [Carl Critchlow] 4p; (10) Big Ben [Dez Skinn/William Simpson and Dave Hine, the story is never concluded] 9p.

Notes: Final issue. The text article "By Any Other Name" carried more legal letters between Marvel and *Warrior*. Skinn acknowledged that much of the reasons for the recent British reprints and Euro artists/stories were because many of the original *Warrior* writers and artists had been snatched up by American comic publishers. He also noted that #22's cover was a good seller for Quality while the covers for #15 and #19 were not. New installments of *Laser Eraser and Pressbutton* and *Twilight World* were promised but, of course, this being the final issue, they never appeared. The *Pressbutton* story promised did appear in the final issue of the color comic *Axel Pressbutton*. Grant Morrison was to have taken over scripting *The Liberators*. There would be a gap of over three and a half years between this *V for Vendetta* episode and the next to appear—published by DC in the *V for Vendetta* mini-series. This was a damn fine anthology title.

Archie

Basically Strange

1. cover: Richard Corben (November 1982)

(1) T.H.U.N.D.E.R. Agents ad [? Manna and Rich Buckler, frontis] 1p; (2) Movie Review:

Bladerunner [Chris Henderson, text article with photo] 1p; (3) The Man Who Tried to Kill Death [Marvin Channing/Alex Toth, reprinted from *Sorcery* #8 (August 1974)] 5p; (4) Tetragrammaton [Tim Ryan/Rick Bryant] 10p; (5) Book Review: Earth Invader [David M. Singer, text article] 1p; (6) Movie Review: Swamp Thing [?, text article with photo] 1p; (7) The Benefactor [T. Casey Brennan/Vicente Alcazar, reprinted from *Sorcery* #7 (June 1974)] 4p; (8) The Ultimate Power! [Wally Wood, reprinted from *Archie's Superhero Comics Digest* #2 (1979)] 6p; (9) Death Is My Love's Name [Marvin Channing/Frank Thorne, reprinted from *Sorcery* #10 (December 1974)] 6p; (10) The Creator [Bruce Jones] 6p; (11) Portfolio [Pepe Moreno, Matthew Staples and Robert Morillo, pin-ups] 3p; (12) Portfolio Bios [?, text article] 1p; (13) Next issue ad [Gray Morrow, the Black Hood (a Red Circle superhero) is featured] ½ p; (14) Red Circle ad [Rich Buckler, The Shield, the Golden Age Shield, the Fly, the Black Hood, Jaguar, Comet and the Web are featured] 1p.

Notes: Publisher: John Carbonaro for John C. Productions (a sister or subsidiary company of Archie Comics). Editor: Chris Adames. It was $1.95 for 48 pages. Corben's cover art originally appeared as a Den poster in 1979. This was largely a reprint magazine and was clearly intended to make additional use of the stories produced for Archie's Red Circle mystery and superhero line from 1973 to 1975. Regardless of the origins, there were some good stories here, carefully chosen to make the best use of the shading and tones added to the artwork. The Toth story in particular actually benefited from the B&W printing. Both Wood's "The Ultimate Power!" and Jones' previously unpublished "The Creator" were done in 1975 and were probably intended for either of the color comics *Sorcery* or *Madhouse*. The lone new story here, Tim Ryan and Rick Bryant's "Tetragrammaton" was an artist showcase with Bryant trying a different art technique for each page. The entire story consisted of either full page or double page spreads and they're beautifully done, with striking images. The portfolio pages are also quite good. The never-published second issue was clearly going to be focused on the Red Circle superhero, the Black Hood. Legend has it that this first issue had only 2000 copies printed and that most of those were destroyed, making it fairly rare. However, if you can find a copy of it, it's usually not priced too high. Nice little item.

Spider-Baby Graphix

Taboo

1. cover: Steve Bissette/ back cover: Rolf Stark (Fall 1988)

(1) Introduction [Clive Barker, text article] 3p; (2) Censortivity pin-up [Steve Bissette] 1p; (3) S. Clay Wilson profile [Steve Bissette, text article] 1p; (4) The Kitty Killer Kids [S. Clay Wilson] 2p; (5) Alan Moore/Bill Wray profile [Steve Bissette, text article] 2p; (6) Come On Down [Alan Moore/Bill Wray] 9p; (7) Charles Vess profile [Steve Bissette, text article] 1p; (8) Scarecrow [Charles Vess] 5p; (9) Tom Sniegoski/Mike Hoffman profile [Steve Bissette, text article] 1p; (10) Tooth Decay [Tom Sniegoski/Mike Hoffman] 10p; (11) Charles Burns profile [Steve Bissette, text article] 1p; (12) Contagious [Charles Burns] 4p; (13) Bernie Mireault profile [Steve Bissette, text article] 1p; (14) Cable [Bernie Mireault] 13p; (15) Jack Butterworth/Cam Kennedy profile [Steve Bissette/various, text article, art reprinted from various 1950s horror comics] 2p; (16) Eyes without a Face [Jack Butterworth/Cam Kennedy] 8p; (17) Tim Lucas/Mike Hoffman profile [Steve Bissette, text article] 2p; (18) Throat Sprockets [Tim Lucas/Mike Hoffman] 12p; (19) Eddie Campbell profile [Steve Bissette, text article] 2p; (20) The Pyjama Girl [Eddie Campbell] 4p; (21) Introduction [Steve Bissette, text article] 1p; (22) Cottonmouth [Steve Bissette, reprinted and expanded from a 3-page story appearing in *Gore Shriek* #1 (1987)] 5p; (23) Chigger and the Man [Keith Giffen and Robert Loren Fleming/Keith

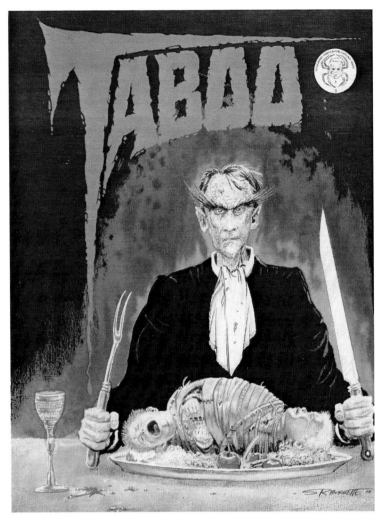

This disturbing image by Steve Bissette for his trade paperback magazine *Taboo*'s first issue gave readers some clue as to the horrific contents within. © Taboo/Steve Bissette/used by permission.

Giffen] 10p; (24) Chester Brown profile [Steve Bissette, text article] 1p; (25) Dirk the Gerbil [Chester Brown, reprinted from *Escape* #7 (?)] 2p; (26) A Late Night Snack [Chester Brown] 5p; (27) Pin-Up [Greg Irons, on the inside back cover] 1p.

Notes: Publishers and editors: Steve Bissette and Nancy O'Connor. It was $9.95 for 112 pages, published in trade paperback form. Both Cerebus artist Dave Sim and Bissette's *Swamp Thing* art partner John Totleben were involved in this first issue. Sim was to have acted as the publisher but he convinced Bissette that self-publishing was the way to go. Totleben was to have been a co-editor but bowed out before this issue appeared. This issue was dedicated to underground artist Greg Irons. *Taboo* was an ambitious attempt to expand past the 1950s EC foundations of horror comics and rewrite the 1960s/1970s Warren templates for graphic horror, as well as meld the style and sensibility of the early underground horror comics of the 1960s–1970s with that of the more mainstream writers and artists of the 1980s. Did it succeed? Perhaps not completely but still far better than anyone had any right to expect at the time. By 1988, when *Taboo* premiered, prose horror was boiling hot. Spurred by the enormous financial and literacy success of Stephen King, Peter Straub, Clive Barker and others, horror fiction was experiencing one of its biggest (even if short-lived) booms ever. Yet in the comic field, where horror had been a strong seller for at least two decades, times were hard. All of the B&W horror magazines were gone. None of the major companies' mystery books were still in print and the independents' color and B&W comics were either gone or rapidly disappearing as well. *Swamp Thing* was still in print but it was in the process of being neutered by DC, who were dismayed over the religious aspects of the current writer/artist Rick Veitch's time-travel storyline, wherein the *Swamp Thing* became the wood of the cross Jesus was nailed to. Neil Gaiman's *Sandman* was still a year away from seeing its first issue. *Taboo* looked much like the last stand and in some way, perhaps it was. It was certainly an ambitious and impressive-looking magazine. Printed in trade paperback form and running 100+ pages for each issue, there was room for a number of different styles and story lengths. Artists and writers certainly made use of that fact with stories that ranged from single-page tales to (in future issues) stories 40 pages and more in length. The quality of the stories was generally high too. Rarely did you see filler. For this first issue, the stories tended not to be as extreme as what appeared in later issues but the horror content wasn't timid in any way. Some of the stories (the Vess effort, for one) could easily have appeared in other horror or fantasy titles but the majority here (and almost entire issues, as time went by) could probably only have only appeared in this magazine. The

proof of that is how very few of these stories have been reprinted, regardless of their quality. To my certain knowledge, only the Vess, Burns, Brown and Campbell stories have been reprinted from this issue, and only in collections of their own works. Best art here would be from Charles Vess on his solo tale and Mike Hoffman's superior effort on "Throat Sprockets." The best story is Tim Lucas' gritty and extremely disturbing "Throat Sprockets" as well. A *very* unsettling tale. Superior work also appeared from Chester Brown, whose "A Late Night Snack" is particularly good; S. Clay Wilson; the team of Robert Loren Fleming and Keith Giffen; Charles Burns and Bissette himself. The Alan Moore/Bill Wray story was originally intended for the Harris revival of *Creepy* and was done in 1985. A nice touch by editor Bissette was an introduction page for nearly every story that would profile the creator, give a short essay on the story itself and provide a bibliographic entry on other work the creator or creators had produced. This was a fine way to spotlight the artists and writers, give the fan something more to look for, and was an inexpensive way to fill pages with useful information without resorting to dreary filler material. It's quite useful for the comics historian as well. This was an impressive debut, followed by even more impressive issues.

2. cover: John Totleben/back cover: Charles Lang (1989)

(1) The Droolies [Clive Barker, frontis] 1p; **(2)** Eddie Campbell profile [Steve Bissette, text article] 1p; **(3)** The Pyjama Girl's Big Night Out [Eddie Campbell] 2p; **(4)** Dave Marshall profile [Steve Bissette, text article] 1p; **(5)** Encore [Dave Marshall] 11p; **(6)** Tim Lucas/Simonida Perica-Uth profile [Steve Bissette, text article] 1p; **(7)** Sweet Nothings [Tim Lucas/Simonida Perica-Uth] 16p; **(8)** James Robert Smith/Mike Hoffman profile [Steve Bissette, text article] 1p; **(9)** Wet [James Robert Smith/Mike Hoffman] 8p; **(10)** Rick Grimes profile [Steve Bissette, text article] 1p; **(11)** Hell's Toupee [Rick Grimes] 6p; **(12)** Sick Animal Pin-Up [Rick Grimes, reprinted from *Parade of Gore* #1 (1977)] 1p; **(13)** Tom Marnick profile [Steve Bissette, text article] 1p; **(14)** Check-Out Time [Tom Marnick] 6p; **(15)** Saying Grace Introduction [Steve Bissette, text article] 1p; **(16)** Saying Grace [Steve Bissette] 4p; **(17)** Mark Askwith/Rick Taylor profile [Steve Bissette, text article] 1p; (18) Sharks [Mark Askwith/Richard G. Taylor] 7p; (19) Cara Sherman Tereno profile [Steve Bissette, text article] 1p; (20) Life with the Vampire [Cara Sherman Tereno] 25p; (21) S. Clay Wilson profile [Tom Veitch, text article] 2p; (22) Black Pages [S. Clay Wilson, pin-ups] 4p; (23) Oh, Baby! Our Love Is *Taboo* [Bernie Mireault] 1p; (24) Michael Zulli profile [Steve Bissette, text article] 1p; (25) Mercy [Michael Zulli] 6p; (26) Richard Sala profile [Steve Bissette, text article] 1p; (27) Hate Mail [Richard Sala] 5p; (28) From Hell Introduction [Alan Moore, text article] 2p; (29) From Hell: Prologue: The Old Men on the Shore [Alan Moore/Eddie Campbell] 9p; (30) From Hell, Chapter One: The Affections of Young Mr. S [Alan Moore/Eddie Campbell] 12p; (31) Concrete Reads *Taboo* [Paul Chadwick] 1p; (32) From Hell Pin-Up [Alan Moore, on the inside back cover] 1p.

Notes: It cost $9.95 for 144 pages. This magazine had to exist, if only to provide an initial home for *From Hell*, certainly the most impressive story/serial that *Taboo* would run. And that's saying something since *Taboo* ran an extremely high number of high-quality stories in its lifetime. *From Hell* gave many readers (including myself) reason to return to *Taboo*, even after the long delays in publication between volumes might have caused the reader's attention to the title to drift. This lack of a timely publishing schedule, coupled with stories or artwork that were extremely offensive to some and pretty much disturbing to everybody, probably hurt the magazine more than the format or cost. For the first installment of *From Hell*, Moore delivers a complex and well researched Jack the Ripper intro while Campbell delivers artwork both disturbing and lucid. In addition to *From Hell*, Tim Lucas delivered another fine story, Mark Askwith and Rick Taylor handed us "Sharks" and Michael Zulli did double duty as writer/artist on his excellent story "Mercy." S. Clay Wilson's gory and horrific pin-up pages caused a great deal of trouble and delays when several printers declined to print the explicit images. There were also printer troubles dealing with the Totleben cover. To his credit, Bissette refused to back down and eventually found a printer to run the presses for the book. However, the controversy surrounding

such events would plague *Taboo* for the remainder of its run. In addition, the long delay between binding the pages and attaching the cover meant that a great many copies of *Taboo* #2 would have the problem of the cover popping loose from the binding within minutes of opening the book.

3. cover: Michael Zulli/frontis: Rolf Stark/back cover: Simonida Perica-Uth (1989)

(1) The Maternity Ward [Jack Venooker/Steve Bissette] ½ p; (2) Santa Sangre Pin-Up [Moebius] 1p; (3) Bernie Mireault profile [Steve Bissette, text article] 1p; (4) Poker Face [Bernie Mireault] 11p; (5) Rick Veitch profile [Steve Bissette, text article] 1p; (6) A Touch of Vinyl [Rick Veitch and Jack Weiner/Rick Veitch] 10p; (7) Phil Elliott/Glenn Dakin profile [Steve Bissette, text article] 1p; (8) Vulnerable [Glenn Dakin/Phil Elliott] 3p; (9) Jim Wheelock profile [Steve Bissette, text article] 1p; (10) One Good Trick [Jim Wheelock] 6p; (11) Tim Lucas/Mike Hoffman profile [Steve Bissette, text article] 1p; (12) Throat Sprockets: Transylvania Mon Amour [Tim Lucas/Mike Hoffman] 30p; (13) Rick Grimes profile [Steve Bissette, text article] 1p; (14) Cactus Water [Rick Grimes] 10p; (15) Rolf Stark /Marlene Stevens profile [Steve Bissette, text article] 1p; (16) Love in the Afternoon... [Rolf Stark and Marlene Stevens/Rolf Stark] 15p; (17) From Hell, Chapter 2: A State of Darkness [Alan Moore/Eddie Campbell] 33p; (18) From Hell pin-up [Alan Moore, on the inside back cover] 1p.

Notes: It was $9.95 for 128 pages. Bissette and O'Connor are actually listed as co-editors for the first time. Best story was the new installment of *From Hell*. Best art was Rolf Stark's work from the haunting "Love in the Afternoon...." Good work also appeared from Rick Veitch and Bernie Mireault while Tim Lucas and Mike Hoffman gave us an excellent follow-up to #1's "Throat Sprockets." Strong, striking issue.

4. cover: Moebius/frontis: Nancy O'Connor/back cover: Brian Sendelbach (1990)

(1) Dreaming and the Law [Phillip Hester] 2p; (2) Phil Hester/Dave Sim profiles [Steve Bissette, text article] 1p; (3) 1963 [Dave Sim, pin-up] 1p; (4) untitled [Charles Burn] 2p; (5) Charles Burns/Neil Gaiman and Michael Zulli profiles [Steve Bissette, text article] 1p; (6) Babycakes [Neil Gaiman/Michael Zulli] 4p; (7)

Michael Zulli's artwork for *Taboo* #3 may have been inspired by Roman Polanski's 1965 film *Repulsion*. © Taboo/Steve Bissette/ used by permission.

owsky, text article with photos] 4p; (**16**) El Topo [Alejandro Jodorowsky/Spain Rodriguez, originally printed in Europe in the 1970s?] 4p; (**17**) S. Clay Wilson profile [Steve Bissette, text article] 1p; (**18**) Retinal Worm [S. Clay Wilson] 5p; (**19**) P. Foerster profile [Steve Bissette, text article] 1p; (**20**) La Fugue (The Escape) [P. Foerster] 5p; (**21**) Tim Lucas/Steve White profiles [Steve Bissette, text article] 1p; (**22**) Blue Angel [Tim Lucas/Steve White] 5p; (**23**) Charles Vess profile [Steve Bissette, text article] 1p; (**24**) Morrigan Tales [Elaine Lee/ Charles Vess] 18p; (**25**) Rick Grimes profile [Steve Bissette, text article] 1p; (**26**) These Things Happen [Rick Grimes] 5p; (**27**) L. Roy Aiken/Mike Hoffman profiles [Steve Bissette, text article] 1p; (**28**) Neither Seen nor Heard [L. Roy Aiken/Mike Hoffman] 11p; (**29**) From Hell, Chapter Three: Blackmail or Mrs. Barrett [Alan Moore/Eddie Campbell] 19p; (**30**) From Hell pin-up [Alan Moore, on the inside back cover] 1p.

Matt Brooker aka D'Israeli profile [Steve Bissette, text article] 1p; (**8**) Cholesterol [D'Israeli] 6p; (**9**) Mark Askwith and Rick Taylor profile [Steve Bissette, text article] 1p; (**10**) Davey's Dream [Mark Askwith/Rick Taylor] 11p; (**11**) Moebius profile [Steve Bissette, text article with photo] 1p; (**12**) Alejandro Jodorowsky profile [Steve Bissette/Moebius, text article with photo] 1p; (**13**) Eyes of the Cat aka Les Yeux Du Chat [Alejandro Jodorowsky/Moebius, originally printed in France in 1978] 50p; (**14**) A History of Alejandro Jodorowsky [Steve Bissette/Moebius, text article with photos] 2p; (**15**) The Creators of Les Yeux Du Chat Discuss the Story's Origin, Its Execution, and Their Thoughts on Today, Twelve Years Later [Jean-Marc Lofficier, Steve Bissette, Moebius and Alejandro Jodor-

Notes: It was $14.95 for 168 pages. Tundra Publishing was credited with co-production. All of the Moebius pages were printed on yellow paper. Charles Vess' "Morrigan Tales" was a redrawn, rewritten and greatly expanded version of the story originally published in *Sabre* #1 (August 1982). The best artwork here was easily from the French master Moebius. Steve White, Charles Vess, Mike Hoffman and Michael Zulli also provided high-quality work. Best story was Alan Moore's latest chapter of *From Hell*, with Tim Lucas, Elaine Lee, Neil Gaiman, Phil Hester and Alejandro Jodorowsky also delivering excellent stories. I find myself really disliking the work of Rick Grimes and P. Foerster. Their stories and art seemed like arid dead zones that blunted the appeal of the stories that book-ended them.

Do [Jeff Jones, text story] 2p; **(13)** Matt Howarth profile [Steve Bissette, text article] 1p; **(14)** Baby's on Fire [Matt Howarth] 6p; **(15)** Rick Grimes profile/ Michael H. Price–Adrian Martinez profile [Steve Bissette, text article] 1p; **(16)** Akimbo [Rick Grimes] 6p; **(17)** Verse from a Viscera Vase II [Michael H. Price/Adrian Martinez, poem] 1p; **(18)** Michael Zulli/Ramsey Campbell profile [Steve Bissette, text article] 1p; **(19)** Again [Michael Zulli, from the story by Ramsey Campbell] 27p; **(20)** S. Clay Wilson profile [Steve Bissette, text article] 1p; **(21)** This Is Dynamite [S. Clay Wilson] 2p; **(22)** From Hell Introduction [Alan Moore, text article] 1p; **(23)** From Hell, Chapter Four: "What Doth the Lord Require of Thee?" [Alan Moore/Eddie Campbell] 38p; **(24)** Dawn at the Crematorium #28 [Rolf Stark, color painting, on the inside back cover] 1p.

Jean "Moebius" Giraud's howling werewolf graced *Taboo*'s fourth issue and demonstrated the international flavor of *Taboo*. © Taboo/ Steve Bissette/used by permission.

5. cover: Jeff Jones/frontis: Melinda Gebbe/ back cover: Michael Zulli (1991)

(1) Seeing Is Not Believing [Douglas E. Winter, text article] 3p; **(2)** Introduction [James Ellroy, text article] 1p; **(3)** 39th and Norton [Tom Foxmarnick/Dennis Ellefson] 11p; **(4)** Pin-Up [Jeff Nicholson] 1p; **(5)** Jeff Nicholson profile [Steve Bissette, text article] 1p; **(6)** Through the Habitrails: It's Not Your Juice [Jeff Nicholson] 1p; **(7)** Through the Habitrails: Increasing the Gerbils [Jeff Nicholson] 4p; **(8)** Through The Habitrails: Jar Head [Jeff Nicholson] 8p; **(9)** Lost Girls Introduction [Steve Bissette, text article] 1p; **(10)** Lost Girls [Alan Moore/Melinda Gebbe, color] 8p; **(11)** Jeff Jones profile [Steve Bissette, text article] 1p; **(12)** Better Things to

Notes: Steve Bissette was now listed as the sole editor. The cost was $14.95 for 130 pages. The frontispiece depicted the Moore/Gebbe *Lost Girls*. The focus this issue was on erotic horror stories and the reader wasn't spared much in the way of twisted, kinky and often disgusting horror fare. This also was a particularly strong issue in terms of story, with even the most disturbing tales being disturbing more for the strong, unsettling quality of the story itself and not for the undeniable sexual shocks contained within. S. Clay Wilson's little two pager was nearly as controversial as his earlier pin-ups from #2. Alan Moore and Melinda Gebbie unwrapped the first chapter of their strikingly beautiful sex novel, *Lost Girls*, which depicted the grown-up escapades of literary characters Dorothy Gale (*The*

Wizard of Oz), Wendy Darling (*Peter Pan*) and Alice Lindell (*Alice's Adventures in Wonderland and Through the Looking-Glass*), years before Moore tried a similar approach with *The League of Extraordinary Gentlemen*. Although Jeff Nicolson is probably an acquired taste, the first chapters of his serial *Through the Habitrails* were quirky and interesting, a trait that lasted throughout the serial. Matt Howarth delivered a fine short story as did the team of Tom Foxmarnick and Dennis Ellefson. Another lengthy and well-done chapter of *From Hell* appeared. However, the best story and art belong to Michael Zulli's superb adaptation of Ramsey Campbell's damn creepy short story "Again." Don't read this one just before dropping off to sleep. I'd like to make special note of Rolf Stark's back-cover painting and his work in general. Stark's interests may have focused solely on the Holocaust but his work was powerful and, while extremely grim and disturbing, beautiful in its intentions.

Taboo Especial

1. cover and back cover: J. K. Potter/frontis: Moebius (1991)

(**1**) "I'll Have a Zombie." A Pit Stop at Bissette's Bar [Philip Nutman/Howard Cruse, text article] 2p; (**2**) Let's Go Shopping pin-up [Mark Martin] 1½ p; (**3**) Mark Martin/Eddie Campbell profiles [Steve Bissette, text article] 1p; (**4**) Horror Story [Eddie Campbell] 1p; (**5**) Glenn L. Barr profile [Steve Bissette, text article with photo] 1p; (**6**) Cliff's Wild Life [Glenn L. Barr] 23p; (**7**) Rick Grime profile [Steve Bissette, text article] 1p; (**8**) Glycerous Aquarium Footstool [Rick Grimes] 3p; (**9**) Wendy Snow-Lang profile [Steve Bissette, text article] 1p; (**10**) Want [Wendy Snow-Lang] 14p; (**11**) Through the Habitrails Introduction [Steve Bissette and Jeff Nicholson, text article] 1p; (**12**) Through the Habitrails: The Doomed One [Jeff Nicholson] 8p; (**13**) Rick McCollum profile [Steve Bissette, text article] 1p; (**14**) Fin de Salome [Rick McCollum] 14p; (**15**) Mark Bode profile [Steve Bissette, text article] 1p; (**16**) I Have a Dream [Mark Bode] 12p; (**17**) Scott McCloud profile [Steve Bissette, text article] 1p; (**18**) A Day's Work [Scott McCloud] 25p; (**19**) Dick Foreman profiles [Steve Bissette, text article] 1p; (**20**) Suburban Autopsies... [Dick Foreman/Pete Williamson] 6p; (**21**) Noel Tuazon profile [Steve Bissette, text article] 1p; (**22**) Obese Obsessor

[Noel Tuazon] 8p; (**23**) Jussi Tuomola profile [Steve Bissette, text article] 1p; (**24**) Neon Spring [Jussi Tuomola] 22p; (**25**) Pin-Up [S. Clay Wilson] 1p; (**26**) "Want" cover [Wendy Snow-Lang, on the inside back cover] 1p.

Notes: While this was technically a special and not a regular issue of *Taboo*, I'm including it in the regular numbering just "cause I want to. It was $14.95 for 152 pages. This issue was dedicated to the then-recently deceased actor Klaus Kinski while the frontispiece depicts Kinski as Jack the Ripper. An insert ad card came with the issue featuring art by Steve Bissette and Michael Zulli from which you could order *Taboo* #4–6 and the *Taboo Especial* from Tundra Publishing. Scott McCloud's work was the first published result of a still ongoing artists' contest to write, draw and complete a 24-page comic in 24 hours. Best art here is Wendy Snow-Lang's elegant effort, yet, while the stories are generally good, there isn't any I'd pick out as a superior effort. I also like Rick McCollum's artwork. This is one of the milder issues of *Taboo* (which means it's still probably grosser than almost any other horror comic ever published). "Neon Spring" is printed sideways.

6. cover: Cru Zen/frontis: Mark A. Nelson/ title page: Steve Bissette/back cover: Mark Martin (1991)

(**1**) Blood Monster [Neil Gaiman/Nancy O'Connor] 4p; (**2**) Through the Habitrails Introduction [Steve Bissette, text article] 1p; (**3**) Through the Habitrails: Escape #1: "El Muerte" [Jeff Nicholson] 8p; (**4**) Through the Habitrails: Futile Love [Jeff Nicholson] 11p; (**5**) Charles Burns profile [Steve Bissette, text article] 2p; (**6**) The Cat Woman Returns [Charles Burns] 20p; (**7**) Lost Girls Introduction/Alan Moore and Melinda Gebbe profiles [Steve Bissette, text article] 2p; (**8**) Lost Girls, Chapters 2 and 3 [Alan Moore/Melinda Gebbe, color] 16p; (**9**) Rick Grimes profile [Steve Bissette/Rick Grimes, text article] 1p; (**10**) Dolly and Withtina [Rick Grimes] 6p; (**11**) From Hell Prologue/The Nemesis of Neglect ad [various, text article] 1p; (**12**) From Hell, Chapter Five: The Nemesis of Neglect [Alan Moore/Eddie Campbell] 40p; (**13**) Holly Gaiman/Michael Zulli profile [Michael Zulli and Steve Bissette, text article] 1p; (**14**) Holly's Story [Holly Gaiman/Michael Zulli] 6p; (**15**) Pin-Ups [S. Clay Wilson, second pin-up on the inside back cover] 2p.

Notes: It cost $14.95 for 122 pages. Charles Burns' disturbing "The Cat Woman Returns" is a fumetti strip and was done in 1979. Holly Gaiman, Neil Gaiman's daughter, was five years old when she wrote "Holly's Story." The latest chapter of *From Hell* is the best story, although "Blood Monster," "Lost Girls" and "The Cat Woman Returns" are also very good. Best art is Melinda Gebbe's beautiful, lush color work on *Lost Girls* with good work also appearing from Michael Zulli, Nancy O'Connor and Eddie Campbell. A Sweeney Todd sampler pamphlet was included with this issue. This 16-page pamphlet provided a historical and artistic overview of the legend of Sweeney Todd, the infamous "Demon Barber of Fleet Street," and was written by Neil Gaiman and illustrated by Michael Zulli. As with the *Taboo Especial*, an insert card/ad with artwork by Steve Bissette and Michael Zulli was also included. The Bissette art is repeated from the previous insert card but Zulli's is a partial reprint of the Sweeney Todd pamphlet's cover. A special offer for pre-ordering *Taboo* #7 was the intended inclusion of the mini-comic *SpiderBaby Comix* #0, which was to feature Steve Bissette's entry, "A Life in Black and White," from the 24-pages-in-24-hours contest. As it turned out, that Bissette tale was included as part of the issue itself for folks who special-ordered it. Everybody else got the issue without the Bissette tale.

7. cover: Joe Coleman/frontis and title page: Paul Komoda/back cover: Brian Sendelbach (1992)

(1) Phil Elliott and Paul Grist profiles [Steve Bissette, text article] ½ p; **(2)** Monsters [Phil Elliott and Paul Grist] 2p; **(3)** Kenneth Smith profile [Steve Bissette, text article] 1p; **(4)** Odradek [Kenneth Smith, from the story by Franz Kafka] 5p; **(5)** From Hell Prologue [various, text article] 1p; **(6)** From Hell, Chapter Six: September [Alan Moore/Eddie Campbell] 25p; **(7)** Joe Coleman profile [Steve Bissette, text article] 1p; **(8)** A Good Christian [Joe Coleman] 4p; **(9)** P. Foerster profile [Steve Bissette, text article] 1p; **(10)** The Music-Loving Spider aka L'Araignee Melomane [P. Foerster, translated by R. and J. M. Lofficier] 7p; **(11)** Jeff Nicholson profile [Steve Bissette, text article] 1p; **(12)** Through the Habitrails: Be Creative [Jeff Nicholson] 7p; **(13)** Through the Habitrails: Escape #2: The Dry Creek Bed [Jeff Nicholson] 6p; **(14)** Lost Girls Introduction [Steve Bissette, text article] 3p; **(15)** Lost Girls, Chapters 4 and 5 [Alan Moore/Melinda Gebbie, color] 16p; **(16)** Rick Grimes profile [Steve Bissette, text article] 1p; **(17)** Breathing Is for Sissies [Rick Grimes] 2p; **(18)** Jack Butterworth/Eric Vincent profiles [Steve Bissette, text article] 1p; **(19)** Bad Things [Jack Butterworth/Eric Vincent] 13p; **(20)** Neil Gaiman/Michael Zulli profiles [Steve Bissette, text article] 1p; **(21)** Sweeney Todd: The Demon Barber of Fleet Street: Prologue [Neil Gaiman/Michael Zulli, story never concluded] 26p; **(22)** Aidan Potts profile [Steve Bissette, text article] 1p; **(23)** After Life [Aidan Potts] 3p; **(24)** SpiderBaby Comix No. O: A Life in Black and White [Steve Bissette] 26p; **(25)** Those Wacky Cartoonists [Steve Bissette/Matt Howarth, Jeff Nicholson, Mark Martin, Jim Woodring and Kenneth Smith, ad for various independent comics and mini-comics] 1p; **(26)** Pin-Up [Tony Salmons, on the inside back cover] 1p.

Notes: The cost was $14.95 for 158 pages. This was the last issue of *Taboo* in its original format. Between this issue and the next, three years passed and the biggest selling points of *Taboo*, the serials by Alan Moore/Eddie Campbell or Moore/Melinda Gebbie, as well as by Neil Gaiman/Michael Zulli, either moved on to their own series or simply went uncompleted. Only early orders had the Bissette *SpiderBaby Comix No. O* included in the issue. The "Sweeney Todd" prologue was gorgeous in both story and art but the story proper never actually appeared.

8. cover: Charles J. Lang/frontis: Moebius/back cover: Michael Zulli (1995)

(1) Introduction [Steve Bissette, text article] 3p; **(2)** All She Does Is Eat! [Jack Butterworth/Greg Capullo] 10p; **(3)** Satan and the Savior [David Sexton/David Sexton and P. Craig Russell] 15p; **(4)** President "Doosh" Quimby [Rick Grimes] 6p; **(5)** The Disaster Area [Tim Lucas/David Lloyd] 12p; **(6)** Revenge [Matt Howarth] 30p; **(7)** Johnny 23 [Al Columbia] 4p; **(8)** Through the Habitrails: Cat Lover [Jeff Nicholson] 29p; **(9)** Twilight [Wladyslaw Reymont/Alec Stevens] 6p; **(10)** Bid Return [Jeff Jones, on the inside back cover] 1p.

Notes: Now published by Kitchen Sink Press. It was $14.95 for 128 pages. These stories were left over after *Taboo* ceased "regular" publication in 1992. Bissette and his then-publishing partner Tundra did not see eye to eye on a great many things and finally things got so bad that Bissette closed down the title. Bissette's exhaustion, even three years later, was evident. Unlike the first eight issues (including the *Taboo Especial*), there are no author profiles or mini-history lessons. In fact, there are no extras at all, something that is highly unusual in every other Bissette-led comic production he's ever done. *Through the Habitrails* finally concluded its run. The best story here is "Satan and the Savior" while the best artwork belongs to David Lloyd. However, I also liked the work by Nicholson, Butterworth/Capullo, Sexton/Russell, Tim Lucas, and Al Columbia. Some high-quality material appears here.

9. cover and back cover: Alan M. Clarke/frontis: Paul Komada/inside back cover: Kenneth Smith (1995)

(1) Introduction [Dave Sim, text article] 1p; (2) Taboo: A Chronology [various] 2p; (3) The Vampire [Alec Stevens, from the story by Jan Neruda] 6p; (4) "Gator Bait: The Crimes of Joe D. Ball [Michael H. Price/ Lamberto Alvarez] 12p; (5) Dr. Miro's Masterpieces [Jeff Dickinson] 6p; (6) ...In the Garden [Stephen Blue] 4p; (7) The Worms Crawl in... [Chet Williamson/Tim Truman] 13p; (8) Grue Love [Rick Grimes] 3p; (9) The New Ecology of Death [James Roberts Smith/Mike Hoffman] 10p; (10) One Day in Hell, God Spoke [Tony Salmons] 4p; (11) After Life [Dave Thorpe/Aidan Potts] 25p; (12) The Coconut Garden [Mark David Dietz] 5p; (13) Hunting and Gathering [Phillip Hester] 5p; (14) The Joys of Childhood [Angela Bocage] 4p; (15) Circumcision [Phillip Hester] 8p; (16) *Taboo* Is *Taboo* [Steve Bissette, text article, reprinted from *Gauntlet* (1990)] 6p; (17) From Hell [Alan Moore, text article, reprinted from a 1989 Fantaco Enterpriese catalog] 1p.

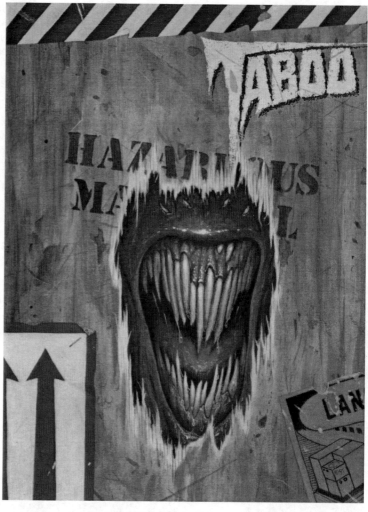

Hazardous material indeed, as the monsters within *Taboo* #9 chew their way out to grab the reader by the throat. Courtesy of cover artist Alan M. Clark. © Taboo/Steve Bissette/used by permission.

Notes: It was $14.95 for 128 pages. Final issue. Best artwork appeared from Stephen Blue and Tim Truman. I don't believe there's any single great story here although there are a number of good ones. I was impressed by the work of Phillip Hester, Aidan Potts, Chet Williamson, Alec Stevens, James Robert Smith/Mike Hoffman and Tony Salmons. The true life story concerning serial killer Joe Ball that was chronicled in "Gator Bait" was also adapted for comics in one of DC's Paradox *Big Book* titles in the late 1990s.

Globe Communications

Monsters Attack!

1. cover: John Severin/back cover: Walter John Brogan (September 1989)

(1) The Boneyard [Michael Delle Femine, text article, all of Delle Femine's stories, artwork and articles were credited to Mort Todd with one exception, noted in #2] 1p; (2) The Sex Vampires from Outer Space [Olivo Vincent/Gray Morrow] 6p; (3) George Romero's Dead: Flower Children of the Apocalypse [Evan Michelson, Charles Victor and Johnny Zhivago, text article with photos] 3p; (4) A Monster for All Seasons! [Pat Boyette] 7p; (5) Return of the Golem [Michael Delle Femine/John Severin, story credited to Mort Todd] 9p; (6) Frankenstein 1990: Resurrection [Jon Loring/Rick Altergott, text story] 6p; (7) Pirate's Plunder Pin-Up [Michael Delle Femine, credited to Mort Todd] 1p; (8) In Solid [Steve Ditko] 6p; (9) Weirdbeard [Rurik Tyler, story and art credited to Madman] 8p.

Notes: Publisher: Globe Communications. Editor: Michael Delle Femine. It was $1.95 for 48 pages. The cover was reprinted in color as a two-page poster on the frontispiece and the inside back cover (this inside color art would remain throughout the series). Boyette's "A Monster for All Seasons!" is a rewritten, redrawn rehash of his 1971 Skywald story "The Geek!" The text story "Frankenstein 1990" was intended as a serial but never had a second installment. This was a rather odd effort to apparently put out a somewhat more kid-friendly B&W horror magazine than either the departed Skywald or Warren books but try to keep the book edgy, too. It never quite made its goal but some interesting

work did appear here. Both Morrow and Boyette's artwork was quite good while Ditko's was a pleasing cross between his Charlton and Warren work. Severin delivered the best art here on his Nazi/Golem story while Rurik Tyler's odd, gory "Weirdbeard" was the best story. Walter Brogan's back-cover art owed a clear debt to Jack Davis, but was still pretty good.

2. cover: John Severin/frontis: Pat Boyette/back cover: Walter John Brogan (October 1989)

(1) The Boneyard [Michael Delle Femine, text article, credited to Mort Todd] 1p; (2) Aquacarnivora [Olivo Vincent/Gray Morrow] 8p; (3) The Mars Attacks Chronicles: The Pulp Paint-

Who would have thought that John Severin could do such a cool Freddy Kruger? The folks at *Monsters Attack!* #2, obviously.

brush of Norman Saunders [Bhob Stewart/Norman Saunders, text article with photos. Saunders' art is reprinted from various sources] 5p; (4) The Cask of Amontillado! [Charles V. Hall/Walter James Brogan, from the story by Edgar Allan Poe] 7p; (5) It's All in His Head! [Steve Ditko/Steve Ditko and Michael Delle Femine, Delle Femine's inks credited to E. O'Brien] 5p; (6) Radical New Pipe Pin-Up [Michael Delle Femine, credited to Mort Todd] 1p; (7) The Outsider [Bhob Stewart/Steve Harper, from the story by H. P. Lovecraft] 6p; (8) "Are You Ready for Freddy, the Man of Your Dreams?" [Kevin McMahon, text article with photos] 6p; (9) Abracadaver [Rurik Tyler, story and art credited to Madman] 8p.

Notes: It cost $1.49 for 48 pages. Severin's cover of Freddy Kruger was reprinted on the inside back cover. It's a pretty good rendering, too! Generally better stories and art than the first issue. Bhob Stewart's excellent article on the *Mars Attack* bubble gum cards is very interesting as well. Best story goes again to the odd "Abracadaver" by Tyler, as does best art. Good issue.

3. cover: John Severin/frontis: Gray Morrow with back cover: Rurik Tyler, credited as Madman (July 1990)

(1) Pin-Up [Pat Redding] 1p; (2) A Boy's Life [Michael Delle Femine/John Severin, story credited to Mort Todd] 7p; (3) Godzilla Pin-Up [Michael Delle Femine, credited to Mort Todd] 1p; (4) Face It [Steve Ditko] 5p; (5) Jason's Body Count: Friday the 13th on Video: An Overview [Kevin McMahon, text article with photos, the last four pages are a checklist of Jason's victims and the methods he used to kill them!] 8p; (6) Cells [Rurik Tyler, story and art credited to Madman] 8p; (7) The Wake of a Monster! [Pat Boyette] 6p; (8) The Daemon [John Arcudi/Gene Colan] 8p.

Notes: The price was $2.25 for 48 pages. A ten-month gap occurred between #2 and 3. Severin's cover portrait of Jason from the Friday the 13th movies was reprinted on the inside back cover. Gray Morrow's frontispiece painting was beautiful. Ditko's artwork on his story is a definite step down from the excellent work he did in #1. Gene Colan's art is reproduced from his pencils (and very well-presented, too) and is the best art appearing here. Tyler's "Cells" is the best story. The letters page begins.

4. cover: John Severin/frontis: Walter James Brogan/inside back cover: Rurik Tyler, credited to Madman (September 1990)

(1) Tag Yer Dead! [Michael Delle Femine/John Severin, story credited to Mort Todd] 9p; (2) Goribis [Pat Boyette] 1p; (3) Akira the Movie [Michael Delle Femine, text article with photos, credited to Mort Todd] 4p; (4) Monster Attack! Bookwork: The Lonely One/Panorama of Hell [Michael Delle Femine, text article, credited to Mort Todd] 1p; (5) Illusion [Steve Ditko] 5p; (6) Godzilla, King of the Monsters! [Michael Delle Femine, text article with photos, credited to Mort Todd] 7p; (7) Circulation: Zero! [Charles E. Hall/Gray Morrow] 8p; (8) Darkman Rising!: An Interview with Sam Raimi [Quelou Parente and Sam Raimi, text article with photos] 4p; (9) Bookworm [Nicola Cuti/Alex Toth] 6p.

Notes: Good issue. Severin's *Godzilla* cover was reprinted on the back cover. Tyler's inside back cover work would have made a fine cover as well. "Bookworm" was done in 1975 and originally intended for a Charlton magazine. For some reason, Toth withheld the artwork and the same story appeared at Charlton with art by Charles Nicholas and Vince Alcasia. One is tempted to award Toth the best artwork in any comic that he appears in but the best artwork here actually belongs to John Severin. Pat Boyette's one-pager is quite nicely done as well.

5. cover: George A. Bush/back cover: Frank Borth (December 1990)

(1) A Job Well Done [Ric Meyers/Alex Toth, reprinted from *Thrilling Adventure Stories* #2 (August 1975)] 7p; (2) Monster Trucks pin-up [Pat Redding] 1p; (3) The Trouble Was [Ron Goulart/Gray Morrow, from the story by Goulart] 7p; (4) The Frankenstein Legend and Karloff [Kevin McMahon/Gene Colan, text article] 7p; (5) Freak Show [Mary Silverstone/Walter James Brogan] 9p; (6) Pin-Up [Pat Redding] 1p; (7) The Creator [Steve Ditko] 6p; (8) Cellar Jelly! [Rurik Tyler] 8p.

Notes: Final issue. Editor: Lou Silverstone and Jerry DeFuccio. The cover was reprinted as a color poster on the frontispiece and inside back cover. Goulart's adaptation of his crime story was very well done. The cover and back cover were illustrating parts of Mary Shelley's *Frankenstein*'s monster mythos, as was Gene Colan's art for the Karloff article. Ditko's story "The Creator" was also a variation on the Frankenstein's monster storyline, but with enough unique quirks to make it interesting. Tyler's story "Cellar Jelly!" had the best story and artwork in this issue. A pretty good magazine with some darn good stories in it.

Bruce Hamilton Publishing

Grave Tales

1. cover: Joe Staton (October 1991)

(1) Pretender to the Throne [Eric Dinehart/Joe Staton] 8p; **(2)** Proper Test for a Demon [Link Yarco/Pat Boyette] 8p; **(3)** Deadly Mistake [Bill Pearson/Gray Morrow] 8p; **(4)** Grave Mails [Leonard Clark?, text article] 2p; **(5)** Physician, Heal Thyself [Russ Miller/John Heebink and Dan Adkins] 8p; **(6)** Maggots/Dread of Night ad [?] 1p; **(7)** Wanna-Be [Nat Gertler/Batton Lash] 8p.

Notes: Publisher and managing editor: Bruce Hamilton. Editor: Leonard "John" Clark. It was $3.95 for 48 pages. *Grave Tales* had its origins in a Bill Pearson-edited/Hamilton-published 1974 independent fanzine with the same title. This version (and its sister magazines, *Maggots* and *Dread of Night*) was clearly an attempt to revive the early style of the *Creepy/Eerie/Vampirella* horror magazines. Instead of one host, however, this issue presented five, with short messages from each of them (supposedly) in the text article that later became the letters page. Each of the five hosts introduced one of the five stories here, beginning with the Grave Digger, an Uncle Creepy look-alike who was also cover-featured; then Obadiah, a rather ugly gnome-like creature; followed by Echo, a female ghost; then the rather sleazy Ed the Window-Washer, who was an ugly Peeping Tom character; and finally, Deadpan, a corpse with maggots crawling out of him who wore, naturally, a battered cooking pan on his head! The stories were a little on the tame side, although Gray Morrow brought in a very nice art job on his story. Pat Boyette and Joe Staton also delivered good work.

2. cover: Gray Morrow (December 1991)

(1) Deadly Developments [Nat Gertler/Sparky Moore] 6p; **(2)** The Jolly Corner [Eric Dine-hart/Joe Staton, from the story by Henry James] 8p; **(3)** The Haunting of Henry James [Geoffrey Blum, text article with photos] 1p; **(4)** Grave Tales History/ad [Bruce Hamilton/Mike Roberts and Don Newton, Roberts art is from the cover of the original *Grave Tales*, Newton's art is from an interior story from the same issue] 1p; **(5)** Maggots #2 Preview Art [various] 2p; **(6)** Black and White and Red All Over [Eric Dinehart/Steve Stiles] 8p; **(7)** Maggots #2 Preview Art [various] 2p; **(8)** Simon's Salvation [Jack C. Harris/John Heebink] 8p; **(9)** The Springfield Werewolf [Bill Pearson/Russ Miller, text story] 2p; **(10)** The Monster Maker [James Van Hise/Tom Sutton] 8p.

Notes: The *Grave Tales* history page notes that 115,000 copies of #1 were printed. The stories took an upturn in quality as both the adaptation of "The Jolly Corner" by Eric Dinehart and Van Hise's original "The Monster Maker" were very good and the remaining stories weren't bad either. "Black and White and Red All Over" is a homage to EC artist Graham Ingels, right down to the lettering of Ingram (Ingels' doppelganger's name) in the style of the ghastly signature that Ingels used on his splash pages. Tom Sutton's art on "The Monster Maker" is quite striking and is easily the best in this solid issue. The actual letters page debuts.

3. cover: Joe Staton (February 1992)

(1) Dog Gone! [John Cochran/Joe Staton] 8p; **(2)** Grave Tales in Color ad [Joe Staton and Gray Morrow] 1p; **(3)** The Vigil [Steve Skeates/John Workman] 6p; **(4)** Sredni Vashtar [Geoffrey Blum/Sparky Moore, from the story by Saki] 8p; **(5)** Salina, part 3 [Nicola Cuti, text story] 2p; **(6)** Dread of Night in Color ad [Joe Staton] 1p; **(7)** Cycle of the Vampire! [Jack C. Harris/Joe Heebink] 8p; **(8)** Maggots in Color ad [Joe Staton and Gray Morrow] 1p; **(9)** Bios of Our Creators: Joe Staton [Leonard Clark?, text article with photo] 1p; **(10)** Role Model [Jeff Bailey and Marty Golia/Joe Staton] 8p.

Notes: Final issue. Pretty darn good issue. "Role Model" is a spoof/takeoff on Bill Watterson's *Calvin and Hobbes* comic strip and is really quite good. The text story *Salina* had its first two sections appear in *Maggots* #2 and *Dread of Night* #2. Joe Staton provides the best artwork here with John Workman coming in close behind. Best story is the *C and H* spoof by Bailey and

Golia although John Cochran and Steve Skeates' stories (both of these guys were Warren Publications veterans) were also quite good. In fact, Cochran's story was written in 1975 and originally intended for the Skywald magazines. Apparently the writing was on the wall for the phase-out of the black and white magazines as Hamilton advertised a planned move to 32-page color comics for all three of their titles, running ads showing the intended covers for all three titles, but those color comics were never published.

Maggots

1. cover: Gray Morrow (November 1991)

(1) The Big Greasy [Matt Wayne/Steve Stiles] 8p; (2) Scary-Go-Round [Gary Leach/Alfredo Alcala] 8p; (3) Maggots Mail [Leonard Clark, text article] 2p; (4) Horror You Today? [John Clark and Bruce Hamilton/Joe Staton] 6p; (5) Sore Spot [Jack C. Harris/Joe Staton] 8p; (6) Don't Touch That Dial [Link Yarco/Russ Miller, text story] 2p; (7) Caged In [Link Yarco/Batton Lash] 8p.

Notes: Publisher and managing editor: Bruce Hamilton. Editor: Leonard "John" Clark. The cost was $3.95 for 48 pages. This magazine had possibly the most disgusting title in horror comics! Like *Grave Tales*, this magazine had not one, but five new horror hosts beginning with the cover-featured sexy bird lady, Madraven Stark, then psychologist Dr. Pocks, talk show host Eval Reising, the alien parasite/human Prof. Zschiesche (whose origin was told in "Horror You Today?") and finally morgue keeper Morgan. "Sore Spot," hosted by Prof. Zschiesche, is an

Gray Morrow presents Madraven Stark as the cover model for the most disgusting title in B&W magazine history—*Maggots!* #1.

alternate version of "Horror You Today?" This issue is a considerable improvement on the contents of *Grave Tales* #1, with generally decent stories and art from all involved.

2. cover: Gray Morrow (January 1992)

(1) A Dinner to Remember! [Al Ryan/John Workman] 6p; (2) *Dread of Night* #2 Preview Pages [various] 2p; (3) Byte of the Wolf [Robert Borski/Howard Bender and Neil Vokes] 8p; (4) Salina, part 1 [Nicola Cuti, text story, continued in *Dread of Night* #2] 2p; (5) Under the Rug! [Donald Markstein/Steve Stiles] 8p; (6) L. A. Flaw [Link Yarco/Terry Tidwell and Bud La Rosa] 8p; (7) Dread of Night Preview Pages [various] 2p; (8) The Puppet Man [Nicola Cuti/Alfredo Alcala] 8p.

Notes: The first actual letters page debuts. Nice two-page spread in the Stiles story.

3. cover: Gray Morrow (March 1992)

(1) Some Kind of Beautiful [Jack C. Harris/ Gray Morrow] 8p; **(2)** Little Sara's Dolls [Nicola Cuti/Dan Day and David Day] 6p; **(3)** Perchance to Dream! [Russ Miller/Steve Stiles] 8p; **(4)** Prima Facie Evidence [Gary Leach/Tony DeZuniga] 8p; **(5)** Chemical Dependents [Janice Lane Miller/Russ Miller, text story] 2p; **(6)** Bios of our Creators: Gray Morrow [Leonard Clark, text article with photo] 1p; **(7)** Identity Crisis [Al Ryan/Joe Staton] 8p.

Notes: Final issue. One of only two painted covers to appear on the Hamilton magazines. This cover is very good. DeZuniga's art on his story looks very rushed and uneven. More like thumbnails than actual finished art. Best art and story comes from the Nicola Cuti/ Day brothers' effort "Little Sara's Dolls."

Dread of Night

1. cover: L. B. Cole (November 1991)

(1) The Familiar [Michael Brewer/Ralph Reese and Gray Morrow] 8p; **(2)** He's a Charmer! [Russ Miller/Batton Lash] 6p; **(3)** *Grave Tales* #2 Preview Pages [various] 4p; **(4)** Upgrade! [Nat Gertler/Howard Bender and Brian Buniak] 8p; **(5)** Dead Write [Leonard Clark, text article and the letters page] 2p; **(6)** Withdrawal [Charles Marshall/Dan Day and David Day] 8p; **(7)** Hell Well [Nicola Cuti, text story] 2p; **(8)** Blood Island [Bill Pearson/Ernie Colon] 8p.

Notes: Publisher and editor-in-chief: Bruce Hamilton. Editor: Leonard "John" Clark. Cost: $3.95 for 48 pages. Cole's painted cover is a redo of the original 1974 fanzine *Grave*

Tales' cover. It's very good. Cole was one of the great pre-code horror cover artists and also did the striking cover for John Stanley's "Tales from the Tomb" in 1962. This first issue is decidedly more gory than the debut issues of either *Grave Tales* or *Maggots*. Count Robespierre is the horror host for three of the stories with the other two featuring hosts coming over from *Maggots* and *Grave Tales.* The Reese/Morrow teamup provides the best art while Bill Pearson's sly vampire tale provided the best story. "Hell Well" has a great story logo, courtesy of writer/artist Nicola Cuti. A pretty good issue.

Legendary cover artist L. B. Cole delivers what may be one of the last of his great horror covers, featuring what he called "poster color," bright primary art over a black or dark surface. This image was based on Mike Roberts' cover for the 1974 fanzine *Grave Tales*.

2. cover: Gray Morrow (January 1992)

(1) The Wolf-Woman of Roxbury [Link Yarco/John Heebink] 8p; **(2)** Jelly [Nicola Cuti/Steve Stiles] 6p; **(3)** Salina, part 2 [Nicola Cuti, text story, continued in *Grave Tales* #3] 2p; **(4)** Grave Tales #3 Preview Pages [various] 2p; **(5)** A Born Werewolf [James Van Hise/James Dean Pascoe] 8p; **(6)** Grave Tales #3 Preview Pages [various] 2p; **(7)** Twisted Channels [Al Ryan/Andrew Paquette and Rick Bryant] 8p; **(8)** Bios of our Creators: Batton Lash [Leonard Clark, text article with photo] 1p; **(9)** Monsters 101 [Nat Gertler/Batton Lash] 8p.

Notes: Final issue. Best art is the superior job by James Dean Pascoe while the best story is the delightful "The Wolf-Woman of Roxbury" by Link Yarco. These books were usually only slightly more graphic than, say, DC's mystery comics but they were generally good and are usually rather cheap to purchase when you can find them.

There's some good stuff here. I wish they'd lasted longer.

To date, *Doomed* is the last newsstand effort at a full-sized B&W horror magazine. The artwork for the first issue features this alternate cover by Jeremy Geddes. © IDW Publishing/used by permission.

IDW Publishing

Doomed (B&W magazine)

1. cover, frontis and back cover: Ashley Wood/alternate cover: Jeremy Geddas (October 2005)

(1) Ms. Doomed's Introduction [Chris Ryall/Ashley Wood] 1p; **(2)** Bloodson [Chris Ryall/Ashley Wood, from the story by Richard Matheson] 15p; **(3)** Cuts [F. Paul Wilson/Ted McKeever, from the story by Wilson] 15p; **(4)** Blood Rape of the Lust Ghouls [Chris Ryall/Eduardo Barretto, from the story by David J. Schow] 15p; **(5)** The Final Performance [Chris Ryall/Kristian Donaldson, from the story by Robert Bloch] 15p; **(6)** Outlawed Legacies: Please Kill Me Now: The Life and Deathwish of David J. Schow [Joshua Jabcuga and David J. Schow, text article with photos] 6p; **(7)** Ms. Doomed's Farewell [Chris Ryall/Ashley Wood] 1p; **(8)** Next issue ad [Ashley Wood, on the inside back cover] 1p.

Notes: It was $6.99 for 72 pages. Publisher: Ted Adams. Editor: Chris Ryall. At last we see a return to the full-size B&W horror magazines of the 1960s–1990s! IDW Publishing makes an admirable effort here, adapting stories from four major horror writers. The best of the bunch is Robert Bloch's "The Final Performance," adapted by editor Chris Ryall and artist Kristian Donaldson. The story does a fine job of conveying the feel of a cross-country drive on very limited funds and the seedy, out-of-the-way diners and motels one might frequent as a result of those low funds. The artwork is crisp and well laid out and I particularly like the idea of leaving the hero's eyes in darkness throughout the story, except for one necessary panel. Best story and art for this premiere issue. The other adaptations are all worthwhile reading as well, with good work from Eduardo Barretto, Chris Ryall, Ted McKeever and some very nice work by Ashley Wood, who doubled as the art director. The influence of the Warren magazines was clear in the cover layout, which closely resembled the old Warren style, and in the use of a sexy hostess to introduce the magazine. However, this hostess, Ms. Doomed, was not the pun-spouting horror host of old, but a decidedly creepy lady with a major hate for men. NOT somebody you'd like to ever actually meet. Her dominatrix-style dialogue was loaded with bitterness. Both covers were quite good, with Geddas' art appearing to be somewhat in the style of Phil Hale's, and greatly resembling a frame from a stop-action animated film. Ashley Wood's artwork also appears to be somewhat of a cross between David Mazzuchelli and Jeff Jones and is quite good. One thing I definitely did like was that, following the interview, a one-page ad appeared for the books of the interviewed writer (in this issue, David J. Schow). Well laid out with informative information on each book, this is a nice touch. The interior ads for IDW's other books were also generally well done. There's a part of me that cringes at the price but, in reality, Warren was selling their books for $1.50 when regular four-color comics sold for 30 cents. So in 1973 the cost of a Warren magazine was five times what the average comic cost. The $7 price tag for this magazine is only double what the average 22-page (I don't count ads) comic sells for today and you're getting 60 pages of story and art here, plus an interview. This was a better buy for your dollar than either the Warren books were in the 1970s or new color comics are today.

2. cover, frontis and back cover: Ashley Wood/alternate cover: Jeremy Geddes (April 2006)

(1) Ms. Doomed Pin-Up [Ashley Wood] 1p; (2) Bagged [Chris Ryall/Ashely Wood, from the story by David J. Schow] 15p; (3) Crickets [Scott Tipton/Mike Hoffman, from the story by Richard Matheson] 15p; (4) Warm Farewell [Dan Taylor/Alex Sanchez, from the story by Robert Bloch] 15p; (5) Slasher [F. Paul Wilson/Tony Salmons, from the story by Wilson] 15p; (6) Outlawed Legacies: F. Paul Wilson Interview [Joshua Jubcuga and F. Paul Wilson, text article] 7p; (7) Ms. Doomed's Farewell [Chris Ryall/Ashley Wood] 1p; (8) Next issue ad [Ashley Wood, on the inside back cover] 1p.

Notes: Four more adapted tales from the same four writers presented in #1. Best artwork was from Mike Hoffman, although his backgrounds (or lack of them) left something to be desired at times. Best stories were the adapted Matheson and Wilson stories although the Schow tale was decent enough. Unfortunately the Bloch adaptation seemed a bit obvious although the art was nice. All in all, a decent issue.

3. cover and frontis: Ashley Wood/alternate cover: Jeremy Geddes (September 2006)

(1) Ms. Doomed Introduction [Chris Ryall/Ashley Wood] 1p; (2) Fat Chance [Ted Adams/Ashley Wood, from the story by Robert Bloch] 15p; (3) The Book Vault: World War Z/Thunderstruck/Harbringers [Ted Adams, text article] 2p; (4) The Children of Noah [Scott Tipton/Nat Jones, from the story by Richard Matheson] 15p; (5) DVD Late Show: Asylum/Shock-O-Rama/It Waits [Christopher Mills, text article] 1p; (6) Pelts [F. Paul Wilson/James A. Owen, Lon Saline, Mary McCray and J. Brundage Owen, from the story by Wilson] 16p; (7) Tales of the Doomed: Circle Seven [Chris Ryall, text story, inspired by Jeremy Geddes cover image] 2p; (8) Visitation [Ivan Brandon/Andy MacDonald, from the story by David J. Schow] 15p; (9) Outlawed Legacies: Robert Bloch [Robert Bloch, Jack Ketchum and Joshua Jabcuga, text article] 3p; (10) Ms. Doomed's Farewell [Chris Ryall/Ashley Wood] 1p; (11) Next issue ad [Ashley Wood, on the inside back cover] 1p.

Notes: Seventy-two pages. I quite liked the Matheson adaptation.

4. cover, frontis and back cover: Ashley Wood/alternate cover: Jeremy Geddes (November 2006)

(1) Ms. Doomed's Introduction [Chris Ryall/Ashley Wood] 1p; (2) Legion of Plotters [Ted Adams/Ashley Wood, from the story by Richard Matheson] 15p; (3) The Book Vault: 20th

Century Ghosts/Blood Lines/Heart-Shaped Box/Weed Species/Love Hurts and Other Stories [Ted Adams, text article] 2p; (4) Faces [F. Paul Wilson/Rufus Dayglo, from the story by Wilson] 16p; (5) DVD Late Show: Frankenhooker/Slither/Silent Hill [Christopher Mills, text article] 1p; (6) Coming Soon to a Theater Near You [Kris Oprisko/T. Cypress, from the story by David J. Schow] 15p; (7) Tales of the Doomed: Twenty Years On [Chris Ryall/Jeremy Geddes, text story, Geddes art is reprinted in B&W from the alternate cover] 2p; (8) Ego Trip [Joshua Jabcuga/Dario Bruzuela, from the story by Robert Bloch] 15p; (9) Outlawed Legacies: Richard Matheson [Stanley Wiater and Matthew R. Bradley, text article] 1½ p; (10) Intrepid Bibliographier and the Richard Matheson Companion Associate Editor [Paul Stuve, text article] 1½ p; (11) Ms. Doom's Farewell [Chris Ryall/Ashley Wood] 1p.

Notes: Final issue. This series closed out much as it began, with decent adaptations of good horror stories and interesting non-fiction reviews and essays. I liked "Legion of Plotters" best, both for story and art but all the stories were interesting and most well drawn. The Wiater/Bradley article was later used as the foreword to the nonfiction book *The Richard Matheson Companion*.

Mike Hoffman and Jason Crawley

Bloke's Terrible Tomb of Terror

1. cover/frontis: Mike Hoffman/inside back cover: Jim Collins (July 2011)

(1) Reflection of Evil [Jason Crawley/Mike Hoffman] 9p; (2) The Art of Dying [Jason Crawley/Fernando Ignatius] 10p; (3) Love Hurts [Jason Crawley/Rock Baker and Jeff Austin] 10p; (4) Sparks Will Fly! [Michael Mitchell] 6p; (5) Tomb of Terror ad [Mike Hoffman] 1p; (6) Face Value [Jason Crawley/Robert Smith] 7p; (7) In Perspective [Mike Hoffman] 8p.

Notes: It was $8.95 for 52 pages. Publishers and editors: Mike Hoffman and Jason Crawley. The cover is repeated sans copy on the back cover. This full-size B&W magazine is not distributed on newsstands. It's only available via internet sales. Bloke is the rather seedy British horror

host, who's recently transplanted himself to the U.S. Mike Hoffman is one of the best horror artists around and he clearly models this magazine on both the Warren magazines and on *Web of Horror*. Oddly enough, for the past decade or so, Hoffman has done a tremendous amount of artwork in the style of Frank Frazetta. Most "imitators" of Frazetta are, frankly, pretty poor, but Hoffman, like Arthur Suydam, has enough of his own style in his art to allow that art to be viewed as "working in the style of" rather than a slavish imitation. All of the covers for this series thus far are in the Frazetta style and all are quite good. The stories aren't bad either, with Hoffman's partner, Jason Crawley, proving to have a nicely macabre and twisted sense of horror. Most of the stories in this issue are a cross between early Warren tales and the more black humor stylings of EC Comics. The best effort in this issue is the lead-off story, "Reflection of Evil," but I also liked "The Art of Dying" and "Love Hurts." A good issue.

2. cover and inside back cover: Mike Hoffman (October 2011)

(1) False Alarm [Jason Crawley/Jason Paulos] 6p; (2) Bee-Witched [Mike Hoffman] 8p; (3) Invasion of the Slag Maggots [Jason Crawley/Maurizio Ercole] 8p; (4) Witness From the Grave [Jason Crawley/Mike Hoffman] 10p; (5) Tomb of Terror ad [Mike Hoffman] 1p; (6) Those Crazy Kids on Vlad 7 [Mike Hoffman] 5p; (7) All The Grooviest Monsters Dig Tomb! [Mike Hoffman] 1p; (8) In the Same Vein [Mike Hoffman] 7p; (9) Epilogue [Mike Hoffman] 1p; (10) Hoffman Publishing ad [Mike Hoffman] 1p.

Notes: A science-fiction themed issue. The stories in this issue seem to be modeled more on the EC sci-fi comics mixed with DC Comics' *House of Mystery* title. Not quite as adult but still entertaining. Hoffman did a great deal more of the artwork this issue. The best story and art is from the last tale, "In the Same Vein," which features a pretty horrific and disquieting ending, although the story itself is a little confusing.

3. cover, frontis and inside back cover: Mike Hoffman (February 2012)

(1) Green Fingers [Jason Crawley/Rock Baker and Mike Hoffman] 8p; (2) Mike Hoffman

website ad [Mike Hoffman] 1p; (3) An Artist's Model [Jason Crawley/Mike Hoffman] 8p; (4) Deja Grue [Jason Crawley/Rock Baker and Mike Hoffman] 8p; (5) Tomb of Terror ad [Mike Hoffman] 1p; (6) The Fear-Leader pin-up [Mike Hoffman] 1p; (7) The Hitch-Hiker [Jason Crawley/Mike Hoffman] 6p; (7) Liver Night! [Jason Crawley?/Mike Hoffman?] 9p; (8) A Stand-Up Guy [?/Mike Hoffman] 5p.

Notes: The story quality slips this issue, with most of the stories being overly familiar, tele-graphing their endings halfway through page 2. The best story and art is from "Liver Night!" which doesn't display any credits. The inking appears to be Hoffman's but I'm not sure about the penciling. I hope the quality picks up for issue #4. The back cover is quite nice, although it reminds me a bit too strongly of an old Fra-zetta painting done for the Mystery Book Club back in the early 1970s.

A Time of Wine-Dark Horrors

The death of Warren Publications and Marvel's nearly simultaneous ending of new horror stories in their B&W magazines occurred in 1983. This is not to say that horror, especially new horror, has vanished from comics themselves. After the long drought of the 1990s, since 2000 Marvel has put out a steady stream of mini-series and one-shot horror comic books. Most are in color but some are in black and white. Their Haunt of Horror revival, with Poe and Lovecraft adaptations done both in B&W and in regular comic book size by Warren vets Rich Margopoulos and Richard Corben are well worth searching for.

IDW Publishing regularly publishes color horror comics, including the excellent *30 Days of Night* and, to date, three separate but connected mini-series by Steve Niles and Warren/DC/Marvel artist Bernie Wrightson. A 2011 collection of those Niles/Wrightson stories was published under the title *Monstrous Collection* and featured the pages reproduced magazine-sized and in B&W. Recent information indicates that Niles and Wrightson are working on a sequel to the *Frankenstein* novel.

Dark Horse Comics publishes Mike Mignola's *Hellboy* and its spin-off titles, *B.R.P.D.*, *Abe Sapien*, *Lobster Johnson* and *Witchfinder*. Mignola's art is an uncanny blend of Alex Toth's play of shadows and light crossed with Jack Kirby's dynamic storytelling. In addition, Mignola has also made room for (among many others) Warren artist Richard Corben, Warren and EC artist John Severin and Marvel artist Herb Trimpe to draw some of these adventures and it is nice to see the connection between the old and the new. All of these *Hellboy* titles are fun to read and well worth your time. Dark Horse has also revived Warren's *Creepy* as a 48-page regular-sized B&W comic anthology. The editors, Shawna Gore and Dave Land, and consulting editors, Dan Braun and Craig Haffner, have managed to touch base with many of the original Warren creators, including Angelo Torres, Gene Colan, Doug Moench, Ken Kelly, Manuel Sanjulian, Richard Corben and others as well as bringing in newer artists and writers. It hasn't reached the heights of the original titles yet but, as I write this, it's only seven issues in. Give it time and who knows? Dark Horse also publishes Steve Niles' *Cal MacDonald* adventures, Eric Powell's *The Goon* and Jan Strnad and Richard Corben's *Ragemoor*—all three good horror titles.

DC Comics published a fabulous novel-length adaptation of William Hope Hodgson's *The House on the Borderland*, with script by Simon Revelstroke and art by Richard Corben. They have also published the single color volume of Alan Moore and David Lloyd's *V for Vendetta* and six volumes of Moore's acclaimed early work on *Swamp Thing* with Steve Bissette, John Totenben, Rick Veitch and many other fine artists and storytellers. Neil Gaiman and Co.'s series of *Sandman* volumes is a powerful collection of books and well worth your time. Under its Vertigo publishing branch, DC has produced a considerable amount of straight horror. Particularly noteworthy are the various collected volumes of the long running *Hellblazer* series, Jeff Lemire's *Sweet Tooth* (currently at four volumes and counting), and the seventeen volumes to date of Bill Willingham and Mark Buckingham's *Fables*.

Fables is perhaps more fantasy oriented than horror but it has moments of uncomfortable horror in all the right ways. It's also beautifully written and illustrated. It is the best comic by far, in any genre, being produced today.

There are also dozens of small publishers producing literally hundreds of horror comics — some good, some bad. Most are not particularly distinguished but every now and then you get one that rises above the crowd. I'd like to recommend the various works of Charles Burns, particularly the creepy *Black Hole*. *Nightmare World*, an excellent three-volume collection of interconnected short stories by Dirk Manning and various artists, is published by Image. The four volumes of *Nightmares and Fairytales* by Serene Valentino and Co., featuring excellent gothic tales, appear from SLG Publishing. Warren, DC and Harvey veteran Ernie Colon recently issued a collection of B&W horror tales under the umbrella title of the old radio show *Inner Sanctum*, said volume being published by NBM Publishing. This hardcover collection clearly shows that Colon still has what it takes to render a chilling story. NBM Publishing also delivers Rick Geary's true-life crime volumes — ten volumes from the 19th century and four (to date) from the 20th century — which contain plenty of horrific events drawn from real life. Especially noteworthy is his retelling of the crimes of Jack the Ripper. Writer-artist Rick Veitch's self-published works from his King Hell Press are often more SF than straight horror but all of his strong work contains elements of horror. Top Shelf Publications publishes the massive collected volume of Alan Moore and Eddie Campbell's Jack the Ripper novel *From Hell* as well as Moore and Melinda Gebbie's sexually explicit *Lost Girls*. Alan Moore's chilling take on the themes of H. P. Lovecraft — 2011's *Neonomicon* — is a frightening book from Avatar Press.

However, for the readers of this volume the main interest is what's available from the B&W titles we've been following. The answer to that is: a lot.

Warren's legacy is split between three different publishers. Dark Horse is publishing the *Creepy Archives*, at this writing coming in at thirteen separate hardcover volumes covering *Creepy*

#1–63 so far. They also publish the *Eerie Archives*, at eleven volumes currently, and covering *Eerie* #1–55. Each volume of these collections is superbly reproduced, with the B&W artwork crisp and dynamic looking, while the color covers and stories are as good looking as the day they first appeared. Each volume also includes an informative foreword (for the sake of full disclosure, I need to admit that I wrote the foreword to *Creepy Archives*, vol. 9) which provides either an overview of the time period or some excellent interviews with major writers or artists appearing in that volume. It would be hard to imagine a better-looking or more comprehensive way to reproduce these issues.

Due to a settlement between James Warren and Harris Publications in the early 2000s, *Vampirella* was split off from *Creepy* and *Eerie*. In turn, Dynamite Entertainment either purchased or leased the rights to the original magazines and is thus the publisher of the *Vampirella Archives*. In style and format they have largely followed the appearance of the Dark Horse volumes. Unfortunately they provide no introductions and their reproduction of the B&W art is not as sharp as Dark Horse's efforts. Still the representation of the artwork isn't terrible either and they do provide more issues per volume than Dark Horse. The *Vampirella Archives* stands currently at four volumes and covers *Vampirella* #1–28.

The publishing rights to *Blazing Combat* were sold by Warren in the 1990s and a one-volume collection of all four original issues has been published in both hardcover and trade paperback by Fantagraphic Books. This volume includes both a foreword and two interviews (conducted in the 1990s) with original publisher James Warren and original editor/writer Archie Goodwin. This was the best war comic ever produced, with beautiful artwork and hard-hitting scripts. If you're genuinely interested in comics at all, this is an essential volume.

To date, Skywald's output has not been collected in any organized fashion. However, editor Al Hewetson finished an autobiography/history of his work at the company shortly before he died. In fact, he finished it the *day* he died. It's called *Skywald: The Illustrated History of the Horror-Mood* and was published by British publisher

THE NEXT DAY, HUNCHED OVER A BOWL OF MY MOTHER'S WATERY OATMEAL IN THE WINTRY CHILL OF OUR KITCHEN, I WOULD **ASK** HER, VERY QUIETLY AND VERY SLOWLY...

WHERE WAS DADDY LAST NIGHT?

SHE WOULD LOOK AT ME AND **SMILE** WITH HER EYES. EYES, ONCE BEAUTIFUL, NOW VERY GREY AND ALMOST SUNKEN COMPLETELY INTO THE DARK CIRCLES THAT HAD FORMED AROUND THEM IN THE PAST SEVERAL MONTHS. SHE NEVER SAID A WORD, BUT THE PAIN AND **TORMENT** IN THOSE EYES SPOKE WITH AN ELOQUENCE THE SPOKEN WORD COULD NEVER MATCH!

I WOULD THEN SET ABOUT THE **RUNNING** OF OUR LITTLE FARM, MUCH NEGLECTED OF LATE BY MY FATHER. I HAD MUCH TIME TO THINK ON THAT CHILL AND WINDY MORNING AS THE FIRST SNOW BEGAN TO FALL!

IN SCHOOL, I THOUGHT LITTLE ON MY **LESSONS**, RECEIVING MANY VARIED AND UNIMAGINATIVE PUNISHMENTS FOR MY LACK OF ATTENTION. I SELDOM HEARD THE JEERING LAUGHTER OF MY CLASSMATES OVER THE ALL ENCOMPASSING ROAR OF MY OWN **THOUGHTS**.

RETURNING **HOME**, I WOULD ARRIVE AT THE PATH LEADING TO OUR HOUSE JUST IN TIME TO SEE MY FATHER DEPART, **AXE** IN HAND. IN RETROSPECT, IT OCCURS TO ME THAT DURING THOSE TUMULTUOUS MONTHS OF LATE FALL AND EARLY WINTER, I SAW **NOTHING** OF MY FATHER DURING DAYLIGHT HOURS AND LITTLE MORE THAN HIS **SHADOW** AT NIGHT.

SIXTH BRUTAL MURDER BEHEADED BODY FOUND IN KITC

IT IS THAT **SHADOW** WHICH DOMINATES MY MOST VIVID RECOLLECTIONS OF THOSE MONTHS.

David Kerekes via his company Headpress. The book not only contains Hewetson's recollections of Skywald circa 1972–1975 but also features nineteen complete stories from the magazines and one previously unpublished tale that was left over after the Skywald collapse. The book is fascinating and the stories serve as an excellent "best of" volume. Perhaps someday there will be a series of Skywald archive volumes as well. Cross your fingers, folks. Headpress has also published *The Complete Saga of the Victims* by Hewetson and Jesus Suso Rego, including the previously unpublished ending to this graphic serial which ran originally in *Scream* magazine. It's a must-buy for a Skywald fan.

DC has published a number of B&W volumes of their mystery/horror color comics from the 1960s and 1970s in their *Showcase Presents* volumes. So far, there have been three *House of Mystery* volumes, two volumes of *House of Secrets*, two volumes of the *Phantom Stranger*, and single volumes each of the *Witching Hour*, *Ghosts*, the *Spectre*, *Secrets of Sinister House* and *Weird War Tales*. In many cases, the excellent B&W reproduction enhances the individual stories, making them seem a far better collection of tales than perhaps they did 40 years ago. In addition, DC recently republished the single issue of Jack Kirby's *Spirit World*, along with as much of the intended second issue as still exists, in a hardcover volume. This is well worth taking a look at.

Marvel has also represented a number of their color comics in their own version of the DC's B&W *Showcase* volumes, called the *Marvel Essentials* collection. Unlike DC, Marvel's storing of original scans and film of the artwork appears to have been rather haphazard and their reproduction suffers as a result, with numerous pages and even entire issues having to be reproduced from the actual color comics themselves, which can muddy the look of the page. Still, these are worthy volumes. Marvel's *Essential* line so far has done four volumes of *Tomb of Dracula*— the last of which features the contents of the B&W

Dracula Lives! magazine, four volumes of *Dr. Strange*, two volumes each of *Werewolf by Night*, *Man-Thing*, *Ghost Rider*, *Vampire Tales* and *Marvel Horror*— this last one covering the color and B&W adventures of *Satana*, the color comic *Son of Satan*, and various adventures of the *Living Mummy*, *Brother Voodoo* and other second-tier supernatural heroes. There are also one volume collections of *Tales of the Zombie* and *The Monster of Frankenstein*. You should be aware that Marvel's reprinting of their B&W magazines suffers from censorship, as any nudity in the original artwork is retouched to cover it up. Still, these reprinting are an affordable way to collect these stories.

Running Press published four volumes of actual comics in their *The Mammoth Book of...* series, including *Best War Comics*, *Best Horror Comics*, *Best Crime Comics* and *Best Zombie Comics*. Each volume runs about 450 pages. These volumes have good introductions and commentaries by the editors, and the *Best Horror*, *War* and *Crime* volumes are very good collections, covering stories from a great number of publishers in both the U.S. and Europe. The *Zombie* title, while showcasing some good material, is more single-minded in theme and tends to get monotonous. Mind you, all of the volumes have problems. Although the titles claim to be the best of their various genres, no stories from Marvel or DC appear. Nor do many from either Warren or EC. You can hardly claim to have a comprehensive collection if you can't reprint the most prominent publishers' stories. In addition, Running Press is a prose book publisher and their inexperience with comics unfortunately shows. All of the volumes seem to have one or more stories with pages out of order. The publishers don't always seem to know how best to reproduce or convert color comics to sharp edged, clear B&W pages. Thus, many of the pages are too dark, especially pages that were originally painted art or have been reduced in size. The *Best Horror* volume reprints an entire story, Scott Hampton's excellent painted adaptation of Robert E.

Opposite: From my favorite issue of *Creepy* comes my personal favorite story— the witty "The Shadow of the Axe" by Dave Sim and Russ Heath. Heath's artwork renders time, place and, most especially, a dysfunctional family in vivid detail. © New Comic Co./used by permission.

Howard's "Pigeons from Hell," with the script missing. Forty-eight pages of far-too-dark and too-small-reprinted artwork and no words! Nonetheless, all of the problems mentioned are ones of sloppy production, not of original quality or story choice. Peter Normanton, the publisher/editor of the British fanzine *From the Tomb*, is the editor for *Best Horror Comics* and he shows remarkably good taste in selections, including the first reprinting in over 30 years of the classic John Stanley/Ed Robbins tale "The Monster of Dread End" from 1962 as well as the first ever reprintings of several stories from *Web of Horror*. The *War* and *Crime* volumes are also most impressive, especially the *Crime* collection, which is chock-full of both great and historically important stories. All of the volumes highlight stories from both traditional color comics, B&W magazine publishers, European comics and underground titles, providing a sweeping collection of comic stories that one person would be hard put to locate on their own.

In 2006, Idea Man Production collected B&W versions of Dick Briefer's excellent pre–Code horror comic *The Monster of Frankenstein*. Briefer's version of the Monster changed from being one of the first horror characters in the 1940s to a humor version in the late 1940s–early 1950s and back to a full-fledged horror character during the horror craze of 1950–1954. Issues #18–33, which featured all of the 1950s horror issues, are included in this book. Briefer's take on *Frankenstein* was unique and not only well drawn but well written as well. One of the stories may well have been the inspiration for Roger Corman's *Little Shop of Horrors*. The B&W artwork is reprinted from old color comics but the book is still worth buying.

All of the titles mentioned are in addition to a massive outpouring in recent years of color archive volumes covering pre–Code and post–Code comics from EC, Marvel, Harvey, Gold Key/Dell and DC titles. Several of these volumes focus on a single artist, such as Alex Toth, Steve Ditko, Wally Wood, Dick Briefer or Bob Powell. Many of these titles are also must-have books for the collector.

You might also like to know about the various books and magazines that provide a history of the B&W horror magazines (as well as the comic field in general). In magazine form, there are (or have been) three modern comic history efforts with probably the best of these being the late *Comic Book Artist*, edited by Jon B. Cooke, which ran for 25 issues from 1998 to 2003 via Twomorrows Publishing and added another six issues from 2003 to 2004 via Top Shelf Comics. *Comic Book Artist* devoted each issue to a particular publisher or theme and provided exhaustive interviews and articles dealing with each theme. These issues also displayed large amounts of rare or exclusive artwork from the time periods discussed. Cooke generally concentrated on comics from the 1960s to the 1980s. Back issues of both publishing incarnations can be found on the original publishers' websites.

The second title is *Alter Ego*, edited by Roy Thomas, who at one point was the editor-in-chief at Marvel Comics as well as an important writer for Marvel, DC and other publishers. *Alter Ego* actually began as a fanzine edited and published by Jerry Bails, a pioneer comic book historian, in 1961. The fanzine was passed on to fan Ron Foss and then to a teenaged Roy Thomas. It ran for ten irregular issues though 1969. An eleventh issue was published by Mike Friedrich's *Star*Reach* Comics in 1978, co-edited by Thomas and Friedrich. Then, in 1998, Jon Cooke began running a mini-version (edited by Thomas) as a flip-book section in the back of *Comic Book Artist* for several issues. In 1999 the title was revived as a full-fledged professional magazine, edited by Thomas. It has been in print ever since and has published more than a hundred issues — a remarkable achievement for any magazine, let alone one dealing with the history of comics. Thomas' approach on Alter Ego is somewhat more scattershot than Cooke's (or less rigid, if you prefer) but he also covers a generally wider spectrum, dealing with comics from the 1930s to 1974, the year when Thomas resigned as the lead editor for Marvel Comics. Each issue generally consists of a lead article or interview that is cover-featured, along with numerous other interviewed creators or topics, often unrelated to the lead article, and closes out each issue with a special segment (similar to the way *Alter Ego* was carried in the back of *Comic Book*

Artist) devoted exclusively to Fawcett's *Captain Marvel* titles. This concluding segment is edited by P. C. Hammerlinck. For our purposes, *AE* usually features a horror issue each year around Halloween time with generous amounts of historical detail and artwork. Current and back issues, both print and jpeg versions, are available from Twomorrows Publishing's website.

The third history magazine, *Back Issue*, is also published by Twomorrows and was originally conceived as a replacement title for *Comic Book Artist* when Cooke moved his magazine to Top Shelf. Edited by Michael Eury, this magazine focuses on comics from 1975 to the early or mid–1990s. Unlike either *Comic Book Artist* or *AE*, *Back Issue* favors articles on comics far more than interviews but does publish the occasional interview as well. In most other respects it greatly resembles *AE* and the original *Comic Book Artist* in layout and artwork, and, like *AE*, it generally publishes a horror themed issue each fall. *Back Issue* has published well over fifty issues since its debut in 2003 and is also available in both print and jpeg versions from the *Tomorrows* Publishing website. All three titles are invaluable resources for both comic history and collecting. Again, for the sake of disclosure, I must mention that I have written articles or provided information for all three magazines.

In addition there have been a few recent fanzines (a fan-generated genre that has, sadly, largely died out as the internet and distribution problems have rendered much of their "special and unique" aspects inert) that have focused on horror. *Spooky*, an English fanzine which focused strictly on the Warren magazines, was published for eight issues by Piers Casimir from 2003 to 2006. Piers also published a fat *Spooky 2010 Yearbook* collection in 2009. Both the fanzine and the yearbook provided interviews, background information and rare art from Warren veterans such as Nicola Cuti and Bill DuBay. I also provided interviews for this fanzine.

Another exceptional British fanzine/magazine was *From the Tomb*, published and edited by Peter Normanton. It started out as a B&W mini-mag effort without covers and progressed to a glossy full-color magazine. It ran for 28 issues, from 2000 to 2009, and focused on both American and British horror magazines and comics. Each issue was generally better in both writing and production than the last and each displayed Normanton's steadily upward learning curve on how to improve his magazine and its contents. Like *Comic Book Artist*, *Alter Ego*, *Back Issue* and *Spooky*, this is a treasure trove for the horror enthusiast and collector, featuring articles and the occasional interview on classic terror tales or rare and obscure horror comics, with information extending from the pre–Code 1950s right up to today. You can locate back issues at www.fromthetombstore.co.nr/. Again, I have written articles for this magazine.

Books that deal with horror comics have begun to swell in recent years. I won't mention all of them but some of the most significant ones follow.

For fans of Warren, the first glimmer of a revival of interest appeared in 2001 with the publication of *The Warren Companion* by David A. Roach and Jon B. Cooke. This book featured all of the interviews and much of the artwork presented in the fourth issue of Cooke's *Comic Book Artist*, which focused on Warren's B&W magazines. Besides the interviews, there is a Warren checklist, lengthy appendixes, a short history of the "Spanish invasion" and brief articles on the B&W efforts of Marvel, Skywald and other publishers. The passage of time has caused some of *The Warren Companion*'s information to be outdated or superseded (in at least some respects by the book you're holding in your hands) but this is an excellent starter volume if you can find it — it's out of print, with copies on amazon.com currently going for north of $600 dollars!

There is also the exceptional 2010 reference book *Gathering Horror*, self-published by author David Horne via his own Phrona Press. This massive volume covers the publishing history of Warren Publications in exhaustive detail. At 688 pages, Horne provides lively and accurate details about all things Warren, including lengthy indexes on foreign versions of the titles. There were only 750 copies of this book printed and I suspect it too will soon soar in value when the available copies are purchased. It's a fine, fine book.

Skywald is represented by the aforementioned *Skywald!: The Illustrated History of the Horror-Mood* by Al Hewetson as well as Stephen Sennitt's *Ghastly Terror!: The Horrible Story of the Horror Comics*, which has lengthy chapters on both Warren and Skywald, as well on chapters on various pre– and post–Code color comics. Sennitt prefers Skywald over Warren and puts up a spirited argument for the horror-mood titles, although his opinion, at times, seems unsupported by the very facts that he's relating. Still, it's a lively book, provocative and entertaining. Thus far, those two books, and this one, are the only titles to focus on the history of the Skywald legacy.

For fans of Myron Fass's *Eerie* Publications, Feral House published *The Weird World of Eerie Publications*, written by Mike Howlett and featuring a introduction by *Taboo* editor Steve Bissette. I'm going on record for thinking these titles to be dismal, low-grade, sloppy messes that trashed the pre-code stories they reworked into boring, bloody garbage, but there are folks I quite respect who very much disagree with me. For those folks as well as the casual reader, this well-researched and written book is certainly worth looking at. It's also about 15,000 times better than any comic magazine that *Eerie* Publications ever put out.

There are also several books dealing with pre–Code color horror comics, the most noteworthy being *Tales of Terror!* by Fred von Bernewitz and Grant Geissman and published by Gemstone. It is the ultimate volume on EC Comics with checklists, credits, articles and rare bits and pieces of information and art. Another excellent EC book is *Foul Play!*, also by Geissman, which focuses on the EC artists and relates some of their post–EC careers. I'd be remiss in not mentioning that the EC comics are also being reprinted in color archive volumes. They'd originally been collected in stunningly beautiful B&W volumes, issued by Ross Cochran in the 1980s. The latter is the version I much prefer but both versions are excellent fare.

Craig Yoe has (to date) edited three fine full color efforts on pre–Code artists — the first fo-cusing on and entitled *Dick Briefer's Frankenstein* and the second focusing on Bob Powell's pre–Code horror tales entitled *Bob Powell's Terror*. The third volume, still upcoming at this writing appears to focus on and is titled *Zombies*.

Two other excellent books are *Four Color Fear: Forgotten Horror Comics of the 1950s* (Fantagraphic Books) by Greg Sadowski and John Benson and *The Horror! The Horror!: Comic Books the Government Didn't Want You to Read* (Abrams Comicarts) by Jim Trombetta and R. L. Stine. Both are well written and interesting discussions of the pre–Code horror comics.

Submitted for Your Approval

The B&W horror magazines of the 1960s–1980s were a unique aspect of the comic market and publishing. Jim Warren found a publishing niche on the newsstands at what may well be the only time that such a venture could have made a breakthrough in that market. He opened the door for at least a halfdozen other publishers who, with varying success, followed in his footsteps.

The comics magazines produced featured some of the best editors, writers and artists that comics had to offer and presented stories that still stand out as some of the most accomplished efforts in the medium nearly 50 years later.

I hope this book, chronicling the successes and failures of those titles, evokes some fond memories for those who read them for the first time when both they and the magazines were young. I also hope that it proves to be of equally interesting reading to those readers who have come along later, finding the stories in handsome hardbound archive volumes or in yellowed, battered original copies. There's a treasure trove of reading and beautiful artwork, of fevered dreams and skin-crawling terror in these magazines and collections. If this book is your doorway to those stories, then welcome. You've already opened the door. The first step is taken. Now go and find your own suitably horrible fun.

The Best Black and White Horror Tales

Warren

1. Landscape (*Blazing Combat* #2) by Archie Goodwin and Joe Orlando
2. Collector's Edition (*Creepy* #10) by Archie Goodwin and Steve Ditko
3. Dark Rider! (*Eerie* #8) by Archie Goodwin and John Severin
4. To Kill a God (*Vampirella* #12) by Wally Wood
5. The Third Night of Mourning (*Creepy* #49) by Jim Stenstrum and Jaime Brocal
6. Bless Us, Father... (*Creepy* #59) by Bill DuBay and Richard Corben
7. Jenifer (*Creepy* #63) by Bruce Jones and Berni Wrightson
8. Nightfall (*Eerie* #60) by Bill DuBay and Berni Wrightson
9. The House on the Sea (*Vampirella* #41) by Jim Stenstrum and Rafael Auraleon
10. 0il of Dog (*Creepy* #67) by Jack Butterworth and Isidro Mones via Ambrose Bierce
11. Gamal and the Cockatrice (*Vampirella* #47) by Bruce Bezaire and Rafael Auraleon
12. Night of the Jackass (*Eerie* #60, 63–65) by Bruce Bezaire and Jose Ortiz
13. Daddy and the Pie (*Eerie* #64) by Bill DuBay and Alex Toth
14. Thrillkill (*Creepy* #75) by Jim Stenstrum and Neal Adams
15. Godeye (*Eerie* #68) by Budd Lewis and Leopoldo Sanchez
16. Deep Brown and Jorum (*Eerie* #68) by Jim Stenstrum and Esteban Maroto
17. Creeps (*Creepy* #78) by Archie Goodwin, Wally Wood and John Severin
18. The Shadow of the Axe (*Creepy* #79) by Dave Sim and Russ Heath
19. Yellow Heat (*Vampirella* #58) by Bruce Jones and Russ Heath
20. In Deep (*Creepy* #83) by Bruce Jones and Richard Corben
21. Process of Elimination (*Creepy* #83) by Bruce Jones and Russ Heath
22. Warrior's Ritual (*Creepy* #112) by Archie Goodwin and John Severin
23. The Night Willa Jane Gronley Went Home (*Vampirella* #82) by Archie Goodwin, Val Mayerik and Jeff Easley
24. Blood on Black Satin (*Eerie* #109–111) by Doug Moench and Paul Gulacy
25. Sight Unseen (*Vampirella* #89) by Bruce Jones and Jose Ortiz

Skywald

1. The Man Who Stole Eternity (*Psycho* #3) by Gardner Fox and Bill Everett
2. Hag of the Blood Basket (*Nightmare* #4) by Al Hewetson and Tom Sutton
3. Sand Castles (*Psycho* #6) by Ed Fedory and Pablo Marcos
4. Limb from Limb from Death (*Nightmare 1972 Annual*) by Al Hewetson and Pablo Marcos
5. Have You Seen The Black Rain? (*Psycho* #8) by Al Hewetson and Juez Xirinius

6. ...Make Mephisto's Child Burn... (*Psycho* #11) by Ed Fedory and Felipe Dela Rosa

7. The Comics Macabre (*Scream* #1) by Al Hewetson and Maelo Cintron

8. The Saga of the Victims (*Scream* #6–9, 11) by Al Hewetson and Jesus Suso Rego

9. Metzengerstein (*Scream* #9) by Al Hewetson and Luis Collado via Edgar Allan Poe

10. The Fiend of Changsha, part 2: Dead by Day, Fiend by Night (*Psycho* #24) by Al Hewetson and Sanho Kim

This back cover art by Rurik Tyler from *Monsters Attack!* #4 seems a nice place to stop. A touching moment for the monster inside us all.

Marvel

1. Conan: The Frost Giant's Daughter (*Savage Tales* #1) by Roy Thomas and Barry Windsor-Smith via Robert E. Howard

2. Solomon Kane: Skulls in the Stars (*Monsters Unleashed!* #1) by Roy Thomas and Ralph Reese via Robert E. Howard

3. Dracula: Lord of Death ... Lord of Hell! (*Dracula Lives!* #3) by Marv Wolfman, John Buscema and Syd Shores

4. Solomon Kane: Castle of the Undead (*Dracula Lives!* #3) by Roy Thomas, Alan Weiss and the Crusty Bunkers via a fragment by Robert E. Howard

5. Satana (*Vampire Tales* #2) by Roy Thomas and John Romita, Sr.

6. A Monster Reborn (*Monsters Unleashed!* #4) by Steve Gerber and Pablo Marcos

7. The Drifting Snow (*Vampire Tales* #4) by Tony Isabella and Esteban Maroto via August Derleth

8. In the Shadows of the City (*Haunt of Horror* #1) by Steve Gerber and Vicente Alcazar

9. Morbius: Where Is Gallows Bend and What the Hell Am I Doing There? (*Vampire Tales* #7) by Don McGregor and Tom Sutton

10. ...A View from Without... (*Unknown Worlds of Science Fiction* #1) by Neal Adams

11. ...Not Long Before the End (*Unknown Worlds of Science Fiction* #3) by Doug Moench and Vicente Alcazar via Larry Niven

12. "Repent, Harlequin!" Said the Ticktockman (*Unknown Worlds of Science Fiction* #3) by Roy Thomas and Alex Nino via Harlan Ellison

13. It! (*Masters of Terror* #1)

by Roy Thomas, Marie Severin, Frank Giacoia and Mike Esposito via Theodore Sturgeon

14. Behold the Man (*Unknown Worlds of Science Fiction* #6) by Doug Moench and Alex Nino via Michael Moorcock

15. Satana: The Damnation Waltz (*Marvel Preview* #7) by Chris Claremont and Vicente Alcazar

16. The Lawnmower Man (*Bizarre Adventures* #29) by Stephen King and Walt Simonson via King

17. Vengeance Is (*Bizarre Adventures* #31) by John Byrne

18. A Frog Is a Frog (*Bizarre Adventures* #31) by Stephen Perry and Steve Bissette

19. Dracula: The Blood Bequest (*Bizarre Adventures* #33) by Stephen Perry, Steve Bissette and John Totleben

20. Dracula: Death Vow! (*The Tomb of Dracula* #4) by Roger McKenzie, John Buscema and Klaus Janson

The Best of the Rest!

1. Feed Me! (*Web of Horror* #3) by Mike Friedrich and Berni Wrightson

2. The President Must Die! (*Spirit World* #1) by Jack Kirby and Vince Colletta

3. V for Vendetta (*Warrior* #1–26) by Alan Moore and David Lloyd

4. Throat Sprockets (*Taboo* #1) by Tim Lucas and Mike Hoffman

5. The Pyjama Girl (*Taboo* #1) by Eddie Campbell

6. From Hell (*Taboo* #2–7) by Alan Moore and Eddie Campbell

7. Again (*Taboo* #5) by Michael Zulli via Ramsey Campbell

8. Cellar Jelly! (*Monsters Attack!* #5) by Rurik Taylor

9. The Monster Maker (*Grave Tales* #2) by James Van Hise and Tom Sutton

10. Role Model (*Grave Tales* #3) by Jeff Bailey, Marty Golia and Joe Staton

Sources

Casimir, Piers, ed. *Spooky* 1 #1 (2003).
_____. *Spooky* 2 #5 (2006).
Cooke, Jon B., ed. *Comic Book Artist* #4 (Spring 1999).
_____. "The Man Called Ploog: Bronco-Busting to Eisner to Frankenstein." *Comic Book Artist* (Summer 1998): 52–56, 61.
_____. "Rise & Fall of Rovin's Empire: A Candid Conversation with Atlas/Seaboard editor Jeff Rovin." *Comic Book Artist* (Dec. 2001): 24–43.
_____, and Gisella Marcos. "Pablo's Amazing Journey: From Peru to Florida, 'Zombie' Artist Pablo Marcos Speaks." *Comic Book Artist* (May 2001): 104–108.
Enfantino, Peter. "The Very Best of Creepy." *From the Tomb* (June 2004): 17–19.
Hewetson, Alan. "...My Days in Horror Comics ... A Skywald Horror-Mood Special Feature...." *Horror-Mood* blog, http://supergggraphics.blogspot.com/2011/11/my-days-in-horror-comics-skywald-horror.html.
_____, ed. *Skywald: The Complete Illustrated History of the Horror-Mood*. Manchester, UK: Headpress, 2004.
Horne, David: *Gathering Horror: A Completist Collector's Catalogue and Index for Warren Publishing*. Concord, CA: Phrona Press, 2010.
Howlett, Mike, and Stephen R. Bissette. *The Weird World of Eerie Publications:* Comic Gore That Warped Millions of Young Minds. Port Townsend, WA: Feral House, 2010.
Jusko, Joe. *The Art of Joe Jusko*. San Diego, CA: IDW, 2011.
Karpas, Peter. *Enjolra's World*. 2003. www.enjolrasworld.com.
Kemp, Earl, and Luis Ortiz, eds. *Cult Magazines: A to Z: A Compendium of Culturally Obsessive & Curiously Expressive Publications*. New York: Nonstop Press, 2009.
Klein, Bob, Tim Stroup, Jon Ingersoll, Tim Tjarks, and Gene Reed. *The Grand Comics Database*. April 2012. www.comics.org.
Normanton, Peter. "The Black and White Horror of Christmas Past." *From the Tomb* (Dec 2005): 22–27.
_____. "The Essential Horror: Skywald Comics and the Legacy of H. P. Lovecraft." *From the Tomb* (Oct 2002): 16–21.
_____. "The Human Gargoyles." *From the Tomb* (Feb 2004): 13–15.
_____. "Web of Horror." *From the Tomb* (Oct 2001): 2, 4–7.
Normanton, Peter, ed. *From the Tomb* #26 (Oct 2008).
"Re: The Warren Report." *Comic Book Artist* (Summer 1999): 5–9, 98. [Letters' page dealing with *CBA* #4.]
Roach, David A., Jon B. Cooke, Richard Corben, and Frank Frazetta, eds. *The Warren Companion*. Raleigh, NC: TwoMorrows, 2001.
Sennitt, Stephen. *Ghastly Terror!: The Horrible Story of Horror Comics*. Manchester, UK: Headpress, 2002.
Stewart, Bhob, and Jim Vadebonocoeur, Jr. *The Wallace Wood Checklist*. Raleigh, NC: TwoMorrows, 2003.
Warner, George E. *The Horror-Mood*. Blog. http://supergggraphics.blogspot.com/2010/11/complete-illustrated-skywald-checklist_27.html.
Warren, James. "He's in Heaven: Jim Warren Remembers Archie Goodwin." *Comic Book Artist* (Spring 1998): 3.

Index

Numbers in **bold italics** indicate pages with photographs.